THE CENTURY PSYCHOLOGY SERIES

Richard M. Elliott, *Editor*

Kenneth MacCorquodale, *Assistant Editor*

THEORIES *of* LEARNING

ERNEST R. HILGARD
Stanford University

THEORIES *of* LEARNING

Second Edition

New *York*

APPLETON-CENTURY-CROFTS, INC.

632-17

Library of Congress Card Number: 56-5144

PRINTED IN THE UNITED STATES OF AMERICA

PREFACE

THE AIM of this edition, as of the first edition, is to provide an understanding of each of the major learning theories in relation to the experiments to which that theory gives rise. The years since the first edition have seen an enormous expansion of psychological research in learning and no dearth of theoretical contributions. The task of providing an introductory exposition that is at once clear and critical becomes increasingly difficult.

I have chosen to deal with the major positions that flourished in the first half of the twentieth century in much the way they were dealt with in the first edition, building the exposition around the psychologists who gave currency to the several theories. Thus the chapters on Thorndike, Guthrie, Hull, Skinner, Tolman, classical gestalt, Lewin, and functionalism are repeated, though each has been thoroughly rewritten. New chapters include one on the learning significance of Freud's psychodynamics, one on mathematical models, and two on other current developments. The over-all result is a book of one-third more pages. Despite the orientation toward historical antecedents of current theory, nearly half the literature cited is new to this edition.

In the effort to keep the book from becoming unduly large, some of the material from the first edition has not been incorporated in the revision. The chapter on Wheeler's views is omitted with the regret that neither he nor any of his followers has revised the position sufficiently to keep it currently active. Much of the material from the dropped chapter on theories influenced by field conceptions has been treated in other ways, but some of it has been lost in the revision. So, too, Hull's 1943 postulates have had to give way to allow a critical exposition of his final 1952 system. For some purposes, therefore, the present edition does not completely replace the earlier one, and occasional references are made in the new edition to non-repeated material in the earlier one.

The two chapters on current developments recognize that the advances in mid-century cannot be confined to the standard positions that became defined in the first half of the century. Younger psychologists who began as students of one or another of the masters have matured as theorists in their own right and can no longer be subordinated as disciples or defenders of older views. In the new chapters I have tried to trace the connections with the earlier positions, while recognizing that we are moving forward, and debate is no longer confined to old issues. Some members of the new generation of theorists no doubt now deserve chapters in their own right; but until the new viewpoints are somewhat better crystallized, the necessary distinctions would undoubtedly prove confusing to the student who is trying for the first time to discover the identifying characteristics of the longer established theories.

It is my hope that this book may assist the student of the psychology of learning and his teachers to find their way into the current experimental and theoretical literature of learning—a literature now increasingly forbidding without a guide. While my task is expository and not polemical, I have not refrained from expressing personal judgments when these seemed appropriate to me. I hope, however, that these personal intrusions will be recognized for what they are, and that they remain distinguishable from the more objective exposition of the theories here considered. In the final chapter on retrospect and prospect I have departed from the expository style of the earlier chapters in order to estimate where we now stand on the more important isssues and to indicate the paths that seem likely to lead to clarification and ultimate agreement.

Suggestions that have changed the second edition have come from many students, colleagues, and critics, most of whom will have to go unnamed. I cannot refrain from mentioning the patient reading and helpful comments of the editors of this series, R. M. Elliott and Kenneth MacCorquodale. Individual chapters benefited through critical reading by Douglas H. Lawrence, Robert R. Sears, Morris I. Stein, Patrick C. Suppes, and Thurlow R. Wilson. I am grateful for permission to use as yet unpublished materials from Neal E. Miller, O. Hobart Mowrer, B. F. Skinner, and Kenneth W. Spence. The typing was done by Miss Irene Payne and the new charts drafted by P. Stanley King.

The following publishers permitted the reproduction of figures or quotations: Appleton-Century-Crofts, Inc., Cambridge University Press, Columbia University Press, Cornell University Press, Duke University Press, Free Press, Harper and Brothers, Harvard University Press, Hogarth Press, Henry Holt and Company, Houghton Mifflin Company, Kegan Paul, Trench, Trubner and Company, Liveright Publishing Corporation, McGraw-Hill Book Company, Inc., The Macmillan Company, National Society for the Study of Education, Prentice-Hall, Rinehart and Company, Ronald Press, Stanford University Press, Teachers College, Columbia University, University of Oregon Press, John Wiley and Sons, Inc., Yale University Press. The publishers of the following journals and monograph series have permitted quotations from these sources: *American Journal of Psychology, American Psychologist, Contributions to Psy-*

chological Theory, Genetic Psychology Monographs, Journal of Abnormal and Social Psychology, Journal of Comparative Psychology, Journal of Comparative and Physiological Psychology, Journal of Experimental Psychology, Journal of General Psychology, Journal of Psychology, Psychological Bulletin, Psychological Review, University of California Publications in Psychology, University of Iowa Studies in Child Welfare. The original source is cited in each case.

Stanford, California

E.R.H.

CONTENTS

CONTENTS

THEORIES *of* LEARNING

Chapter 1

THE NATURE OF LEARNING THEORIES

THE scientific study of learning is carried on primarily by psychologists. Psychology's claim to the field was staked in part by masterly pioneers such as Ebbinghaus (1885),[1] Bryan and Harter (1897, 1899), and Thorndike (1898). Those who have followed in their footsteps have been primarily psychologists. Professional educators have welcomed educational psychology as a foundation science upon which to build their practices, and studies of learning have gone on concurrently in laboratories of general psychology and laboratories of educational psychology, with interplay between the pure and applied fields. Under the circumstances, it is very natural for psychologists to feel that the study of learning belongs to them.

In addition to historical reasons, there is another basis on which to account for the psychologist's interest in learning. This is the centrality of learning in the more general systems of psychological theory. A scientist, along with the desire to satisfy his curiosity about the facts of nature, has a predilection for ordering his facts into systems of laws and theories. He is interested not only in verified facts and relationships, but in neat and parsimonious ways of summarizing these facts. Psychologists with a penchant for systems find a theory of learning essential because so much of man's diverse behavior is the result of learning. If the rich diversity of behavior is to be understood in accordance with a few principles, it is evident that some of these principles will have to do with the way in which learning comes about.

Many psychologists make explicit acknowledgment of the centrality of learning in their broader systems. Three examples may be cited.

1. In his definition of behavior as *molar* rather than as *molecular* (a

[1] References cited can be found by author and date in the list at the end of the book.

distinction that lies at the very heart of his system), Tolman[2] lists docility ("teachableness") as the crowning characteristic of such behavior. All molar behavior is docile. Hence learning becomes for Tolman an identifying character of that which he wishes to include as behavior.

2. Guthrie makes of learning the mark of mind. As he puts it:

> The ability to learn, that is, to respond differently to a situation because of past response to the situation, is what distinguishes those living creatures which common sense endows with minds. This is the practical descriptive use of the term "mind."[3]

3. Hull,[4] in introducing his theory of the behavior sciences, finds it natural to devote the first volume of his series to learning theory. He scarcely distinguishes between a theory of learning and a theory of behavior, so important is learning in his conception of behavior. While his books are primarily about learning, their titles reflect the intended generality: *Principles of behavior, A behavior system.*

Although not all psychologists give this same prominence to learning in their theories, the fact that others do makes it imperative for all to treat the problems of learning in one way or another. Hence the systematic aspects of learning theory have come to be important to all psychologists interested in more general theories.

THE DEFINITION OF LEARNING

What Learning Includes

There are many activities which everyone will agree count as illustrations of learning: acquiring a vocabulary, memorizing a poem, learning to operate a typewriter. There are other activities, not quite as obviously learned, which easily classify as learned, once you have reflected upon them. Among these are the acquiring of prejudices and preferences and other social attitudes and ideals, including the many skills involved in the social interplay with other people. Finally there are a number of activities whose acquisition is not usually classifiable as a gain or improvement because their utility, if such there be, is not readily demonstrable. Among these are tics, mannerisms, autistic gestures.

Such a pointing to illustrations of learning serves very well as a first approximation to a definition. It is, in fact, extremely difficult to write an entirely satisfactory definition. Although we are tempted to define

[2] Tolman (1932b), pages 14–16.
[3] Guthrie (1952), page 3.
[4] Hull (1943).

learning as improvement with practice, or as profiting by experience, we know very well that some learning is not improvement, and other learning is not desirable in its consequences. To describe it alternatively as any change with repetition confuses it with growth, fatigue, and other changes which may take place with repetition. The following definition may be offered provisionally:

> Learning is the process by which an activity originates or is changed through reacting to an encountered situation, provided that the characteristics of the change in activity cannot be explained on the basis of native response tendencies, maturation, or temporary states of the organism (e.g., fatigue, drugs, etc.).

The definition is not formally satisfactory because of the many undefined terms in it, but it will do to call attention to the problems involved in any definition of learning. The definition must distinguish between (1) the kinds of changes, and their correlated antecedents, which are included as learning, and (2) the related kinds of changes, and their antecedents, which are not classified as learning. We can now go on to consider some of the changes that are excluded by our provisional definition.

Native Response Tendencies versus Learning

The older catalogs of innate behavior usually included among unlearned activities the reflexes (such as pupillary constriction to light), the tropisms (such as a moth's dashing into a flame), and the instincts (such as a bird's nest-building). We may continue to acknowledge such activities as species characteristics. After a period during which it was rather emotionally tabooed, the term "instinct" is again part of the psychologist's vocabulary, referring to complex unlearned activity characteristic of a species.[5]

The problem of instinct versus learning is not solved by attempting to classify some behavior as instinctive in its entirety and other behavior as learned in its entirety. The in-between nature of behavior with large instinctive components is well illustrated by the experiments on *imprinting.*[6] A young duckling, for example, is prepared instinctively to accept a certain range of mother-figures, characterized by size, movement, and vocalization. Once such a mother-figure has been accepted and followed about, only this *particular* mother now satisfies the instinctive demand. The selected mother (who may be Professor Lorenz crawling on hands and knees) has become imprinted, and is the only "mother"

[5] Tinbergen (1951).
[6] E.g., Lorenz (1952), Ramsay (1951).

the duckling will now follow. Imprinting is then a form of learning, but a form very closely allied to the instinctive propensities of a particular kind of organism of a particular age. (We lack at present evidence for imprinting except in fowls and other birds.) The problem of distinguishing between the instinctive and learned components of the behavior illustrated by imprinting is an experimental problem, depending for its clarification upon the ingenuity of the experimenter in designing appropriate control experiments.

Maturation versus Learning

Growth is learning's chief competitor as a modifier of behavior. If a behavior sequence matures through regular stages irrespective of intervening practice, the behavior is said to develop through maturation and not through learning. If training procedures do not speed up or modify the behavior, such procedures are not causally important and the changes do not classify as learning. Relatively pure cases like the swimming of tadpoles and the flying of birds can be attributed primarily to maturation. Many activities are not as clear-cut, but develop through a complex interplay of maturation and learning. A convenient illustration is the development of language in the child. The child does not learn to talk until old enough, but the language which he learns is that which he hears. In such cases it is an experimental problem to isolate the effects of maturation and of learning. The ambiguity in such cases is one of fact, not of definition.

Fatigue versus Learning

When activities are repeated in rapid succession, there is often a loss in efficiency commonly attributed to fatigue. Such changes in performance are called work decrements in the experimental laboratory. The units of a work curve are like those of a practice curve: performance plotted against trials or repetitions. Hence the experimental arrangements in obtaining a work curve are essentially those of a learning procedure and, at first sight, it appears to be a form of question-begging to define the processes involved by the results obtained. It would be question-begging, however, only if we were to equate learning or fatigue with the change in performance. Actually *both* learning and fatigue are *inferences* from the performances, and it is permissible to make such inferences as the obtained performances require or suggest. Fatigue curves tend to show decreasing proficiency with repetition and recovery with rests. Learning curves ordinarily show gains with repetitions and forgetting over rests. These typical differences between learning effects and fatigue effects are evident enough, but the inferences from performance are made on somewhat more complex evidence. It is because of the complexity of these inferences that it is difficult to state a concise definition of learning which will conserve the learning inferences from performance while eliminating the fatigue inferences. The problem is logically the same as distinguishing changes due to maturation and to learning. But again the ambiguity is one of fact, not of definition.

Learning always must remain an inference from performance, and only confusion results if performance and learning are identified. A clear illustration is provided by performance under the influence of drugs or intoxicants. The fact that learned behavior fails when the organism is in such a state does not mean that forgetting has occurred. When the normal state has been restored, the performance may return to normal levels although there has been no intervening training.

Learning and the Nervous System

Some definitions of learning avoid the problem of performance by defining learning as a change in the central nervous system. So long as this change in the nervous system persists, temporary changes in state, such as those in fatigue and intoxication, affect performance but not learning. This definition asserts that learning is an inference, but it goes on to make a particular sort of inference about the role of the nervous system in learning. In view of the lack of knowledge of what actually does take place inside the organism when learning occurs, it is preferable not to include hypothetical neural processes in the definition of learning. We know that learning takes place. We should therefore be able to define what we are talking about without reference to any speculation whatever. This position does not deny that what we are calling learning may be a function of nervous tissue. It asserts only that it is not necessary to know anything about the neural correlates of learning in order to know that learning occurs.

Learning, Problem-Solving, and Reasoning

After you have learned, there are many things which you are able to do. If you can add and subtract, you can solve many novel problems without learning anything new. Where the solution of problems is relatively mechanical (as in addition and subtraction), the problem may be thought of as merely the exercise or utilization of a learned bit of behavior. When, however, there is greater novelty, more putting of things into relationship, as in reasoning or inventiveness, the process is interesting in its own light, and is not to be described simply as the running off of old habits.

The question has been raised, especially by Maier,[7] as to the appropriateness of including processes like reasoning within the same classification as other kinds of learning. My preference is for including them. Leaving them in does not prejudge their explanation. There may be several kinds of learning from the simpler to the more complex, not all following the same principles. If so, we have no assurance that the only sharp break comes when "reasoning" appears. Leaving the doubtful processes in simply asserts that a complete theory of learning must have something to say about reasoning, creative imagination, and inventiveness, in addition to what may be said about memorizing and retaining or about the acquisition of skill.

Definition Not a Major Source of Disagreement Between Theories

While it is extremely difficult to formulate a satisfactory definition of learning so as to include all the activities and processes which we wish to include and eliminate all those which we wish to exclude, the difficulty does not prove to be embarrassing because it is not a source of controversy as between theories. The controversy is over fact and interpretation, not over definition. There are occasional confusions over definition, but such confusions may usually be resolved by resort to pointing, to denotation. For the most part it is satisfactory to continue to mean by learning that which conforms to the usual socially accepted meaning that is part of our common heritage. Where distinctions have to be made with greater precision, they can be made through carefully specified types of inference from experiments.

SOME TYPICAL PROBLEMS CONFRONTING LEARNING THEORIES

The preferences of the theorist often lead him to concentrate upon one kind of learning situation to the neglect of the others. His theory is then appropriate to this situation, but becomes somewhat strained in relation to other problems of learning. A comprehensive learning theory ought to answer the questions which an intelligent non-psychologist might ask about the sorts of learning which are met in everyday life.

[7] Maier (1931).

A few such questions will be listed here, and then used later in appraising the theories which different writers present.

1. *What are the limits of learning?* Here is raised the question of the capacity to learn, of individual differences among learners of the same species and of unlike species. There are questions not only of persistent differences in capacity, but of change in capacity with age. Who can learn what? Are the limits set at birth? Do people get more or less alike with practice? These are the sorts of questions which it is natural to raise.

2. *What is the role of practice in learning?* The old adage that practice makes perfect has considerable racial wisdom behind it. Surely one learns to roller skate or to play the piano only by engaging in the activity. But what do we know about practice in detail? Does improvement depend directly on the amount of repetition? If not, what are its conditions? What are the most favorable circumstances of practice? Can repetitive drill be harmful as well as helpful to the learner?

3. *How important are drives and incentives, rewards and punishments?* Everybody knows in a general way that learning can be controlled by rewards and punishments, and that it is easier to learn something which is interesting than something which is dull. But are the consequences of rewards and punishments equal and opposite? Is there a difference between intrinsic and extrinsic motives in their effect upon learning? How do goals and purposes affect the process?

4. *What is the place of understanding and insight?* Some things are learned more readily if we know what we are about. We are better off as travelers if we can understand a timetable or a road map. We are helpless with differential equations unless we understand the symbols and the rules for their manipulation. But we can form vowels satisfactorily without knowing how we place our tongues, and we can read without being aware of our eye movements. Some things we appear to acquire blindly and automatically; some things we struggle hard to understand and can finally master only as we understand them. Is learning in one case different from what it is in the other?

5. *Does learning one thing help you learn something else?* This is the problem of formal discipline, as it used to be called, or of transfer of training, to use a more familiar contemporary designation. Some transfer of training must occur or there would be no use in developing a foundation for later learning. Nobody denies that it is easier to build a vocabulary in a language after you have a start in it, or that higher mathematics profits from mastery of basic concepts. The question is really

one of how much transfer takes place, under what conditions, and what its nature is.

6. *What happens when we remember and when we forget?* The ordinary facts of memory are mysterious enough, but in addition to familiar remembering and forgetting, our memories may play peculiar tricks on us. Some things we wish to remember are forgotten; some things we would be willing to forget continue to plague us. In cases of amnesia there are often gaps in memory, with earlier and later events remembered. Then there are the distortions of memory, in which we remember what did not happen, as is so strikingly demonstrated in testimony experiments. What is taking place? What control have we over processes involved?

These six questions will serve as useful ones to ask of each of the major theories. They suffice to illustrate the kinds of questions which give rise to theories of learning.

ISSUES ON WHICH LEARNING THEORIES DIVIDE

In the preceding section we asked certain common-sense questions about learning, on the assumption that a good learning theory should have something to say about each of them. Such questions can be raised before we know anything about actual learning theories. Now we wish to turn, however, to certain issues that have arisen in the formulation of actual theories. By alerting us in this way to what is to follow, we are better prepared for some of the differences in flavor that we shall meet as we review one theory after another.

Learning theories fall into two major families: *stimulus-response* theories and *cognitive* theories, but not all theories belong to these two families. The stimulus-response theories include such diverse members as the theories of Thorndike, Guthrie, Skinner, and Hull. The cognitive theories include at least those of Tolman, the classical gestalt psychologists, and Lewin. Not completely and clearly classifiable in these terms are the theories of functionalism, psychodynamics, and the probabilistic theories of the model builders. The lines of cleavage between the two families of theories are not the only cleavages within learning theories; there are other specific issues upon which theories within one family may differ.

General Issues Producing a Cleavage Between Stimulus-Response and Cognitive Theories

The cleavages between the theorists of opposing camps are difficult to understand because many of the distinctions which at first seem to contrast sharply later are found to be blurred. All reputable theorists accept a common logic of experimentation, so that disagreements over experimentally obtained facts are readily arbitrated. In the end, all the theorists accept a common body of demonstrated relationships, at the factual or descriptive level; any theorist who denied an established fact, a reproducible experimental finding, would lose status among his scientific colleagues, and his theories would no longer command respect. The first rule that we must be prepared to accept, as we judge the relative merits of different theories is this: *All the theorists accept all of the facts.* Some experimental findings are doubted when they are first announced and the status of findings *as fact* may for a long time be doubted; but once the status as fact is established, all accept the fact as true. Hence the differences between two theorists are primarily differences in interpretation. Both theories may fit the facts reasonably well, but the proponent of each theory believes his view to be the more fruitful. We shall be better prepared later on to discuss the ways in which theories get validated or modified after we are acquainted with them in more detail. For the present, we must be prepared to accept the historical truth that opposing theories have great survival value, and that an appeal to the facts as a way of choosing between theories is a very complex process, not nearly as decisive in practice as we might expect it to be.

We may begin by examining three kinds of preferences on which stimulus-response theorists tend to differ from cognitive theorists.

1. *"Peripheral" versus "Central" Intermediaries*

Ever since Watson promulgated the theory that thinking was merely the carrying out of subvocal speech movements, stimulus-response theorists have preferred to find response or movement intermediaries to serve as integrators of behavior sequences. Such movement-produced intermediaries can be classified as "peripheral" mechanisms, as contrasted with "central" (ideational) intermediaries. The stimulus-response theorist tends to believe that some sort of chained muscular responses, linked perhaps by fractional anticipatory goal responses, serve to keep a rat running to a distant food box. The cognitive theorist, on the other hand, more freely infers central brain processes, such as memories or expectations, as integrators of goal-seeking behavior. The differences in preference survive in this case because both kinds of theorists depend upon *inferences* from observed behavior, and the inferences are not directly verified in either case. It is potentially easier to verify tongue movements in thinking than it is to discover a revived memory trace in the brain, but in fact such verification is not offered with the precision necessary to compel belief in the theory. Under the circumstances, the choice between the peripheral and the central explanation is not forced, and favoring one or the other position depends upon more general systematic preferences.

2. *Acquisition of Habits versus Acquisition of Cognitive Structures*

The stimulus-response theorist and the cognitive theorist come up with different answers to the question, What is learned? The answer of the former is "habits"; the answer of the latter is "cognitive structures." The first answer appeals to common sense: we all know that we develop smooth-running skills by practicing them; what we learn is *responses.* But the second answer also appeals to common sense: if we locate a candy store from one starting point, we can find it from another because we "know where it is"; what we learn is *facts.* A smooth-running skill illustrates a learned habit; knowing alternate routes illustrates cognitive structure. If all habits were highly mechanical and stereotyped, variable nonhabitual behavior would force us to admit cognitive structures as part, at least, of what is learned. But the stimulus-response psychologist is satisfied that he can deduce from the laws of habit formation the behavior that the cognitive theorist believes supports his interpretation. Hence we cannot choose between the theories by coming up with "decisive" illustrations of what we learn, for both groups of theorists will offer explanations of all our examples. The competing theories would not have survived thus far had they been unable to offer such explanations.

3. *Trial and Error versus Insight in Problem-Solving*

When confronted with a novel problem, how does the learner reach solution? The stimulus-response psychologist finds the learner assembling his habits from the past appropriate to the new problem, responding either according to the elements that the new problem has in common with familiar ones, or according to aspects of the new situation which are similar to situations met before. If these do not lead to solution, the learner resorts to trial and error, bringing out of his behavior repertory one response after another until the problem is solved. The cognitive psychologist agrees with much of this description of what the learner does, but he adds interpretations not offered by the stimulus-response psychologist. He points out, for example, that granting all the requisite experience with the parts of a problem, there is no guarantee that the learner will be able to bring these past experiences to bear upon the solution. He may be able to solve the problem if it is presented in one form and not solve it if it is presented in another form, even though both forms require the same past experiences for their solution. According to the cognitive theorist, the preferred method of presentation permits a perceptual structuring leading to "insight," that is, to the understanding of the essential relationships involved. The stimulus-response psychologist tends, by preference, to look to the past history of the learner for the sources of solution, while the cognitive psychologist, by preference, looks to the contemporary structuring of the problem. His preference for the past does not require the stimulus-response psychologist to ignore the present structuring of the problem, nor does his preference for the present require the cognitive psychologist to ignore the past. One must not assume because there is a difference in preference that either theorist is blind to the totality of the learning situation. The facts of the insight experiment are accepted by both theorists, as are the facts of skill learning. We may remind ourselves again that no single experiment will demolish either the interpretation according to trial and error or the interpretation according to insight.

These three issues—peripheral versus central intermediaries, acquisition of habits versus acquisition of cognitive structures, and trial and error versus insight in problem-solving—give something of the flavor of the differences between these two major families of theories.

Specific Issues Not Confined to the Major Families

Some issues lie outside the conflict between the stimulus-response and the cognitive theories. Thus two stimulus-response psychologists may differ as to the role of reinforcement in learning, and two cognitive theorists may differ as to the necessity for a physiological explanation of learning. Three of these issues will suffice to alert us to the many problems that learning theorists face.

1. *Contiguity versus Reinforcement*

The oldest law of association is that ideas experienced together tend to become associated. This has come down in one form or another to the present day as the principle of association by contiguity, although it is now more fashionable to describe the association as between stimuli and responses rather than as between ideas. Several of our contemporary theorists accept the principle of contiguous association, notably Guthrie (a stimulus-response psychologist) and Tolman (a cognitive psychologist). Other theorists insist that learning does not take place through contiguity alone, unless there is some sort of reinforcement, some equivalent of reward or punishment.

2. *One or More Kinds of Learning?*

The contiguity-reinforcement dilemma may be resolved by accepting both, thus defining two varieties of learning. This solution has appealed to theorists such as Thorndike and Skinner and Mowrer. But these two varieties are not the only possibilities. Perhaps by using the common name "learning" to cover the acquisition of motor skills, the memorization of a poem, the solving of a geometrical puzzle, and the understanding of a period in history, we are deceiving ourselves by looking for common laws explanatory of processes that have little in common.

Hence the theorist has to choose between a single-factor theory and a multi-factor one. Tolman at one time pointed to the possibility of seven kinds of learning.

3. *Intervening Variables versus Hypothetical Constructs* [8]

We have already considered a contrast between two types of intermediary, the peripheral and the central types. But as theories become more refined, additional problems arise over the way in which inferred intermediaries should be specified. One kind of intermediary found in theories is a mathematical constant that reappears in various contexts, such as the acceleration of a free-falling body (g) that appears in equations describing the movement of a pendulum, the path of a projectile, or the way in which balls roll down inclined planes. Such an integrating intervening variable need have no properties other than those expressed in its units of measurement, that is, it need have no independent existence, apart from the functional relationships it has in its systematic context. This kind of integrating intermediary, without surplus meanings, is called an *intervening variable.* By contrast, some kinds of intermediaries are concrete, tangible, palpable, with properties of their own. Suppose, for example, we describe the behavior that results when a cat is confronted with a barking dog. The cat arches its back, hisses, its hair stands on end, and numerous changes take place within its digestive and circulatory system. Many of the internal changes can be *explained* by the

[8] MacCorquodale and Meehl (1948), Marx (1951b), Ginsberg (1954), Maze (1954).

use of a demonstrable intermediary, adrenin, the hormone of the adrenal glands. Suppose that before adrenin was isolated a theorist had inferred that some substance in the blood stream was causing the internal changes. This would have been a *hypothetical construct* at this stage, an inferred intermediary with palpable qualities. The discovery of adrenin would have then confirmed the hypothesis that such a substance in the blood stream was, in fact, causing many of the changes. Adrenin, as a substance, has other properties than those inferred from bodily changes in emotion. In this it differs from a mere intervening variable, which has no further properties beyond its systematic ones.

Those who hold with intervening variables in their learning theories are free to choose such variables as they wish, provided they serve their systematic purposes of producing a more coherent and parsimonious theory than can be produced without them. Those who prefer hypothetical constructs must seek either demonstrable movements or secretions (if they are peripheralists), or some physiological brain processes (if they are centralists). Again, the issue over intervening variables or hypothetical constructs is not confined to one or the other of the major theoretical families.

One extreme position is that we can do away with intermediaries entirely (Skinner). Thus, on this issue as on the others, we have nearly all possible views represented.

This brief introduction to three contrasts between stimulus-response theories and cognitive theories, and three issues that are not confined to the two major families, should make it clear that what seem to be diametrically opposed points of view may turn out to be based on differences in preference, each being possible of persuasive statement, and to a point justifiable. The opposed cases are each made by intelligent men of good will. We shall have to wait until later to consider how a more unified outlook may eventually be achieved.

THE PLAN OF THIS BOOK

The student of learning, conscientiously trying to understand learning phenomena and the laws regulating them, is likely to despair of finding a secure position if opposing points of view are presented as equally plausible, so that the choice between them is made arbitrary. He may fall into a vapid eclecticism, with the general formula, "There's much to be said on all sides."

This is not a necessary outcome of a serious attempt to understand opposing points of view. Science ought to be systematic, not eclectic, but a premature systematic position is likely to be dogmatic and bigoted just as an enduring eclecticism is likely to be superficial and opportunistic. It is possible to have systematization of knowledge as the goal without permitting the desire for system to blind the seeker after it to the truths unearthed by those with views unlike his own.

Throughout the chapters that follow, in presenting one after the other a variety of systematic positions, with illustrative experiments testing their assertions, the effort is made to show that there is something to be learned from each of them. Each has discovered phenomena which move us forward in our knowledge about learning. At the same time, no one has succeeded in providing a system invulnerable to criticism. The construction of a fully satisfactory theory of learning is likely to remain for a long time an uncompleted task.

SUPPLEMENTARY READINGS

GENERAL SOURCES ON THE PSYCHOLOGY OF LEARNING

DEESE, J. (1952) *The psychology of learning.*

HILGARD, E. R., and MARQUIS, D. G. (1940) *Conditioning and learning.*

McGEOCH, J. A., and IRION, A. L. (1952) *The psychology of human learning.* Revised.

OSGOOD, C. E. (1953) *Method and theory in experimental psychology.* Chapters 8–16.

STEVENS, S. S., ed. (1951) *Handbook of experimental psychology.* Chapters 13, 15–21, 34.

WOODWORTH, R. S., and SCHLOSBERG, H. (1954) *Experimental psychology.* Revised. Chapters 18–26.

CONTRASTING POINTS OF VIEW TOWARD LEARNING

ESTES, W. K., KOCH, S., MACCORQUODALE, K., MEEHL, P. E., MUELLER, C. G., Jr., SCHOENFELD, W. N., and VERPLANCK, W. S. (1954) *Modern learning theory.*

McCONNELL, T. R., and others (1942) *The psychology of learning.* Natl. Soc. Stud. Educ., 41st Yearbook, Part II.

MARX, M. H., ed. (1951) *Psychological theory: contemporary readings.* Chapter 11.

STOLUROW, L. M., ed. (1953) *Readings in learning.*

THORPE, L. P., and SCHMULLER, A. M. (1954) *Contemporary theories of learning, with applications to education and psychology.*

The *Annual Review of Psychology,* appearing first in 1950, each year reviews critically the current experimental and theoretical literature on learning. The reviewers up to the time of writing have been A. W. Melton (1950), C. E. Buxton (1951), H. F. Harlow (1952), B. J. Underwood (1953), E. C. Tolman and L. Postman (1954), and K. MacCorquodale (1955). The reviews are valuable not only as indexes to the literature but for the trends in experiment and theory detected by the reviewers.

Chapter 2

THORNDIKE'S CONNECTIONISM

FOR nearly half a century one learning theory dominated all others in America, despite numerous attacks upon it and the rise of its many rivals. It is the theory of Edward L. Thorndike (1874–1949), first announced in his *Animal intelligence* (1898). Its pre-eminence has been aptly assessed by Tolman:

> The psychology of animal learning—not to mention that of child learning—has been and still is primarily a matter of agreeing or disagreeing with Thorndike, or trying in minor ways to improve upon him. Gestalt psychologists, conditioned-reflex psychologists, sign-gestalt psychologists—all of us here in America seem to have taken Thorndike, overtly or covertly, as our starting point.[1]

The basis of learning accepted by Thorndike in his earliest writings was association between sense impressions and impulses to action. Such an association came to be known as a "bond" or a "connection." Because it is these bonds or connections which become strengthened or weakened in the making and breaking of habits, Thorndike's system has sometimes been called a "bond" psychology or simply "connectionism." As such it is the original stimulus-response or S-R psychology of learning.

CONNECTIONISM BEFORE 1930

There were few changes in Thorndike's theory between 1898 and 1930. During these years Thorndike devoted himself largely to applications of his established theory to problems of educational and social importance. Because of the stability of the concepts during these years, it is possible to select any one of Thorndike's many publications to serve as a guide to his theory. The major work, from which most of the quotations in what follows have been taken, is the three-volume *Educational*

[1] Tolman (1938a), page 11.

psychology (1913–1914), which represents the system at the height of its popularity.

The most characteristic form of learning of both lower animals and man is identified by Thorndike as trial-and-error learning, or, as he preferred to call it later, learning by selecting and connecting. The learner is confronted by a problem situation in which he has to reach a goal such as escape from a problem-box or attainment of food. He does this by selecting the appropriate response from a number of possible responses. A trial is defined by the length of time (or number of errors) involved in a single reaching of the goal. Thorndike's earliest experiments were of this kind, done chiefly with cats, although some experiments with dogs, fish, and monkeys were included.[2] The typical experiment is that of a hungry cat confined in a box with a concealed mechanism operated by a latch. If the cat correctly manipulates the latch, the door opens, and the cat gains access to the food outside. The first trials are characterized by a great amount of clawing, biting, and dashing about before the latch is moved. The score, as measured in elapsed time, is high. On succeeding trials the time scores get lower, but slowly and irregularly. It is this gradualness which suggests that the cat does not really "catch on" to the manner of escape, but learns it instead by the stamping in of correct responses and the stamping out of incorrect ones.

Experiments like this have become so commonplace that the importance of their introduction by Thorndike is easily overlooked. By contrast with the other laboratory arrangements within which learning was studied, the problem-box brought to the fore the problems of motivation, of rewards and of punishments. The typical laboratory experiments on learning before Thorndike were either the experiments introduced by Ebbinghaus on the memorization and recall of verbal materials or the experiments on acquistion of skill exemplified by the Bryan and Harter studies of learning telegraphy. In both of these, motivation remains in the background as one of the contextual features, along with learning capacity and other factors not entering as manipulated variables. In his "law of effect" Thorndike brought motivation into the foreground. Trials were defined not by a repetition of a list (Ebbinghaus) or by so many minutes of practice (Bryan and Harter) but by the performance prior to successful (or unsuccessful) goal attainment.

Thorndike saw that in his law of effect he had added an important supplement to the familiar law of habit formation through repetition:

[2] Thorndike (1898) (1911).

But practice without zeal—with equal comfort at success and failure—does *not* make perfect, and the nervous system grows *away* from the modes in which it is *exercised with resulting discomfort.* When the law of effect is omitted—when habit-formation is reduced to the supposed effect of mere repetition—two results are almost certain. By the resulting theory, little in human behavior can be explained by the law of habit; and by the resulting practice, unproductive or extremely wasteful forms of drill are encouraged.[3]

The interest in rewards and punishments which grew out of his experiments with animals continued naturally enough as he turned his attention to learning as it occurs in schools. There the arguments over punishment, promotion, school marks, and other incentive devices were rife, even though academic psychologists had not yet awakened to the centrality of motivational concepts.

Thorndike's experiments on animals had a very profound influence upon his thinking about human learning. He became convinced, contrary to the then popular beliefs, that animal behavior was little mediated by ideas. Responses were said to be made directly to the situation as sensed. While he did not go so far as to deny ideation among animals, he was convinced that the great bulk of their learning could be explained by the direct binding of acts to situations, unmediated by ideas. A comparison of the learning curves of human subjects with those of animals led him to believe that the same essentially mechanical phenomena disclosed by animal learning are the fundamentals of human learning also. Although always aware of the greater subtlety and range of human learning, he showed a strong preference for understanding more complex learning in terms of the simpler, and for identifying the simpler forms of human learning with that of animals.

Both theory and practice need emphatic and frequent reminders that man's learning is fundamentally the action of the laws of readiness, exercise, and effect. He is first of all an associative mechanism working to avoid what disturbs the life-processes of the neurones. If we begin by fabricating imaginary powers and faculties, or if we avoid thought by loose and empty terms, or if we stay lost in wonder at the extraordinary versatility and inventiveness of the higher forms of learning, we shall never understand man's progress or control his education.[4]

The systematic position is best understood through the three laws to which he refers: readiness, exercise, and effect. It is in accordance with these laws that animal and human learning takes place.

[3] Thorndike (1913b), page 22.
[4] Thorndike (1913b), page 23.

The Law of Readiness

The law of readiness is an accessory principle which describes a physiological substratum for the law of effect. It states the circumstances under which a learner tends to be satisfied or annoyed, to welcome or to reject. There are three such circumstances: [5]

1. When a conduction unit is ready to conduct, conduction by it is satisfying, nothing being done to alter its action.
2. For a conduction unit ready to conduct not to conduct is annoying, and provokes whatever response nature provides in connection with that particular annoying lack.
3. When a conduction unit unready for conduction is forced to conduct, conduction by it is annoying.

Although "conduction units" were referred to in his earlier writings as though he were talking about actual neurones, Thorndike did not, in fact, pay much attention to neuroanatomical details. He talked about neurones to be clear that he was talking about direct impulses to action, and not about "consciousness" or "ideas." It must be remembered that his system antedated behaviorism, even though its emphasis was definitely toward an objective account of behavior. The physiological language was the most available vocabulary for the objectivist prior to the rise of behaviorism. Actually Thorndike's "conduction units" have no precise physiological meaning. It would be difficult, for example, to understand how a physiological unit unready to conduct could be made to conduct.

If for "conduction unit" a term such as "action tendency" is substituted, the psychological meaning of Thorndike's law of readiness becomes clearer. When an action tendency is aroused through preparatory adjustments, sets, attitudes, and the like, fulfillment of the tendency in action is satisfying, non-fulfillment is annoying. Readiness thus means a preparation for action. Thorndike uses the illustration of an animal running after its prey, getting ready all the while for jumping upon it and seizing it. He describes a child seeing an attractive object at a distance, getting ready to approach it, seize it, and manipulate it. He says that it is the neurones which prepare prophetically for later actions in the sequence. This somewhat objectionable manner of describing what goes on need not detract from the reality of the psychological observation that satisfaction and frustration depend upon what the organism is prepared to do.

There is another kind of readiness familiar to educators. This is

[5] The wording follows Thorndike (1913a), page 128.

illustrated by the use of "reading readiness" to refer to the child's reaching a maturity level appropriate to the beginning of reading. Thorndike did not use his law of readiness in this way, and it would be historically inaccurate to construe his law of readiness as an anticipation of maturational readiness. There is, of course, a logical relationship between the two kinds of readiness, because interests and motives mature along with capacities. But Thorndike's readiness was a law of preparatory adjustment, not a law about growth.

The Earlier Law of Exercise

The law of exercise refers to the strengthening of connections with practice (Law of Use) and to the weakening of connections or forgetting when practice is discontinued (Law of Disuse). Strengthening is defined by the increase in probability that the response will be made when the situation recurs. This probability may be either a *greater* probability of occurrence if the situation is repeated immediately, or an *equal* probability persisting longer in time. That is, a stronger connection is in a favored competitive position relative to other habits, either at the time of its strengthening or if tested after there has been opportunity for forgetting.

The definition of strength by probability of occurrence[6] has a very contemporary ring. It is acceptable in itself to those who might go on to reject the structural basis assigned by Thorndike to changes in strength of connections. Although changes were said to occur in neurones and synapses, even in his earlier writings the precise properties attributed to neurones were cautiously stated and not actually essential to the theory.

The kinds of phenomena falling under the law of exercise are chiefly those of repetitive habits, as in rote memorizing or the acquiring of muscular skills. Learning curves in which performance is plotted against trials represent the quantification of the law of use; forgetting curves give quantitative details for the law of disuse. During the period under discussion, Thorndike accepted uncritically the prevailing principle of learning by doing, even though he had criticized the use of the principle independent of the law of effect. He later altered his position and greatly reduced the emphasis upon the law of exercise.

The Earlier Law of Effect

The law of effect refers to the strengthening or weakening of a connection as a result of its consequences. When a modifiable connection

[6] Thorndike (1913b), page 2.

is made and is accompanied by or followed by a satisfying state of affairs, the strength of the connection is increased; if the connection is made and followed by an annoying state of affairs, its strength is decreased.

Two chief objections have been made to the law of effect by its critics. At the height of behaviorism it was objected that satisfaction and annoyance were subjective terms, inappropriate for use in describing animal behavior. But Thorndike was in reality ahead of his critics, for he had early stated what he meant by such states of affairs in what would today be called operational terms:

> By a satisfying state of affairs is meant one which the animal does nothing to avoid, often doing things which maintain or renew it. By an annoying state of affairs is meant one which the animal does nothing to preserve, often doing things which put an end to it.[7]

These definitions are not circular, so far as the law of effect is concerned. That is, the states of affairs characterized as satisfying and as annoying are specified independently of their influence upon modifiable connections. The law of effect then states what may be expected to happen to preceding modifiable connections which are followed by such specified states. The objection that Thorndike was lacking in objectivity in the statement of the law of effect is not a valid one.

The second objection was that the backward effect of a state of affairs on something now past in time is not conceivable. The past is gone, effects can be felt only in the present, or perhaps revealed in the future. The criticism, like the first, is a faulty one. The effect is revealed in the probability of occurrence of the response when the situation next occurs; whether or not such an effect occurs is a matter of observation and experiment, not something to be denied on a priori grounds. In fairness to his critics, it must be said that Thorndike's insistence on a backward influence upon neurones encouraged such objections to the law of effect. Some of his statements were indeed objectionable, but the objectionable statements never did express the essence of the law of effect, which is essentially an empirical matter.

Translated into more familiar words, Thorndike is saying in this law that rewards or successes further the learning of the rewarded behavior, whereas punishments or failures reduce the tendency to repeat the behavior leading to punishment, failure, or annoyance. So much would merely be a reassertion of common observations. But he went further and insisted that the action of consequences is direct and need

[7] Thorndike (1913b), page 2.

not be mediated by ideas. In this insistence his law of effect anticipates the reinforcement principle adopted in many conditioned-response theories. The later changes in theory reduced the importance of annoyers relative to satisfiers and added some new phenomena, but the central importance of a modified law of effect persisted in Thorndike's final statements of his position.

Subordinate Laws

The major laws of readiness, exercise, and effect were said to have five subsidiary laws applicable to both animal and human learning.[8] Among these occurs one, associative shifting, which is so similar to one variety of conditioned response theory that it deserves special mention.

In a short account of Thorndike's views, the impression may be given that Thorndike was a very systematic writer. His "system," apart from a few persistent preferences, is in fact a rather loose collection of rules and suggestions. What was called a "law" at any one time was a statement which at the time apeared to Thorndike to have some generality of application. No effort was made to retain internal coherence among the concepts used, or to establish any genuine relationship of co-ordination or subordination among the laws. The five "subordinate laws" to be discussed are principles which seemed to Thorndike somewhat less important than the major laws of readiness, exercise, and effect. They are not related to the major laws in any clear manner, and in later writings they were occasionally omitted, occasionally revived.

1. *Multiple response.* The first of the five principles is that of multiple response or varied reaction. In order for a response to be rewarded, it must occur. When he faces a problem the learner tries one thing after another. When the appropriate behavior is stumbled upon, success follows and learning is possible. Were the organism unable to vary its responses, the correct solution might never be elicited.

2. *Set or attitude.* The second principle is that learning is guided by a total attitude or "set" of the organism. Responses are determined in part by enduring adjustments characteristic of individuals raised in a given culture. But they are also influenced by more momentary tendencies. The attitude or set determines not only what the person will do, but what will satisfy or annoy him. Thorndike says that a more ambitious golfer will be annoyed by shots which the more modest would cherish. This principle is related to a series of conceptions coming to prominence later in discussions of level of aspiration.

[8] Thorndike (1913b), pages 23–31.

3. *Prepotency of elements.* The third principle states that the learner is able to react selectively to prepotent elements in the problem. That is, a man can pick out the essential item and base his responses upon it, neglecting other adventitious features which might confuse a lower animal. This ability to deal with the relevant parts of situations makes analytical and insightful learning possible.

4. *Response by analogy.* The fourth principle is that of assimilation, or response by analogy. How does man react to novel situations? He responds to a new situation as he would to some situation like it, or he responds to some element in the new situation to which he has a response in his repertory. Responses can always be explained by old acquisitions, together with inborn tendencies to respond; there is nothing mysterious about responses to novelty.

5. *Associative shifting.* The fifth of these subsidiary laws is called associative shifting. The fundamental notion is that if a response can be kept intact through a series of changes in the stimulating situation, it may finally be given to a totally new stimulus. The stimulating situation is changed first by addition, then by subtraction, until nothing from the original situation remains. Thorndike illustrates by the act of teaching a cat to stand up at command. First a bit of fish is dangled before the cat while you say, "Stand up." After enough trials, by proper arrangement, the fish may be omitted, and the oral signal will alone evoke the response. The most general statement of the principle of associative shifting is that we may "get any response of which a learner is capable associated with any situation to which he is sensitive." [9] This is obviously related to that type of conditioning in which the process is described as substituting a conditioned stimulus for an unconditioned one. Thorndike noted the similarity, but believed the conditioned response to be a more specialized case under the broader principle of associative shifting. While in his earlier writings associative shifting was but the fifth of the subordinate laws, in later books it was "promoted," becoming a kind of learning second to that by selecting and connecting.[10]

Controlling Learning

There is always some danger of misunderstanding a systematic writer's influence if attention is confined to the more abstract and generalized laws which he proposes, to the neglect of some of the accessory details which give both flavor and body to his teaching. Thorndike as

[9] Thorndike (1913b), page 15.
[10] Thorndike (1935), pages 191–197.

early as 1913 was giving much more attention to the dynamics of learning than a formal consideration of his laws suggests.

Within the framework of his primary laws, he saw three considerations which affected the teacher's problem in using them in the classroom.[11] These were: (1) ease of identification of the bonds to be formed or broken; (2) ease of identification of the states of affairs which should satisfy or annoy; and (3) ease of application of satisfaction and annoyance to the identified states of affairs. The teacher and the learner must know the characteristics of a good performance in order that practice may be appropriately arranged. Errors must be diagnosed so that they will not be repeated. When there is lack of clarity about what is being taught or learned, practice may be strengthening the wrong connections as well as the right ones. At the same time, needed connections may be weakened by disuse. It is especially hard to teach imagination, force, and beauty in literary expression because it is difficult to be specific about the conduct which should be made satisfying at the time it occurs. The importance of specificity runs throughout Thorndike's writings. As we shall see later, this is at once a source of strength in his system and one of its points of vulnerability.

But Thorndike's advice is not limited to the application of his major laws. He refers also to a number of motivational features not readily deducible from the laws of readiness and effect. Five aids to improvement he lists as the interest series.[12] These he believes to be commonly accepted by educators:

1. Interest in the work
2. Interest in improvement
3. Significance
4. Problem-attitude
5. Attentiveness

To these five he added two more which he felt were open to some dispute. They were the absence of irrelevant emotion and the absence of worry. In his emphasis upon satisfiers and annoyers he is not talking about "crude emotional states," which he believes are to be avoided.

> In the case of improvement in skill, the balance turns again toward freedom from all the crude emotional states and even from all the finer excitements, save the intrinsic satisfyingness of success and a firm repudiation of errors which can hardly be called exciting.[13]

[11] Thorndike (1913b), pages 213–217.
[12] Thorndike (1913b), pages 217–226.
[13] Thorndike (1913b), pages 226–227.

Thus to his rather harsh and brittle doctrine of specificity of connections he adds informal considerations which do much to temper it. The active role of the learner, who comes to the learning situation with needs and problems which determine what will be satisfying to him, is recognized implicitly in the commentary on the laws, although it lacks explicit statement in the laws themselves. It is probably these accessory features which have commanded ardent support by Thorndike's followers, while it is the more abstract features which have been the focus of attack by those who have disagreed with him.

The Identical-Elements Theory of Transfer

Schools are publicly supported in the hope that more general uses will be made of what is learned in school. To some extent all schooling is aimed at a kind of transfer beyond the school. Whether the proper way to achieve this end may turn out to be to teach more formal subject matter, like mathematics and the classics, or to give more attention to practical subject matter like manual training and social studies, the problem is a central one for educators.

Thorndike early interested himself in the problem. His theory began to take form in an experimental study done in collaboration with Woodworth [14] and was formally stated in his early *Educational psychology* (1903). The theory proposes that transfer depends upon the presence of identical elements in the original learning and in the new learning which it facilitates. These may be identities of either substance or procedure. Thus the ability to speak and write well are important in all schoolroom classes and many tasks of ordinary life. Hence mastery of these skills will serve in different pursuits, and transfer will be effected through what the different situations require in common. The substance of what is required in different situations may be unlike, but there may be procedures in common. The procedures of looking things up in such diverse sources as a dictionary, a cookbook, and a chemist's handbook have much in common, despite the unlike contents of the three kinds of book. If an activity is learned more easily because another activity was learned first, it is only because the two activities overlap. Learning is always specific, never general: when it appears to be general, it is only because new situations have much of old situations in them.

Intelligence as measured by tests may be thought of as to some extent a measure of the transfer-capacity of an individual. That is, the test measures the ability to give right answers in relatively novel situations.

[14] Thorndike and Woodworth (1901).

It is logically sound that Thorndike's theory of intelligence is, like his theory of transfer, a matter of specific connections. The more bonds the individual has which can be used, the more intelligent he is.

Thorndike's specificity doctrines of transfer and of intelligence have been highly influential and have led to a great deal of experimental work. Although the problems of the nature of and measurement of intelligence lie outside the scope of this volume, there will be occasion later to consider some of the alternative explanations of transfer.

During the stable period of Thorndike's system there were many changes in psychological climate, but these left him unruffled. The rise of behaviorism and the new importance attributed to the conditioned response affected him but little, because the new enthusiasts were talking a congenial language, even when they included him in their sweeping attacks on everything which preceded them. The attacks by the gestalt psychologists in the '20's were more telling, and he began later to meet some of their criticisms. But it was his own experiments which led him to come before the International Congress of Psychology in New Haven in September, 1929, with the statement, "I was wrong." He there announced two fundamental revisions in his laws of exercise and effect which became the basis for a number of publications dating from 1930.

CONNECTIONISM AFTER 1930

The revisions of his fundamental laws were reported by Thorndike in a number of journal articles and monographs with various collaborators, the main results being gathered in two large volumes under the titles *The fundamentals of learning* (1932a) and *The psychology of wants, interests, and attitudes* (1935). The law of exercise was practically renounced as a law of learning, only a trivial amount of strengthening of connections being left as a function of mere repetition. The law of effect remained only half true, the weakening effects of annoying consequences being renounced. For the two central laws there was substituted half the original law of effect.

Disproof of the Law of Exercise

The type of experiment used to disprove the law of exercise was that in which repetition went on under circumstances in which the law of effect could not be applicable. For example, repeated attempts to draw a line exactly 3 inches long while blindfolded did not lead to improvement, no matter how frequent the repetitions. Practice brings improvement only because it permits other factors to be effective; practice itself does nothing. Thorndike intended that his "repeal" of the law of exercise should be a safeguard against its misuse, not a denial of the importance of controlled practice. The laws of habit strengthening must be those of the conditions under which practice takes place; mere repetition of situations is not enough. If the person is informed each time after his attempt to draw a 3-inch line that his product is too long or too short, he will improve with repetition.[15]

The law of exercise was not, in fact, fully repealed. It is said that repetition of *situations* produces no change in strength of connections, but repetition of *connections* may produce a small advantage for that connection as against competing connections attached to the same situation. The strengthening is almost negligible; for all practical purposes, connections get strengthened by being rewarded, not by just occurring. In one of those curious and optimistically quantitative summaries which Thorndike occasionally made, he concluded that a single occurrence followed by reward strengthens a connection about six times as much as it would be strengthened by merely occurring.[16]

The Truncated Law of Effect

A number of experiments yielded data showing that the effects of reward and punishment were not equal and opposite, as had been implied in earlier statements of the effects of satisfiers and of annoyers. Instead, under conditions in which symmetrical action was possible, reward appeared to be much more powerful than punishment. This conclusion, if confirmed, is of immense social importance in such fields of application as education and criminology.

One of these experiments was done with chicks.[17] A simple maze gave the chick the choice of three pathways, one of which led to "freedom, food, and company"—that is, to an open compartment where there were other chicks eating. The wrong choices led to confinement for 30 seconds. Statistics were kept on the tendencies to return to the preceding choice if it had led to reward, and to avoid the preceding choice if it led to punishment. Thorndike interpreted his findings as follows: "The results of all comparisons by all methods tell the same story. Re-

[15] Trowbridge and Cason (1932). There is indeed more regularizing of performance in his own experiments than Thorndike believed, according to recomputation of his data by Seashore and Bavelas (1941).

[16] Thorndike (1940), page 14.

[17] Thorndike (1932b).

warding a connection always strengthened it substantially; punishing it weakened it little or not at all." [18]

The corresponding experiment with human subjects consists of a multiple-choice vocabulary test. For example, a Spanish word is given with five English words, one of which is its correct translation. A second and a third word follow, and so on through a list, each word with alternative translations arranged in the same manner. The subject guesses the word which is correct, underlines it, and then hears the experimenter say *Right* ("rewarded" response) or *Wrong* ("punished" response). How will he change his responses the next time through the list? As with the chicks, reward leads to repetition of the rewarded connection, but punishment does not lead to a weakening of the punished connection. In six experiments of this general sort, Thorndike concluded that the announcement of *Wrong* did not weaken connections enough to counterbalance the slight increase in strength gained from just occurring.[19]

Thorndike and his staff went on to collect a series of testimonials about the relative efficacy of rewards and punishments from published biographies and other sources, going back many years. The almost universal evidence of the greater beneficial effect of reward than of punishment gives practical support to the findings of the experiments, which otherwise would be criticized as too far removed from ordinary life.[20]

There were some statistical difficulties in Thorndike's interpretations of his data which caused him to underestimate the significance of punishment. On the whole, however, he probably did a service through calling attention to the asymmetry of the effects of reward and of punishment.

As in the disproof of the law of exercise, the repeal of the principle of weakening by annoying after-effects is not absolute. It is only direct weakening which is denied. Punishments do, according to Thorndike, affect learning indirectly. Thorndike says that their indirect effect comes chiefly from leading the animal to do something in the presence of the annoyer which makes him less likely to repeat the original connection. But this is not necessarily the case.

> An annoyer which is attached to a modifiable connection may cause the animal to feel fear or chagrin, jump back, run away, wince, cry, perform the same act as before but more vigorously, or whatever else is in his repertory as a response to that annoyer in that situation. But there is no evidence that it takes

[18] Thorndike (1932b), page 58.
[19] Thorndike (1932a), page 288.
[20] Thorndike (1935), pages 135–144; 248–255.

away strength from the physiological basis of the connection in any way comparable to the way in which a satisfying after-effect adds strength to it.[21]

Thorndike was less successful in his attempts to explain the action of effect than in demonstrating that there are phenomena to which his principles apply. He distinguished between a direct *confirming influence* and the *informative influence* of rewards. Control of behavior according to the information supplied by its consequences implies mediation by ideas of the sort, "If I do this, I get fed; if I do that, I get slapped." Thorndike believed that he kept this kind of deliberation at a minimum in his experiments, so that what he had to explain was the direct confirmatory reaction which he said was responsible for the strengthening of responses through reward. This confirming reaction is vaguely described as an "unknown reaction of the neurones" which is aroused by the satisfier and strengthens the connection upon which it impinges.[22] The confirming reaction is said to be independent of sensory pleasures, and independent of the intensity of the satisfier. It is highly selective, depending upon aroused drives or "overhead control in the brain." While such an account is far from satisfactory, it at least helps to show where Thorndike stood. He was against mediation by ideas, as an interpretation of effect according to information would imply. At the same time, he recognized the complexity of the reinforcement process and was not committed to a simple hedonism. The law of effect was for him no longer a law of affect, as Hollingworth once named it.[23]

Belongingness

In addition to the revisions of the laws of exercise and effect, several new terms entered as Thorndike's system was revised. One of these, *belongingness,* by its recognition of an organizational principle foreign to the structure of Thorndike's theory of specificity and mechanical action, made concessions to the gestalt psychologists.[24] According to this principle, a connection is more easily learned if the response belongs to the situation, and an after-effect does better if it belongs to the connection it strengthens. Thus a series of sentences may be read, each of the form "John is a butcher. Henry is a carpenter." The association John-butcher is a stronger one following such a reading than the association butcher-Henry, even though the latter connection is based on more nearly contiguous items. The reason is that a subject and predicate belong to-

[21] Thorndike (1932a), pages 311–313.
[22] Thorndike (1933c).
[23] Hollingworth (1931).
[24] The point was made early by Brown and Feder (1934). See also Guthrie (1936b).

gether in a way in which the end of one sentence and the beginning of another do not. The belongingness of a reward or punishment depends upon its appropriateness in satisfying an aroused motive or want in the learner, and in its logical or informative relationship to the activities rewarded or punished. Thus to be rewarded by having your thirst quenched when you lift a glass of cool water to your lips is reward with belonging. If the same series of movements led sporadically to an electric shock on your ankle, that would be punishment without belonging. Although Thorndike states that after-effects are influential without either belongingness or relevance, he points out at the same time that they are more effective when they do belong and when they are relevant.[25]

While the principle of belongingness may be interpreted as something of a concession, the principle of *polarity* is emphasized as defying gestalt principles.[26] The principle of polarity is that connections act more easily in the direction in which they were formed than in the opposite direction. If you have learned the items of a German-English vocabulary, it is easier to respond to the German word by its English equivalent than to the English word by its German equivalent. If a connection is thought of as a new whole, Thorndike contends, the polarity principle ought not be important. It ought then to be as easy to dissociate parts from the whole in one direction as in another.

Other new terms introduced, such as "impressiveness," "identifiability," "availability," and "mental systems," represent informal extensions of notions already latent in the earlier writings.

Discovery of the Spread of Effect

In 1933 a new kind of experimental evidence was offered in support of the law of effect, evidence described as the *spread of effect*.[27] The experiments purported to show that the influence of a rewarding state of affairs acts not only on the connection to which it belongs but on adjacent connections both before and after the rewarded connection, the effect diminishing with each step that the connection is removed from the rewarded one. The effect acts to strengthen even punished connections in the neighborhood of the rewarded one. The experiments lent support to the automatic and mechanical action of effect. A characteristic experiment was that in which the subject was asked to state a number from 1 to 10 following the announcement of a stimulus word by the

[25] Thorndike (1935), pages 52–61.
[26] Thorndike (1932a), page 158.
[27] Thorndike (1933a) (1933b).

experimenter. The experimenter then called his response *Right* or *Wrong*, these "rewards" and "punishments" conforming either to a prearranged assignment of correct numbers to each word, or to some systematic pattern of "rights" or "wrongs." In either case, the assignment of numbers from the point of view of the subject is arbitrary, and the cue to repeat the number first assigned or to change it comes from what the experimenter says following each word. The lists are so long that the subject cannot recall on the second trial just what was done on the first one.

After the list has been read a number of times in this manner, the responses of the subject are classified to find the number of times the response was repeated. Not only are the rewarded responses repeated more often than the others, but responses called *Wrong* are repeated beyond chance expectancy if they occur near in time to a response called *Right*. To some extent the phenomena included in the spread of effect come nearest to a "discovery" in the whole of Thorndike's work. Because of the novelty of the phenomena and their systematic relevance, typical experiments in support of and critical of the spread of effect are reviewed below as illustrative of Thorndike's influence upon experimentation in the field of learning.

EXPERIMENTS ON THE SPREAD OF EFFECT

The spread of effect is the most characteristic feature of contemporary connectionism. It illustrates at once both the relative potency of rewards and punishments and the semi-automatic manner in which effects act upon connections, whether or not they "belong." To the extent that the phenomena of the spread of effect stand upon firm ground, Thorndike's basic conceptions are buttressed against attacks by his critics.

Punishment More Effective Than Thorndike Believed

Thorndike had already changed his mind about the effectiveness of annoyers in weakening connections before the spread-of-effect experiments were announced. He interpreted his results on the spread of effect as confirming his recently acquired belief in the relative ineffectiveness of punishments in weakening connections. The spread of effect is then, to him, a spread of positive effects, a gradient of reward. Reward is said to strengthen even neighboring punished connections.

In several of his experiments, Thorndike made a faulty assumption about the baseline of chance expectation. He assumed that one alternative in a series of multiple possibilities was as likely to occur as another.

That is, if there were four choices, by chance each should occur 25 per cent of the time. When the opportunity is given to repeat the responses, the same one chosen last time should be chosen again in 25 per cent of the cases, if the tendency to respond has been neither strengthened nor weakened during the first occurrence. In practice this chance repetition seldom occurs, for whatever predisposition leads to a preference for one of the choices the first time tends to favor that same choice the next time. Suppose there are four alternatives, and the series is presented twice. If there is a 35 per cent agreement on choices between the first and the second time, this does not mean that the gain over chance resulted from repetition. The above-chance preference may have been there on the first trial. This criticism has been made by Stephens (1934) and Hull (1935d), among others, and empirical results show that punishment does in fact lead to fewer repetitions. The result of Thorndike's use of too low a base for chance repetition was automatically to assign too much strengthening to rewards and too little weakening to punishments. The asymmetry could be entirely a statistical artifact.

Tilton, a former associate of Thorndike, repeated the spread-of-effect experiment with careful controls to determine what the empirical level of repetition would be without the saying of *Right* and *Wrong*, and then proceeded to plot the spread of effect on either side of a rewarded and a punished response.[28] He made a correction also for a serial position effect, that is, for a tendency to repeat the same response to items near the beginning and the end of the list. When correction is made, it is found that the effects of *Right* and *Wrong* are about alike, the announcement of *Wrong* decreasing repetitions about as much as *Right* increases them. A replotting of Tilton's results is shown in Figures 1 and 2.

Tilton's study shows that there is a tendency for punished responses in the neighborhood of reward to be repeated more frequently than such responses remote from reward. Their punishment (being called *Wrong*) suffices however, even one step from reward, to lead to *less* repetition than would occur if the response were neither rewarded nor punished (Figure 1). Similarly, when a response called *Wrong* (punished) occurs in the midst of a series of rewarded responses, the neighboring rewarded responses are repeated less frequently than they would have been had they not been in the neighborhood of the punished response. Again, however, their reward (being called *Right*) is enough to lead to their repetition at a *greater* frequency than that represented by the neutral baseline (Figure 2).

[28] Tilton (1939) (1945).

Because Tilton used the conventional method of obtaining spread of effect, repeating lists over and over again, and allowing right responses and wrong responses to appear with any degree of separation, he had to make a rather elaborate analysis in order to exhibit just what was in fact happening within his experiment. Martens (1946) introduced a corrective by arranging the experimental situation so that each position before and after reward has an equal opportunity to be represented in the final spread of effect pattern. This she did by limiting the training and testing to one trial each on each list. That is, on one trial through

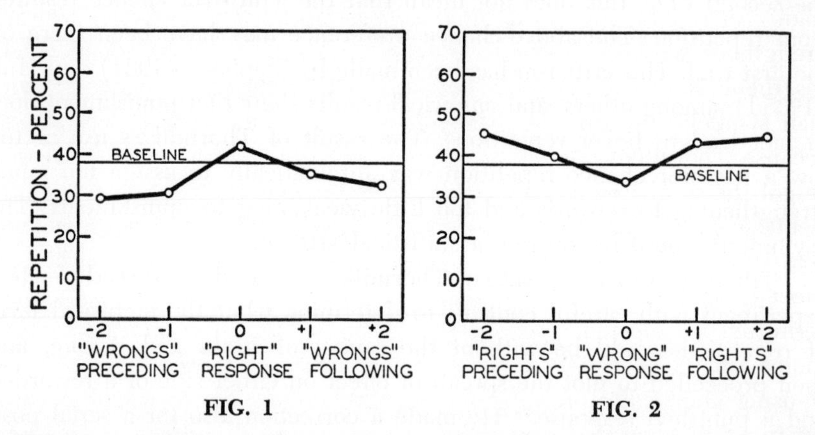

FIGURE 1. Gradient of effect around a *Right* response. Calling a response *Right* increases its repetition, calling a response *Wrong* decreases its repetition; but the decrease is less when the *Wrong* is near to an isolated *Right*. Redrawn from Tilton (1945).

FIGURE 2. Gradient of effect around a *Wrong* response. Calling a response *Wrong* decreases its repetition, calling a response *Right* increases its repetition, but the increase is less when the *Right* is near to an isolated *Wrong*. Redrawn from Tilton (1945).

a list of words the subject arbitrarily assigned numbers and was informed each time whether the number was right or wrong. The experimenter was able to assign the word *Right* to prearranged positions, all other positions being assigned the word *Wrong*. Then a single additional trial was used to determine the extent to which the subject would repeat the numbers called *Right* and repeat or change the numbers called *Wrong*. The statistical handling and interpretation of the effects of *Right* and *Wrong* are greatly simplified, for according to the prearranged pattern there are an equal number of opportunities to give the same response or a different response to each of several positions before and after the rewarded connection. The control situation consisted in the subject's assigning numbers as in a free association experiment, with the list repeated twice, no announcements of *Right* or of *Wrong* being used.[29] Her results in this modified situation supported Tilton's, so far as the effect of a rewarded response imbedded in the midst of punished responses is concerned. That is, the effect of *Wrong*, even adjacent to the rewarded connection is greater than whatever influence can be attributed to the spread of the effect of *Right*. The direct effects of both *Right* and of *Wrong* are greater than any spread from one to the other.

Stephens (1941), like Tilton, a former student of Thorndike, has made an interesting mediating suggestion that "symbolic" reward strengthens weak connections more than "symbolic" punishment weakens them, but symbolic punishment weakens strong connections more than symbolic reward strengthens them. According to this view, it was because Thorndike tended to work mostly with weak connections that he got the results he did. Stephens' experiment was done by using statements such as appear on attitude scales to determine certain convictions held strongly by the subjects, others held less strongly. Then a law-of-effect experiment was arranged, in which multiple-choice answers were permitted to selected statements, and the subject was informed which choice was correct. The method of information was the ingenious one of using chemically prepared paper so that the correct response came out in color when it was marked by the instrument provided. This permitted the experiment to be done with groups. When the experiment was then repeated, it was possible to see which tendency was the greater, to repeat the response answered correctly or to change from the response answered incorrectly. The change was found to be correlated with the conviction represented by the answer. The better-established replies were more influenced by punishment, the less-well-established by reward.

There is a difficulty of interpretation in this experiment which may help to account for uncertainty in other experiments about the relative influence of reward and punishment. There is a logical difference between responding in the intelligent direction to *Right* and to *Wrong*. The intelligent response to *Right* is to do again what was last done. This

[29] The "empirical chance" or "neutral" level of repetition depends upon the instructions within the control period. Martens' method, which sought "natural" associates between words and numbers, as in the free-association experiment, led to a higher baseline of repetition than Wallach and Henle's (1941) method, which may have mildly discouraged repetitions. The problem of level of repetition within different kinds of tasks was later studied by Sheffield and Jenkins (1952), whose results are reported further on. The interpretation of the relative efficacy of reward and punishment depends upon the assumed baseline, and if there is arbitrariness about the baseline there must be arbitrariness in the interpretation of positive and negative effects.

makes possible immediate rehearsal; the task is clear. The intelligent response to *Wrong* is to do something different, but what to do is less clear. It is necessary both to remember what not to do and to form some sort of hypothesis as to what to do. Under time pressure this vagueness might well produce an asymmetry between responses following *Right* and *Wrong*. In the case of poorly established convictions, it may be harder to remember what was said that was called *Right* than in the case of well-established convictions to remember what was said that was called *Wrong*. If that were true, Stephens' results would follow. Anything which makes it easier to make the necessary discriminations in one case than in another will effect the relative potency of hearing *Right* or *Wrong*, and of modifying subsequent behavior accordingly. In other words, the situation is not nearly as mechanical and stupid as it appears; in fact, the results can be best understood on the assumption that the individual is doing his best to act intelligently under somewhat confusing circumstances.

The Theory of Discrete Connections Probably Faulty

The spread of effect as Thorndike describes it presupposes a series of stimulus-response connections with no other organization among them than succession in time. What is strengthened (or weakened) is the tendency for a stimulus to be followed by the response which accompanied it the last time. Other experimenters have given evidence that additional principles of organization do apply, and the automatic spread of the influence of reward to neighboring connections is either incorrect or a gross oversimplification.

Zirkle (1946a), by changing the order of stimulus words on successive trials, showed that what was repeated was a neighboring response, not a stimulus-response connection. That is, a tendency to repeat the response "five" given originally to the word "youthful" two steps removed from reward, was found on the next trial to be given to "supports" as the stimulus word in the corresponding position. There was no increase in the tendency to say "five" after "youthful" unless it appeared in its old place. Under the usual arrangements of the experiment on spread of effect, it would be impossible to distinguish between strengthening a response or a connection, but under the special circumstances of Zirkle's experiment it is clear that response is the more important beneficiary of the reward.

This suggestion by Zirkle that it is the response rather than the connection which enters prominently into spread-of-effect data receives further support from the experiments of Jenkins and Sheffield (1946). They show that guessing habits are important in the usual spread-of-effect experiments. Guessing habits refer to patterns of response, not to isolated stimulus-response preferences. They found that if a rewarded response was repeated, other responses following it were also repeated; if a rewarded response was not repeated, other responses in its neighborhood were not repeated beyond chance levels. Hence the *repetition* of a rewarded response appears to be more important than the fact of reward. The major effect of reward is to lead to repetition of the correct response; once this success is achieved, the repetition of responses after the reward depends upon guessing habits.[30]

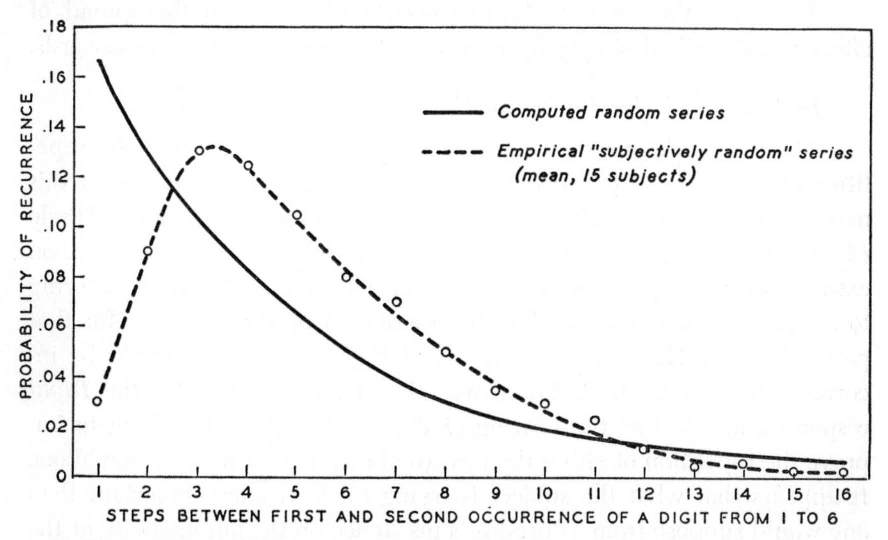

FIGURE 3. Distribution of steps from the first to the second occurrence of a digit from "one" through "six" in a random series and in a "subjectively random" series produced by 15 subjects. Note that the subjects typically avoid using the same digit a second time until other digits have been used. From Smith (1949), page 360.

A related but supplementary suggestion has been made and verified by M. H. Smith, Jr. (1949). In what he calls the "probability-bias hypothesis," he points out that subjects in attempting to respond with a random series of digits tend to avoid using the same digit over again until most of the digits have been used up. In a chance series, the digit has an equal chance of coming up on each trial; its appearance on any one trial is not influenced by the fact that it may have occurred on the

[30] The guessing sequence hypothesis has been amply supported through additional work by the same authors, their collaborators, and others: e.g., Jenkins and Cunningham (1949), Sheffield (1949b), Fagan and North (1951), Sheffield and Jenkins (1952).

preceding one. Intervals between two occurrences of the same digit in a "random" series are plotted in Figure 3 along with the intervals between two occurrences in a "subjectively random" series. The striking difference between the curves arises because the subjects, in attempting to produce a random series, postpone the recurrence of a digit once used. How can this bias against repetition produce a spread of effect? The chance of repeating a digit used on the preceding trial following a correct (*Right*) response is enhanced by the *avoidance* of the digit just used as the "correct" response. While this effect is slight, so is the amount of the spread of effect as commonly found. A consistent slight bias of this kind is enough to produce statistically significant results.

There are thus seen to be organizational factors in the spread of effect not described simply by remoteness of connections from rewards.

Is "Reward" the Basis for the Enhancement Effect?

The presumption is made in Thorndike's experiments that the repetition of the response called *Right* results directly from reward. That this may not be the case is shown in the experiments of Wallach and Henle (1941, 1942). The subject believed himself to be in an experiment on extrasensory perception, so that as he went through a list he was trying to assign the number which had been assigned by someone else for that particular trial. Hence a response called *Right* on one trial might be incorrect on the next trial. There was thus no intent to learn the *Right* responses, and in fact the hearing of the word *Right* did nothing to improve the repetition of either the rewarded response or its near neighbors. It appears that what the subject is trying to do is more important than one would suppose from Thorndike's insistence on the automaticity of the effect of reward.

Another of Zirkle's experiments [31] bears importantly on the question of what causes the repetition of the response called *Right*. Influenced by the possibility that something like a figure-ground relationship may be effective in these situations, Zirkle arranged to have three degrees of isolation of the response called *Right*. It was his conjecture that with greater isolation there would be greater repetition of this response, and perhaps of its near neighbors also. The degrees of isolation were obtained by inserting within a list of black lower-case words as the words to be called *Right* (*a*) a nonsense syllable in red capital letters, the highest degree of isolation, (*b*) a word in black capital letters, the next degree of isolation, and (*c*) a word printed the same as all the other

[31] Zirkle (1946b).

words, in black lower-case letters, but isolated solely by being called *Right* in the midst of consecutive words called *Wrong*. The results are plotted from Zirkle's data in Figure 4. His prediction was fully confirmed. Not only was the most isolated response most regularly repeated, but its repetition was followed by the enhanced repetition of the words immediately following. Because the spread of effect was not demonstrated for the words immediately preceding the isolated word, it is

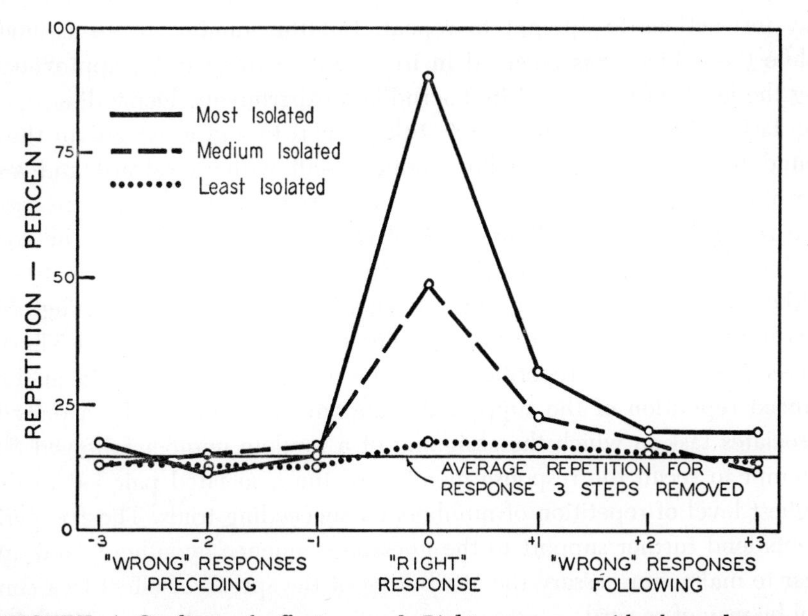

FIGURE 4. Gradient of effect around *Right* responses with three degrees of isolation. All isolated responses called *Right*, all neighboring items called *Wrong*. The differences among the three curves depend upon the differences in degree of isolation of the items called *Right*. The most isolated item, a nonsense syllable in red capital letters; the medium isolated item, a word in black capital letters; the least isolated item, a word printed like all other items, in black lower-case letters, isolated only by being called *Right* in the midst of words called *Wrong*. Plotted from Zirkle (1946b).

probable that isolation led to the repetition of the isolated word, and that guessing habits then produced the after-gradient. This conjecture is indirectly supported by the experiments of Jenkins and Postman (1948), in which they found no gradient around an isolated stimulus when guessing sequences were eliminated.

In his experiment on spread of effect when there was neither reward nor opportunity for learning, Sheffield (1949b) found the typical "spread," but the level of repetition was lower than in the usual Thorndike experiment. While Thorndike [32] had found the average per cent of repetition for the position following reward to be 20.4, the corresponding per cent in Sheffield's experiment was 13.3. Was there after all some effect of "reward," or can the difference in level be accounted for on other grounds?

Sheffield and Jenkins (1952) set out to determine whether or not the reward was responsible for the enhancement in Thorndike's experiments. They continued to use Sheffield's procedure of having subjects assign numbers at random, without any statement of *Right* or *Wrong* or any instructions to attempt to repeat. But the numbers were assigned while the subject was engaged in irrelevant learning tasks, approximating the kinds of tasks used in Thorndike's experiments. Depending upon the task used, percentages of repetition equal to and greater than those found by Thorndike could be produced—all without reward and any learning related to the number sequences. A few of the results are summarized graphically in Figure 5. A change in instructions, and the concealing of the record of previous replies, raised the level of repetition, without any new task being introduced; when an irrelevant learning task was used, with a fixed order of stimulus presentation (typical of Thorndike's practice), the repetition of other ordered stimuli led to an enhanced repetition of the supposedly random numbers; finally, a paired-associates task in which the assigning of a random number followed the attempt to recall the response member of the associated pair led to the highest level of repetition of numbers on succeeding trials. These experiments lend further support to the guessing-sequence hypothesis, and appear to make unnecessary the attributing of the spread of effect to a control by way of reward.

One dissent in recent years from the negative findings on the spread of effect is that of Duncan (1951). Aware of the many criticisms of the spread of effect, he designed an experiment in which the *stimulus*-member of the associated items would again be important. (It must be remembered that most of the criticisms center around the fact that the spread of effect is generated by response-habits having little to do with the nature of the stimuli presented.) To this end he used two sets of stimulus words. One set consisted of unrelated adjectives ("ancient," "downcast," "mutual") while the other consisted of adjectives very similar in meaning ("superb," "choice," "unique"). Duncan suggested that saying *Right* to a number assigned to one of the similar adjectives might very well lead to a repetition of a number assigned to another similar adjective.

[32] Thorndike (1933b). The experiments averaged for comparison with Sheffield's are Experiments F, H, and I.

In other words, the generalization tendencies might lead to an enhancement of the spread of effect, through uncertainty as to the exact locus of the reward. By the use of the control adjectives of dissimilar meanings, presumably guessing tendencies and the like would be balanced out. His results were largely ambiguous, but the one statistically significant

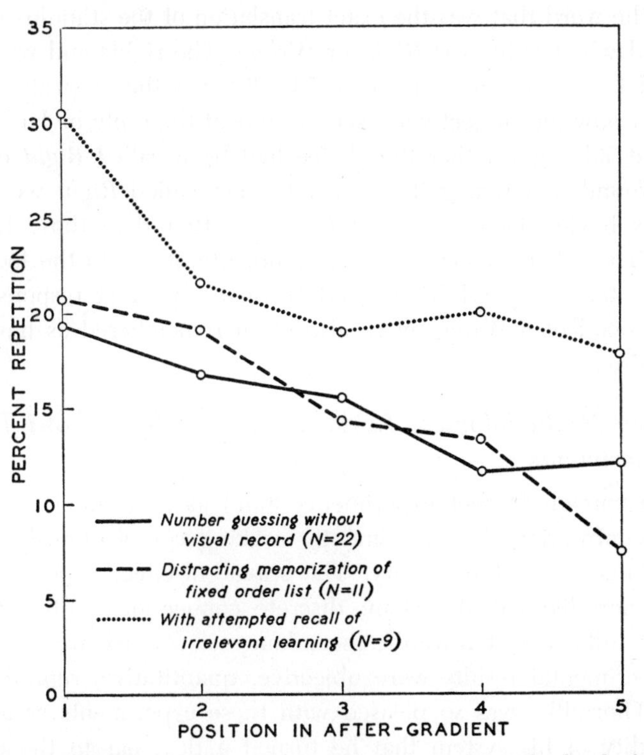

FIGURE 5. Modified conditions of experimentation raising the level of repetition in a "spread-of-effect" type of experiment without reward or relevant learning. Plotted from the data of Sheffield and Jenkins (1952).

difference he found favored his hypothesis and thus gave some slight support to Thorndike's position. Perhaps the main lesson to be learned is that it is very difficult to design the finally decisive experiment, and despite all its critics the spread of effect is not yet permanently demolished.[33]

The suggestion from Duncan's experiment that uncertainty as to

[33] There are some unfortunate weaknesses in Duncan's experiment that prevent its making a strong case for keeping the spread of effect alive. For example, he finds more of a gradient (more repetition, and more difference between the two adjacent positions) following a "rewarded" response *not* repeated than following a "rewarded" response that *is* repeated. Perhaps his too-similar adjectives have *displaced* the action of reward rather than *spread* it!

what was rewarded may have something to do with the spread of effect receives indirect confirmation from experiments by Nuttin (1949) (1953). The subject was given a list of 40 well-known stimulus words. Each word was followed by five two-syllable words of an "unknown language" (actually artificially constructed nonsense words). He was asked to choose the word that was the exact translation of the stimulus-word, and then told whether he was *Right* or *Wrong*. The rights and wrongs were assigned in a prearranged manner. The list was then repeated a second time, but now the subject was asked to repeat the reply he had given the first time, adding whether the choice had been called *Right* or *Wrong*. Nuttin found that wrong items next to ones called *Right* were remembered as having been called *Right* more often than those farther removed. There is thus some subjective uncertainty as to the locus of the experimenter's assigned *Rights* and *Wrongs*. (Correct responses in the neighborhood of a *Wrong* were also often remembered as having been called *Wrong*.)

Some Methodological Lessons from the Spread-of-Effect Experiments

The spread-of-effect experiments stand as a warning of the many pitfalls confronting the experimenter seeking conscientiously to design experiments relevant to theory. The spread-of-effect experiment epitomized Thorndike's final system: discrete connections, automatic ("biological") influence of rewards, ascendancy of reward over punishment. The experimental results were objective, quantitative, reproducible by others. Thorndike was so pleased with these experiments as a proof of the validity of his system that he turned a deaf ear to the critics. In preparing the collection of his papers for his final book he inserted this comment regarding the criticisms of the spread-of-effect experiments: "There are a few recent dissenters, but if they will repeat the original experiments in full I prophecy that they will be convinced." [34]

The causal factors in any learning experiment are complex. The positive contribution of the experiments critical of Thorndike has been to call attention to a number of these factors that he either overlooked or slighted in his description and explanation of the spread phenomenon. Some of these are:

1. The phenomena are influenced by the set or instructions that determine what the subject is trying to do.[35]

[34] Thorndike (1949), page 27.
[35] Wallach and Henle (1941).

2. The learning task undertaken may be irrelevant to the spread phenomena, yet influence the level of repetition.[36]

3. An isolation or emphasis effect is as important as reward in determining which response is most frequently repeated.[37]

4. Guessing habits result in a gradient of response around the focal response that is repeated for any reason whatever.[38]

5. A probability bias operates so that a subject repeats a digit at less than chance frequency when attempting to respond in random fashion. This avoidance of one or more previously used digits leads to a beyond-chance repetition of the remaining digits.[39]

6. Integration of serial acts through anticipatory responses, remote associations, etc., produces types of gradient superficially similar to, but not causally identifiable with, the spread of effect.[40]

If errors enter because of these six causal factors, they are errors in explanation or interpretation. They do not in themselves imply poor experimentation, for the factors may themselves be systematically varied and their effects studied.

There are, in addition, errors in the treating of data that led to systematic distortions of the results as these results were reported from many of the earlier experiments on spread of effect that attempted to do just what Thorndike recommended, that is, to repeat his experiments in full. Three of these are worth noting:

1. A faulty baseline of chance was selected, on the assumption that empirical chance levels are equal to computed random levels.[41] This error led to an underestimation of the influence of punishment (saying *Wrong*).

2. Improper weighting of steps in the gradient by scoring responses between two rewarded responses (*Rights*) as *both* preceding and following a *Right*.[42] This error led to a greater symmetry in the "before" and

[36] Sheffield and Jenkins (1952).

[37] Zirkle (1946b). The possible role of emphasis was earlier suggested by Tolman, Hall, and Bretnall (1932). The isolation effect came to Zirkle's attention through the work of von Restorff (1933). Strengthened response through isolated punishment, noted by Zirkle, has been confirmed by Stone (1953).

[38] Jenkins and Sheffield (1946). The suggestion was earlier made by Tolman (1936), in a review of one of Thorndike's books, but he did not follow it up.

[39] Smith (1949).

[40] Jenkins (1943) found data apparently supporting the spread of effect in a maze experiment with rats, but anticipatory and perseverative tendencies make unsuitable an interpretation in terms of spread of effect to discrete connections. We shall later meet other gradients, such as the gradient of reinforcement, which have only a family resemblance to spread of effect.

[41] Pointed out by Stephens (1934), Hull (1935d), Tilton (1939).

[42] Pointed out especially by Tilton (1939) (1945).

"after" gradients than has been found in later experiments avoiding this error.

3. Repeating lists many times in the same order, thus increasing the proportion of *Right* responses through learning and reducing both the prevalence of *Wrong* responses and their distance from the nearest *Right*. As a consequence the *Wrong* responses that remain are predominantly those which (for any reason) are stereotyped and resistant to change. Because late in practice these are necessarily near to *Right* responses, it will appear statistically (but spuriously) that *Wrong* responses are repeated *because* of their proximity to *Right* ones.[43]

It is seldom that a single variety of experiment is as crucial to a systematic theoretical position as the spread-of-effect experiment was to Thorndike's. For that reason its criticisms have been more pertinent than the criticisms of less important experiments. That the criticisms have also been more devastating is merely a matter of fact. Had the spread of effect been confirmed by repeated experiments under appropriate conditions, its explanation would have been accepted as an impressive contribution to psychological theory.

ESTIMATE OF THORNDIKE'S POSITION

Before proceeding to an appraisal of the contemporary significance of Thorndike's position, his answers to the standard problems of learning will be summarized. By attempting such a summary for each of several leading learning theorists it will be easier to keep perspective on their similarities and differences.

Thorndike's Position on Typical Problems of Learning

Thorndike's answers are briefly summarized according to the six typical problems discussed in the first chapter.

1. *Capacity.* Learning capacity depends upon the number of bonds and their availability. The differences between bright and dull are quantitative rather than qualitative, although intelligence has dimensions of altitude as well as of breadth.[44] The theory of intelligence is consonant with the identical-elements theory of transfer.

2. *Practice.* Repetition of situations does not in itself modify connections. Repetition of connections leads to a negligible increase in

[43] This criticism, although fairly obvious, was first noted in the earlier edition of this book.

[44] Thorndike and others (1927).

strength, unless the connections are rewarded. Practice is important because it permits rewards to act upon connections.

3. *Motivation.* Reward acts directly on neighboring connections to strengthen them; punishment has no corresponding direct weakening effect. Punishment may work indirectly, however, through making the learner do something else which may confront him with a reward. "Ideas" need not intervene; connections may be strengthened directly, without awareness.

4. *Understanding.* The role of understanding is minimized, not because it is undemonstrable, but because it grows out of earlier habits. The best way to get understanding is to build a body of connections appropriate to that understanding. When situations are understood at once it is a matter of transfer or assimilation, that is, there are enough elements in common with old situations to permit old habits to act acceptably.

5. *Transfer.* The theory of identical elements is espoused. Reaction to new situations benefits by the identity of these new situations, in part, with old situations, and also by a principle of analogy described as assimilation.

6. *Forgetting.* The original law of disuse assumed forgetting to take place without practice in accordance with the empirical findings of studies such as those of Ebbinghaus. Later books did not deal with the problem in any detail; the law of disuse was not mentioned, but some decay with no practice was still implied.

The flavor of Thorndike's theory was all along that of the automatic strengthening of specific connections—directly, without intervening ideas or conscious influences. While Thorndike was not an avowed behaviorist, and was willing occasionally to use subjective terms, his emphasis was certainly behavioral. It would be unfair to leave the discussion of Thorndike without referring again to his insistence on measurement, and through that insistence his contribution to the improvement of the learning of skills in the schools. There was an energetic empiricism about Thorndike's experimenting and theorizing which compensated for its lack of systematic elegance.

The Specificity Doctrine a Source Both of Strength and of Weakness

Thorndike gave great impetus to what has sometimes been called the scientific movement in education—the movement which suggests that educational practices be regulated according to verified outcomes of specific practices. His tremendous drive led to enormous output in fields as varied as handwriting scales, dictionary-writing, methods in teaching arithmetic and spelling, intelligence tests, and vocational guidance. But the secret of his output was not only energy: the output stemmed also from his matter-of-fact conception of science, that in order to do something about anything you have to know specifically what you are about.

The specificity doctrine helps you to roll up your sleeves and get to work. Consider, for example, all the complications involved in the teaching of reading. What is it that the child is to be taught? Philology? Grammar? Semantics? It took a Thorndike to give the simple answer: "Words." With that answer he proceeded to count the frequency with which each word occurs in English, by tabulating millions of printed words from all manner of sources. He then arrived at the most common words. These are the words which must surely be understood. He made available lists and dictionaries to facilitate teaching the most needed words. A specificity theory like Thorndike's tells the educator where to look and how to measure in a baffling field such as schoolroom practices.

The specificity doctrine is also a source of weakness, and it has been the target of the most severe attacks upon Thorndike. The illustration above shows the kinds of criticisms which Thorndike invites. Is language no more than words? Are the most frequent words really what we wish to teach? Perhaps we need to think of language as a means of expression, as logic in action, and must therefore equip the child with the minimum set of tools necessary for adequate communication. That this approach is a possible one has been shown by the development of Basic English, wherein the central vocabulary of 850 words overlaps only in part with Thorndike's most frequent words.[45] The approach of Basic English takes into account the organized character of language as an instrument of meaning. Thorndike, true to association tradition, tended to think of language as a collection of words, which he set out to treat quantitatively.

In Thorndike the analytical emphasis of all association theory also pervaded the conception of rewards and punishments, and weakened somewhat the analysis of these phenomena. The notion that the law of effect works mechanically on all connections in the neighborhood of the rewarded one makes of reward something extrinsic to the activity in question, something pinned on adventitiously. In showing that the law

[45] E.g., Richards (1943). The basic list of 850 words includes some words in the seventh thousand of Thorndike's count, such as *advertisement* and *sneeze*.

of effect may work this way, he slighted the internal relationships between success and what the individual is trying to do, goals which satisfy aroused motives or needs. Again, texts may be cited in proof of the fact that Thorndike knew all this—he early quoted the "interest series" as we have shown and later added the notion of "belongingness"—but that does not alter the conclusion that his scientific preoccupations led him away from the internal relations of effort and success to the external relationship of any satisfying state of affairs strengthening any connection which happened to be near it.

Perhaps more heat has been generated over Thorndike's subordination of insight and understanding to drill and habit than over any other aspect of his writings. While he thought insight very rare in animals—perhaps rarer than it actually is—he did not deny insight in man. He was not awed by it, and thought it best understood by the same associative laws applying in other situations. Just as erroneous inferences are made because of habitual associations which throw the learner off his course, so the insights of the genius are made by appropriate habitual associations and analogies. He had this to say of reaction to novel situations:

> There is no arbitrary *hocus pocus* whereby man's nature acts in an unpredictable spasm when he is confronted with a new situation. His habits do not then retire to some convenient distance while some new and mysterious entities direct his behavior. On the contrary, nowhere are the bonds acquired with old situations more surely revealed in action than when a new situation appears.[46]

Although this comment is true enough, Thorndike's failure to give real concern to the way in which past habits are utilized in problem solution, to consider what arrangement makes a problem hard, what easy, when the same essential bonds are involved, is a genuine limitation. The difference is a real one for school practice. It is possible to teach number combinations first (establish the "bonds"), then expect some glimmer of understanding later, or it is possible to achieve some understanding of what numbers are for, to comprehend the situation as a problem, and then to learn the combinations in this context. In the end you come out at the same place, knowing the tables and knowing how to use them, but it is not a foregone conclusion that the one method of teaching will be more efficient than the other, either for knowing precisely what has been taught or for being able to apply it in new situations. Thorndike's preoccupation with bonds has insured that we turn to others, not Thorndike's followers, for a more careful appraisal of the role of meaning and understanding.

[46] Thorndike (1913b), page 29.

SUPPLEMENTARY READINGS

BOOKS

Thorndike was a prolific writer. His bibliography appears in two parts in the *Teachers College Record:* for the years 1898 to 1940 in volume 41 (1940), pages 699–725; for the years 1940 to 1949 in volume 51 (1949), pages 42–45. The total comes to more than 500 items.

The following books contain his major contributions to learning theory, with much supporting experimental data:

THORNDIKE, E. L. (1911) *Animal intelligence.*

THORNDIKE, E. L. (1913) *The psychology of learning* (*Educational psychology,* Vol. II).

THORNDIKE, E. L. (1922) *The psychology of arithmetic.*

THORNDIKE, E. L. and others (1928) *Adult learning.*

THORNDIKE, E. L. (1932) *The fundamentals of learning.*

THORNDIKE, E. L. (1935) *The psychology of wants, interests, and attitudes.*

THORNDIKE, E. L. (1949) *Selected writings from a connectionist's psychology.*

SHORTER INTRODUCTIONS

GATES, A. I. (1942) Connectionism: Present concepts and interpretations. Chapter 4 in *The psychology of learning.* Natl. Soc. Stud. Educ., 41st Yearbook, Part II, 141–164.

ROCK, R. T., Jr. (1940) Thorndike's contributions to the psychology of learning. *Teach. Coll. Rec.,* 41, 751–761.

SANDIFORD, P. (1942) Connectionism: Its origins and major features. Chapter 3 in *The psychology of learning.* Natl. Soc. Stud. Educ., 41st Yearbook, Part II, 97–140.

THORNDIKE, E. L. (1940) The ABC of human behavior. Chapter 2 in *Human nature and the social order,* 5–20.

CRITICAL REVIEWS

BROWN, J. F., and FEDER, D. D. (1934) Thorndike's theory of learning as gestalt psychology. *Psychol. Bull.,* 31, 426–437.

CASON, H. (1932) Review of Thorndike's *Human learning. J. abnorm. soc. Psychol.,* 27, 214–222.

HULL, C. L. (1935) Special review of Thorndike's *The fundamentals of learning. Psychol. Bull.,* 32, 807–823.

MCGEOCH, J. A. (1933) Review of Thorndike's *The fundamentals of learning. J. gen. Psychol.,* 8, 285–296.

TOLMAN, E. C. (1936) Connectionism; wants, interests, and attitudes. *Character and Pers.,* 4, 245–253.

REPRESENTATIVE EXPERIMENTS

A scientific theory can best be judged by its consequences in experimentation. This requires an appraisal of the kinds of experiments to which the theory leads and a review of the interpretations offered for the obtained data. A preferred theory ought to lead to cogent experiments and to suggest convincing interpretations.

Following this and succeeding chapters there will be short lists of experiments, useful in estimating the theories in this way. Many other references would be equally satisfactory for this purpose. The items marked with an asterisk are reproduced in large part in Thorndike (1949).

LORGE, I. (1936) Irrelevant rewards in animal learning. *J. comp. Psychol.*, 21, 105–128.

POSTMAN, L., and JARRETT, R. F. (1952) An experimental analysis of 'learning without awareness.' *Amer. J. Psychol.*, 65, 244–255.

ROCK, R. T., Jr. (1935) The influence upon learning of the quantitative variation of after-effects. *Teach. Coll. Contr. Educ.*, No. 650.

STONE, G. R. (1953) The effect of negative inventives in serial learning: VII. Theory of punishment. *J. gen. Psychol.*, 48, 133–161.

THORNDIKE, E. L. (1908) The effect of practice in the case of a purely intellectual function. *Amer. J. Psychol.*, 19, 374–384.

THORNDIKE, E. L. (1910) Practice in the case of addition. *Amer. J. Psychol.*, 21, 483–486.

THORNDIKE, E. L. (1924) Mental discipline in high school studies. *J. educ. Psychol.*, 15, 1–22; 83–98.

*THORNDIKE, E. L. (1927) The influence of primacy. *J. exp. Psychol.*, 10, 18–29.

*THORNDIKE, E. L. (1932) Reward and punishment in animal learning. *Comp. Psychol. Monogr.*, 8, No. 39, 65 pp.

*THORNDIKE, E. L. (1933) An experimental study of rewards. *Teach. Coll. Contr. Educ.*, No. 580, 72 pp.

THORNDIKE, E. L., and LORGE, I. (1935) The influence of relevance and belonging. *J. exp. Psychol.*, 18, 574–584.

THORNDIKE, E. L., and ROCK, R. T., Jr. (1934) Learning without awareness of what is being learned or intent to learn it. *J. exp. Psychol.*, 17, 1–19.

FINAL NOTE

For notices of the first edition of this book, disagreeing with my interpretation of some aspects of Thorndike's system, see:

STONE, G. R. (1948) Hilgard on the dominant laws of learning. *Psychol. Rev.*, 55, 342–344.

WOODWORTH, R. S. (1949) Review of Hilgard's *Theories of learning*. *J. abnorm. soc. Psychol.*, 44, 124–129.

The following reviews bear importantly on the law of effect as a central feature of Thorndike's system:

MEEHL, P. E. (1950) On the circularity of the law of effect. *Psychol. Bull.*, 47, 52–75.

NUTTIN, J. (1953) *Tâche, réussite et échec.* Especially Chapter V, pages 247–304.

POSTMAN, L. (1947) The history and present status of the Law of Effect. *Psychol. Bull.*, 44, 489–563.

Chapter 3

GUTHRIE'S CONTIGUOUS CONDITIONING

IN some respects, Edwin R. Guthrie's system is very much like Thorndike's. It is a stimulus-response association psychology, objective and practical. But in other respects the systems are very different. It is such similarities and differences which define the problems of contemporary learning theory.

Thorndike accepted two kinds of learning: selecting and connecting (under the law of effect), and associative shifting. For him, associative shifting was originally the fifth of some subsidiary principles, and by far the major burden was carried by selecting and connecting. For Guthrie, on the contrary, a conception very like associative shifting is made the cornerstone of his system, and learning of the trial-and-error sort is derivative and secondary. Guthrie does not accept the law of effect in Thorndike's sense, and this is the basic cleavage between their systems.

THE BACKGROUND OF BEHAVIORISM AND OF CONDITIONING

Guthrie is a contemporary behaviorist who lays much stress upon conditioning as the characteristic form of learning. Before turning to his own theories it may prove helpful to consider the background against which they have emerged.

Watson's Behaviorism

Behaviorism as a "school" of psychology is usually thought of as originating with Watson (1913), who became its most vigorous spokesman. There were other varieties of behaviorism, however, and Guthrie was led to his position by way of Singer (1911), with whom he had studied. The behaviorists have in common the conviction that a science of psychology must be based upon a study of that which is overtly observable: physical stimuli, the muscular movements and glandular secretions which they arouse, and the environmental products which ensue. The behaviorists differ somewhat among themselves as to what may be inferred in addition to what is measured, but they all exclude self-observation (introspection) as a legitimate scientific method. Partly as a protection against an indirect use of introspection, the behaviorists have tended to prefer experimentation on animals and infants.

Watson's *Behavior: An introduction to comparative psychology* (1914) was the first book to follow the announcement of his new position. In it occurred his attempted refutation of Thorndike's law of effect and the substitution of the laws of frequency and recency. He believed that animal learning, as in the maze or problem-box, could be explained according to what the animal had most often been led to do in the situation, with the most recent act favored in recall. Because the successful act was both most frequent and most recent, its recurrence could be explained without recourse to an added principle of effect. This denial of effect was part of his program of getting rid of the residual subjectivity which he felt was implied in Thorndike's concepts of satisfiers and annoyers. While the frequency-recency theory did not survive its criticisms,[1] it serves to point up Watson's desire to find objective laws to substitute for those with even a tinge of subjective flavor.

The behaviorist knows that other events intervene between measured stimuli and the responses to them. In order to preserve a systematically coherent position, these intervening events are posited to be much like the observed ones, that is, *implicit* or *covert* stimulus-response sequences. In his early studies on the control of the maze habit, Watson (1907) had attributed great importance to kinesthetic stimuli as integrators of the habits involved. Because kinesthetic stimuli are aroused as a result of the organism's movements, they fit well into a behavioral or reaction psychology. Even the unobserved processes inferred to be going on between stimuli and responses are said to be comprised of movements and movement-produced stimuli. This emphasis upon kinesthesis as the integrator of animal learning served Watson well when he became puzzled about human thought processes. He decided that thought was merely implicit speech, that is, talking to oneself. Sensitive enough instruments, he conjectured, would detect tongue movements or other movement accompaniments of thinking. He was thus able to hold to his consistent behaviorist position without denying that thinking goes on.

[1] Peterson (1922); Gengerelli (1928).

It was somewhat later that Watson discovered that the conditioned reflex of Pavlov and Bekhterev might serve as a useful paradigm for learning.[2] Because it grew out of the objective tradition that had happened to develop within Russian physiology, it fitted his temper and he adopted it enthusiastically. In Watson's later writings the conditioned reflex was central to learning, as the unit out of which habits are built.

Watson's general textbook, *Psychology from the standpoint of a behaviorist,* appeared in 1919. It was soon followed by other books written from an avowedly behavioristic standpoint. Among these was Smith and Guthrie's *General psychology in terms of behavior* (1921). Like Watson's book, it treated all of psychology from a behavioral viewpoint and made use of conditioning principles. It, too, laid great stress upon movement-produced stimuli. Hence there is a family relationship between the two books, although they differ greatly in expository style. Watson laid far more stress upon the details of physiology and anatomy, and upon appropriate methods for the behavioral study of psychological relationships. Smith and Guthrie showed less concern for experimental and neurophysiological detail, but instead gave a plausible interpretation of ordinary experience as described consistently from the new standpoint. Guthrie's contemporary writings preserve the flavor of the Smith and Guthrie book. Despite their similarities, Guthrie's point of view must be considered as something other than a working out of Watson's position.[3]

The Conditioned Reflex or Conditioned Response

The conditioned-reflex principle is conceptually so simple as to make an attractive prototype for learning. Certain stimuli lead regularly to reflex responses. A light flashed into the eye causes pupillary constriction, a tap on the patellar tendon leads to a knee jerk, chemicals on the tongue produce salivation. Such natural reflexes are called *unconditioned reflexes* and the stimuli which produce them are called *unconditioned stimuli.* If a second stimulus, not originally leading to the response, is frequently presented slightly before or accompanying the unconditioned stimulus, it presently comes to elicit the response. Such a stimulus is called a *conditioned stimulus* and the learned response is called a *conditioned reflex.* Because of the desire to extend the principle to responses not obviously reflex, later writers have usually preferred the less specific

[2] Watson (1916).

[3] It is suggested in Chapter 5 that Hull's position is another kind of descendant of Watson's.

word "response" to the word "reflex," so that the movements involved are called conditioned and unconditioned responses, whether or not they conform to the definition of a reflex.

The study of conditioned salivary responses in dogs was carried out systematically by Pavlov [4] over many years, and he discovered most of the relationships which later studies have more fully explored. The translations of his terms have become common in the literature of learning.

The appearance or strengthening of a conditioned response is said to take place through *reinforcement.* Reinforcement may refer to the experimental *arrangement* of following the conditioned stimulus by the unconditioned stimulus, although the word is sometimes used to refer to the implied *process* of strengthening of the conditioned response. When the conditioned stimulus is presented alone, unaccompanied by the unconditioned stimulus, the conditioned response is said to be *non-reinforced.* Under repeated non-reinforcement there is a tendency for the conditioned response to weaken or even to disappear completely. This is referred to as *experimental extinction,* or, more simply, *extinction.* By extinction may be meant either the experimental arrangement of non-reinforcement, or the weakening process itself. Extinction is not, in fact, a destruction of the conditioned response, for when the animal is returned to the laboratory after a rest following extinction, the conditioned response is usually found to have reappeared, though commonly at reduced strength. This return of response strength after extinction, without intervening reinforcement, is called *spontaneous recovery.* The simple history of a conditioned response is then its strengthening through reinforcement, its weakening through extinction, and its partial recovery with rest.

Two additional concepts are extremely important in the extension of conditioning principles. These are *generalization* and *discrimination.* A new conditioned stimulus, not previously reinforced, may elicit a conditioned response the first time it is presented. The probability that it will do so is increased if it is similar to the conditioned stimulus which has been reinforced. Thus if a conditioned stimulus is obtained to one tone, another tone, at a slightly different frequency, will also produce a conditioned response, with lesser magnitude the further the separation of the tones. This process whereby a novel stimulus produces a response learned to another similar stimulus is known as *generalization.* If the two stimuli are sufficiently distinguishable, the organism can be taught to respond to one of them and to cease responding to the other. Such a dis-

[4] Pavlov (1927) (1928).

crimination is produced by the method of contrasts. That is, one of the stimuli is regularly reinforced, the other regularly non-reinforced. The selective extinction which results is known as *conditioned discrimination*, because the organism has learned to react differentially to the two stimuli which at first evoked more nearly the same response. Discrimination may be between patterns of stimuli as well as between single stimuli.

Pavlov's paradigm of conditioning has come to be called *classical conditioning* to distinguish it from a variety known as *instrumental conditioning*. Instrumental conditioning is epitomized by an experiment to be described more fully in the next chapter: lever-pressing by the rat, rewarded by a pellet of food. Because pressing the lever is causally related to the appearance of food the learned response is an *instrumental* one, that is, it acts upon the environment to produce a given change. The two chief differences between classical conditioning and instrumental conditioning lie in the relationships between the conditioned response and the reinforcing event:

1. *Classes of response.* In classical conditioning, the conditioned and unconditional responses fall in the same class. That is, conditioned salivation is reinforced by presenting an unconditioned stimulus that elicits unconditioned salivation. In instrumental conditioning, the two responses fall into different classes: conditioned lever-pressing is reinforced by food, and unconditioned eating responses have little in common with lever-pressing.

2. *Contingent relationship between conditioned and unconditioned stimuli.* In classical conditioning, reinforcement is under the control of the experimenter. The unconditioned stimulus (e.g., food) appears after a standard time interval whether or not the dog responds to the conditioned stimulus (e.g., bell). In instrumental conditioning the reinforcement is controlled by the behaving organism. That is, the rat receives the reinforcing stimulus (food) only if it gives the conditioned response of pressing the lever.

Despite these differences in experimental arrangements, the general laws of reinforcement, extinction, spontaneous recovery, generalization, and discrimination are so similar within classical and instrumental conditioning that a common terminology has come to be used for both varieties,[5] and it is a matter for theoretical discussion whether or not separate principles of learning apply to the two classes.

In choosing to use what has been learned from conditioned-response

[5] A glossary of terms used in conditioning experiments may be found in Hilgard and Marquis (1940), pages 341–353.

experiments, Watson and Guthrie selected somewhat different alternatives. Watson used the Pavlov experiment as the paradigm of learning, made of the conditioned reflex the unit of habit, and built his system on that foundation. Guthrie, unlike Watson, starts with a principle of conditioning or of associative learning, a principle which is not dependent strictly upon the Pavlov kind of experiment. To Guthrie, Pavlov's experiment is a highly artificial one, useful for the relationships it exhibits, but itself requiring explanation according to more general principles. For Watson, the classical conditioning experiment provided the answers he sought as to how learning takes place; for Guthrie, the classical conditioning experiment raises as many questions as it answers.

CONTIGUITY OF CUE AND RESPONSE: THE ONE LAW OF ASSOCIATION

The Lowest Common Denominator of Learning

Guthrie's one law of learning, from which all else about learning is made comprehensible, is stated by Guthrie as follows: "A combination of stimuli which has accompanied a movement will on its recurrence tend to be followed by that movement." [6]

There is an elegant simplicity about the statement, which avoids mention of drives, of successive repetitions, of rewards or of punishments. Stimuli and movements in combination: that is all. This one principle serves as the basis for a very ingenious and intriguing theory of learning.

A second statement is needed to complete the basic postulate about learning: "A stimulus pattern gains its full associative strength on the occasion of its first pairing with a response." [7]

This somewhat paradoxical statement, in view of undeniable improvement with practice, is a very necessary adjunct to the theory, because it makes possible a number of derivative statements about learning and forgetting. It can be thought of as a kind of *recency principle*, for if learning occurs completely in one trial, that which was last done in the presence of a stimulus combination will be that which will be done when the stimulus combination next recurs.[8]

[6] Guthrie (1935), page 26; Guthrie (1952), page 23. Where the quotations from Guthrie remain unchanged between the 1935 and the 1952 editions of his book, the earlier only will be cited hereafter.

[7] Guthrie (1942), page 30.

[8] Because it refers to the last response of a succession rather than to recency in time, Voeks (1948) (1950) suggests that it be called the *principle of postremity*.

How can Guthrie demonstrate that more complicated forms of learning conform to these simple principles? As in the case of other sophisticated theorists, he does not proceed by denying familiar forms of learning. His problem is that of showing that learning as we know it can, in fact, be shown not to contradict these basic principles. He does not deny that there is learning which may be described as insightful or purposive or problem-solving. It is Guthrie's task to show that each of these forms requires no new principles of explanation beyond the primary law of association by contiguity.

Why Strict Contiguity of Measured Stimulus and Response Is Not Essential

One of the standard experiments in the literature of conditioning is that showing the importance of the time interval between the conditioned stimulus and unconditioned response. The empirical results suggest a gradient, with a most favorable interval and less favorable intervals on either side of this optimal interval.[9]

Guthrie is able to hold out for strict simultaneity of cue and response in the face of these data by proposing that the true cue being conditioned is not the stimulus as measured. An external stimulus may give rise to movements of the organism. These movements in turn produce stimuli. When associations appear to be made between stimuli and responses separated in time, it is because these intervening movements fill in the gap. The true association is between simultaneous events.

There is a strong preference for *movement-produced stimuli* as the true conditioners in Guthrie's system. They permit the integration of habits within a wide range of environmental change in stimulation, because these stimuli are carried around by the organism. It appears that some of this preference dates from the early emphasis of Watson (1907) on kinesthesis as the basis of control of the maze habit, a position no longer tenable.[10] Such covert movement-produced stimuli provide ever-present explanations for conduct which cannot be inferred from external stimulus-response relationships.

[9] Hilgard and Marquis (1940), pages 158–173. Additional determinations of this stimulus-separation gradient include Reynolds (1945a), Kimble (1947), White and Schlosberg (1952), McAllister (1953). For somewhat discordant results, see also Libby (1951).

[10] Honzik (1936) found kinesthesis to be one of the least useful of several sensory controls of the maze habit.

Why Repetition Brings Improvement

The reason that practice brings improvement is that improvement, and other forms of success, refer to acts, to outcomes of learnings, rather than to *movements.* Guthrie believes that his interest in movements, and the prediction of movements, is almost unique among learning theorists; others, he says, are interested in goal achievements, and results of one sort or another. One difference between him and Thorndike is that Thorndike is concerned with scores on tasks, with items learned, pages typed, or correct responses attained. Guthrie is concerned only with the movements of the organism, regardless of whether they lead to error or success.

A skill, such as getting the ball into the basket in a game of basketball, is not one act but many. It does not depend upon a single muscular movement, but upon a number of movements made under a number of different circumstances. Any one movement may be learned in any one trial, but to learn all the movements demanded by the complicated skill calls for practice in all the different situations: while near the basket and far away, on one side and on the other, with and without a guard nearby. Practice is necessary; but it produces its consequences, not in accordance with a law of frequency, but according to the simple principle of the attachment of cues to movements. The more varied the movements called for in a given act of skill, and the more varied the cues which must become assimilated to these movements, the more practice is required. There is no mystery about the length of time it takes to learn to operate a typewriter: there are so many keys in so many combinations, calling for the attachment of a great many cues to a great many responses. It is concomitantly necessary to get rid of the faulty associations which lead to what, from a product point of view, is an error. This is done by having the correct behavior occur to the cue which previously gave rise to the faulty behavior. When finally all the cues lead to acceptable behavior, the task is mastered. The apparent contradiction of single-trial learning with actual experience of painstaking fumbling before success is achieved is resolved when the skilled task is seen to be composed of a large number of habits.

Associative Inhibition, Forgetting, and the Breaking of Habits

The fact of extinction is one of the findings of conditioning experiments that is in need of explanation. Because cues should remain faithful to their responses, Guthrie cannot agree to extinction as a decay due to mere non-reinforced repetition. According to him, extinction always occurs as associative inhibition, that is, through the learning of an incompatible response. His is an interference theory and hence requires no new principles, because the original learning and the interfering learning follow the same rules.

Forgetting is explained in the same way. If there were no interference with old learning there would be no forgetting. It has been shown, for example, that conditioned responses, even though in some respects they appear fragile, are actually quite resistant to forgetting.[11] The long-lasting character of these conditioned responses is to be understood because they represent learning highly specific to cues not confronted in daily life. If the learners lived in the laboratory, their responses would be subject to more interferences. Guthrie's position is but an extreme form of the retroactive inhibition theory of forgetting, to be discussed in greater detail later.

If it is desired to break up a habit (that is, to accelerate its forgetting), it is only necessary to cause other movements to occur in the presence of the cues to the habit. The problem of locating the cues and substituting other behavior often takes time, because many cues may lead to the undesirable habit.

> Drinking or smoking after years of practice are action systems which can be started by thousands of reminders. . . . I had once a caller to whom I was explaining that the apple I had just finished was a splendid device for avoiding a smoke. The caller pointed out that I was at that moment smoking. The habit of lighting a cigarette was so attached to the finish of eating that smoking had started automatically.[12]

Guthrie suggests three ways in which activities are commonly weakened: [13]

1. The first method is to introduce the stimulus which you wish to have disregarded, but only in such faint degree that it will not call out its response. This is the method of training a horse to the saddle by starting with a light blanket, and gradually working up to full equipment, at no time permitting the horse to become so startled that it plunges or struggles.

2. The second method is to repeat the signal until the original re-

[11] E.g., Hilgard and Campbell (1936); Wendt (1937); Skinner (1950).
[12] Guthrie (1935), page 139.
[13] Paraphrased from Guthrie (1935), pages 70–73.

sponse is fatigued, and then continuing it, so that new responses are learned to the signal. The "broncho-busting" of the western ranches followed essentially this technique.

3. The third method is to present the stimulus when other features in the situation inhibit the undesirable response. One illustration given by Guthrie is that of training a dog not to catch and eat chickens by tying a dead chicken about its neck. As it struggles to get rid of the corpse it develops an avoidance response to chickens at close quarters. Another example, illustrating undesirable learning, is the disobedience learned by the child whose mother calls him when he is too occupied with what he is doing to obey.

SOME DERIVATIVE EXPLANATIONS AND APPLICATIONS

In his two books *The psychology of learning* (1935) (1952) and *The psychology of human conflict* (1938), Guthrie finds it unnecessary to make any formal additions to the basic principles of learning in order to apply his theory to practical learning problems and to the handling of personality disorders.[14] While the basic principles remain, there are some ingeniously derived supplementations which, once accounted for, play an important role in the further discussions. Among these are explanations of the place of motives, the action of reward and punishment, and the origin of anticipatory responses as important substitutes for ideas and intentions.

Motives

The motivational state of the organism, its hunger, thirst, or state of comfort or discomfort, has no formal place in Guthrie's learning theory; the motivational state is important only because it determines the presence and vigor of movements that may enter into associative connection. The motive is important only for what it causes the organism to do. The movements that occur get associated; if a hungry cat acts differently from a well-fed cat, her movements are different and so her learning may be different. She learns what she does; what she does is more important than what her motivational state happens to be. In the

[14] The same comments apply to his collaborative books as well: Smith and Guthrie (1921), Guthrie and Horton (1946), Guthrie and Edwards (1949), Guthrie and Powers (1950).

Guthrie and Horton (1946) experiments the cat often did not eat the salmon provided in the dish outside the cage. This did not matter, for *leaving the cage* was the important behavior.

Motives are, however, important in one of the derivations from the basic theory of contiguous association: they are important in providing *maintaining stimuli,* keeping the organism active until a goal is reached. The goal removes these maintaining stimuli, and brings the activity to an end.[15] We shall see how these maintaining stimuli, along with movement-produced stimuli, tend to keep a series of acts integrated, and account for anticipation, for behavior characterized by intent.

Reward

While Guthrie believes as everyone else does that rewards influence outcomes, his rejection of the law of effect and of the principle of reinforcement in conditioning is based on the position that nothing new is added to associative learning by reward except a mechanical arrangement. This mechanical arrangement, which places reward at the end of a series of acts, removes the organism from the stimuli acting just prior to the reward. Hence, being removed from the stimuli, the behavior to these stimuli is preserved intact. Instead of behavior being strengthened by reward, reward preserves it from disintegration. It was just as strong before the reward occurred, but, if there had been no reward, behavior in the same situation would have been changed. The act leading to the reward, being the last act in the problematic situation, is the one favored when the situation next repeats itself. Guthrie is very explicit about this. Of an animal's excape from a problem-box he says:

> *The position taken in this paper is that the animal learns to escape with its first escape.* This learning is protected from forgetting because the escape removes the animal from the situation which has then no chance to acquire new associations.
>
> [Of latch-opening followed by food.] *What encountering the food does is not to intensify a previous item of behavior but to protect that item from being unlearned.* The whole situation and action of the animal is so changed by the food that the pre-food situation is shielded from new associations. These new associations can not be established in the absence of the box interior, and in the absence of the behavior that preceded latch-opening.[16]

Although this is the fundamental position with respect to reward, and frequently reiterated in refutation of the law of effect and related interpretations, the action of reward is found to be somewhat more com-

[15] Guthrie (1942), page 18.
[16] Guthrie (1940), pages 144–145. Italics in the original.

plicated when one examines the totality of Guthrie's system. The first (and primary) role of reward is to remove the animal from the problem and thus prevent unlearning. But by the principle of association the animal also learns the activity that he carries on in the presence of the reward (chewing and salivating to food, for example), and this behavior tends to be invoked by renewed hunger and by any of the cues from the problem that may have persisted while the rewarded behavior was going on.

> . . . There is one act, however, to which hunger may remain a faithful conditioner. That is the act of eating; and the faithfulness of hunger to this association derives from the fact that hunger dies when eating occurs. As Stevenson Smith and I pointed out in our *General Psychology,* elements of the consummatory response tend to be present throughout a series of actions driven by a maintaining stimulus.[17]
>
> Not only do general movements of eating tend to be aroused by hunger contractions, but the specific movements demanded by the peculiar nature of the food are possibly in evidence. Hence when the rat runs the maze he is ready for whatever reward has been received in the past, sunflower seed or bran mash. This readiness is an actual muscular readiness. . . .[18]

A theoretical problem arises when Guthrie holds at once (*a*) that the reward removes the learner from all the cues prior to the reward, and (*b*) that these prior cues are somehow reward-attached. He could resolve this dilemma in one of two ways. He could retreat from the all-or-nothing removal of cues by reward: perhaps reward acts by *changing* the situation somewhat, even though not entirely. Or he could define the "true" reward as coming at a stage later than eating, perhaps consummation through food digestion. The animal is still hungry while eating, hence hunger produces anticipatory eating responses. Then, however, the act of eating does not remove the animal from the cues to which he has been exposed, because he has been exposed to eating-response cues all along. What finally changes the situation and brings the end of hunger (and presumably other cues) is satiation. Although this sounds like something of a quibble, the distinction between the theory of contiguous association and the theory of reinforcement is so slight that only the utmost clarity of statement will permit a choice between them.

One illustration may serve to show how important it is to know exactly what the theory states. The experiment of Sheffield and Roby (1950) shows that the non-nutritive taste of saccharin may serve as a reward. The result is used as a refutation of the need-satiation theory of reinforcement and as support for the theory of contiguous associa-

[17] Guthrie (1935), pages 151–152.
[18] Guthrie (1935), page 173.

tion (as well as some other theories). The empirical support for Guthrie derives from the fact that the rat's behavior changes strikingly after the saccharin is ingested. The authors conclude:

> It is suggested that elicitation of the consummatory response appears to be a more critical *primary* reinforcing factor in instrumental learning than the drive reduction subsequently achieved.[19]

While this consummatory response is the final one in a series, it has not yet taken the learner out of the situation. It must itself be part of the series, otherwise there could be no anticipatory responses reflecting it. What *really* takes the animal out of the situation? What is *really* reinforcing? Is it the new behavior that takes place after the consummatory response is over? But if it is this new behavior, does that not occur *after* some sort of stimulus-reduction has taken place?

Guthrie's general standpoint is clear enough: reward does not strengthen prior behavior, it merely protects it from unlearning. But the more precise questions about the relation of this position to his interpretation of anticipatory response remain unanswered.

Punishment

The primary interpretation of punishment is that of all associative learning: you tend to do what you did under the same circumstances:

> . . . Sitting on tacks does not discourage learning. It encourages one in learning to do something else than sit. It is not the feeling caused by punishment, but the specific action caused by punishment that determines what will be learned. To train a dog to jump through a hoop, the effectiveness of punishment depends on where it is applied, front or rear. It is what the punishment makes the dog do that counts or what it makes a man do, not what it makes him feel.[20]
>
> What we can predict is that the influence of stimuli acting at the time of either satisfaction or annoyance will be to re-establish whatever behavior was in evidence at the time.[21]

If one were to stop with statements such as these, it would appear that Guthrie treats reward and punishment in a symmetrical fashion. Certainly punishment changes a situation very strikingly, as reward does. Hence one might infer that all antecedent behavior would remain intact, being protected from new learning by the altered conditions of punishment as much as by the altered conditions of reward. Sometimes this does actually appear to be the case. Running responses leading to charged grills, with safety beyond, may prove resistant to extinction.[22]

[19] Sheffield and Roby (1950), page 481.
[20] Guthrie (1935), page 158.
[21] Guthrie (1935), page 154.
[22] Gwinn (1949), F. D. Sheffield (1949a).

The symmetry in treatment of reward and punishment, as implied in the foregoing quotations, is somewhat illusory, for "doing what you last did" refers to very different parts of the behavior cycle when the reference is to reward than when the reference is to punishment. "What you last did" that remains in your behavior repertory because of reward is what you did *just before* the reward appeared; "what you last did" in the case of punishment refers to what you did *just after* the punishment, leading to escape. Punishment produces "maintaining stimuli" relieved by a later movement that brings relief:

> . . . An animal on a charged grid, a barefoot boy on a hot pavement, a man sitting on a tack have as their goals mere escape from the intense stimulation that causes general tension and restlessness as well as specific movement. These stimuli continue to act as what Stevenson Smith and I called maintaining stimuli until some movement carries the subject away from the source of stimulation, or the source of stimulation away from the subject.[23]

When these stimuli are removed, we have the circumstances defining reward, and so, if that were the whole story, the prior behavior should remain intact. This kind of relief from punishment has come to be known as *escape learning* to distinguish between it and *avoidance learning.* To move from escape learning to avoidance learning we require an anticipatory response, conditioned to some cue, so that the punishment is circumvented. As we saw in relation to reward, Guthrie's system makes provision for anticipatory responses, and these can, of course, be made use of to explain avoidance learning. The animal merely makes the escape response to some cue present at the time of punishment—a cue which, fortunately, makes its appearance before the threatened punishment. Hence what happens at the end of a sequence of acts leading to punishment does something *in addition to* and *other than* removing the organism from the scene: it also sets up some conditioned anticipatory responses.

Noxious stimuli may lead not only to escape and avoidance learning but to a third subvariety, more properly called punishment, that is, to the inhibiting of otherwise rewarded behavior. We may try to stop the child's doing something he enjoys; we may try to break a "bad habit." Punishment of this kind always involves conflict.

Guthrie's position with respect to this subvariety of punishment has been aptly summarized by Sheffield:

> (*a*) Punishment works only if the last response to the punished situation is incompatible with the response that brought on the punishment.

[23] Guthrie (1935), page 165.

(*b*) Punishment works only if the cues present when the incompatible response is performed are present when the punished response is performed.

(*c*) Punishment that produces only emotional excitement will tend to fixate the punished response.[24]

The main point is that punishment wins out in a conflict with behavior that is otherwise motivated only if there is conflict. The statement about the presence of cues is not as decisive as it sounds, in view of Guthrie's acceptance of anticipatory responses and movement-produced stimuli as cues. In other words, there are always plenty of cues, if one needs them. The third point is a useful one: In some cases, what appears to be punishing to the trainer may not be punishing to the learner; in other cases, punishment, even though annoying, may accentuate stereotyped behavior.

Intentions

Conduct is organized into sequences in which people make plans and carry them out, or at least start to carry them out. Guthrie is aware of this and devotes a chapter to learning with and without intention.[25]

He and Smith had earlier followed the lead of Sherrington and Woodworth in considering sequences of behavior as composed of precurrent or preparatory responses and consummatory responses.[26] Such acts appear from the outside to be intentional, for the earlier adjustments clearly are in readiness for the consequences that are to follow. These anticipatory responses or readiness reactions are said to be conditioned to maintaining stimuli.

The typical case is that of the hungry rat running down an alleyway to food at the end. The activity is maintained by the internal stimuli aroused by food deprivation to which running and eating behavior have been conditioned in the past. That is, the rat found food at some previous time after running while hungry. These internal stimuli, plus the stimuli from the runway (if it has been previously a path to food), maintain the running of the animal against competing responses, such as stopping to explore. Anticipatory salivation or chewing movements give directional character to the behavior. All this food anticipation is fulfilled if there is food at the end of the maze. Because the stimuli of hunger and anticipation are now removed, and the animal is out of the maze, all the learning is intact for a new trial at a later time. This is about as complex a description as Guthrie ever indulges in, and the details are not taken

[24] F. D. Sheffield (1949).

[25] Guthrie (1935), pages 202–211.

[26] Smith and Guthrie (1921); Sherrington (1906); Woodworth (1918).

as seriously as Hull, for example, takes them. But the paradigm provides a way of talking about human intentions and purposes also.

> The essence of an intention is a body of maintaining stimuli which may or may not include sources of unrest like thirst or hunger but always includes action tendencies conditioned during a past experience—a readiness to speak, a readiness to go, a readiness to read, and in each case a readiness not only for the act but also for the previously rehearsed consequences of the act. These readinesses are not complete acts but they consist in tensions of the muscles that will take part in the complete act.[27]

This statement goes a long way toward the point of view which those with very different theories of learning accept. The only feature which keeps it within the bounds of Guthrie's theory is that all the readinesses, including the readiness for the "previously rehearsed consequences of the act," are said to consist in tensions in the muscles. This assumption, characteristic of the behaviorist position, remains in the realm of conjecture rather than of demonstration.

The Control of the Learning Process

It is part of the charm of Guthrie's writing that it is closely in touch with life and provides amusing but cogent suggestions for meeting the problems of animal training, child-rearing, and pedagogy. This practicality is not a necessary characteristic of the system, for if one seriously attempted to provide evidence for the theory he would be buried in the midst of the precise movement correlates of measurable stimuli and the muscular tension accompaniments of preparatory adjustments. But the system is not intended to be taken seriously in that sense. As long as a convenient way of talking about things can be found without seeming to contradict the system, quantitative precision is not essential. It is Guthrie's conviction that scientific laws to be useful must be approximately true, but they must also be stated coarsely enough to be teachable to freshmen.[28]

Most of the practical advice which Guthrie gives is good advice, and he succeeds in making it flow from the theory. Consider the following example:

> The mother of a ten-year-old girl complained to a psychologist that for two years her daughter had annoyed her by a habit of tossing coat and hat on the floor as she entered the house. On a hundred occasions the mother had insisted that the girl pick up the clothing and hang it in its place. These wild ways were changed only after the mother, on advice, began to insist not that the girl pick up the fallen garments from the floor, but that she put them on, return to the

[27] Guthrie (1935), pages 205–206.
[28] Guthrie (1936a).

street, and re-enter the house, this time removing the coat and hanging it properly.[29]

Why was this advice given? Behavior is in response to stimuli. Hanging up the coat and hat was in response to her mother's pleading and the sight of the clothing on the floor. In order to attach the desired behavior to its proper cues, it was necessary to go outside and come into the house, so that entering the house became the cue for hanging up the coat and hat.

The following statements represent the kind of suggestions which recur in his writings:

1. If you wish to encourage a particular kind of behavior or discourage another, discover the cues leading to the behavior in question. In the one case, arrange the situation so that the desired behavior occurs when those cues are present; in the other case, arrange it so that the undesired behavior does not occur in the presence of the cues. This is all that is involved in the skillful use of reward and punishment. A student does not learn what was in a lecture or a book. He learns only what the lecture or book caused him to do.[30]

2. Use as many stimulus supports for desired behavior as possible, because any ordinary behavior is a complex of movements to a complex of stimuli. The more stimuli there are associated with the desired behavior, the less likely that distracting stimuli and competing behavior will upset the desirable behavior. There would be fewer lines confused in amateur theatricals if there were more dress rehearsals, since the cues from the stage and the actors are part of the situation to which the actor responds. Another way of putting this is to rule that we should practice in the precise form later to be demanded of us.

EXPERIMENTS ON THE PUZZLE-BOX

One of the serious lacks in the early history of Guthrie's proposals was the failure to set convincing experiments. Such an experiment[31] was completed between the two editions of his book on learning and provides a much more tangible ground on which to come to grips with both the strengths and the weaknesses of Guthrie's position.

It is fitting that Guthrie and Horton should have chosen as a characteristic experiment the behavior of the cat in escaping from a puzzle-

[29] Guthrie (1935), page 21.
[30] Guthrie (1942), page 55.
[31] Guthrie and Horton (1946).

box, because this situation had already been the occasion for both experiment and theory. Thorndike's classical experiment has already been cited (page 16). This gave the send-off to Thorndike's theory by convincing him that little of the cat's behavior was mediated by ideas and much of it controlled by the influence of rewards. Adams' (1929) repetition of Thorndike's work gave much more evidence for ideas. These two experiments represent extremes of theory in addition to providing detailed descriptions of behavior as background for the Guthrie and Horton experiment.

Adams' Repetition and Supplementation of Thorndike's Work

Adams (1929) repeated Thorndike's experiment as faithfully as possible, noting details of the cat's behavior instead of relying solely on time curves. He also designed some other experiments, of which the following is typical.

A piece of liver is suspended from the top of a wire cage, so that the liver rests on the floor inside the cage, loosely held by the thread. A hungry cat in the room with the cage, but outside it, sees the liver and walks over to the cage. It hesitates for a time and its head moves up and down as though it is studying the string. Then it jumps on top of the cage, catches the string in its mouth, raises the liver by joint use of mouth and paw, and leaps down with the stick at the end of the string in its mouth. The liver is pulled to the top of the cage, but it is unfortunately torn off. In another trial the cat is successful in obtaining the liver by pawing the stick, taking it in its mouth and jumping down again. This time the liver has been more securely fastened, and the response is successful.

Adams argues that this kind of behavior is very different from the random slashing about described by Thorndike and appears by analogy to be controlled by ideas. If the cat has used its past behavior and habits, it has used them in a new situation in a remarkably appropriate manner.

The Guthrie and Horton Experiment

Because of their wish to record details of movement rather than to score achievement in some other manner, a special problem-box was designed which permitted the cat to be fully observed during the period prior to solution and its exact posture to be recorded photographically at the moment it activated the release. The release mechanism was a small pole set in the midst of the floor of a glass-covered cage with exit door in the front. The animal entered through a starting box and tunnel at the rear. If it touched the pole in any manner at all, the front door was opened and the animal could escape into the room. A camera was operated as the door was opening, so that a photograph of the animal was obtained at the moment of release, while it was still in contact with the pole.

In each of three preliminary trials the animal entered the box through the tunnel and made its way out the front door, which was left ajar, to find a bit of salmon on the table top in front of the box. The first of the regular trials followed. During the regular trials, the experimenters kept notes of the animal's behavior as it entered the box through the tunnel at the rear, and the camera recorded the exact time and position when it struck the release mechanism.

The results are remarkable for the amount of repetitiousness in each cat's successive release. A cat which bites the pole may do so time after time; one which has escaped by backing into the pole may back almost endlessly in its efforts to escape by the same movement. Others use front paws or hind paws, or roll against the pole. The cat, in full agreement with the theory, learns the method of escape in the first trial and then repeats what is essentially the same solution time after time. Some cats have several modes of escape which they use at different times, or they have one type of escape for a long time and then shift to another. These exceptions to the principle of doing what was done the last time are accounted for on the basis of a different entrance, which changes the stimulating conditions; the result of accidental distractions; or, having been in the box a long time and failing to operate the release by a familiar method, some new method may have superseded the familiar one. The fact that the last movement—the movement at the time of release—is the most stereotyped is in agreement with the principle that such an act will remain intact because nothing can interfere with it, the cat leaving the situation as soon as he strikes the release mechanism. The fact that the food reward is inconsequential is shown by the cat's often failing to eat the fish or to lick the milk provided for it.

Guthrie and Horton say that they have seen in the behavior of their cats all that Adams and Thorndike report. But they have also seen a degree of stereotypy which points strongly to the tendency for behavior to repeat itself under similar conditions. Some of the tracings of photographs of Guthrie and Horton's cats are shown in Figure 6.

This behavior is so convincing that it has to be acknowledged. It is coherent with all that Guthrie has been proposing in his theory. That is surely as much as could be wished for by a theorist from a series of experiments.

Why did these cats learn so much more easily than Thorndike's? The answer given is plausible. These cats always found the release mechanism available in exactly the same form, and readily operable. Thorndike's release mechanism was more difficult to operate and was probably not always in precisely the same position. Hence Thorndike's cats had to

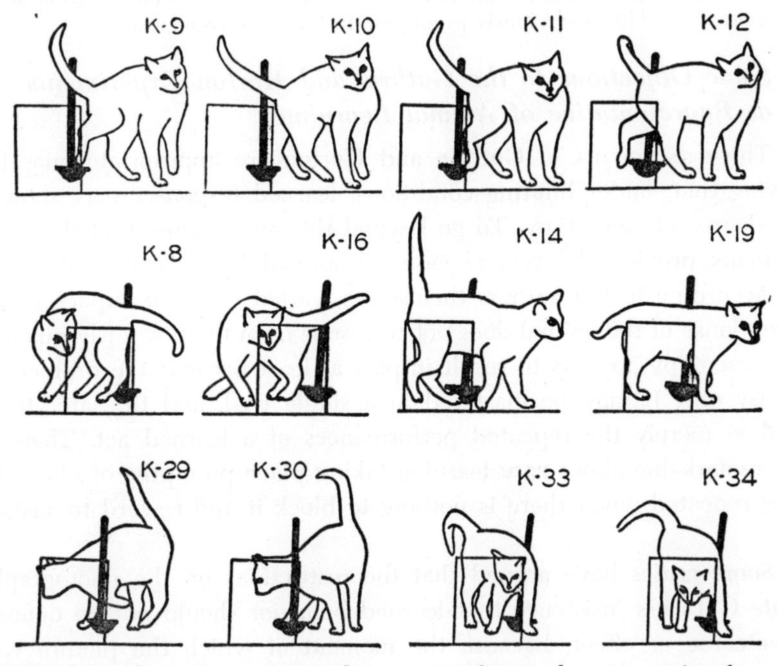

FIGURE 6. Alternative stereotyped responses of a single cat escaping from the puzzle box by touching the pole. Responses K-9 through K-12 illustrate one type of response used frequently by cat K. The remaining pairs of pictures show four other response types used by the same cat. Reproduced from tracings of photographs taken automatically at the time of release. From Guthrie and Horton (1946).

learn a series of habits rather than a single habit. When Guthrie and Horton's cats failed to operate the mechanism by a familiar method they, too, adopted a new method. Stereotypy was shown because stereotypy worked.

Guthrie and Horton are clear that they are not proposing a test of the cat's intelligence. They could easily have devised an experiment in which there would have been much less stereotypy. But the point is that as far as the learning of movements is concerned, the animal tends to do what it last did in the situation. If the situation forces it to do something else, it will do something else. Cats do not jump at the place where a bird was previously caught if there is no bird there, though they may lie in wait at the same spot.

The experiments are accepted by the authors as fully justifying the theory which Guthrie has all along expounded:

> It has been our conclusion from our observation of this series of experiments that the prediction of what any animal would do at any moment is most securely based on a record of what the animal was observed to do *in that situation at its last occurrence*. This is obviously prediction in terms of association.[32]

Some Objections to the Guthrie and Horton Experiments as Representative of Animal Learning

The experiments of Guthrie and Horton are appropriate ones for showing that, under limiting conditions, learned responses may show a high degree of stereotypy. To go beyond this and assume that these experiments provide the typical case for animal learning is misleading.

According to the authors themselves, varied behavior supervenes if the response of the animal does not release it from the box fairly quickly. The stereotypy appears to result in part at least because the problem is an easy one. It may be mastered in a single trial, and the later trials are then merely the repeated performances of a learned act. There is little remarkable about easy learning taking place promptly, or about its being repeated when there is nothing to block it and reward to sustain it.[33]

Some critics have argued that the restrictions on the photographs violate Guthrie's insistence that learned behavior should not be defined by outcome or effect, because the moment at which the picture was snapped was defined by the consequences of the activity: releasing the door.

> The effect of this restriction in picture taking could be seen more clearly in an experiment that required the animal to stand on his hind legs and reach out of the upper corner of the cage in order to press a button to release the door and take the picture. In this way we further restrict the set of possible responses and achieve added stereotypy. On the other hand, other experimental situations could be constructed, which would reduce stereotypy. In either case, however, what is procured are data concerning responses defined in terms of effect.[34]

It is not quite clear how much Guthrie and Horton wish to make of the amount of stereotypy they observed. Commenting on an earlier and

[32] Guthrie and Horton (1946), page 42.
[33] Baffling situations also lead to stereotypy. E.g., Hamilton (1916).
[34] Mueller and Schoenfeld (1954), page 358.

related experiment done with guinea pigs by Muenzinger, Koerner, and Irey (1929), Guthrie writes:

> These authors conclude that the mechanization of habitual movement "is still accompanied by variability of its pattern . . ." and that accessory movements, "while on the whole exhibiting much plasticity, show some mechanization of a brief and unstable kind."
>
> The account given by Muenzinger, Koerner, and Irey is quite consistent with what Horton and I observed in our cats. We were interested in the routinizing, they in the exceptions and new behavior. We were convinced that whole segments of movement appear and are repeated all-or-none on succeeding trials.[35]

Guthrie and Horton certainly succeeded in showing a considerable amount of repetitiveness and stereotypy in learned behavior. This leads them to conclude, as indicated in the earlier quotation, that prediction is best made on the basis of the last prior occurrence, and that such a prediction is obviously one in terms of association. We may question this last conclusion. To prophesy that a man who owns and wears only blue ties will wear a blue tie tomorrow is an actuarial prediction pure and simple, with no theory in it. It is logically similar to the prediction of an insurance company that a given percentage of people will die at a given age. The only assumption is a certain uniformity of events when taken *en masse*—an assumption scarcely attributable to associationism.

To account for learning, rather than for the repetition of learned acts, one has to account not for uniformity but for change. Upon learning in this sense the Guthrie and Horton experiments throw little light. Most of the change in behavior took place in the neglected early trials in which the cats learned to find their way out of the box through the glass door. There was, to be sure, the supplementary learning to use the pole to open the door. A harder but possibly clearer problem, like the string-pulling problems studied by Adams, perhaps would be solved by fewer animals, but those which solved them could use the solutions in novel situations. Thus the chosen learning situation has a great deal to do with what aspects of behavior will be revealed. The problem-box of Guthrie and Horton, which at first blush appears to lay bare the primitive nature of learning, may in fact be a highly specialized situation poorly designed to show the behavior of the cat as it would solve a problem which, while harder for it, was more appropriate to it in clarity of cue-response relationships.

[35] Guthrie (1952), pages 271–272.

STEPS TOWARD FORMALIZATION AND ADDITIONAL EXPERIMENTAL TESTING

Since the first edition of this book appeared, some of Guthrie's students have undertaken the task of clarifying and formalizing his theory, and of designing new experiments crucially related to it. The theory has gained support also from other quarters, and has now become a serious contender among contemporary learning theories, as it was there suggested that, with such help, it might become.

Guthrie's statements have been collected and cast into postulational form by Voeks (1950). She goes on to state eight theorems open to experimental test, and has herself provided some confirming experimental results. Her four basic postulates are here quoted verbatim:

Postulate 1: Principle of Association

(*a*) Any stimulus-pattern which once accompanies a response, and/or immediately precedes it (by ½ seconds or less), becomes a full-strength direct cue for that response. (*b*) This is the only way in which stimulus-patterns not now cues for a particular response can become direct cues for that response.

Postulate 2: Principle of Postremity

(*a*) A stimulus which has accompanied or immediately preceded two or more incompatible responses is a conditioned stimulus for only the last response made while that stimulus was present. (*b*) This is the only way in which a stimulus now a cue for a particular response can cease being a cue for that response.

Postulate 3: Principle of Response Probability[36]

The probability of any particular response's occurring (P) at some specified time is an increasing monotonic function (x) of the proportion (N) of the stimuli present which are at that time cues for that response. ($P = N^x$).

Postulate 4: Principle of Dynamic Situations

The stimulus-pattern of a situation is not static but from time to time is modified, due to such changes as result from the subject's making a response, accumulation of fatigue products, visceral changes and other internal processes of the subject, introduction of controlled or uncontrolled variations in the stimuli present.

These four postulates (and the theorems related to them) deal with isolated responses as the essential core of Guthrie's theory. Unfortunately, Voeks's theorem system has not yet been extended to deal systematically with the puzzling problems posed by various arrangements of reward and

[36] Some of the subscripts have been omitted from the symbols in Postulate 3 as unnecessary here.

punishment, with anticipatory responses, with the integration of acts through movement-produced stimuli. Nevertheless, the start made by Voeks is a very useful one, and her experimental tests are cogent.

Her first experimental test [37] (completed before the system was formalized, but consistent with the formalization) deals with the prediction of behavior in a maze. She studied the individual responses at each choice-point of 57 human subjects learning a raised relief finger maze and a punch-board maze. She tested which of two predictions was the more accurate: (1) prediction based on the *frequency* of prior choices at the point of choice, and (2) prediction based on *postremity* (i.e., the last choice that was made). Postremity won out easily. The success of prediction by postremity was most striking when the prediction disagreed with that on the basis of frequency. For 56 of the 57 subjects, postremity predicted better than frequency for those choices in which the predictions disagreed. The difference was statistically highly significant. These results are, of course, in agreement with Guthrie's theory, especially as stated in Voeks's Postulate 2.

The major puzzle is why the maze was learned at all. Why was not the last trial chiefly a repetition of the first, with some minor fluctuations according to Postulate 4? The explanation is not very difficult for the high-relief maze, for the last response was always leaving the choice-point by the true path. The explanation is more difficult for the punch-board maze, because a "non-correction" method was used. That is, if the "wrong" hole was punched, this was signalled to the subject, but he went on to the next choice without punching the "right" hole. Let us look at Voeks's explanation of the learning of the punch-board maze:

> . . . Now, in the learning of the punch-board maze, S may insert his stylus into the wrong hole of a pair, e.g., pair 8. A stimulus then is presented (the sound of the buzzer in our experiment, E saying "wrong" in others, etc.) which may cause S to withdraw his stylus and make additional responses on that trial to that choice point. These responses may involve, for instance, the S's saying to himself "Eight, not this hole, that one is right," or even making incipient or possibly overt movements toward the other correct hole while looking at the pair. If this has been the case, the next time S comes to the pair of holes, he will say "Eight" (as instructed), and it is expected he will start toward the incorrect hole, draw his stylus back, say "No, not this hole; that one is right," and then make the previously established conditioned response to the stimulus "That-is-right," i.e., the response of inserting his stylus into the hole at which he has just looked and said "That is right." Thus another error may be eliminated. This again is in accordance with the principle of postremity.[38]

[37] Voeks (1948).
[38] Voeks (1948), page 505.

In fairness to the experimenter it must be pointed out that this change of response would have been *recorded* as a failure of prediction by postremity, although on the basis of her theoretical analysis it was no failure at all. Hence her successful predictions by postremity are on the conservative side. The explanation offered for the actual learning (the elimination of an error) seems to come very near to an explanation according to knowledge of results or effect, and gives somewhat specialized meaning to the concept of "doing what you last did."

The second experiment [39] studies conditioned eyelid responses of human subjects, measuring both the occurrence of the responses and their amplitudes. The question asked is this: "Is a stimulus-response connection gradually strengthened by reinforcement, or is a stimulus-response connection established suddenly, in all-or-none fashion?" Hull is said to favor gradual strengthening, Guthrie all-or-none appearance of responses, according to Voeks's postulates 1 and 2.

Two tests were made of the theory of gradual strengthening, the first studying amplitude, the second frequency. Beginning with the first conditioned response (CR), succeeding responses for each subject were divided into fourths. For only 6 of 32 subjects was there a progressive increase in *amplitude* of CR from quarter to quarter. In general, increases from quarter to quarter were not statistically significant, although for 25 of the 32 subjects the last CR was larger than the first (a significant difference). Amplitude changes thus gave little support to Hull's theory of gradual increase in strength with repeated reinforcement. The *frequency* results were more strikingly in Guthrie's favor, because a response was acquired in all-or-none fashion. No subject showed an increase in frequency of CR from quarter to quarter following his first CR. Half the subjects gave CR's on every trial after their first one, and there were only a few lapses for the others.

How do Voeks's results square with the many acquisition curves published for CR's? It is well known that curves for groups of subjects show characteristics very different from curves for individual subjects. Voeks has very convincingly shown that response acquisition may be all-or-none, and yet a group learning curve will show a gradual slope. The accompanying learning curve (Figure 7) results, for example, when the probability of response is plotted as a group function for 15 subjects all of whom had jumpwise curves, that is, all of whom responded consistently with CR's after the first CR was made. The form of the curve

[39] Voeks (1954).

is determined solely by the trial on which the first CR happened to appear for different subjects.[40]

Voeks predicted jumpwise curves of learning under the very uniform conditions of stimulation that she arranged to produce, and her predictions were well borne out. A jumpwise curve is, of course, ideal for a test of the postremity principle: if there is an unbroken run of no responses, the prediction by postremity is perfect during the course of this run; if this is followed by an unbroken run of conditioned responses,

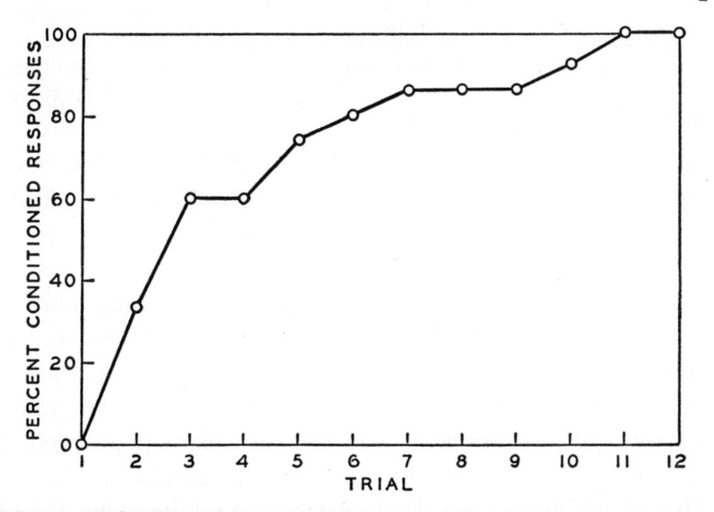

FIGURE 7. Misleading effect of combining individual learning curves. The group curve results from combining the curves of 15 subjects all of whom had jumpwise curves, i.e., a run of no responses followed by consistent responding. After Voeks (1954), page 145.

prediction by postremity is perfect then, too. The prediction fails for only one trial (that on which the conditioning occurs!). By the test of postremity prediction, Guthrie's theory was beautifully confirmed. Of the total predictions made, 84.6 per cent were correct.

What are we to do with the fact that an unconditioned response of the eyelid *did* occur (within ½ second of the conditioned stimulus) on every trial from the beginning? Does not Voeks's Postulate 1 lead us to expect a conditioned response right away? Why does the CR wait for several trials (as many as 10) before it makes its appearance? Perhaps there is something to the group curve after all, showing that the probability of giving the *first* CR increases with the number of reinforcements.

[40] Not all individual conditioning curves are of Voeks's jumpwise type. Many acquisition curves showing gradual acquisition have been published for single learners: dogs, rats, human subjects. For individual curves of eyelid conditioning (the response Voeks studied) see Hilgard (1931), page 14, Cohen, Hilgard, and Wendt (1933), page 64.

The postremity principle cannot predict when the first CR appears, because its appearance *always* violates the principle (at least, so far as *recorded* responses are concerned).

This leads us to consider another postulate. There is a frequency principle in Guthrie's system, stated in Voeks's Postulate 3. It is the principle that cues are assimilated to a response with practice, and, conversely, cues are alienated during forgetting. According to Guthrie:

> The strengthening of an S-R connection with repetition may very possibly be the result of the enlistment of increasing numbers of stimuli as conditioners.[41]
>
> But why should practice make the effect increasingly certain? Is it not quite possible that on successive practice periods more and more conditioners are enlisted, so that after twenty periods there is a high probability that the cue will have enough support to be effective? [42]

Although this interpretation is very plausible, it makes it difficult to find a crucial test of Guthrie's theory. If one-trial learning suffices, then either the basic principle of association, or the related principle of postremity, is confirmed; if learning is gradual, then the principle of probability is confirmed. Only as the principles are made more precise will it be possible to find exceptions and hence improve the theory. Estes (1950) has given a more precise statement of Guthrie's probability principle and worked it out in a form suitable for critical testing. He regards a stimulus, or stimulating situation, as a finite population of relatively small, independent, environmental events, of which only a sample is effective at any given time. Each occurrence produces conditioning of the momentary effective sample of stimulus elements. Estes acknowledges that the line of argument is the one developed by Guthrie.[43] We shall return to the details of Estes' theory later, as we consider other mathematical and probabilistic theories.

The work of Voeks and of Estes well illustrates the steps needed to make Guthrie's theory more suitable for experimental testing. While the theory is itself undergoing formalization, a number of aspects of it are undergoing experimental tests. It is difficult to summarize these briefly, because most of the experiments require, in addition to the presentation of their data, the elaboration of an argument to show how the data lead to a preference for one interpretation over another. A few representative studies are listed in Table 1 merely to indicate the kind of work that is going on, and to provide a "search-pattern" for those who wish to seek out the newer studies that are appearing right along.

[41] Guthrie (1930), page 420.
[42] Guthrie (1935), page 100.
[43] Estes (1950), page 100.

TABLE 1. Some Experimental Results Bearing on Guthrie's Theory

Experimenter and Date of Report	*General Nature of Experiment and Findings*	*Relationship to Guthrie's Theory as Stated by Experimenter*
Seward (1942)	Rats learned to press a bar more readily when rewarded by food than when merely removed after pressing the bar.	"The superiority of the rewarded animals was marked. . . . In this respect Guthrie's theory appears inadequate."
Seward, Dill, and Holland (1944)	Human subjects given task of finding a correct button in response to each of a series of colors. Some colors shown twice paired with different buttons. In recall, with new order of stimuli, subjects more often responded with first response than with second (postreme) response.	". . . These findings challenge the general validity of Guthrie's proposition and call for an examination of the conditions under which it does or does not hold."
V. F. Sheffield (1949)	In alley experiment with rats, after massed training resistance to extinction was greater for 50 per cent reinforcement group than for 100 per cent; groups did not differ, however, after spaced training.	"These results verify a prediction from a hypothesis utilizing stimulus-response learning concepts" ("such as those used by Guthrie and Hull").
Kimball and Kendall (1953)	Rats learned to avoid shock by turning a wheel when a light came on preceding the shock. Extinction was either by a "toleration" method, in which the conditioned stimulus came on gradually, or by the usual "exhaustion" method, with non-reinforcement of conditioned stimulus presented at full strength. Extinction was more rapid by toleration method.	"This result confirms one of Guthrie's theoretical ideas and necessitates a reformulation of Hull's theory of extinction."
Zeaman and Radner (1953)	Rat learns response that turns off light but not one that turns on light.	"Guthrie's theory as formalized by Voeks is not directly confirmed. The crucialness of the data for Guthrie's theory is seen to be dependent upon the outcome of further research on the nature of the rat's unlearned response to light."
Wickens and Platt (1954)	Finger withdrawal for one group conditioned to tone that ceased when .450 sec. shock began; for other group tone continued with shock. Difference in conditioning not significant.	"The results of this experiment would seem to be predicted more readily by the type of theory advanced by Mowrer than by Guthrie's strict contiguity theory. . . . It is likely, however, that Guthrie's theory could handle the results through the use of the concept of movement-produced stimuli."

Enough of the current studies favor Guthrie's theory to insure that it will be given serious attention as an active contemporary theory of learning.

ESTIMATE OF GUTHRIE'S POSITION

Guthrie's Position on Typical Problems of Learning

By way of comparative summary, how Guthrie stands on the several representative problems of learning will be briefly stated.

1. *Capacity.* Problems of capacity are not formally treated, although species differences are recognized and allowance is made for maturation as a determiner of many classes of acts.[44] Presumably any response which the organism can make can become associated with any stimulus to which he is sensitive—a generalization about the possibility of learning which is reminiscent of what Thorndike says about associative shifting. If pressed, Guthrie could find a basis for differences in capacity both in the differentiation of movement and in the discrimination among proprioceptive cues. All animals are not equally versatile and equally equipped with receptors.

2. *Practice.* Practice assimilates and alienates cues, until a whole family of stimulus combinations comes to evoke a whole family of responses which lead to the outcome socially described as successful performance. Because skill represents a population of habits, learning appears to accumulate with repetition, although basically each individual habit is learned at full strength in a single repetition.

3. *Motivation.* Motivation affects learning indirectly through what it causes the animal to do. Reward is a secondary or derivative principle, not a primary one as in Thorndike's system. Reward works because it removes the animal from the stimulating situation in which the "correct" response has been made. It does not strengthen the "correct" response, but prevents its weakening because no new response can become attached to the cues which led to the correct response. Thus there is a relative strengthening, because responses to other cues get alienated.

Punishment does at once several different things. In general, its effects for learning are determined by what it causes the organism to do, according to the principle that the best predictor of learning is the response in the situation that last occurred. We may distinguish four cases:

[44] Guthrie (1935), pages 18, 38.

a. Mild punishment may be merely exciting, and enhance ongoing behavior without disrupting it.

b. More intense punishment may break up a prior habit by leading to incompatible behavior in the presence of the cues for the earlier habit.

c. Continuing punishment acts like a drive, producing maintaining stimuli that keep the organism active until it finds relief. Then the consequence for learning is really that of reward: the act that leads to safety is rewarding because it terminates the punishment and by removing the maintaining stimuli protects from unlearning the activities carried on in the presence of those stimuli.

d. Stimuli that have previously accompanied the punishment produce behavior that formerly occurred following the punishment itself. Here we have an illustration of anticipatory response, essential to avoidance behavior. The cues to avoidance must earlier have been present at the time of punishment for this anticipation to occur.

4. *Understanding.* Concepts like "insight" are handled in a derisive manner, although it is recognized that learning with foresight of its consequences may occur. The tendency is to talk down such learning, however, just as Thorndike did, and to emphasize the mechanical and repetitious nature of most human as well as animal learning. Such learning with intention and foresight as does occur is explained on the basis of conditioned anticipatory or readiness reactions, based upon past experience and hence not contradicting association principles.

5. *Transfer.* Learning transfers to new situations because of common elements within the old and new. In this the position is rather like Thorndike's. Stress is laid, however, on the identity being carried by way of common responses evoked, the proprioceptive stimuli being sufficiently similar from responses to a variety of stimuli to evoke common conditioned responses. The emphasis upon movement-produced stimuli thus represents Guthrie's supplementation to Thorndike.

Because of his principle of responses being conditioned to all adventitious contiguous stimuli, Guthrie expects rather little transfer and is, in fact, rather extreme about it. The only way to be sure to get desired behavior in a new situation is to practice in that new situation as well. To be able to perform in a variety of situations, you have to practice in a variety of situations.

6. *Forgetting.* Learning is said to be permanent unless interfered with by new learning. Hence all forgetting is due to the learning of new responses which replace the old responses. It may take place gradually

for the same reason that skills may be acquired gradually: remembering depends upon many habits to many cues, and subhabits may drop out gradually as subcues become attached to new responses.

By contrast with Thorndike, Guthrie is an avowed behaviorist who makes it a matter of some importance to get rid of subjective terms, to refer, for example, to inner speech instead of to thinking. The emphasis upon movement-produced stimuli is part of this older behaviorist tradition which Guthrie carries into the present. While an orthodox behaviorist in these respects, his is an informal behaviorism, with little of the brittleness of earlier Watsonianism.

Invulnerability of the Theory a Cause for Skepticism

The uncertainty that exists in practically all learning experimentation makes the fact-minded psychologist suspicious of a finished system at this stage of our knowledge. While scientific truth must eventually have exceptionless validity—if its laws are truly lawful—the history of our most advanced sciences shows that their theories move by successive approximations, and the most advanced theories do not emerge full blown from the head of the theorist. Even as loose a system as Thorndike's went through revisions on the basis of evidence regarding the effects of punishment; Hull's system, the most carefully worked out of any, was continuously being revamped to meet experimental fact. One of the sources of uneasiness about Guthrie's system lies in its assured answers to the problems of learning—answers that have remained unchanged through a quarter of a century of the most active psychological experimentation we have ever known. Experimental controversies finally get resolved as we learn more about the independent variables that modify the measured consequences. No matter how these issues get resolved, Guthrie's system remains unchanged. Either the theory is a miraculously inspired one or it is not stated very precisely, and hence is not very sensitive to experimental data.

Criticism of Guthrie's position is rendered somewhat difficult by the nature of the task which he sets himself. It is not quite clear whether he believes his system to have any responsibility with respect to details.

> The principle of association or conditioning is not an explanation of any instance of behavior. It is merely a tool by which explanation is furthered. A tool is not true or false; it is useful or useless.[45]

The paradox of the theory lies in the kind of sophistication implied in this statement, combined with a casualness which baffles the critic. It

[45] Guthrie (1935), page 232.

is not unfair to ask of the position that it substantiate its claims, which are, indeed, far-reaching and are competitive with the claims of others.

Of the opposing points of view to which he objects, Guthrie generously admits that their phenomena and the terms used to describe them are correct and useful for certain purposes.[46] What he says in essence is that what they do is all right for limited purposes, but it is not very helpful so far as understanding ordinary learning is concerned. All other writers are said to be concerned with outcomes, in the form of success or goal achievement. Under their theories, he says, the teacher must be a mere passive element in the situation and cannot be told how to influence the outcome.[47] This *non sequitur* indicates a failure to take opposing claims seriously. Insight, if not predicted on the basis of past experience, must be in the category of luck, and hence lie outside of science.[48] While many of Guthrie's observations are astute, a cavalier handling of serious alternatives to his own gives an impression of immutability inappropriate in a growing science.

The Simplicity of the Theory May Be Illusory

Certainly much of the fascination of Guthrie's theory rests upon his ability to deduce a wide range of phenomena from the single principle of one-trial contiguous association. Parsimonious scientific theories are attractive, and this is the ultimate in reductionist theories. Although Voeks found it convenient to state four postulates, with proper definitions of the stimuli and responses entering into association, she would have found one to be enough, with the other three as corollaries.

A painstaking search through Guthrie's writings for careful definitions of stimulus and response, for distinctions between observables and constructs, for statements taking the form of predictions and those taking the form of a posteriori explanations, has led recent critics to conclude:

> While the principles of conditioning which he expands seem to have a parsimony that would be desirable in a theoretical formulation of behavior, a closer analysis reveals that a formidable set of additional assumptions and constructs are required if his theory is to possess any real applicability to experimental data.[49]

[46] See Guthrie's comments on Tolman, Hull, Skinner and others, Guthrie (1952), pages 189–252. These pages are new to the revised edition of the book, although the orientation is unchanged from views expressed much earlier, e.g., Guthrie (1942), page 57.

[47] Guthrie (1942), page 57.

[48] Guthrie (1935), page 25.

[49] Mueller and Schoenfeld (1954), page 377.

It is undoubtedly true that many reviews of Guthrie in the literature have mistaken incompleteness for simplicity.[50]

Guthrie's Contributions

Despite his formal concern with the more hard-boiled aspects of scientific observation and scientific logic, Guthrie is without a peer in the use of anecdote and illustration to make pertinent comments about the activities of everyday life, including the symptoms found in the psychological clinic. This complicated material is talked about in dramatically simple terms, and his theory makes this kind of talk possible. The difference between plausibility and proof is one of the differences that hounds psychological science, and a theory that is not sensitive to experimental data will not be sensitive either to those clinical patients who do not get well following good advice. Nevertheless, there is something to be learned from Guthrie's type of psychologizing, and it is not a sufficient explanation to remark that he is a wise and experienced person, a shrewd observer of human beings. His kind of psychologizing is appealing enough to have led many promising young men and women to enter upon careers in psychology—a contribution to the field not to be overlooked.

At the experimental level, Guthrie's greatest contribution is to call attention to the large element of repetitiveness and stereotypy in behavior when the opportunities are favorable to such monotonous behavior. The tendency toward smugness is easily overlooked, especially by those who choose to study the changes in behavior called learning.

There are enough well-trained younger psychologists friendly to Guthrie's ideas to undertake the task of increasing the rigor of his system beyond that yet attained. The promise of the system is great enough to make the effort worth while.

SUPPLEMENTARY READINGS

BOOKS

GUTHRIE, E. R. (1935) (1952) *The psychology of learning.*

GUTHRIE, E. R. (1938) *The psychology of human conflict.*

SHORTER INTRODUCTIONS

GUTHRIE, E. R. (1930) Conditioning as a principle of learning. *Psychol. Rev.*, 37, 412–428.

GUTHRIE, E. R. (1942) Conditioning: A theory of learning in terms of stimulus, response and association. Chapter 1 in *The psychology of learning.* Natl. Soc. Stud. Educ., 41st Yearbook, Part II, 17–60.

[50] Mueller and Schoenfeld (1954), page 368.

CRITICAL REVIEWS

ADAMS, D. K. (1948) Review of Guthrie and Horton's *Cats in a puzzle box. Psychol. Bull.*, 45, 548–550.

CARMICHAEL, L. (1936) Review of Guthrie's *The psychology of learning. J. gen. Psychol.*, 14, 490–492.

HILGARD, E. R. (1935) Review of Guthrie's *The psychology of learning. Psychol. Bull.*, 32, 306–309.

SEARS, R. R. (1939) Review of Guthrie's *The psychology of human conflict. Psychol. Bull.*, 36, 829–830.

REPRESENTATIVE EXPERIMENTS

CARTER, L. F. (1936) Maze learning with a differential proprioceptive cue. *J. exp. Psychol.*, 19, 758–762.

CARTER, L. F. (1941) Intensity of conditioned stimulus and rate of conditioning. *J. exp. Psychol.*, 28, 481–490.

GUTHRIE, E. R. (1933) Association as a function of time interval. *Psychol. Rev.*, 40, 355–367.

SHEFFIELD, F. D. (1948) Avoidance training and the contiguity principle. *J. comp. physiol. Psychol.*, 41, 165–177.

SHEFFIELD, F. D., and TEMMER, H. W. (1950) Relative resistance to extinction of escape training and avoidance training. *J. exp. Psychol.*, 40, 287–298.

SHEFFIELD, F. D., WULFF, J. J., and BACKER, R. (1951) Reward value of copulation without sex drive reduction. *J. comp. physiol. Psychol.*, 44, 3–8.

SHEFFIELD, V. F. (1950) Resistance to extinction as a function of the distribution of extinction trials. *J. exp. Psychol.*, 40, 305–313.

SMITH, S., and FITCH, E. E. (1935) Skill and proprioceptor pattern. *J. genet. Psychol.*, 46, 303–310.

VOEKS, V. (1954) Acquisition of S-R connections: a test of Hull's and Guthrie's theories. *J. exp. Psychol.*, 47, 137–147.

YACORZYNSKI, G. K., and GUTHRIE, E. R. (1937) A comparative study of involuntary and voluntary conditioned responses. *J. gen. Psychol.*, 16, 235–257.

FINAL NOTE

For a searching criticism of the corresponding chapter in the first edition of this book, see:

SHEFFIELD, F. D. (1949) Hilgard's critique of Guthrie. *Psychol. Rev.*, 56, 284–291.

The following critical review of Guthrie's contributions from the point of view of the logic of science and system-making goes into greater analytical detail than the present chapter:

MUELLER, C. G., Jr., and SCHOENFELD, W. N. (1954) Edwin R. Guthrie. In W. K. ESTES and others. *Modern learning theory*, 345–379.

Chapter 4

SKINNER'S OPERANT CONDITIONING

IN a series of papers beginning in 1930, B. F. Skinner proposed a formulation of behavior which arose out of observations of animal performance in a type of experiment that he invented: the bar-pressing activity of a rat in a specially designed box called (by others) the Skinner box. The experiments and theories were first brought together in book form in his *Behavior of organisms* (1938). Experimentation has continued, much of it using a new organism (the pigeon) and a new equivalent of bar-pressing (the pigeon's pecking at a spot). The principles have become the basis for two textbooks of general psychology, Keller and Schoenfeld's *Principles of psychology* (1950) and Skinner's *Science and human behavior* (1953). As an avowed behaviorism making use of conditioning principles, the system can be understood as a development of the ground broken by Thorndike, just as Guthrie's system can be so understood. But if Guthrie's theory is thought of as a development of Thorndike's associative shifting, Skinner's operant conditioning is a development more along the lines of Thorndike's learning by selecting and connecting under the law of effect. As we shall see, Skinner acknowledges two kinds of learning, just as Thorndike did, but, like Thorndike, he places more emphasis upon that kind of learning which is under the control of its consequences.

RESPONDENT AND OPERANT BEHAVIOR

The greatest break with conventional stimulus-response psychology within Skinner's system is the distinction between respondent and operant behavior. Conventional stimulus-response psychology enforced the dictum "no stimulus, no response" by assuming the presence of stimuli when a response occurred though no stimuli were identifiable. Although it was often convenient to talk about "random" or "spontaneous" responses, it was not doubted that stimuli were present to elicit them, if the experimenter only had means of detecting them. Skinner finds this method of forcing facts both undesirable and unnecessary. He proposes that two classes of response be distinguished, a class of *elicited* responses and a class of *emitted* responses.

Respondent and Operant Distinguished

Responses which are elicited by known stimuli are classified as *respondents.* Pupillary constriction to light and the knee jerk to a blow on the patellar tendon serve as convenient illustrations. There is a second class of responses which need not be correlated with any known stimuli. These *emitted* responses are designated *operants,* to distinguish them from respondents. While the conventional treatment of such responses is to consider them as respondents with unknown stimuli, Skinner holds the conviction that the stimulus conditions, if any, are irrelevant to the understanding of operant behavior. Because operant behavior is not elicited by recognized stimuli, its strength cannot be measured according to the usual laws of the reflex, which are all stated as functions of stimuli. Instead, rate of response is used as a measure of strength.

An operant may, and usually does, acquire a relation to prior stimulation. In that case it becomes a *discriminated operant;* the stimulus becomes an occasion for the operant behavior, but is not an eliciting stimulus as in the case of a true reflex. Skinner formerly extended the term "reflex" to cover the operant, although this proved somewhat awkward because several of the laws of the reflex do not apply. A simple illustration of an operant co-ordinated with a stimulus would be a reaction-time experiment as commonly conducted in the psychological laboratory. The correlation between stimulus and response may easily be changed, as by instructions to depress the key instead of lifting the finger from it. The relationship of latency of response to changes in stimulus intensity is very different for a discriminated operant from what it is for an elicited response, say the lid reflex to sound—a respondent. Such a comparison between a discriminated operant and a respondent has been made by Peak (1933). Although the characteristics of voluntary and reflex eyelid responses both were changed in response to sounds differing in loudness, the magnitudes of changes differed for the two kinds of response.

Most human behavior is operant in character. The behavior of eating a meal, driving a car, writing a letter, shows but little of respondent character. The emphasis which Skinner places upon operant behavior is appropriate if he is going to have something to say that applies in principle to the commonest forms of human (and animal) behavior.

Two Types of Conditioning

Related to the two types of response there are said to be two types of conditioning.

The conditioning of respondent behavior is assigned to Type S, because reinforcement is correlated with stimuli. The conditioned stimulus (e.g., a tone) is presented together with the unconditioned stimulus (e.g., food) and thus comes to elicit the response (e.g., salivation). The reinforcing event that interests Skinner is the presentation of the unconditioned stimulus, not the response to it. Pavlov's classical conditioning experiment is said to be of Type S. Its two laws are the Law of Conditioning of Type S, and the Law of Extinction of Type S.[1] The law of conditioning makes such conditioning depend upon the approximate simultaneity of stimuli. The evidence for the existence of Type S conditioning is actually quite slim, because much that by experimental arrangement conforms to classical conditioning is better understood as a consequence of factors other than contiguity of stimulus and response. Hull, as we shall see, denied the existence of conditioning of Type S; Skinner admits that it does not appear experimentally in pure form.[2] But Skinner does not attribute much importance to Type S in any case. Whether or not there is such conditioning does not matter too much to his system.

Type R he believes to be much the more important. This is the conditioning of operant behavior, and the letter R is used to call attention to the important term in the correlation with reinforcement. In this case it is a *response* which is correlated with reinforcement. The experimental example which he originally used was lever-pressing. This response may be strengthened by following it with food. It is not the *sight* of the lever which is important; it is the *pressing* of the lever. The conditioned response does not resemble the response to the reinforcing stimulus; its relationship to the reinforcing stimulus is that it causes it to appear. In operant conditioning, conditioning of Type R, reinforcement cannot follow unless the conditioned response appears; reinforcement is *contingent upon* response. The two laws of Type R are not unlike those of Type S, including a law of conditioning and a law of extinction. The law of conditioning of Type R may be compared to Thorndike's law of effect: *If*

[1] Skinner (1938), pages 18–19.
[2] Skinner (1938), page 238.

the occurrence of an operant is followed by presentation of a reinforcing stimulus, the strength is increased.[3] Note that the reinforcing situation is defined by its stimulus; nothing is said about satisfying after-effects or about drive reduction. What gets strengthened is not a stimulus-response connection, because the operant requires no stimulus; this statement is unlike Thorndike:

> This dependence upon the posterior reinforcing stimulus gives the term operant its significance. . . . The operant . . . becomes significant for behavior and takes on an identifiable form when it acts upon the environment in such a way that a reinforcing stimulus is produced.[4]

The mechanical arrangement under which Type R conditioning is usually demonstrated is that suggested by the quotation, a situation in which the response of the organism produces the reinforcing agent. This is what has been called instrumental conditioning to distinguish it from the arrangements of classical conditioning.[5]

One suggestion offered quite tentatively by Skinner[6] is that conditioning of Type S may be limited to autonomic responses, Type R to skeletal behavior. The crucial question is whether Type S occurs at all; if it does, it may well be limited to autonomic responses. That Type R occurs is evident, and most skeletal responses, including those obtained under the arrangements of classical conditioning, can easily be shown to conform to the pattern of discriminated operants. Actual experiments in which autonomic conditioning takes place (salivation, galvanic response) are full of indirect accompaniments of Type R. When the circumstances seem almost ideal for demonstrating Type S conditioning, as in attempts to condition pupillary constriction by presenting a tone along with a light, it is extremely difficult to obtain any conditioning at all.[7]

REINFORCEMENT OF AN OPERANT

In order to get at the quantitative relationships within operant conditioning, Skinner designed a special apparatus suitable for use with

[3] Skinner (1938), page 21.

[4] Skinner (1938), page 22.

[5] Hilgard and Marquis (1940), pages 51–74. For Skinner's laboratory methods, see Ferster (1953).

[6] Skinner (1938), page 112.

[7] Recent attempts at pupillary conditioning have been most unsuccessful, e.g., Wedell, Taylor, and Skolnick (1940), Hilgard, Dutton, and Helmick (1949), Young (1954). Some success has been reported, however, by Kotake and Mihama (1951) and Mihama and Kotake (1954), so the matter is still open. "Pure cases" of Type S conditioning are hard to find. The heart-rate conditioning of Notterman, Schoenfeld, and Bersh (1952) includes the possibility of operant intermediaries.

white rats. It consists essentially of a darkened sound-resisting box in which the rat is placed. There is a small brass lever within the compartment which, if pressed, delivers a pellet of food. The lever is connected with a recording system which produces a graphical tracing of the number of lever pressings plotted against the length of time that the rat is in the box. By a carefully controlled handling of the animals, remarkably consistent and "lawful" results can be obtained. Modifications of the experiment can be introduced so that food is not delivered every time the lever is depressed. The consequences of doing this and of making other changes in the situation have been systematically reported.

The evident consequence of the reinforcement of an operant is to increase the rate with which the operant response is emitted. This increase in rate of responding is an indicator of the increased probability of response, which is the appropriate measure of *operant strength*, substituting for such measures as amplitude and latency, more appropriate for measuring the strength of a respondent. While the expression *reflex strength* was originally used for both respondent and operant behavior,[8] in Skinner's later writings he tends to restrict the word "reflex" to its ordinary meaning of elicited reflexes (salivation, knee-jerk), and to conditioned reflexes based on them, that is, to respondent behavior.[9]

Extinction as a Measure of Operant Strength

When an operant is regularly reinforced, the rate of responding is interrupted by the activity of eating. Because the time-consuming act of eating does not occur during extinction, responses within extinction serve better than responses during conditioning as measures of the consequences of reinforcement. Two measures of responses within extinction are commonly used: *rate of responding*, and the *total number of responses* before responding returns to its normal rate prior to conditioning. The total number of responses during extinction now often described as resistance to extinction was formerly called the *reflex reserve*,[10] a figure of speech to describe a kind of reservoir of responses ready to be emitted during extinction. Skinner no longer believes the concept of a reflex reserve to be very useful, although he appears to reject it because of his later interpretation of appropriate scientific concepts rather than because of any change in the factual relationships described.[11]

[8] Skinner (1938), page 20.

[9] Skinner (1938), pages 45–59.

[10] Skinner (1938), page 26.

[11] Skinner (1950), page 203. The original concept was not without its critics, e.g., Ellson (1939).

A single reinforcement suffices to produce a number of conditioned operant responses in extinction. After receiving a single pellet of food following one pressing of the bar, a rat may respond 50 or more times, yielding a typical extinction curve. Additional reinforcements add slowly to the number of responses during extinction. An extinction curve following a single reinforcement and one following 250 reinforcements are reproduced in Figure 8. The curves are cumulative ones, not to be confused with learning curves as usually plotted. As the curve levels off it means that responses have stopped; as the curve is constructed it is not possible for it to fall.

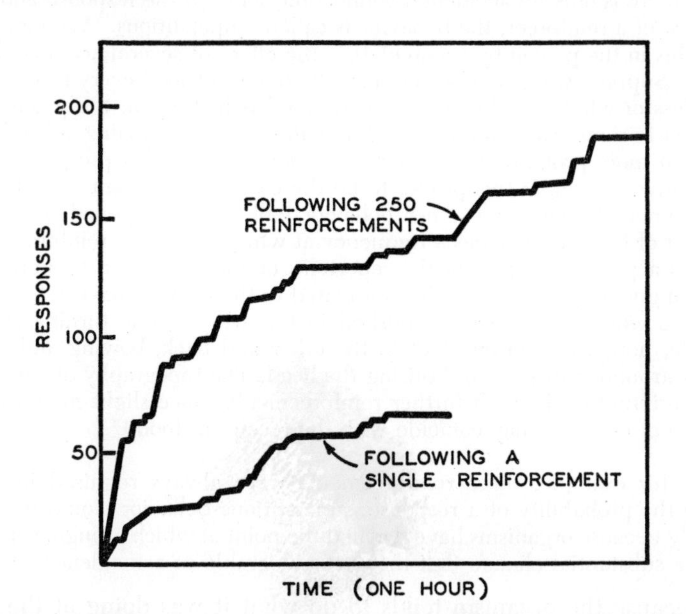

FIGURE 8. Extinction of lever-pressing by rats following a single reinforcement and following 250 reinforcements. Although several times as many responses are emitted after 250 reinforcements as after a single reinforcement, it is evident that the total number of responses in the "reserve" does not increase in direct proportion to the number of reinforcements. Data from Skinner (1933) and F. S. Keller and A. Kerr (unpublished data), replotted from Skinner (1938), pages 87 and 91. Both curves have been moved back so that time is here shown as measured from the first response.

The considerable influence of a single reinforcement leads Skinner to conjecture that, if we were able to isolate a single operant, we might find an instantaneous change to a maximum probability.[12] This conjecture, we may note, is very similar to that of Guthrie with respect to one-trial learning. The further conjecture that actual conditioning is

[12] Skinner (1953a), page 68.

found to be gradual because several component operants are involved is also not unlike Guthrie. The residual difference is that the single event for Skinner is a reinforcement, whereas for Guthrie it is a mere occurrence.

The importance of single reinforcements ("one-trial learning") is brought out in two arrangements which have come to prominence in Skinner's later work. The first of these is the development of "superstitious" behavior. The second is the control of behavior through successive approximations.

If there is only an accidental connection between the response and the appearance of a reinforcer, the behavior is called "superstitious." We may demonstrate this in the pigeon by accumulating the effect of several accidental contingencies. Suppose we give a pigeon a small amount of food every fifteen seconds regardless of what it is doing. When the food is first given, the pigeon will be behaving in some way—if only standing still—and conditioning will take place. It is then more probable that the same behavior will be in progress when the food is given again. If this proves to be the case, the "operant" will be further strengthened. If not, some other behavior will be strengthened. Eventually a given bit of behavior reaches a frequency at which it is often reinforced. It then becomes a permanent part of the repertoire of the bird, even though the food has been given by a clock which is unrelated to the bird's behavior. Conspicuous responses which have been established in this way include turning sharply to one side, hopping from one foot to the other and back, bowing and scraping, turning around, strutting, and raising the head. The topography of the behavior may continue to drift with further reinforcements, since slight modifications in the form of response may coincide with the receipt of food.[13]

If, for example, three reinforcements were always required in order to change the probability of a response, superstitious behavior would be unlikely. It is only because organisms have reached the point at which a single contingency makes a substantial change that they are vulnerable to coincidences.[14]

Because the organism tends to do what it was doing at the time of the reinforcement, it is possible to lead an organism to do very much what the experimenter wishes by "baiting" each step of the way. Skinner and his collaborators have demonstrated great skill and ingenuity in animal training through the use of this method. Some of the reports have appeared in the popular picture magazines, an early account showing a rat using a marble to obtain food from a vending machine, another showing pigeons playing a modified game of table tennis, a third in which a dog learns to retrieve a bone from a pedal-operated refuse can. The animal-training possibilities are almost unlimited.[15] How do single rein-

[13] Skinner (1953a), page 85.

[14] Skinner (1953a), page 87.

[15] The accounts have appeared many places, such as: *Life*, May 31, 1937; *Science Newsletter*, June 17, 1950; *Newsweek*, May 7, 1951. See also Breland and Breland (1951), Skinner (1951).

forcements bring such diverse behavior under control? Here is one demonstration:

An effective classroom demonstration of the Law of Effect may be arranged in the following way. A pigeon, reduced to 80 per cent of its *ad lib* weight, is habituated to a small, semi-circular amphitheatre and is fed there for several days from a food hopper, which the experimenter presents by closing a hand switch. The demonstration consists of establishing a selected response by suitable reinforcement with food. For example, by sighting across the amphitheatre at a scale on the opposite wall, it is possible to present the hopper whenever the top of the pigeon's head rises above a given mark. Higher and higher marks are chosen until, within a few minutes, the pigeon is walking about the cage with its head held as high as possible. In another demonstration the bird is conditioned to strike a marble placed on the floor of the amphitheatre. This may be done in a few minutes by reinforcing successive steps. Food is presented first when the bird is merely moving near the marble, later when it looks down in the direction of the marble, later still when it moves its head toward the marble, and finally when it pecks it. Anyone who has seen such a demonstration knows that the Law of Effect is no theory. It simply specifies a procedure for altering the probability of a chosen response.[16]

Positive and Negative Primary Reinforcers

A reinforcer is defined by its effects. Any stimulus is a reinforcer if it increases the probability of a response. The stimuli that happen to act as reinforcers fall into two classes: [17]

1. A *positive reinforcer* is a stimulus which, when added to a situation, strengthens the probability of an operant response. Food, water, sexual contact, classify as positive reinforcers.

2. A *negative reinforcer* is a stimulus which, when *removed* from a situation, strengthens the probability of an operant response. A loud noise, a very bright light, extreme heat or cold, electric shock, classify as negative reinforcers.

Notice that the effect of reinforcement is always to *increase* the probability of response. Punishment is something other than negative reinforcement as here defined. While a reinforcer is defined by its effects, this is not true for punishment. Punishment, according to Skinner and his followers, is defined as an experimental arrangement whose effects remain to be investigated empirically. The *arrangement* is the opposite of reinforcement (although the *effects* are not opposite), so that two main cases arise: (1) the presentation of a negative reinforcer, and (2) the removal of a positive reinforcer. We shall return later to a consideration of the consequences of punishment.

Why is a reinforcer reinforcing? One possibility is that reinforcement

[16] Skinner (1950), page 200.
[17] Skinner (1953a), page 73.

reduces a state of deprivation, that is, it meets a need, as when a hungry animal eats. The hungrier a bird, the greater the rate of its responses as a consequence of food reinforcement. Skinner recognizes, however, that reinforcement does not always reduce deprivation. Conditioning may occur before any substantial change can take place in the internal state of the learner.

All we know is that the *type* of event which reduces deprivation is also reinforcing.

Skinner rather tentatively accepts an explanation in terms of evolutionary biology, but he does not find it of much help in the detailed functional analysis of what actually occurs.[18]

Schedules of Reinforcement

The reinforcement of operant behavior in ordinary life is not regular and uniform. The fisherman does not hook a fish with every cast of the line; the crop the farmer sows does not always yield a harvest. Hence the problem of maintaining or strengthening a response through *intermittent reinforcement* is more than a laboratory curiosity.[19] Skinner has explored extensively two main classes of intermittent reinforcement, now called *interval reinforcement* and *ratio reinforcement.*

By *interval reinforcement* he means reinforcement given at fixed intervals of time, every 3 minutes or every 10 minutes, at the discretion of the experimenter. In the experiment itself this means the reinforcement of the first response that occurs after that interval of time, so there is actually some slight variation in the time of reinforcement depending upon the activity of the learner. This arrangement, also called periodic reconditioning, or periodic reinforcement, delivers a standard amount of reinforcement per hour. It results in lawful rates of responding, the rate being proportional to the interval between reinforcements, the shorter intervals yielding more rapid response rates. Under standard conditions of experimentation and drive, for example, Skinner found about 18 to 20 responses per reinforcement, over a considerable range of intervals. The uniformity of rates of responding is illustrated in Figures 9 and 10.

The uniform number of responses per reinforcement is called the *extinction ratio,* that is, the ratio of unreinforced to reinforced responses. The size of the ratio does not change much from one length of interval to another, provided drive remains constant.

[18] Skinner (1953a), pages 81–84.

[19] The expression "intermittent reinforcement" is a better descriptive term than "partial reinforcement," an earlier name for the same arrangement (Hilgard and Marquis, 1940, page 347).

Although curves drawn in the scale of Figures 9 and 10 appear uniform, there is actually a stepwise character to response when reinforcement is given at regular intervals. This follows because a response is never reinforced shortly after a prior reinforcement, and so, after a time, the rate of responding is low following a reinforcement. This minor fluctua-

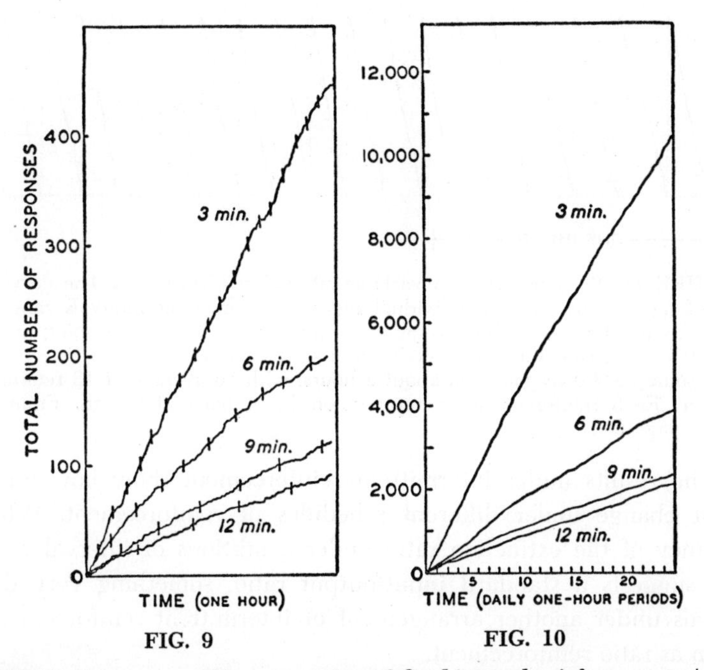

FIGURE 9. Responses within one session of fixed-interval reinforcement. A pellet was delivered every 3, 6, 9, and 12 minutes, respectively. The more frequent the reinforcement, the more rapid the rate of responding, although each rate is relatively uniform. After Skinner (1938), as reproduced by Hilgard and Marquis (1940), page 151.

FIGURE 10. Responses within repeated sessions of fixed-interval reinforcement. Responses of the same rats whose records are given in Figure 9 are here accumulated for successive daily sessions. The uniformity of rate persists throughout. When expressed as number of responses per reinforcement this rate is decribed as the "extinction ratio." After Skinner (1938), as reproduced by Hilgard and Marquis (1940), page 151.

tion or scalloping of the curves can be corrected by a modification known as *variable-interval reinforcement* (also called aperiodic reinforcement.) Under this arrangement, an *average* interval is substituted for a fixed interval, so that, while a response may be reinforced every 5 minutes on the average, in some cases the second reinforcement follows immediately upon an earlier reinforcement, and at other times it is longer delayed.

Under such a schedule, performance is remarkably stable and uniform, and highly resistant to extinction. An illustration is found in Figure 11. A pigeon has given as many as 10,000 unreinforced responses in extinction following such variable-interval reinforcement.

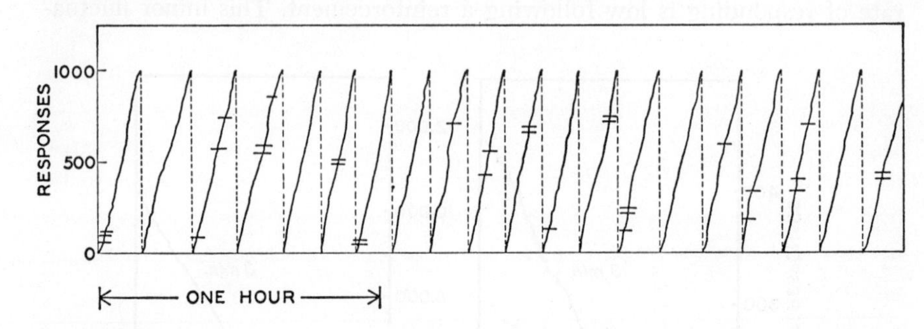

FIGURE 11. Responses within variable-interval reinforcement. The curves are of the pecking responses of an individual pigeon reinforced at intervals ranging from 10 seconds to 21 minutes, but averaging 5 minutes. Each of the sloping lines represents 1,000 responses; the pen resets to zero after each 1,000. The whole record represents some 20,000 responses in about 3 hours, with an average of 12 reinforcements per hour. Each reinforcement is represented by a horizontal dash. From Skinner (1950), page 208.

The results under intermittent reinforcement show how input and output change under different schedules of reinforcement. While the constancy of the extinction ratio under conditions of interval reinforcement suggests a standard input-output ratio, something very different happens under another arrangement of intermittent reinforcement, that known as ratio reinforcement.

In *ratio reinforcement,* instead of delivering a pellet of food at standard intervals of time, a pellet is delivered after a standard number of responses. In one study they were delivered after 16, 24, 32, 48, 64, 96, or 192 responses. These ratios have to be approached gradually, for such occasional reinforcements can maintain responses only if responses are already being emitted at a rapid rate. The end-products of such training are shown in Figure 12. The somewhat paradoxical finding now is that the less frequent the reinforcement, the more rapid the response! The extinction ratio has changed from the order of 20:1 under interval reinforcement to 200:1 under ratio reinforcement.

The steplike character of performance, mentioned in connection with reinforcement at fixed intervals, is pronounced with reinforcement at fixed ratios. After the burst of responding just before reinforcement there follows a period of very slow responding just after reinforcement. If the ratio is made too high, there develop long periods of no response following reinforcement, a condition likened by Skinner to "abulia," the inability to expend effort. He points out the analogy with the student who has finished a term paper, perhaps in a burst of speed as the deadline approaches, and then finds it difficult to start work on a new assignment.[20]

The pause after reinforcement may be eliminated by adopting *variable-ratio reinforcement,* that is, using a range of ratios around a mean value. Because the probability of reinforcement at any moment remains approximately constant, a uniform rate of responding ensues; because this probability is increased with rapid responding, the rate tends to be high. A pigeon may respond as rapidly as five times per second and keep up this rate for many hours. (This rate corresponds to that of the ticking of a watch.)

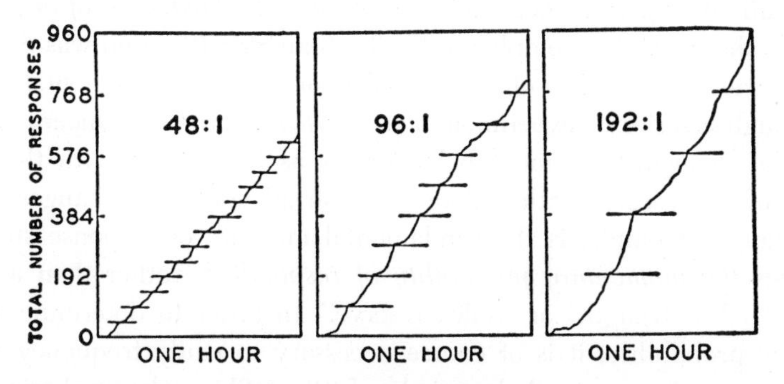

FIGURE 12. Responses within ratio reinforcement. Responses from individual rats reinforced every 48, 96, and 192 responses, as indicated by the horizontal lines. Under these circumstances very high rates of responding develop, the highest rate being found with the lowest frequency of reinforcement. After Skinner (1938), as reproduced by Hilgard and Marquis (1940), page 152.

Schedules can also be brought under multiple control. For example, by selecting one of three colors to be projected on the key that the pigeon pecks, the pigeon can be put on fixed-interval, fixed-ratio, or variable-interval reinforcement, and will behave as it has learned to behave under each of these schedules alone. Skinner has trained a pigeon up to nine different performances under nine different conditions of stimulation.

Another variation is a *mixed* schedule—a multiple schedule without external stimulus control. That is, the pigeon has no differential external stimulus to determine whether it will be reinforced after responding

[20] Skinner (1953a), page 104.

30 times *or* after the passage of 15 minutes. These conditions are alternated more or less at random. The characteristic stable performance is thus described by Skinner:

> The bird runs off a number of responses at a high rate. If the current schedule is a ratio schedule, it will then be reinforced. If it is, however, an interval schedule, the bird will run somewhat past the number reinforced as a ratio and then will break suddenly to a zero rate of responding from which emerges a smooth interval scallop extending over the rest of the 15-minute period. That is, the bird "tests" the schedule by running off a number of responses sufficient to achieve reinforcement if the schedule is a ratio; if no reinforcement is forthcoming, the performance "primes" the bird into the interval scallop.[21]

It is evident that the bird's own behavior can function as a discriminative stimulus in controlling schedule performances.

These more recent experiments, while belonging to the same general family of experiments as those reported in *The behavior of organisms* (1938), show a shift of emphasis. Earlier Skinner's attention was directed to the general course of a change in behavior over an experimental period or through a series of experimental sessions. His primary concern is now with the moment-to-moment behavior, or as he puts it, with the "fine grain" of the records rather than the over-all course of changes. With this change of emphasis the fundamental measure of response strength becomes *the momentary probability of responding*, rather than a more global "habit strength" or "reflex reserve." In order to determine a momentary probability, it is of course necessary to study frequency of response over more extended periods of time. Skinner's emphasis upon frequency of response has persisted from his earliest writings, and he has recently ably defended his choice of this measure.[22]

Secondary Reinforcement

The principle of secondary reinforcement is simply this:

> A stimulus that is not originally a reinforcing one . . . can become reinforcing through repeated association with one that is.[23]

That is, through conditioning, a stimulus acquires the power to condition. Consider, for example, the acquisition of reinforcing power by the light in the following experiment. When a rat presses a bar, a light comes on. After 1 second a pellet of food falls into the tray, reinforcing the bar-pressing. The light remains on for two seconds after the food appears. Several groups of animals are conditioned in this way, for 10, 20, 40, 80,

[21] Private communication dated December 28, 1954.
[22] Skinner (1953b).
[23] Keller and Schoenfeld (1950), page 232.

and 120 reinforcements, respectively. After conditioning, the rate of responding is reduced to a low level by extinction in the dark. Then pressing the bar again turns on the light for 1 second, but does not deliver food. Under these circumstances responses again appear, showing that the light has acquired reinforcing properties. The number of responses emitted in a 45-minute period increased with the number of prior pairings of light and food.[24]

Other experiments suggest that the light will acquire secondary reinforcing properties only if it appears *before* the reinforcing stimulus, and is thus either part of a chain or a discriminative stimulus.[25]

The following summary of secondary reinforcement shows its systematic importance in operant behavior:

1. A stimulus that occasions or accompanies a reinforcement acquires thereby reinforcing value of its own, and may be called a conditioned, secondary, or derived reinforcement. A secondary reinforcement may be extinguished when repeatedly applied to a response for which there is no ultimate primary reinforcement.
2. A secondary reinforcement is positive when the reinforcement with which it is correlated is positive, and negative when the latter is negative.
3. Once established, a secondary reinforcement is independent and nonspecific; it will not only strengthen the same response which produced the original reinforcement, but it will also condition a new and unrelated response. Moreover, it will do so even in the presence of a different motive.
4. Through generalization, many stimuli besides the one correlated with reinforcement acquire reinforcing value—positive or negative.[26]

One of the most important consequences of the development of secondary reinforcement is the emergence of a class of *generalized reinforcers*.[27] This generalization comes about because some secondary reinforcers tend to accompany a variety of primary reinforcers. Money is a convenient illustration, because money provides access to food, drink, shelter, entertainment, and thus becomes a generalized reinforcer for a variety of activities. The so-called needs (need for attention, need for affection, need for approval) lead to the kinds of persistent behavior best understood as a consequence of intermittent reinforcement, and the kinds of reinforcement sought are the generalized ones implied in the words "attention," "affection," and "approval." Language behavior, such as calling objects by their correct names, tends to be reinforced by the generalized reinforcement from the listeners, who show in indirect ways whether or not they understand and approve. According to Skinner, even-

[24] Bersh (1951).
[25] Schoenfeld, Antonitis, and Bersh (1950a); Webb and Nolan (1953).
[26] Keller and Schoenfeld (1950), page 260.
[27] Skinner (1953a), page 77–81.

tually generalized reinforcers are effective even though the primary reinforcers on which they are based no longer accompany them.[28] This is close to the functional autonomy of motives, as proposed by Allport.[29]

OTHER INFLUENCES AFFECTING OPERANT STRENGTH

In the effort to remain descriptive and positivistic, Skinner has attempted to avoid the postulating of intermediaries not observed in his experiments, and to deal instead with a procedure that he calls *functional analysis.* A functional analysis is concerned with the lawfulness of relationships and the manner in which these relationships fluctuate under specified conditions. We have just reviewed one very important class of events in the functional analysis of behavior: reinforcements, as they affect operant strength. Two other classes of events are significantly correlated with responses in the problems that Skinner studies. These are the classes known as *drive* and *emotion.*

Drive

Hours of food deprivation are important in determining the rate of responding in a Skinner box. The variable actually plotted is exactly that: hours of deprivation. Is it necessary to say anything further? Is it important to talk about physiological needs, or hunger? Let us first cite some typical experimental results and then return to these questions.

Eight rats learned to press a lever under interval reinforcement. They practiced daily but received the main portion of their rations on alternate days. The correlation between responding and hours of deprivation showed up in high and low rates on successive days. Two subgroups were created, matched according to their response rates during conditioning. They were now extinguished on alternative days, one group when hunger was high, the other when hunger was low. The high hunger group yielded nearly double the responses of the low group on successive daily periods, although the two extinction curves showed similar curvature.[30]

Does deprivation affect the amount of contribution of each reinforcement, or does it merely affect the rate of responding during extinction? In a test of these relationships, rats were reinforced after different amounts of food deprivation, from one-half hour to 47 hours. Various sub-

[28] Skinner (1953a), page 81.
[29] Allport (1937).
[30] Skinner (1950), pages 201–202.

groups of animals received 1, 10, and 30 reinforcements, respectively. Then the strength of conditioning was tested by resistance to extinction, at a common level of deprivation (23 hours). Resistance to extinction was throughout correlated with the number of prior reinforcements, but *not* with the level of deprivation within reinforcement.[31]

These two studies suffice to illustrate the kinds of relationships between drive and operant conditioning that are open to investigation. In a narrative account of the results we tend to move back and forth between describing the rats as "deprived of food" or as "hungry." The two expressions are operationally equivalent, though when we assign the results to "hunger" instead of to "hours without food" we tend to imply a theory. This leads us back to the problem of the status of "drive" as a concept.

Skinner is quite clear that he means by "drive" merely a set of operations (such as the withholding of food for a certain number of hours), which operations have an effect upon rate of responding. He is interested in the lawfulness of these effects under various circumstances. He objects to most of the current uses of "drive" by supporting the following assertions:[32]

A drive is not a stimulus.
A drive is not a physiological state.
A drive is not a psychic state.
A drive is not simply a state of strength.

By these negatives he makes it clear that he does not accept the stimuli from stomach contractions as the prototype of drives, nor does he accept physiological needs, or pleasures or pains, or desires or wishes. For the purposes of the systematic study of behavior, the word "drive" is used only to acknowledge certain classes of operation which affect behavior in ways other than the ways by which reinforcement affects it. He does not believe inference to an intermediary (intervening variable or hypothetical construct) to be necessary in order to carry out the functional analysis.

Emotion and Punishment

Just as drives are inappropriately classified as stimuli, so, according to Skinner, emotions are often unwisely classified as responses. Weeping at a bruised shin or over the loss of a game is ordinarily said to be an emotional response, but weeping because of a cinder in the eye is not.

[31] Strassburger (1950).
[32] Skinner (1953a), pages 144–146.

This way of treating emotion is rejected in favor of referring it to a set of operations, in many ways like drive. Its importance arises because of the accompanying or ensuing changes in response.

The effects of punishment are often emotional by this definition. Punishment might act dynamically as negative conditioning, as though reinforcement were being subtracted, but in fact it does not serve in this way. If at the beginning of extinction the rat is slapped on its feet when it presses the lever, its rate of responding is depressed, but it eventually recovers. The total responses to extinction have not been reduced by the punishment, as they should be if the punishment were negative conditioning.[33] Such a temporary effect upon rate but not upon total resistance to extinction is emotional. There is here some support for Thorndike's belief that punishments do not act opposite to rewards.

Because of the importance of the problem of punishment, Estes' (1944) study, carrying further Skinner's earlier explorations, will be reviewed later as an exemplification of Skinner's system.

DISCRIMINATION AND DIFFERENTIATION

In situations which require more than a change in rate of responding, two features stand out. One is the discrimination between stimuli, so that a given response may be made to one of a pair of stimuli and not to the other member of the pair. A second feature is differentiation of response, so that response form or topography is altered or adjusted appropriately to the situation. The complexities of behavior can be understood according to discriminations and differentiations arranged into appropriate chains or patterns.

Discrimination of Stimuli

The standard lever-pressing experiment may serve the purposes of discriminatory conditioning if the lever-pressing delivers a pellet of food in the presence of a positive, supporting stimulus (e.g., a 3 c.p. light) and fails to deliver in the absence of this discriminatory stimulus. The rat learns to respond only when the light is on, but the light does not actually elicit the response. The difference between a discriminatory stimulus as an occasion for a response and as eliciting it is clarified by an example. I reach for a pencil lying on the desk, but I reach only when the pencil is there, and I do not reach for it just *because* it is there. While the pencil does not *elicit* reaching, it has something to do with my reach-

[33] Skinner (1938), page 154.

ing. If it were dark and there were no pencil there, I might grope for it because the discriminatory stimuli would be lacking. The pencil does not elicit reaching in the light any more than in the dark. It is only the *occasion* for reaching.[34]

When the food is delivered only in the presence of the light, the situation is a sort of controlled intermittent reinforcement, for lever-pressing is reinforced only part of the time. Eventually response occurs almost exclusively when the light is on, so that nearly every response is reinforced. The resistance to extinction that is built up at this stage is not that of interval reinforcement, but that of ordinary every-trial reinforcement. There are two operants with the same form of response, one with the light on, one with the light off; they are selectively reinforced and extinguished. There is an interaction called *induction* by Skinner which corresponds to Hull's generalization; whatever happens to one operant affects the other to some extent.

The following statements are offered to clarify this somewhat complex situation: [35]

1. Responses accumulated in the presence of the positive stimulus are available in the presence of the negative stimulus. This is the principle of inductive conditioning or generalization.

2. Responses emitted in the presence of the negative stimulus are no longer available under the positive stimulus. This is the principle of inductive extinction.

3. Selective reinforcement and extinction increase the number of responses available chiefly in the presence of the positive stimulus. This is the positive half of the principle of discrimination.

4. Responses acquired in the presence of the positive stimulus may become less readily available under the negative stimulus. This is the negative half of the principle of discrimination—the breakdown of induction.

The discrimination experiment is always complicated by an additional fact of importance. The positive stimulus which acts as the occasion for the response and for the reinforcement becomes itself a secondary reinforcing agent.

Skinner believes that his arrangement for obtaining discrimination is superior to that usually used, in which a choice of responses confronts the animal. His rats may either respond to the lever or not respond. They do not have to choose between two levers, or between a right and a

[34] Skinner (1938), page 178.
[35] Skinner (1938), page 229.

left turn. He believes that the discrimination box is a "crude instrument" for studying the nature of the process,[36] and finds Tolman's (1938a) dependence upon choice-point behavior a severe limitation.[37] The objection is that in the choice situation no measure of strength is obtained—only a measure of relative strength.

Differentiation of a Response

Among a number of novel and useful distinctions made by Skinner is that between discrimination of stimuli and differentiation of response. In operant conditioning, reinforcement can be made contingent on either (*a*) the properties of accompanying stimuli (when the result is a discrimination), or (*b*) the properties of the response (when the result is a differentiation).

The rat may be taught, for example, to press the lever with a given force, or to hold it down for a given duration, in order for the pellet to be delivered. The basic rule of operant conditioning applies: that the response must occur before it can be reinforced. Extreme forms or values may be obtained by successive approximations. Operant responses are emitted with an original range of form or intensity (Hull's response oscillation). If only the more extreme values are reinforced, the whole distribution shifts, so that higher and higher values may be obtained. The training method of successive approximations permits the finally learned behavior to be very different from that originally emitted.

> Animal trainers are well versed in this method. As a sort of *tour de force* I have trained a rat to execute an elaborate series of responses suggested by recent work on anthropoid apes. The behavior consists of pulling a string to obtain a marble from a rack, picking the marble up with the fore-paws, carrying it to a tube projecting two inches above the floor of the cage, and dropping it inside. Every step in the process had to be worked out through a series of approximations, since the component responses were not in the original repertoire of the rat.[38]

Response novelty is one of the features rather badly accounted for in most stimulus-response systems. Thorndike's law of assimilation, Guthrie's principle of compromise movements, and Skinner's successive approximations are all attempts to deal with the problem. The concept of emitted behavior has advantages over that of elicited behavior. It has always been embarrassing for theories of the conditioning type to try to find original stimuli to produce the responses called for in singing a

[36] Skinner (1938), page 231.
[37] Skinner (1938), page 437.
[38] Skinner (1938), pages 339–340.

song or in writing a poem. Such stimuli need not be specified for emitted behavior.

THE SEARCH FOR A UNIT OF BEHAVIOR

In the foregoing account of some of the kinds of data which Skinner collects and of the concepts used in describing them, his more general theory has been implied rather than made explicit. Skinner is definitely interested in supporting a scientific theory of a specific kind. He favors what he calls a purely descriptive system, and a frankly analytical one. How he goes about system-making is best illustrated in his discussion of the *reflex* and its laws.

Early Reliance on the Reflex as the Unit

Skinner believes that a purely descriptive system, in order to be scientific and not a mere "botanizing" of behavior, must choose an appropriate natural unit of behavior. A real unit will not be an artificial bit of behavior taken improperly out of context, nor will it be something too complex to enter into orderly relations as a descriptive unit. The level of specification found to be necessary is not something a priori, but is the level found in experience "marked by the orderliness of dynamic changes." [39] Skinner believed, especially at the outset, that his system had a merit not possessed by other stimulus-response systems—the discovery of this appropriate unit: the *reflex,* as he defined this term.

By a reflex Skinner means a lawful correlation between a class of stimuli and a class of responses. The reflex is not to be identified with the spinal reflex, which is defined topographically; its reference is solely to behavior and not to anatomy or neurology. The definition rests on a dynamic relationship. What a stimulus is, what a response is, what a reflex is can be defined only according to the lawful experimental consequences when the reflex unit is isolated.

> The reflex as an analytical unit is actually obtained in *practice.* The unit is a fact, and its validity and the validity of the laws describing its changes do not depend upon the correctness of analytical assumptions or the possibility of a later synthesis of more complex behavior.[40]

The laws of the reflex. There are static laws, dynamic laws, and laws of interaction.[41]

The static laws refer to the quantitative properties of representa-

[39] Skinner (1938), page 40.
[40] Skinner (1938), page 29.
[41] Skinner (1938), pages 12–33.

tive reflexes. They are reminiscent of the laws of spinal reflexes: the law of threshold, the law of latency, the law of magnitude of response as a function of intensity, the law of after-discharge, and the law of temporal summation.

The dynamic laws include "classical examples," which means, presumably, that they too derive from the study of spinal reflexes: the law of refractory phase, the law of reflex fatigue, the law of facilitation, the law of inhibition. In addition there are other examples, logically similar but differing in the nature of the operations affecting reflex strength: the laws of conditioning, extinction, drive, and emotion. These have already been considered.

The laws of interaction give an answer to the part-whole problem. They are: the law of compatibility, the law of prepotency, the law of algebraic summation, the law of blending, the law of spatial summation, the law of chaining, and the law of induction.

There is a family resemblance between the topics covered in Skinner's laws and in Hull's postulates, although as they are given by Skinner the laws are defining principles and are not stated so as to be used to deduce behavior. Skinner's laws are unlikely to be found false because they are worded in such a form that they are true at the level of general observation. They provide a framework for further specification and quantification. They enter exposition quite differently from Hull's postulates. Actually, there is little reference to the laws as the data from experiments are discussed.

How laws of this kind define a descriptive system and lead to experiments might be illustrated by a parallel example from plant growth. Preliminary observation would soon establish the fact that growth varies with the amount of water in the soil, the range of temperature, and the amount of sunlight. Before proceeding to further experimental work it would be possible to state a series of growth laws: one law relating growth to moisture, another to temperature, another to illumination, together with some presumptive laws of their interaction. For example, it is plausible that with more moisture in the soil the plant could thrive at somewhat higher room temperatures. An experimental program might easily be motivated by the search for the precise form of these laws. One can imagine the greenhouse with thermostats, moisture controls, shades, and sunlamps. The laws of growth could be worked out according to these and similar variables without any regard for the physiology of cells or for the chemistry of growth hormones. The observations would, in fact, be governed largely by the descriptive system implied in the laws, but their aim is not to prove or disprove these laws, for as far as it goes each law merely describes experimental findings. This way of investigation is essentially what Skinner has proposed and what he has succeeded in doing. There is this difference, that the isolation of a reflex to be studied and the selection of units of measurement is a more perplexing problem than defining plant growth.

The Functional Unit Studied Is Not Necessarily the "Atom" of Behavior

While Skinner continues to search for the appropriate unit of analysis, the basic datum, he appears no longer to be confident that he has found the unit either in the reflex or in the measured operant. Three terms enter into the characterization of a conditioned operant: the discriminative stimulus that is the occasion for the response, the response, and the reinforcement. The "same" response is not the "same" operant if correlated with different stimuli or with different reinforcers. The operant under study is perhaps not a "single" operant.

A somewhat modified suggestion as to an "element" of behavior emerges in the following passage which follows a discussion of the problem of transfer:

> This leads us to identify the element rather than the response as the unit of behavior. It is a sort of behavioral atom, which may never appear by itself upon any single occasion but is the essential ingredient or component of all instances. The reinforcement of a response increases the probability of all responses containing the same elements.[42]

> We lack adequate tools to deal with the continuity of behavior or with the interaction among operants attributable to common atomic units. The operant represents a valid level of analysis, however, because the properties which define a response are observable data. A given set of properties may be given a functional unity. *Although methods must eventually be developed which will not emphasize units at this level,* they are not necessary to our understanding of the principal dynamic properties of behavior.[43]

These quotations suggest that Skinner believes we are still at a very preliminary stage in the development of behavioral science. Perhaps his objection to theory (as theory is used by others) arises because of his strong conviction that we need to discard old concepts and make a fresh start. We are not far enough along this new road to begin the more detailed analysis called for in matured theory.

[42] Skinner (1953a), page 94.
[43] Skinner (1953a), page 95. Emphasis added.

Chained Responses as Illustrative of Functional Units

What is the practical meaning of assigning "functional unity" to a given set of properties? Some light can be thrown on this by an analysis of chaining, for actual behavior as we know it comes in sequences larger than those of bar-pressing or spot-pecking.

Even the bar-pressing operant is in reality a chain:

> The use of a chain cannot be avoided in operant behavior because the very act of reinforcement implies it.[44]

In their discussion of chaining, Keller and Schoenfeld give a lucid account of the problem of determining the degree of analysis desirable in order to remain at the level of experimental specification.[45] They begin with six distinct operants describing what the rat actually does in a Skinner box:

Operant Number	*Discriminative Stimulus*	*Response of the Rat*
1	Bar-location	Approach of rat to front of box
2	Visual bar	Rising on hind legs; placing paws on bar
3	Tactual bar	Pressing of bar, thus activating food-magazine
4	Apparatus noise	Lowering foreparts to food-tray
5	Visual pellet	Seizing of pellet by teeth and paws
6	Pellet-in-mouth	Chewing of pellet

It would be possible, as they suggest, to lengthen this list, including the several responses making up the approach from the door to the bar-location, and the several ingestion responses that follow upon the chewing of food. Instead, however, they find it equally legitimate to reduce the list, as follows:

Operant Number	*Discriminative Stimulus*	*Response of the Rat*
1	Visual bar	Rising
2	Tactual bar	Pressing
3	Apparatus noise	Lowering
4	Visual pellet	Seizing

The advantage of this reduction lies in the clearly observable and regularly recurring sequence or chain of responses, with identifiable (and

[44] Skinner (1938), page 43.
[45] Keller and Schoenfeld (1950), pages 197–208.

controllable) stimuli. In this chain each response produces the discriminative stimulus for the next response.

Does the chain operate as a unit? The well-conditioned rat makes the transitions so smoothly that it seems to be giving one response, not four. But the independence of the units of the chain can be tested experimentally.

1. If we eliminate only the stimulus for the final unit of the chain (the pellet), as in extinction, the first three links of the chain are gradually weakened, but the last is unaffected. The rat will seize and eat a pellet exactly as before.

2. If we now eliminate both the third and fourth links in the chain (the apparatus noise as well as the pellet), and carry out extinction, we can find out more about the chain. Reintroducing the noise after extinction is well along again reinforces bar-pressing. Hence, during conditioning, the third link had become a secondary reinforcer. Furthermore, the extinction of the preceding two links in the chain did not extinguish the reinforcing properties of the third link.

This kind of functional and experimental study isolates units of the chain which preserve some independence in the whole. These units are part of a chain, and their distinctiveness as units is not entirely arbitrary. It would be possible to record the separate responses, and not only the final one. It is suggested not only that future investigations will undoubtedly employ such procedures, but that exploratory attempts have already been made.[46]

The unit appropriate for experimental study turns out, in fact, to have a measure of arbitrariness about it. If it is a matter of convenience whether to measure one response of the chain, or four responses, or many more than that, there is evidently some selectivity exercised by the experimenter. This is always true: *all* description is partial description. The nature of events is such that description of them cannot be exhaustive. The functional unit, for Skinner, as for other experimenters, is not given completely by the processes under investigation. Sometimes the functional unit is a simple response, sometimes a complex act, sometimes a rate of responding. The unit no longer has the clean dimensions of a correlation between a class of stimuli and a class of responses as implied in the original concept of a reflex. The atom of behavior proves to be evasive.

[46] Keller and Schoenfeld (1950), page 203. The attempts cited are those of Arnold (1947).

EXTENSION AND APPLICATION OF OPERANT CONDITIONING

The generality of Skinner's approach to problems of behavior is suggested by the titles chosen for his books: *The behavior of organisms* (1938) and *Science and human behavior* (1953). Neither title betrays that the precise data derive largely from experiments on rats and pigeons. Although the data are now being supplemented by experiments with human subjects, both children and adults, normal and disturbed, in these books the extension of the theory is by analogy rather than by experimentation. From a scientific point of view (using the word "science" as Skinner uses it) the extensions merely explore the kinds of variables which may eventually be brought under scientific control. The ultimate possibilities, as Skinner envisages them, are boundless: one chapter he includes is entitled "Designing a culture." [47] We are not here concerned with the larger political and ethical aspects of the society he presents. Instead, our problem is to see the steps by which laboratory learning is extended to encompass learning in a larger context. For our purposes we may therefore select some typical problem areas and see how they are handled. Three such problem areas are schoolroom learning, verbal behavior, and psychotherapy.

Schoolroom Learning

Skinner has announced, and embarked upon, a program of investigation designed to increase the efficiency of teaching of arithmetic, reading, or spelling, by using a mechanical device expected to prove far superior to the usual teacher.[48] One form of device presents number combinations for the teaching of addition. The child punches the correct answer in a kind of adding-machine keyboard; if the answer is correct, "reinforcement" occurs by having the problem move on. The machine has two advantages: (1) the timing of the reinforcement is prompt, thus embodying our knowledge of favorable arrangements for reinforcement, and (2) the order of problems is determined by an exact understanding of generalization, interference, and the need for spaced review. No teacher can be as skilled a reinforcer as the machine, for the teacher cannot be with every child at once, commending proper responses and correcting erroneous ones. Furthermore, the teacher cannot be as skilled

[47] Skinner's novel *Walden Two* (1948) is a sketch of a modern Utopia portraying the possibility of a scientific culture.
[48] Skinner (1954).

in determining the proper order of presentation. We can learn about schedules of reinforcement from precise experiments and then build them into our machines. Because some schedules yield far more in the way of stability of response than other schedules, we can hope to save a great deal of time in the teaching of our children.

While as described here, the new technique can serve only to teach a "skill," it must be acknowledged that a great deal of time and effort goes into such teaching, and that failures entail great social cost. If the new methods prove promising, they deserve a try, though their limitations must of course be understood. Schoolroom learning is a social experience as well as an opportunity to learn the multiplication tables. No new machine will make the teacher superfluous!

Verbal Behavior

Language most clearly distinguishes human behavior from that of other mammals. Knowledge of how we acquire language, and how we use it, is essential to an understanding of human learning. Skinner has long been interested in verbal behavior. As early as 1936 he produced a phonograph record composed of chance groupings of speech sound, which because they were chance were inherently meaningless. The record, called a "verbal summator," was used to study the words "read into" sounds by the listener. It was a kind of projective technique, similar in the auditory field to the ink-blots used in the visual field.[49] Within the next few years Skinner reported studies of word association, alliteration, and other kinds of sound patterning.[50] His William James Lectures, delivered at Harvard University in 1948, are to appear eventually in revised form as a volume entitled *Verbal behavior.* We can see that verbal behavior has been taken seriously as an empirical problem.

The main point of the analysis is that speech sounds are emitted (and reinforced) as any other bits of behavior.[51] Some speech utterances make demands upon the hearer and get reinforced as the hearer complies. This function (called the "mand" function) appears early in the language behavior of the child. A second function is concerned largely with naming (the "tact" function). The tact function leads to the richness and versatility of language. Its reinforcement by the hearer is

[49] Skinner (1936c); Shakow and Rosenzweig (1940).
[50] Skinner (1937), Cook and Skinner (1939), Skinner (1939) (1941).
[51] The best available treatment at the time of writing is the section on verbal behavior in Keller and Schoenfeld (1950), pages 376–399, on which the following brief digest is based. A few suggestions and illustrations are to be found in Skinner (1953a), pages 210–216.

more general than mand reinforcement. The reciprocal relationship between the speaker and the hearer, involving mutual reinforcement, is complex, but subject to straightforward analysis. The analysis calls for no new principles, however, beyond those familiar in operant conditioning.

Psychotherapy[52]

The need for psychotherapy is said to result from the by-products of excessive control by other people (especially through punishment), whereby the individual is either incapacitated or rendered dangerous to himself or to others. Excessive control has by-products that are either emotional (fear, anxiety, anger or rage, depression) or revealed in operant behavior (drug addiction, excessively vigorous or restrained behavior, defective discrimination of stimuli, defective self-knowledge, aversive self-stimulation).

The patient turns to the therapist because any relief (or promise of relief) is positively reinforcing. Psychoanalytic therapy can be characterized most simply, according to Skinner, as follows: the therapist constitutes himself a non-punishing audience. Under these circumstances, responses repressed by punishment tend to return. Forgotten experiences may be recovered, the patient may act aggressively (or at least verbalize aggressive impulses), the patient may exhibit strong emotion. The appearance of previously punished behavior in the presence of the non-punishing therapist makes possible the extinction of some of the effects of punishment. This Skinner believes to be the principal result of such therapy.

This plausible account calls for no "explanatory fictions"—no id, ego, or superego, inhabiting a psychic or mental world.

> What is "wrong" with the individual who displays these by-products of punishment is easily stated. A particular personal history has produced an organism whose behavior is disadvantageous or dangerous. In what sense it is disadvantageous or dangerous must be specified in each case by noting the consequences both to the individual himself and to others. The task of the therapist is to supplement a personal history in such a way that behavior no longer has these characteristics.[53]

Psychotherapy rests on the direct investigation and redirection of behavior itself. Behavior is itself the subject matter of therapy; the behavior is not the symptom of some other subject matter.

These conjectures are based on analogies between human behavior and experimental studies largely on lower forms. More recently, however, the methods have been extended to the study of human patients

[52] Skinner (1953a), pages 359–383.
[53] Skinner (1953a), page 372.

hospitalized with psychoses. Preliminary results show that vending machines with candy or cigarettes or pictures as reinforcing stimuli can sustain operant behavior over long periods of experimentation lasting an hour a day. It is supposed that results will be even more satisfactory with food reinforcement, and this is being tried. The therapeutic implications thus far have not been of primary concern, but periods of psychotic activity within the experimental hour appear reduced in frequency and duration, at least for some patients.[54]

The foregoing discussion of teaching, verbal behavior, and psychotherapy suffices to show the flavor of Skinner's theory as applied to a broader range of problems. The steps from the present knowledge of behavior to these broader fields are largely matters of technique and engineering, rather than of the discovery of new scientific principles. Nothing new in the way of dynamic principles is expected to emerge as the broader subject matter is investigated.

THE CONSEQUENCES OF PUNISHMENT AS ILLUSTRATIVE OF EXPERIMENTS WITH OPERANT BEHAVIOR

Some of the suggestions about the action of punishment which Skinner had earlier made were more extensively studied by Estes (1944) under his direction. Estes' work serves as a convenient example of the experimental approach to a problem by an investigator adopting Skinner's general point of view. Estes chose a more conventional terminology than Skinner, avoiding words like "operant" or "reflex" or "emitted," but the experiments could have been described in Skinner's words. It is of some interest that Estes found the more usual vocabulary satisfactorily precise for his purposes.

On the assumption that punishment does have effects, the two chief possibilities are that it weakens the habit or that it merely suppresses response. If the habit is weakened, punishment acts as a negative reinforcement, or as an agent hastening extinction. If the response is merely suppressed, the response has not been eliminated from the organism's repertory. Skinner's preliminary experiments favored the latter alternative, that punishment suppresses the rate of responding without eliminating responses from the total of responses to appear in extinction. Estes points out that the alternatives are genuine ones in the light of clinical experience. It is familiar that behavior may be repressed, and not overtly expressed, although the tendencies continue to exist at considerable strength.

[54] Skinner, Solomon, and others (1954)

Punishment Does Not Act as a Negative Reinforcement

In agreement with Skinner (and the later Thorndike), Estes finds that punishment does not lead to a reduction in the total number of responses given during extinction, even though there is temporary suppression of response following the punishment. Some characteristic findings are shown in Figure 13.

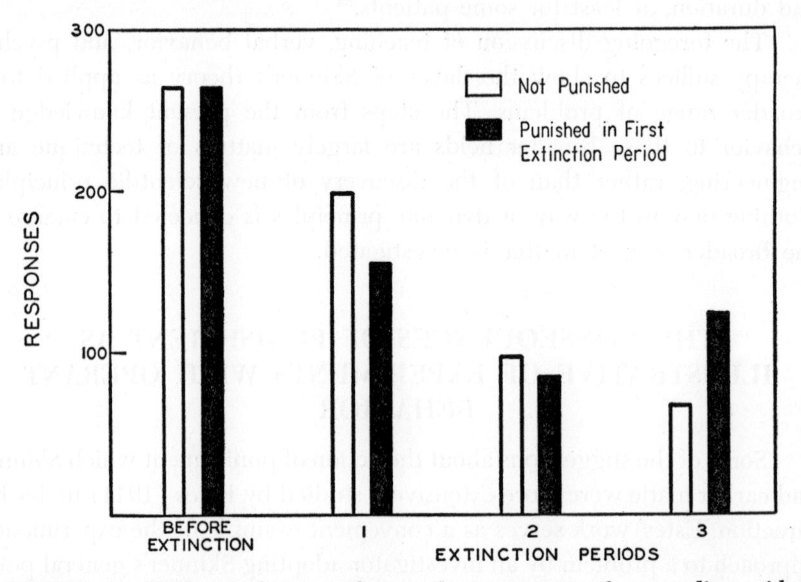

FIGURE 13. Evidence that punishment depresses rate of responding without decreasing the total responses within extinction. Responses of two groups of 8 rats each are compared. While the groups were not alike in their response frequency prior to extinction, their rates have been equated, and other comparisons are based upon this adjustment. Within the first extinction period one group of rats received an average of 9 punishments (electric shocks while pressing the lever). This punishment reduced the number of responses on the first day, and perhaps on the second, but by the third day there was a compensatory increase in the number of responses so that the total responses of the group punished on the first day and of the group not punished are the same over the three days of extinction. Data from Estes (1944), Experiment A, corrected for differences prior to extinction.

On the basis of additional experiments in the series, Estes concludes that the total number of elicitations of the response necessary for extinction may be reduced somewhat by punishment, but the time required for complete extinction of the response will not be affected by the punishment. More generally, the conclusion is reached that a response cannot be eliminated from an organism's repertory by the action of punishment alone.

Punishment More Importantly Associated with Stimuli Than with Responses

If punishment were a reinforcing agent similar to reward, it would act on responses, in accordance with Skinner's principle of Type R conditioning. That its more significant correlation is with discriminative stimuli is pointed out by Estes on the basis of several kinds of evidence.

In one experiment[55] the animals of the experimental group were shocked at intervals of approximately 30 seconds, care being taken not to shock them during or immediately after a response to the lever. Recovery from the effects of punishment follows the same course (i.e., the same mathematical function fits the course) as the course following punishment of the response itself. It is argued therefore that the effect must be due to the contiguity of the disturbing stimuli with stimuli in the box which normally act as occasions for lever pressing.

This conjecture was tested in another experiment[56] in which the rat was left in the box for an adaptation period following punishment. During this time the lever was withdrawn, so that response to it was impossible. The effects of the short period of severe punishment were almost completely dispelled, confirming the interpretation that punishment was related to the stimulating situation rather than specifically to the response.

Intermittent Punishment More Effective than Punishment at Every Occurrence

If punishment is delivered every time the response is made, the rate of responding is seriously depressed. While it is not depressed as much if punishment is given only occasionally, the effects of punishment persist longer in the latter case.[57] This is shown in two experiments, in one of which the test is made by simple extinction, the other in which the extinction follows an adaptation period. The results are most striking following adaptation. Adaptation does not bring recovery after intermittent punishment as it does after every-trial punishment. The results are shown in Figure 14.

Estes offers some conjectures in explanation of these results. He accepts a twofold theory of the effect of punishment. One principle, already referred to, is that punishment creates an emotional state which depresses

[55] Estes (1944), Experiment I.
[56] Estes (1944), Experiment J.
[57] Estes (1944), Experiments E and K. The average number of punishments received by each rat turns out to be about the same for both groups. Hence it is legitimate to compare the long-time effects of the two types of punishment.

responses while the state is aroused. This consequence of punishment does not lower the resistance to extinction. It is recovered from by adaptation or during subsequent extinction trials. The second principle is one congruent with Hull's interpretation of punishment, that is, an interpretation of the cessation of shock as reinforcing. Estes believes that the withdrawal responses are positively conditioned by the termination of the shock de-

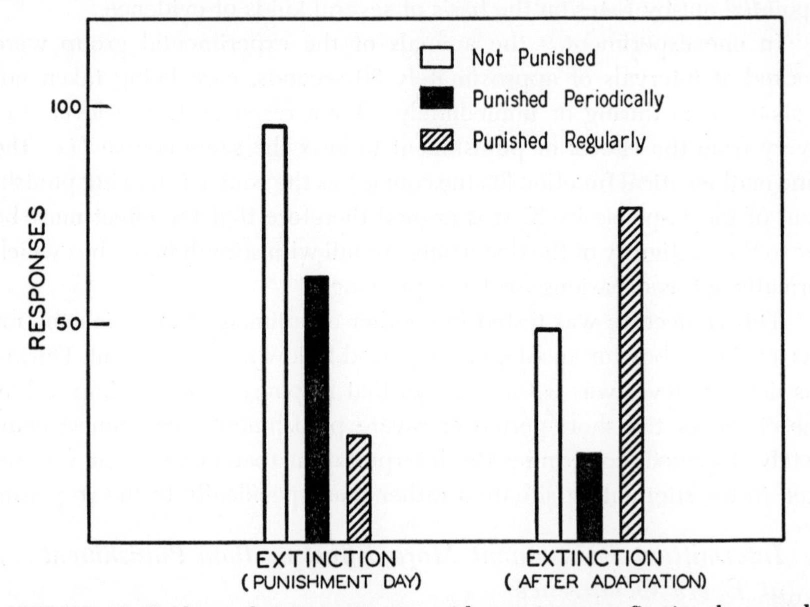

FIGURE 14. Evidence that intermittent punishment is more effective than regular punishment. The mean numbers of responses of three groups are shown, a control group extinguished in the usual manner, a group punished for responding whenever response occurred, and a group punished periodically, for responses occurring within every fourth minute of the 40-minute extinction period. Following the experimental day there were two adaptation days, when the animals were placed in the boxes with the levers retracted. The results for extinction are for the first day with the exposed lever, after these adaptation days. The adaptation period has almost completely eradicated the results of regular punishment, but the consequences of periodic punishment persist. Each group consisted of 6 rats. Data from Estes (1944), Experiment K, corrected for differences prior to extinction.

livered by the lever. He believes, further, that such withdrawal responses are conditioned more strongly through intermittent reinforcement than through ordinary continuous reinforcement, consistent with Skinner's findings for conditioning in general.

Punishment in the Practical Control of Behavior

Estes suggests several practical implications of his study.

The main finding is that a response cannot be eliminated from the organism's repertory more rapidly with the aid of punishment than without it. Permanent weakening comes about only by non-reinforced elicitation—and this weakening process may be prevented if punishment suppresses the response. This is in line with clinical findings about forms of aggressive or hostile responses which have come under parental or other social punishment. They are not eliminated until they can be brought to free expression, when the behavior can be appropriately redirected.

Another disadvantage of punishment lies in the concomitant emotional state which is aroused. This state will suppress other responses in addition to the one punished. The lack of specificity of its target is a weakness of punishment.

On the positive side, there are several "rules" which serve to show when and how punishment may be useful:

1. Punishment may be used to hold a response at low strength. Under these circumstances, punishment has to continue indefinitely, as it does not eliminate the response. The continuing punishment is equally or more effective if administered occasionally than if it is given every time the objectionable behavior occurs.

2. It is possible to take advantage of the period of suppressed response following punishment in order to strengthen some other response by reinforcement.

3. It is important that punishment be given in the presence of the discriminative cues for the response. Delayed punishment is likely to prove ineffective because it is given at a time when the discriminative stimuli leading to the undesired conduct are absent.

The series of experiments by Estes, with their interpretations, show how, within the experimental and theoretical framework of Skinner's system, it is possible to experiment upon problems genuinely relevant to the practical control of learning situations. The challenging difficulty remains of finding appropriate ways to test the implications in a social context.

ESTIMATE OF SKINNER'S SYSTEM

Skinner's Position on Typical Problems of Learning

Now that we have available general textbooks written from the standpoint of Skinner's position, it is possible to make a summary in relation to problems that do not fit directly into his conceptual scheme.

1. *Capacity.* In a descriptive system, it is to be expected that the laws will contain empirical constants differing for various species and for different members of each species. The eating rate, for example, cannot be expected to remain the same for young and old animals, and for

animals unlike in their food preferences. Because *lawfulness* rather than *laws* is what the systematist insists upon, differences in capacity are not of central importance. There is no suggestion that at higher capacity levels the laws are essentially any different; verbal behavior in man, for example, is said to conform to the general principles of operant behavior.

Skinner argues against the usefulness of a "trait" description in studying individual differences. A trait-name does not refer to any unit of behavior suitable for study through the functional analysis that he recommends.[58]

2. *Practice.* Something like a simple law of exercise (practice under conditions of contiguity of stimulus and response) is accepted for Type S conditioning. The conditioning that occurs under Type R depends upon repeated reinforcement. The possibility is favored that maximum reinforcement may occur in a single trial for the single operant, but the single operant is not achieved experimentally. In the usual case, the accumulation of strength with repeated reinforcement depends upon a population of discriminated stimuli and the related operants, more or less after the manner of Guthrie's explanation of the interpretation of the acquisition of skill with practice.

The effect of a single reinforcement is greatly enhanced by the secondary reinforcement deriving from it. Hence there is no direct correspondence between the number of responses yielded in extinction and the number of responses reinforced. The schedule of reinforcements is very important, with the greatest yields in the way of resistance to extinction coming from intermittent reinforcement (interval or ratio reinforcement).

3. *Motivation.* In agreement with Thorndike, reward is found to increase operant strength, while punishment has no corresponding weakening influence. Although there are several ways in which punishment enters, one is to create the variable called emotion, which reduces the rate of responding without reducing the number of responses yielded in extinction.

Drive level (determined by degree of deprivation) affects the rate of responding, but its level does not influence the effectiveness of a reinforcing stimulus in producing resistance to extinction. There is an unresolved problem of a lower limit here, for there must be enough drive to maintain responding and to make the reinforcer relevant.[59]

[58] Skinner (1953a), pages 194–203.

[59] We shall meet this same problem in the next chapter, when Hull's interpretation of reinforcement is under consideration.

4. *Understanding.* The word "insight" does not occur in the indexes of Skinner's books. Keller and Schoenfeld identify insight with rapid learning, and then explain it on the basis of (1) *similarity* of the present problem to one earlier solved, or (2) the *simplicity* of the problem.[60]

Because solving a problem means only the appearance of a solution in the form of a response, Skinner believes that the technique of problem-solving is merely that of manipulating variables which may lead to the emission of the response. No new factor of originality is involved. This makes it possible to teach a child to think.[61]

5. *Transfer.* Skinner prefers to use the term "induction" for what is commonly called generalization in the literature of conditioning. Such induction is the basis of transfer. The reinforcement of a response increases the probability of all responses containing the same elements. Similarly, the control acquired by a stimulus is shared by other stimuli with common properties. This interpretation of transfer is, in spirit, very similar to Thorndike's.

6. *Forgetting.* There is no special theory of forgetting proposed, although the distinction between extinction and forgetting is carefully maintained. Conditioning is long remembered. A pigeon showed sizable extinction curves six years after the response had been last reinforced. Extinction, too, is retained. Spontaneous recovery does not mean that extinction is forgotten, for successive extinctions show the results of earlier ones.

True forgetting appears to be a slow process of decay with time. Other kinds of response decrement are better subsumed under extinction or interference by incompatible responses. The latter interpretation applies to so-called Freudian forgetting.

The Reflex No Longer a Satisfactory Unit

When he first committed himself to the reflex as his unit (Skinner, 1931), he referred to the correlation between a class of stimuli and a class of responses. If this correlation was lawful, he believed the term "reflex" to be appropriate. A case could be made for his position, but the consequence was no more than to discover as his unit what Thorndike had earlier named the "connection" or "bond." Thorndike, too, accepted the correlation between situations and responses as the basis for his unit.

When Skinner developed the notion of emitted behavior, his earlier unit was no longer appropriate. The discriminated operant, which is the

[60] Keller and Schoenfeld (1950), page 60.
[61] Skinner (1953a), pages 252–256.

basis of experiment and theory in the newer writing, he early referred to as a *pseudo-reflex*.[62] He pointed out that it would be a great mistake to suppose that the correlation established between a discriminated stimulus and an operant followed the laws of the reflex. Thus the systematic correlation between stimuli and responses, a legitimate extension of the historical term "reflex," was no longer appropriate in dealing with operants. The terms which enter a reflex relationship should be those of "stimulus" and "response." Skinner's concern has appropriately shifted to mere lawfulness of behavior. The reflex proper (the basis for respondent behavior) is limited to autonomic and postural responses; the operant can just as well run under its own name, and not be confused with these reflexes. Instead of insisting on the analysis into reflex units, Skinner now appears somewhat less sure about the ultimate unit, and is temporarily satisfied with a functional analysis at the level of experimental convenience.

Co-ordination with Other Systematic Viewpoints

Skinner's "fresh start" approach to psychology has made it difficult for him to use the data collected by others, and, on principle, he rejects their concepts. His role in reference to the theories of others—insofar as he has paid any attention to their claims—has been chiefly that of a trenchant critic. He has felt no responsibility for the task of inter-investigator co-ordination. In his book *Science and human behavior* (1953), written as a textbook, he used no literature citations, and he mentions by name, among writers with some place in learning theory, only Thorndike, Pavlov, and Freud.

That some co-ordination is possible is shown by Keller and Schoenfeld (1950), who made a serious effort to bridge the gap between the data collected by Skinner and his followers and by others interested in learning. They were able to find much that they could use, even though they remained within the conceptual structure of Skinner's system.

The almost exclusive preoccupation with animal experiments (except for the studies of verbal behavior, and work with abnormal human subjects thus far only sketchily reported) raises some interesting questions. Presumably a functional, descriptive psychology of this kind must ultimately design experiments at the level at which scientific statements are to be made. As Verplanck points out, it is somewhat anomalous that a systematist who refuses to predict what a rat or pigeon will do—because such prediction does not belong in a scientific study of behavior—is willing

[62] Skinner (1935).

to make confident assertions about the most complex forms of human behavior, economic, political, religious.[63] The intervening steps appear to be missing, and the theory makes no formal provision for them.

The Anti-Theory Argument

Skinner's espousal of a descriptive, positivistic position and his opposition to a hypothetico-deductive system have frequently been reasserted, nowhere more clearly than in his presidential address before the Midwestern Psychological Association, entitled: "Are theories of learning necessary?"[64]

The theories he opposes are of at least two kinds. One kind is that which would find its explanations at a different level of discourse, using, for example, a physiological explanation for psychological events. There is no real objection to such a theory, unless it is overly insisted upon. The independence of the behavioral subject matter must be permitted, and explanatory mechanisms, especially explanatory fictions, are to be avoided. He challenges another kind of theory, commonly called hypothetico-deductive, which stresses the formulation of hypotheses and their testing. This kind of theory Skinner objects to as a futile and extravagant exercise. The argument can be stated simply enough. The end result of scientific investigation, whether the investigation is descriptive or an effort to confirm a theory, is a described functional relationship demonstrated in the data. Because the end result is the same, the only point at issue is really which method more efficiently directs the inquiry. Skinner is firmly of the opinion that theories are wasteful and misleading. They usually send the investigator down the wrong paths, and even if the scientific logic makes them self-correcting, the paths back are strewn with discarded theories. Once the data are in order, the theories tend to drop out. "If the theories have played no part in the design of the experiment, we need not be sorry to see them go."

Criticism of existing hypothetico-deductive systems in psychology is easy. This does not mean that their scientific logic is wrong. It may mean that some particular efforts have been premature or misdirected. Perhaps Skinner is right in criticizing unripe theorizing, but surely he is wrong if he means that we should return to a Baconian conception of science. The power achieved by other sciences through theoretical formulation is too convincing for such formulation not to serve at least as a long-range goal

[63] Verplanck (1954), page 311.
[64] Skinner (1950).

for those trying to create a science of behavior. That Skinner's approach is a fruitful one need not lead to the conclusion that other approaches are futile.

One of the next steps for a science, after lawful relationships have been discovered and appreciable amounts of data collected, is to represent the data in a kind of shorthand summary, using a minimal number of terms, and mathematical representation. This kind of systematic science Skinner can support, because it does not call for inferences alien to the data of observation. But he says of it:

> We do not seem to be ready for a theory in this sense. At the moment we make little use of empirical, let alone rational, equations. A few of the present curves could have been fairly closely fitted. But the most elementary preliminary survey shows that there are many relevant variables, and until their importance has been experimentally determined, an equation that allows for them will have so many arbitrary constants that a good fit will be a matter of course and cause for very little satisfaction.[65]

It is not surprising that a recent critic has found it appropriate to remark that Skinner's is "a highly formal, but not a highly formalized, theory." [66]

Success of the System

Two major achievements give the system a firm place in contemporary psychology.

At the level of data, the most novel and interesting data are those deriving from the various schedules of intermittent reinforcement. Only the sketchiest of experiments have been done by other workers in this fascinating field,[67] and the kind of operant behavior studied by Skinner has lent itself beautifully to this kind of investigation. It is a far cry from pointing out that rewards influence learning to achieving the kind of control whereby several thousands of responses are yielded at a uniform rate during extinction following a particular pattern of rewarding.

At the level of practical behavior the most striking results have been obtained in animal training. While these have not been of very great theoretical interest, it is not wise to dismiss them as merely signs of cleverness on the part of the trainers. These practical demonstrations serve as important empirical supports for certain aspects of the system—a kind of support very much needed for learning theories, and notably lacking thus far. No other learning theorist has been able to train an animal before

[65] Skinner (1950), page 216.
[66] Verplanck (1954), page 295.
[67] For a critical review of the literature, see Jenkins and Stanley (1950).

an audience in a prompt and predictable manner, while at the same time epitomizing the principles of his theory. There have long been public demonstrations of learned behavior—of conditioned responses, of maze learning, of discrimination—but these demonstrations have usually relied upon exhibiting the results of earlier training. By contrast, Skinner's pigeons can be brought before a class and taught various "stunts" before the eyes of the students. The empirical demonstration that learning is under the experimenter's control is important, and if what happens can be described in terms of the system, so much the better for the system.

The practical use of the system is based on the complementary principles of control through presenting and withholding food reward for a hungry animal. The supplementary principles of stimulus discrimination and response differentiation suffice to inaugurate the method of successive approximations. Beyond that, all that is needed is the experimenter's ingenuity. It is not necessary to worry about anything precise in the way either of experimental data or of correlated principles. From the point of view of a theoretical achievement this is really a pretty modest extension of Thorndike's law of effect. Whether or not a child can be taught to write a limerick by the same methods can only be known when the limerick gets written. The theory does not propose to predict!

SUPPLEMENTARY READINGS

BOOKS

KELLER, F. S., and SCHOENFELD, W. N. (1950) *Principles of psychology.*
SKINNER, B. F. (1938) *The behavior of organisms.*
SKINNER, B. F. (1953) *Science and human behavior.*

SHORTER INTRODUCTIONS

KELLER, F. S. (1954) *Learning (Reinforcement theory).* New York: Doubleday.
SKINNER, B. F. (1950) Are theories of learning necessary? *Psychol. Rev.*, 57, 193–216.
SKINNER, B. F. (1953) Some contributions of an experimental analysis of behavior to psychology as a whole. *Amer. Psychologist*, 8, 69–78.

CRITICAL REVIEWS

FINAN, J. L. (1940) Review of Skinner's *The behavior of organisms. J. gen. Psychol.*, 22, 441–447.
FINGER, F. W. (1954) Review of Skinner's *Science and human behavior. Psychol. Bull.*, 51, 86–88.
HILGARD, E. R. (1939) Review of Skinner's *The behavior of organisms. Psychol. Bull.*, 36, 121–125.
KRECHEVSKY, I. (1939) Review of Skinner's *The behavior of organisms. J. abnorm. soc. Psychol.*, 34, 404–407.

REPRESENTATIVE EXPERIMENTS

DINSMOOR, J. A. (1950) A quantitative comparison of the discriminative and reinforcing functions of a stimulus. *J. exp. Psychol.*, 40, 458–472.

ESTES, W. K. (1949) A study of motivating conditions necessary for secondary reinforcement. *J. exp. Psychol.*, 39, 306–310.

ESTES, W. K., and SKINNER, B. F. (1941) Some quantitative properties of anxiety. *J. exp. Psychol.*, 29, 390–400.

FERSTER, C. B. (1954) Use of the blackout in the investigation of temporal discrimination in fixed-interval reinforcement. *J. exp. Psychol.*, 47, 69–74.

FRICK, F. C. (1948) An analysis of an operant discrimination. *J. Psychol.*, 26, 93–123.

GRAHAM, C. H., and GAGNÉ, R. M. (1940) The acquisition, extinction, and spontaneous recovery of a conditioned operant response. *J. exp. Psychol.*, 26, 251–280.

HERON, W. T., and SKINNER, B. F. (1940) The rate of extinction in maze-bright and maze-dull rates. *Psychol. Rec.*, 4, 11–18.

KELLER, F. S. (1941) Light-aversion in the white rat. *Psychol. Rec.*, 4, 235–250.

NOTTERMAN, J. M. (1951) A study of some relations among aperiodic reinforcement, discrimination training, and secondary reinforcement. *J. exp. Psychol.*, 41, 161–169.

SCHOENFELD, W. N., ANTONITIS, J. J., and BERSH, P. J. (1950) Unconditioned response rate of the white rat in a bar-pressing apparatus. *J. comp. physiol. Psychol.*, 43, 41–48.

SKINNER, B. F. (1948) "Superstition" in the pigeon. *J. exp. Psychol.*, 38, 168–172.

STRASSBURGER, R. C. (1950) Resistance to extinction of a conditioned operant as related to drive level at reinforcement. *J. exp. Psychol.*, 40, 473–487.

FINAL NOTE

The following review deals with such systematic problems as Skinner's definitions of stimulus and response, and the nature of the concepts he employs. (The latest reference to Skinner's work is 1950).

VERPLANCK, W. S. (1954) Burrhus F. Skinner. In W. K. Estes and others. *Modern learning theory.*

Two books under Skinner's authorship that are forthcoming but not available at the time of writing are: *Verbal behavior* (William James Lectures at Harvard), and (with C. B. Ferster) *Schedules of reinforcement.*

His novel *Walden Two* (1948) is worth reading along with *Science and human behavior* (1953) for a comparison between the scientific system and its imaginary application in an experimental Utopia.

Chapter 5

HULL'S SYSTEMATIC BEHAVIOR THEORY

CLARK L. HULL (1884–1952), greatly impressed by the appearance of Pavlov's *Conditioned reflexes* (1927), began thereafter a long series of theoretical and experimental studies that in their totality comprise the best example of hypothetico-deductive system-making to appear during the first half of the century. The system is a behaviorism, and as such falls into the family of theories to which Guthrie's and Skinner's also belong. Each of these three systems represents in its own way a fulfillment of the behavioristic program originally proposed by Watson. Like Watson's, Hull's theory is avowedly mechanistic and studiously avoids reference to consciousness. Its central concept is habit, and it derives most of its information about habit from experiments with conditioned responses. Complex behavior, furthermore, is derived step by step from what is known about more elementary forms of learning. In these respects the theories of Watson and Hull are alike, but in other respects Hull's system represents a great advance over Watson's. Hull took the detailed findings of conditioning experiments much more seriously than Watson, who was satisfied to make use of the general paradigm provided by conditioned responses. Hull adopted (and adapted) Thorndike's law of effect, whereas Watson rejected it. For Watson's policy of denials and negations, Hull substituted a positive program of trying to explain purposes, insights, and other phenomena difficult for a behaviorism to encompass.

THE BASIC ORIENTATION

Before turning to the more formal system, expressed in postulates, corollaries, and theorems, we may do well to examine the broad framework within which the system operates.

Intervening Variables and Their Anchorage in Observables

In the first revision (1929) of his widely used textbook Woodworth suggested that we substitute the formula S-O-R for the earlier recommended S-R formula. The stimulus (S) affects the organism (O), and what happens as a consequence, the response (R), depends upon O as well as upon S. Hull's system may be thought of as a herculean elaboration of this S-O-R formula.[1]

In our experiments we measure environmental influences upon the organism (the input), and then measure the organism's responses (the output). These measures provide firm anchorage for our data in the environment, where objectivity can be achieved and maintained. Input and output are not comprised exclusively of the experimentally studied stimuli and responses. Other influences upon the organism can be treated as experimental variables, such as prior history of training, deprivation schedules, injection of drugs, and these influences can be described as objectively as stimuli and responses. What goes on within the organism we have to infer, and in the course of making these inferences we postulate certain *intervening variables* or *symbolic constructs.* If we tie these inferences firmly to the input-output terms by way of quantitative mathematical statements, we lose nothing in objectivity, and gain something in convenience, understanding, and fertility of deducing new phenomena. This is the basic logic of the system.

Reinforcement the Primary Condition for Habit Formation

In his choice among the three major possibilities (contiguity alone, reinforcement alone, or a dual theory), Hull stood firmly for a reinforcement theory. As early as 1935 he suggested that the Pavlov experiment might be considered a special case under Thorndike's law of effect, and in 1937 he published a formal derivation of Pavlovian conditioning on the basis of a reinforcement principle.[2] Although some modifications were made in his interpretation of reinforcement, he held to the end to the one principle as central to learning.

Reinforcement theory of the kind Hull espoused requires, in the specification of a primary reinforcing state of affairs, either drive reduction, as in need satisfaction, or drive-stimulus reduction, as in the satisfaction of a craving rather than a need. Hull earlier held to the drive-reduction theory, most clearly exemplified in escape from a continuing noxious

[1] Spence (1952a), page 646.
[2] Hull (1935a) (1937).

stimulus, such as an electrically charged grid. The activity that terminates the noxious stimulus is reinforced because the need to escape injury is satisfied in the escape. Later, under the influence of the Miller-Dollard theory of drive-stimulus reduction,[3] Hull went over to the drive-stimulus reduction theory and abandoned the drive-reduction interpretation of reinforcement. The example of escape from a noxious stimulus was equally cogent, though now the reduction in pain (the consequence of stimulation) is theoretically the basis for reinforcement instead of the escape from injury (the underlying need). In primary reinforcement the two events (drive and drive-stimulus) are so closely associated that it does not matter very much which is assumed to be reduced. But needs may require time for their satisfaction (as in the time required to digest food) whereas incentives (including food) work promptly as reinforcers, more as stimuli might be expected to work. Furthermore, as secondary reinforcement came into greater and greater prominence in reinforcement theories, the stimulus-reduction theory became even more attractive. This follows because secondary reinforcement is a function of stimuli rather than of needs.

Integration of Behavior Sequences Through Anticipatory Responses

Most of the primary behavioral laws in Hull's system were derived from either classical or instrumental conditioning (both interpreted as illustrations of learning under the control of reinforcement). But the appeal of the system rests upon the comprehensive explanation that it provides of many phenomena of learning in experiments not classifiable as simple conditioning: more complex trial-and-error and discriminatory learning, maze learning, rote memorization, tool using, and so on. In order to make these further deductions, Hull proposed a number of intermediate mechanisms, derivable from the basic laws of his system, but, once derived, of very wide applicability. At this point the intent is merely to give something of the flavor of these intermediaries; more detailed illustrations will be presented later in this chapter.

Many of the stimuli present at the time the goal is reached are also present earlier. These include the stimuli from the drive (what Guthrie called maintaining stimuli), environmental stimuli present both earlier and during reinforcement, traces from earlier stimuli persisting to the goal, as well as stimuli aroused by the animal's own movements. Hence in repeating a sequence of acts leading to a goal, as in running through a maze, there are always enough of these stimuli conditioned to the goal

[3] Miller and Dollard (1941).

response to elicit fractions of the goal response prior to reaching the goal. These *fractional antedating goal-responses* (r_G's) are very important integrators in Hull's system, and he made very ingenious use of them. While they were prominent all along in Guthrie's system, Guthrie never did formalize their use as Hull did.

The fractional anticipatory responses give rise to stimuli (s_G). These stimuli sometimes serve as surrogates for directing ideas. In that case the r_G is a "pure-stimulus act," that is, an act that serves functionally merely to produce a stimulus that maintains a steering role in behavior.[4]

These same stimuli (s_G) are very important in secondary reinforcement, permitting reinforcement originating in food at the end of the maze to move back and reinforce turns far from the goal.[5]

Furthermore, it is these same stimuli (s_G) that generate the *gradient of reinforcement* and the *habit-family hierarchy*, important intermediate mechanisms, which we shall meet later on.

Thus, on the basis of primary behavioral postulates, Hull deduced types of mechanism that led to wide generality in his deductions.

The Requirements for a Quantitative, Deductive System

Hull knew very clearly what he wanted in the way of a formal system. Such a system should begin with adequately defined terms, and then state a few (as few as possible) basic postulates. These postulates may either be very general empirical findings, and thus independently verifiable, or, if not directly testable, they must be subject to indirect verification. Their purpose is to relate the fundamental intervening variables by strict logic (and quantifiable mathematical equations) to each other and to their anchorages in environmental events. These postulates, taken together with the definitions, will generate new testable deductions or predictions. These are the corollaries and the theorems of the system.

The progress of science comes about through the experimental testing of theorems. When agreement is found, the postulate system generating the theorem remains in the running; when disagreement is found, a search is made for the faulty postulate, if such there be, and the postulate is then revised. Possibly, if no faulty postulate can be found, a new postulate may have to be added. Thus the system is self-correcting, and only those features survive that have stood the scrutiny of meticulous experimental testing.

Systems of this kind begin as "miniature" ones. That is, they encom-

[4] Hull (1931).
[5] Hull (1952a), page 14.

pass at first only a limited range of data. Even these limited data put the early system under strain, and the next steps consist in trying to secure a better fit between the theory and these data. Then additional data are incorporated through extensions of the system. Sometimes two or more "miniature systems" may be combined, as appropriate bridging concepts are developed. There may be major shifts in the systematic formulations, as when, in physics, Newtonian theory became a special case under Einstein's more general theory. Thus theory construction proceeds by successive approximations, and finality in a theory is often a sign that the theory is faulty.

Did Hull succeed in producing a good system, according to these criteria? A satisfactory answer may perhaps have to wait for the verdict of history. If a generally acceptable theory of learning eventually emerges with convincing evidence of its ancestry in Hull's earlier formulations, he will have succeeded. If the direction in which he moved turns out to have been a blind alley, and greater success comes from a fresh start in new directions, then his success will not have been as great. Even so he will have done a profoundly valuable service in showing what a mature system might look like, and in insisting that it was not too early to attempt to systematize psychology in rigorous fashion.

THE FINAL SYSTEM

Earlier Sets of Postulates

Hull's theoretical system evolved gradually. He habitually wrote down various conjectures and plans for experiments in bound notebooks, twenty-five volumes between 1915 and 1951.[6] Many of his later publications were foreshadowed in these notes and in the frequent mimeographed memoranda that he circulated. His first paper addressed specifically to the subject matter of his final system was in 1929, entitled "A functional interpretation of the conditioned reflex." In it he acknowledged his great indebtedness to Pavlov and began on an informal basis to make the kinds of deductions he later sought to formalize. Another important influence upon his later theorizing arose out of a summer's teaching at Harvard in 1930, when he was invited to lecture on aptitude testing because of the favorable reception of his recent book on that topic (1928). He there met C. I. Lewis and other philosophers, and asked them why philosophers had neglected his doctoral dissertation on concept formation.[7] Their answers are no

[6] Hull (1951), page 120.
[7] Hull (1920).

longer available to us, but in any case he added to his library, and read, Newton's *Principia,* and Whitehead and Russell's *Principia Mathematica.* These raised his sights as to the kind of theory to which he might aspire. The first formal system, using definitions, postulates, and theorems, appeared in 1935.[8] It was what he called a "miniature system" concerned with rote learning, to be elaborately worked over later in the most detailed of Hull's formal systematic efforts, the collaborative book entitled *Mathematico-deductive theory of rote learning.*[9]

The true ancestor of the final postulate set, however, was contained in Hull's presidential address before the American Psychological Association at Dartmouth in 1936.[10] This new "miniature system" was concerned with adaptive behavior of the kinds reflected in the later postulate sets in *Principles of behavior* (1943),[11] *Essentials of behavior* (1951),[12] and *A behavior system* (1952a). The final book was completed only a few weeks before Hull's death and appeared posthumously. It was written while he was suffering from a heart condition and could work only a few hours a day. It is a tribute to his devotion to his work that it was finished at all. Some of the changes in the latest version may very well turn out not to have been improvements. The system was by no means a finished one, and Hull was the first to acknowledge this. The promised books on individual differences and on social behavior did not get written, and the final book is full of qualifications and reservations. If therefore we base the exposition on the final book, and have some faults to find, this need not be taken as disparaging to Hull. The book carries the flavor that he intended, and the details would have to be filled in and corrected in any case. Such was the kind of system Hull envisaged.

In the pages to follow we shall trace through the postulates and corollaries of the final system one at a time, and then summarize the system, before turning to some of the deductive consequences of the system. There are a total of 17 postulates and 17 corollaries. An introduction to these postulates and corollaries necessarily has to be somewhat detailed if it is to be at once expository and critical. The effort has been made to keep the discussion within bounds by reducing the statement

[8] Hull (1935a).

[9] Hull and others (1940).

[10] Hull (1937).

[11] For an introduction to the postulate set of 1943, see the earlier edition of this book, Hilgard (1948), pages 80–91.

[12] This short book contains, with a few slight differences, the postulates in the final book. Essentially the same postulates were listed in an earlier journal article, Hull (1950a).

of the postulates and corollaries to their essentials through paraphrasing and eliminating some of the quantitative mathematical expression.

The Sensitive and Responding Organism

The organism, before it learns, brings with it certain tendencies to respond and the necessary sensory equipment to be affected by the environment. Hull's first postulates acknowledge these starting points for a stimulus-response theory.

Postulate 1. Unlearned stimulus-response connections

Organisms at birth possess a hierarchy of need-terminating responses that are aroused under conditions of stimulation and drive. The responses activated by stimulation under conditions of need are not a random selection of the organism's responses, but are those most likely to terminate the need.[13]

The first postulate recognizes a kind of biological trial and error favoring survival, based presumably on evolution. It actually plays little role in the system.

Postulate 2. The molar stimulus trace and its stimulus equivalent

A. Stimuli impinging upon a receptor give rise to afferent neural impulses. These constitute a "self-propagating molar afferent trace impulse," providing the equivalent of an increasing stimulus, reaching its maximum in about .450 seconds.

B. A new phase follows the maximum. This subsiding phase of the molar afferent trace impulse gives rise to a second stimulus equivalent. The subsiding phase endures longer than the first (recruitment) phase.

C. The intensity of the molar stimulus trace (s) (i.e., the effective stimulus in associative learning) is a logarithmic function of the molar stimulus equivalent of the trace.[14]

The second postulate sets the stage for one of the asserted fundamental conditions for associative learning: the contiguity between stimulus and response. As with Guthrie, the contiguity that counts is inside the organism—in Hull's terms the coincidence between the molar stimulus trace and effector activity. Hence the second postulate is introduced to define the effective intensity of the process initiated when an external stimulus impinges upon a receptor. The argument leading to parts A and B

[13] Paraphrased from Hull (1952a), page 5; (1951), page 4; (1943), page 66.

[14] The three parts of this postulate are paraphrased from Hull (1952a), page 5; (1951), page 11. The earlier postulate, Hull (1943), page 47, has been considerably revised in order to make use of quantitative data from the experiments of Reynolds (1945a) and Kimble (1947). How he uses their data can be found in Hull (1952a), pages 101–104. Because the equations stated in quantitative form in Hull's postulates are not essential to understanding the postulate set, the essence is here reported in verbal paraphrases.

of the postulate is as follows. If stimulus and response must be coincident in time for conditioning to occur, the most favorable interval between conditioned and unconditioned stimuli must be that at which the maximum after-effect of the conditioned stimulus coincides with the beginning of the unconditioned response. From the experiments of Kimble and of Reynolds this is known to be at an interval of about .450 seconds. Hence this interval appears in postulate 2A as the interval of maximum molar afferent trace impulse. The form of recruitment and of subsidence is the form of the curves obtained by Kimble and Reynolds with various intervals between conditioned and unconditioned stimuli.

The introduction of the logarithmic term in 2C is apparently a concession to psychophysics. The Weber-Fechner law taught us to expect a roughly logarithmic relationship between the sensory response and the physical stimulus. This logarithmic transformation may conceivably take place within the receptor, within the afferent processes, or within the cortex. Hull has rather casually assigned the transformation to the afferent process—the molar stimulus trace bearing a logarithmic relationship to the molar stimulus *equivalent* of the trace.[15]

Motivation and Reinforcement

We now come close to the heart of the theory, which is unified around the conception that learning takes place only as a consequence of reinforcement.

Postulate 3. Primary reinforcement

When a response (R) is closely associated with a stimulus trace (s) and this stimulus-response conjunction is associated with a rapid decrease in drive-produced stimuli (S_D) there will result an increase in the tendency for that stimulus trace (s) to evoke that response (R).

The rapid decrease in the goal stimulus (s_G) is also reinforcing.[16]

We may note that the association which gets strengthened is alike for both Guthrie and Hull: a contiguous stimulus-response connection.

[15] Placing the logarithmic transformation where he does would perhaps classify Hull with those favoring "outer" psychophysics, as contrasted with Fechner's "inner" psychophysics. See Dodge (1911); Boring (1950), pages 291–292.

[16] Paraphrased from Hull (1952a), pages 5–6; (1951), page 20. See also (1943), page 80. The decrease in S_D as the basis of primary reinforcement is the more usual statement of the postulate, the choice having been made between decrease in drive (D) and in the drive stimulus (S_D). The insertion of s_G into the postulate on primary reinforcement appears to be an after-thought, based on the possibility that even when responses are reinforced by food it is not the drive that is satisfied but some derivative of the drive (i.e., some s_G), such as taste or appetite. Because r_G and s_G are central to secondary reinforcement, it would probably be wise, in considering the system as a whole, to forget that Hull included s_G in Postulate 3. See the discussion of Corollary xv, page 148.

But for Guthrie it gets fixed merely because it occurs; for Hull it gets strengthened *only because it occurs in association with reinforcement.* Primary reinforcement is brought about, according to the postulate, by the decrease in the stimuli produced by a drive, for example, the removal of a noxious stimulus, the reduction of hunger pangs (or by a decrease of stimuli associated with the anticipated satisfaction of these drives). Hull notes that he has vacillated somewhat in his earlier discussions between a reduction in need or drive (D), and a reduction in drive stimuli (S_D). He ends up with the latter, but with some reservations, and, in fact, leaves the matter open for revision.[17]

Corollary i. Secondary drive

When a neutral stimulus trace (*s*) has been closely associated with the evocation and rapid decrease of drive-produced stimuli (S_D), the hitherto neutral stimulus trace (*s*) acquires a tendency to bring about these drive stimuli (S_D), so that the previously neutral stimulus trace (*s*) becomes the occasion for a secondary drive ($s \longrightarrow S_D$).[18]

This corollary expresses an association between two stimuli: the neutral stimulus trace (*s*), and the drive stimulus (S_D). Such an association is foreign to Hull's system, for learning must always involve a response term. Actually a response intermediary is implied, even though not stated. This may be illustrated by the acquisition of fear as a secondary drive. The primary drive is pain, producing the original drive stimulus (S_D). Neutral stimuli associated with pain give rise to "fear" responses, very similar to responses to pain, and the proprioceptive consequences of these learned *responses* produce the drive stimulus (S_D) that serves the secondary drive.[19] The corollary, however, asserts nothing about this response intermediary.

Corollary ii. Secondary reinforcement

When a neutral stimulus trace (*s*) has been closely associated with a rapid diminution in drive produced stimuli (S_D), the hitherto neutral stimulus trace (*s*) acquires a tendency to bring about the reduction of S_D, so that the previously neutral stimulus trace (*s*) acquires "the power of acting as a reinforcing agent." [20]

Despite the seeming formality of his exposition, Hull used many variations in wording when stating his postulates, so that precise meanings are sometimes hard to infer. I have restated the two corollaries in closely parallel form, which he did not do. Then it becomes evident that a neutral

[17] Hull (1952a), page 153.
[18] Paraphrased from Hull (1952a), page 6; (1951), page 25; (1943), page 98.
[19] N. E. Miller (1948a) (1951b).
[20] Paraphrased from Hull (1952a), page 6; (1951), page 28; (1943), page 95.

stimulus trace associated consistently with a reinforcing state of affairs acquires two functions (and both at once!): (1) the power to arouse a secondary drive (Corollary i), and (2) the power to reduce drive stimuli, and hence act as a secondary reinforcing agent (Corollary ii).

The distinction between secondary drive and secondary reinforcement is an important one, and practical examples can be found to make the distinction clear. For example, fear and anxiety easily classify as secondary drives, and their reduction is reinforcing. Similarly, distinctive food-boxes, or poker-chips used as tokens, readily classify as secondary reinforcing agents. A chimpanzee will work for a token only when hungry: the drive remains the usual hunger drive, but the secondary reinforcing agent is not itself hunger-satisfying. Hull intended to preserve this distinction in the corollaries, but the formal statements do not specify when the neutral stimuli will *evoke* S_D (then serving as secondary drives), or when they will *reduce* S_D (then serving as secondary reinforcers). The only hint of a difference is that for the acquiring of a secondary drive the neutral stimulus must be present at the time of drive evocation as well as drive reduction, while, for the acquiring of secondary reinforcement, the neutral stimulus has to be present only at the time of drive reduction.

The attempt to interpret the actual events in secondary reinforcement came late in Hull's theorizing, and he probably had not developed a theory fully satisfactory to himself. That he was attempting to hold to a consistent drive-stimulus reduction theory of secondary reinforcement (as well as of primary reinforcement), is clear from the following statement:

> It follows that any stimulus consistently associated with a reinforcement situation will through that association acquire the power of evoking the conditioned inhibition, i.e., a reduction in stimulus intensity, and so of itself producing the resulting reinforcement. Since this indirect power of reinforcement is acquired through learning, it is called *secondary reinforcement.*[21]

It can be pointed out that all conditioned stimuli must develop some secondary reinforcing powers because they must necessarily be associated with a reinforcing state of affairs.

While as paraphrased the corollaries deal only with *secondary* drives and reinforcements, they are applicable also to higher-order derivatives, so that tertiary drives can be built upon secondary ones, and higher-order reinforcements can be based upon higher-order drives.

[21] Hull (1951), pages 27–28.

The Law of Habit Formation

Having chosen contiguous association under reinforcement as the basic *qualitative* condition for habit strengthening, Hull had an additional basic choice to make regarding the *quantitative* influence of reinforcement. Either reinforcement could contribute its maximum influence on one trial (the possibility accepted as a genuine one by Skinner, and corresponding to Guthrie's one-trial learning), or reinforcement could add an increment to habit strength on each occurrence. Hull chose the latter alternative.

Postulate 4. Habit strength ($_SH_R$) *as a function of reinforcement*

Habit strength (the tendency for a stimulus trace to evoke an associated response) increases as a positive growth function of the number of trials, provided that trials are evenly spaced, reinforcement occurs on every trial, and everything else remains constant.[22]

The function described as a positive growth function is of the form:

$$_SH_R = 1 - 10^{-aN}$$

where N is the number of trials from absolute zero, and a is an empirical constant of the order of .03 as stated in the original postulate. Such a function is used throughout Hull's quantitative formulations. It can be understood as a function with a maximum at 1.00, this maximum being approached in such a manner that each unit of reinforcement increases habit strength by a constant fraction of the possible habit strength as yet unrealized. This is, of course, a curve of decreasing gains. Because the total range is 1.00, the unit of habit was originally defined as a *hab,* a centigrade unit extending by steps of .01 to 1.00.[23]

While the postulate shows habit strength to be a function solely of the number of reinforcements, we cannot tell from this postulate alone what other influences there may be upon habit strength. Because it is specified that everything else is constant, it might be that habit strength would be different with a given number of reinforcements if, say, drive were different. We may anticipate a little, however, and point out that *there are no systematic influences upon* $_SH_R$ *other than the number of reinforced trials.* It would actually have been unnecessary to state in the postulate that everything else is constant, for nothing else can affect $_SH_R$ directly.[24]

[22] Paraphrased from Hull (1952a), page 6; (1951), page 32; (1943), page 114.

[23] Hull (1951), page 32. The *hab* is dropped in Hull (1952a), and $_SH_R$ becomes a multiplying factor without any units.

[24] One of the important changes between 1951 and 1952 is the dropping of the influence upon $_SH_R$ of stimulus intensity during learning. See footnote 28.

This is a radical departure from the earlier system, because now most of the influences, as we shall see, are upon reaction potential ($_SE_R$) rather than upon habit strength ($_SH_R$). The distinction between performance and learning, so long insisted upon by Tolman, was formally accepted in the 1943 postulates, but by now has greatly reduced the quantitative influence of reinforcement upon associative learning. We would expect the magnitude of each reinforcement to be pertinent in determining the contribution of reinforcement to habit strength, but we are now told that this is not the case, so long as some unspecified minimum of reduction in S_D occurs.

Non-associative Factors Affecting Reaction Potential

Reaction potential ($_SE_R$) is Hull's term for the inferred process close to response evocation. It can be inferred only from response, but is not to be identified with response. Reaction potential and response are not identical because reaction potential may be below threshold, hence not lead to response, or it may interact with competing tendencies and hence be incompletely revealed in response.

We may conveniently think of $_SH_R$ as signifying associative strength and of $_SE_R$ as signifying the strength of the tendency to respond. At a given level of habit strength ($_SH_R$) the magnitude of the reaction potential ($_SE_R$) depends in addition upon three chief non-associative [25] factors operative at the time of response evocation. These are specified in the next three postulates.

Postulate 5. Primary drive (D)

A. A primary drive (at least that resulting from food deprivation) consists of two components: (1) the drive proper, which increases with the number of hours of food deprivation, and (2) an inanition component which reduces drive as starvation continues.

B. Each drive condition generates a characteristic drive stimulus (S_D) which is an increasing function of the drive condition.

C. Some drive conditions may motivate into action habits set up on the basis of different drive conditions.[26]

According to Spence, drive (D) is conceived by Hull as "a nonspecific state or general condition of the nervous system to which all the specific needs contribute." [27] Hence the general drive level is due not only to the

[25] Spence (1951a).

[26] Paraphrased from Hull (1952a), pages 6–7; (1951), pages 28–40; (1943) page 253. The postulate as stated by Hull has four parts, one of which is introduced for illustrative purposes only. It describes the course of hunger drive as measured in one experiment (Yamaguchi, 1951), and is omitted here as unnecessary to the argument.

[27] Spence (1951a), page 249.

relevant drive but to all needs coexisting at the time. The drive stimulus (S_D) is more nearly specific to a given drive, so that it can provide for discrimination between drives as well as for reinforcement. There is some interchangeability among drives as acknowledged in the final part of the postulate.

Drive activates habit strength into reaction potential. The simplest form of statement is:

$$_SE_R = D \times {_SH_R}$$

This means that a habit of given strength will yield responses of greater or less magnitude, depending upon the level of drive operating at the time the response is evoked. For the sake of simplicity, this and the two following postulates assume that the levels of the non-associative factors have remained the same during learning and testing, in order to avoid the complications that ensue when a different level of drive is used in learning and in testing. This assumption makes it possible to provide quantitative expressions for the postulates with greater ease. The intent is, however, that drive strength has its true influence at the time of response evocation, that is, that it is a non-associative factor.

The concept of drive is very important in Hull's system. It has three distinct functions:

1. Without drive there could be no primary reinforcement, because primary reinforcement requires the rapid diminution of S_D. There could, of course, be no secondary reinforcement either, for secondary reinforcement originates in the association of a stimulus with primary reinforcement.

2. Without drive there could be no response, for drive activates habit strength into reaction potential. Drive is the most important multiplier of $_SH_R$.

3. Without the distinctiveness of the drive stimuli S_D there could be no regulation of habits by the need state of the organism, no way to learn to go one place for water when thirsty, another place for food when hungry.

The first and third of these functions together determine *which* incentive is reinforcing, as well as *why* it is reinforcing; the second function is that of a goad to action in the direction of need satisfaction; the third also gives drive a discriminative or steering role.

Postulate 6. Stimulus-intensity dynamism (V)

The greater the intensity of the stimulus, the greater the reaction potential for any given level of habit strength. The magnitude of the stimulus-intensity dynamism (V), as a component of reaction potential, is an increasing logarithmic function of the stimulus intensity.[28]

The basic equation parallels that for drive:

$$_S E_R = V \times {_S H_R}$$

Postulate 7. Incentive motivation (K)

The greater the magnitude of the incentive used in reinforcement, the greater the reaction potential for any given level of habit strength. The incentive motivation (K), as a component of reaction potential, is a negatively accelerated increasing function of the weight of food or quantity of other incentive.[29]

Again it must be noted that the influence of amount of the reinforcing agent during learning is upon reaction potential and not upon habit strength:

$$_S E_R = K \times {_S H_R}$$

We are dealing here with constant values of K within training and testing, so that the question of shift of incentive between learning and testing (as in latent learning experiments) must wait for further discussion. So, too, the problem of the influence of the perceived incentive, as part of response evocation, will be discussed later.

Postulate 8. The constitution of reaction potential ($_S E_R$)

When conditions have been constant throughout learning and response-evocation, the reaction potential ($_S E_R$) is determined by the habit strength ($_S H_R$) multiplied by (1) the drive (D), (2) the stimulus-intensity dynamism (V), and (3) the incentive motivation (K).[30]

The general equation becomes:

$$_S E_R = D \times V \times K \times {_S H_R}$$

This postulate merely combines the results of the preceding three into one equation. Several statements need to be made about this equation, especially about the implication of the multiplication signs and the resulting problem of units of measurement.

The major magnitude in the determination of $_S E_R$ turns out to be D rather than $_S H_R$. The maximum values of D, in the sigma units by which $_S E_R$ is measured, may be as great as twice the maximum of $_S E_R$.[31] Hence D

[28] Paraphrased from Hull (1952a), page 7; (1951), page 46. The concept does not appear in Hull (1943). A change occurred between 1951 and 1952, in that in the 1952 version V_1, the V during learning, no longer affects $_S H_R$.

[29] Paraphrased from Hull (1952a), page 7; (1951), page 51; (1943), page 129.

[30] Paraphrased from Hull (1952a), page 7; (1951), page 8, but with the omission of J and a changed role for V. The relations are considerably altered from Hull (1943), e.g., page 178.

[31] Hull (1951), page 58, states that the maximum hunger drive ranges "uncertainly from 6 to 12 σ." The maximum assumed for $_S E_R$ is 6 σ.

is measured in the units of $_SE_R$. The other multiplying terms are merely decimal multipliers or weights, without units, each with a maximum of 1.00. Were $_SH_R$, V, and K all at the maximum, $_SE_R$ would be equal to D. Any other values of $_SH_R$, V, and K make $_SE_R$ less than D. A zero value for any multiplier (including D) makes $_SE_R$ assume a value of zero. We shall return later to a discussion of the measurement of $_SE_R$. For the present, we may note that the *forms* of the functions underlying $_SH_R$, D, V, and K have some degree of independent determination, but their *units* are entirely arbitrary. For $_SH_R$, V, and K the arbitrary maximum is 1.00, and they are pure numbers, without any kind of unit. Both the maximum value and the units of D are obtained by working backwards from $_SE_R$. Had D been treated symmetrically with $_SH_R$ (as it was when the unit called *mote* was assigned, paralleling *hab*) [32] then any one of the other terms could just as well have taken on the larger range of values. It is important to note how a *tour de force* of this kind makes possible the multiplication of four quite disparate quantities without causing the systematist major difficulties. A preferable solution (and an equally simple one) would have been to preserve the uniform (arbitrary) scale for each of the factors, and then to introduce an arbitrary constant to convert to the scale used for $_SE_R$. This would have made no difference in the end, and would have avoided the illusion that D was assigned more importance than the others on the basis of some kind of empirical evidence. It turns out to be merely the residual legatee of the constant required to convert to the units of $_SE_R$.

Corollary iii. Delay in reinforcement (*J*)

A. For a response in a chain, the greater the delay in reinforcement, the weaker the reaction potential leading to that response.

B. For a single response, the greater the delay in reinforcement, the weaker the reaction potential, according to a gradient that falls off rapidly at first and then more slowly, approaching the asymptote at about 5 seconds.[33]

The delay-in-reinforcement gradient has been very important in Hull's theorizing ever since his early paper on the goal gradient.[34] The simple delay-in-reinforcement gradient (Part B of Corollary iii) became shorter

[32] Hull (1943), page 243. At that time the decimal was omitted, so that both $_SH_R$ and D had maximum values of 100.

[33] Paraphrased from Hull (1952a), pages 7–8. The equation stated by Hull is based on a complicated determination, (1952a), pages 126–133. Hull himself had serious doubts about some of the assumptions involved, (1952a), page 131 (footnote), page 133. The status as a corollary is a change from (1951), page 56, where J was a multiplier equivalent to D, V and K. It was then a modification from (1943), pages 145, 178.

[34] Hull (1932).

as Hull's system evolved. The earlier gradient for a single reinforced response extended for 30 to 60 seconds, while the final one extends but 5 seconds.[35]

The shortening of the gradient came about as secondary reinforcement gained more prominence in the generation of the longer gradients. By placing the gradient in a corollary rather than a postulate, Hull accepted Spence's suggestion that the primary gradient is probably absent altogether, all gradients being generated through secondary reinforcement or other intermediate mechanisms.[36]

Corollary iiiA has the logical status of a theorem, extending the gradient to cover links in a chain of responses.

Behavioral Summation and Withdrawal

The next four corollaries deal with a complication of habit strength and reaction potential when two stimuli (along a continuum) have been associated with the same response through reinforcement.

Corollary iv. The summation of habit strengths when two stimuli S and S′ have been separately associated with a response through reinforcement
Corollary v. The summation of reaction potentials when two stimuli S and S′ have been separately associated with a response through reinforcement
Corollary vi. The withdrawal of habit strength when S′ is withdrawn from the combination of S and S′ as in Corollary iv
Corollary vii. The withdrawal of reaction potential when S′ is withdrawn from the combination of S and S′ as in Corollary v [37]

These four corollaries all revolve about the same basic assumption. The combined habit strength is said to be composed of (1) the primary habit strength ($_SH_R$) to the stimulus more frequently followed by a reinforced response, and (2) the additional habit strength to this stimulus ($_S\bar{H}_R$) generalized from the habit strength acquired by the second stimulus ($_{S'}H_R$). The sum is less than that obtained by direct addition of these two components. To compute the sum you may first convert both of these habit strengths ($_SH_R$ and $_S\bar{H}_R$) to the number of reinforcements that must follow response to S in order to reach these strengths. Add these two N's and from this sum compute the equivalent habit strength. This will be the combined habit strength you seek. An algebraic simplification

[35] For the earlier gradient, see Hull (1943), page 145, for the later one, Hull (1952a), page 131.
[36] Spence (1947).
[37] Corollaries iv through vii appear in Hull (1952a), pages 8–9, and in (1951) pages 63, 65, 67, and 69. The earlier discussion appeared in (1943), page 223.

reduces the computational complexity and permits computation directly from the habit strengths:

$${}_SH_R \dotplus {}_S\bar{H}_R = {}_SH_R + {}_S\bar{H}_R - {}_SH_R \times {}_S\bar{H}_R \qquad \text{(Corollary iv)}$$

The same argument applies to the computation of the combined reaction potential, and the steps are reversed in the withdrawal of habit strength and reaction potential.

Corollary viii. Behavioral summation of incentive substances [38]

The corollary as Hull states it indicates a method of determining the relative weights to be assigned different incentive substances (e.g., water and food) in order to compute a combined value of K, the incentive reinforcement, when both substances are used together.

Inhibition

The fundamental form of inhibition in most conditioning theories is represented by experimental extinction—the reduction in response with repeated non-reinforcement. One interpretation is that extinction is a result of competing response tendencies. This interpretation requires no new principle, and no negative response tendencies have to be computed. It is the position we have met in the views of both Guthrie and Skinner. The second interpretation calls for a special theory of inhibition, producing a negative reaction potential. Hull adopts this second kind of theory. The empirical and theoretical background for Hull's theory rests on Hovland's earlier recognition of inhibition-of-reinforcement,[39] on Neal Miller's analysis of the role of muscle strain, fatigue, and pain in extinction and spontaneous recovery, and in "anticipatory relaxation," [40] and on Mowrer's experimental test of effortfulness of task in relation to experimental extinction.[41]

With this background, Hull suggests that two kinds of inhibitory potential compete with excitatory potential to weaken it: reactive inhibition (I_R) and conditioned inhibition (${}_SI_R$). These both act as negative reaction potentials. They summate to produce a total inhibitory potential that can neutralize positive reaction potential.

Reactive inhibition (I_R) is generated whenever a response occurs, and

[38] The corollary is stated in mathematical form in Hull (1952a), page 9; (1951), page 72.
[39] Hovland (1936). Sometimes continued reinforcement leads to a decline in response resembling experimental extinction, e.g., Hilgard (1933).
[40] Miller and Dollard (1941), pages 40–43; Miller (1951b), pages 451–452.
[41] Mowrer and Jones (1943).

is akin to tissue injury, fatigue, or pain. As such, it acts as a barrier to repetition, directly inhibiting reaction potential. It has a second aspect in addition, in that it acts (just as pain does) as a drive, strengthening any activity associated with its reduction.[42] The activity that reduces I_R is rest ("non-activity"), and it is this conditioned non-activity that is known as conditioned inhibition ($_SI_R$).

Postulate 9. Inhibitory potential

A. The occurrence of a response produces reactive inhibition (I_R) which both inhibits reaction potential and acts as a negative drive.

B. Reactive inhibition (I_R) dissipates spontaneously with the passage of time as a simple decay function of elapsed time.

C. As a given response is repeated, increments of reactive inhibition summate. The resulting I_R also summates with conditioned inhibition ($_SI_R$) to produce the aggregate inhibitory potential ($\dot{I}_R$).

D. When non-reinforced responses follow each other at short intervals, the aggregate inhibitory potential ($\dot{I}_R$) increases as a positive growth function of the number of non-reinforced trials, thus yielding the phenomena of experimental extinction.

E. Because the aggregate inhibitory potential ($\dot{I}_R$) increases with the magnitude of the work involved in each response, the greater the work involved the fewer the number of unreinforced responses to a criterion of experimental extinction.[43]

Portions of this postulate (especially parts C, D, and E) are intimately related to the three following corollaries.

Corollary ix. Conditioned inhibition

Stimulus traces closely associated with the cessation of a response, in the presence of I_R (which is assumed to decrease also when the response ceases) become conditioned to the particular non-activity. This conditioned non-activity is known as conditioned inhibition ($_SI_R$), and opposes reaction potential ($_SE_R$). The amount of $_SI_R$ generated increases with the amount of I_R present.[44]

The systematic considerations here are actually very complex, and they are treated rather sketchily by Hull. Because $_SI_R$ is a habit, it ought to have two components, the equivalents of $_SH_R$ and $_SE_R$. Actually, Hull treats only the reaction potential ($_SE_R$) equivalent. Conditioned inhibition ($_SI_R$) is said to be a function of the amount of I_R because the more I_R there is the more rapidly it can diminish and hence the more reinforcing it can be.[45] This argument reflects outmoded features of the system. A form

[42] Hull did not follow up all the implications of treating I_R as a drive. He did not subtract it from D, which as a matter of course his system requires; he did not use it in conjunction with D as a multiplier in the determination of reaction potential.

[43] The five parts of Postulate 9 are paraphrased from Hull (1952a), pages 9–10; (1951), pages 74–81. Antecedents occur in (1943), especially page 300.

[44] Paraphrased from Hull (1952a), page 10; (1951), page 75; (1943), page 300.

[45] Hull (1951), page 75; Kimble (1949), page 22.

of the theory more consistent with the current system would simply make a stronger drive (I_R) a larger multiplier, with the same result—a larger $_SI_R$ resulting from larger values of I_R.

In Corollary ix, conditioned inhibition is derived from the principle of reinforcement (Postulate 3) by interpreting inactivity as a response and I_R as a drive. Hence it is legitimately a corollary rather than a postulate, although Hull is not always clear about his basis for classifying the several principles. The corollary is necessary to provide a definition of conditioned inhibition ($_SI_R$) already made use of in Postulate 9C.

Corollary x. Aggregate inhibitory potential as a function of work

The aggregate inhibitory potential that is generated through complete extinction requiring a fixed number of trials is an increasing function of the magnitude of the work involved in each response.[46]

Corollary xi. Aggregate inhibitory potential as a function of the number of responses

The aggregate inhibitory potential that is generated through complete extinction requiring a fixed magnitude of work per response is an increasing function of the number of trials.[47]

Corollary x follows from Postulate 9E, but restates the postulate for *a constant number of trials* to complete extinction, instead of a constant reaction potential. A good guess as to the reason for this and the following corollary is that scaled data were available from experiments based on responses to extinction.[48]

Corollary xi bears a corresponding relation to Postulate 9D. The postulate states the number of trials to extinction when reaction potential is constant and the work per response varies, while the corollary states the number of trials to extinction *when work is constant* and reaction potential varies. This implication of the corollary is not self-evident, until we remember that the total amount of inhibition generated during extinction must equal the total amount of reaction potential that it must neutralize. Hence with constant work, the only independent variable implied in Corollary xi is the amount of reaction potential to be overcome through the generation of inhibition during extinction.

Equivalence and Interaction of Stimuli

We now come to two postulates concerned with stimulus interrelationships, the first with *generalization*, when one stimulus is to some degree

[46] Paraphrased from Hull (1952a), page 10; (1951), page 84; (1943), page 279.
[47] Paraphrased from Hull (1952a), page 10; (1951), page 85.
[48] The experiments are those of Mowrer and Jones (1943), Perin (1942), and Williams (1938).

equivalent to another, the second with *afferent stimulus interaction* when two or more stimuli are active at once. The earlier corollaries that dealt with interaction effects (Corollaries iv through viii) considered the summation and withdrawal of reaction potential, once habits have been set up. Here the concern is with the properties of *stimuli* and with the changes in stimulus traces when more than one stimulus is active at once.

Postulate 10. Stimulus generalization

A. The generalized habit strength ($_{s_2}\bar{H}_R$) associated with a stimulus trace s_2 differing in *quality* from the stimulus trace s_1 involved in the habit $_{s_1}H_R$) depends upon the remoteness of s_2 from s_1 on a qualitative continuum in units of discrimination thresholds (j.n.d.'s).

Provided D, K, and V remain constant, the generalized reaction potential ($_{s_2}\underline{E}_R$) will vary directly with $_{s_2}H_R$.

B. The generalized habit strength ($_{s_2}\bar{H}_R$) associated with a stimulus-trace (s_2) differing in *intensity* from the one (s_1) involved in the prior learned habit ($_{s_1}H_R$) likewise depends upon the remoteness of s_2 from s_1. Because the difference is one of intensity, log units may be used instead of j.n.d.'s in determining the stimulus separation. The amount of generalization, furthermore, is a function of V_1, the stimulus-intensity dynamism of s_1 during conditioning.[49]

Provided D and K remain constant, the generalized reaction potential ($_{s_2}\underline{E}_R$) will vary directly with $_{s_2}\bar{H}_R$ and V_2, the stimulus-intensity dynamism of s_2 during testing.

C. Generalized conditioned inhibition ($_{s_2}\underline{I}_R$) follows the same principles of generalization from $_{s_1}I_R$ along qualitative and quantitative stimulus continua as generalized habit strength and generalized reaction potential.[50]

The postulate means essentially that the more alike two stimuli are, the more nearly one can substitute for the other in arousing conditioned responses. The differences between stimuli along a dimension permit description of a *gradient of generalization* along this dimension. Such a gradient is implied in each of the three parts of the postulate. A number of closely related attempts have been made to derive the form of the gradient from empirical data, and to apply the results to problems of stimulus equivalence and to discrimination.[51]

Corollary xii. The generalization of habit strength and reaction potential with change in strength of drive

When a response is learned under one intensity of drive and tested under another, both generalized habit strength ($_s\bar{H}_R$) and generalized reaction poten-

[49] This use of V_1 appears to be a "hangover" from the 1951 postulate set. This is the only place in the final postulates where habit strength is any longer a function of stimulus intensity. See footnote 28.

[50] The postulate in its three parts is paraphrased from Hull (1952a), pages 10–11, (1951), pages 88–92 (with minor systematic differences); (1943), pages 199, 264.

[51] E.g., Spence (1936) (1937) (1939) (1942); Hull (1939a) (1947b) (1949) (1950b). For related papers of his own, and a critical review of the Hull-Spence formulations, see Razran (1949).

tial ($_{S}\underline{E}_{R}$) will be decreased, their strengths following a gradient based upon the amount of difference in drive strength during learning and during testing.[52]

The meaning of this corollary is not clear without some explanation. Drive-stimulus habit strength ($_{S_D}\bar{H}_{R}$) is always a component of the total habit strength resulting from learning. (We have not met this in exactly this form before, but S_D is always present with the response that is being reinforced, and so enters into association with it.) Hence under a new drive intensity, the total generalized habit strength will have as a component a *reduced* generalized drive-stimulus habit strength ($_{S_D}\bar{H}_{R}$). The reduction follows from Postulate 10, the new drive stimulus being at some distance from the original one. It follows that as a consequence of the change in the drive stimulus, the resulting total generalized habit strength or reaction potential will be less under a new drive intensity than under the original drive conditions, the amount less depending on how far apart the drive conditions of learning and testing happen to be.

It comes as something of a surprise to learn that D, as a multiplier of habit strength, holds during learning and testing *when D remains constant,* but at the time of testing a change in D always *reduces* reaction potential, *even though D is increased.* This is all the more surprising because the other multipliers (V and K) continue to operate as multipliers with changed intensity, increasing reaction potential as they increase, and decreasing reaction potential as they decrease.

The empirical data which give general support to the corollary are those of Yamaguchi (1952). He found that with starvation periods ranging from 3 to 72 hours, with tests at various in-between periods of food deprivation, tested responses tended to be at minimum latency when the testing and training drives were alike. When tested at other intervals of deprivation, either greater or less than the training interval, responses tended to be of longer latency. These results are in agreement with the corollary, or, to put it the other way, these results gave rise to the corollary.

A related experiment by Strassburger (1950), perhaps unfamiliar to Hull, yielded results conforming better to what one would expect from Hull's general postulate system, but disagreeing with this corollary. After training under various conditions of food deprivation from ½ to 47 hours, then testing under a uniform deprivation of 23 hours, he found no differences in the number of responses to extinction that could be attributed to differences in the drive level at the time of original learning, but he did

[52] Paraphrased from Hull (1952a), page 11; (1951), page 90; (1943), pages 235–236.

find differences attributable to the number of prior reinforcements. This is just what Hull's Postulate 4 would lead us to expect. It is not consistent with Corollary xii, however, because change of drive at time of testing did not of itself reduce responsiveness.

Postulate 11. Afferent stimulus interaction in external inhibition

When a response has been conditioned to a stimulus (S_1) and one or more previously neutral stimuli (S_2, S_3, . . .) are presented along with S_1, the afferent impulses from this combination of stimuli interact to yield a new molar impulse ($\check{s}$). This new impulse is equivalent to a stimulus at a greater or less distance from S_1 on a qualitative continuum. The resulting generalized reaction potential to $\check{s}$ will be smaller than that to s_1, depending upon their remoteness from each other.[53]

The equation defining the amount of reduction in ${}_sE_R$ is:

$$d \text{ (in j.n.d.'s)} = \frac{\log \frac{{}_sE_R}{{}_{\check{s}}E_R}}{j}$$

where ${}_sE_R$ is the original reaction potential, ${}_{\check{s}}E_R$ the reaction potential reduced by external inhibition because of the presence of the added stimuli, and j a constant determined by the form of the gradient of generalization.

It is clear that the equation attempts to quantify the effects, while asserting nothing at all about the kind of patterning or other relationship among stimuli responsible for these effects. Furthermore, as presented it quantifies merely the limited form of interaction found in external inhibition, and does not cover the many other varieties of stimulus interaction. Parallel equations could have been developed covering some of the other matters that Hull discussed less formally, and he intended that a research program would determine the circumstances producing the kinds of changes he was ready to quantify.

This postulate permitted Hull to acknowledge the properties of patterned stimuli—the essence of the gestalt perception problem. He believed that in this postulate he had achieved a rapprochement with gestalt psychology, a sign of the maturing of psychological science.[54]

Random Variability of Reaction Potential

Organisms vary from moment to moment in their ability to perform well-established habits. In memorizing nonsense syllables, a syllable correctly anticipated on one trial may be missed on the next trial. A stimulus threshold is never at a fixed value. The threshold is instead some measure of central tendency, with a dispersion of values about it. This body of

[53] Paraphrased from Hull (1952a), page 11; (1951), page 95. An earlier, somewhat more general statement, is in Hull (1943), page 47.

[54] Hull (1942), page 77.

facts pointing to momentary variation is encompassed in the following postulate.

Postulate 12. Behavioral oscillation ($_{S}O_{R}$)

A. Reaction potential ($_{S}E_{R}$) varies from moment to moment, the standard deviation of the fluctuations serving as a measure of behavioral oscillation ($_{S}O_{R}$). The distribution in leptokurtic.

B. Behavioral oscillation ($_{S}O_{R}$) begins with zero dispersion at absolute zero of $_{S}H_{R}$, then rises to an unsteady maximum as $_{S}H_{R}$ increases.

C. The oscillations of competing reaction potentials are assumed to be asynchronous.[55]

The concept of behavioral oscillation, as finally embodied in this postulate, intrigued Hull as early as 1917,[56] and it has had a place in each of his formal systems. It is instructive to note the changes that have occurred, because these changes tell us something about the provisional nature of system-making at this stage in the history of learning theories.

1. In 1940 it was the response threshold that oscillated. Hence a given reaction potential might suffice to bring a response above threshold on one trial, and then (without change in the reaction potential) the response might fall below the oscillating threshold on the next.[57]

2. In 1943 behavioral oscillation became an inhibitory appendage to reaction potential. Thus the amount of $_{S}O_{R}$ present at the moment of responding was always *subtracted* from the $_{S}E_{R}$ present at that moment. The distribution of $_{S}O_{R}$ was assumed to be normal, that is, Gaussian.[58]

3. By 1952, the oscillation was incorporated into reaction potential, and no systematic reason existed any longer for the symbol $_{S}O_{R}$, it having become simply the standard deviation of $_{S}E_{R}$, and, incidentally, the unit according to which reaction potential was quantified. The detailed efforts to quantify reaction potential led to several of the refinements reflected in the postulate, notably (1) the statement that the distribution of $_{S}E_{R}$ is leptokurtic rather than Gaussian, and (2) the discovery that the dispersion of $_{S}O_{R}$ is not constant, but changes with the number of reinforcements.

The deductive use of the concept of behavioral oscillation was also extended in 1952 to account for alternation cycles in trial-and-error learning. We shall return to this deduction later in this chapter.

[55] The whole postulate is paraphrased from Hull (1952a), pages 11–12. A typographical error in his book makes part B of the postulate refer to subthreshold reinforcements where superthreshold reinforcements are intended. See also Hull (1951), pages 97, 99; (1943), page 319.

[56] Hull (1917). For a note on the history of the use of the concept, see Hull (1952a), pages 56–57.

[57] Hull and others (1940), page 74.

[58] Hull (1943), pages 314 and 319.

Corollary xiii. Response generalization

A. Response-intensity generalization. When a muscular contraction of given intensity has been reinforced, that muscle will contract on successive trials with varying intensities in a distribution about the central reinforced region.

B. Qualitative-response generalization. When the contractions of several muscles produce a given habitual act, the combination of the independent variation of each produces a qualitative change from the central result originally reinforced.[59]

We have met qualitative change in response in Skinner's treatment of response differentiation and in his use of spontaneous changes to move by successive approximations from one response to another. Hull had something of this sort in mind in this corollary.

Hull mentioned the corollary specifically three times in the 1952 book. He referred to it first by showing how, through reinforcing only the responses of appropriate intensity, you can shift response intensity along a continuum. He pointed out, second, that locomotion is a highly generalized form of response. Walking to one point in space does not differ fundamentally from walking to any other point. Third, he referred to the principle in accounting for the shift from moving toward a goal to dragging the goal-object toward the subject, as in stick and hoe experiments.[60]

Reaction Potential and Evoked Response

The postulates have moved gradually from stimulus-traces through habit strength, drive, and other intervening variables determining reaction potential, until now we are ready to consider the emergence of the observable, recordable response. Reaction evocation requires, first of all, that reaction potential must be above the threshold of response.

Postulate 13. Absolute zero of reaction potential (Z) *and the reaction threshold* ($_SL_R$)

A. The reaction threshold ($_SL_R$) lies above the absolute zero (Z) of reaction potential ($_SE_R$).

B. Response evocation occurs only when the momentary reaction potential exceeds the reaction threshold.[61]

The "absolute zero" referred to here is a "relative" absolute, for it is based empirically on the number of reinforcements which must be delivered experimentally before there is indication of learning. In the illustrations used by Hull, the order of magnitude of reinforcements between

[59] Paraphrased from Hull (1952a), page 12; (1943), page 319. The corollary does not appear in Hull (1951).

[60] These three mentions can be found in Hull (1952a), pages 200, 218, and 324.

[61] Paraphrased from Hull (1952a), page 12; (1951), page 102; (1943), page 344.

"absolute zero" and the reaction threshold is two reinforcements of bar-pressing. This says nothing of the transfer from prior learning of other manipulatory skills or eating habits, and so can scarcely be thought of as a true absolute zero of habit strength. In fact, careful experiments have shown that the bar-pressing tendency has appreciable strength prior to reinforcement.[62]

Corollary xiv. The competition of incompatible reaction potentials

When reaction potentials to two or more incompatible responses occur in an organism at the same instant, each in a suprathreshold magnitude, only that reaction whose momentary reaction potential is greatest will be evoked.[63]

The corollary is convenient in the derivation of trial-and-error learning, where the choice is, say, between turning right or left. The organism will then make the response that has the higher momentary reaction potential. This corollary now accounts for probability of occurrence as a measure of response strength for competing responses. As a broad generalization the corollary is by no means self-evident. Antagonistic muscles may both be contracted at once. Then, while either flexion or extension may occur, the muscles will be under heightened tension, and the response will differ from what it would have been had only one muscle set been active. The possibility of compromise response—much emphasized by Guthrie—must also not be overlooked.

Postulate 14. Reaction potential as a function of reaction latency

Reaction potential (${}_{S}E_{R}$) can be inferred from reaction latency (${}_{S}t_{R}$); the shorter the latency the greater the reaction potential.[64]

The logic of the system, as a causal chain, is that latency is a function of reaction potential, and the postulate was so stated in early versions of the system. However, Hull's desire to emphasize the anchorage of the system to observables led him in his later versions to turn the matter around, and to indicate how the strength of the reaction potential could be inferred from latency. The form of the function he expressed as follows:

$$ {}_{S}E_{R} = a\,({}_{S}t_{R})^{-b} $$

The effort to quantify ${}_{S}E_{R}$ in some absolute manner, independent of the special units of measurement used in experiments, occupied a great deal of Hull's attention during his last years. One of his close associates has stated that he believes it "almost certain" that Hull considered the

[62] Schoenfeld, Antonitis, and Bersh (1950b).

[63] Paraphrased from Hull (1952a), pages 12–13; (1951), page 104; (1943), page 344.

[64] Paraphrased from Hull (1952a), page 13; (1951), page 107; (1943), page 344.

articles on the quantification of habit strength (and reaction potential) to be the most significant of his theoretical papers.[65]

The method used in quantification consisted of a paired-comparison technique based on one of Thurstone's scaling procedures. The basic assumption is that latency directly reflects excitatory potential, and the comparisons used are between latencies on successive trials for groups of animals trained under comparable conditions. Beyond this basic assumption of decreasing latency with increasing reaction potential, the remaining assumptions are essentially statistical ones, having to do with the deriving of an equal-unit scale. The unit, as previously mentioned, is that of σ, the standard deviation of ${}_{S}E_{R}$. Because this unit is very general (not in grams, millimeters, seconds, or any other measure specific to experiments), it serves Hull's purposes very well. Having devised this scale, Hull was able to co-ordinate other aspects of response to it, and the final postulates were based on the assumption that other measures could best be stated in terms of the unit derived from the study of latency.

Postulate 15. Reaction potential as a function of reaction amplitude

Reaction potential may be inferred from reaction amplitude. In the case of the Tarchanoff galvanic skin reaction in man, the relationship between reaction potential and amplitude is a linear one.[66]

The reinforcements in a galvanic skin response experiment with human subjects were converted to the new units of ${}_{S}E_{R}$ derived from the latency of bar-passing responses in rats. These scaled values of ${}_{S}E_{R}$ turned out to bear a linear relationship to the amplitude of the conditioned galvanic skin responses as recorded on an uncalibrated apparatus in millimeters of deflection. This is the empirical basis for the postulate.[67]

Hull felt that he was on safe ground in confining the amplitude postulate to autonomic conditioning (as represented specifically by the Tarchanoff phenomenon). Amplitude in striate muscle conditioning is complicated by the possibility of limiting amplitude through conditions of reinforcement (Corollary xiii), a complication Hull felt to be inapplicable to autonomic responses.[68]

[65] Hovland (1952), page 349. The major papers are: Hull, Felsinger, Gladstone, and Yamaguchi (1947), Felsinger, Gladstone, Yamaguchi, and Hull (1947), Gladstone, Yamaguchi, Hull, and Felsinger (1947), Yamaguchi, Hull, Felsinger, and Gladstone (1948).

[66] Paraphrased from Hull (1952a), page 13; (1951), page 109; (1943), page 344.

[67] It may be noted, however, that the same argument from the same data was possible in 1943, before the more elaborate scaling method was devised. Compare Hull (1943), Figure 78, page 340, with Hull (1951), Figure 25, page 109. Original data from Hovland (1937b).

[68] Hull (1943), page 339. He knew, of course, that the same complication was possible with latency, but he disregarded it on the assumption that the necessary ex-

Postulate 16. Total responses to extinction as a function of reaction potential

A. The reaction potential ($_SE_R$) acquired following massed reinforcements can be inferred from the number of massed unreinforced evocations (n) required to produce experimental extinction.

B. The reaction potential ($_SE_R$) acquired following quasi-distributed reinforcements can be inferred from the number of massed unreinforced evocations (n) required to produce experimental extinction, but for any given value of n the inferred $_SE_R$ will be higher than under the conditions of Part A, and the forms of relationship differ for Parts A and B.[69]

Hull gave equations for both of these functions, but because he had a tendency, especially in the final system, to select any convenient illustration for purposes of quantitative statement, it is not at all clear how general he expected these relationships to be. That of Part A might conceivably have some measure of generality; that for Part B is surely merely illustrative, for "quasi-distributed reinforcements" during training followed by "massed trials" during extinction yield a whole family of functions. The particular function presented as an equation in the statement of the postulate 16A expressed reaction potential as a function of trials to extinction. If inverted to state the causal order of events, the equation implies after massed reinforcements a curve of *increasing* gains for number of responses to extinction with increments in reaction potential. For example, a reaction potential of 2.0 σ will be followed by 20 non-reinforced responses in massed extinction, while one of 3.0 σ will be followed by nearly 50 non-reinforced responses. After distributed reinforcements (Postulate 16B), the corresponding curve is one of *decreasing* gains with increases in reaction potential. While for $_SE_R$ of 4.0 σ there will follow 20 non-reinforced responses to extinction, even at the near-maximum of 6 σ there would be less than 25 non-reinforced responses to extinction. It is doubtful if the contrast between these two functions does more than point to the complexity of the relationships involved with varying schedules of reinforcement—a point amply demonstrated by Skinner.

Individual Differences

Hull offered the suggestion that the "constants" appearing in his equations may vary with the learner, and hence serve as a kind of index to individual differences. If, for example, rate of human learning were found in some context to be a function of measured intelligence, then the in-

perimental precautions could be taken. For criticism of latency as a measure see Mueller (1950), Skinner (1950).

[69] Paraphrased from Hull (1952a), page 13; (1951), pages 112–114. The relationship between $_SE_R$ and n had earlier been assumed to be linear (1943), page 344, while in 1951–1952 the functions are both curvilinear.

dividual IQ (or some equivalent of it) might appear as a parameter in the equation relating the number of reinforcements to the achieved reaction potential.

Postulate 17. Individual differences

The "constant" numerical values appearing in the equations stated in the basic postulates and corollaries vary from species to species, from individual to individual, and from some physiological states to others in the same individual at different times.[70]

The treatment of individual differences was purely programmatic, for the postulates and corollaries as stated were based on responses from groups of subjects. Furthermore, the constants were usually obtained from curve-fitting, and hence do not have the rational status desirable in interchangeable constants subject to independent measurement.

The problem sensed by Hull is an important one, and could be faced provisionally with groups of subjects tested under several conditions. Consider, for example, the constants in the curve for serial-position effects, worked out in the rote learning system. The three constants are L (the reaction threshold), ΔK (the amount of inhibition generated by each repetition of each nonsense syllable), and F (a factor of reduction whereby inhibition is progressively reduced at syllables more remote from the point of origin of the inhibition). If the same learners participate throughout, and everything else is kept constant through appropriate experimental controls, then the constants should change in some systematic way for groups of learners of different ages. For any one group of learners the constants should not change when new conditions are introduced, such as length of list, which have no bearing on the constants. We have no evidence of this kind at the present time to support the adequacy of constants as measures of individual differences. The logical possibilities are clear enough, and it is these possibilities to which Hull called attention in the postulate.

The Antedating Goal Reaction and Its Role in Secondary Reinforcement

Hull ended his final set of postulates and basic corollaries with the following one.

Corollary xv. Secondary reinforcement by fractional antedating goal reactions

When a response (R) is associated with a stimulus trace (s) and this stimulus-response conjunction is accompanied by an antedating goal reaction

[70] Paraphrased from Hull (1952a), page 13; (1951), page 117. The matter was first dealt with systematically in Hull (1945).

(r_G) and by the stimulus resulting from it (s_G), there will result an increase in the tendency for that stimulus (s) to evoke that response (R).

The reinforcement comes about because of the secondary reinforcing powers of s_G.[71]

In this corollary and in the discussion of it, Hull says nothing more about the role of s_G in primary reinforcement (Postulate 3). This omission supports the earlier interpretation that the addition of s_G to Postulate 3 was an afterthought. The secondary reinforcing power of s_G in Corollary xv is that of any stimulus that has been closely associated with primary reinforcement (see Corollary ii).

We have now completed a summary of the postulates and corollaries presented in the first chapter of Hull's last book as the basic "laws" of his system. In later chapters he added only two more principles given the status of corollaries, although he stated 133 theorems. The corollaries must have had special meaning for him, as somehow fundamental, and they therefore merit discussion here.

Corollary xvi. Generalization between reaction potentials to positive and negative stimuli in simple trial-and-error learning

A. When an organism acquires two reaction potentials ${}_SE_{R+}$ and ${}_SE_{R-}$ to similar stimuli S_+ and S_- in the evoking of responses R_+ and R_-, which, while different, use substantially the same muscles, a gain in ${}_SE_{R+}$ through reinforcement will be accompanied by a generalized gain in ${}_SE_{R-}$.

B. When the reaction potential to the negative stimulus (${}_SE_{R-}$) loses strength through extinction, a generalized loss in ${}_SE_{R+}$ will accompany this loss in ${}_SE_{R-}$.[72]

The relationships in this corollary follow rather directly from stimulus and response generalization (Postulate 10 and Corollary xiii).

Corollary xvii. Experimental extinction

In non-reinforced trials following regular reinforcement, the evoking stimulus (1) for a time will continue to evoke the response, (2) sometimes will evoke the response for a time with a rise in reaction potential, (3) the rise (if any) will be followed by a progressive fall in reaction potential, and (4) the course of the fall in reaction potential is the reverse of a positive learning curve.[73]

Why a new corollary, when the same facts were covered in Postulates 9A and 9D? Except for the statement about an occasional rise in reaction potential with non-reinforcement, there is nothing new in the corollary itself. The novelty rests instead in some of the thinking that lies behind the corollary. Hull, renewing an earlier suggestion,[74] described the realiza-

[71] Paraphrased from Hull (1952a), pages 14 and 125.
[72] Paraphrased from Hull (1952a), page 23.
[73] Paraphrased from Hull (1952a), page 134.
[74] Hull (1937).

tion of an anticipation as occurring when actual eating ($S_G \longrightarrow R_G$) follows upon the antedating sequence ($r_G \longrightarrow s_G$). When the anticipated S_G is omitted, as in non-reinforcement, the anticipation is frustrated. Frustrated anticipation may lead to more intensified activity (heightened ${}_SE_R$) through aroused emotion (hence heightened D). This accounts for that portion of the corollary suggesting temporary increase in reaction potential early in extinction. In the end, the accumulation of I_R will lead to diminished ${}_SE_R$. The decay process is enhanced, however, by the conditioning of inhibition to s_G, yielding ${}_{s_G}I_R$. Because this is learning, we have reason to expect the form of the extinction curve to reflect ordinary learning, though in reverse.

In this corollary we have a good indication of unfinished business, as Hull, clear to the end, was attempting to rethink his systematic formulations.

The System Summarized

The set of postulates and corollaries became somewhat formidable, and in places somewhat fragmented as Hull attempted to work into the basic principles not only all manner of quantitative relationships found to hold in classical and instrumental conditioning, but other kinds of phenomena needed to deal with types of problems beyond these reference experiments. Even so, it is possible to cut through some of the specific detail, and to summarize the system in rather direct fashion as a chain of anchored constructs beginning with the antecedent conditions (input), moving through the intervening variables to response (output). Such a summary is given in Figure 15.

In Column I we have input conditions, all except ${}_{S'}H_R$ defined by objective experimental conditions. (${}_{S'}H_R$ is habit strength from a related habit, to become expressed as generalized habit strength, ${}_S\bar{H}_R$.)

In Column 2 we find the intervening variables most closely tied to the antecedent conditions. In Column 3 we assemble, in an intermediate step, the consequences of the simultaneous presence of the variables in Column 2. We are now (in Column 4) close to response evocation, but we must first take into account the oscillation of reaction potential (${}_SO_R$) and the threshold of response (${}_SL_R$). Finally (in Column 5) the response emerges, with the measurable characteristics of latency (${}_St_R$), amplitude (A), or number of non-reinforced evocations to extinction (n). Formerly, probability of response was also used as a response measure, but in the final system the probability measure was felt by Hull to be appropriate

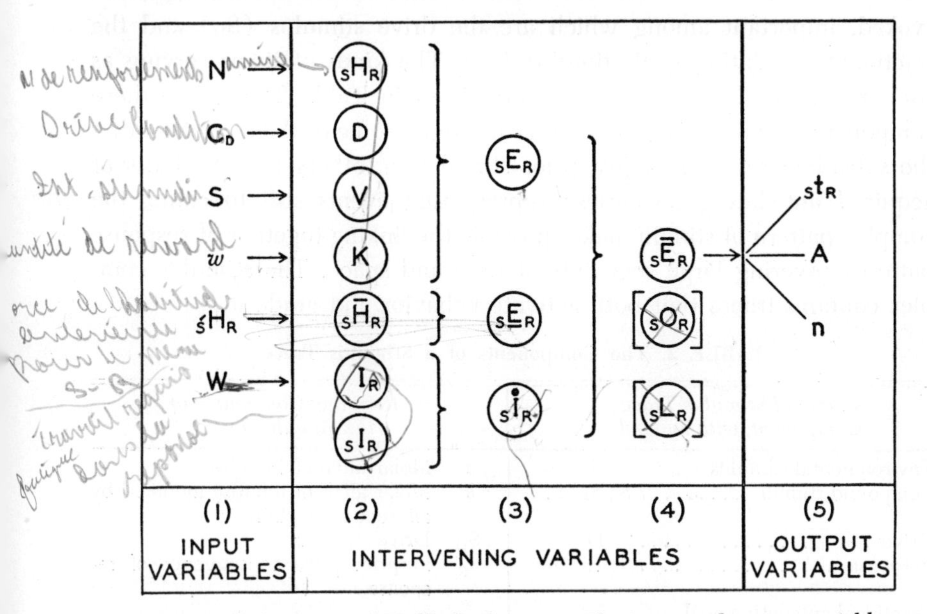

FIGURE 15. Summary of Hull's final system. The input and output variables, and the intervening variables, are symbolized as follows in the figure:

Column (*1*)

N, number of prior reinforcements
C_D, drive condition
S, stimulus intensity
w, amount (weight) of reward
$_{S'}H_R$, strength of a habit based on same response conditioned to another stimulus
W, work required in responding

Column (*2*)

$_{S}H_{R}$, habit strength
D, drive
V, stimulus-intensity dynamism
K, incentive motivation
$_{S}\bar{H}_{R}$, generalized habit strength from related habit
I_R, reactive inhibition
$_{S}I_{R}$, conditioned inhibition

Column (*3*)

$_{S}E_{R}$, reaction potential
$_{S}\underline{E}_{R}$, generalized reaction potential
$_{S}\dot{I}_{R}$, aggregate inhibitory potential

Column (*4*)

$_{S}\bar{E}_{R}$, net reaction potential
$_{S}O_{R}$, oscillation of reaction potential
$_{S}L_{R}$, reaction threshold

Column (*5*)

$_{S}t_{R}$, reaction latency
A, reaction amplitude
n, number of non-reinforced responses to extinction

only when conflicting responses were involved, and hence probability is inappropriate as a measure from which to infer $_{S}E_{R}$.[75]

The diagram falls short in not listing the several important stimulus components making up the complex of traces present when a response is

[75] The original probability postulate occurs in Hull (1943), page 344. The discussion of reasons for withdrawing it may be found in Hull (1951), page 126. Corollary xiv permits use of the empirical data formerly included in the probability postulate.

evoked, important among which are the drive stimulus (S_D) and the fractional antedating goal stimulus (s_G). The kinds of items serving as components of the stimulus trace are listed in Table 2. Because these components are not all contemporary in origin, some of them representing the subsiding residues of just prior stimulation, others (on the basis of acquired antedating responses) representing events still to come, the complex pattern of stimuli makes possible the linking together of response patterns covering large segments of time and space. The stimulus complex contains traces that both activate behavior and guide it.

TABLE 2. The Components of a Stimulus Trace

Origin of Stimulus-Trace Component, with Symbol		*Resulting Component of the Stimulus Trace*	
Environmental stimulus	S	s	Molar afferent impulse
Compound stimuli	S_1, S_2 ...	$\check{s}$	Molar afferent impulse modified by afferent interaction
Drive	D	S_D	Drive stimulus
Response	R	s_R	Proprioceptive consequence of response
Fractional antedating goal response	r_G	s_G	Fractional antedating goal stimulus

DERIVED INTERMEDIATE MECHANISMS

Hull's system is characterized by him as molar, by which he means non-physiological. That is, the inferences to intervening variables do not depend upon the discovery of the physiological substratum which is causal in a "molecular" way. The assertions about molar stimulus traces, or afferent interaction, need not include specification in terms of the constitution of nerve bundles or the characteristics of the nervous impulse. Hull vacillated somewhat by including physiological *language* in his postulates. In any case, Hull's system classifies as a *reductive* system, in that more complex phenomena are deduced on the basis of presumably simpler, more basic phenomena and relationships. In this sense the more complex are "reduced" to the simpler through analysis. It is characteristic of all systems of this kind *that they intend to explain behavior that is superficially unlike the behavior from which the postulates are derived.* In other words, Hull did not intend merely to systematize the account of rat lever-pressing, from which most of the data for his later set of postulates derived. He intended to arrive at the basic laws of behavior, at least the laws of the behavior of mammalian organisms, including the social behavior of man.

In order to bridge the gap between the simple laboratory experiments furnishing the constants in the postulates and corollaries, and the more familiar behavior of organisms adapting to a complex environment, he derived *intermediate mechanisms.* Once these mechanisms were available, they opened the way to the explanation of many more varieties of behavior. We shall consider two of these mechanisms: the gradient of reinforcement (originally the goal gradient), and the habit-family hierarchy.

We have to distinguish between the historical and the logical order of postulates and intermediate mechanisms. Many of Hull's most brilliant deductive accounts of complex phenomena were made in early papers, prior to the postulate systems.[76] Many of these accounts were essentially unchanged when they were reworked for the 1952 book, even though in the meantime the postulate system underwent substantial revision. From a logical point of view, however, *once the system has been constructed,* the postulates take priority. The same applies, of course to predictions. An experimental fact may be "predicted" by a system, even though the fact has long been known. The only advantage in predicting new (unknown) facts is that, in predicting them, there is less temptation to include the facts in the postulates used as a basis for their prediction.

The Gradient of Reinforcement (the Goal Gradient)

There are two chief kinds of time gradients involved in conditioning experiments. The first (found primarily in classical conditioning) is based on the time between the conditioned stimulus and the unconditioned stimulus, short forward intervals being found most satisfactory. Hull took this interval into account in developing his postulate regarding the stimulus trace (Postulate 2B). The assumption is that conditioning is actually simultaneous, but the gradient is produced by a rising and falling molar trace set into motion by the external stimulus. The second kind of time gradient (found chiefly in instrumental conditioning) is based on the time between the response to be strengthened and the reinforcement. This second gradient is considered in the corollary concerned with delay in reinforcement (Corollary iiiB). As pointed out earlier, the simple gradient (a single response reinforced) is assumed to extend for about 5 seconds; if a reinforcement is delayed more than 5 seconds, its effectiveness must depend upon other mechanisms.

The measurement of the gradient of reinforcement depends upon experiments of the instrumental conditioning type, in which an act such

[76] For an introduction to the deductions available before 1940, see the summaries in Hilgard and Marquis (1940): maze learning, 216–221; serial verbal learning, 221–226; reasoning experiments, 236–241; circumventing a barrier, 242–243.

as pushing a lever or running down an alley leads to the goal-object and reinforcement. Delay may be introduced between the act to be rewarded and the goal-object which provides the reinforcing state of affairs. Thus the delivery of the pellet of food which is the reward for lever-pressing may be postponed for an arbitrary number of seconds in order to study the effect upon rat learning of such a delay. The gradient of reinforcement is derived from such delayed reinforcement experiments, as distinguished from the stimulus-response separation experiments of classical conditioning. Hull at first believed, on the basis of a delayed reinforcement experiment done with rats in the lever-pressing box, that the basic gradient of reinforcement was fairly short, in the case of the rat, "possibly no more than thirty seconds and very probably less than sixty seconds."

Other experiments on the effect of delayed reward, such as those of Wolfe (1934), show that in a simple alley maze the reward is effective for learning with much longer delays, at least as long as 20 minutes, the longest delay tested. A gradient is shown here, also, with the longer intervals less effective for learning than the shorter ones.

Let us see how these gradients are related, before we turn to the manner in which they are used to derive other forms of behavior. The final theory somewhat unclearly implied four steps:

1. The influence of reinforcement is solely upon the immediately concurrent stimulus and response units. There is no genuine primary gradient of reinforcement. In this Hull follows Spence (1947), and he has eliminated delay in reinforcement from his postulate set.

2. For a single stimulus-response conjunction followed by delayed reinforcement there is a short gradient of reinforcement, extending about 5 seconds. This is expressed in Corollary iiiB. The delay is derived on the basis of r_G and its s_G, especially via the secondary reinforcement role of s_G.

3. For links in a chain of responses, with terminal reinforcement, the links farther removed from reinforcement are less strongly reinforced. This is a longer gradient than that for the unchained single response, and it depends upon the secondary reinforcement provided by the environment and by the organism's own movements. This is the principle to account for the gradients in *minutes* rather than in *seconds*. It is described qualitatively in Corollary iiiA, but is not derived. While later it is treated quantitatively, the quantities are assigned *on the assumption that the gradient exists in appropriate magnitudes.* Nowhere is it linked quantitatively with the gradient of Corollary iiiB just described.

4. In any actual chain of responses as observed and recorded, the gradients of reinforcement affecting individual links in the chain summate

in complex fashion to produce *empirical gradients*[77] bearing little resemblance to any single inferred underlying gradient of reinforcement.

To be strictly elegant in system construction, we ought to be able to move by formal steps from each one of the foregoing numbered propositions to the next. We can follow Hull's attempt to get from (1) to (2), though his derivation involved outmoded features of his system.[78] He moved from (2) to (3) very informally, without attempting to construct a sound bridge between them. He made a more serious, and more successful, effort to move from (3) to (4). To that step we now turn.

This is our first illustration, in any detail, of how Hull proceeded to use an intermediate mechanism in accounting for concrete behavior in a complex situation. Beginning with the assumption of the long gradient of reinforcement of point (3) above (an assumption already involving many steps from the basic postulates), the problem is to account for the actual latencies of response at each step of a four-response chain, leading to reinforcement at the end.

Let us begin with the empirical data that we wish to derive. They come from an experiment by Arnold.[79] A rat learns to press a button presented outside the window of its restraining cage, whenever the shutter is opened. Pressing the button is rewarded by a pellet of food. Now the experiment proper begins. A clever device presents to the rat a chain of four stimulus-response possibilities by means of a car running by his window on a track. In this experiment, there are four parts of the car, all alike, all with buttons exactly like the one he already learned to press. When the shutter is opened, button B_1 is presented. He presses it, and starts the car in motion, though no pellet appears. Three seconds later the second button B_2 has come into view as the car stops with it before the window. He presses it; now button B_3 appears. In three more seconds he has the opportunity of pressing B_4. Because the response was well learned, there is not enough extinction in these few non-reinforced trials to prevent the response. Having made the four responses in order, the shutter falls, and the food reward appears, giving terminal reinforcement to the whole linked series. The series of events is presented once a day, and a measure of reaction latency taken at each button. The results for trials

[77] The term "empirical gradient" is a convenient term for the gradients actually found. At one time the distinction was made between the gradient of reinforcement as the gradient of habit strengthening, and the goal gradient as the effect upon performance, a distinction first suggested by Miller and Miles (1935). But when the gradient of reinforcement came itself to be derived rather than basic, the former distinction between it and the goal gradient was no longer maintained by Hull.

[78] Hull (1952a), pages 127–128.

[79] Arnold (1947). Additional experiments in the series were also considered by Hull.

2–10 are shown in Figure 16. While there is a kind of gradient of reinforcement, with latency getting shorter nearer to the goal, there is a striking upturn at B_4. The theoretical problem is to derive this empirical gradient from the overlap of gradients, all of which fall off from the point of reinforcement.

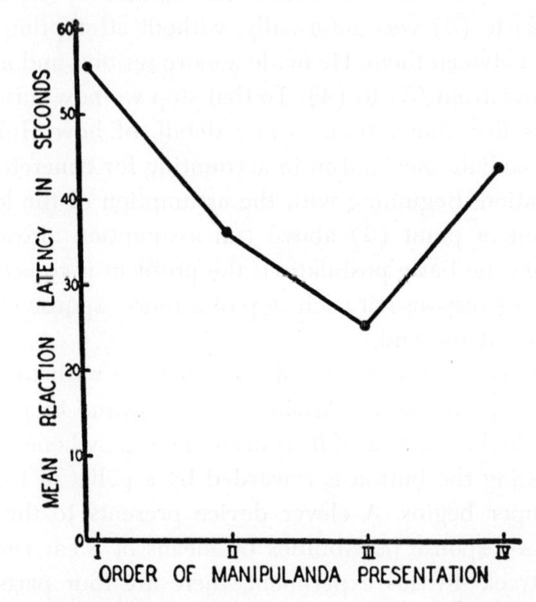

FIGURE 16. Reaction latency of responses to each of the four stimuli in a behavior chain with terminal reinforcement. Adapted from Arnold (1947), page 356, and Hull (1952a), page 164.

The steps involved are as follows:

1. On the basis of prior learning, there is the original $_SE_R$ available equally to B_1, B_2, B_3, and B_4. Some initial value must be assumed. (Hull arbitrarily assumed 2.0 σ.)

2. The general form of the gradient of reinforcement with time is assumed, and both its form and the number of trials required to generate it are arbitrary, though the form is consistent with gradients of generalization. The resulting increments of reaction potential at each of the stimuli turn out to be: B_1, .234; B_2, .380; B_3, .617; B_4, 1.000 σ. This conforms to our expectation of greater gains nearer to reinforcement, because reinforcement follows B_4.

3. The original $_SE_R$ (2 σ) and the increment through reinforcement must be added for each link in the chain, according to the principle by

which reaction potentials are combined. The sum will, of course, be less than the arithmetical sum. The result turns out to be: B_1, 2.16; B_2, 2.25; B_3, 2.41; B_4, 2.67. These values Hull calls the *gradient-of-reinforcement* values in this context, because they are the values at each link before we consider the interaction of the different links.

4. We must now take into account the fact that a stimulus does not cease to operate when it is withdrawn, but its trace persists. Hence that persisting stimulus trace will derive reinforcement from each of the subsequent secondary reinforcements along the route to the goal, and through generalization the effect will be felt at the next onset of the stimulus. Similarly, each response along the way contributes strength to the links preceding it (whose traces are represented when it is being reinforced) and to the responses following it (because its stimulus trace will be part of the stimulus complex when these succeeding responses occur). This two-way contribution of each link to the others is computed, again through arbitrary formulas whose exponents have no relationship quantitatively to those given in the postulates, though the form of the equations is as postulated. The results are given in Table 3.

TABLE 3. Steps Used by Hull in Computing the Theoretical Mean Reaction Latencies at the Response Points of a Four-Link Response Chain. The gradient of reinforcement values, from which the remaining values in the table are generalized, are shown in bold type. See text. From Hull (1952a), page 162.

	Components of Reaction Potential $({}_SE_R)$			
Assumed d values (in j.n.d.'s)	4	2	1	
Response number	B_1	B_2	B_3	B_4
Values based on delay in reinforcement				
9 seconds delay	**2.16**	.14	.03	.02
6 seconds delay	.57	**2.25**	.57	.28
3 seconds delay	.30	1.21	**2.41**	1.21
0 seconds delay	.24	.95	1.89	**2.67**
Behavior sums (+) of ${}_SE_R$	2.82σ	3.54σ	3.78σ	3.46σ
Reaction latencies (${}_St_R$)	3.51″	2.19″	1.91″	2.30″

5. Now we add up the various components of reaction potential at each link in the chain. The addition is again by formula, and not straight arithmetic. The sums are given in the row second from the bottom of Table 3.

6. The final step is to convert these ${}_SE_R$'s to latencies (${}_St_R$'s). Here again an arbitrary formula, with new constants but familiar form, is used,

and the latencies computed, as shown in the bottom row of Table 3. This is the end of the determination, and the results are plotted in Figure 17, for comparison with Figure 16.

The general agreement between the two figures is striking enough to indicate Hull's ingenuity. There is some disagreement in the absolute magnitudes, however, and this led Hull to assert:

> This degree of agreement between experiment and theory is, perhaps, as close as may reasonably be expected in the present early stage of the science.[80]

The agreement lies in the form of the function. The failure lies in the latency measure—a matter of really great importance to the system because of the reliance on latency for quantifying ${}_SE_R$. Hull had earlier,

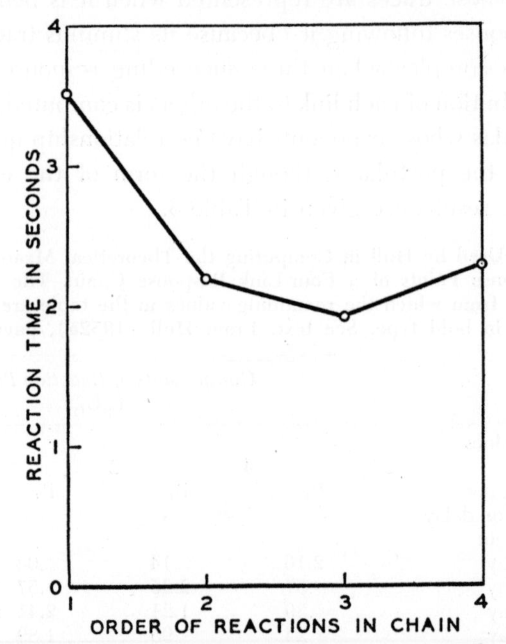

FIGURE 17. Theoretical reaction latency of responses to each of the four stimuli in a behavior chain with terminal reinforcement. Compare with the empirical results shown in Figure 16. Adapted from Hull (1952a), page 163.

in choosing the equation for the computation of latency, multiplied the values derived from Postulate 14 by an arbitrary constant (3+) because he noted that the values would otherwise have been too small,[81] then two pages later he finds that he had not boosted the latency enough. He could easily have chosen a constant to make the values correspond much more

[80] Hull (1952a), page 165.
[81] Hull (1952a), page 163.

closely, by multiplying by 50 instead of multiplying by 3. Possibly he worked the matter out independently, and then felt it would be deceptive to work backwards from the result, or thought a 50-fold correction was too great. Because the constants are arbitrary anyhow, he might as well have worked backwards, and achieved as good a fit as possible. Had the constants been independently determined, there would have been some point in seeing how much discrepancy remained. As it stands, the prediction of the form of the function is an achievement. Everything else is arbitrary, and consequently the achievement itself has much that is *ad hoc* in it.

The main point of this detail with respect to the derivation of the gradient for a chain of responses has been to point out how the derivation depends primarily upon the intermediate mechanism (the gradient of reinforcement), but then uses other principles (e.g., generalization, summation of reaction potentials, conversion of reaction potential to latency) to achieve a predicted result, an empirical curve that bears little resemblance to the principles used in its deduction, but corresponds closely in form to the results of a complex learning experiment. The deduction points out also how deceptive is the apparent quantitative rigor of the system. The quantities in the postulates are mere illustrations of quantities, and are not, in fact, made use of in any consistent manner in later derivations.

While the gradient of reinforcement is not the primary one it was earlier considered to be, it is a derivative or intermediate principle, which, once established, again serves its former purposes in the explanation of more complex learning. The original application was to the maze. The principle mediated the deduction that responses nearer to the goal would be more strongly conditioned than those farther removed, so that short paths would be preferred to longer ones, blinds near the goal would be eliminated more readily than blinds farther away, longer blinds would be more readily eliminated than shorter ones, and so on.[82] The goal gradient principle was later applied to field-force problems as studied by Lewin.[83] For example, in experiments involving the circumventing of barriers between the learner and a visible goal, Hull proposed that the reaction to the perceived goal-object should behave in accordance with the goal gradient. That is, the nearer the learner came to the goal, the

[82] Hull (1932). For an introductory exposition, see Hilgard and Marquis (1940), pages 216–221. For the earlier history of the problem of the goal gradient, see Hull (1943), pages 159–160.

[83] Hull (1938). The problems were such as proposed by Lewin (1933a) (1935). The deductions are repeated with little change in Hull (1952a), pages 262–268.

stronger should be its response-evoking power. Thus Hull, by way of the gradient of reinforcement, came to conclusions similar to those described by Lewin as goal-attraction in relation to distance.

The Habit-Family Hierarchy

A second derived principle is that of the habit-family hierarchy. This is not included among the postulates because, like the gradient of reinforcement, it is a principle at intermediate level, being itself derived from more basic principles. It carries great weight, however, in the deduction of further behavioral phenomena.

Because there are multiple routes between a starting point and a goal, the organism learns alternative ways of moving from a common starting point to a common goal-position where it finds need satisfaction. These alternatives constitute a habit family because of an inferred integrating mechanism. The integration into a family is by way of the *fractional antedating goal reaction,* present as each alternative is active. The fractional anticipatory goal reaction provides a stimulus (s_G) to which all overt responses are conditioned. Through the differential action of the gradient of reinforcement, some responses are less strongly conditioned to s_G than others. The starting responses of longer routes, for example, are more remote from reinforcement than the starting responses of shorter routes. Hence the latter are more strongly reinforced, and more strongly conditioned to s_G. As a consequence, the alternative behavior patterns are arranged in a preferred order. The less favored routes are chosen only when the more favored are blocked. It is this set of alternative habits, integrated by a common goal-stimulus, and arranged in preferential order, that constitutes a *habit-family hierarchy.*

It is further deduced by Hull that if one member of a habit-family hierarchy is reinforced in a new situation, all other members of the family share at once in the tendency to be evoked as reactions in that situation.[84] This makes possible the explanation of response equivalences and other appropriate reactions in novel or problematic situations, such as those found in insight and reasoning experiments.

The principle was first applied to maze learning,[85] serving chiefly to explain the tendency for the rat to enter goal-pointing blinds, even though such entrances had never been reinforced in the maze situation. Goal orientation was taken to represent an inappropriate transfer of spatial habits acquired in free space. Another application was in relation to the

[84] Formal deduction was first given by Hull (1937), page 27.
[85] Hull (1934a).

detour experiments.[86] The difficulty of turning away from a perceived goal beyond a barrier depends on the presence of habit-family hierarchies as well as upon goal gradients. In the usual experience of free space, the favored path is the straight line between the learner and the goal. The next-favored starting response is that making least angle with the goal. The greater the angle, the less favored is the starting response in that family of habits built up in previous experience. Hence, when blocked, the learner prefers a path which goes off at a right angle to one which requires that he turn his back on the goal. In some objective situations he may come to choose a longer path to a shorter one, if the habit-family hierarchy proves to be misleading.

SOME REPRESENTATIVE DEDUCTIONS AND THEIR EXPERIMENTAL TESTS

We have met one illustration of Hull's deductive procedure in his computation of reaction latencies at each link of a four-link reaction chain with terminal reinforcement. His system commanded its initial attention because of his skill in carrying out corresponding computations in a variety of fields of experimentation. Summaries of many of his earlier deductions are already available.[87] A number of these deductions were repeated in the final book, with moderate changes to conform to the new system. The three illustrations chosen for discussion in what follows are, in substance, new to the final book (response alternation in trial-and-error learning, latent learning, and adient-abient conflict). Although they represent but a small sample of the total available deductions in the final system, they will serve to demonstrate Hull's method of arriving at new phenomena with the help of familiar postulates.

Response Alternation in Trial-and-Error Learning

Thorndike was impressed by the gradualness of trial-and-error learning. The gradualness implied that a response, once correct, was not consistently repeated thereafter, and that an incorrect response, once eliminated, must have cropped up occasionally. Hull attempted to come to closer grips than Thorndike did with this problem of response alternation in trial and error.

It will make the problem more concrete to begin first with the em-

[86] Hull (1938).
[87] In addition to the summaries on serial learning and problem-solving in Hilgard and Marquis (1940), on rote memorization and related phenomena, see the first edition of this book, Hilgard (1948).

pirical results, and then to turn to the deduction. In one of his own experiments Hull (1939b) used a modified Skinner box, as sketched in Figure 18. The experimenter could present either the vertical or the horizontal bar alone, or both together. The rat first learned to operate the vertical bar alone, and continued to operate it for 15 food-reinforced responses. The following day the experimenter presented only the

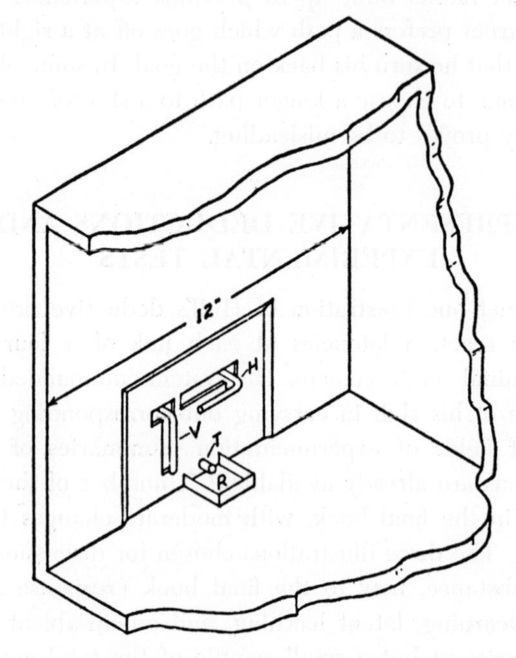

FIGURE 18. Diagrammatic representation of box used to study trial-and-error in the two-lever problem. Either the horizontal bar (H) or the vertical one (V) could be made positive; that is, when the appropriate bar was pressed a pellet of food fell through the tube (T), into the food-dish (R). After Hull (1939b), page 237.

horizontal bar, and the rat learned to operate it for 60 food-reinforced responses. The crucial test came the next day. The experimenter first allowed a warm-up by permitting four reinforcements of the already strong *horizontal* bar habit. Then he presented both bars at once, but set the apparatus so that only response to the *vertical* bar led to reinforcement. This became a simple trial-and-error experiment, requiring a reversal from the stronger and more recently reinforced to the weaker and earlier reinforced habit.

All 76 animals that finally mastered the trial-and-error learning met the criterion of learning gradually, responding now to the horizontal bar, now to the vertical bar. Sometimes the rat would respond to one bar for several trials, then respond to the other for a run of trials. Hull grouped these vacillating runs into what he called *alternation cycles.* He defined a cycle as including two phases, a run of responses to the vertical and a run of responses to the horizontal, such runs being preceded and followed by changes of response. Thus the cycle lasts from a

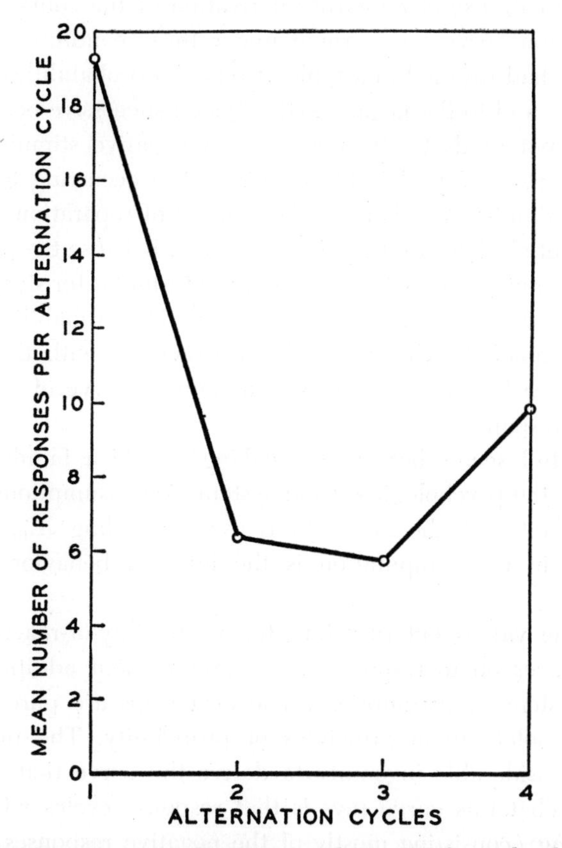

FIGURE 19. Responses per alternation cycle in simple trial-and-error learning when the incorrect response was originally more strongly conditioned than the correct one. Data from Hull (1939b), as plotted in Hull (1952a), page 52.

shift in a given direction (say from horizontal to vertical) through the shift in the opposite direction (from vertical to horizontal) and continues until the original shift occurs again. This corresponds to the usual definition of a two-phase cycle. The length of the cycle is determined by the number of responses in the runs making up the two phases of the cycle.

In order to exaggerate the effect somewhat, Hull selected the data from the 25 animals (among the 76) which yielded from four to six complete response-alternation cycles. His plot of the number of responses per alternation cycle for the first four cycles is reproduced as Figure 19.

Can such a curve be predicted on the basis of the postulates of the system? Here is how Hull went about it.

He first made use of an earlier derivation of the course of a probability-of-reaction curve for learning under these conditions. His earlier computations had resulted in a table of reaction-probabilities of response to the positive and to the negative stimulus on successive occasions. First the reaction potentials to the positive and negative stimuli were computed in σ units. The probability of a response occurring to one or the other of the stimuli depends upon the amount of separation of these two reaction potentials, because they are in conflict. Because the potentials are based upon σ units, he could use the familiar formulas for significance of a difference and determine a critical ratio, d/σ_d. The probability of reaction can be determined by the probabilities associated with this ratio. The result of this earlier computation was a sigmoid curve of acquisition of the positive response.[88]

While Hull seems here to be making simply a familiar statistical computation, the psychological (and systematic) assumptions underlying it are consonant with the assumptions used in scaling ${}_{S}E_{R}$, because the σ unit used in the computation is the inferred behavioral oscillation (${}_{S}O_{R}$).

From the values entering into the probability-of-reaction learning curve, he moves on to response alternation without additional psychological or systematic assumptions. The next steps are purely statistical, and depend solely upon principles of probability. The principles are used with considerable ingenuity to derive the curve that is plotted as Figure 20. What this curve says is that response cycles will at first be relatively long (consisting mostly of the negative responses, not yet extinguished), that they will fall to some minimum length, and then increase in length again (at the end consisting largely of positive responses, now overcoming through reinforcement their original handicap relative to negative responses).

Hull has now, by way of a number of steps consistent with his theory, supplemented by probability considerations, derived a theoretical curve that shows a strong family resemblance to the empirical curve of Figure 19. The abscissa units are not alike, and precise comparison is not

[88] Hull (1952a), pages 30–33.

possible; but the resemblance is strong, and the deduction is in this case an unusually rigorous one.

The plotting of response-alternation cycles exhibits another of Hull's strengths—an ingenuity he showed in discovering or inventing new ways to summarize the data from familiar types of experiment. The theoretical basis for the curve shown in Figure 20 permits other deductions under different conditions of experiment, so that this figure is but one of a

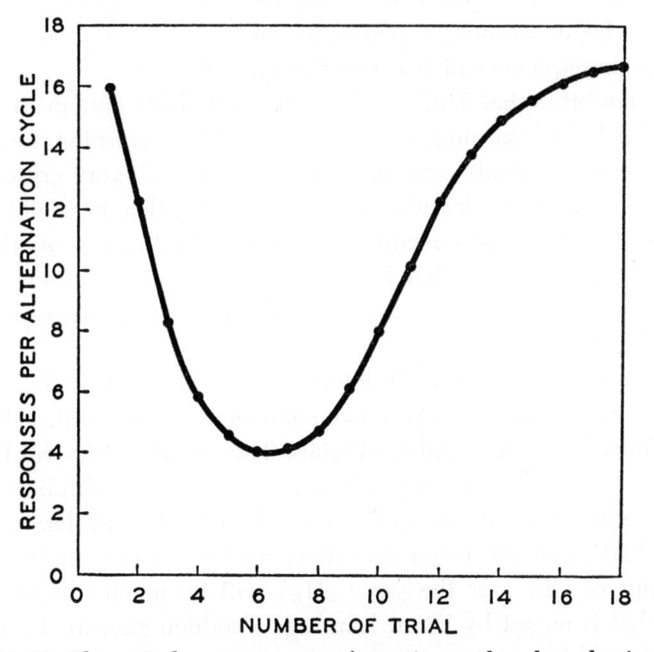

FIGURE 20. Theoretical responses per alternation cycle when the incorrect response was originally more strongly conditioned than the correct one. Compare with empirical curve of Figure 19. After Hull (1952a), page 48.

family of curves. Mathematical formulation has the advantage that shifts in the form of functions can be predicted when the parameters change. These shifts are often very different from those that might be guessed or intuited. If they are then confirmed experimentally, the theory receives a genuinc support.

Latent Learning

Sometimes, when a new incentive is introduced, animals performing at a very mediocre level without the incentive make sudden gains, bringing them abreast of animals trained all along with the favored incentive. Because the new incentive seems to bring out concealed or unused learning, experiments of this kind, when successful, are said to reveal *latent learning.* Such experiments were formerly a source of controversy between reinforcement theorists and cognitive theorists. The cognitive theorists cited these experiments in support of their position and pointed out the difficulties for the reinforcement theorist. In the type of theory Hull held in 1943 they were indeed difficult to account for, because $_SH_R$ then depended upon the magnitude of the reinforcement. With the change in emphasis from $_SH_R$ to $_SE_R$, Hull no longer had difficulty with latent-learning experiments and proceeded to deduce their results as consequences of his new theory.

It is doubtful that Hull deliberately shifted his system in order to account for latent learning, for the facts of latent learning were at the time very much in doubt, and his followers were still very critical of the results of earlier latent-learning experiments. Another possibility is that the shift from $_SH_R$ to $_SE_R$ occurred because of Hull's preoccupation with quantification. He found that he could quantify $_SE_R$, but was far from quantifying $_SH_R$. Hence it was preferable to write more equations in terms of $_SE_R$.[89]

The method by which Hull derived latent learning is simplicity itself. So long as there exists a modicum of reinforcement, $_SH_R$ builds up as a function of the number of trials. The revealed $_SE_R$ will be small, and the revealed learning slight, because one of the multipliers (K, the incentive reinforcement) is small. Now when K is made large, through the introduction of the major incentive, we have a new multiplier, and the amount of $_SE_R$ (for the same $_SH_R$) will be much greater. This is largely what is meant by latent learning: a sudden gain in $_SE_R$ with the introduction of incentive.

Hull's deduced latent learning is shown schematically in Figure 21. Shifts of incentive, either upwards or downwards, within a few trials place the organism on the learning curve characteristic of animals trained all along with the new incentive. Hull accepts the familiar latent-learning data of Tolman and Honzik (1930) as supporting his prediction.[90]

Adient-Abient Conflict

The postulates and corollaries include references to anticipatory goal responses and to a factor (K) having to do with the magnitude of incentives used in prior reinforcements. They assert nothing, however, about *perceived* incentives. Hence Hull saved the problems of perceived in-

[89] This is also Koch's interpretation, Koch (1954), page 106, footnote 29.
[90] We shall meet latent learning again in the next chapter.

centives to be treated through theorems derived from the more basic postulates.

Perceived incentives are very important in ordinary behavior. Consider a cat lying in wait to pounce upon a bird, or a buzzard circling in search of carrion, or a male dog attracted by a female in heat. The ongoing behavior is very much influenced by the perceived incentive.

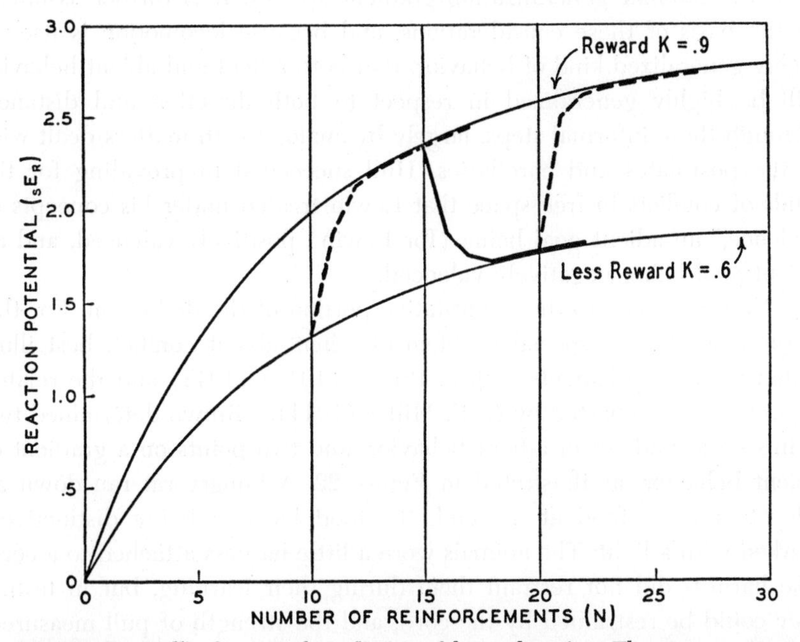

FIGURE 21. Hull's theoretical prediction of latent learning. The upper curve represents the course of learning with a large incentive (K = .9) throughout. The lower curve shows the course of learning with a smaller incentive (K = .6). The first curve that crosses between the two predicts what will happen if the incentive is increased at trial 10 for animals previously trained with the smaller incentive (the typical latent learning result). The next two crossings represent the result of a decrease in incentive at trial 15, and an increase at trial 20. After Hull (1952a), page 144.

Perceived incentives are of two kinds: those, such as food, which invite approach; and those, such as noxious stimuli, which invite avoidance. Hull, selecting some older terms, called approach behavior *adience* or *adient behavior,* and withdrawal *abience* or *abient behavior.*

Hull takes the major steps from the postulates to the basic theorems of adient and abient behavior informally, that is, without quantitative reference to the postulates (except for similarities in the forms of function chosen). In the first step, he accepts it as plausible that approach responses to an attractive incentive near at hand have been conditioned according to familiar principles. The same is implied, but in reverse, for withdrawal responses. At a distance, an incentive object, whether adient or abient, will produce a stimulus pattern resembling the one close to the object, so that responses conditioned to the object itself will be conditioned to the object at a distance, at an intensity corresponding to the difference between the stimulus patterns for the near and far object. Thus the familiar generalization gradient applies. It is further assumed, on the basis of these considerations, and because locomotion is itself a highly generalized kind of behavior, that both adient and abient behavior will be highly generalized in respect to both direction and distance. Through these informal steps, largely by analogy with matters dealt with in the postulates and corollaries, Hull succeeded in providing for the kinds of conflicts in free space that Lewin treated under his concepts of "valence," an adient goal being (for Lewin) positively valenced, and an abient goal being negatively valenced.

Now we come to the quantitative portion of the deduction. For this purpose we take a special problem of adient-abient conflict, best illustrated in the experiments of J. S. Brown (1942) (1948) and the related experiments as reported by N. E. Miller (1944).[91] Brown determined two points on a gradient of adient behavior, and two points on a gradient of abient behavior, as illustrated in Figure 22. A hungry rat ran down an alley to receive food at the end, the food location being distinctively marked with a light. The animals wore a little harness attached to a cord. The harness did not restrain them during their learning, but in testing they could be restrained by the cord, and the strength of pull measured. This is the pull in grams as recorded in Figure 22 at the two points of the approach gradient. Other animals, instead of receiving food at the end of the alley, received electric shock. When restrained near the point of shock, they pulled hard to get away from the shock zone, but if restrained at a distance they pulled away only slightly. These two points make up the avoidance gradient, which is seen to be much steeper than the approach gradient. Miller and his associates predicted that if animals were both fed and shocked at the end of the alley, they would be placed in conflict. When placed at the end of the alley farthest from the ambivalent goal, they should approach part way and then stop, the point of stopping being related to the point at which the two gradients cross, because here the opposite pulls are equal. By strengthening the hunger or weakening the shock, the animals could be made to approach nearer to the goal

[91] The important evidence for the theorem under study is from an unpublished study by Miller, Brown, and Lipofsky (1943), discussed by N. E. Miller (1944), page 437.

before stopping. Hence the experimental results agreed with the interpretation that the two independent gradients measured by Brown would interact when both food and shock occurred together.

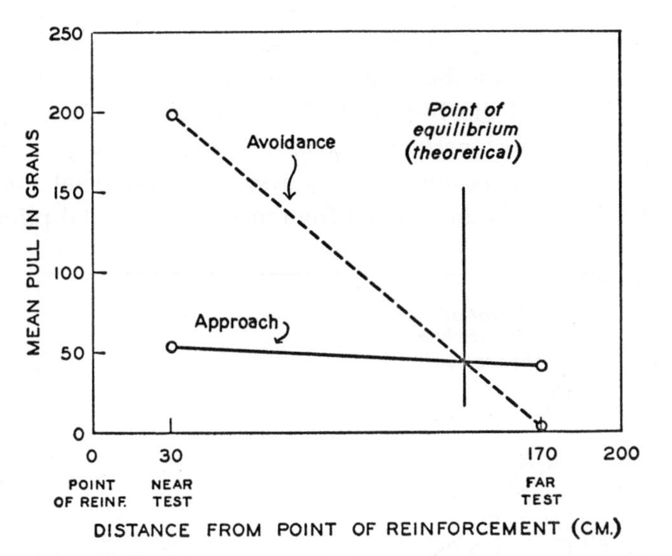

FIGURE 22. Empirical form of approach and avoidance gradients. The straight-line gradients are based on two points determined by J. S. Brown for each gradient separately, as reproduced by Miller (1944), page 434. The theoretical point of equilibrium has been added.

Now let us see how Hull, with these facts before him, ties them into his system. This is a good illustration of prediction after-the-fact, but such prediction is, of course, entirely permissible in a deductive system.

The theorem with which Hull comes out is stated as follows: [92]

Theorem 86. Other things equal, with moderately sophisticated subjects, when an adient object and an abient object occupy nearly the same point in space and the maximum abient reaction potential is greater than the maximum adient potential, there will be a point of stable equilibrium at a j.n.d. distance from the adient-abient object amounting to

$$d = \frac{\log_{10} \frac{{}_{S}E'_{R}}{{}_{S}E_{R}}}{j' - j}$$

Miller's conclusion is thus given a precise mathematical form. The derivation here will serve to provide a step-by-step illustration of the method Hull used much more generally.

First, for the straight-line gradients of Figure 22, Hull substituted

[92] Hull (1952a), pages 249–250.

the curved gradients of Figure 23, in order to use curves of the same form that he used in generalization gradients (Postulate 10). The adience exponent he made half that of the abience exponent, simply because Brown and Miller had found the two gradients to differ in slope.

This tampering with the exponents, in order to agree with the results of experiments, is allowable, but it should follow some of the rules of the system. In strict logic, because Hull does not *deduce* these differences in exponents, he must *postulate* them. Therefore he has added a new but unacknowledged postulate to his system at this point (until such time as the differences are derived from more fundamental principles).

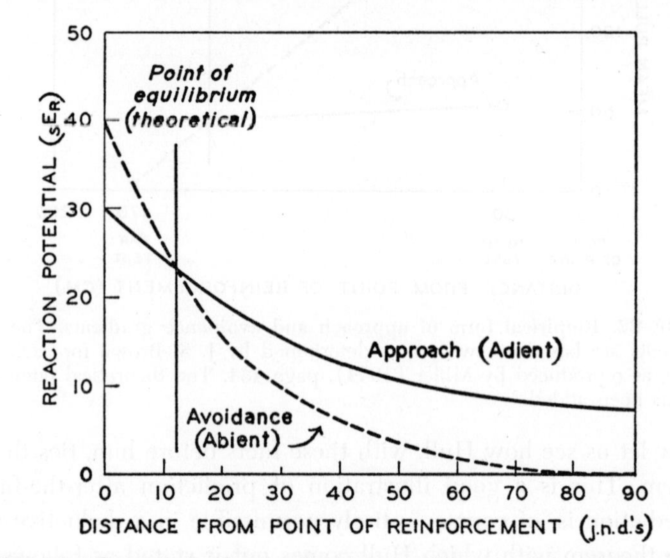

FIGURE 23. Theoretical adient and abient gradients used by Hull in predicting the point of equilibrium in an adient-abient conflict. Compare with the empirical results of Figure 22. Replotted from Hull (1952a) to conform with the conventions of Figure 22.

The point of equilibrium in Figure 23, like that in Figure 22, is the point at which the two curves cross. What Theorem 86 states is merely the algebraic solution of the problem solved graphically in Figure 23.

For adient behavior, we assume the gradient to be of the form:

$$ {}_S\underline{\bar{E}}_R = {}_SE_R \times 10^{-jd} \quad (1) $$

Where ${}_S\underline{\bar{E}}_R$ is the generalized reaction potential at any point on the gradient at a distance d in j.n.d.'s from the point of reinforcement.

The corresponding gradient for abience is:

$$ {}_S\underline{\bar{E}}'_R = {}_SE'_R \times 10^{-j'd} \quad (2) $$

To derive the equation required for the theorem we find that value of d at which the two gradients will balance each other, where $_S\underline{E}_R = {_S\underline{E}'_R}$. This is a matter of simple algebra, which looks more forbidding than it is partly because the subscripts S and R are appendages without any mathematical meaning.

We know that, at the value of d which we seek

$$_S\underline{E}_R = {_S\underline{E}'_R} \tag{3}$$

Hence, from (1) and (2)

$$_SE_R \times 10^{-jd} = {_SE'_R} \times 10^{-j'd} \tag{4}$$

Eliminating the negative exponents, we may write

$$\frac{_SE_R}{10^{jd}} = \frac{_SE'_R}{10^{j'd}} \tag{5}$$

Transposing terms, we have

$$\frac{10^{j'd}}{10^{jd}} = \frac{_SE'_R}{_SE_R} \tag{6}$$

Taking the logarithm of both sides,

$$j'd - jd = \log_{10} \frac{_SE'_R}{_SE_R} \tag{7}$$

Solving for d, the value we are after,

$$d = \frac{\log_{10} \frac{_SE'_R}{_SE_R}}{j' - j} \tag{8}$$

Equation (8) is the one appearing in the theorem. It results solely from selecting as the form of the gradient the form earlier adopted for generalization gradients, with the added assumption (similar to Miller's) that there is an equilibrium point where the two gradients coincide.

To prepare a plot as in Figure 23, it is necessary to make computations, using actual values for the terms entering into equation (8). Let us see how Hull did this. He assumed the following values, which, while arbitrary, are of an order of magnitude used elsewhere in the system:

$_SE'_R = 4\ \sigma$
$_SE_R\ = 3\ \sigma$
} The greater magnitude of the abient reaction potential $_SE'_R$ is assumed in Theorem 86.

$j' = .02$
$j\ = .01$
} The greater steepness of the abient gradient ($j' > j$) is assumed to be a fundamental characteristic.

Substituting these values in Equation (8), we have

$$d = \frac{\log \frac{4\sigma}{3\sigma}}{.02 - .01} = \frac{\log 1.333}{.01}$$

Looking up the value of log 1.333 in a table of logarithms, we find log 1.333 = .1248, hence

$$d = \frac{.1248}{.01} = 12.48 \text{ j.n.d.'s}$$

By examining Figure 23, we see that the algebraic and graphical solutions agree (as indeed they should!).

What do we learn from these computations? When we follow Hull's computational technique, we find that very often the results are obtained, as in this example, through assigning equations to simultaneous functions, and then solving the simultaneous equations. The tie-in with the total system is often very slight. In this case, the forms of the gradients are the same as those used in generalization gradients, and the constants are similar in meaning. But the accuracy of the deductions does not depend upon these similarities, and, in fact, some of the correspondence between the system and the deductions is purely gratuitous. For example, no operational meaning is given to a difference in j.n.d.'s along a gradient of this kind, so that there is no check whatever on the use of these units. An accurate use of empirically defined j.n.d. units might very well change the slope of the gradient. Furthermore, the puzzling problems of the relative effectiveness of reward and punishment, which ought to be dealt with as central features of a reinforcement theory, are here glossed over by the very molar assumption that the exponent for the gradient of abience is double that for adience. For a genuinely precise deduction it would be necessary also to show that strength of pull when restrained has a determinate relationship to reaction potential as quantified in the system. Despite the appearance of precision, and of tie-in with his system, Hull's deduction is by no means rigorous and represents little, if any, advance over the simpler presentation of Figure 22.

Proceeding in somewhat similar manner, now that the general principles of adience and abience were accepted and in some sense justified, Hull was able to combine the principle of the habit-family hierarchy with that of the gradient of reinforcement to explain the attraction of goals beyond barriers, and of the paths taken around such barriers. These are the kinds of problems in open space emphasized in field theories such as Lewin's. Hull was willing to go so far as to borrow portions of the physical analogies used by the field theorists:

> Assuming as a first approximation that behavioral vectors in quite naive subjects operate roughly as physical vectors, even a slight movement to one side of the line will unbalance the otherwise completely opposed reaction tendencies. . . .[93]

Because adience and abience operate in two-dimensional space, Hull acknowledged that he had developed a field theory of sorts:

> The theory of adient and abient behavior thus involves examples of bona fide field theory, though this theory must not be confused with physical field theories, from which the present theory differs in most respects.[94]

Hull referred to two chief differences between his kind of field theory and physical field theory: first, the organism is not propelled, as a physical particle is, by external forces from the field, but the energy for its movements comes primarily from the food it eats; second, the distances important in physics are actual distances (centimeters or meters) while the distances in his system are in j.n.d.'s, hence defined according to the organism's reactions. The residual difference between Hull and Lewin on these points appears to be almost purely linguistic, for Lewin would not have objected to the substance of either of Hull's two points.

Success in Prediction

Eventually a self-correcting hypothetico-deductive system must be judged by its successes, that is, the agreements between predictions and observed events, and by its adjustments to its failures.

On any kind of tabulation, Hull's several postulate systems have fared very well.

A tabulation of the material in the rote-learning book showed evidence bearing on 71 of the 110 theorems and corollaries. The evidence gave clear support in 39 cases (55 per cent), was somewhat ambiguous in 20 cases (28 per cent), and disagreed with the prediction in the remaining 12 cases (17 per cent).[95]

The successes represent a substantial achievement, but the failures, too, are achievements, in that they show Hull's statements to have been made clearly enough that data could contradict them.

[93] Hull (1952a), page 242.
[94] Hull (1952a), page 269.
[95] Hilgard (1940).

Hull presented his own summary of successes in prediction in the final book.[96] He classified the evidence bearing on 121 of 178 theoretical propositions in that book. Of these, he found 106 (87 per cent) substantially validated, 14 (12 per cent) probably valid, but uncertain, and only one (1 per cent) definitely invalid.

This very high agreement is somewhat disturbing at this stage in science, even though the ultimate aim is exceptionless validity. Too high agreement, when the system is as unfinished as this one, suggests either (1) low standards with respect to what constitutes agreement, or (2) too great reliance on working backward from data, with *ad hoc* assumptions to guarantee agreement. Guaranteed agreements should not be tabulated as verifications. Working backwards is not, in itself, a defect in a theoretical system. In fact, there is no real alternative, for the improvement in a system comes precisely through "working backwards" to obtain better agreement with reality. But there are rules by which the deductions remain coherent and internally consistent, and these are often difficult to apply. As Hull pointed out, the 55 predictions in his book not covered by known relevant evidence will provide a good test of the fertility of his system, because they are free of the charge of working backward from the known.

ESTIMATE OF HULL'S POSITION

Hull's Position on Typical Problems

Because he was willing to face the problems of learning posed by others as well as those which he set himself, it is possible to assign Hull a position on the representative problems chosen as the basis for comparing the different points of view.

1. *Capacity.* A volume on individual differences on which Hull had been working was not completed by the time of his death. He published but a single paper on the problem [97] and did not carry the analysis much further in his final book. Individual differences in capacity will be reflected in the constants that appear in the behavioral laws. Once these are under control, it will be possible to make fundamental attacks on such problems as that of the relationship between learning and persistent individual differences.

2. *Practice.* Mere contiguous repetition does nothing but generate inhibition; all improvement depends upon reinforcement. Hull is in this

[96] Hull (1952a), 351–353.
[97] Hull (1945).

respect in agreement with Thorndike and Skinner, and opposed to Guthrie. Because the *amount* of reinforcement does not affect habit strength, provided some minimum amount is present, the number of reinforcements is the basic variable in acquiring habit strength.

3. *Motivation.* The basic paradigm for reinforcement lies in need reduction, as when food relieves the body's need for sustenance, or when escape saves the organism from injury. Thus the primary reinforcing quality of reward and of punishment is the same: food reward relieves hunger tension, escape from shock reduces shock tension. While these are the underlying biological facts, the reinforcement itself is mediated by stimulus reduction, that is, by reducing the stimuli associated with the drive, rather than by satisfying the drive itself. Secondary reinforcement can be provided by any stimulus regularly associated with primary reinforcement.

Drive is complexly related to learning: (1) it provides the basis for both primary and secondary reinforcement, (2) it activates habit strength into reaction potential, and (3) it provides differential internal stimuli that guide behavior.

More complicated relationships involving anxiety, avoidance, expectation, frustration, conflict, may be derived from the more primitive principles of primary and secondary reinforcement. Important intermediate derivations include adient (approach) behavior to perceived positive incentives and abient (withdrawal) behavior to perceived negative incentives.

4. *Understanding.* The organism's own responses furnish the surrogates for ideas. The fractional antedating goal response (r_G) provides stimuli (s_G) whose sole function, in some instances, is to guide behavior. Responses that provide such stimuli are called "pure stimulus acts." Ideas thus have the substantive quality that Guthrie also assigns to them. Two intermediate mechanisms emerge as important in meeting the problems of behavior in space, and in problem-solving generally. These are the principle of the gradient of reinforcement, extended to include objects perceived at a distance, and the habit-family hierarchy, which permits the maximum utilization of past experience in the solving of present problems. Both principles depend for their effectiveness upon aroused fractional anticipatory responses, and upon discriminations among the stimuli that these responses produce.

5. *Transfer.* There are two aspects to transfer: equivalence of stimuli and equivalence of responses. Hull explains equivalence of stimuli either on the basis of generalization, or via intermediate reactions. Equivalence

of responses depends in part upon response oscillation, and the generalization there involved; it depends also on the organization of responses into hierarchies by way of the habit-family hierarchy. All responses in the hierarchy have in the past led to the same goal, so that they are in that respect equivalent.

6. *Forgetting.* In the volume on rote learning, the decay of excitation is postulated by Hull and his associates to occur according to a kind of law of disuse, making forgetting a function of time. He reaffirmed this position in one of the corollaries of the 1943 book, but did not provide for it in his postulate set.[98] I find no reference to forgetting as such in the 1952 book, the only references being to the *rise* in the curve of reminiscence, without discussion of the subsequent fall. The only acquired function that decays systematically with the passage of time is reactive inhibition (I_R).

It is pertinent to refer here to Hull's own summary of the basic principles as he perceived them, after completing the system reported in his final book. He listed and described eight *automatic adaptive behavior mechanisms.*

1. Inborn responses tendencies (${}_SU_R$) provide the first automatic mechanism for adapting to emergency situations.

2. The primitive capacity to learn is the second mechanism, "a slightly slower means of adaptation to less acute situations."

3. The antedating defense reaction, arising through learning combined with stimulus generalization, provides the third adaptive mechanism.

4. The extinction of useless acts, negative response learning, is the fourth mechanism.

5. Trial-and-error learning is the fifth mechanism.

6. Discrimination learning is the sixth mechanism.

7. A second type of antedating defense reaction, depending upon the persistence of stimulus traces (rather than upon generalization, as in the case of a perceived dangerous object), is the seventh mechanism.

8. The fractional antedating reaction (r_G) with its proprioceptive stimulus correlate (s_G), provides for the "automatic (stimulus) guidance of organismic behavior to goals." This eighth and final mechanism is the crowning achievement of the system.

Further study of this major automatic device presumably will lead to the detailed behavioral understanding of thought and reasoning, which constitute

[98] Hull (1943), page 296.

the highest attainment of organic evolution. Indeed the $r_G \longrightarrow s_G$ mechanism leads in a strictly logical manner into what was formerly regarded as the very heart of the psychic: interest, planning, foresight, foreknowledge, expectancy, purpose, and so on.[99]

The Status of Hull's Final Reinforcement Theory

Hull's theory is not a highly integrated one, so that no one concept is truly central to it. If one accepts his own summary, according to the foregoing eight mechanisms, the fact of learning is important, but the particular mechanism of learning is not crucial. Perhaps the most crucial concept is that of the r_G-s_G mechanism, which has only a tangential relationship to reinforcement theory. Nevertheless, the most controversial issue among the S-R theories concerns the status of reinforcement.

Hull's vacillation between the items to be reduced in primary reinforcement led him to reject D, to turn to S_D, then to add s_G as an afterthought. There was no finality to his interpretation of primary reinforcement. We shall return to this issue again in Chapter 12, when we consider the views of some of his followers, and some recent experiments.

He was also quite unclear as to what lay beneath secondary reinforcement, although he was clear as to its importance. A stimulus associated with primary reinforcement became at once (1) a conditioner of secondary drive, hence a producer of S_D, and (2) a secondary reinforcer, and hence the equivalent of reduced S_D. Hull was not really clear about this, because he seems not to have thought about both secondary drive and secondary reinforcement at the same time. His thinking was particular, not general. When he thought of secondary drive, he thought of what Miller and Mowrer talk about as fear or anxiety. When he thought of secondary reinforcement, he thought of such things as distinctive end-boxes, or tokens substituting for food. But when he wrote his formal propositions, they implied that a stimulus associated with reinforcement could become at once *both* a drive and a reinforcing agent, for the conditions necessary to become a secondary drive appear to be the same as the conditions for becoming a secondary reinforcing agent (Corollaries i and ii). The literary form of the two corollaries differs somewhat, and it may be that Hull intended a difference, but if he did he was not clear.

Hence these fundamental matters—the nature of primary and secondary reinforcement—he really left for others to settle.

[99] Hull (1952a), page 350.

The Quantification of Reaction Potential

Just what did Hull achieve in the effort to quantify reaction potential, a task to which he devoted much effort, and in the success of which he took some satisfaction?

It is worth taking a look at what he did, because the problem of assigning quantities to intervening variables is one that other theorists who use such variables (e.g., Tolman) must eventually face.

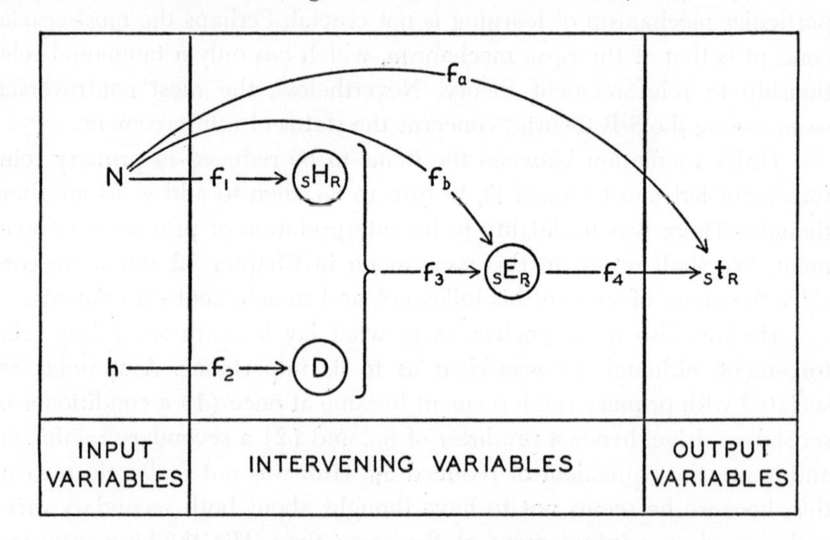

FIGURE 24. The logical problem of measuring intervening variables.

A simplified version of Hull's system is presented in Figure 24. It omits generalization effects, K, V, and inhibition, but it includes the most important intervening variables $_SH_R$, D, and $_SE_R$, circled in the diagram to distinguish them from the input and output variables. The problem is to get from the external world of input and output to these intervening variables, in terms of which the most important equations are to be written. If we assume everything else constant, our fundamental equation is:

$$_SE_R = f_3(_SH_R, D) \qquad (1)$$

As a first approximation Hull assumed the equation to be of the form:

$$_SE_R = {_SH_R} \times D \qquad (2)$$

But while we are about the problem of strict quantification, we cannot make this assumption. It is part of our empirical-theoretical problem to determine the form of the f_3 function. We cannot move from equation (1) to equation (2) without proof.

Now, in general, we have three helpful contributions to determining the f functions, because each of the intervening variables is anchored to input or output. We have the three functions:

$$_SH_R = f_1\,(N),\text{ where N is the number of reinforcements} \qquad (3)$$
$$D = f_2\,(h),\text{ where } h \text{ is hours of food deprivation} \qquad (4)$$
$$_SE_R = f_4\,(_St_R),\text{ where } _St_R \text{ is the latency of response} \qquad (5)$$

Were we able to determine f_1, f_2, and f_4, we should have some chance of determining f_3. We can find equations in Hull's system for each of these functions, so we might assume that he had followed out this program. Actually he did nothing of the kind.

The only function indicated in Figure 24 that is actually given in the data is f_a, which can be stated:

$$_St_R = f_a\,(N) \qquad (6)$$

That is, we know from experiments that in some instances latency of response becomes progressively shorter as the number of reinforcements increases, and we can fit curves to our results, or scale our results, if we wish. Hull and his collaborators proceeded to scale this function, and then named the scaled value $_SE_R$. That is, the f_4 function is determined on the assumption that reaction potential bears a one-to-one correspondence to scaled latency. Then

$$_SE_R = f_4\,(_St_R) \qquad (7)$$

Now we are able to make an algebraic manipulation between equations (6) and (7), substituting $_SE_R$ for $_St_R$ in equation (6), and we appear to have measured an intervening variable:

$$_SE_R = f_b(N) \qquad (8)$$

This is really the extent to which Hull, strictly speaking, quantified intervening variables. The f_3 function was never determined from *independent* computations of $_SH_R$, D, and $_SE_R$ by way of the appropriate f_1, f_2, and f_4 functions.

A further step was taken to complete the picture by using the data from Perin (1942), in which a functional relationship was established between hours of food deprivation and latency of response. Again by using the f_4 function shown in Figure 24, it was possible to state a relationship between hours of food deprivation (h) and reaction potential ($_SE_R$). But this depended solely on the relation between (h) and ($_St_R$) and still did not solve the problem of the f_1, f_2, and f_3 functions, which is really the heart of the problem of assigning quantities to intervening variables. Hull was rightly aware of the task that needed to be done, but he failed to accomplish it.

The quantification task that was carried out so carefully—the scaling of latency—was not a total loss, for in the process some contributions were made to scaling theory; and the new position given behavioral oscillation in the system led to some interesting implications, as we saw in the example of predicted alternation sequences.

How Satisfactory a System Did Hull Leave?

Hull's system has many points of superiority over any other existing psychological system. It is at once comprehensive and detailed, theoretical, yet empirically quantitative. It is easy to locate faults within it because it is so carefully worked out, so explicit and mathematical that its errors of incompleteness or inconsistency are easily brought into focus. A theory expressed solely in the ordinary literary language may sound very plausible because the gaps in the theory are glossed over through cogent illustrations. A theory such as Hull's calls attention to itself whenever it jumps a gap. In criticizing Hull's theory we must not lose sight of the fact that, with all its weaknesses, it is a major achievement.

We do well to think of Hull's system as really twofold. On the one hand, he was embarked upon a bold and comprehensive theory of behavior, a theory he hoped would serve as a basis for much of social science. On the other hand, he was experimenting with a very precise miniature system, with determinate constants based upon controlled experimentation. He attempted to combine these two enterprises at once, and was not very skilled at distinguishing between what he accomplished on a large scale and on a small scale, for he wanted the whole to be one system.

On a large scale, when dealing with behavior in free space, problem-solving, and ideas, Hull made skillful use of peripheral mechanisms, particularly the hypothesized r_G—s_G sequence. By interlocking these goal anticipations into other features of his system, particularly through the gradient of reinforcement and the habit-family hierarchy, he was able to make large-scale deductions of familiar forms of behavior. When moving on this large-scale level, the theory was very "molar" indeed, and almost no efforts were made to pin down precisely the kinds of anticipatory movements (chewing movements, bodily postures) that would serve as the tangible base for the important fractional antedating response. The choice of this mechanism was made (as a surrogate for ideas) because it was ponderable, and hence, in principle, at least, subject to measurement. One can easily think of possible experiments to test aspects of the r_G mechanism, especially the grosser aspects.[100] If experiments cannot be designed to test the subtler r_G mechanisms, then one might as well deal with "ideas" as with "pure-stimulus acts." The argument that the characteristics of these acts can be inferred, if not measured, has some appeal, but it is possible to infer discriminations between ideas or engrams, too. Perhaps r_G need have no more tangible reality than ${}_SH_R$, but the system always implies that it is a genuine response, with proprioceptive consequences. It may be noted also that the large-scale deductions, built on r_G, do not require any one special theory of learning, so long as goal anticipation can be achieved by that theory.

When Hull was operating on a smaller scale, and attempting to become precise and quantitative, he became highly particularistic, confining many of the postulates and corollaries to the results of single experiments done with rat bar-pressing in a Skinner box modified so that a latency measure could be secured. Hull became so preoccupied with this quantification that he failed to distinguish between this exercise in miniature-system construction and the larger task on which he was simultaneously engaged. He therefore began to write into his *basic postulates* what were really *exercises in quantification.* Surely a set of laws of mammalian behavior ought not reflect in the constants of its basic postulates such specialized information as the most favorable interval for human eyelid conditioning (Postulate 2), how many days without food weakens a rat (Postulate 5), the weight in grams of food needed to condition a rat (Postulate 7), a rat's reaction time (Postulate 13), or the amplitude in millimeters of galvanometer deflection in human conditioning (Postulate 15).

It would have been preferable to distinguish between the tentative generalization and then separately to offer the quantitative evidence as illustrative. An alternative would have been to limit the miniature system to the rat in the bar-pressing box, with every effort to be systematic and to make the various constants interchangeable, to make a determined effort to measure intervening variables within this one limited universe. Then the particularistic postulates would have been appropriate, as other postulates were appropriate to rote learning.

The source of these deficiencies in the system cannot easily be specified. It is difficult to distinguish between weaknesses inherent in the system, and problems that were Hull's as a theorist and system-maker.

[100] An early example was given by N. E. Miller (1935).

We have two illustrations in his career of systems beginning with a large sweep and then, after heroic quantitative effort, ending so particularistic as to be much less inviting than they were before the effort was made. The first was the rote-learning theory, which, in its grosser form [101] appeared more inviting than in its better worked-out form.[102] So many *ad hoc* assumptions had to be made in the more precise formulation that little has been heard from this since. Now we find a similar progression in the theory of adaptive behavior. The early papers, in the 1930's, gave a new outlook upon the systematic prediction of behavior in a great variety of situations. The postulates were based largely upon the interpretation of maze behavior (simple trial and error, and serial learning). Now, as the system became more precise, these larger predictions were mostly carried over from the past; the new postulates in both 1943 and 1952 became so tied to a limited kind of experiment (chiefly rat bar-pressing) that they are little likely to survive. It may be that particularism is an inevitable consequence of seeking precise quantitative prediction in the present stage of behavioral science. If so, it means that the theorist, at least for a time, will have to be modest in what he attempts to do, and may have to be satisfied to remain within a miniature system. If particularism is not the inevitable result of the scientific logic used, then it may be that something was wrong with the kind of concepts employed. The additional possibility is that some limitation in Hull as a systematist led him to particularism. Whatever the reason, Hull's followers will undoubtedly be able to build on his foundation to produce a more satisfactory postulate set than he left.

It must be acknowledged that Hull's system, for its time, was the best there was—not necessarily the one nearest to psychological reality, not necessarily the one whose generalizations were the most likely to endure—but the one worked out in the greatest detail, with the most conscientious effort to be quantitative throughout and at all points closely in touch with empirical tests. Furthermore, it may well be said to have been the most influential of the theories between 1930 and 1950, judging from the experimental and theoretical studies engendered by it, whether in its defense, its amendment, or its refutation. Its primary contribution may turn out to lie not in its substance at all, but rather in the ideal it set for a genuinely systematic and quantitative psychological system far different from the "schools" which so long plagued psychology.

[101] Hull (1935a).
[102] Hull and others (1940).

SUPPLEMENTARY READINGS

BOOKS

HULL, C. L., HOVLAND, C. I., ROSS, R. T., HALL, M., PERKINS, D. T., and FITCH, F. B. (1940) *Mathematico-deductive theory of rote learning.*

HULL, C. L. (1943) *Principles of behavior.*

HULL, C. L. (1951) *Essentials of behavior.*

HULL, C. L. (1952) *A behavior system.*

SHORTER INTRODUCTIONS

HULL, C. L. (1942) Conditioning: Outline of a systematic theory of learning. Chapter 2 in *The psychology of learning.* Natl. Soc. Stud. Educ., 41st Yearbook, Part II, 61–95.

HULL, C. L. (1950) Behavior postulates and corollaries—1949. *Psychol. Rev.,* 57, 173–180.

LAMBERT, W. W. (1954) Stimulus-response contiguity and reinforcement theory in social psychology. In G. Lindzey, ed. *Handbook of social psychology.* 65–71.

SPENCE, K. W. (1951) Theoretical interpretations of learning. In C. P. Stone, ed. *Comparative psychology.* Third edition. 239–291.

SPENCE, K. W. (1951) Theoretical interpretations of learning. In S. S. Stevens, ed. *Handbook of experimental psychology.* 690–729.

CRITICAL REVIEWS

HILGARD, E. R. (1940) Review of *Mathematico-deductive theory of rote learning:* The psychological system. *Psychol. Bull.,* 37, 808–815.

KOCH, S. (1944) Review of Hull's *Principles of behavior. Psychol. Bull.,* 41, 269–286.

LEEPER, R. (1944) Dr. Hull's *Principles of behavior. J. genet. Psychol.,* 65, 3–52.

LEEPER, R. (1952) Review of Hull's *Essentials of behavior. Amer. J. Psychol.,* 65, 478–491.

MARHENKE, P. (1940) Review of *Mathematico-deductive theory of rote learning:* The logical system. *Psychol. Bull.,* 37, 815–817.

RITCHIE, B. F. (1944) Hull's treatment of learning. *Psychol. Bull.,* 41, 640–652.

SCHOENFELD, W. N., and BERSH, P. J. (1952) Review of Hull's *Essentials of behavior. Psychol. Bull.,* 49, 628–636.

SEWARD, J. P. (1954) Hull's system of behavior: an evaluation. *Psychol. Rev.,* 61, 145–159.

SKINNER, B. F. (1944) Review of Hull's *Principles of behavior. Amer. J. Psychol.,* 57, 276–281.

REPRESENTATIVE EXPERIMENTS

BROWN, J. S. (1948) Gradients of approach and avoidance responses and their relation to levels of motivation. *J. comp. physiol. Psychol.,* 41, 450–465.

ELLSON, D. G. (1938) Quantitative studies of the interaction of simple habits. I. Recovery from specific and generalized effects of extinction. *J. exp. Psychol.,* 23, 330–358.

GRICE, G. R. (1949) Visual discrimination learning with simultaneous and successive presentation of stimuli. *J. comp. physiol. Psychol.,* 42, 365–373.

HULL, C. L. (1935) The influence of caffeine and other factors on certain phenomena of rote learning. *J. gen. Psychol.,* 13, 249–274.

Hull, C. L. (1947) Reactively heterogeneous trial-and-error learning with distributed trials and terminal reinforcement. *J. exp. Psychol.*, 37, 118–135.

Kendler, H. H. (1946) The influence of simultaneous hunger and thirst drives upon the learning of two opposed spatial responses of the white rat. *J. exp. Psychol.*, 36, 212–220.

Kimble, G. A. (1949) An experimental test of a two-factor theory of inhibition. *J. exp. Psychol.*, 39, 15–23.

Perin, C. T. (1942) Behavior potentiality as a joint function of the amount of training and the degree of hunger at the time of extinction. *J. exp. Psychol.*, 30, 93–113.

Spence, K. W. (1942) The basis of solution by chimpanzees of the intermediate size problem. *J. exp. Psychol.*, 31, 257–271.

Spence, K. W., Bergmann, G., and Lippitt, R. A. (1950) A study of simple learning under irrelevant motivational-reward conditions. *J. exp. Psychol.*, 40, 539–551.

Woodbury, C. B. (1950) Double, triple, and quadruple repetition in the white rat. *J. comp. physiol. Psychol.*, 43, 490–502.

Yamaguchi, H. G. (1952) Gradients of drive stimulus (S_D) intensity generalization. *J. exp. Psychol.*, 43, 298–304.

FINAL NOTE

If at some points the reader believes that I have been more severely critical of Hull's system than is objectively justified, he should perhaps be warned that at least one competent reviewer detected a bias against S-R theories in the earlier edition of this book:

Miller, N. E. (1949) Review of Hilgard's *Theories of learning*. *Psychol. Bull.*, 46, 529–532.

For a detailed and searching criticism of Hull's system from the standpoint of the logic of science, see:

Koch, S. (1954) Clark L. Hull. In W. K. Estes and others. *Modern learning theory*. 1–176.

To achieve a balanced view of Hull's earnestness, and his modesty about his attainments, his autobiography is well worth reading:

Hull, C. L. (1952) Autobiography. In H. S. Langfeld and others. *A history of psychology in autobiography*. Volume 4. 143–162.

Chapter 6

TOLMAN'S SIGN LEARNING

THE theory of Edward C. Tolman was called purposive behaviorism in his major systematic work, *Purposive behavior in animals and men* (1932). Since then he (and others) have called it a sign-gestalt theory, a sign-significate theory, or an expectancy theory. These later terms all emphasize the *cognitive* nature of the theory, which distinguishes it in certain respects from the stimulus-response theories of Thorndike, Guthrie, Skinner, and Hull. The designation *sign learning* provides a satisfactory short name, abbreviating sign-gestalt and sign-significate, while calling attention to the cognitive reference within the theory.

Tolman acknowledged the complex affiliations of his system—with Watson's behaviorism, McDougall's hormic psychology, Woodworth's dynamic psychology, gestalt psychology (in both classical and Lewin's forms). He later recognized a number of parallels between his system and the probabilistic functionalism developed independently by Brunswik.[1] Still later, the influence of psychoanalysis began to be noticeable.[2] Because of these complex affiliations it is appropriate to consider his system after our familiarity with the other behaviorisms, and before turning to the non-behavioristic theories.

Despite some shifts in vocabulary, Tolman has held firm to his main tenets during the more than twenty years since his book appeared:

1. His system is a genuine *behaviorism*, and as such rigidly rejects introspection as a method and "raw feels" as data for psychological science. When he makes reference to consciousness, to inventive ideation, and the like, he is talking about interpretations of observed behavior. He does not accept "verbal report" as a dodge by which to smuggle consciousness in through the back door.

2. The system is a *molar*, rather than a *molecular*, behaviorism. An

[1] Tolman and Brunswik (1935).
[2] Tolman (1942) (1943).

act of behavior has distinctive properties all its own, to be identified and described irrespective of whatever muscular, glandular, or neural processes underlie it. The molecular facts of physics and physiology upon which behavior rests have identifying properties of their own, which are not the properties of behavior as molar. This means for Tolman an independence from physiology, a characteristic which he shares with several of the writers whom we have considered.

3. The system is a *purposivism,* but of a sort to avoid the implications of a teleological metaphysics. It is a purposivism because it recognizes that behavior is regulated in accordance with objectively determinable ends. It is not mentalistic; purposes are not those of a self-conscious mind. It is not in agreement with teleological points of view which make effects take precedence over and determine their causes.

The strongest rejection is of American structuralism, because structuralism was dependent upon introspection of the most offensive sort, that known as *Beschreibung.* Watsonian behaviorism is almost as vigorously rejected, because it was not only molecular but tended to neglect the problems of goal-seeking behavior.

THE SYSTEMATIC POSITION

Behavior as Molar

The descriptive properties of molar behavior are the most general characteristics of behavior which would impress themselves upon an intelligent onlooker without prepossessions and before any attempt to explain how the behavior comes about.

First, behavior is goal-directed. It is always a getting-toward something, or a getting-away from something. The most significant description of any behavior is what the organism is doing, what it is up to, where it is going. The cat is trying to get out of the box, the carpenter is building a house (or earning a living), the musician is seeking acclaim for his virtuosity. The particular movements involved are less descriptive of the molar behavior than is the goal toward which or away from which the movements lead. This feature characterizes molar behavior as *purposive.*

Second, the behavior makes use of environmental supports as means-objects toward the goal. The world in which behavior goes on is a world of paths and tools, obstacles, and by-paths with which the organism has commerce. The manner in which the organism makes use of paths and tools in relation to its goals characterizes molar behavior as *cognitive* as well as purposive.

Third, there is a selective preference for short or easy means-activities as against long or difficult ones, called the *principle of least effort.*

Fourth, behavior, if it is molar, is *docile.* That is, molar behavior is characterized by teachableness. If it is mechanical and stereotyped, like a spinal reflex, it belongs at the molecular level. Docility is said to be a mark of purpose.[3]

Intervening Variables

The complete act of behavior is initiated by environmental stimuli and physiological states. Certain processes intervene, and behavior emerges. Programmatically, this is the formula which Hull took over from Tolman. The problem of psychological analysis at the molar level is to infer the processes which intervene between the initiation of action in the world of physics and physiology and the resulting observable consequences, again in the world of physics and physiology. Because all of the data are rooted in this world, the system remains a behaviorism.

In spite of his methodological behaviorism, Tolman is clearly bent on making a "psychological" as against a "physiological" analysis. The intervening variables include such processes as cognitions and purposes, so that, on one side of its ancestry, Tolman's position belongs with the gestalt psychologists who have been characterized as "centralists," rather than with the stimulus-response psychologists characterized as "peripheralists."[4]

The precise variables entering into behavior determination have not remained fixed in Tolman's later discussions, but his logic of system-making has remained the same. The set of terms used in his presidential address before the American Psychological Association in 1937[5] may serve as illustrative.

The background of physiology and physics with which choice-point behavior begins is defined by environmental and individual difference variables:

I. *Environmental Variables*

M—Maintenance schedule
G—Appropriateness of goal object
S—Types and modes of stimuli provided

[3] In this Tolman follows Perry (1918).
[4] Murray (1938); Leeper (1944).
[5] Tolman (1938a).

R—Types of motor response required
Σ (OBO)—Cumulative nature and number of trials [6]
P—Pattern of preceding and succeeding maze units

II. *Individual Difference Variables*

H—Heredity
A—Age
T—Previous training
E—Special endocrine, drug or vitamin conditions

It is possible to study the effect of such variables on resulting behavior. The usual learning curve is a plot of the functional relationship under stated conditions. These are the behavioral "facts" about learning. It is the effort to explain the facts which leads to theories.

Tolman's explanation rests on *intervening variables.* These are inferred processes between the independent variables (stimuli, etc.) and the dependent variables (responses, etc.). The preliminary list as presented co-ordinates one intervening variable with each of the environmental variables.

Intervening Variable		*Environmental Variable*
Demand	correlated with	Maintenance schedule
Appetite	" "	Appropriateness of goal object
Differentiation	" "	Types and modes of stimuli provided
Motor skill	" "	Types of motor response required
Hypotheses	" "	Cumulative nature and number of trials
Biases	" "	Pattern of preceding and succeeding maze units

Although the intervening variables may sound subjective, in principle each can be given objective definition and measurement through a defining experiment in which everything else is held constant except the correlative environmental variable while that one is systematically varied. Demand, for example, may be expected to increase with the number of hours since feeding, but the relationship between food deprivation and demand is not a simple one. It must be studied empirically. The same holds for each of the intervening variables.

Having thus established a basis for inferring the value of the intervening variable from the antecedent conditions, the next stage in theory construction is to find the equations relating intervening variables to behavioral outcomes, as these intervening variables are simultaneously varied.

[6] Σ(OBO) is a shorthand formula which means some consequence or summation of previous experiences in which one occasion (O) has led through behavior (B) to another occasion (O). The occasions are such features as a choice point, a goal at the left, and so on.

In spite of the clear outline of what a systematic theory ought to be, Tolman has nowhere attempted quantitative predictions paralleling those of Hull, so that his conjectures have not in that sense been put to the test.[7] This does not mean that his experiments are unrelated to his theory. There are, in fact, many predictions, but they assert that one path will be preferred to another, that under one set of circumstances the problem will be easier than under another set, and so on. The dimensional analysis which completes the function is not provided, and Hull's conscientious efforts are instructive in showing how difficult that task is likely to be.

Recent Formulations in Relation to Earlier Ones

There have been no radical revisions in Tolman's systematic thinking, although various schemes have been tried out for classifying the phenomena of learning, and a number of diagrams have been prepared to provide models for thinking about learning and other aspects of behavior. The confident insistence upon building all principles so as to be derivable from and applicable to rat behavior (possibly to guarantee that the system remained a behaviorism) seems to have been somewhat relaxed. Some of the later papers attempt to generalize the interpretation of motivation and cognition in a way useful to social science generally. In these later papers more illustrations come from child-rearing and human behavior than in the earlier writings.

The most elaborate model since the first book holds to the original pattern of independent variables, intervening variables, and dependent (action) variables.[8] The changes from earlier to later models do not reflect any fundamental reorientation, although there are some vocabulary differences. The three chief intervening-variables in the 1951 model are (*a*) the need system, (*b*) the belief-value matrix, and (*c*) the behavior space.

The *need system* bears a family resemblance to the drive theories with which we are already familiar. The needs arise either through physiological deprivation or through psychologically defined drive conditions.

The *behavior space* in which "locomotion" takes place is a space of objects in various places, with distance and direction, *as perceived by the actor* at a given moment. These objects have positive or negative "valences" on them, and the actor is attracted or repelled by them. The behavior space is very similar to Lewin's life space. We shall consider

[7] Some starts have been made, e.g., Tolman (1939) (1941).
[8] Tolman (1951b) (1952b).

this kind of construct when Lewin's views are discussed in Chapter 8.

If we have become accustomed to stimulus-response language, we are likely to be confused initially by some of the language the cognitive theorist uses, especially his physical or geometrical metaphors. When the stimulus-response psychologist refers to an object in space, he means that physical object, or at least those aspects of it which, as stimuli, can impinge upon the subject's receptors. When the cognitive theorist refers to an object in space, he is commonly talking about that object *as perceived*, or *as it is expected to be when perceived.* It is important to remember that perception and perception-like processes are central for him. Thus when Tolman assigns *valence* to an object he does not mean that some mysterious attracting or repelling force has been added to a physical object. He means only that the object as perceived or as expected is as an object-to-be-sought or as an object-to-be-avoided. We may recall William James' description of a nestful of eggs as perceived by a broody hen: "the utterly fascinating and precious and never-to-be-too-much-sat-upon object." For the hen, the nestful of eggs has positive valence.

The *belief-value matrix* holds most interest as a possible supplementation to learning theory. This matrix (or, really a set of matrices) includes learned categorizations and differentiations concerning environmental objects. Objects categorized in a common class have gradients of generalization built up, so that the objects come to have a preferential or hierarchical order, similar in effect to Hull's gradients of generalization or his habit-family hierarchy. Tolman points out how little information we have about any of these gradients, except for simple sensory qualities. What he has in mind is something more complex. He uses as an illustration the functional dimension described by Sears and his coworkers for fantasy aggression in the doll-play of children.[9] These investigators found that doll-figures showed a consistent order of "psychological distance" from the child, as revealed by the amount of aggression either attributed to them, or addressed to them. The order—from near to far—is the child itself, then the parent doll of the same sex, the parent doll of the opposite sex, the child doll of the same sex, the child doll of the opposite sex, then the baby doll, then puppets or imaginary forces. Tolman assumes that such a gradient would be learned in our culture and would constitute then one item in the belief-value matrix.

To carry further with this system, Tolman points out that it would be necessary to provide operational definitions for all the following terms:

[9] E.g., Sears (1951).

VARIABLES TO BE OPERATIONALLY DEFINED [10]

Need Systems

a. List of needs
b. Magnitude of a given need at a given moment

Belief-Value Matrices

c. The magnitude of the gratification and deprivation "values" of the given matrix at a given time.
d. The shape of the cathexis belief attaching the various types of goal object (arrayed along a given generalized dimension) to the gratification end of a given matrix.[11]
e. The shape of the means-end belief attaching types of means object (arrayed along a given generalization dimension) to a given type of goal object or subgoal object.

Behavior Spaces

f. Perceived qualities, distances, and directions in the behavior space.
g. The strength of a need-push.
h. The strength of a positive or negative valence.
i. The strength and direction of a field force.
j. The identification of a locomotion.

It is evident enough from the unfinished business implied in this list that, whatever new directions are proposed for the model, the new model is not yet ready for detailed critical appraisal.

SIGN LEARNING

Sign Learning as an Alternative to Response Learning

Stimulus-response theories, while stated with different degrees of sophistication, imply that the organism is goaded along a path by internal and external stimuli, learning the correct movement sequences so that they are released under appropriate conditions of drive and environmental stimulation. The alternative possibility is that the learner is following signs to a goal, is learning his way about, is following a sort of map—in other words, is learning not movements but meanings. This is the contention of Tolman's theory of sign learning. The organism learns sign-significate relations; it learns a behavior route, not a movement pattern. Many learning situations do not permit a clear distinction between

[10] The list is reproduced verbatim from Tolman (1951b), page 334.

[11] A *cathexis belief* is a preference or selective appetite whereby one goal object is valued above another as a means of obtaining gratification. The geometrical concept ("shape of cathexis belief") refers to some sort of scaling of a series of possible goal-objects (e.g., foods) on a preference dimension, some of them being closer together some farther apart. (Tolman, 1951b, pages 337–338.)

these two possibilities. If there is a single path with food at the end and the organism runs faster at each opportunity, there is no way of telling whether his responses are being stamped in by reinforcement or whether he is guided by his immanent purposes and cognitions.

Because both stimulus-response and sign learning so often predict the same behavioral outcome, it is necessary to design special experiments in which it is possible to favor one theory over the other. Three situations give strong support to the sign-learning alternative. These are experiments on reward expectancy, on place learning, and on latent learning.

1. *Reward expectancy.* One of the earliest and most striking observations on reward expectancy was that of Tinklepaugh (1928). In his experiment, food was placed under one of two containers while the monkey was looking but prevented from immediate access to the cans and food. Later the monkey was permitted to choose between the containers and showed skill in choosing correctly. The behavior which is pertinent here occurred when, after a banana had been hidden under one of the cups, the experimenter substituted for it a lettuce leaf (a less preferred food). The monkey rejected the lettuce leaf and engaged in definite searching behavior. Somewhat the same sort of behavior was found by Elliott (1928) when the food in the goal-box of a rat maze experiment was changed from bran mash to sunflower seed. More systematic experiments have been carried out since with chimpanzees.[12] There is little doubt that animals have some sort of precognition or expectancy of specific goal objects. Under those circumstances, other goal-objects produce signs of behavior disruption. Such behavior means that the sign-learning theory is appropriate; it does not, of course, mean that other theories may not attempt to deduce the behavior from other principles.

2. *Place learning.* Experiments on place learning are designed to show that the learner is not moving from start to goal according to a fixed sequence of movements, such as would be predicted from reinforcement theories, but is capable of behavior which is varied appropriately to changed conditions, as though he "knows" where the goal is. There are three subtypes of these experiments.

The first subtype of the place-learning alternative to response learning leaves the form of the path intact but interferes with the movement sequences in getting from start to goal. In one experiment, rats that had learned to run a maze straight on, after surgically produced cerebellar

[12] Cowles and Nissen (1937).

damage were unable to run the maze except in circles, but even so were able to run without error.[13] They could not have been running off the earlier learned sequences of kinesthetic habits. In another, rats were able to demonstrate what they had learned by swimming the correct path after having been trained in wading it.[14]

The second subtype of place-learning experiment sets a movement habit against a spatial habit and determines which is the more readily learned. Tolman and his collaborators[15] arranged an elevated maze in the form of a cross, as shown in Figure 25. The response-learning group was started in random alternation from either S_1 or S_2, always finding food by turning to the right. That is, food was at F_1 when the start was

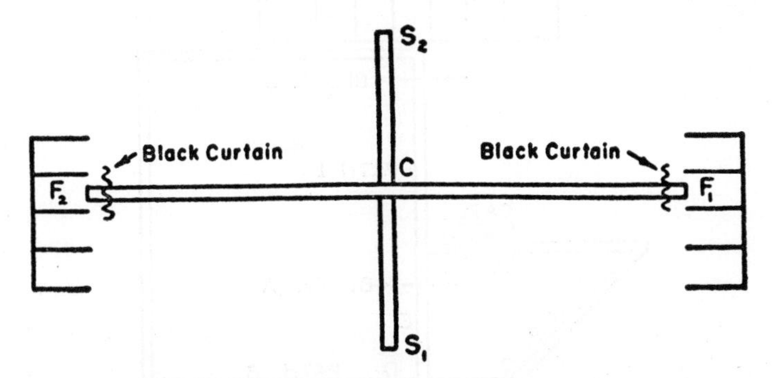

FIGURE 25. Maze used to test the relative ease of learning either a response which brings reward or the place at which reward is found. By starting irregularly at S_1 and S_2, but finding reward at the same food box each time, one group of rats turns now to the right, now to the left, to find food always at the same location. These are the place learners. By starting at either S_1 or S_2, but always finding food as a result of turning the same way (right or left), another group is taught always to make the same response, but to find food at different places, depending upon the starting point. Place learning, under the conditions of the experiment, is found to be easier than response learning. From Tolman, Ritchie, and Kalish (1946), page 223.

S_1 and at F_2 when the start was S_2. The place-learning group, by contrast, always went to the same place for food. This meant that if running to F_1, a right turn would be required when starting from S_1 and a left turn when starting from S_2. The place-learning group was much the more successful. The eight rats of the place-learning group all learned within 8 trials, so that the next 10 trials were without error. None of the eight rats of the response-learning group learned this quickly, and five of them did not reach the criterion in 72 trials. Under the circumstances of an

13 Lashley and Ball (1929).
14 Macfarlane (1930).
15 Tolman, Ritchie, and Kalish (1946) (1947).

elevated maze with many extra-maze cues, it is clearly demonstrated that place learning is simpler than response learning.[16]

The third subtype of place-learning experiment involves the use of alternative paths when a practiced path is blocked. An early form of the blocked-path experiment is that of Tolman and Honzik (1932a) which is said to demonstrate inferential expectation, or insight. The main features of the arrangement are as follows. There are three paths (1, 2, and 3),

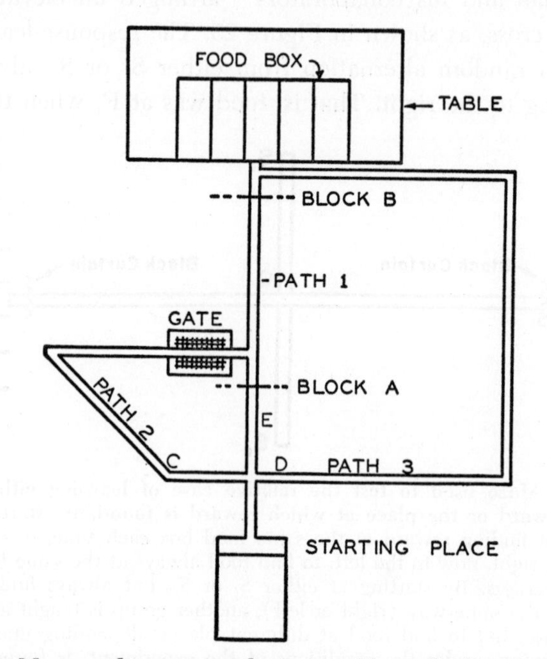

FIGURE 26. Maze used to test insight in rats. The paths become established as a hierarchy according to length, Path 1 preferred to Path 2, Path 2 to Path 3. If Path 1 is closed by Block A, the rats run by Path 2. If Path 1 is closed by Block B, the rats run by Path 3 if they have "insight" that the barrier closes Path 2 as well as Path 1. From Honzik and Tolman (1930a), page 223.

in that order of length from shortest to longest, and hence in that order of preference (Figure 26). In preliminary training, when path 1 was blocked, a preference was established between paths 2 and 3 for the shorter of these paths. Only when path 2 was blocked also, did they run by path 3. We may somewhat oversimplify by saying that a familiarity with all paths and a preference for them in the order 1, 2, 3 was estab-

[16] The importance of the extra-maze cues has been demonstrated by Blodgett and McCutchan (1947) (1948), who have other criticisms of the experiment cited. See the experimental reply, Ritchie, Aeschliman, and Peirce (1950). For other criticisms of space-learning experiments see Gentry, Brown, and Kaplan (1947).

lished in preliminary training. An important feature of the maze design, crucial for the test, was that paths 1 and 2 had a common segment leading to the goal. Previously the block in path 1 had been placed before this common path; then the rat, after backing up from the block, ran to path 2. Now in the test the block was placed farther along path 1, so that it fell in the common path. Would the rat in backing out again run by the second preference, path 2, and be frustrated, or would it "see" that path 2 was also blocked? What the rats did, predominantly, was to avoid path 2, and to take the path ordinarily least preferred, the long path 3, but the only one open. Again the hypothesis is supported that the rat acted in accordance with some sort of "map" of the situation, and not according to blind habit, or according to the automatic running off of habits in hierarchical order.[17]

One of the several later experiments using blocked paths also involved rotation of the starting table through 180° on test trials, as illustrated in Figure 27.[18] The original T-maze used in training is diagrammed at the left. From the table-top A the F_1 rats learned to turn left, in the direction of the light L_1. They were rewarded by food at the end of the run, in the place signallized by the light. The F_2 rats learned to turn right, in the direction of the light L_2. The figure on the right shows how the table was moved from the test trials. It was not only moved, but provided with 10 radiating paths, in addition to the original straight-ahead path, now blocked. You would predict from a naive place-theory that the rats, knowing their way around, would take that path leading most directly toward the light where they had been fed. With rare exceptions they failed to choose the dircct path. Thcy did, however, show a direction reversal, the F_1 rats now predominantly turning right rather than left, the F_2 rats turning left rather than right. They responded to the rotation of the starting point all right, but they tended to choose the extreme paths running most directly toward the appropriate wall rather than directly to the place where they had been fed. While the results thus lend some support to a directional-orientation theory, they show that a rat's "cognitive map" (if it exists) does not correspond in any simple or direct manner to the rat's experienced spatial reality.

3. *Latent Learning.* In addition to the experiments on reward ex-

[17] The Tolman and Honzik experiment has been criticized by other experimenters who have shown that the results, while reproducible, are easily disturbed by the manipulation of experimental variables such as alley width which would not be expected to make insight impossible. See Evans (1936), Harsh (1937), Keller and Hill (1936), Kuo (1937).

[18] Ritchie (1948).

pectancy and on space learning, a third variety of experiment bears importantly on sign learning. These are the latent-learning experiments to be described more fully later in this chapter. The latent-learning experiments show that an animal can learn by exploring the maze, without food reward, so that, when reward is later introduced, performance is better than that of rats without this exposure, and sometimes as good as that of rats with many previously rewarded trials. The "latent learning" consists of knowledge of the maze, not revealed in choice of the

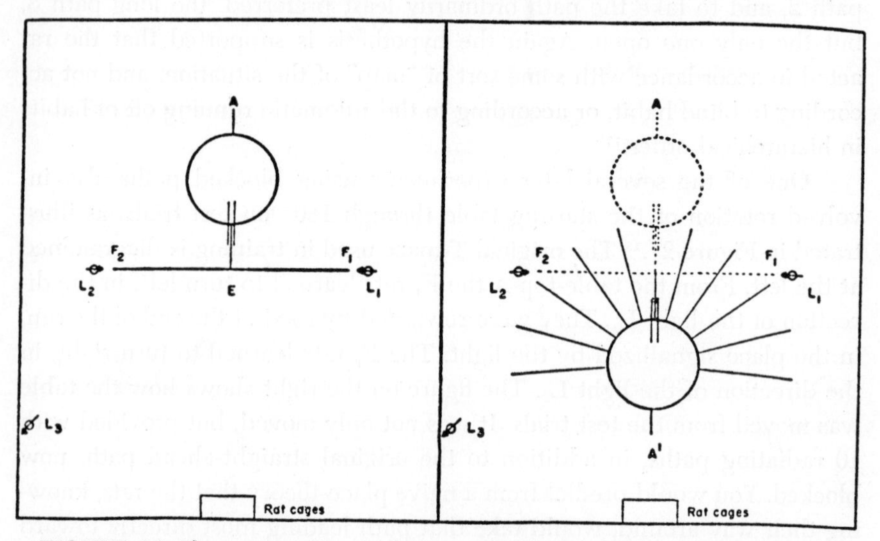

FIGURE 27. Place orientation in the rat. The dotted figure on the right shows the T-maze used in training, the solid figure the rotated maze, with radiating paths, as used in testing. In testing, the direct path from the table-top to the original choice-point was blocked. After Ritchie (1948), page 664.

shortest path from entrance to exit until the rat is motivated to make that choice. The experiments, beginning with those of Blodgett (1929), have been interpreted as critical of reinforcement explanations of learning, although, as we have seen, the issue has been somewhat dulled by changes in Hull's interpretation of reinforcement.

In his own summarization of the experimental work supporting his theory, Tolman (1948b) lists two additional varieties as significant: the experiments on "hypotheses" in rats,[19] and the experiments on vicarious trial and error (VTE).[20] The experiments on hypotheses led to the conclusion that in a four-choice maze the animals adopted systematic modes

[19] Krechevsky (1932a).

[20] Muenzinger (1938), Tolman (1939), Geier, Levin, and Tolman (1941), Jackson (1943).

of solution, such a choice being somewhat tentative, so that one mode would be rejected for another. These experiments furnished the background for a controversy over "continuity" and "discontinuity" in discrimination learning, the hypothesis experiments furnishing support for the "discontinuity" interpretation.[21] Vicarious trial and error refers to the vacillation at a choice-point before the animal is "committed" to one or the other choice. This active comparing of stimuli appears to Tolman to support his viewpoint that perceptual or cognitive processes are prominent in controlling behavior at a choice point.

Expectancy versus Habit

Can a more precise formulation be made of the sign-learning theory —the theory to which the results of all of these experiments are said to conform? It has sometimes been characterized as a theory of "what leads to what," a theory of signs, significates, and behavior routes. There are really two central problems in a theory of this kind: first, how is the expectation acquired that a given sign will lead to its significate, and, second, how is this expectation translated into action? We begin with the problem of acquiring the expectation.

The theory is that with repeated experience of a sequence of events leading to a goal the probability is discriminated that the given behavior will eventuate in the expected end result. The result (for behavior) is faster running and blind-alley elimination, exactly as if a habit were being strengthened by reward. Hence some ingenuity is required to isolate circumstances in which the expectancy interpretation is more appropriate than the habit-strengthening one. While the foregoing account of experiments gives qualitative support to a cognitive interpretation of learning, if expectancies conform to probabilities, a more quantitative approach should be possible. In a very stimulating paper Tolman and Brunswik (1935) proposed that the causal texture of the environment is not such as to permit firm expectations but that predictions must often be made on the basis of probabilities. In an experimental test of the proposal, Brunswik (1939) presented his rats with such a contingent environment, in which food might sometimes be found on the right, sometimes on the left. He found that there was some measure of agreement between the choices of the rat and the probability that food would be where he went for it.

An important supplementary finding in Brunswik's experiment is that the nature of the goal provides *an emphasis* that makes a great dif-

[21] For a further discussion of this issue, see Chapter 12.

ference in the behavioral response to the discriminated probability. He found, for example, that rats rewarded on one side of a T-maze 100 per cent of their runs to that side, and on the other side in 50 per cent of their runs to that side, showed a preference for the two sides in roughly the 2:1 ratio of these reward schedules. This preference was tested during the last eight trials of training. During these trials, the rats ran to the 100 per cent rewarded side in 72 per cent of the runs, and to the 50 per cent rewarded side in 28 per cent of the runs. If, however, the partial reward side was also "dangerous" on half the trials (a shock being used instead of non-reward), this cancelled the effect of the intermittent reward, and learning was equivalent to that in a conventional T-maze experiment in which one side only was rewarded. This, and related results, led Brunswik to state:

> Discrimination of probabilities tends to increase with the rate of the probability of *emphasis* on the two sides of the probability discrimination problem.[22]

Common experience amply justifies this supplementation to a simple probability theory. One might walk into a store to try to make an unusual purchase even though the probability was only 1:10 that the store carried the merchandise sought. But one would not buy a ticket on an airline where the probability of a crash was 1:10. Discriminated probabilities are *weighted* before they emerge in action.

In order to compare an expectancy theory with a reinforcement theory, Humphreys performed several experiments of the conditioned-response type. In human eyelid conditioning, it had already been shown that conditioned discrimination was more rapid when subjects knew which stimulus of a pair was to be positive, which negative, than when the probabilities had to be established through experience with the stimuli.[23] The conjecture that the subjects were responding according to their expectations was a plausible one. Humphreys went on to show that random alternation of reinforcement and non-reinforcement led not only to as much conditioning as reinforcement every trial, but was followed also by greater resistance to extinction.[24] During extinction, responses increased in frequency at first, and then fell off. This would be anticipated on an expectancy theory because the likelihood of reinforcement was great after a non-reinforcement during the body of the experiment, and greater still after two non-reinforcements because there were never more than two successive non-reinforcements during the

[22] Brunswik (1939), page 185.
[23] Hilgard, R. K. Campbell, and W. N. Sears (1938).
[24] Humphreys (1939a).

training sessions. But even after this high point, extinction was gradual. Humphreys conjectured that a shift from intermittent reinforcement to uniform non-reinforcement must have led with difficulty to the hypothesis of uniform non-reinforcement. Because the experiment was done with human subjects, a direct test was possible on the verbal level, and Humphreys designed and carried out a simple experiment which confirmed his conjecture.[25]

For the study of verbal expectations, two lights were arranged on a board. When one of these lights was turned on, the subject was asked to guess whether or not it would be followed by the other light. Half the subjects were "trained" with the second light invariably following the first. They came gradually to guess in a high percentage of the cases that the first light would be followed by the second, in agreement with their experience. The other half had the second light turned on only in random alternation, so that half the time it did not appear. They guessed at chance level. Within the conditioning experiment, the intermittent-reinforcement group performed like the group uniformly reinforced; but in the verbal experiment, the groups behaved entirely unlike. Does this difference not invalidate the comparison? On the contrary, it is an essential part of it, because it is necessary to distinguish between performance and expectation. In the conditioning experiment, uncertainty leads to conditioned responses as well as certainty because it is a "danger" situation; blinking is as easy as refraining from blinking, and there is no penalty for an "erroneous" response, that is, for blinking to the conditioned stimulus alone. In the verbal experiment, response is more nearly representative of "pure" expectation, because a false guess is subjectively interpreted as a mistake in a way in which a false conditioned response is not.

The crucial portion of the experiment is that in which extinction is simulated, that is, in which the first light is never again followed by the second. Humphreys' results are plotted in Figure 28. It is seen that the group which had been trained on the every-trial "reinforcement" quickly developed the hypothesis of uniform non-reinforcement, and ceased to expect the second light. The group trained with intermittent "reinforcement" showed the rise in expectation which the theory demands, and the slow acceptance of the hypothesis that there would be no more second lights.[26]

[25] Humphreys (1939b).

[26] The results of intermittent reinforcement, both within conditioning experiments and within verbal experiments, have proved to be of considerable theoretical interest,

A provisional expectancy is an hypothesis. When a situation is not yet structured so that path-goal relationships become clear, behavior in relationship to the situation may either be "random" or "systematic." If it is systematic, it may be said to accord with an hypothesis. Score averages from groups of animals tend to conceal the differences between chance approaches and more orderly approaches, because one animal's responses cancel another's unless they happen to correspond to the

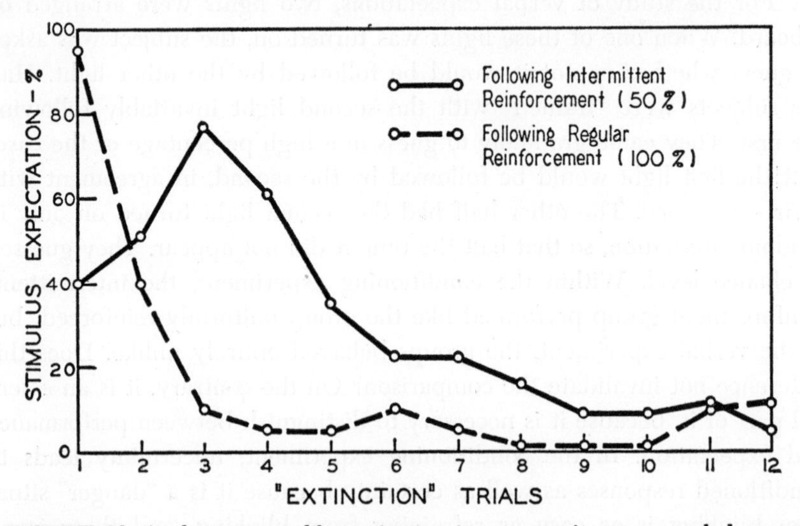

FIGURE 28. A phenomenon like extinction in an experiment on verbal expectations. Prior to yielding the data in this figure, one group had regularly experienced a second light following a signal light, and had developed the expectation that a second light would regularly follow. This condition simulates 100 per cent reinforcement in a conditioning situation. For the second group, the signal light had been followed by the "expected" light only half the time. This condition is like 50 per cent reinforcement in conditioning, and leads to uncertainty as to whether or not the signal will be followed by a second light. Beginning with the trials shown in the figure, the signal light was never followed by the second light, thus simulating extinction. What is recorded is the per cent of subjects guessing on each trial that the second light would occur. Following regular reinforcement the change to the expectation of regular non-reinforcement occurs more readily than following intermittent reinforcement. After Humphreys (1939b).

experimenter's plan as to what will be counted correct. By studying the presolution behavior of individual animals, systematic attempts at solution can often be discovered, solutions of the order: "turn right," "alternate," "go to the dark." These are not mere fixed preferences, because after one pattern has been used for a while, the animal learner may shift

and the experimental literature is now sizable. For a useful summary, see Jenkins and Stanley (1950). On verbal experiments similar to Humphreys', see Grant, Hake, and Hornseth (1951), Hake, Grant, and Hornseth (1951).

to another one. Krech named such systematic attempts at solution "hypotheses," and studied them under a number of conditions.[27]

The full-fledged conception of expectancy thus includes at least the following aspects: (1) The organism brings to a problematic situation various systematic modes of attack, based largely on prior experiences. (2) The cognitive field is provisionally organized according to the hypotheses of the learner, the hypotheses which survive being those which best correspond with reality, that is, with the causal texture of the environment. These hypotheses or expectancies are confirmed by successes in goal achievement. (3) A clearly established cognitive structure is available for use under altered conditions, as when a frequently used path is blocked.[28]

Confirmation versus Reinforcement

Because Tolman has been at such pains to protest against the law of effect and the principle of reinforcement as essential to learning, it is in order to inquire what role he assigns motivation in learning.

One role assigned to motivation is in relation to performance. Learning is *used* when drives are active. When drives are aroused, a state of tension ensues, leading to demands for goal-objects.[29] These tensions lead to activity, guided by the expectancies or cognitive structures available. In this role, then, motivation is not really a factor in learning at all. It is related to performance, not to acquisition. Because this role of motivation is made much of in the criticisms of reinforcement theories, the impression is given that learning, the acquiring of cognitive structures, is independent of motivation. This is not true in fact, nor is it true in Tolman's theory.

The second role of motivation is in the acquisition of cognitive structures. In one of the experiments critical of the law of effect, the suggestion was made that what appeared to be the principle of effect might better be considered the influence of *emphasis*.[30] That is, motivation determines which features of the environment shall interest the learner, and those to which he pays attention. Such factors are influential in perceptual acquisitions, which are the genuine substance of place learning. Causal sequences of the environment are not all spatial. Some

[27] Krechevsky (1932a) (1932b) (1933a) (1933b).

[28] We postpone until Chapter 12 consideration of the attempts of others to systematize expectancy theory.

[29] The parallel may be noted with Hull's interpretation of drive as activating habit strength into reaction potential.

[30] Tolman, Hall, and Bretnall (1932).

are temporal; some are logical or systematic or arbitrary. The goal-object, by its presence or absence, verifies or refutes hypotheses. Hence the goal-object is essential for the establishment of some features of cognitive structure. Latent learning, which dramatizes a relatively unmotivated, incidental type of learning, is an extreme instance of the relationship of goal-behavior to learning and is probably not a typical case.

The importance of something like emphasis is well brought out in the series of experiments by Muenzinger and his associates,[31] in which punishment or obstacles to be overcome, even on the side of the correct choice, aid learning. Whether or not punishment will be an aid to learning thus depends upon what influence it has on the cognitions of the learner. It may be helpful as an emphasizer or harmful as a distractor.

The principle in Tolman's system that most nearly replaces reinforcement is the principle of *confirmation.* If an expectancy is confirmed, its probability value is increased; if an expectancy is not confirmed, its probability value is decreased (i.e., it undergoes extinction). Tolman distinguishes between confirmation and reinforcement in a passage describing the building up of preferences for one restaurant over another:

> Such learning takes place, I believe, not primarily through reinforcement in the Hullian sense but merely by the *repeated "confirming"* experiences of finding what restaurants lead to what foods by what costs and with what degrees of gratification.[32]

The regulatory role of reward is not very different in Hull's system from this role in Tolman's, though the interpretations differ. According to Tolman, the learner acquires knowledge of a means-end relationship; according to reinforcement theory, he learns behavior which is followed by reward. In any case, it would be most misleading to interpret Tolman's position as if reward influenced performance only, and not learning. All that he insists upon is that learning and performance cannot be equated, and the role of motivation in learning differs in some respects from its role in performance. This conclusion, originally proposed by Lashley (1929), can scarcely be doubted.

VARIETIES OF LEARNING AND THEIR LAWS

The 1932 Version

Learning theorists commonly select one kind of learning problem or situation as typical and then proceed to develop a theory appropriate to this reference situation. Having constructed a set of principles in this

[31] Muenzinger and others, 1934–1952.
[32] Tolman (1952b), page 396.

way, they attempt to show by a logical process that other kinds of learning are really at base like the typical one, and hence explicable in the same terms. Recognizing this tendency, Tolman selected for review three kinds of learning experiments, with their three corresponding doctrines. These were conditioned-reflex learning (Pavlov), trial-and-error learning (Thorndike), and inventive learning (Köhler). He then gave a sign-gestalt interpretation of each of the three kinds of learning as alternative to the usual theory associated with each. He found it useful to preserve the typical experiments, which represent a kind of hierarchy from stupidity to intelligence. The laws applicable to the more stupid situations have to be supplemented by additional laws for the higher forms of learning.

In the 1932 version there are three groups of laws: capacity laws, laws relative to the nature of the material, and laws relative to the manner of presentation.

1. *Capacity laws.* Only organisms can learn. It is evident, therefore, that what the organism can learn must depend on what kind of an organism it is. That is the reason for capacity laws.

The list of capacity laws is as follows: [33]

a. Formal means-end-capacities
b. Discriminating and manipulating capacities
c. Retentivity
d. Means-end-capacities needed for alternative routes, detours, etc.
e. Ideational capacities
f. Creative instability

In order to learn conditioned reflexes, the learner must have the necessary capacities to form and act in accordance with "sign-gestalt-expectations." That is, the conditioned stimulus serves as a sign that the unconditioned stimulus is about to appear and the conditioned behavior is appropriate to the sign. This capacity is named a "means-end-capacity." In his later writings Tolman has dropped a number of the hyphenated terms which made his book clear, entertaining, but also somewhat forbidding. In the list of laws which we have given above, his terms have been freely paraphrased to make for easier reading, although there may be some loss involved. In addition to the general capacity for sign learning, conditioning requires special capacities for discriminating and manipulating features of the environment. Finally retentivity is implied, if the results of earlier conditioning trials are to influence later ones. Only capacity laws *a*, *b*, and *c* apply to conditioning.

The capacities needed for trial-and-error learning are the same as

[33] Tolman (1932b), pages 376–377.

those required for conditioning, except that additional means-end-capacities are needed because more alternatives are open to the learner. The field relationships of alternate routes, detours, final common paths, are involved. Additional capacities of ideational sort, permitting comparison of alternatives (a mental "running-back-and-forth"), are probably helpful in trial-and-error learning.

Inventive learning requires all the capacities of the other varieties of learning plus *creative instability.* This is a capacity to break out into new lines of activity which have never occurred to the learner before.

The need for capacity laws seems evident enough, once they are proposed, though they have been neglected in most learning theories. Even Thorndike, strongly identified with the study of individual differences, neglects capacity laws in his learning theory. Such a statement as "Any response of which the organism is capable can become attached to any stimulus to which it is sensitive" [34] implies only sensitivity capacity and response capacity, and neglects any capacity to establish relations between them. It would be grossly unfair to say that Thorndike did not recognize differences in learning ability, but it is true that he slighted the different kinds of capacities needed for different kinds of learning, because all learning was merely the forming of bonds. Hull, who also in one of his earlier research interests contributed to the psychology of individual differences,[35] only late in his career began to consider individuality as something to enter into his learning theory.[36]

2. *Laws relating to the nature of the material.* In Tolman's discussion of these topics, he calls attention to certain "gestalt-inducing-conditions" and suggests that they are of the sorts emphasized in gestalt studies of perception.

The list follows: [37]

a. Togetherness
b. Fusibility
c. Other gestalt-like laws
d. Interrelations among the spatial, temporal and other characters of the alternatives
e. Characters in the material favoring new closures and expansions of the field

In relation to conditioned-reflex learning, these laws suggest that there must be a "togetherness" of essential signs and their means-end-relationship to the thing signified. Tolman states that this is about what

[34] Thorndike (1913b), page 15.
[35] Hull (1928).
[36] Hull (1945).
[37] Tolman (1932b), pages 378–385.

Thorndike has called "belongingness." Tolman adds a somewhat similar law of fusibility of sign, significate, and signified means-end-relationship by which he means a certain naturalness about the situation which makes it easier to form a gestalt of the whole. He provides in a third law for the possibility of new discoveries. He adds one law (*d*) for trial-and-error learning and one for inventive learning (*e*), to suggest that some arrangements must be easier than others. He points to Köhler's observation that the ape could learn to use the stick more easily to rake in the food if the stick and food were perceived together.

These laws show great catholicity, but there is no ordering principle among them. "Spatial, temporal, and other" can scarcely be said to arrange things dimensionally. They do make a definite bow to the important fact that perceptual principles must be understood if the relative ease or difficulty of problematic situations is to be made comprehensible.

3. *Laws relative to the manner of presentation.* These are the laws inherited largely from association psychology, the ones for which abundant evidence can be found recorded in McGeoch and Irion's book (1952). The list is as follows: [38]

a. Frequency, recency
b. Revival after extinction, primacy, distributed repetition, etc.
c. Motivation
d. Not "effect" but "emphasis"
e. Temporal orders and sequences in the presentation of alternatives
f. Temporal relations between the presentation of certain of the already given alternatives and the true solution

Of these, the first four belong to conditioned-reflex learning, the first five to trial-and-error learning, and all six to inventive learning.

The principles of frequency and recency are accepted in the following form: "The more frequently and more recently the actual sequence of sign, means-end-relation and significate have been presented, the stronger, other things being equal, this resulting sign-gestalt will tend to be." [39] That is, only in a situation favorable to sign-gestalt formation will frequency be effective. The other laws provide opportunity again to raise the question of the law of effect, and to make some observations descriptive of favorable conditions in trial-and-error and multiple-choice experiments.

As a set, the laws are rather disappointing. They serve as a useful reminder of the main tenets of the point of view and of its criticisms of prevailing doctrines. They leave much to be asked for on the positive

[38] Tolman (1932b), pages 385–389.
[39] Tolman (1932b), page 386.

side in their lack of sufficient precision of statement so that they can be called true or false.

Leaving the laws in this form makes everything a matter of correlations between situation and behavior and does not get at the formal problem of rigorous definition and measurement of intervening variables. This lack has not yet been made up, in spite of later reworkings of the list of laws.

The 1949 Version

New sets of laws have been proposed by Tolman from time to time.[40] The "laws" do not have the centrality within his system that Hull's postulates have within his, so the revision of the list of laws requires little reinterpretation of earlier experimentation. For purposes of understanding the restatement of the theory, however, it is useful to review one of these later revisions. The one selected for review appeared 17 years after the first.[41]

In this later paper, Tolman distinguished six "types of connections or relations" that get learned, and then proceeded to indicate what was known about the "laws" applying to each.

1. *Cathexes.* Tolman borrowed the word "cathexis" (plural, cathexes) from psychoanalytic theory, where it refers metaphorically to the energy charge with which an activity is invested. He gives it a related but more restricted meaning, almost equivalent to Lewin's valence. A cathexis is an acquired relationship between a drive and an object. If a hungry child wants a banana, you know that the child has a learned cathexis between its hunger drive and a banana as a preferred goal-object. This is a positive cathexis, for the child is led to seek bananas. A negative cathexis works the other way. If a burned child fears a hot stove his fear is connected, as a negative cathexis, to the stove, and the cathexis is negative because he shuns the stove.

Tolman believes that drive reduction (reinforcement) is probably valid as an explanation for the acquiring of cathexes, but he believes we need more experimental evidence.

Both positive and negative cathexes, he believes, are very resistant to forgetting.

2. *Equivalence beliefs.* This is Tolman's substitute for secondary reinforcement, whereby an organism reacts to a subgoal (or a subdisturbance, in the case of negative cathexes), as it would in the presence of

[40] Tolman (1934) (1937) (1949a).
[41] Tolman (1949a).

the goal or actual disturbance. In social behavior, and especially in the psychological clinic, we see many evidences of faulty equivalence beliefs. These are often engendered by traumatic experiences. Hence Tolman concludes that the reinforcement principle is valid for equivalence beliefs as for cathexes, but it needs to be supplemented by an awareness of the importance of traumatic experience.

3. *Field expectancies.* These are the rechristened sign-gestalt-expectations of the earlier system. They permit the organism to take shortcuts, roundabout routes, and make possible latent learning. Tolman reasserts his contention that reinforcement per se is not valid in the explanation of field expectancies, although he acknowledges the importance of motivation.

> The presence of reinforcement in a particular locus makes the locus a goal which determines what performance will take place but it does not stamp in S-R connections though it probably does give a special vividness to that locus in the total field expectancy.[42]

Although we know little at present about laws of the formation of field expectancies, when we do work them out we shall have to take into account perceptual sensitivity, memory, and inference abilities.

The forgetting of field expectancies is probably more rapid than the forgetting of cathexes and equivalence beliefs. Such forgetting, Tolman believes, probably follows the sorts of laws the gestalt psychologists have uncovered.

4. *Field-cognition modes.* These modes are of higher order than the field expectancies. A field-cognition mode makes a given expectancy-formation possible. The mode is based in part upon innate capacities and in part on previously established field expectancies. Hence a field-cognition mode represents a disposition or readiness to acquire field expectancies of one of three varieties: perceptual, memorial, or inferential.

Tolman has no laws to suggest. Such laws will arise out of at present non-existent types of transfer experiment.

5. *Drive discriminations.* Tolman here refers to experiments such as those of Hull (1933) and Leeper (1935), in which the animal learned to go one way when hungry, another way when thirsty. Tolman has no laws to suggest.

6. *Motor patterns.* Because his behaviorism is not of the stimulus-response variety, Tolman recognizes that he needs some special principles governing the acquisition of motor patterns. For these, Tolman was in 1949 prepared to accept Guthrie's simple conditioning explanation.

[42] Tolman (1949a), page 151.

It is evident that these laws have not moved toward precision over the initial set. Tolman states his own estimate of what he has done here:

> And, although, as usual, I have been merely programmatic and have not attempted to set up, at this date, any precise system of postulates and deduced theorems, I *have* made some specific suggestions as to some of the conditions and laws for the acquisition, de-acquisition, and forgetting of these relationships.[43]

While Tolman has made very thoughtful observations on learning, and has been responsible for much original experimentation, he has not proposed a system clearly enough defined so that successive approximations succeeded in making it more exact and testable. We find, in this statement of six kinds of learned relationships, two explained by reinforcement (Hull, Skinner), one explained by simple conditioning (Guthrie), and three not explained at all. This is characteristic of Tolman's role. In addition to making concessions to other interpretations, he has consistently pointed out relationships difficult for stimulus-response theorists to explain, without himself being able to offer much in the way of detailed explanation for these discovered relationships.

EXPERIMENTS ON LATENT LEARNING

Reinforcement theory proposes that habits are strengthened by reinforcement; sign-learning theory says that expectancies become established, and that performance is secondarily correlated with expectancy. Experiments on latent learning have been used all along to argue against reinforcement as an essential principle of learning.[44] The arguments against reinforcement theory had more cogency before Hull modified his theory to minimize the amount of necessary reinforcement and to emphasize the factors activating habit into performance. All that can be said with confidence, now that Hull has quoted the original latent-learning experiments as evidence in support of his predictions, is that the *details* of latent-learning experiments place reinforcement theory under strain. But it is equally true that the details of latent-learning experiments likewise place cognitive theories under strain, for an adequate theory (whether a reinforcement theory or a sign-learning theory) has to account for *both* the positive *and* the negative results with which the literature abounds. Because the latent-learning experiment has proved such a fertile area for testing theories, it is worth examining the evidence in some detail.

[43] Tolman (1949a), page 154.
[44] E.g., Tolman (1938b); Thistlethwaite (1951b).

Tolman and Honzik's Experiment

Following up the work started by Blodgett (1929), Tolman and Honzik (1930b) studied the effect of introduction of reward in a rat-maze experiment after the animals had run several days without food. The control group, fed each day in the maze, reduced their error and time scores much more rapidly than the non-fed group, but when food was introduced for the latter group, error scores and time scores abruptly became alike for both groups. Thus the non-fed group had apparently profited as much by its earlier trials as the fed group. Since this profiting did not show in performance, the learning taking place is said to be "latent." The results for error elimination are shown in Figure 29.

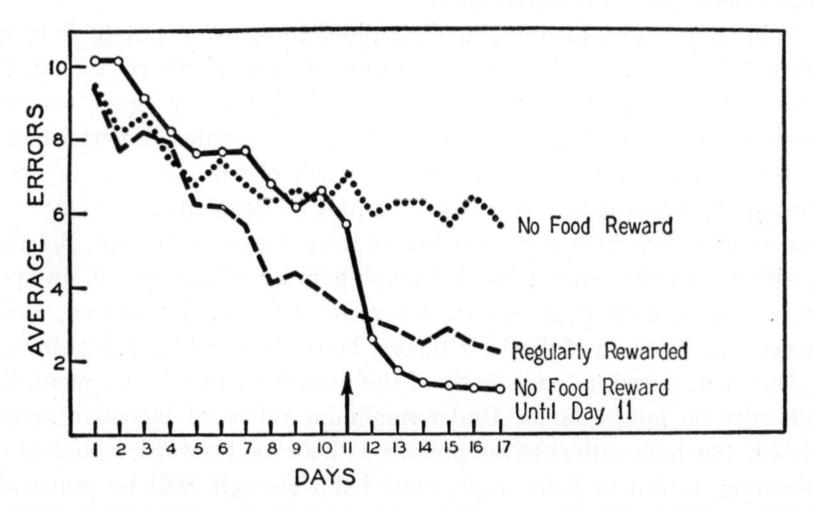

FIGURE 29. Evidence for latent learning in the maze. With no food reward there is some reduction in errors, but not as great a reduction as with regular food reward. Despite the higher error scores prior to the introduction of food, the group rewarded only from the 11th trial immediately begins to do as well as the group that had been regularly rewarded. The interpretation is that some learning went on within the first 10 trials which did not show in performance until the food incentive activated it. After Tolman and Honzik (1930b).

There were three groups: two control groups, one rewarded throughout, the other non-rewarded throughout, and the experimental group, non-rewarded until the eleventh trial. On the twelfth day, the experimental group, having been fed but once in the maze, made as few errors as the group which had received food in the maze each of the preceding days.

There are several comments to be made on this situation, in its bearing on other theories as well as Tolman's. The maze used was a 14-unit one of multiple-T type,[45] arranged with doors between each unit to prevent retracing. The rat without food at the end still progressed through the maze, so that, according to such a theory as Guthrie's, learning conditions were ideal. The rat had no opportunity to unlearn what it last did in each segment, which was of course to go through the door to the next one. The results are critical of Guthrie's theory not because the rat shows latent learning but because it does not show enough learning when there is no food at the end of the maze. (It is to be recalled that the Guthrie and Horton cats often did not eat when they left the problem-box; their behavior was said to be fixed because they left the box.) The Guthrie explanation is not sufficient, because the fed rats learned much better than the unfed ones.

Reinforcement theories, in their older form, were put to it to explain latent learning. In the older forms of "law of effect" theory, the presumption was that reinforcement worked directly upon response strength, so that all that was learned should be revealed in performance. Reinforcement theorists usually made much of the decrease in errors during non-rewarded trials in latent-learning experiments as evidence that *some* reinforcement was present before reward was introduced. But they could really only account for *that much* gain by reinforcement, any previously concealed gain, shown when reward was introduced, being unaccounted for. In Hull's later theory, however, in which habit strength ($_SH_R$) is acquired independently of the magnitude of reinforcement, this difficulty no longer holds. Under minimum values of incentive magnitude K (such incentives as are present without food reward, including exploration, return to home cage, etc.) habit strength will be practically "latent," to be revealed in reaction potential when large values of K′ are created by introducing the food reward.

Tolman's explanation is that the non-reward situation was a good one for learning the spatial relations of the maze. Every unit had one dead end and another end with a door. The last thing done in each case was to go through the door. Recency (which is accepted as favoring sign-gestalts) would strengthen the cognition that the door was the way from one segment to the next, though under non-reward conditions there were no reasons for the rat to show what it "knew." The substitution of the food at the end of the maze, a highly demanded goal-object, led the rat to use its cognitive map, to take the turns which led from one unit to the next. Hence the sudden reduction in errors. That the group with

[45] Stone and Nyswander (1927).

late introduction of reward had a tendency to do even better than the regularly rewarded group may conceivably have been due to a more thorough exploration of the maze in the early trials by the non-rewarded group, with consequent better orientation when finally running toward the goal.

Five Varieties of Latent-Learning Experiment and Their Results

An upsurge of interest in latent learning led to many experimental reports, of which 48 have been classified by MacCorquodale and Meehl into five categories.[46] Their classification is followed here, as well as their scoring of the experiments as yielding positive or negative results.

1. *Unrewarded trials with later introduction of relevant reward.* This is the type of experiment that Blodgett performed and Tolman and Honzik followed up. Of nine studies cited, seven are interpreted as positive, two as negative.[47]

2. *Free exploration followed by relevant reward.* The animal is permitted to run around in the maze for some time. Then it is either fed in the goal-box prior to the test runs, or runs the maze as usual to food at the end. In either arrangement a control group is necessary for comparison. Of five experiments of this kind, all were positive.[48]

It has been reported that in free exploration animals tend to reduce their entrance into culs, thus producing latent learning through a kind of "satiation" of blind-alley entrances.[49] But the problem turns out not to be that simple, for more recent workers have found the most successful latent learners to be the ones that made the *largest* number of cul entries during exploration. They did not decrease their cul entrances during exploration.[50]

3. *Location of incentives learned under satiation and tested under relevant drive.* In this third variety of experiment, animals satiated for

[46] MacCorquodale and Meehl (1954), pages 199–213. The last of the latent learning experiments cited is dated 1952. These writers leaned heavily upon a review by Thistlethwaite (1951a), both for earlier experimental citations and for the major classificatory scheme. Thistlethwaite's review led to two replies, Kendler (1952) and Maltzman (1952), to which he responded, Thistlethwaite (1952a).

[47] Positive results: Blodgett (1929), Elliott (1929), Herb (1940), Simmons (1924), Tolman and Honzik (1930b), Wallace, Blackwell, and Jenkins (1941), and Williams (1929). Negative results: Meehl and MacCorquodale (1951), Reynolds (1945b).

[48] Positive results: Buxton (1940), Daub (1933), Haney (1931), Karn and Porter (1946), Lashley (1918).

[49] MacCorquodale and Meehl (1951).

[50] Kimball, Kimball, and Weaver (1953). Unfortunately, they used different alley widths and younger rats than MacCorquodale and Meehl.

food and water run a T-maze or a Y-maze with food and water in opposite arms, or in one arm. Then, under test conditions, the "hungry" or "thirsty" animal demonstrates latent learning if it can choose the appropriate turn to reach the relevant incentive. Of nine reports of this variety, seven yielded positive results, two negative results.[51]

To explain this kind of learning, the reinforcement theorist falls back upon Hull's fractional antedating goal response (r_G). This is, of course, the reinforcement theorist's equivalent of "cognition." [52] The issue, when a reinforcement theorist invokes r_G, is not over whether or not the "expectancy" language is appropriate, for such language is always appropriate when r_G's are involved. The issue is over the scientific precision and fertility of the "expectancy" interpretation as contrasted with the r_G one. Because r_G's have the dimensions of ordinary responses they can be treated with a quantitative precision. Because cognitions lack such dimensions, similar treatment is not feasible. Critics of the r_G concept do not deny the possibility of precision, but they believe that precision in the use of r_G has not been achieved, and that some of the suggested uses of r_G are faulty. For example, if there are cases in which palpable r_G's do not exist, then the r_G theory is insufficient.

4. *Location of incentives learned under strong irrelevant (competing) drives.* If food is present in one arm of a T-maze and water in the other, a thirsty animal, through a forced-run procedure, sometimes encounters the dry food, without eating it, and sometimes encounters the water, and drinks it. Under these arrangements, will the animal, if made hungry, run to the side where food had been encountered? This is the only variety of experiment in which the negative results outweigh in numbers the positive ones. Of eighteen studies, only seven are positive, and eleven are negative.[53]

These experiments point to complexities that call for detailed analy-

[51] Positive results: MacCorquodale and Meehl (1951), Meehl and MacCorquodale (1948), Seward, Levy, and Handlon (1950), Spence, Bergmann, and Lippitt (1950), Spence and Lippitt (1940), Szymanski (1918), Thistlethwaite (1951b). Negative results: Kendler (1947a), Maltzman (1950). Kendler and Levine (1953) have added some positive results.

[52] A defense of the r_G concept in the interpretation of irrelevant motivation-incentive experiments can be found in Spence, Bergmann, and Lippitt (1950), Kendler, Karasik, and Schrier (1954). Some difficulties with the r_G concept are pointed out by Thistlethwaite (1951b). See also Heron (1949).

[53] Positive results: Bendig (1952), Christie (1952), Diesenroth and Spence (1941), Strange (1950), Thistlethwaite (1952b), Walker (1951), Walker, Knotter, and DeValois (1950). Negative results: Christie (1951), Fehrer (1951), Gleitman (1950), Grice (1940), Kendler (1947b), Kendler and Mencher (1948), Kendler and Kanner (1950), Littman (1950), Shaw and Waters (1950), Spence and Lippitt (1946), Walker (1948).

sis of what is happening. There is an asymmetry, for example, between a hunger-food sequence and a thirst-water sequence. One might suppose that a hungry and thirsty animal would be more likely to drink water than to eat dry food. Yet Heron (1949) found that hungry and thirsty animals chose the *food* side in a familiar apparatus in 100 per cent of their choices, where the other side led to water! Animals that were satiated, that is, that had all they would eat or drink, chose the water side in 92 per cent of the trials. Heron's conjecture that perhaps the choice was made on the basis of full or empty stomach, rather than on the basis of drive discrimination, was supported by the choices of animals whose stomachs were full of water. They, like the food-and-water satiated animals, chose the *water* side, insofar as they made any choices at all.

Another complexity is introduced because under strong drive some of the animals have to be *forced* down the alley leading to the irrelevant incentive. Walker, Knotter, and DeValois (1950) showed that animals that had to be forced demonstrated latent learning less frequently than animals not forced. They showed also that animals with strong position preference during the early runs were less likely to show latent learning in the test runs.

When all of these complexities are unravelled, the focus of the controversy over theory may very well change, just as it has already changed from the *existence* of latent learning to the *circumstances* under which latent learning occurs.

5. *Exploration of paths leading to distinctive goal-boxes, followed by prefeeding in one goal-box prior to the test run.* This design differs from the second type (exploration of a maze) in that discriminable goal-boxes are used. It is in reality a variant of Maier's (1929) reasoning experiment, in which many of the same arrangements are involved. Hence Maier's experiment, and the successful repetitions of it, give some additional supporting evidence. The typical experiment with this design uses a T-maze with two easily distinguishable end-boxes. After the rat is familiar with the arms of the maze and the end-boxes to which these lead, it is fed in one of the end-boxes. It demonstrates latent learning if, when placed at the entrance, it chooses the side leading to the appropriate goal-box. Of seven studies of this kind, four are classified as positive, three as negative.[54]

What conclusions can we draw from this array of contradictory

[54] Positive results: Gilchrist (1952), Iwahara and Marx (1950), Seward (1949), Tolman and Gleitman (1949). Negative results: Denny and Davis (1951), Seward, Datel, and Levy (1952). (In the last study, one of three replications came out positive.)

evidence? So far as sheer "score" is concerned, of the studies reviewed by MacCorquodale and Meehl, thirty were reported as positive, eighteen as negative. There is no longer any doubt but that, under appropriate circumstances, latent learning is demonstrable.

Other Varieties of Latent-Learning Experiment

Because the possibilities of learning under irrelevant motivation-incentive conditions are enormous, the five foregoing experimental varieties are not exhaustive.

An ingenious and novel test of latent learning has been proposed by Muenzinger and Conrad (1954). They suggest that latent learning can be tested by its *interference* with a novel task as well as by its acceleration of learning in the original task. The interference ("negative transfer") method permits a distinction between two phases of latent learning. In the first phase the non-rewarded animal becomes "maze-wise" without learning the true path. If in this phase the animal is moved to a new maze that is the mirror-image of the first, and run with reward, he shows *positive transfer,* that is, learns more successfully than control rats without the prior non-rewarded experience. In the second phase, "true-path" learning occurs, and produces *negative transfer* when the rat is run in the mirror-image maze with reward. This second phase demonstrates genuine latent learning of the true path. In the reported experiments the first phase lasted for 10 trials (five on each of two days), and the last phase began only on the third non-rewarded day. If the reward is introduced earlier (on the first or second day) true-path learning sets in earlier, and negative transfer is demonstrable in the mirror-image maze.[55] These findings suggest several important supplementations to the previous interpretation of latent learning—both as to what is happening in the non-rewarded runs and what happens when the reward is introduced.

There has been a long history of experimentation on "incidental learning" in human subjects, that is, on the learning of something tangentially related to an ongoing task upon which attention is directed. These experiments have recently been assimilated to latent learning, for they are appropriately classified as learning under low degrees of relevant motivation, such learning being followed by more direct testing. For example, Stevenson (1954) finds striking increase in latent-learning ability with age during the preschool years. Postman and Thuma (1954)

[55] Kanner (1954) also shows that rewarded animals learn somewhat more than unrewarded ones.

distinguish between the subject's recognition of the *presence* of the incidental stimuli and his recall of their *location*.

Following their review of the latent-learning literature, MacCorquodale and Meehl conclude:

> In spite of the preceding difficulties of interpretation, it seems safe to say that the current state of the evidence is at least encouraging to the theorist oriented to some form of expectancy theory. We were, frankly, somewhat more impressed by the overall trend of the evidence than we had expected to be.[56]

They have suggestions for both the major competing theories. First, they say, cognitive theorists have rested too often with attempts to confound the opposition by posing the question "How do you explain that one?" The cognition theorist must take seriously the accounting for negative results as well as taking satisfaction in the positive results. Second, reinforcement theorists have tended to use an "elastic" explanation based on r_G. They must use the r_G concept rigorously if they wish to assert the superiority of their type of explanation.

ESTIMATE OF TOLMAN'S SIGN LEARNING

Tolman's Position on the Typical Problems of Learning

Because it is a system with some aspirations toward completeness, there are statements within Tolman's writings relevant to most of the problems raised by other writers.

1. *Capacity*. Tolman has recognized the need for capacity laws. The matter interests him chiefly because of the possible gradation of learning tasks from those requiring least to those requiring most intelligence. It is natural that one who makes predictions about what animals will do in problem-solving situations is confronted with the limitations of one organism as compared with another. Tolman believes that the high degree of specificity of capacities in the rat is due to the lack of influence of a culture which prizes certain behaviors over others. Hence one of the contributions of animal studies may be to show processes at a subcultural level.[57]

2. *Practice*. The law of exercise is accepted in the sense of the frequency with which the sign, the significate, and the behavioral relation between the two, have been presented. Exercise is not the cause of the initial selection of the right response. Mere frequency without "be-

[56] MacCorquodale and Meehl (1954), page 213.
[57] Tolman (1945).

longing" does not establish a connection. After a response has been learned, overexercise tends to fix it, making it unduly resistant to change.[58]

3. *Motivation.* Rewards and punishment tend to regulate performance, rather than acquisition, although they are related to acquisition also because they serve as "emphasizers" and because goal-objects confirm or refute hypotheses. Because of the demonstration of latent learning, the law of effect in its usual sense (reward as a strengthener of response tendencies) is not accepted.

4. *Understanding.* Cognitive processes are of the very essence of molar behavior and learning. Hence Tolman is friendly to learning by creative inference, inventive ideation, and so on. He repeatedly states, however, that he does not wish to imply "introspectively get-at-able conscious contents." The prototype of learning is sensible, reasonable adjustment according to the requirements of the situation; stupid learning occurs as a limiting case when the problem is unsuited to the learner's capacities or is set up in inaccessible form. Insightful learning is not limited to the primates; it is characteristic of rat behavior as well.

5. *Transfer.* The problem of transfer of training as such has been of relatively slight interest to those experimenting with animals. To some extent all the experiments on change of reward, change of drive, place learning, and latent learning are experiments on problems related to transfer, that is, the ability to use something learned in one situation in relation to another. All cognitive theories expect a large measure of transfer, provided the essential relationships of the situation are open to the observation of the learner.

6. *Forgetting.* Having earlier experimented in the field of retroactive inhibition,[59] it is probable that Tolman is friendly toward some theory of retroactive inhibition, and he has indicated that he accepts the Freudian mechanism of repression.[60]

He has also asserted the resistance of cathexes and equivalence beliefs to forgetting, and the susceptibility of field expectations to the kind of forgetting emphasized by gestalt psychologists.

Molar Behavior as a Field Concept

The student of molar behavior contends that there can be a psychological science or behavioral science in its own right, not waiting for

[58] Krechevsky and Honzik (1932).
[59] Tolman (1917).
[60] Tolman (1942), pages 63–64.

its progress upon advances in other sciences. While there is some controversy about this, it is a position which can be defended by both stimulus-response and cognition psychologists. Hull too, was able to adopt a concept of molar behavior by this definition.

Beyond the matter of level of discourse there lies the question as to whether molar behavior is essentially a field concept. The question might be put another way. To what extent is Tolman's sign-gestalt theory a true gestalt psychology? Koffka, in his review of Tolman's book, welcomed the friendliness to gestalt, but deplored some limitations which he detected in Tolman's variety of gestalt.[61] He believed that the distinction between molar and molecular did not go far enough, because the reality of the molecular was acknowledged. Koffka would wish field principles applied to physiology as well as to psychology, so that all explanatory concepts should be molar. Furthermore, Tolman's preoccupation with behavior sequences and historical interpretations makes sign-gestalts only a limited illustration of the variety of possible gestalts.

This disadvantage, from Koffka's point of view, makes it easier to compare Tolman's experiments with those done under the influence of other theories. Since the experiments are done with rats in mazes and discrimination situations, they are directly comparable to the experiments in the typical American animal laboratory. Therefore Tolman challenges prevailing conceptions such as those of Thorndike and Guthrie and Hull more vividly than the more orthodox gestalt writers, whose situations are often so different as to be incommensurate.

Tolman makes so many generous acknowledgments to Lewin that there is no doubt of the affiliations between their systems, as third parties have made clear.[62] Their differences became adjusted in a brief and friendly controversy.[63]

The conception of molar behavior is consonant with prevailing conceptions of science, in which some degree of arbitrariness is recognized in the abstractions to be made from the totality of natural events for the purposes of any given science. Natural laws can be formulated in many different ways to cover aspects of occurrences. Tolman has undoubtedly done a service to psychology in joining with those who see the importance of a "psychological" psychology, that is, one whose concepts are appropriate to the level of its descriptions and predictions.

[61] Koffka (1933).
[62] E.g., White (1943).
[63] Tolman (1932a), Lewin (1933b). For his appreciation of Lewin, see Tolman (1948a).

The Status of Intervening Variables

The distinction between performance and learning, which must be accepted in one form or another, requires that learning be inferred from performance. These inferences are always being made, even in the most "objective" sorts of observations, because only "relevant" physical or physiological occurrences are recorded. There is nothing especially new about Tolman's intervening variable, except that he points out clearly and insistently that the intervening variable is there, and is not out of place in a behavioral science. The logical mistake is easily made of supposing that the physical and physiological terms to which the intervening variables are anchored are themselves independent of theories, which they are not. The kinds of experiments which are performed, the kinds of measurements which are taken, always involve selection by the experimenter. The data, even though reproducible, are not "pure" facts of nature. The question may therefore be raised whether the intervening variables are going to be anything not found in the experimental relationships directly. It is doubtful whether a satisfactory answer can be given until the intervening variables are identified with quantities. If there are derived constants, interchangeable from one situation to another, then the intervening variable becomes a scientific construct of some importance.[64]

As previously pointed out, Hull has adopted the intervening variable also, so that the logic is common to the differing points of view. The remaining difference lies in the sorts of intervening variables chosen.

A distinction has been made by MacCorquodale and Meehl (1948) between two kinds of symbolic intermediaries: "intervening variables" and "hypothetical constructs." A pure "intervening variable" is a mere convenience in system-making, and has no properties or dimensions other than those specified in the equations that define it. A "hypothetical construct" is an entity with properties attributed to it beyond those of the functional equations in which it appears. Hull's r_G is an example of a hypothetical construct because it has all the properties of a muscular response and is said to give rise to proprioceptive stimuli (s_G) as any muscular response does. While it is hypothesized, rather than observed, it is potentially observable and need not always have the status of a metaphor. Although Tolman's system appears to be built around "intervening variables" in the MacCorquodale and Meehl sense (demands, cognitions, etc.), Tolman denies this and asserts not only that all theories

[64] Seward (1955).

use both types of intermediary, but that hypothetical constructs are desirable.[65]

The distinction made by MacCorquodale and Meehl is a useful one, but it is a mistake to jump to the conclusion (which they did not suggest) that one of the types of intermediary is invariably preferable to the other. Possibly what we need is a clearer specification of the rules under which each should be used. Consider the gene theory in biology. If the gene is believed to be "a something" that has its place on the chromosome, it is a hypothetical construct, and its added properties are such as may be revealed eventually under the microscope or by chemical analysis. If it were merely a pawn to be used in the study of the statistics of unit characters and their genetic transmission, the gene would be a pure intervening variable. In this case, the status of hypothetical construct has seemed to be a useful one, as one considers chromosome maps, crossovers, and so on. The gravitational constant (g) used in the law of falling bodies is another kind of intervening variable, for it is merely a constant defining the acceleration of a free-falling body under specified conditions, with no other status beyond that. It is a convenience in harmonizing free-falling bodies, balls rolling down inclined planes, and the period of a pendulum, and as such justifies itself even though it has no independent existence as an entity. Precisely what kinds of intervening variables prove useful in psychology will depend upon what we can do with them. The test comes in their clarity, specificity, and fertility in system-making. If a hypothetical construct is used, its surplus meanings should be reasonable, and ideally a search should go on for its independent verification.

What Kind of Behaviorism?

When Tolman announced his purposive behaviorism [66] American psychology was still excited over the new behaviorism of Watson. It was Tolman's contribution then to show that a sophisticated behaviorism can be cognizant of all the richness and variety of psychological events, and need not be constrained by an effort to build an engineer's model of the learning machine.

With the diversification of behaviorism under the influence of Tolman and others, the old brittleness of Watsonian behaviorism has largely disappeared, and what virtues there are in the behavioristic position

[65] Tolman (1951b), pages 282–283. For a further discussion of the issues, see Marx (1951b), Ginsberg (1954), Maze (1954).

[66] Tolman (1922). His system was already ten years old when his major book appeared.

have now become part of the underlying assumptions of most American psychologists—without most of them thinking of themselves as behaviorists at all.[67]

Tolman's catholicity and his friendliness to new ideas have prevented his developing a "tight" or "elegant" system, even though he has all along made suggestions as to what such a system would be like. He has kept his prominent place in the forefront of learning theorists by his sensitivity to important problems, by his inventiveness in experimentation, and by keeping others on their mettle.

SUPPLEMENTARY READINGS

BOOKS

TOLMAN, E. C. (1932) *Purposive behavior in animals and men.*
TOLMAN, E. C. (1942) *Drives toward war.*
TOLMAN, E. C. (1951) *Collected papers in psychology.*

SHORTER INTRODUCTIONS

SPENCE, K. W. (1951) Theoretical interpretations of learning. In C. P. Stone, ed. *Comparative psychology.* Third edition, 239–291. Tolman's position is summarized on pages 256–261.
TOLMAN, E. C. (1948) Cognitive maps in rats and men. *Psychol. Rev.*, 55, 189–208.
TOLMAN, E. C. (1952) A cognition motivation model. *Psychol. Rev.*, 59, 389–400.

CRITICAL REVIEWS

ADAMS, D. K. (1933) Three theories of learning. *J. gen. Psychol.*, 8, 485–497.
KOFFKA, K. (1933) Review of Tolman's *Purposive behavior in animals and men. Psychol. Bull.*, 30, 440–451.
MACLEOD, R. B. (1952) Review of Tolman's *Collected papers in psychology. Psychol. Bull.*, 49, 274–276.
YOUNG, P. T. (1933) Review of Tolman's *Purposive behavior in animals and men. Amer. J. Psychol.*, 45, 177–178.

REPRESENTATIVE EXPERIMENTS

BLODGETT, H. C. (1929) The effect of the introduction of reward upon the maze performance of rats. *Univ. Calif. Publ. Psychol.*, 4, 113–134.
BUEL, J., and BALLACHEY, E. L. (1934) Choice-point expectancy in the maze running of the rat. *J. genet. Psychol.*, 45, 145–168.
CRUTCHFIELD, R. S. (1939) The determiners of energy expenditure in string-pulling by the rat. *J. Psychol.*, 7, 163–178.
GEIER, F. M., LEVIN, M., and TOLMAN, E. C. (1941) Individual differences in emotionality, hypothesis formation, vicarious trial and error, and visual discrimination learning in rats. *Comp. Psychol. Monogr.*, 17, Serial No. 87.

[67] Spence (1948). The contemporary designation of *behavioral scientist* is noncommittal on the issues of Watsonian behaviorism.

Honzik, C. H., and Tolman, E. C. (1936) The perception of spatial relations by the rat: A type of response not easily explained by conditioning. *J. comp. Psychol.*, 22, 287–318.

Hudson, B. B. (1950) One-trial learning in the domestic rat. *Genet. Psychol. Monogr.*, 57, 173–180.

Krechevsky, I. (1932) "Hypotheses" versus "chance" in the presolution period in sensory discrimination learning. *Univ. Calif. Publ. Psychol.*, 6, 27–44.

Ritchie, B. F., Hay, A., and Hare, R. (1951) Studies in spatial learning: IX. A dispositional analysis of response-performance. *J. comp. physiol. Psychol.*, 44, 442–449.

Thistlewaite, D. L. (1952) Conditions of irrelevant incentive learning. *J. comp. physiol. Psychol.*, 45, 517–525.

Tolman, E. C., and Gleitman, H. (1949). Studies in learning and motivation: I. Equal reinforcements in both end-boxes, followed by shock in one end-box. *J. exp. Psychol.*, 39, 810–819.

Tolman, E. C., Hall, C. S. and Bretnall, E. P. (1932) A disproof of the law of effect and a substitution of the laws of emphasis, motivation and disruption. *J. exp. Psychol.*, 15, 601–614.

Tolman, E. C., and Minium, E. (1942) VTE in rats: Overlearning and difficulty of discrimination. *J. comp. Psychol.*, 34, 301–306.

FINAL NOTE

At the time of writing, the most ambitious attempt of Tolman to provide a systematic undergirding for social science generally, in terms of his theoretical constructs, is the following:

Tolman, E. C. (1951) A psychological model. In T. Parsons and E. A. Shils, eds. *Toward a general theory of action*, 279–361.

The reader interested in the further outreaches of his thinking will find much in his discussion not touched upon in the text of this chapter.

Tolman's self-appraisal can be found in his autobiography:

Tolman, E. C. (1952) Autobiography. In H. S. Langfeld and others, eds. *A history of psychology in autobiography*. Vol. IV.

For a thorough review of Tolman's position, with some suggestions as to possible steps in systematization, see:

MacCorquodale, K., and Meehl, P. E. (1954) Edward C. Tolman. In W. K. Estes and others. *Modern learning theory*, 177–266.

Chapter 7

CLASSICAL GESTALT THEORY

DURING the first quarter of the century in America the quarrels within academic psychology lay chiefly inside the framework of association psychology. Structuralism, functionalism, and behaviorism were all members of the association family. A few dissident voices, such as Freud and McDougall, got little hearing. This complacency was disturbed by the new gestalt doctrine which influenced American learning theories chiefly through the appearance in English of Wolfgang Köhler's *Mentality of apes* (1925) and Kurt Koffka's *Growth of the mind* (1924). The theory had been developing in Germany since it was first announced by Max Wertheimer in 1912, but these books, and the visits of Köhler and Koffka to America about the time of their publication, brought the new theory vividly to the attention of American psychologists.

Koffka's book had an important effect upon American learning theory because of its detailed criticism of trial-and-error learning as conceived by Thorndike—a thrust at the very heart of the currently popular theory. The vigorous attack upon Thorndike (and upon behaviorism, although Thorndike was not, strictly speaking, a member of the school) was supported by Köhler's well-known experiments on apes, described in detail in his book which appeared close in time to Koffka's. Köhler's book brought the notion of insightful learning into the foreground, as an alternative to trial and error. He showed how apes could obtain rewards without going through the laborious processes of stamping out incorrect responses and stamping in correct ones, as implied in Thorndike's theories and as displayed in the learning curves of Thorndike's cats. Apes could use sticks and boxes as tools; they could turn away from the end of the activity toward a means to the end.

Köhler's experiments with apes were done in the years 1913–1917, on the island of Tenerife off the coast of Africa. His book about these experiments [1] appeared in English a few years later and immediately was

[1] Köhler (1917).

widely read and quoted. Two main series of experiments interested the American psychological public in the problems of insight. These were the box problems and the stick problems.

In the single-box situation, a lure, such as a banana, is attached to the top of the chimpanzee's cage. The lure is out of reach but can be obtained by climbing upon and jumping from a box which is available in the cage. The problem is a difficult one for the chimpanzee. Only Sultan (Köhler's most intelligent ape) solved it without assistance, though six others mastered the problem after first being helped either by having the box placed beneath the food or by watching others using the box. The problem was not solved by direct imitation of others. What watching others use the box did was to lead the observer to attempt to use the box as a leaping platform, but sometimes without making any effort whatsoever to bring it near the lure. When the problem was mastered, a chimpanzee alone in a cage with box and banana would turn away from the goal in order to seek the box and to move it into position. This "detour" character of insightful behavior is, according to Köhler, one of its important features.

The box-stacking problem, requiring that a second box be placed upon the first before the banana can be reached, is much more difficult. It requires both the incorporation of the second box into the pattern of solution, and a mastery of the gravitational problem of building a stable two-box structure. While the emphasis in secondary accounts of Köhler's work is usually upon the intelligence which his apes displayed, he himself is at pains to account for the amount of apparent stupidity. In the box-stacking experiment, for example, he believes that the apes have shown insight into the relationship of "one-box-upon-another," but not into the nature of a stable two-box structure. Such physical stability as was achieved in later structures was essentially a matter of trial and error.

The stick problems required the use of one or more sticks as tools with which to rake in food out of reach beyond the bars of the cage. The beginning of insight occurs as the stick is brought into play, although often unsuccessfully, as when it is thrown at the banana and lost. Once it has been used successfully, it is sought after by the chimpanzee and used promptly. The most dramatic of the stick-using experiments was in a problem mastered by Sultan, in which eventually two sticks were joined together after the manner of a jointed fishing pole in order to obtain a banana which could not be reached with either stick alone. The process was a slow one, and the first placing of the sticks together appeared to be more or less accidental. Once having seen the sticks in this relationship, however, Sultan was able to "get the idea" and to repeat the insertion of one stick into the end of the other over and over again.

Although the attack by Köhler and Koffka was chiefly upon Thorndike, it came at a time when American psychology was in the grips of a confident but somewhat sterile behaviorism. It is hard to see at this distance why such a common-sense and familiar notion as insight in learning should have created such a stir. But at the time Watsonian behaviorism had, in fact, won support for a fairly "hard-boiled" view of learning, according to which the organism was played upon by the pushes and pulls of the environment and reacted in ways essentially stupid. Lloyd Morgan's canon which had seriously undercut the attributing of higher mental processes to animals had fairly well succeeded via behaviorism in excising them from man also. Therefore the return to a more balanced view, represented by the insight experiments, gave new hope to teachers and others who saw thinking and understanding returned to respectability. Insight was not a new discovery—it was a return to a conception laymen had never abandoned. Nobody uninfluenced by peculiar doctrines would ever have denied insight as a fact—yet it took Köhler to restore it as a fact in American psychology. It was, in some respects, time for a change, and Köhler's experiments dramatized release from the negatives of Thorndikian and Watsonian thinking.

That the more enthusiastic reception for the new learning theories should have come first from the educators is not surprising.[2] There had already been a rift growing between Thorndike and the more progressive group within education, who, under Dewey's leadership, had made much more than he of the capacity of the individual for setting and solving his own problems. The new insight doctrine fitted nicely their slogan of freeing intelligence for creative activity.

Animal psychologists like Yerkes, who had never espoused behaviorism, welcomed the new movement as a natural development. Yerkes himself had done experiments on insightful learning independent of gestalt influences,[3] and the intelligence demonstrated by Köhler's apes did not surprise him. Curiously enough, insightful learning in subhuman animals was less threatening to theorists than learning by understanding in man, chiefly because it was still the rather rare and unusual behavior among animals. Rats still learned mazes, it was thought, without in-

[2] It was an educator-psychologist, R. M. Ogden, who translated Koffka (1924).
[3] E.g., Yerkes (1916)

sight. So the animal experimenters added insight experiments to their list and continued both old and new experiments. But if the insight doctrine were to be accepted in human learning, the field would be wide open for destroying all the familiar laws of learning as they applied to man. It is not surprising that those who were at the time concerned more largely with human learning, such as Thorndike, Robinson, and Guthrie, should all have been cool to the insight concept.

The visible opposition between Köhler and Thorndike was over insight and trial and error, that is, over intelligent learning as contrasted with blind fumbling. But the opposition between gestalt psychology and association psychology goes much deeper. In order to understand this opposition, it will be necessary to examine the gestalt views in greater detail.

There are a number of variants within the gestalt movement and among those strongly influenced by gestalt conceptions. Köhler and Koffka were closest to Wertheimer, the official founder of the school. This chapter is devoted to their treatment of learning. Lewin, while originally from Berlin and definitely within the ranks, broke enough new ground so that a separate chapter is devoted to his position. All four of these men, originally German, eventually settled in America, where three of them (Koffka, Lewin, and Wertheimer) have since died. They are the leaders of what is historically gestalt psychology.

Their views were picked up and considerably modified by Wheeler (1929) (1932) (1940) under the name of *organismic psychology,* but his position deviated too much from classical gestalt psychology for him to be counted within the core group.[4]

The fullest and most systematic treatment of the problems of learning from the gestalt viewpoint is found in Koffka's *Principles of gestalt psychology* (1935). It was written after a period of acclimatization to America, and so meshes somewhat better than earlier writings with the concerns of American psychologists. Most of the direct references will be made to this source.

[4] Wheeler's views were elaborated, with Perkins, in a widely used textbook on educational psychology, Wheeler and Perkins (1932). For an account of the organismic position, see the first edition of this book, Hilgard (1948), pages 234–260. Because Wheeler's theory is no longer influential, the chapter has been dropped from this edition, despite some provocative ideas contained in the theory.

THE LAWS OF ORGANIZATION

Gestalt psychology had its start and has achieved its greatest success in the field of perception. Its demonstrations of the role of background and organization upon phenomenally perceived processes are so convincing that only an unusually stubborn opponent will discredit the achievement. The primary attack upon association theory was an attack on the "bundle hypothesis" sensation theory—the theory that a percept is made up of sensation-like elements, bound together by association.

When the gestalt psychologists turned later to the problems of learning, the equipment brought to the study of learning was that which had succeeded in the field of perception, and the arguments previously used against the sensation were turned against the reflex. In spite of the attention which Köhler's ape experiments received, gestalt psychologists can be fairly said to have been only moderately interested in learning. This does not mean that their few experiments are without significance; it means only that they have considered the problems of learning secondary to the problems of perception. Perhaps in America the shoe is on the other foot, and in preoccupation with learning we have too long neglected the relationship between the two fields.[5]

The starting point for Koffka's treatment of learning is the assumption that the laws of organization in perception are applicable to learning. This applicability is enhanced because of the prominence in learning given in his theory to the initial adjustment, to the discovery of the correct response in the first place. Since this discovery depends upon the structuring of the field as it is open to the observation of the learner, the ease or difficulty of the problem is largely a matter of perception. In some sense, Köhler's apes were presented with perceptual problems; if they literally "saw" the situation correctly, they had "insight."

The application of the laws of organization to learning problems is done too casually by Koffka to be very convincing, but if he had been more systematic about it, the development of the argument might have gone along the following lines. There would be a guiding principle (the Law of Prägnanz) and four laws of organization subordinate to it: the laws of similarity, proximity, closure, and good continuation.

[5] The point was made some years ago by Leeper (1935b).

The Law of Prägnanz

The law of *Prägnanz*[6] suggests the direction of events. Psychological organization tends to move in one general direction rather than in other directions, always toward the state of *Prägnanz,* toward the "good" gestalt. The organization will be as "good" as prevailing conditions allow. A "good" gestalt has such properties as regularity, simplicity, stability, and so on.

Because of the dynamic properties of "fields," the conditions of equilibrium are necessarily important. In physics, processes which terminate in stationary distributions are characterized by certain maxima and minima, as by a minimum of energy capable of doing work. This minimum for the whole sometimes requires a part to absorb a maximum of energy. The law of *Prägnanz* is a law of equilibrium like the principles of the maximum or minimum in physics. It ought to correspond to them in reality, since it is the phenomenal representation of physiological processes which obey physical laws. In effect, however, it is used as an analogy. When organization moves toward a minimum, it is characterized phenomenally by the simplicity of uniformity; when it moves toward a maximum, it is characterized by the simplicity of perfect articulation.[7] "We might say, sacrificing a great deal of the precision of the physical proposition, that in psychological organization either as much or as little will happen as the prevailing conditions permit."[8]

Learning situations are problematical. They therefore give rise to tensions and to disequilibria. Some such principle as the law of *Prägnanz* becomes appropriate to them, although Koffka does not develop the point, except by way of the other laws, each of which, in its own way, is an illustration of the more general principle.

1. *The law of similarity.* The law of similarity or of equality is the counterpart of association's law of similarity. This and the other laws all derive from Wertheimer (1923). He used it as a principle determining the formation of groups in perception, such as groups of lines or dots. Similar items (e.g., alike in form or color) or similar transitions (e.g., alike in the steps separating them) tend to form groups in perception. In a series of experiments with nonsense syllables, two-place numbers, and nonsense two-dimensional figures, Köhler (1941) showed quite conclusively that similar (homogeneous) pairs were much more

[6] The German word is inadequately translated as "pregnancy." It has the meaning of "*knapp, und doch vielsagend*" (compact but significant).
[7] Koffka (1935), pages 171–174.
[8] Koffka (1935), page 108.

readily learned than dissimilar (heterogeneous) ones. Homogeneous pairs illustrate the law of similarity. He denied that his results supported simple association theory, preferring instead to attribute the results to "interaction" producing a unitary trace rather than a "connection" between similar items.

The law of similarity was applied by Koffka to the selection of a memory trace by a process active at the time of recall. That trace will be selected by an excitatory process which possesses the same wholeness character. The meaning of trace selection will be considered later. The meaning is conveyed sufficiently by the process of recognition, where a face present now recalls the same one seen earlier and results in the feeling of familiarity.

2. *The law of proximity.* Perceptual groups are favored according to the nearness of the parts. Thus if several parallel lines are spaced unevenly on a page, those nearer together will tend to form groups against a background of empty space. Because whatever favors organization will also favor learning, retention, and recall, the law of proximity becomes the gestalt equivalent of association by contiguity. Patterning through proximity holds also within audition, as in the grouping of successive clicks. Then the proximity is a temporal one. As it applies to memory, the law of proximity becomes also a law of recency. Old impressions are less well recognized and recalled than new ones because the recent trace is nearer in time to the present active process.[9]

3. *The law of closure.* Closed areas are more stable than unclosed ones and therefore more readily form figures in perception. As applied to learning, closure is an alternative to the law of effect. The direction of behavior is toward an end-situation which brings closure with it. It is in this manner that rewards influence learning.

> So long as activity is incomplete, every new situation created by it is still to the animal a transitional situation; whereas when the animal has attained his goal, he has arrived at a situation which is to him an end-situation.[10]

In a problematic situation the whole is seen as incomplete and a tension is set up toward completion. This strain to complete is an aid to learning, and to achieve closure is satisfying. This is the meaning of the above quotation, and shows how closure is an alternative to effect.

4. *The law of good continuation.* This is the last of Wertheimer's principles taken over by Koffka, although Wertheimer had several more.

[9] Koffka (1935), page 464.

[10] Koffka (1924), page 102. From *The growth of the mind* by K. Koffka, Kegan Paul, Trench, Trubner & Co., Ltd., London, 1924.

Organization in perception tends to occur in such a manner that a straight line appears to continue as a straight line, a part circle as a circle, and so on, even though many other kinds of perceptual structuring would be possible. Closure and continuation are aspects of articulate organization. Oragnization applies to learning as well as to perception.

Köhler (1941) demonstrated, for example, that the learning of paired figures was facilitated when the figures "fitted," that is, when the cue and response items formed a regular pair. Pairs fitting less well were harder to learn.

In each of the foregoing laws we have a principle from perception applied to learning.

THE SPECIAL PROBLEMS OF LEARNING

The general point of view of gestalt psychology is expressed in the statement that the laws of organization apply equally to perception and to learning. There are, however, special problems within learning to which Koffka devoted considerable discussion. Because of his anti-empiricist [11] position, he had to find some way of dealing with the evident influence of earlier experiences on present performance. The problem is best approached via memory, in which the past is represented somehow in the present. A second problem concerns the gradual transformation which takes place as skills of the trial-and-error sort are mastered. Finally, of course, there is the problem of restructuring the present field, as implied in insightful learning and in productive thinking.

The Role of Past Experience: the Trace Theory

Because modification by and through experience is part of the very definition of learning, the gestalt attitude toward experience is important.

The gestalt preference is distinctly for conceiving psychological processes as the function of the present field, and the explanatory role of past experience is denied in situation after situation in which to others it seems to be important. Examples include the perceptual constancies—whereby a man looks man-size at a distance, a red coat looks equally red in sunshine and shadow. The illusions of movement and perception of third dimension are also included. Koffka, in spite of a vigorous objection to empiricism, takes a moderate view toward the role of past experience in learning.

[11] Koffka was *anti-empiricist*, objecting to an explanation of present perception solely on the basis of past experience. This did not make him a *nativist*, however, for he believed that gestalt laws of organization provided a *third* solution to the problem of space perception. See Koffka (1935), pages 160–161; Luchins (1951), pages 83–86.

It will not be necessary to point out that an anti-empiristic attitude does not mean the denial of the enormous value of experience. Not *that* it makes use of experience causes our objection to empiricism, but *how* it makes use of it.[12]

A favorite experiment repeatedly cited by gestalt psychologists in order to disprove the role of experience is that of Gottschaldt (1926). For example, if a picture of a letter E is presented 1000 times, and then a church window is exposed, are you any more likely to notice that some of the leaded lines in the windows could form a letter E than if E had been presented only once? We may doubt if a jury of association psychologists or anyone else would expect experience to tear down a percept into the thousand and one possible parts unless there were some kind of search involved. If you looked for the hidden part, and found it, the finding would be easier the next time. Gottschaldt accepts this conclusion, and had evidence that the results of previous discovery were evident in later tests. In the newspaper puzzles with faces hidden in the trees, once the face has been found it is more easily found again. Gottschaldt's experiment reduces to the demonstration that camouflage hides familiar objects as effectively as it hides unfamiliar ones—provided we have no reason to be looking for the familiar objects. Gottschaldt's experiments are cited by gestalt psychologists as very damaging to associationist or empiricist positions. Because of the difference in conception as to what is important, the experiment has not impressed association psychologists as being a crucial refutation of their position.[13]

By the very nature of the case, it is not as easy for the gestalt psychologist to dismiss the role of experience in memory as it is to dismiss its role in perception. Memory so obviously depends upon prior experience that it would be foolhardy to deny it. Koffka is as puzzled as a nongestalt psychologist over Wheeler's attempt to get rid of memory traces.[14] Koffka believes some trace theory essential and proceeds to consider how the traces of past experiences can be reactivated by present processes.

The trace hypothesis is an involved one, and its full exposition requires over 100 pages of text.[15] The essential features of the theory are (1) a trace is assumed which persists from a prior experience, so that it represents the past in the present; (2) a present process is also posited, one which can select, reactivate, or in some manner communicate with the trace; and (3) there is a resulting new process of recall or recogni-

[12] Koffka (1935), page 639n.

[13] Moore (1930) Braly (1933) and Henle (1942a) dispute Gottschaldt's interpretations.

[14] E.g., Wheeler (1932), pages 167–169.

[15] Koffka (1935), pages 423–528.

tion. The process and the trace are to be distinguished; they are localized in different parts of the brain. The trace system is organized according to the same laws applying in other fields, and the communication between process and trace follows these laws.

The trace concept was further elaborated by Köhler (1938) and by Katona (1940). Katona made a distinction between *individual* traces, referring to specific items, and *structural* traces, derived from the wholeness character of a process. The structural traces are said to be more adaptable and flexible, to be formed more quickly, and to persist longer than individual traces.[16]

By way of the doctrine of traces, the gestalt psychologist is able to represent a past event in the present. That is, of course, all that the association psychologist proposes to do. But the trace system, if it is a system organized under gestalt laws, must undergo changes according to the law of *Prägnanz*. If these changes are of a systematic sort it will be evidence against a theory of mere connections weakening in time or inhibited by new learning.

The experiments of Wulf (1922) and later experiments following up his suggestions will be reviewed among the illustrative experiments. The main point is that perceived figures are reproduced differently from the original model, and that the differences are systematic and progressive rather than random. The changes with successive reproduction correspond to the laws of organization, and move toward the "good" gestalt. A circle with a small break in it tends to be reproduced as a whole circle, and an asymmetrical figure tends to become more symmetrical in a drawing of it from memory. There are two chief tendencies noted by Wulf: *leveling* and *sharpening*. The leveling tendency is that already described, a tendency to move according to the intrinsic character of the figure into symmetry and uniform relations of parts. Sharpening consists in the accentuating of details which serve as the discriminatory features of the pattern. For example, a saw-toothed figure may be reproduced with deeper and more striking teeth. Against the theory that memory leads to decay and fuzziness, the gestalt theory is that it leads to change but in the direction of greater clarity. A third tendency pointed out by Wulf is called *normalizing*. A figure which looks something like a familiar object tends on reproduction to be drawn more like such an object. All these changes (leveling, sharpening, and normalizing) are in the direction of a "good" gestalt.

To the extent that these systematic changes occur in the trace, there

16 Katona (1940), pages 194–195.

is a real addition which gestalt theory makes to other theories of memorial change.

New Learning: the Formation of Traces

What happens as new traces get formed? It is to be recalled that Koffka distinguishes between the process and the trace. The process is that which goes on because of the present stimulating situation; the trace is the result of earlier processes.

1. Some processes are directly dependent upon stimuli. When such stimuli are presented a second time, the processes differ from those present the first time because the stimuli have been reacted to before. For example, the second exposure may be recognized as "familiar." This difference suffices to show that learning took place with the first exposure. His illustrations are limited to perceptual ones, and it is apparently perceptual responses to which Koffka refers when he speaks of processes directly dependent upon stimuli.[17]

2. Processes may undergo transformation within a single sustained presentation. For example, when a series of sentences about mathematics is finally "understood" as a demonstration or proof, such a transformation has occurred. The insight experiments also illustrate such transformations.[18]

3. Some processes are transformed by their consequences. This amounts to an acceptance by Koffka of the empirical "law of effect," but the explanation differs from Thorndike's. The transformation of process is at base the same as in the insight experiments, but it often occurs piecemeal as a consequence of the experimental arrangements. In the insight experiments all the data necessary for the transformation of process are present simultaneously, so that restructuring can take place at once. In the typical trial-and-error experiment, by contrast, the situation cannot be understood until the animal's activity has itself led to consequences—to food, to freedom, and so on. Once success is achieved, the process leading to success is transformed. It has a new meaning, a new role in the goal-directed activity.[19]

The Effects of Repetition: the Consolidation of Trace Systems

The aggregate trace system resulting from repetition is always being transformed. With each repetition the trace organization left from pre-

[17] Koffka (1935), pages 549–550.
[18] Koffka (1935), pages 555–556.
[19] Koffka (1935), page 552.

ceding processes interacts with the present process to create something new. According to the principle of retroactive inhibition (which Koffka accepts), preceding individual traces are disrupted by the new learning. Repetition can still be beneficial, however, because the trace system becomes consolidated even while individual traces are destroyed. As the trace system becomes more fixed, it becomes pre-eminent over process and exerts more influence on future processes than such processes affect it. Such a trace system is said to become increasingly available; that is, it corresponds to what associationists think of as a habit system ready to function. A precaution is needed in the interpretation of availability, for conditions which make a trace more and more available for mere repetitions of one process may make it less available for other processes.[20] This is one of the dangers of too much drill in the school subjects, because drill may have a narrowing or "blinding" influence.[21]

The treatment of the acquisition of skill by Koffka is sketchy and conjectural, for the problem has not been experimentally attacked by members of the gestalt group. But skill is made coherent with the process-trace theory through a line of thought somewhat as follows. The trace, as part of the field of a process, exerts an influence on the process in the direction of making it similar to the process which originally produced the trace.[22] This is close to Guthrie's statement that we tend to do what we last did in the same situation. Highly perfected skills can be repeated after periods of disuse because the process communicates with a stable trace system to which it then conforms. While the skill is being learned the trace is less stable. Through the interaction of trace and process, greater stability is achieved. This achievement of greater stability is what is meant by improvement in the skill. Because the trace system, obeying dynamic laws, also undergoes stabilizing changes over a period of no practice, the greater improvement with distributed practice than with massed practice is explained.

Restructuring the Present Field: Insight

The contrast between trial and error and insight is a subject of some misunderstanding because there are empirical facts on the one hand and theories about these facts on the other. So far as empirical situations are concerned, there are experiments which demonstrate a maximum of fumbling, with gradual improvements and little understanding of how improvement takes place. These may be classified as experiments in

[20] Koffka (1935), page 547.
[21] Luchins (1942).
[22] Koffka (1935), page 553.

which learning is by trial and error, without prejudging the processes to be invoked in explaining the learning. There are also experiments in which the learner obviously perceives a relationship which leads to a problem solution, and the experiment may be classified as an insight experiment. And there are situations which fall between, where there is partial insight combined with rather blind trial and error. The empirical grading of situations does not mean that the interpretations have to be so graded, that is, that the trial-and-error behavior must be explained by a trial-and-error theory, insight by an insight theory, and mixed behavior by appropriate mixtures of the theories. This impression is occasionally given by writers taking a middle-of-the-road position. The theorist, recognizing these empirical differences, tries to account for the differences on the basis of a unified set of principles.

Descriptive Characteristics of Insightful Learning

We may distinguish between what goes on in an actual experiment investigating insightful learning and the distinctive criteria of insight, for what goes on is by no means limited to insight, and overlaps greatly with other forms of learning.

1. A more intelligent organism is more likely to achieve insight, just as it is more likely to be successful at other forms of complex learning. Thus older children are more successful at insight problems than younger ones (e.g., Richardson, 1932), and apes more successful than guinea pigs.

2. An experienced organism is more likely to achieve insightful solution than a less experienced one (e.g., Birch, 1945b). To some extent insight depends on past experience, as other forms of learning do. Thus a child cannot get insight into a mathematics problem stated symbolically unless he understands the conventional signs, even if the problem is otherwise suited to his capacity.

The difference between association theories and gestalt theories lies in the implication of association theories that the possession of the necessary past experience somehow guarantees the solution.[23] While gestalt theorists would agree that past experience will facilitate solution, they object to explanations in terms of previous experience without taking organization into account. More is needed than the necessary amount of information. Just knowing enough words does not cause you to write a poem. The necessary experience alone does not solve the prob-

[23] The issue is discussed again (Chapter 12) in connection with the experiments and theories of Harlow (1949).

lem. In one of his early experiments, Maier (1930) provided his subjects with all the experience necessary for solving a problem, but only one of thirty-seven solved it. The past experience had to be used appropriately before solution would occur.

3. Some experimental arrangements are more favorable than others for the elicitation of insightful solution. Organization is contributed both by processes inherent in the organism and by structural patterning in the environment, and, of course, basically through the interaction of organism and environment. Insight is possible only if the learning situation is so arranged that all necessary aspects are open to observation. If a needed tool is hidden, its use in solution is made unlikely, or at least more difficult. In one form of the puzzle-box it is necessary for the rat to dig through a sawdust floor to discover a concealed tunnel which permits exit. Because the entrance to the tunnel is concealed beneath a uniform bed of sawdust, insight is impossible, and the first solution necessarily occurs almost by chance—being aided only by the fact that sawdust-digging is within the rat's habitual action pattern. The parts which need to be brought into relationship for solution are assembled more easily if they are simultaneously present in perception; for example, it is harder for an ape to learn to use a stick which lies on the side of the cage opposite the food than one which lies on the same side as the food (Jackson, 1942).

Skilled teachers are well aware of differences between situations in which understanding is arrived at easily and those in which it is achieved with difficulty—even though the same ultimate steps are involved and the same end stage reached. In the favored arrangement the problem is so structured that significant features are perceived in proper relationship, and distracting or confusing features are subordinated. Some mathematics teachers make problem solution difficult to grasp because they go through derivations step by step without an overview of where the steps are leading or what the articulating principles are. They teach the necessary operations, but the final insight eludes the students because of the manner in which the proof is arranged.

4. Trial-and-error behavior is present in the course of achieving insightful solution. In the presolution period the learner may make many false starts and be engaged in activity which can be characterized as trial and error. When insight will come (if it does come) is not predictable. These two features (initial fumbling and lack of predictability) have been used by opponents of insight either to assimilate it to associative learning because trial and error occurs, or to characterize it as

mystical, non-scientific, or accidental because the moment of solution cannot be predicted.

The reply to those who find trial and error in insight experiments, and therefore wish to make insightful solution continuous with ordinary associative learning, is that fumbling in problem-solving is not *mere* trial and error. Even those who tend to favor trial-and-error interpretations have come to speak in terms of approximation and correction [24] or in other ways to indicate that the "try" is a real try and not just any old action in the behavior repertory. In the case of adult insight experiments, the "try" is often a plausible hypothesis which has to be rejected. A succession of such hypotheses may be tried before the appropriate one is hit upon. The more intelligent reasoner may actually take longer to solve a given problem because he commands a greater variety of hypotheses to bring to its solution. There is a theoretical distinction which ought to be made between blind fumbling and intelligent searching. Merely varied behavior is one thing; behavior testing hypotheses is varied also, but according to a different type of organization.

That random behavior and luck may further solution is illustrated by some behavior which I observed one summer while assisting Yerkes in an insight experiment with a young chimpanzee. The problem set the animal was to obtain a banana from a long hollow box, open at both ends.[25] The box, essentially a rectangular tube, was firmly fastened to the floor of a large cage. The banana was inserted through a trap door in the middle of the box under the watchful eye of the animal, then the trap door was securely padlocked. The chimpanzee, after a number of unsuccessful efforts to obtain the banana by direct attack—reaching in either end of the tube with hands and with feet, attempting to lift the tube from the floor—seemed to give up temporarily, or, as gestalt psychologists say, to "go out of the field." This extraneous behavior took the form of playful cavorting. In this mood the animal incorporated into her play the hoe handle which was standing in the corner of the room, climbing it, and throwing it. Once the handle fell with its end near the open tunnel. The chimpanzee stopped her play, became calm, looked reflective, and, for the first time in her history used the pole as a tool to push the banana out of the far end of the tube.

The lucky position of the hoe handle structured the situation perceptually to make solution easier. It brought the hoe handle in as a possibility and gave direction to the problem-solving behavior. It did not

[24] Dodge (1931).

[25] The box is illustrated in Yerkes (1943).

add to the chimpanzee's past experience, but it made it easier to assemble the experiences appropriate to solution. Out of what was superfluous activity there thus developed a "hint" as to the direction of solution. An illustration of the way in which direct hints may aid solution is provided by Maier's (1930) experiment previously referred to. By giving a few "hints," in addition to the necessary past experiences, solutions were obtained to the same problem by a much larger fraction of his subjects.

The objection to insight that it is unpredictable and therefore outside of science is lacking in force. The moment of insight is not the important feature in any case. Other features, such as reproducibility of the behavior and applicability to new situations are more important. But even though the moment of insight for a given animal confronted with a given problem is not predictable, it is possible to arrange problems in an order of difficulty so that the *degree of probability* that insight will occur is predictable. To assume that all predictions based on past occurrences (empirical probabilities) imply associative learning[26] is to make of association a term so broad as to be meaningless.

The four characteristics described (effects of capacity, prior experience, experimental arrangements, and trial and error) are not distinctive for insight, although in the course of discussion certain suggestions were made of differences in interpretation when the solution is viewed in stimulus-response-association terms and when it is viewed as the achievement of insight.

Distinctive Criteria of Insight

Because of the overlap of what happens in trial and error and in insightful learning, can we specify a few defining criteria by which insight can be clearly differentiated from other kinds of problem solution?

An early list of evidences of insight was provided by Yerkes (1927), based upon his analysis of photographic records of the problem-solving of a young gorilla, following upon earlier experiences with the orang-utan and chimpanzee.

> In acts which by us are performed with insight or understanding of relations of means to ends, we are familiar with certain characteristics which are important, if not differential. The following is a partial list of features of such behavior. It is presented here with the thought that the comparative study of behavior with insight, in different organisms, may reveal common characteristics.
>
> (1) Survey, inspection, or persistent examination of problematic situa-

[26] The assumption is made by Guthrie (1935), page 193, and by Guthrie and Horton (1946), page 42.

tion. (2) Hesitation, pause, attitude of concentrated attention. (3) Trial of more or less adequate mode of response. (4) In case initial mode of response proves inadequate, trial of some other mode of response, the transition from the one method to the other being sharp and often sudden. (5) Persistent or frequently recurrent attention to the objective or goal and motivation thereby. (6) Appearance of critical point at which the organism suddenly, directly, and definitely performs the required adaptive act. (7) Ready repetition of adaptive reasponse after once performed. (8) Notable ability to discover and attend to the essential aspect or relation in the problematic situation and to neglect, relatively, variations in non-essentials.[27]

On the basis of his observations of the young gorilla Congo, Yerkes went on to say that these observations confirmed his suspicion "that the conventional formula for habit-formation is incomplete, and the process of 'trial and error' wholly inadequate as an account of anthropoid adaptations."

The three types of evidence for insight most convincing to the experimenter seem to me to be three: *First,* the interruption of movement for a period, referred to by Yerkes as one of survey, inspection, attention, followed by the critical solution. This combines Yerkes' points (1), (2), (5) and (6). In the chimpanzee experiment described above, this stage was initiated following the "lucky" fall of the hoe handle near to the opening of the box. *Second,* the ready repetition of the solution after a single critical solution. This is Yerkes' point (7). The ape in the illustration given was returned to the experimental room on the following day. Everything was arranged as before. When the banana was locked into position and the chimpanzee released, there was a single flip of the lock (it *might* have been unfastened!) and then the animal went directly for the hoe handle, carried it over a shoulder in a manner very different from the day before, and proceeded to use it appropriately as a tool. There was no byplay, no dropping it on the floor. This was convincing to the experimenters as evidence that the previous day's solution was accompanied by insight. (There might be some argument as to *when* the insight came, whether *before* or *after* the previous day's success, although the pause before solution of the first day strongly suggested that insight came before the first solution.) *Third,* solution with insight should be generalized to new situations that require mediation by common principles, or awareness of common relationships. While this is not specified in Yerkes' list, it is implied in the multiple-choice experiment, a kind of insight experiment that Yerkes invented. Here insight is indicated by a perceived relationship such as "the middle one of the open doors" "the second from the

[27] Yerkes (1927), page 156. For other criteria of insight, see Pechstein and Brown (1939).

right of the open doors." In human subjects these generalizations are often put into words when the problem is solved.

These three types of evidence are not entirely clear-cut and unambiguous, but they serve reasonably well when the whole context of the problem is considered. A rat pauses, too, before making a jump in the Lashley discrimination apparatus. How, one may ask, do you distinguish this pause from the kind Yerkes speaks of? The answer lies partly in the greater freedom of Yerkes' animals to move about and to do other things. Interrupted behavior is more readily observed when the possibilities of varied behavior are rich. So too the repetition of a first solution can be made without insight, as shown by the Guthrie and Horton cats. However, when the release pole was moved a few inches they were unable to use their prior pole-pushing habits, thus failing to live up to the third kind of evidence for insight.[28] But a chimpanzee or gorilla that has learned to obtain a banana with a stick will *search* for a stick when a banana is out of reach, or will improvise a stick substitute out of bundled straw. Having reacted to the more abstract relationship of stick-as-a-tool-to-obtain-banana, it is not disturbed by a slight change in the environment.

Such applications of a perceived relationship to another situation in which it is applicable is the equivalent of transfer of training. The gestalt writers prefer to speak of it as *transposition,* on the pattern of a transposed melody. What is transferred is a relationship or a generalization, although the contents in the two situations may be entirely changed.

Stimulus-response psychologists recognize a corresponding application of old learning to new problems through stimulus generalization. While there is some overlap between the theories at all points (hesitation, repeated solution, transposed solution) there is no denying that, descriptively, behavior characterized as insightful occurs. The residual differences between the two theories lie more in their theoretical interpretations of what happens than in the descriptive overlap between the simpler forms of trial-and-error learning and the more convincing illustrations of insight. At the level of observation, insight is not the *explanation* of problem solution for a gestalt psychologist any more than for a stimulus-response psychologist.

Köhler complains about the misinterpretations to which his book on apes led:

> When I once used this expression [insight] in a description of the intelligent behavior of apes, an unfortunate misunderstanding was, it seems, not entirely

[28] Guthrie and Horton (1946), page 17.

prevented. Sometimes the animals were found to be capable of achievements which we had not expected to occur below the human level. It was then stated that such accomplishments clearly involved insight. Apparently, some readers interpreted this formulation as though it referred to a mysterious agent or faculty which was made responsible for the apes' behavior. Actually, nothing of this sort was intended when I wrote my report. . . . No question of inventions or other outstanding intellectual achievements is here involved, and, far from referring to a mental faculty, the concept is used in a strictly descriptive fashion.[29]

To the gestalt psychologist, insight exemplifies rather more clearly than other forms of learning the applicability of the laws of organization. It is these laws that explain insight, and it is the gestalt contention that the same laws explain other forms of learning. Only in that sense is insight for them the typical or characteristic kind of learning.

Productive Thinking

Wertheimer had lectured on thought processes for many years, but had published only a few fragmentary papers during his lifetime. He had, however, completed the manuscript of a small book just before his death. This was edited by his friends and appeared under the title *Productive thinking* (1945). In it a number of his experimental studies are summarized in his characteristic way, with penetrating qualitative analysis of simple situations serving to illustrate the differences between his approach and other approaches to which he is objecting.

The two chief competing alternatives to adopting the gestalt approach to thinking and problem-solving are said to be formal logic on the one hand and association theory on the other. Both of these alternatives are believed to be too limited to encompass what actually happens when an individual confronted with a problem finds a sensible solution.

The distinction is made throughout between a blind solution in which the learner applies a formula, and a sensible solution in which the learner understands what he is doing in relation to the essential structure of the situation. The blind solution is often an unsuccessful application of the formula to a situation not seen to be inappropriate. Experiments are cited, for example, in which school children are taught to find the area of a parallelogram by dropping lines from two corners perpendicular to the base, thus converting the figure to a rectangle, whose area can be found. Children who could do the examples perfectly were baffled, however, when a parallelogram was presented in a new orientation, so that the "correct" steps of the procedure led to confusing results. They had learned the solution according to a blind pro-

[29] Köhler (1947), pages 341–342.

cedure. By contrast, the solution of a five-and-one-half-year-old child is reported.

Given the parallelogram problem, after she had been shown briefly how to get at the area of the rectangle, she said, "I certainly don't know how to do *that.*" Then after a moment of silence: "This is *no good here,*" pointing to the region at the left end; "and *no good here,*" pointing to the region at the right.

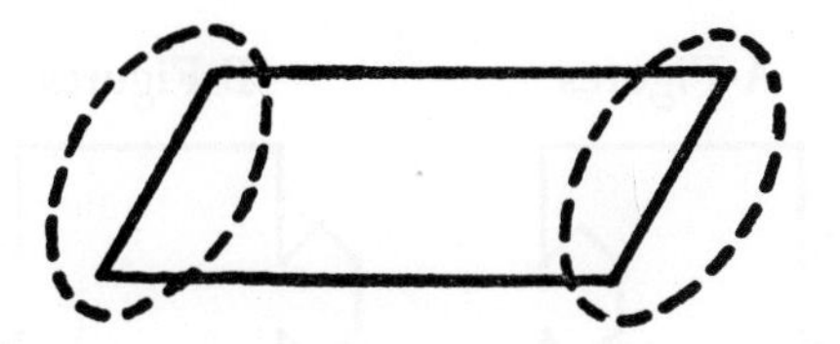

FIGURE 30. Troublesome parts in child's attempt to apply rectangle theory to parallelogram. After Wertheimer (1945), page 48.

"It's troublesome, here and there." Hesitatingly she said: "I could make it right here . . . but . . . ." Suddenly she cried out, "May I have a scissors? What is bad there is just what is needed here. It fits." She took the scissors, cut vertically, and placed the left end at the right.[30]

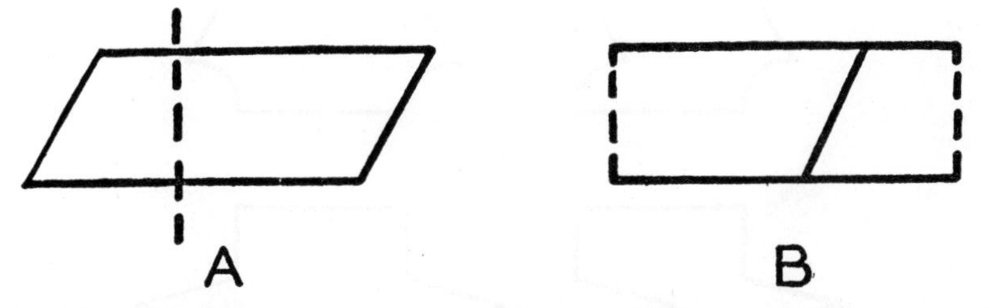

FIGURE 31. Child's solution of parallelogram problem with a scissors. After Wertheimer (1945), page 48.

Another child, given a long parallelogram cut out of a piece of paper, remarked early that the whole middle was all right, but the ends—. She suddenly took the paper and made it into a ring. She saw that it was all right now, since it could be cut vertically anywhere and made into a rectangle.

In cases such as these the solutions appear in an orderly way, in line with the true "structure" of the situation. It is this structural approach which Wertheimer emphasizes.

Children readily grasp such "structural" solutions unless they are badly taught in an atmosphere of blind repetitive drill. Given figures such as those on the left in Figure 32 and those on the right, they can easily sort out the unsolvable ones from the solvable ones. It is futile to

[30] Wertheimer (1945), page 48.

argue, says Wertheimer, that these distinctions are made on the basis of familiarity, as the associationist seems to believe. Children make the distinctions because they know the essential nature of the solution. The structural features and requirements of the situation itself set up strains and stresses which lead in the direction of improving the situation, that is to say, to solving the problem.

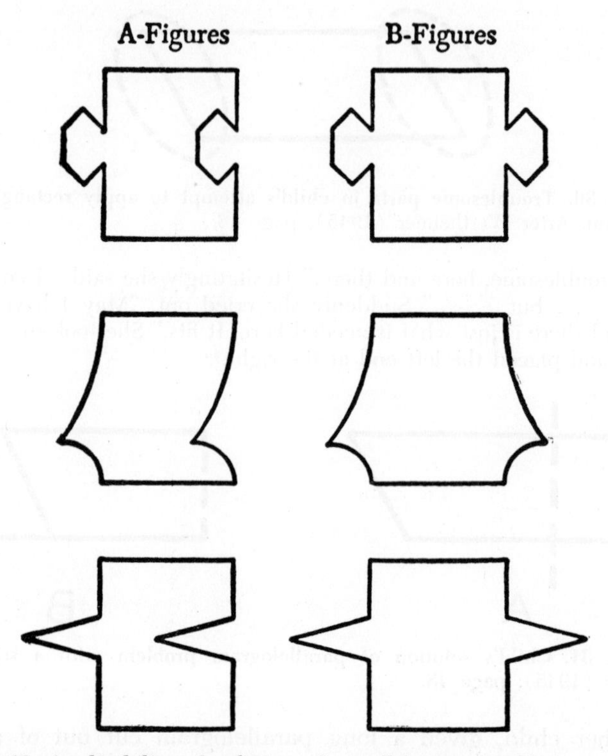

FIGURE 32. Applicability of solution of parallelogram problem to new figures. It is possible to change the A-figures sensibly so that they form rectangles. It is not possible to change the B-figures in this way. The ability of school children to solve the A-figures and to reject the B-figures is said to depend on something other than the familiarity of the figures. From Wertheimer (1945), page 20.

The implications of Wertheimer's point of view for teaching are fairly clear. It is always preferable to proceed in a manner which favors discovery of the essential nature of the problematic situation, of the gaps which require filling in, so that, even at the cost of elegance or brevity, the proof is "organic" rather than "mechanical." [31]

[31] Duncker (1945), page 45.

EXPERIMENTS ILLUSTRATIVE OF GESTALT THEORY OF LEARNING

Three sets of experiments have been selected as representative of the topics stemming from the interests of Köhler, Koffka, and Wertheimer. These are: (1) experiments devised to test the hypothesis that memory traces change in a systematic manner with time, (2) experiments contrasting organization with association in retroactive inhibition and related phenomena, and (3) experiments testing the relative roles of understanding and rote learning in memorization, retention, and transfer. The familiar insight experiments have already been referred to.[32]

Does the Memory Trace Undergo Systematic Change?

The position first advanced by Wulf (1922), that memory traces change according to the dynamic principles of organization, received early support from the experiments of Allport (1930) and Perkins (1932). Gibson (1929) found verbal factors a strong influence in producing what Wulf called normalizing, that is, each reproduction's becoming more like a real object on successive attempts to reconstruct what was seen.[33] He therefore was somewhat critical of the theory of intrinsic factors within the memory trace producing the change.

There is no doubt but that reproductions are often inaccurate and often exhibit the kinds of changes that Wulf suggested. But these changes are often found in the very first reproduction, so that the change may belong more to *perception* than to *memory*. The crux of the matter lies in the finding of progressive changes with lapse of time.

Most of the experiments that have shown changes demanded by the theory have used the method of successive reproductions, which introduces the disturbing factor that the second reproduction is affected by the first, the third by the second, and so on. An extreme illustration of changes which can be made from one reproduction to another is that shown in Figure 33, where each person made one reproduction based on perceiving what the person before him had drawn. Mere lapse of time between seeing the original and reproducing it would scarcely have resulted in, say, the tenth reproduction.

In order to remedy the defect that experiments testing the theory

[32] Review of additional experiments on insight may be found in Woodworth and Schlosberg (1954). A useful summary of the gestalt theory of insightful learning and its conditions may be found in Osgood (1953), pages 605–610.

[33] Gibson's results were extended and confirmed by Carmichael, Hogan, and Walter (1932), Brown (1935).

FIGURE 33. Changes in figures within the method of serial reproduction. Each person views the reproduction by the person preceding him, and then passes his reproduction to the next person. There are progressive changes and elaborations, as in the series illustrated. From Bartlett (1932), pages 180, 181, by permission Cambridge University Press, England, and The Macmillan Company, N.Y.

used successive reproduction predominantly, Hanawalt (1937) had different subjects reproduce the same figures after various intervals of time, with but a single time interval for any one subject. Under these conditions, no progressive change was found. Such changes as occurred were commonly present on the first reproduction, and even might be present when the subject copied the figure present before him.[34]

[34] Related experiments, with primarily negative results, are those of Irwin and Seidenfeld (1937), Irwin and Rovner (1937), Seidenfeld (1938), Goldmeier (1941), Hanawalt and Post (1942), Tennies (1942), Hanawalt (1952).

Hebb and Foord (1945), in a carefully controlled experiment, used the method of recognition rather than that of reproduction, asking the subject to select from a series of figures the one that had been originally presented. There was only one retest for each figure learned by a subject, but the retest was made after a lapse of time differing from one subject to another. The objects presented visually were a circle with a small portion of its circumference incomplete and an arrowhead figure. Presumably there would be a change either toward closure (leveling) or toward emphasizing the broken part (sharpening). The circle may be used for illustration. Testing was done by selecting from a series of broken circles the one which was said to have been seen before. Although there was some variability, the trends were not in support of Wulf's theory, and there were no progressive changes evident with the passing of time.

The conclusions to be reached from these experiments are certainly damaging to the gestalt interpretation of spontaneous changes in the memory trace. They do not deny the gestalt interpretation of changes in perception, or of progressive changes in successive reproduction, where successive perception is involved.

Bartlett's (1932) experiments on repeating stories over long intervals are perhaps more instructive in some ways than the experiments repeating line drawings. They reveal rather striking tendencies toward structuring the story so that it "makes sense," and as the story grows older it also gets shorter and irrelevant details dropped out. This led Bartlett to speak of the *productive* nature of memory as contrasted with its *reproductive* nature. However, the gestalt claim with respect to changes in the trace was based on the experiments of Wulf, and the refutations have been based on experiments using very similar materials. A common-sense use of Wulf's classification of changes into leveling, sharpening, and normalizing has been made by social psychologists,[35] but these uses probably do not require confirmation of spontaneous changes in the trace. Krech and Crutchfield state, for example, that successive reproduction is characteristic of "real life," that is, "an occasional recall (without checking on the accuracy of the recall) of an event that has occurred in the past." [36]

These experiments illustrate how a theory leads to a particular variety of experiment not suggested by other theories. Despite the negative results, the experiments are useful. Experimentation is not intended merely to confirm theories; an equally important role is to refute, to correct,

[35] E.g., Allport and Postman (1947).
[36] Krech and Crutchfield (1948), page 127, footnote 1.

and to delimit the claims of a theory. The by-products have given some support for gestalt perceptual theory while almost invariably refuting the claims respecting the nature of spontaneous changes in the memory trace over time.

The methodological possibilities have not yet been exhausted. Osgood[37] points out a failure to use figures whose perceptual dynamics are known on the basis of actual perceptual experiments (after-images, interpretation of the figure in dim light, etc.). Whether reproduction or recognition tests should be used cannot be given an easy answer. Using several figures at once causes a number of confusions in reproduction, not attributable to the spontaneous changes in a single trace. Possibly more subtle methods should be used in testing individual subjects repeatedly; one suggestion made by Osgood is the use of hypnosis.

Organization versus Associative Interference in Retention

In a series of experiments published between 1933 and 1937, Köhler and his associates found results interpreted by them as interactions implying a field relation between a particular process and a particular trace.[38]

In her first study, von Restorff (1933) showed a relationship between perceptual laws and the recall of nonsense materials. She showed that in the recall of nonsense material, part of the difficulty lies in the homogeneity of the material. If lists of paired associates are constructed so that one pair is of very heterogeneous material, this pair will be retained much better than the pairs of items representing materials more frequently repeated within the list. The interpretation is that the heterogeneous items stand out like a figure on the ground, exactly as in perception. This favorable structuring in perception turns out to be favorable also for recall. Müller (1937) went on to show that the recall of isolated or unique material was favored even when the unique items were distributed over eight separately learned and recalled lists. The final task was the unexpected recall of whatever could be remembered from the eight lists. Six of the eight lists contained one kind of unique item, while two of the lists contained another kind of unique item. Recall favored the rarer unique items found only in two of the eight lists.

In the study of Köhler and von Restorff (1935) an ingenious arrangement was used to test "spontaneous recall" when there was a mini-

[37] Osgood (1953), pages 590–591.

[38] von Restorff (1933), Köhler and von Restorff (1935), Bartel (1937), Müller (1937). Aspects of these experiments were reviewed by Köhler (1938) (1940).

mum of induced "set" to recall. The laws of dynamics are best revealed when the results of process-trace interaction emerge naturally, without any special instruction to "search" for relationships.

All subjects first worked on the following computational problem:

$$x = 21\,(91/7 + 6) + 14$$

Most subjects went through the usual steps:

$$\text{First, } 91/7 = 13 \qquad (1)$$

Therefore,

$$x = 21\,(13 + 6) + 14 \qquad (2)$$

$$= 21\,(19) + 14 \qquad (3)$$

Performing the major multiplication:

$$\begin{array}{r} 21 \\ \times\, 19 \\ \hline 189 \\ 21 \\ \hline 399 \end{array} \qquad (4)$$

Hence,

$$x = 399 + 14 = 413 \qquad (5)$$

At this point the experimenter pointed out, somewhat casually, that the subjects might have noticed a somewhat easier way of multiplying 21×19, using the formula $(20 + 1)(20 - 1) = 20^2 - 1 = 400 - 1 = 399$. The later retention test required recalling the pertinence of the principle that $(a + b)(a - b) = a^2 - b^2$.

After this exercise in computation, and the casual suggestion of another solution, half the subjects went on to do problems in arithmetical computation, while the other half worked on matchstick problems. Then both groups were again assigned a problem related to the one outlined above. The prediction was that the new problem would be detected as similar to the first one more frequently by those working on matchsticks than by those who had continued to work on arithmetic. That is, the computation problem would be more distinctive for those for whom it had been the *only* computation problem, and the new process would therefore be more likely to communicate with the memory traces from the first problem.

The prediction was borne out. The "short-cut" method was used more frequently by those whose intervening activity was with matches than by those whose intervening activity was additional arithmetic. (See Table 4.) Upon questioning, the other subjects could easily remember having been told about the short cut. This bears out the importance of arranging the experiment so as to test *spontaneous* recall if the dynamics of the process are to be exposed. Bartel (1937) continued with related experiments, with consonant results.

Müller (1937) also studied a problem familiar in the history of retroactive-inhibition experiments, the problem of the point in the interval between learning and recall at which the interpolated material produces the greatest amount of interference. Müller's findings supported the view that retroactive inhibition was at a maximum near the point of reproduction, suggesting that the action was really proactive rather than retroactive.

TABLE 4. Spontaneous Recall as Affected by Homogeneous and Heterogeneous Intervening Activity (Köhler and von Restorff, 1935, page 79)

	Continued with Arithmetic (Homogeneous Activity)	*Worked with Matchsticks (Heterogeneous Activity)*	*Total Subjects*
Recalled short cut	9	27	36
Failed to recall short cut	25	10	35
Total subjects	34	37	71

Chi square = 15.3
P less than .001

All of these experiments show a resemblance in design to experiments done in the tradition of associative learning. What is unique about them, or about the theories used to explain them?

First, the experiments commonly employ both homogeneous and heterogeneous materials, in order to point to principles of organization from perception as applying also to retention and recall. Added cogency is given to these arguments by later experiments of Werner (1947), where he showed that boundary phenomena which, in perception, prevent the confusion of forms, also operate in proactive inhibition. Material that was strongly "bounded" did not intrude as erroneous responses in a second list, and produced less interference with the retention of the second list.

Second, the conception of process-trace interaction is said to differ from explanations according to associative connections. Köhler notes, for example, that in the usual retroactive-inhibition experiment traces are poorly distinguished and are densely crowded, so that they no longer function according to their intrinsic natures. Köhler points out that the experiments on spontaneous recall do not have these objections, for they permit the traces to function more normally, with results as predicted from principles of organization.[39]

Drill versus Understanding in Memorization and Retention

In his book on *Organizing and memorizing* (1940), Katona reports a number of experiments inspired by Wertheimer, who contributed the foreword to the book.

Katona attempts experimentally to define and characterize two types of processes leading to recall: rote memorizing and understanding. When a list of nonsense syllables is memorized, the learner is forced to use the former process, because there are no organizing principles which will permit understanding to help. On the other hand, there are many kinds of problems which illustrate principles; in such cases learning by understanding will have advantages. Simple and ingenious experiments were designed in which it was possible to commit the same material to memory with or without understanding, and then to test the results on new learning.

One experiment consisted in the teaching of simple match tricks of the kind illustrated in Figure 34. The problem is to move 3 lines and in so doing to have only 4 squares left. The possible solutions are shown in the figure. There is a simple principle involved in all solutions, which is that no side must be used for more than one square. (There are 16 matches making the original 5 squares; because these 16 matches are now to make 4 squares it is evident that each side can be used but once.) A number of different tasks were used, all ringing changes on the same general pattern.

In his Experiment A, three groups were used, a control group, a memorization group, and a group practiced on examples. No preliminary practice was given the control group. The memorization group was shown the first problem (that of Figure 34), with one of its solutions. Then this same problem was presented in rotated form and the same solution shown. The memorization group was thus shown essentially the same solution four times, with the problem very slightly rearranged geometrically. The group which had practiced on examples experienced six different transitions from one situation to another in their preliminary practice period, although no general principle was enunciated. Following this preliminary practice, each of the three groups was given four tasks to solve; these were all new to the control group, but one of the four

[39] Köhler (1940), page 155.

tasks was familiar to the memorization and examples group. There was a retest four weeks later, with a new control group. In this retest three new tasks were presented along with one of the originally practiced tasks. Successes on the practiced task were about alike for the two groups, in

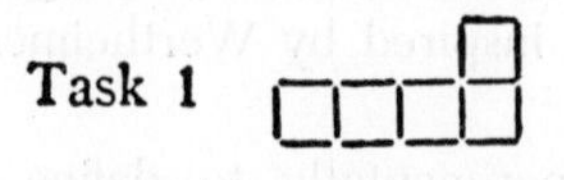

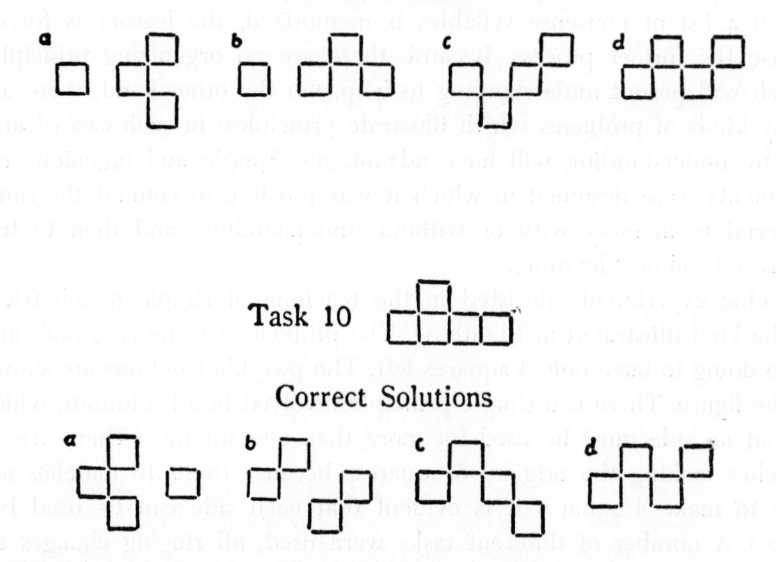

FIGURE 34. Match-stick problems. The assigned problem is to make 4 squares instead of 5 by moving 3 matches (all matches to be used in the solution). Four solutions are shown for each of two tasks. From Katona (1940), page 120.

spite of the fact that the practiced task for the examples group was only one of three tasks practiced, while the memorization group had spent all of its practice period on this one task. The advantage of the examples group was more pronounced on new tasks, as shown in Table 5.

TABLE 5. Comparison of Scores * on New Tasks of Groups Practiced in Different Ways (Katona, 1940, page 86)

	Immediate Test	*Retest After 4 Weeks*
Control Group	1.06	2.20
Memorization Group	1.79	2.84
Group Practiced on Examples	3.92	6.24

* Weighted scores, with possible score of 10. The differences between the examples group and the others are statistically significant.

Why was the group practiced on examples superior? Presumably because the more varied experience had produced some measure of understanding. Verbal reports showed that this understanding was fragmentary, taking such forms as "filling up holes increases the number of squares"; "spreading it out decreases the number of squares." In any case, the method produced a more varied attack, and alternative solutions to the familiar problems were used in a way not true for the memorization group. Memorization sometimes tends to narrow rather than to increase the range of problem-solving.

Katona concludes that learning with understanding not only improves retention of that which is learned, but better qualifies the learner to move forward to new learning. Thus understanding is important for transfer. Some of Katona's conclusions have been criticized by Melton [40] on statistical grounds, but Melton accepts as demonstrated the following points on transfer following learning by understanding:

1. A group which has learned by rote memorization is little better than an unpracticed control group in the learning of new tasks, while a group which has learned with understanding learns new tasks much more readily.

2. When once tasks have been learned with understanding, repeated tests with new tasks result in progressive improvement in performance. By contrast, if the repeated tests are done with practiced tasks, the efficiency of performance on new tasks is reduced.

Katona concludes from all this that there is a real difference in what happens when meaningless memorization goes on and when learning takes place with understanding. He believes that the two kinds of learning are genuine and should be distinguished. This does not mean that he believes that there are two fundamental prototypes of learning, corresponding to the two types of arrangement under which learning takes place. According to him, the underlying factor is organization. Only when better organization fails do you get the extreme picture of rote learning, which is itself a special form of organization resorted to with comparatively incoherent materials. The distinction in kind is not one of ease or of difficulty, for it is sometimes easier to learn by rote than to learn by understanding. The advantages of learning by understanding are that meaningful learning is applicable to new situations and is more enduring.

[40] Melton (1941). For a reply see Katona (1942). Some features of Katona's experiments have been satisfactorily repeated and extended by Hilgard, Irvine, and Whipple (1953), Hilgard, Edgren, and Irvine (1954).

ESTIMATE OF GESTALT THEORY OF LEARNING

Gestalt Theory and the Typical Problems of Learning

The gestalt psychologists find a somewhat distorted emphasis in conventional treatments of learning, so that the problems typically emphasized are not the most natural selection of problems from their standpoint. In order to maintain the symmetry of comparative study of the different positions, however, the same list will be followed which was used to summarize the stimulus-response positions.

1. *Capacity.* Because learning requires differentiation and restructuring of fields, the higher forms of learning depend very much upon natural capacities for reacting in these ways. Poor methods of instruction, however, may be responsible for some inability to face new situations, for a "blindness" which might be confused with stupidity.

2. *Practice.* Changes go on within repetition, not as a result of repetition. Practically all psychologists now agree that this is so, but they differ with regard to the pertinent processes which go on within the repetitions. From the gestalt point of view, repetitions are successive exposures, bringing to light relationships to enter into restructurization. To Koffka, they also make possible the consolidation of trace systems, which is as near as any gestalt psychologist comes to saying that responses become fixed by repetition.

3. *Motivation.* Goals represent end-situations, and as such modify learning through the principle of closure. The processes leading to the successes or failures get transformed by their consequences. The empirical law of effect is accepted, but Thorndike's interpretation of the blind action of effect is denied.

4. *Understanding.* The perceiving of relationships, awareness of the relationships between parts and whole, of means to consequences, are emphasized by the gestalt writers. Problems are to be solved sensibly, structurally, organically, rather than mechanically, stupidly, or by the running off of prior habits.

5. *Transfer.* The gestalt concept most like that of transfer is *transposition.* A pattern of dynamic relationships discovered or understood in one situation may be applicable to another. This is in some respects like Judd's generalization theory of transfer.[41] There is something in common between the earlier learning and the situation in which transfer is found, but what exists in common is not identical piecemeal elements

[41] Judd (1908).

but common patterns, configurations, or relationships. One of the advantages of learning by understanding rather than by rote process is that understanding is transposable to wider ranges of situations, and less often leads to erroneous applications of old learning.

6. *Forgetting.* Koffka relates forgetting to course of changes in the trace. Traces may disappear either through gradual decay (a possibility hard to prove or disprove), through destruction because of being part of a chaotic, ill-structured field, or through assimilation to new traces or processes. The last possibility is familiar as a form of theory of retroactive inhibition. Traces which continue to exist may at a given moment be unavailable. While little is known about this, Koffka believes it must have something to do with ego organization.[42] Finally, there are instances of forgetting in which a process fails to communicate with an otherwise available trace. The forgetting of an intention [43] would presumably classify here. This is also an ego problem.

In addition to such forgetting, there are the dynamic changes which take place in recall, so that what is reproduced is not earlier learning with some parts missing, but a modified trace which is productive as well as reproductive.

General Aspects of Gestalt Theory

In discussing gestalt psychology solely as a theory of learning, some of its more general features have been sidestepped, especially its philosophical orientation and its relation to biology.

The objection to association theory of learning is part of the *holistic* emphasis within the general theory, and coherent with the opposition to "atomistic" explanations according to connections between parts. The objection to sensations as elements of perception ("the bundle hypothesis") is carried over in the objection to stimulus-response connections as elements of habits.

The *phenomenological* standpoint, often stated by gestalt psychologists as opposed to the prevailing *positivistic* position, is not easy to characterize satisfactorily in limited space. Phenomenal observation is more "subjective" than behaviorism, but less sophisticated and specially trained than the introspection recommended by Titchener. The recommended variety of observation is natural and childlike, appreciative rather than analytical. For example, Köhler's later accounts of insight depend upon such a phenomenological description of events. Insight in this context in-

[42] Koffka (1935), pages 525–527.
[43] Birenbaum (1930).

cludes such everyday experiences as enjoying a cool drink. We refer the pleasures we feel to the taste of the drink and to our thirst, through a natural "requiredness" of the relationships. We do not attribute our pleasure to accidental accompaniments, "not, for instance, to the spider on the wall, nor to the size of the chair before me, nor to the thousands of other things in my environment." [44] These everyday experiences of the determination of events, here called insight, are said to refute the theory of chance contiguous associations.[45]

The interpretation of gestalt psychology as a *field theory* rests largely on the evidence assembled by Köhler in his *Physischen Gestalten* (1920), showing the relationship between gestalt laws of organization and well-established principles in physics and biology. The biological emphasis within gestalt has been carried forward by Gelb and Goldstein.[46]

Köhler has all along held *isomorphism* to be central to the understanding of gestalt psychology. This is the principle that the underlying brain fields correspond in their dynamic aspects to phenomenal experience. He believes psychophysical isomorphism follows from the principles of evolution, so that mental events are not alien to physical events, but are rooted in the laws of nature:

> Some fundamental properties of nature rather than any special arrangements in the organism are, I believe, the counterparts of essential mental facts.[47]

We shall return later (Chapter 12) to Köhler's more specific hypotheses about brain fields, and his experiments related to them.

The Interrelationship Between Perception and Learning

Any estimate of the classical gestalt position would be incomplete which did not appraise the success with which the basic thesis has been defended that the dynamic laws of perception and of learning are alike. For the most part, these conjectures have been programmatic rather than worked out in convincing experiments. The point of view has been helpful to the extent that it has brought emphasis upon organization, mean-

[44] Köhler (1947), page 346.

[45] For further discussion of the phenomenological position as interpreted by gestalt psychologists, see MacLeod (1947) (1951). The phenomenology of Snygg and Combs (1949) does not belong within the classical gestalt tradition.

[46] The collaboration between Gelb and Goldstein began in the study of brain-injured soldiers of World War I, Gelb and Goldstein (1918). Goldstein's matured views are presented in book form in Goldstein (1939) (1940) (1948). Wheeler's organismic psychology picked up and extended the biological emphasis, and assimilated embryological studies, but it must be considered an offshoot of gestalt psychology rather than part of the central core of development. So, too, many gestalt-affiliations can be found in Werner (1948), but he is not, strictly speaking, one of the gestalt group.

[47] Köhler (1938), page 400.

ingfulness, and understanding, and has called attention to the importance of the structure of the problematic situation. The laws of similarity (or equality), of proximity, of closure, and of good continuation, are not very convincing as laws of learning, and the attempts made by Koffka to summarize his point of view on learning in terms of them is not very successful. As we shall see in later chapters, the reintroduction of cognitive features into learning has been important, whatever one's judgment of the importance of the laws of organization may be.

Insight as an Alternative to Trial and Error

It is implied in gestalt theory that a learner acts as intelligently as he can under the circumstances which confront him, so that insightful solution of problems is the typical solution, if the problem is not too difficult and the essentials are open to inspection. Fumbling and trial and error are resorted to only when the problem is too difficult, either intrinsically, or because of the way in which it is presented to the learner. This reverses the associationist position that trial and error is the typical method of attack and that reasoning is essentially "mental" trial and error. The empirical facts of insight are as satisfactory as the empirical facts of trial and error. Learning theorists are not yet in agreement on one of the three possibilities: (1) that all learning is of one kind, basically like trial and error, from which insightful learning can be derived; (2) that all learning is basically of one kind, like insightful learning, with trial and error a derivative form; or (3) that more than one kind of learning occurs, of which trial and error and insight are two illustrative examples. A strong case can be made for the gestalt point of view that blind learning is not the prototype of all learning. But this is one of the unresolved issues, to face us in succeeding chapters of this book.

In any case, the gestalt psychologists have sharpened the lines of cleavage in thinking about problems of learning, and by questioning most of what was conventionally accepted they have been of real service, regardless of whatever verdicts or compromises the future may produce.

SUPPLEMENTARY READINGS

BOOKS

ELLIS, W. D. (1938) *A source book of gestalt psychology.*
HARTMANN, G. W. (1935) *Gestalt psychology.*
KOFFKA, K. (1924) *Growth of the mind.*
KOFFKA, K. (1935) *Principles of gestalt psychology.*
KÖHLER, W. (1925) *The mentality of apes.*

KÖHLER, W. (1929) (1947) *Gestalt psychology.*
KÖHLER, W. (1940) *Dynamics in psychology.*
WERTHEIMER, M. (1945) *Productive thinking.*

SHORTER INTRODUCTIONS

HARTMANN, G. W. (1942) The field theory of learning and its educational consequences. Chapter 5 in *The psychology of learning.* Natl. Soc. Stud. Educ., 41st Yearbook, Part II, 165–214.
HEIDBREDER, E. (1933) *Seven Psychologies,* 328–375.
KOFFKA, K. (1925) Mental development. In C. Murchison, ed. *Psychologies of 1925,* 130–143.
KÖHLER, W. (1930) Some tasks of gestalt psychology. In C. Murchison, ed. *Psychologies of 1930,* 143–160.
WOODWORTH, R. S. (1948) *Contemporary schools of psychology,* 120–151.

CRITICAL REVIEWS

BORING, E. G. (1930) The gestalt psychology and the gestalt movement. *Amer. J. Psychol.,* 42, 308–315.
PRATT, C. C. (1936) Review of Koffka's *Principles of gestalt psychology. Amer. J. Psychol.,* 48, 527–531.
ROBINSON, E. S. (1930) Review of Köhler's *Gestalt psychology. J. genet. Psychol.,* 37, 431–450.
SPENCE, K. W. (1941) Review of Köhler's *Dynamics in psychology. Psychol. Bull.,* 38, 886–889.
VERNON, P. E. (1935–1936) Review of Koffka's *Principles of gestalt psychology. Character and Pers.,* 4, 92–94.

REPRESENTATIVE EXPERIMENTS

ADAMSON, R. E. and TAYLOR, D. W. (1954) Functional fixedness as related to elapsed time and set. *J. exp. Psychol.,* 47, 122–126.
BIRCH, H. G. (1945) The role of motivational factors in insightful problem-solving. *J. comp. Psychol.,* 38, 295–317.
BIRCH, H. G. (1945) The relation of previous experience to insightful problem-solving. *J. comp. Psychol.,* 38, 367–383.
DUNCKER, K. (1945) On problem-solving. *Psychol. Monogr.,* 58, No. 270, ix, 113 pp.
DURKIN, H. E. (1937) Trial-and-error, gradual analysis, and sudden reorganization: An experimental study of problem solving. *Arch. Psychol.,* N.Y., No. 210.
GOTTSCHALDT, K. (1926) Über den Einfluss der Erfahrung auf die Wahrnehmung von Figuren, I. *Psychol. Forsch.,* 8, 261–317. Translated and condensed as "Gestalt factors and repetition" in Ellis (1938), pages 109–122.
HANAWALT, N. G. (1952) The method of comparison applied to the problem of memory change. *J. exp. Psychol.,* 43, 37–42.
KÖHLER, W. (1918) Nachweis einfacher Strukturfunktionen beim Schimpansen und beim Haushuhn. *Abb. d. königl. Preuss. Ak. d. Wissen,* Phys. Math. Klasse, Nr. 2, 1–101. (Translated and condensed as "Simple structural functions in the chimpanzee and in the chicken" in Ellis (1938), pages 217–227.)
KÖHLER, W., and RESTORFF, H. von (1935) Analyse von Vörgangen im Spurenfeld. *Psychol. Forsch.,* 21, 56–112.

Newman, E. B. (1939) Forgetting of meaningful material during sleep and waking. *Amer. J. Psychol.*, 52, 65–71.

Perkins, F. T. (1932) Symmetry in visual recall. *Amer. J. Psychol.*, 44, 473–490.

Wertheimer, M. (1925) Über Schlussprozesse im produktiven Denken. *Drei Abhandlungen zur Gestalttheorie*. Berlin: Erlangen, 164–184. Translated and condensed as "The syllogism and productive thinking" in Ellis (1938), 274–282.

Wulf, F. (1922) Über die Veränderung von Vorstellungen (Gedächtnis und Gestalt). *Psychol. Forsch.*, 1, 333–373. (Translated and condensed as "Tendencies in figural variation" in Ellis (1938), pages 136–148.)

FINAL NOTE

No very satisfactory recent account can be found on the gestalt theory of learning. The following small book on gestalt psychology has gone through two German editions and has been very widely translated. Its 29 chapters, many of them of only two or three pages, give the range of applicability of gestalt thinking, but the book is not very satisfactory on critical issues. The word "insight," for example, is not used as a technical term, and does not appear in the index.

Katz, D. (1950) *Gestalt psychology, its nature and significance.*

The following thoughtful summary treats the major issues in terms of the contrast between cognition and stimulus-response theories:

Scheerer, M. (1954) Cognitive theory. In G. Lindzey, ed. *Handbook of social psychology,* 91–137.

Chapter 8

LEWIN'S FIELD THEORY

ALTHOUGH a member of the Berlin gestalt group, Kurt Lewin (1890–1947) early began to break new ground, especially in studies of motivation. After a number of productive years in Germany, he spent his last years in the United States, teaching from 1932 successively at Stanford, Cornell, Iowa, and the Massachusetts Institute of Technology, with a term also at Harvard. He became widely known and highly influential, and because of a warmth and infectious quality of personality developed a devoted following. Although his theory is not, strictly speaking, a psychology of learning, much of it is relevant. His doctoral dissertation, in 1917, was critical of the then current association theory of memorization and retention. The theory that he developed as a corrective was called by various names as it progressed, such as *topological* psychology, but it is now usually referred to by its friends and adherents as a *field-theoretical position.* It is satisfactory to call it simply a field theory, without implying that it resembles in detail the field theories of modern physics.

THE BEGINNINGS OF LEWIN'S THEORY

The Lewin-Ach Controversy

Ach belonged to the Würzburg school which had supplemented conventional association with sets, determining tendencies, and the like, thus adding something more dynamic to the standard theory of strengthening associations through repetition. He designed a series of experiments in which a habit of reproducing nonsense syllables was set up through repeated exposure, and then a determining tendency was introduced which might either facilitate or hinder the tendency created by practice. Thus "will" was set against "habit," and a possible quantitative measure of will proposed.[1]

[1] Ach (1910).

There were three arrangements of nonsense syllables in the original learning experiments of Ach. One was the usual or normal arrangement of heterogeneous pairs, such as *bol-pid;* another arrangement called for a rhyming syllable, as *rik-tik;* the third called for inversion, as *kep-pek.* The subject learned one series of eight pairs of each of these kinds. The stimulus syllable of each pair was later used in test situations. In the test series, instructions were to reproduce what had been practiced, or to rhyme, or to invert. Thus the determining tendency could either sum with or contradict the associative reproductive tendency, or the reproductive factor could be present alone. Strength of reaction was inferred from latency of response. Ach found some results coherent with his theory, that the shortest reaction times were in the cases in which the associative (reproductive) tendency coincided with the determining tendency superimposed by instructions. His other results were somewhat irregular, but were interpreted by him as giving general support to his position.

Lewin's objection to Ach's work was not that he introduced the determining tendency, which Lewin essentially accepted, but that he added it to the conventional association theory without seeing that it was a foreign intrusion and led logically to the abandonment of the simple association theory. Lewin argued that the conflict which appeared in the experiment —and, indeed, conflict was convincingly demonstrated—was not between association and determining tendency, but between two determining tendencies. It was his belief that there is no "force" within mere association to lead to reproduction, that reproduction itself must be motivated and implies a set to reproduce.

Lewin's experiments [2] were much like Ach's, but a few modifications greatly changed the resulting interpretations. First a series of eight pairs of nonsense syllables was learned in which the second syllable rhymed with the first, *dak-tak, ged-ked.* Then a list of eight pairs was learned in which the response syllable was the stimulus syllable spelled backward. Note that the only change in response syllables was in the consonants, the vowels being alike in both the rhyming and the reversed pairs.

The first test series consisted in instructing the subjects to respond to a set of syllables by changing the vowel. Syllables from the previously practiced series were inserted among unfamiliar syllables. If Ach's theory were sound, there should have been some conflict between "habit" and "determining tendency," but none was found. There were no wrong reactions, and the latent times for control and critical syllables were alike.

A second test, however, produced conflict and retardation, such as

[2] Lewin (1917) (1922).

Ach found. When the subjects were told to rhyme a series including both syllables previously rhymed and syllables previously reversed, mistakes were made on the syllables previously reversed. Similarly, with instructions to reverse, errors were made in response to syllables previously rhymed when they were presented in the midst of syllables previously reversed. The interpretation is that the instruction to rhyme to syllables previously learned as rhymes was acted upon as though it had been an instruction to reproduce. When, then, a previously reversed syllable appeared, the faulty self-instruction to reproduce conflicted with the correct instruction to rhyme, and interference was shown.

The occurrence of conflict in one case and not in the other, although the prior habits fixed by association were equally strong before both tests, confirmed Lewin in his belief that the existence of an association (or, in his later terms, a cognitive structure) does not provide the "motor" for mental activity. There is always a tension system necessary for activity, including the activity of reproducing previously learned nonsense syllables.

Lewin's contention, while it remains cogent, has lost some of its force as interest has shifted from the artificially motivated habit of rote learning to habits more intimately tied up to need and tension systems. For example, a conditioned avoidance response, strengthened through repeated reinforcement, has a certain urgency about it, so that it breaks through instructions to inhibit response. It is possible to treat the conflict between "habit" and "determining tendency" in this case much as Ach did, and to find results which seem to support Ach's position.[3] The findings do not contradict Lewin's position, however, because in the case of conditioned avoidance responses there is a "motor" in the threat of punishment which is set against the verbal instructions not to respond. This "habit" is more than mere contiguous association leading to reproduction of associated items.

This early recognition of the dynamic organization of reproductive tendencies is reflected in later experiments on the relationship between tension and retention, as shown in memory for finished and unfinished tasks,[4] and the tendency to resume unfinished tasks when the opportunity arises.[5]

Psychological Tension Systems

Much that foreshadowed his later systematic writings appeared in an important paper by Lewin in 1926, shortly after Köhler's and Koffka's

[3] Hilgard (1938).
[4] Zeigarnik (1927).
[5] Ovsiankina (1928).

views were becoming known in America. Lewin's position was first introduced to American audiences by J. F. Brown (1929), three years after this paper appeared.

For one thing, Lewin set himself squarely in favor of a psychological analysis of the actual situation, and against what he called *accomplishment* concepts. The practice curve for typewriting, scoring typing according to words typed per minute or some other convenient unit, rises, shows a plateau, reaches a limit, and so on—as though all that happened could be described as "typewriting." A more psychological analysis would show that what the beginner is doing and what the skilled typist is doing are entirely different: the beginner's process is one of searching, but the searching process drops out as skill is mastered. This objection to accomplishment is to be compared with Guthrie's objections expressed in much the same way, several years later.[6] The difference is that Guthrie wishes to restrict his measurements to movements, which Lewin would class with accomplishments as lacking in sufficient psychological meaning.

The typical non-gestalt conception of psychological causation, says Lewin at this time, is *adhesion.* One thing is attached to another so that revival of the first brings forth the second. Gestalt psychology is sometimes misunderstood as correcting association by accepting the adhesion principle but permitting it to apply only to parts of wholes. This notion is flatly rejected. No mere coupling principle can provide the energy for psychical activity. Psychological behavior depends upon energy related to psychological tension systems.

Perception of the world of meaningful things and events does not provide the energy for activity, although activity aroused under need-tension systems may be *steered* by perception. This is not unlike Skinner's later notion of the role of the discriminated stimulus in operant behavior: the stimulus does not elicit the behavior, but it does set the occasion for it. The sequence of events from perception to satiation is as follows. The perception of an object or event may give rise to a psychological tension (e.g., a desire), or it may communicate with a state of tension already existing in such a way that this tension system thereupon assumes control over motor behavior. The aroused "valences" (attractions and repulsions of perceived goal objects) act as environmental forces steering subsequent behavior. This behavior then leads to satiation or to the resolution of tension so that a state of equilibrium is approached.

At this early date (1926) Lewin went to some pains to point out the ridiculousness for scientific purposes of saying that "everything depends

[6] Guthrie (1935), page 163.

upon everything else." While as a gestalt psychologist he was concerned with wholes, he recognized as the most important problem the isolation of the "specific psychical units, personality spheres, and behavior wholes" in which one's activities, emotions, intentions, wishes, and hopes are embedded. Whatever psychical unity there may be in the "ego" system, it is a "weak" gestalt, and we are dealing in the personality with a great number of "strong" gestalts which in part are in communication with each other, in part disclose no genuine unity at all. In adults the possibility of organized behavior depends upon a relatively complete segregation of a number of different tension systems.

He devoted a number of pages to an analysis of "intentions," how they are fulfilled, why they are forgotten. He arrives at the conclusion that they are quasi-needs, because their satisfaction is like the satisfaction of other needs, not dependent upon particular occasions or particular actions. Substitute satisfactions may be found for intentions as for needs.

This paper introduced many of the concepts to be developed in the later attempts to formalize and metricize the system. There are the needs and quasi-needs; the tension systems; perception (cognitive structure) as steering, but not as providing energy; valences; boundaries; a differentiated and complexly structured ego system. It is a natural development to the later more formal system.

TOPOLOGICAL, VECTOR, AND HODOLOGICAL PSYCHOLOGY

The more abstract and formal characteristics of Lewin's system were detailed in a book and a monograph, *Principles of topological psychology* (1936), and *The conceptual representation and measurement of psychological forces* (1938). He later stated the relationship of his viewpoint to problems of learning.[7]

The words "topological" and "vector" refer to types of geometry borrowed because they appear to provide the mathematics appropriate to the structure of psychological situations. Any mathematics, like any language or any system of logic, may be used in science if it happens to fit. Plane geometry and trigonometry do for surveying, and spherical geometry is useful for navigation, but Einstein had to turn to a geometry of four dimensions to handle relativity problems. The problem of selecting appropriate mathematical tools is familiar in choosing the proper statistical formulas

[7] Lewin (1942).

for a given set of data. In looking for a "fit" to his conception, Lewin hit upon topology and upon vectors.

Topology is a non-metrical geometry of spaces, in which concepts such as "inside" and "outside" and "boundary" are used. Lewin believes that many psychological situations are structured in that way. Sociologists have long talked of "in-groups" and "out-groups." It is such a usage which Lewin is trying to formalize in topological concepts.

Vectors are borrowed from the mathematical system used in mechanics to describe the resolution of forces. Unlike topology, vectors are metrical. A vector is usually represented by an arrow, the length representing its force, the direction representing the line of application. The point of application may also be shown as a matter of convenience, but it does not belong as a property of the vector. Because much dynamic psychology can be described in terms of conflict and the resolution of conflict, the geometry of vectors finds appropriate application.

His desire for a "qualitative" geometry having some of the characteristics of topology with a "quantitative" geometry of vectors led Lewin to suggest that a new geometry was needed to fit the problems of psychology. He specified some of its characteristics, and named it the geometry of *hodological space.* The root is from the Greek word *hodos,* meaning "path." Hence hodology is to be a geometry of paths, somewhat as topology is a geometry of spaces.

What Lewin intended by borrowing from topological and vector geometries is clear. He was searching for a mathematics which would be appropriate to psychological structure as he understood it. He has been attacked for using these mathematics incorrectly and for drawing improper analogies from them.[8] His system is no doubt vulnerable in some of these respects, but the relevance of his theories for the purposes of the present discussion does not rest upon the validity of his quantitative representations.

The Psychological Field: Life Space

The selection of geometry as an appropriate mathematics is natural because the psychological field is thought of as a space in which the person moves. This space is psychological, not physical; it is represented mathematically by a spatial diagram, but that does not mean that it exists in physical space.

The conception of life space is a plausible one. It signifies that two

[8] London (1944).

people walking down the same street are going different places, and the worlds in which they are walking are to them different worlds. Or as I sit in reverie and make plans for tomorrow, I move in a world very different from that in which I sit. My life space is the space in which I live psychologically, as seen from my own viewpoint. It includes each and every object, person, idea, that I have anything to do with. It corresponds in many ways to the world about me, to the world of things, people, and ideas, being my selection from these, but it becomes my world always in edited and distorted forms. It is possible to distinguish between me and my life space, for I move about in my psychological space as others do in theirs. We interact in the real world, all the while producing changes in our respective psychological worlds. Because of correspondences between the psychological world and the real world, Lewin spoke of life space as quasi-physical, quasi-social, and quasi-conceptual. Life space is conditioned and influenced by the physical, social, and conceptual environment but cannot be identified with that environment.

Life space may be inferred; it does not depend upon subjective report. That is, although life space is psychological, it is not strictly a private affair available only through introspection. A person is not always able to introspect about the forces acting in his life space at a given moment. Life space is a construct, like other scientific constructs, designed to account for the psychological situation at a given moment.

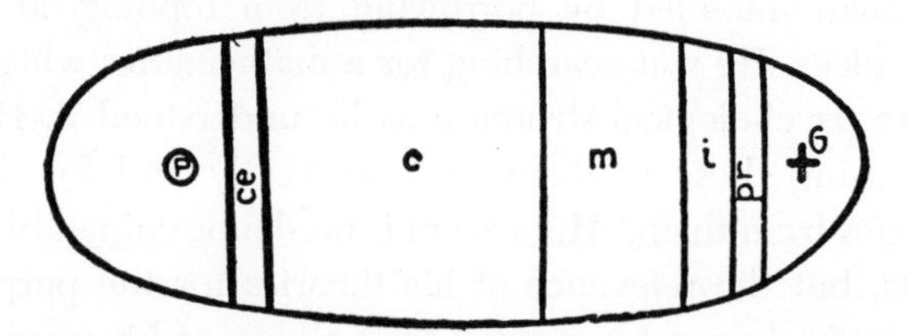

FIGURE 35. Life-space. The situation represented is that of a boy who wants to become a physician. The person (P) is shown separated from the goal region (+ G) by a number of regions with boundaries between them. The regions are college entrance (*ce*), college (*c*), medical school (*m*), internship (*i*), establishing a practice (*pr*). While the locomotion through these regions may take place in the future, they are in the present life-space as obstacles to the attainment of a goal which is now in view. By permission from *Principles of topological psychology*, by K. Lewin, Copyright 1936 by McGraw-Hill Book Co., Inc.

Locomotion in life space is delineated by a geometrical representation of the selection of alternatives, the examining of possibilities, the setting out toward goals, the experiencing of frustration, and the like. It may or may not involve locomotion in the real world. If I move toward an object of choice in the real world, I am also moving in my life space, but the two motions are not to be identified; in life space we represent the psychological significance for the person of the motion in physical space. A typical life-space diagram is shown in Figure 35.

Occasionally life space corresponds very closely to the real world with which the person is in commerce. In that case he is said to be in touch with reality. At the other extreme, we find individuals living in a world of fiction and fantasy—out of touch with reality. In order to describe these differences, Lewin proposes reality-irreality as a dimension of life space. The very young child may not distinguish between his hopes and wishes and the actual circumstances of life. Presumably there is a greater differentiation between reality and irreality as we grow older, although normal adults are still capable of wishful thinking.

The Person in Life Space

The person is often represented as a point moving about in his life space, affected by the pushes and pulls upon him, circumventing barriers in his locomotion in his own life space. If the person is to be treated as a particle in a field, this representation as one point in space is a convenient one.

The person is also represented in a different way, as a differentiated region in life space, the person having a structure of its own. There are more superficial and deeper (less accessible) layers of the personality; there are different degrees of complexity of organization and differentiation; some parts are in communication, while other parts have strong barriers between them. The structure of the person is sometimes diagrammed as in Figure 36. As Leeper [9] points out, a great deal of the experimental work of Lewin and his students has dealt with constructs related to the person, including studies of interrupted tasks, satiation, anger, and rigidity.

Lewin was not very clear about the exact relationship between the person and his life space. Deutsch [10] believes that Lewin used the term "person" in three ways, though Deutsch thinks Lewin might not have agreed with his analysis. One use is as *the behaving person* in life space, essentially a geometrical point upon which the forces diagrammed in life space impinge, determining its locomotion. A second use makes the properties of the person, in interaction with the environment, *produce* life space. His needs, beliefs, and values, determine how life space will be

[9] Leeper (1943), page 62. A summary of earlier work was called *A dynamic theory of personality* (Lewin, 1935).
[10] Deutsch (1954), pages 190–191.

structured for him. The third possibility is that the person and life space are *equivalent,* being two ways of representing the same facts. That is, the diagram of Figure 35 represents the changes in the psychological environment concurrent with the changes in the tension systems shown in Figure 36, and these are two aspects of the psychological situation at the time. Lewin's own preference would probably have been to combine the first and third of these ways of considering the person, that is, he would conceive the "person" as the behaving person, but he would have the behaving person represent at once a differentiated region in life space.

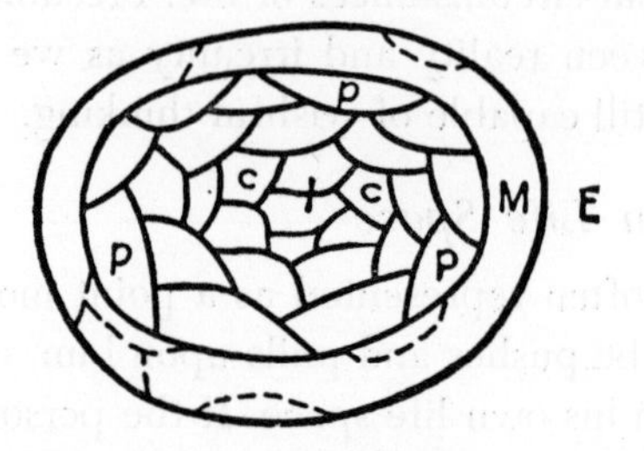

FIGURE 36. Representation of the person. The motor and perceptual regions, because they have commerce with the environment (E), are represented at the boundary zone (M). The portion lying within represents the inner-personal region (I), which has more central parts (*c*) and more peripheral parts (*p*). Under different circumstances of stress, the inner-personal region undergoes differentiation or dedifferentiation ("primitivation"). By permission from *Principles of topological psychology,* by K. Lewin, Copyright 1936 by McGraw-Hill Book Co., Inc.

Valence

When a person is attracted by an object that object is said to have *positive valence,* an analogy with the valence between atoms in chemistry. The person tends to move toward a region in life space that has positive valence, that is, toward an attractive goal or into a region where satisfying activity is possible. To use an older vocabulary, as adopted by Hull (1952), positive valence leads to *adient* activity. By contrast, negative valence refers to an object, or region in life space, from which the person is repelled. That is, objects and activities that a person avoids have negative valence, and they lead to *abient* activity.

Because life space may contain regions with several valences active at once, these give rise to conflict, especially when the opposing forces are approximately in balance. Lewin specified three chief kinds of conflict: [11]

1. Two positive valences. A child has to choose, for example, between going on a picnic and playing with his comrades.

[11] Lewin (1935), pages 88–91. The examples cited are his.

2. A simultaneous positive and negative valence. A child is offered a reward for a school task he does not wish to perform.

3. Two negative valences. A child is threatened by punishment if he does not do a task assigned to him.

The experimental analysis of conflicts of these types has proven fruitful.[12]

The assigning of the valence to the object represented in life space does not, of course, imply that the valence actually inheres in the object. While something like an inverse-square law applies to valence ("the force of attraction varies inversely as the square of the distance"), the theory requires that the distance must be measured psychologically, just as the object carrying valence is the object as perceived by the person. The same object will carry different valences for different people because each of them perceives it differently.

Distance and Direction

Life space is quasi-physical, so sometimes there is a gross correspondence between locomotion in life space and in physical space. A conflict between two objects of which one is on the person's right and one on his left, inviting locomotion in opposite directions, will be represented in a life-space diagram by regions and paths in opposite directions. When physical space and life space are in close correspondence, physical distances and directions may be used for experimental purposes as approximations of distances and directions in life space (that is, Euclidean space is used then to represent hodological space).

But life space often does not correspond to physical space. A choice that is arrived at through reflective thinking is a locomotion in life space quite as genuine as a locomotion involving gross muscular movement. In such cases, where there is no physical counterpart of locomotion, the specification of distance and direction becomes very difficult.

Lewin had little to say about distance. If one path includes another on the way to a goal, it is evident that the included path is shorter than the entire path.[13] That is all that we can say about distance, except in cases in which we assume a correspondence between environmental (physical) space and life space.

Lewin gave a fuller treatment to direction. The direction of a path is defined by the start of the path, "by the beginning step of the distin-

[12] See the early experiments of Fajans (1933a) (1933b), and the later ones by Hovland and Sears (1938), Sears and Hovland (1941), Barker (1942) (1946).

[13] Lewin (1938), page 50.

guished path."[14] There are four possible directions of locomotion. The letter *d*, with appropriate subscripts, serves to symbolize the path whose direction is defined:

(1) The direction of the distinguished path from A to G would be $d_{A,G}$. To indicate a particular route from A to G, the expression might be $d_{A,B,G}$, the additional intermediate letter or letters indicating distinctive portions of the path.

(2) Sometimes the person tends to stay in the present region (continue his present activity). The direction of this tendency is $d_{A,A}$.

(3) Conversely, the direction of a tendency to leave the present region in so far as this tendency involves a disregard of what other regions are moved toward, or the direction of a tendency not to enter the region A, would be $d_{A,-A}$.

(4) Finally, the tendency sometimes is to increase the distance from a not-present region. This tendency has the direction $d_{A,-G}$.[15]

Lewin showed the applicability of his method of representation to a variety of experiments often studied in the learning laboratory: maze learning (familiar and unfamiliar mazes, mazes with one-way doors, T-mazes), the roundabout-route experiments, the use of tools, the obstruction box, extinction of lever-pressing, goal-gradient behavior, various conflict problems. Whether or not his theory is a "learning theory" its relevance to learning is established by these applications.

An Example of the Representation of Experimental Results

Hull (1933) and Leeper (1935a) performed similar experiments in which they taught rats to turn one way through a maze when hungry, another way when thirsty. A rather slight difference in physical arrangements made an enormous difference in the ease of acquiring the habit. Hull's rats took 25 periods of 8 days each (a total of 1000 trials at 5 trials per day) before achieving about 80 per cent correct choices. Leeper's rats performed as well after a single 8-day period (a total of 40 trials). Hull's animals ran to food or water in a common goal-box, finding the door closed if approached from the wrong side. When hungry they could enter the goal-box and find food only if they ran to the left; when thirsty they could find the door open and water in the goal-box only if they ran to the right. (I am disregarding the appropriate balancing out of right and left in the careful design of the experiment.) Leeper's rats ran instead to separate end boxes on the food days and the water days. Both boxes were open, so that if they ran the wrong way on a water day they found food in the end-box they entered; conversely, if they took the wrong path on a food day, they found water in the box entered.

[14] Lewin (1938), page 27.
[15] The summary is quoted from Leeper (1943), page 125.

Let us now see how Lewin diagrammed this difference.[16]

Lewin chose to represent the two experiments by diagrams spatially similar to the actual experimental arrangements, slightly stylized by converting mazes with right-angle turns into circular ones (Figures 37 and 38). There is great freedom in the construction of topological or hodological representations. Hull's problem has to be represented, however, as

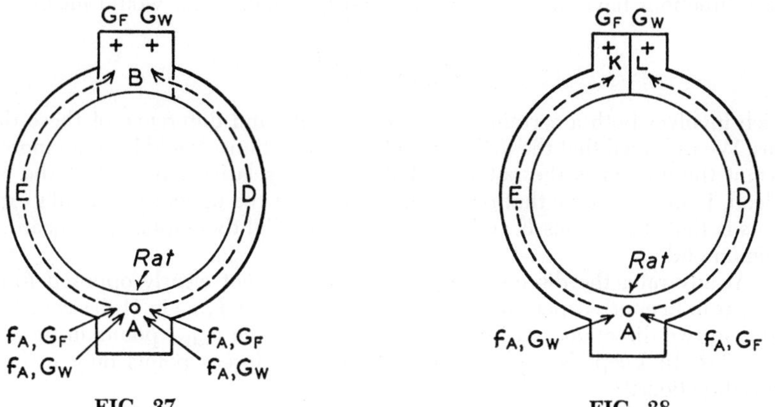

FIGURE 37. Representation of the situation in Hull's experiment (Hull, 1933). A, entrance box; B, goal box; G_F, food goal, reached on hunger day by path A, E,B; G_W, water goal, reached on thirst day by path A,D,B; $f_{A,G}$, force generated by valence of food; f_{A,G_W}, force generated by valence of water. Entrance from the incorrect side was blocked off by a closed door at the goal-box. (Modified slightly from Lewin, 1938, page 182.)

FIGURE 38. Representation of the situation in Leeper's experiment (Leeper, 1935a). A, entrance box; K, goal box in which food was also present, whether the animal was hungry or thirsty; L, goal box in which water was always present, whether the animal was hungry or thirsty; G_F, food goal, reached by path A,E,K; G_W, water goal, reached by path A,D,L; f_{A,G_F}, force generated by valence of food; f_{A,G_W}, force generated by valence of water. Entrances to both goal-boxes always open. (Modified slightly from Lewin, 1938, page 182.)

two paths to a common goal (Figure 37), while Leeper's must be represented as two paths to different goals (Figure 38). Leeper's problem could have been diagrammed as a T-maze or a Y-maze without doing violence to its hodological representation. The important difference between the two figures lies in the forces set up by the highly valenced goals.

[16] Lewin (1938), pages 179–184. It is instructive to compare his explanation with that by Leeper (1935a), pages 31–32, and that by Hull (1952a), page 140. Both Leeper and Hull attribute some influence to the "latent learning" resulting from seeing food when not hungry and water when not thirsty. In his more formal treatment, Hull wrote as though the Hull-Leeper results were alike, thus ignoring the 25:1 difference in difficulty between the two experimental arrangements.

Of the differences between the experiments, Lewin writes:

> For determining the direction of the forces f_{A,G_F} and f_{A,G_W} at the point A in the experiment of Hull, there remains the question of determining the relation between the directions $d_{A,D}$ and $d_{A,E}$. In Leeper's experiment both are clearly opposed. In Hull's experiment we have to deal with a rather complicated relation between the directions of two paths from the same starting region to the same end-region. By discussing the geometry of the situation we have seen that those directions have to be considered "partly equal." That would mean in our case:
>
> $$d_{A,D} \, (=) \, d_{A,E}$$
>
> which involves both a certain amount of equality and difference of these directions. We expected that the *difference* of both directions should become more important the greater is the potency of the means, relatively to that of the ends. Indeed, I would assume that one of the reasons for the difficulty in Hull's experiments is that the regions E and D are relatively slightly emphasized means to a common end.
>
> At any rate, the directions $d_{A,D}$ and $d_{A,E}$ are not clearly opposed to each other, as in Leeper's experiments. In addition, the force f_{A,G_F} in Hull's experiment points in two directions, $d_{A,D}$ and $d_{A,E}$. Also the force f_{A,G_W} points in these two directions. In Leeper's experiment each of these forces points only in one of these directions.[17]

Apart from pointing out the obvious differences in experimental arrangements, Lewin proposes two explanations for the greater ease of learning by Leeper's rats than by Hull's: (1) the two paths are less differentiated for Hull's rats, and (2) the forces determining the choice at the starting point are more nearly in balance for Hull's rats. Unfortunately, Lewin's explanation fails to tell us how he would propose to handle a number of features of the experiments:

> How does experienced goal satisfaction or frustration affect the cognitive structure on the next trial?
>
> How does the state of hunger or thirst modify the cognitive structure of the rat, or the forces or valences operating?
>
> Of what importance are the closed doors in Hull's experiment?[18]
>
> If the forces acting on Hull's rats are in balance, why do the rats eventually solve the problem?

Lewin succeeded in making it plausible that there should be greater difficulty for Hull's rats than for Leeper's, but he clearly did not account in any detail for the findings. One can only conclude that, if other ex-

[17] Lewin (1938), page 183.

[18] Lewin noted their importance, and gave an illustration from human behavior to make the difference between Hull's experiment and Leeper's seem less paradoxical, Lewin (1938), page 181. But the closed doors do not appear in the *formal* treatment of the experiment.

planations are as incomplete as this one, distance and direction are left in an unsatisfactory state.[19]

Behavior as a Function of the Present Life Space

Perhaps even more forcefully than his gestalt colleagues, Lewin insisted that behavior depends upon the present, not upon the past or the future. Past events, like future events, do not exist now, and therefore in his sense, cannot have effects now. While past psychological fields are part of the origin of the present field, their relationship to the present is so indirect that their explanatory value is slight.

As pointed out earlier, the notion of contemporary causation is a sound one, and need not lessen the importance of a knowledge of the past in contributing to an understanding of the present. It is true, however, that in adopting a logical position there often go along with it certain overtones of interest and preoccupation not essential to the position. Lewin's whole-hearted insistence on the importance of the present accentuated his interest in conflict and other contemporaneous motivational situations, and lessened his interest in progressive changes, such as those studied in conventional learning situations or in the psychological clinic.

Lewin justifies his neglect of learning on different grounds. He says that learning (i.e., the influence of the past on the present) has been much overemphasized as a reaction against earlier prescientific teleology (i.e., the influence of the future on the present). Field theory's emphasis on the present he believes to be a necessary corrective, establishing a preferred balance of interest.[20]

The Time Dimension

Despite his preference for dealing with present causes, Lewin was not, of course, oblivious to the time dimension. Because learning theorists tend to be preoccupied with changes that take place in time, it is of interest to examine Lewin's position.

In a discussion defending the principle of contemporaneous causation, at the same time showing that he was aware of historical factors, Lewin had this to say:

> Without altering the principle of contemporaneity as one of the basic propositions of field theory, we have to realize that to determine the psychological direction and velocity of behavior (i.e., what is usually called the "meaning" of the psychological event), we have to take into account in psychology as in

[19] This conclusion was reached also by Leeper (1943), who then suggested improvements that would require major changes in Lewin's system.

[20] Lewin (1942), page 222.

physics a certain time-period. The length of this period depends in psychology upon the scope of the situation. As a rule, the more macroscopic the situation is which has to be described the longer is the period which has to be observed to determine the direction and velocity of behavior at a given time.[21]

Lewin accepted from L. K. Frank (1939) the dimension of life space called "time-perspective," which includes the psychological past and the psychological future. The small child lives largely in the present, and as

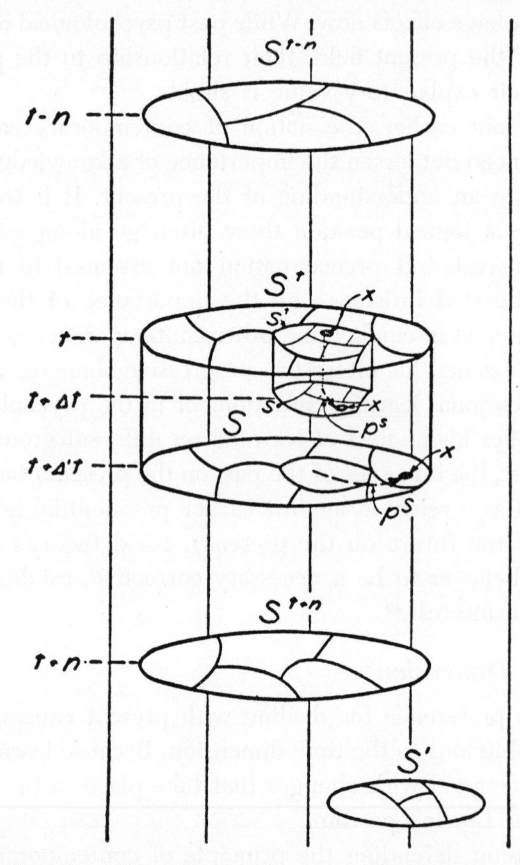

FIGURE 39. The time dimension in life space. The sequence of events starts at the top and moves downward. Note the movement of the person (x) along path p^s in a small segment of time, and along path p^S in a larger segment of time. Lewin (1943), page 302.

he grows he conforms his behavior to events in the more remote future. Part of the overemotional reactions of adolescents may be due to their attempt to face adult problems before they have sufficient time-perspective. Then they interpret a momentary frustration as an enduring defeat.

[21] Lewin (1943), page 301.

No very satisfactory diagrammatic device was found for adding the time dimension to life space. One kind of diagram resembles those used to show the pathways through the spinal cord. Then the time dimension can be thought of as the long axis of the cord, the cross sections corresponding to momentary life space. Such a diagram is given in Figure 39.

Another diagram presents life space captured at various segments of time, as though life space moves along on a continuous belt and can be examined at any moment. Such a diagram, for life space in relation to a planned future event, is given in Figure 40. In this diagram there appears also a vertical dimension, indicating the difference between life space on

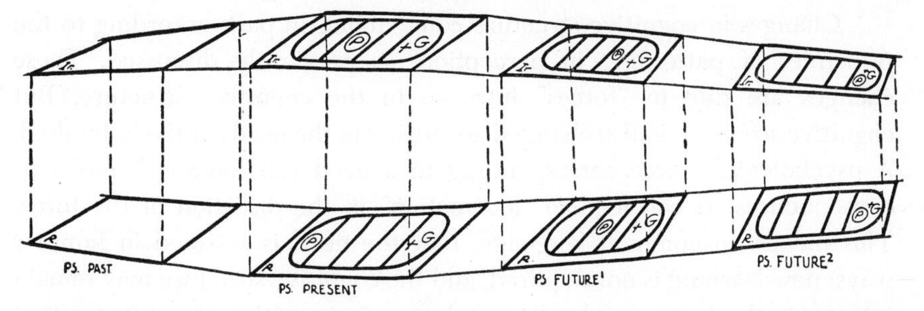

FIGURE 40. Time perspective in planning. The sequence of events starts at the left and moves to the right. Each segment is as seen by the person *at the time represented.* The vertical dimension is that of irreality (wish; fantasy). The coming together of the two levels in the future means that there is less difference between reality and irreality as something planned is more nearly achieved. Note that at earlier stages the wish makes the person appear to be nearer to the goal in irreality than in reality. From Barker, Dembo, and Lewin (1941), page 210.

the plane of irreality (fantasy), and on the level of reality. Note that the future, as now perceived, appears in present life space, but life space itself changes as time moves on.

APPLICATIONS TO LEARNING

Learning as a Change in Cognitive Structure

As one learns, one increases in knowledge. What does it mean to know more? It means to have a more highly differentiated life space, in which there are more subregions connected by defined paths. That is another way of saying that we know facts in their relationships; we know what leads to what.

A problematical situation represents an unstructured region of life space. We do not know how to get from the givens to the goal. We feel insecure until the region becomes structured. When it does become structured so as to permit problem solution, we have learned.

A change in the structure of knowledge (cognitive structure) may occur with repetition. The situation may require repeated exposures before the structure gets changed. The important thing is that the cognitive structure gets changed, not that the repetitions occur. With better arrangements of the problem the structure may get changed with fewer repetitions. This is the lesson of the insight experiments. Too much repetition does not aid learning; on the contrary, repetition may lead to psychological satiation [22] with accompanying disorganization and dedifferentiation of the cognitive structure.

Changes in cognitive structure come about, in part, according to the principles of patterning in perception, as previously discussed. These changes are due to "forces" intrinsic to the cognitive structure. But cognitive structure is also changed according to the needs of the individual. A psychological force corresponding to a need can have either of two consequences. It can lead to "locomotion" in the direction of the force. This means, in common language, that the need is satisfied in familiar ways; new learning is not required, and the cognitive structure may remain intact. Or the force can lead to a change in cognitive structure so that such a "locomotion" may be facilitated. That is, the relationships within the situation are seen in new ways, so that the need may be satisfied. In the latter case, motivated learning may be said to have taken place.

Reward and Punishment

Those who accept law of effect or reinforcement theories have seldom analyzed in detail what the circumstances are which force the learner to confront the reward or the threat of punishment. Lewin's treatment of the conflicts involved is recognized by at least one of his critics as an advance over traditional law-of-effect thinking.[23]

The usual arrangement in punishment is illustrated in Figure 41. The threat of punishment (Pu) is used to keep the learner at an intrinsically disliked task (T). A conflict is set up so that the individual is forced to choose between one or the other of the disagreeable possibilities. Under these circumstances, the tendency is to "leave the field," to avoid both of the tasks. In order to keep the learner in the field of the conflict it is necessary to erect barriers (B). These in actual life are usually authoritarian; it is necessary to "police" a learning situation controlled by punish-

[22] Karsten (1928).
[23] Estes (1954b), page 340.

ment. Because association psychologists have tended to perform their experiments in confining runways or with subjects strapped to the apparatus, they have usually overlooked important dynamic arrangements of their experiments. The importance of the barrier is not incorporated in their theories.

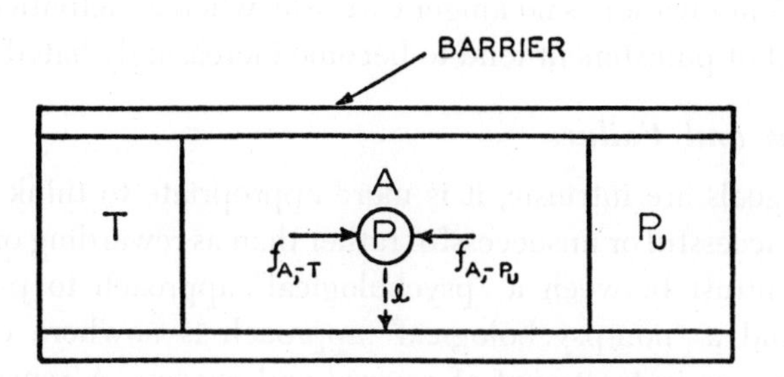

FIGURE 41. Life space in threatened punishment. The person is caught between the tendency to avoid an unpleasant task (T) and the threat of punishment (Pu). Because of the conflict there will be a tendency to leave the situation (1) unless there are strong barriers to prevent this. Hence the punishment situation to be effective, is necessarily prison-like. After Lewin (1942), page 233, by permission of the National Society for the Study of Education.

In a reward situation it is not necessary for the learner to be "walled in" because the attractiveness of the reward keeps him in the field. It is necessary, however, to keep a barrier around the reward, to prevent access by any route (such as W) other than by going through (performing) the disliked but requested activity (Figure 42). Because the reward is externally related to activity T, there will always be a tendency to take

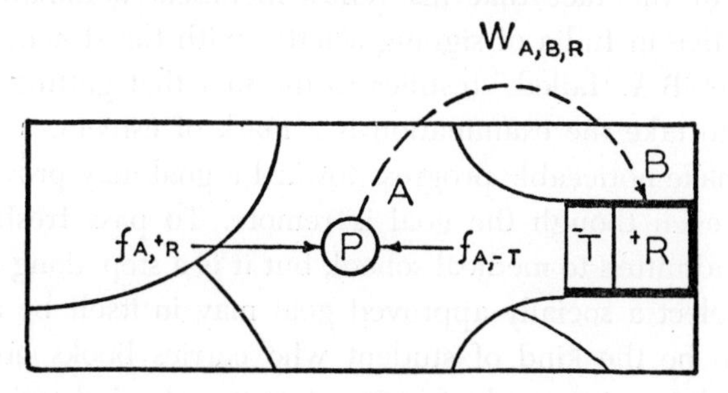

FIGURE 42. Life space in offered reward. The person is in conflict because the approach to reward (R) is by way of the unpleasant task (T). While the tendency to leave the field is not present as it is in punishment, there is a tendency to approach the reward by way of a shortcut so as to avoid T, as by path $W_{A,B,R}$. Hence it is necessary to guard access to the reward to prevent approach by any path other than that through T. Some policing is necessary, but the situation is less prison-like than in the case of control by punishment. After Lewin (1946), page 811, reproduced by permission from *Manual of child psychology* edited by L. Carmichael, published by John Wiley & Sons, Inc.

short cuts, if possible. Cheating by school children is such an effort to obtain the reward without performing the demanded work.

The differences in structure between reward and punishment situations are real. One consequence of the different amounts of constraint in the two situations is that rewarded activities often become interesting and liked, so that motivation is no longer extrinsic, whereas activities controlled by the threat of punishment tend to become increasingly hated.[24]

Success and Failure

When goals are intrinsic, it is more appropriate to think of the goal activity as successful or unsuccessful rather than as rewarding or punishing.

The contrast between a "psychological" approach to psychological problems and a "non-psychological" approach is nowhere clearer than in the difference in treatment of *reward* and *success.* A reward is something tangible and external, which merely terminates a situation (Guthrie) or is associated with need reduction (Hull). A success experience has to be understood according to what the learner is trying to do, and the relationship between success and goal-achievement is a somewhat complex affair. Psychological analysis of success from the point of view of the learner shows at least the following possibilities: [25]

1. To reach a goal constitutes success. This is the usual interpretation of success. It is obviously satisfying to try for something and to achieve it.

2. To get within the region of the goal may be a success experience. Some goals are less well defined than others. A student may hope for an A grade, but be satisfied with a B; a person may wish an office, but take satisfaction in the fact that his fellow-members nominated him. The curious practice in India of signing a letter with the statement following the signature "B.A., failed," testifies to the fact that getting near enough to the goal to take the examination is a mark of esteem.

3. To make noticeable progress toward a goal may provide a success experience, even though the goal is remote. To pass freshman physics is not to be admitted to medical school, but it is a step along the way.

4. To select a socially approved goal may in itself be a success experience. To be the kind of student who carries books home over the Christmas holidays is a mark of serious intent and is bolstering to the ego, even though the books remain unopened. To own an encyclopedia is to

[24] Lewin (1942), page 233. For a fuller discussion of promised reward and threatened punishment, see Lewin (1935), pages 114–170.

[25] Hilgard (1942).

be the kind of person you would like to be, whether or not the encyclopedia is consulted.

If such matters are talked about in the language of primary and secondary reinforcements, some of the vividness of the learner-goal relationship is bound to be lost. It is to Lewin's credit that he made a serious effort to deal with psychologically real problems, and then, as a second step, tried to find a mathematics appropriate to them. Too often the alternative is chosen of looking first for something which can be measured and counted, hoping that psychologically more interesting relationships can be deduced from them later on. This leads to preoccupation with nonsense syllables, mazes, and conditioned responses, to the neglect of the problems of behavior in freer life situations in which the learner selects his own goals and redefines them as he goes along.

The experiments which pointed up the concepts used by Lewin and his students in discussing success and failure were those of Hoppe (1930) which introduced the companion notions of *ego involvement* and *level of aspiration.*

Psychological success and failure depend upon ego involvement in the task at hand. That is the goals must be real to the learner, so that, if achieved, there is the elation of significant accomplishment; if not achieved, there is a chagrin or humiliation of defeat. As William James put it, our self-esteem may be expressed as the ratio between our success and our pretensions.[26]

Hoppe pointed out that there is a restricted region of difficulty within which success and failure are possible (Figure 43). Some tasks are much too easy. To succeed in them is not to experience success. A school child is insulted if asked to spell words which are too easy or to make computations interpreted as "baby stuff." Some tasks are much too hard. If we are asked to give a construction in Russian grammar—and we make no pretense of knowing Russian—this is not a psychological failure. It is only within the range of uncertainty—where both success and failure are possible—that we can really succeed or really fail. Experienced teachers know how hard it is to keep tasks at an appropriate level of difficulty so that the learners remain ego-involved.

Individuals tend to set momentary goals within the range of activities in which there is ego involvement. The momentary goal is referred to as the *level of aspiration.* It is set according to the learner's interpretation of his own achievement, but there are wide individual differences in

[26] James (1890), page I, 310.

the manner of such goal-setting. Some learners are realistic, and set their goals near to what they have shown themselves capable of doing. Those who are unrealistic may depart in either direction from their past achievements. Some are self-protective, and to avoid the possibility of failure set goals too low; others are hopeful, and set goals unrealistically too high.[27]

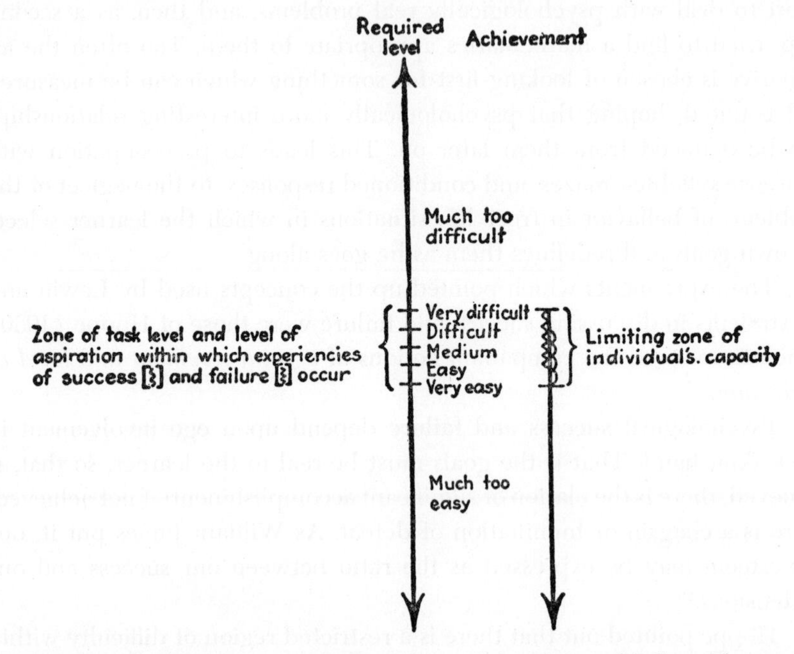

FIGURE 43. Difficulty-level and the experience of success and failure. The psychological experience of success and failure can occur only in the region in which there is some possibility of objective achievement or lack of achievement. By permission from *A dynamic theory of personality,* by K. Lewin, Copyright 1935 by McGraw-Hill Book Co., Inc.

The interrelationships among past achievements, momentary goals, social atmosphere, and individuality, set a number of inviting experimental problems.[28] The flavor of these studies is legitimately compared with that of studies on reward, punishment, and reinforcement, which represent the approach to the same subject matter taken by the stimulus-response psychologists. Regardless of how one may view the conceptual system within which the level-of-aspiration studies are framed, it is evident that they call attention to aspects of goal-directed activities which have been neglected by those preoccupied with reward and punishment.

[27] P. S. Sears (1940) (1941).

[28] For reviews of experiments concerned with level of aspiration, see J. D. Frank (1941) and Lewin, Dembo, Festinger, and P. S. Sears (1944).

Learning as a Change in Motivation

The repetition of an activity brings changes both in the cognitive structure and in the need-tension systems. Often a desirable outcome is a change in the interests or values of the learner, that is, a change in the relative attractiveness of one goal over another. This goal-attractiveness is what Lewin calls *valence,* and valences change.

The following three cases of valence-change as a result of repetition are to be distinguished:

1. Attractive goals may lose their attraction if the activity related to them is repeated to the point of satiation. Monotony and boredom are familiar enough experiences, but their dynamics are by no means simple. The suggestion that every activity presents a barrier to its own repetition (one of Hull's postulates) does not suffice to account for the details that are found. For example, when tasks are graded as pleasant, unpleasant, or indifferent and then repeated excessively, the unpleasant tasks, as might be expected, are first satiated.[29] But it is the pleasant tasks which next become impossible to repeat, and the indifferent tasks are consistently last. Because of less ego involvement in the indifferent tasks, their endless repetition does not develop the resistances found for either pleasant or unpleasant activities. Psychological satiation is not to be confused with fatigue, even though fatigue symptoms are prominently present. Karsten showed that the symptoms often disappeared with a change of set, even though the same muscular activities might be involved in the new task. For example, a subject who had to quit a line-drawing task because of inability to hold the pencil any longer was asked to write out a description of the psychological processes which had been involved in the performance, and was able to pick up the pencil and write about the performance with ease, including demonstrations of the task which no longer could be performed!

2. Goals originally unattractive may become acceptable through a change in the meaning of the goal-related activity. There are many teaching techniques which depend upon this principle. Lewin gives a number of examples.[30] One is the changing of food preferences by telling a story in which the disliked food is the favorite for the hero.[31] This is a common radio device for selling breakfast food. Another illustration is the changing of ideologies, as in the experiment of Bavelas (1942) in which relatively

[29] Karsten (1928).
[30] Lewin (1942), pages 235–236.
[31] Duncker (1938).

autocratic recreation leaders were changed into democratic ones. It was necessary for the cognitive structure of the field, "leadership behavior," to undergo changes so that what they were trying to do as leaders became changed.

3. The choice of goals is influenced by previous experiences of success and failure. This is most clearly shown in the experiments of Sears [32] in which she found that realistic goal-setting was characteristic of those who had experienced success. It is possible to attenuate the bad consequences of failure by teaching more appropriate adjustments to it, thus raising children who can tolerate frustration.[33] But this does not alter the fact that in addition to the problem of how goals affect behavior there exists the very important problem of how goals are chosen.

MEMORY FOR FINISHED AND UNFINISHED TASKS AS ILLUSTRATIVE OF EXPERIMENTS SUGGESTED BY LEWIN'S THEORY

The facts of amnesia show that forgetting and retention are incompletely understood according to our ordinary theories of forgetting through disuse or retroactive inhibition. That there are motivational and emotional factors at work has been emphasized in the Freudian theory of repression.[34] It is in this context that Zeigarnik's (1927) experiment on the recall of finished and unfinished tasks is to be considered, for the experiment dramatically relates forgetting to tension systems within the individual as a demonstration of Lewin's (1926) theory.

The subjects (variously students, teachers, children, 256 in all) were given simple tasks to perform. In the individual experiments there were usually 18 to 22 such tasks: modeling a figure from clay, laying out playing blocks in certain forms, solving simple puzzles, and so on. The experimenter interrupted the subject on half the tasks, waiting until the subject was deeply engrossed in it so that it would be a psychologically real interruption. Which tasks were interrupted differed from subject to subject according to conventional experimental practice.

After "tidying up" in order to remove all tools and other reminders of specific tasks, the experimenter asked the subject: "Please tell me what the tasks were upon which you worked during this experiment." Often a number of tasks were mentioned, then a pause would occur. After

[32] P. S. Sears (1940) (1941).
[33] Keister (1937).
[34] E.g., R. R. Sears (1936a), Rapaport (1942) (1950).

considerable effort a few more tasks might be recalled. For purposes of scoring, only those tasks were counted which were readily recalled, that is, before the pause. The difficulty of such recall is greater than might be supposed. In one series, 32 subjects recalled between 7 and 19 tasks out of 22 worked on, averaging 11, or just half the total; in another series, 14 subjects recalled between 7 and 16 of 20 tasks, averaging 10, again half the total.

When the relative success of recall for completed or interrupted tasks was examined, it was found that of the first 32 subjects, 26 remembered interrupted tasks better than completed ones, 3 remembered both equally well, and 3 remembered the completed tasks better.

A scoring ratio was devised to indicate the relative superiority of interrupted tasks recalled (I) over completed tasks recalled (C). If both were equally recalled, the ratio would be $I/C = 1.00$. In the first experiment the ratio turned out to be 1.9, indicating that the interrupted tasks were recalled 90 per cent better than the completed ones.[35] Most of the other ratios obtained from groups were in the same direction, that is, above 1.0, although there were wide individual differences.

Zeigarnik went on to test several hypotheses to account for the greater retention of the unfinished tasks, and also to determine the circumstances under which finished tasks would be better recalled.

The first hypothesis tested was that the attention value of the task might be enhanced by the shock of interruption. When, however, the task was interrupted early in the hour and completed later, it was forgotten like any other completed task, thus contradicting the hypothesis.

A second hypothesis was that the subjects expected the interrupted tasks to be resumed and therefore made special note of them. However, a test situation in which one group was told that the tasks would be resumed, and another that they would not, failed to result in a difference between the groups.

The remaining hypothesis, the one accepted, is that a task not completed leaves a state of tension, a quasi-need. Completing the task means resolving the tension or discharging the quasi-need. The advantage in memory of the unfinished task is due to the continuation of the tension.

The advantage of unfinished tasks is not to be universally expected. Zeigarnik pointed out at least eight conditions under which the relative advantage is lost:

1. If a task, finished to the experimenter's satisfaction, is considered

[35] Marrow (1938) has pointed out that the ratio of 1.9 is too high because it is an average of ratios. Corrected as a ratio of tasks recalled it is reduced to 1.6.

inadequately completed by the subject, it may be recalled as well as an interrupted task.

2. Tasks which are without a clear-cut completion stage, such as marking X's on a sheet of paper, have no advantage in memory following interruption. Interruption is in such cases not a psychological incompleteness; it is the mere calling of a halt to an endless activity.

3. Subjects who do not become at all involved in the individual tasks, but act according to command, remember finished and unfinished tasks equally well. A group of visiting school children who were set to work when they had come merely to see the laboratory were obedient in this way, and their recall ratio was $I/C = 1.03$.

4. If the tasks are seen as leading to the satisfaction of a single need, so that the boundaries between them are weakened, the individual effects of interruption are lost. One small group of subjects became engrossed in discovering the meaning of the experiment, so that the individual tasks were imbedded in this search for the secret of the experiment. The ratio was $I/C = 1.12$. Another group of subjects was shown in advance all the tasks that were to be solved in the hour. By reducing the separateness of tasks the difference between interruption and completion was lost, with $I/C = 0.97$.

5. If subjects were very tired when performing the experiment and rested when tested, or rested while performing and tired when tested, the memory advantage of unfinished tasks was lost; in fact, for the tired-fresh group, the finished tasks were better recalled ($I/C = 0.61$). An ingenious explanation is offered. It is said that the tension-system cannot be maintained in a loosened, relatively fluid medium, hence memory for the uncompleted tasks is poor in a tired condition. On the other hand, under such circumstances relatively stable systems (finished tasks) persist in spite of the state of fatigue.[36]

6. After delays of 24 hours, the I/C ratio drops to about 1.00, so that there is no longer an advantage for the interrupted task. This is interpreted as due to intervening activity, not to time alone, because of the next observation.

7. If a highly emotional episode is introduced between the tasks and the retest, the same distortion occurs as with the passage of time. Six subjects tested in this way all showed better recall of finished tasks.

[36] The tests were made after 13–15 hours, when the relative advantage of the interrupted task might have been lost in any case. If the conjecture holds, immediate retention after performing while tired should favor the completed tasks.

8. A task which the subject found too difficult was often forgotten, even though it had been interrupted. The situation is considered to favor repression.[37]

The practical implications of Mrs. Zeigarnik's findings are somewhat obscure. In the first place, the memory for the tasks performed is a very different matter from memory for what was learned or how to perform the task next time. It would be a mistake to assume that children should not be permitted to complete assignments, lest they forget them. They might forget what they *did* in the library on Tuesday afternoon and still remember what they *found out* there.[38] In the second place, the phenomenon is so temporary, and so easily disturbed by other experiences, that its practical meaning is uncertain. It may be that the temporary nature of the effects is due to the triviality of the tasks; if that is so, it is important to have a comparable demonstration made with more significant tasks.

One of the more revealing of the later studies concerned with the problem of recall of the task is that of Marrow (1938). He explained that he was trying out different sorts of materials, and that if he saw the subject was getting along all right he would stop him and give him a new task. Only if the subject was taking unusually long, or having trouble, would he be permitted to finish the task. Under these circumstances, interruption was psychologically interpreted as success, non-interruption as failure. Recall was found to be higher for the *completed* tasks, that is, those which caused feelings of failure. While wholly in agreement with the position that ego-related aspects of the performance are important in the recall, the tension set up is not quite that of task completion, although it may be related to it in the form: "If only I had another chance at it!"

The type of investigation started by Zeigarnik has proved a stimulus to a great deal of future work.[39] Some of the subsequent studies have been concerned with a slightly different problem—the resumption of the interrupted tasks. It is evident from these studies that correlated with the memory for the task is a tendency to resume it when the opportunity next

[37] For a list of 11 variables affecting the results in experiments of this kind, see Prentice (1944), page 338.

[38] McKinney (1935), however, found a tendency for the *substance* of an interrupted task (maze learning) to be better retained than the substance of a completed task. Nuttin (1953), pages 341–351, also has shown memory for the substance of the unfinished tasks rather than retention for the *names* of the tasks.

[39] For useful summaries see Prentice (1944), Glixman (1948), McGeoch and Irion (1952), pages 390–394, Alper (1952). Representative studies include Abel (1938), Alper (1946) (1948), Atkinson (1953), Glixman (1949), Martin (1940), Pachauri (1935), Rosenzweig (1933) (1941) (1943), Rosenzweig and Mason (1934), Sanford (1946).

arises.[40] These studies are consonant with the Lewin interpretation that a quasi-need has been set up as a result of the interruption.

ESTIMATE OF LEWIN'S POSITION

Lewin on the Typical Problems of Learning

Because his was not essentially a psychology of learning, it is difficult to assign Lewin a position on each of the standard problems. A large measure of conjecture necessarily enters.

1. *Capacity.* The life space of an adult is more highly differentiated than that of a child. Similarly, the life space of an intelligent person is structured more highly than that of a less intelligent person. There are also differences in fluidity or rigidity.[41]

2. *Practice.* Learning may take place with repetition because the change in cognitive structure or in motivation may require repetition. There is, however, no one-to-one relationship between number of trials and the changes which constitute learning.

3. *Motivation.* The differences between reward and punishment are well represented in life-space diagrams, which point out the difference in the amount of policing required in the two situations. This aspect of reward and punishment has been neglected by all the other writers considered. For some purposes it is preferable to speak about success and failure rather than about reward and punishment. Then the concepts of ego-involvement and level of aspiration become important. Cognitive structure is both activated by and changed by aroused needs or tensions. Motivation is therefore of central importance within the theory.

4. *Understanding.* Because one of the chief characterizations of learning is change in cognitive structure, knowledge and understanding lie at the heart of learning.

5. *Transfer.* Probably the gestalt concept of transposition is acceptable to Lewin.

6. *Forgetting.* Motivated forgetting is important. The dynamics are rather complicated, with interruption in an ego-involved task leading usually to better retention and to attempts at resumption when the opportunity is offered. However, something like repression is accepted, in the forgetting of too difficult tasks.

[40] Related studies include Adler and Kounin (1939), Cartwright (1942), Nowlis (1941), Ovsiankina (1928), Rethlingshafer (1941), Rickers-Ovsiankina (1937).
[41] Kounin (1941).

The Emphasis upon Motivation

The relationship of motivation to learning has been increasingly recognized by stimulus-response theorists, but their usual solutions of the problem have not been well adapted to deal with the complexities of goal-setting, conflict, and problem-solving. The two common solutions have been that of the law of effect (and related reinforcement theories), and the addition of set and determining tendencies to ordinary associative processes. Lewin has made a real contribution by his more dynamic, in some real sense more "psychological," approach to the problem.

Historically there were others making similar proposals. Lewin was undoubtedly influenced by Freud, whose work he thought brilliant but methodologically unsound.[42] In America, McDougall [43] was the arch opponent of behaviorism until gestalt psychology came upon the scene. McDougall often inveighed against the errors of hedonism (in which he classed the law of effect) in placing too much emphasis on what happened in the presence of the goal, and too little on the satisfaction which derived from the striving. Woodworth, whose *Dynamic psychology* (1918) gave currency to the notion of drives, included the conception of activity itself becoming a drive. This is an anticipation of Lewin's tension theory, although Lewin probably was not influenced by it. While McDougall and Woodworth were not gestalt psychologists, they saw some of the limitations in contemporary learning theory which Lewin also saw and attempted to meet through his experiments and theories.

A satisfactory psychological theory of motivation is almost certain to include some kind of ego reference, that is, some incorporation of the present activity within the larger goals, values, or ambitions of the learner.[44] Lewin's motivational theories definitely take account of such problems.

Other Aspects of Lewin's System

The problems of learning can no longer be neatly segregated from the other problems of psychology and limited to the kinds of data that can be plotted in the form of learning and retention curves. Hence it becomes increasingly difficult to determine what aspects of a psychological system may become relevant for learning. In the foregoing account of Lewin's work, emphasis has been placed upon those features that overlap, at least

[42] Lewin (1937).
[43] E.g., McDougall (1923).
[44] The problem was discussed by the contributors to a symposium on the ego and the law of effect, Allport (1946), Mowrer (1946), and Rice (1946).

in topic, with what other learning theorists discuss. Here brief notice will be taken of certain other features of his system, more remote from the usual topics dealt with in the psychology of learning.

One set of Lewin's interests might be designated as *the dynamics of child behavior*. This led to the inclusion of chapters by him in successive editions of handbooks of child psychology [45] and the collection of a book of readings on child development by authors much influenced by him.[46] With prominence given to childhood as a period of learning, interest in child development becomes increasingly important for learning psychologists.

A second set of interests was social psychology, especially *group dynamics*. An early disciple wrote a social psychology using many topological diagrams.[47] A number of Lewin's own papers were collected in a posthumous volume (1951). Again, as the influence of the group upon the learning of the individual comes more into focus, studies of this kind may become more significant for learning.

Related to the interest in group dynamics was a methodological interest in *action research*, a technique for getting things done, while at the same time criticizing the process along the way. His papers in this field have also been collected and published in a small volume with the title *Resolving social conflicts* (1948). The applied psychology of learning can profit from the adaptation of some of the principles of action research, for example, in encouraging teachers to use newer methods and in gaining the support of the community for these methods.[48]

Is Field Theory in Learning Related to Physical Field Theory?

Critics of Lewin have objected to a certain gain for the prestige of his theory because he used words such as "dynamic" and "field," which bring with them implications that the theory is unusually up-to-date and modern, and that other theories are old-fashioned and stodgy.

There are two major criticisms of his identifying his theory as a field theory:

1. If he means simply that he recognizes multiple causation, then his theory is no more a field theory than anyone else's. Any sophisticated theory recognizes that behavior is a function at once of a number of variables.

[45] Lewin (1933a) (1946).
[46] Barker, Kounin, and Wright (1943).
[47] J. F. Brown (1936).
[48] E.g., Hilgard (1953).

2. If he means that his theory is a field theory similar to a physical field theory, then his mathematics ought to correspond more nearly to that used by physicists.

Lewin answered the first criticism by saying that "the recognition of a multitude of factors as determining an event, and even their representation as a phase space, does not presuppose field theory." [49] He points out that Thurstone's factor analysis fits the notion of multiple causation but is not a field theory.

Lewin believed that his theory did correspond closely to field theory in physics. As it applies to psychology, he stated:

> One of the basic statements of psychological field theory can be formulated as follows: Any behavior or any other change in a psychological field depends only upon the psychological field *at that time*.[50]

He believed that the equivalent of the differential in physics (dx/dt) was his concept of "behavior," which, for him, covered any change in the psychological field. But this is an inexact statement, for his equations do not actually make use of differentials. Hence the precise relationship between psychological fields and physical fields is indeterminate. As Estes has put it:

> The main conclusion from our analysis of Lewin's methodology is not that field theory has been found unsuitable in the treatment of learning but rather that the issue is still open because Lewin did not construct a field theory.[51]

His mathematical representations have been criticized, apart from their relationship to field physics. Lewin's use of vectors and valences leading to locomotion in life space represents a courageous attempt to find a mathematics with a natural "fit" to the kind of data with which he deals. The rather unsatisfactory state of this mathematical structure has been pointed out not only by those impatient with his approach,[52] but by those friendly to his point of view.[53] But the difficulties are inherent in the early stages of theory construction and need not prevent appreciation of Lewin's positive suggestions.

His general conception of the relationship between mathematics and the data of a science is sound. There is no question that some forms of mathematics are more appropriate than others. The geometry of spaces does usefully represent alternative routes, conflict, ambivalence, barriers, and many other psychologically real situations. It is the incorporation of

[49] Lewin (1943), page 293.
[50] Lewin (1943), page 295.
[51] Estes (1954b), page 342.
[52] E.g., London (1944).
[53] E g., Leeper (1943).

metrical concepts of distance, direction, and the like which causes the most trouble. The usual diagram also best represents the momentary life space. The conversion of this diagram into a third dimensional figure showing the changes in time—with which learning theories are commonly concerned—introduces some awkwardness. As in the case of Hull's mathematical model, a great deal of tinkering is possible in smoothing out the difficulties without destroying the essence of what it is trying to convey.

SUPPLEMENTARY READINGS

BOOKS

LEWIN, K. (1935) *A dynamic theory of personality.*

LEWIN, K. (1936) *Principles of topological psychology.*

LEWIN, K. (1938) *The conceptual representation and the measurement of psychological forces.*

LEWIN, K. (1948) *Resolving social conflicts.*

LEWIN, K. (1951) *Field theory in social science.*

SHORTER INTRODUCTIONS

LEEPER, R. (1943) *Lewin's topological and vector psychology, a digest and a critique.*

LEWIN, K. (1942) Field theory and learning. Chapter 6 in *The psychology of learning.* Natl. Soc. Stud. Educ., 41st Yearbook, Part II, 215–242.

LEWIN, K. (1946) Behavior and development as a function of the total situation. In L. Carmichael, ed. *Manual of child psychology.* 791–844.

CRITICAL REVIEWS

HEIDBREDER, E. (1937) Review of Lewin's *Principles of topological psychology. Psychol. Bull.*, 34, 584–604.

LEEPER, R. (1943) *Lewin's topological and vector psychology, a digest and a critique.*

SEARS, R. R. (1936) Review of Lewin's *A dynamic theory of personality. Psychol. Bull.*, 33, 548–552.

REPRESENTATIVE EXPERIMENTS

BARKER, R. G. (1942) An experimental study of the resolution of conflict by children. In Q. McNemar and M. A. Merrill, eds. *Studies in personality, Contributed in honor of Lewis M. Terman.* New York: McGraw-Hill, 13–34.

BARKER, R. G., DEMBO, T., and LEWIN, K. (1941) Frustration and regression: a study of young children. *Univ. Ia. Stud. Child Welf.*, 18, No. 1.

BIRENBAUM, G. (1930) Das Vergessen einer Vornahme. *Psychol. Forsch.*, 13, 218–284.

DEMBO, T. (1931) Der Ärger als dynamischen Problem. *Psychol. Forsch.*, 15, 1–144.

FESTINGER, L. (1942) Wish, expectation, and group standards as factors influencing level of aspiration. *J. abnorm. soc. Psychol.*, 37, 184–200.

GLIXMAN, A. F. (1949) Recall of completed and incompleted activities under varying degrees of stress. *J. exp. Psychol.*, 39, 281–295.

Hoppe, F. (1930) Erfolg und Misserfolg. *Psychol. Forsch.*, 14, 1–62.

Karsten, A. (1928) Psychische Sättigung. *Psychol. Forsch.*, 10, 142–254.

Lewin, K., Lippitt, R., and White, R. K. (1939) Patterns of aggressive behavior in experimentally created "social climates." *J. soc. Psychol.*, 10, 271–299.

Ovsiankina, M. (1928) Die Wiederaufnahme unterbrochener Handlungen. *Psychol. Forsch.*, 11, 302–379.

Rosenthal, D., and Cofer, C. N. (1948) The effect on group performance of an indifferent and neglectful attitude shown by one group member. *J. exp. Psychol.*, 38, 568–577.

Schwarz, G. (1927) Über Rückfälligkeit bei Umgewöhnung. *Psychol. Forsch.*, 9, 86–158.

Zeigarnik, B. (1927) Das Behalten erledigter und unerledigter Handlungen. *Psychol. Forsch.*, 9, 1–85.

FINAL NOTE

For a searching critique of the formal aspects of Lewin's theory, see:

Estes, W. K. (1954) Kurt Lewin. In W. K. Estes and others. *Modern learning theory*, 317–344.

For a friendly summary of Lewin's field-theoretical position as a whole, with an extensive bibliography, see:

Deutsch, M. (1954) Field theory in social psychology. In G. Lindzey, ed. *Handbook of social psychology*, 181–222.

For a personal appreciation of Lewin by a fellow learning-theorist, see:

Tolman, E. C. (1948) Kurt Lewin, 1890–1947. *Psychol. Rev.*, 55, 1–4.

Chapter 9

FREUD'S PSYCHODYNAMICS

SIGMUND FREUD (1856–1939) so influenced psychological thinking that a summary of theoretical viewpoints, even in a specialized field such as the psychology of learning, is incomplete without reference to him. In the context of the history of psychology, Boring has this to say of Freud's place:

> It was Freud who put the dynamic conception of psychology where psychologists could see it and take it. They took it, slowly and with hesitation, accepting some principles while rejecting many of the trimmings. It is not likely that the history of psychology can be written in the next three centuries without mention of Freud's name and still claim to be a general history of psychology.[1]

It is no simple task to extract a theory of learning from Freud's writings, for while he was interested in individual development and the kind of re-education that goes on in psychotherapy, the problems whose answers he tried to formulate were not those with which theorists in the field of learning have been chiefly concerned. Psychoanalytic theory is too complex and, at least at the present time, too little formalized, for it to be presented as a set of propositions subject to experimental testing. Therefore, instead of attempting an orderly exposition of a psychodynamic theory of learning, we shall rest content with examining in somewhat piecemeal fashion suggestions from psychoanalysis that bear upon learning. Some of the suggestions have already influenced experimentation in learning, and some of them may be more influential in the years ahead.

PARALLELS BETWEEN PSYCHOANALYTIC THEORY AND CONVENTIONAL INTERPRETATIONS OF LEARNING

One can find in Freud's writings a number of statements that parallel very closely statements made by contemporary learning theorists little

[1] Boring (1950), page 707.

influenced by him. The common topics within psychoanalysis and learning theory serve usefully to show how relevant psychoanalysis is to learning.

The Pleasure Principle and the Law of Effect

Hedonistic theories—that man seeks pleasure and avoids pain—are among the oldest interpretations of human conduct, and any theory of learning must come to grips with the facts to which they refer. There is no doubt that we can control learning by way of reward and punishment. The details sometimes elude us, but the gross facts cannot be doubted.

Freud's pleasure principle is in accord with these facts, and his interpretation of the pleasure principle represents one of the first points of correspondence between his views and those of learning theorists. The corresponding principle in contemporary learning theory is more likely to go under the names of the *law of effect* or *reinforcement theory.* The broad conception, common to both psychoanalysis and learning theory, is that a need state is a state of high tension. Whether we describe this in terms of instincts seeking gratification or of drives leading to consummatory responses, we are talking about the same sequence of events. What controls the direction of movement is a tendency to restore a kind of equilibrium, thus reducing tension. Freud talked about a return to a constant state, and the physiologists, after Cannon, refer to homeostasis. The principle goes back at least to Claude Bernard, but in any case it is shared by Freud and the learning theorists whose views have already been considered.

One of Freud's concise statements of this position is found in the introductory paragraph of his *Beyond the pleasure principle:*

> In the theory of psychoanalysis we have no hesitation in assuming that the course taken by mental events is automatically regulated by the pleasure principle. We believe, that is to say, that the course of those events is invariably set in motion by an unpleasurable tension, and that it takes a direction such that its final outcome coincides with a lowering of that tension—that is, with an avoidance of unpleasure or a production of pleasure.[2]

Freud speculated about the relationship between pleasure and quantity of excitation. Unpleasure, he said, corresponded to an *increase* in excitation and pleasure to a *diminution,* although he allowed some importance to the *rate of change* of excitation. In this he followed a classical psychologist, Fechner, who wrote along the same lines much earlier.[3]

Until lately, American psychologists have preferred to talk about tension and its reduction without bringing in the term "pleasure." More

[2] Freud (1920b), page 1. From *Beyond the pleasure principle* by Sigmund Freud, by permission of Liveright Publishers, New York.

[3] Fechner (1873).

recently, however, attention is again being paid to affectivity.[4] McClelland and his associates (1953) have proposed a quantitative theory of pleasantness and unpleasantness, somewhat along the lines suggested by Freud. They propose that a slight departure from the level of stimulation to which the organism is adapted is usually pleasurable, while an extreme departure is unpleasant or annoying. Thus if one adds salt to distilled water, small quantities make the taste more acceptable, but large quantities make it less acceptable. Freud suggested that this was a field open to experimentation, and indeed it is.[5]

If we are to move to more sophisticated and refined theories of learning, it is imperative that we pay attention to the differences between proposals as well as to their similarities. There is an important aspect of Freud's tension-reduction theory less well represented in contemporary law-of-effect discussions. This is the basic principle that an aroused need that remains unsatisfied produces a fantasy of the goal-object that could satisfy the need. That is, tension reduction that is not accomplished through actual gratification is accomplished through *wish fulfillment,* in the form of a hallucination of the satisfying object. At the id level this fantasy is confused with reality, just as the thirsty man on the desert confuses the mirage with a true oasis. In the *primary process,* under the control of the pleasure principle, wish fulfillment is hallucinatory; the later, more realistic expectation of future events comes with the development of the *secondary process,* when memory images become substituted for hallucinations.

The problem of hallucinations has not been entirely neglected by learning theorists. Mowrer (1938) proposed the study of hallucinations as a means of investigating certain aspects of expectancy. Dollard and Miller, treating perception as a response, and a hallucination as a learned perception in the presence of minimal or ambiguous cues, accept the fact that hallucinations are more likely if drives are strong. They cite evidence for their position.[6]

The first area of correspondence, then, between learning theories and psychoanalysis, is the family resemblance between the tension-reduction interpretation of the law of effect (reinforcement theory in one of its forms) and the pleasure principle, with the caution, however, that learning

[4] E.g., Young (1952).

[5] Freud (1920b), page 2.

[6] Dollard and Miller (1950), pages 178–181. The evidence is from McClelland and Atkinson (1948) that images are influenced by drives, and from Holmberg (1950) that hallucinatory images in dreams are influenced by motivation.

theories have not fully incorporated the fantasy-production feature of the Freudian principle.

The Reality Principle and Trial-and-Error Learning

Freud's first supplementation of the pleasure principle was by way of the *reality principle,* whereby the organism instead of insisting upon immediate gratification takes the "long indirect road to pleasure." [7] Because the pleasure is found at the end of the path, we may think of the psychologist's rat, winding its way through a tortuous maze, eliminating the blind alleys along the way, as being under the control of a reality principle.

There is some ambiguity here, for Freud's reality principle is bound up with the developing ego, and it would be a big jump to assign the rat an ego because it avoids blind alleys on the way to food.

Psychologists have been unclear in trying to find the correspondences between their principles and Freud's reality principle.

Dollard and Miller definitely relate the pleasure principle to the law of effect, but they have no direct counterpart to the reality principle. Ego strength (related, of course, to mastery of reality) they treat in the familiar psychological terms of higher mental processes, learned drives and skills. Reality, they say, is elaborated according to the physical and social conditions of learning.[8]

Mowrer takes a different position. He believes that the law of effect is related to the pleasure principle, in agreement with Miller and Dollard, but he would relate trial-and-error problem solution to this principle also, rather than to the reality principle. He believes the reality principle to be appropriate instead to simple Pavlovian (classical) conditioning, because he believes Pavlov's dogs learn "not what is pleasurable and relieving, but what is actual, true, real." [9] He goes on to infer that such conditioning is limited to the autonomic nervous system, and thus leads himself into what appears to be a most unusual position, namely, that reality learning is under the control of the autonomic system, whereas pleasure-pain learning is under the control of the central nervous system. To some it will seem more plausible to assign instinctive, impulsive functions to the autonomic system (though I would not go that far) and to assign reality-regulated functions, ego functions, to the cognitive apparatus: to the central nervous system and its related structures.

[7] Freud (1911).
[8] Dollard and Miller (1950), pages 9–10.
[9] Mowrer (1950), pages 5–6.

Let us return to animal learning as possibly representing the reality principle because there are many events intervening between the aroused tension and its ultimate resolution. A white rat can learn the true path in a maze, and in a discrimination apparatus it can learn to jump to a triangle and not to a circle. Thus it learns permitted and unpermitted behavior, much in the way a child learns to behave in accordance with the dictates of its culture as transmitted by those in authority over him. The rat can learn probabilities also. If rewarded more frequently on the right than on the left he learns to turn more often to the right, as though to equate the response-reinforcement ratio on both sides.[10] This conforming of behavior to reality, even to a contingent reality, surely has some resemblance to the earliest ego functions. Learned discrimination always involves conflict, and the conflict is resolved through the weighting of the choices by reward and punishment. These weights become available through the accumulation of experiences with the environment. Sometimes, when discrimination is difficult, the rat mobilizes his experience through what Muenzinger and Tolman call "vicarious trial and error" (VTE), that is, a sampling of both choices by looking back or forth, or by making short runs first to one side and then to the other before the animal is committed to a choice. This appears to be a kind of symbolic reality-testing, an analogue of ego-type behavior.

Academic psychologists and psychoanalysts spend a good deal of their time studying the approach to and solution of reality problems. We may conclude that there is some gross correspondence in *topic* between what Freud calls the reality principle and the studies in which behavior is regulated largely by experienced success and failure. What is lacking in the co-ordination is a clear ego psychology in academic psychology to be co-ordinated with the ego theory in psychoanalysis. The ego psychology of psychoanalysis is itself only now undergoing clarification.[11]

Repetition-Compulsion in Relation to Theories of Habit Strength

In his *Beyond the pleasure principle,* Freud introduced a number of highly speculative notions, with awareness that he was trying out ideas to which he did not wish fully to commit himself. One of the suggestions most closely bound to evidence from his clinical experience was that of

[10] E.g., Brunswik (1939).

[11] For developments within psychoanalytic ego-theory, see Erikson (1950), A. Freud (1936), H. Hartmann (1950), Loewenstein (1954).

a *repetition-compulsion.* These repetition-compulsions are believed to be beyond the pleasure principle, for Freud says:

> The greater part of what is re-experienced under the compulsion to repeat must cause the ego unpleasure, since it brings to light activities of repressed instinctual impulses. . . . The compulsion to repeat also recalls from the past experiences which include no possibility of pleasure, and which can never, even long ago, have brought satisfaction even to instinctual impulses which have since been repressed.[12]

Freud recognized that sometimes repeating unpleasant activities yields pleasure, possibly through the sense of mastery that is achieved. These cases he believed to be genuine, but they are still under the control of the pleasure principle, and are not what Freud meant by acts not under the control of the pleasure principle. He was not talking about secondary or derived pleasure; he referred to behavior that he believed to be independent of, and disregarding, the pleasure principle.

In the effort to understand these repetition-compulsions, especially as they appeared in traumatic neuroses, Freud was led to posit a destructive instinct ("death instinct") existing alongside of *Eros* (the "life instinct," comprising self-preservation, self-love, and object-love). This is one of the more controversial topics within psychoanalysis itself, and some relatively orthodox analysts find Freud's formulation unsatisfactory.[13]

This is not the place to enter into a detailed critique of psychoanalytic theory, and in relating the work of academic psychologists to Freudian theory we must be satisfied to review some of the points of correspondence. In general, academic psychologists who have discussed repetition-compulsion have confined themselves to the kinds of behavior resistant to the usual principles of extinction. Mowrer, for example, notes the parallel between Hull's interest in acts that do not extinguish and the repetition-compulsion, and he sees a relation between repetition-compulsion and functional autonomy.[14] Dollard and Miller indicate that the repetition-compulsion is a result of cues provided by emotions that are themselves aroused by meaningless shreds of memories that recur in free association. Instrumental acts (the tendencies to repeat) are conditioned to these cues.[15]

Learning theorists have offered three suggestions to explain acts unusually resistant to extinction:

[12] Freud (1920b), page 21. From *Beyond the pleasure principle* by Sigmund Freud, by permission of Liveright Publishers, New York.

[13] E.g., Fenichel (1945), pages 59–61.

[14] Mowrer (1950), pages 9, 112.

[15] Dollard and Miller (1950), page 253.

1. All compulsions may conform to ordinary principles of tension-reduction learning. They may involve subtle forms of anxiety reduction, as in the defense mechanism known as "undoing." It is admitted that available data are insufficient to demonstrate that this explanation holds in all cases.[16]

2. Overlearned activities may be resistant to change, hence lead to excessive repetition. Rats trained to jump a gap in order to be rewarded, if they repeat the activity often enough, will fail to take a direct path when one is provided.[17] A kind of "canalization" takes place, so that the familiar is preferred and the behavior remains stereotyped.[18] This has a family resemblance to compulsive behavior, but because the behavior was once a source of gratification it does not fit Freud's specifications for repetition-compulsion.

3. Behavior acquired under excessive frustration may become "abnormally fixated," and thus resistant to change. This suggestion is elaborated by Maier (1949) on the basis of extensive experiments conducted by him and his students and collaborators. If rats in the familiar Lashley jumping apparatus are rewarded for jumping to a cross and punished for jumping to a circle, they soon learn to jump to the correct figure, whether it is presented on the right or on the left, and the habit is flexible and can be reversed if reward and punishment are reversed. If, however, they are given an insoluble problem, with reward now on the right, now on the left, with no systematic relationship between the cards in the windows and the rewards and punishments, they develop highly stereotyped behavior, such as jumping to the left, no matter what happens. The response occasionally persists for hundreds of trials, even though every trial is punished. It appears that the response is no longer under control of the reality principle. Accessory evidence shows that the discrimination between the cards may be learned without affecting the fixated response. Even when the opposite window is left open with the food clearly in view, the rat, fixated on the left, will continue to jump to the left, bump its nose, and fall into the net. This is the nearest we come to an experimental analogue of compulsive behavior.

The experimental problem has been reopened by Wilcoxon (1952), who repeated Maier's experiments with a number of controls. He found the main cause of the excessive fixation to be the the learning of an act that was occasionally punished, occasionally rewarded, when the alter-

[16] Mowrer (1950), page 112.

[17] Gilhousen (1931).

[18] The possible significance of "canalization" has been treated by Murphy (1947), pages 161–191.

native was invariably punished. While he interpreted his results as conforming to ordinary principles of associative learning, the causal factors are complex.

Compulsive behavior is a profitable field for further investigation, apart from trying to test in detail Freud's hypotheses. Fenichel lists three types of compulsion.[19] The first type rests on the periodicity of drive states (instincts), so that derivatives of these states may be expected also to occur periodically. He believes that manic-depressive phenomena fit this type. The second type is a repetition due to the tendency of the repressed to find an outlet. In the so-called "neuroses of destiny" the patient periodically evokes or endures the same experience. The symptoms are sometimes set off by "anniversaries" of significant events.[20] Compulsive rituals, such as compulsive counting, are said by Fenichel to fit this type. The third type consists in the repetition of traumatic events for the purpose of achieving a belated mastery. Children who have been the passive victims of frustration may seek in their games an active repetition of the event at a time of their own choosing, in order to gain comprehension and mastery. The dreams and repeated symptoms in traumatic neurosis fit this pattern.

It is evident that there are problems here that have not been fully represented in learning experiments, although again there is overlap in topic, that it, between repetition-compulsion and overlearning, abnormal fixation, and resistance to extinction.

These three principles from Freud (the pleasure principle, the reality principle, and repetition-compulsion) have been selected to show that there are at least some parallels between Freudian theory and the discussions by learning theorists. It would no doubt prove fruitful to try to achieve greater clarity with respect to these parallels, for the interrelationships are by no means obvious and direct.

PSYCHOANALYTIC CONCEPTIONS THAT HAVE INFLUENCED LEARNING EXPERIMENTS AND THEORIES

In the foregoing account of parallels between Freudian theory and the work of academic psychologists it should be evident that the two lines developed rather independently. That is, studies of the law of effect, of overlearning, and of problem-solving were not undertaken to test

[19] Fenichel (1945), pages 542–543.
[20] E.g., J. R. Hilgard (1953).

Freudian theory, and Freudian theory was not developed in order to "explain" the results obtained by experimental psychologists. There have been a number of topics within Freudian theory, however, that have definitely set problems for the experimental psychologist. We now turn to a review of some of these.

Anxiety as a Drive

Freud's views about anxiety evolved along with other aspects of his theory.[21] At first he thought that attacks of anxiety in his patients gave evidence of repressed instinctive (libidinal) excitation. That is, repressed libido, he thought, was transformed into anxiety.[22] Later, as he developed the theory of id, ego, and superego, he assigned anxiety production to the ego. When the ego perceives danger this perception arouses anxiety, and then steps are taken to reduce anxiety. Symptom formation may be one of these steps. Repression may also be one of the devices adopted by the ego, so that, instead of repression causing anxiety, we now have anxiety causing repression.[23]

Anxiety is closely related to fear, though fear usually has a real object, while anxiety may be a vague apprehension of unknown danger. Three kinds of anxiety can be distinguished, of which the first is indistinguishable from fear:

1. *Objective anxiety* (also called real or true anxiety) depends upon real or anticipated danger whose source lies in the external world. To be afraid of a poisonous snake or a holdup man is to be anxious in this way. True anxiety implies a real known danger.

2. *Neurotic anxiety* is in regard to an unknown danger. Upon analysis it is found that the danger is, as Freud put it, an instinctual one. That is, a person is afraid of being overpowered by some impulse or thought that will prove harmful to him. Sometimes there is a real or threatened danger but the reaction to it is excessive, thus revealing the neurotic element in the anxiety.[24]

3. *Moral anxiety* is aroused by a perception of danger from the conscience (superego). The fear is that of being punished (belittled, degraded) for doing or thinking something that is contrary to the ego ideal. Moral anxiety is experienced as feelings of *guilt* or *shame*.[25]

[21] A useful account of the changes in Freud's conceptions is given by R. May (1950), pages 112–127.

[22] Freud (1920a), pages 347–349.

[23] The new views can be found in Freud (1926).

[24] For the distinction between these first two types of anxiety, see Freud (1926), pages 112–117.

[25] For a discussion of the three kinds of anxiety, see Hall (1954), pages 59–69. On shame and guilt, see Piers and Singer (1953).

Anxiety in later life was said to have two modes of origin: one, involuntary and automatic, whenever a danger situation arose, the second "produced by the ego when such a situation merely threatened, in order to procure its avoidance." [26]

Mowrer (1939) was the first of the experimenters on learning to see the possibility of studying an analogue of anxiety in experiments on avoidance conditioning. He proceeded to show experimentally how rats that had experienced pain in the presence of certain cues could be led to make avoidance responses in the presence of those cues, that is, when the pain was merely threatened.[27] Thus he believed the anxiety-fear response to be the conditioned form of the pain response. Just as pain can be used as a drive to produce learning through escape, so anxiety can be used to produce learning. The anxiety can be reduced by appropriate avoidance responses just as pain can be reduced by escape responses. Hence these anxiety-reducing responses are learned by the ordinary reinforcement principle of tension reduction. Conceivably defense reactions or neurotic symptoms might be acquired through this familiar learning pattern. This kind of acquired fear or anxiety has been extensively studied as a drive in animal learning, especially by N. E. Miller.[28]

Mowrer's views changed somewhat as he began to consider those features of human behavior less represented in rat behavior, especially man's capacity to consider the future consequences of his acts.[29] He gradually arrived at his own position on anxiety, at variance with Freudian theory. He developed what he called a "guilt theory" as contrasted with Freud's "impulse theory." [30]

The problems of anxiety, shame, and guilt lead far afield from present-day learning theory. The main point of contact at present is in the treatment of acquired fear as a drive. The importance of fear as a drive is thus summarized by Dollard and Miller:

> One of the most important drives of all is fear, or "anxiety" as it is often called when its source is vague or obscured by repression (Freud, 1926). There are three main reasons why fear is so important: because it can be so strong, because it can be attached to new cues so easily by learning, and because it is the motivation that produces the inhibiting responses in most conflicts.[31]

A somewhat different, yet related, use of the concept of anxiety in learning experiments was introduced by Taylor (1951), when she classi-

[26] Freud (1926), page 109.
[27] Mowrer (1940b).
[28] Miller (1948a). For a review of other related studies see Miller (1951b), Farber (1954).
[29] Mowrer and Ullman (1945).
[30] Mowrer (1950), page 537.
[31] Dollard and Miller (1950), page 190.

fied human subjects in an investigation of eyelid conditioning according to their scores on a verbal "anxiety scale" derived from the Minnesota Multiphasic Personality Inventory. She found that the more anxious subjects conditioned more rapidly than the less anxious ones, and interpreted anxiety as drive—as the multiplier D in Hull's theory. A number of additional experimenters have used her scale in testing various hypotheses about the relationship between anxiety and conditioning.[32]

Our review shows us that in the course of experimentation theories of anxiety have diverged from the testing of Freud's interpretations. But the original introduction of anxiety concepts into learning theory was by those who were interested in Freudian theory, and they indicated indebtedness to Freud's writings.

Unconscious Influences upon Word Associations

The free-association technique of psychoanalysis has found its representation in psychological experimentation chiefly through the diagnostic word-association test introduced by Jung. Many experiments have been done, acknowledging the importance of the emotional processes behind word associations, leading quantitatively to the recognition of a number of "complex indicators." [33] Although these have not had much influence within learning experiments, lawful relations can be found, as between the frequency of response words and the reaction times with which they are given.[34]

Word recognition, which is also a form of associative reaction to the printed word, has been studied in relation to the affective significance of the words. These studies, often referred to as studies of perceptual defense, are reviewed later in this chapter.

Repression, Forgetting, and Recall

Ever since Ebbinghaus, psychologists have made quantitative study of memorization and recall part of their laboratory practice. It was natural, therefore, that Freudian interpretations of memory lapses should have been seized upon as appropriate for experimental testing. At first, psychologists grasped only the forgetting aspect of repression, failing to take into account the motivational aspects. This was due, in part, to the re-

[32] Bindra, Paterson, and Strzelecki (1955), Bitterman and Holtzmann (1952), Farber and Spence (1953), Hilgard, Jones, and Kaplan (1951), Montague (1953), Ramond (1953), Spence and Farber (1953) (1954), Spence and Taylor (1951) (1953), Taylor and Spence (1952). For a valuable review of both experiment and theory, see Farber (1954). The scale itself is described in Taylor (1953).

[33] E.g., Hull and Lugoff (1921).

[34] Schlosberg and Heineman (1950).

jection of the psychoanalytic theory of instincts, in part to the absence of motivational concepts in prevailing studies of memory and forgetting.[35]

Freud distinguished between a *primal repression* and a second phase called repression proper.[36] The primal repression consists in "a denial of entry into consciousness to the mental (ideational) presentation of the instinct." The ideational content then remains unaltered and the instinct remains attached to it. "The second phase of repression, *repression proper*, concerns mental derivatives of the repressed instinct-presentation, or such trains of thought as, originating elsewhere, have come into associative connection with it." The tendency to ward off these secondary derivatives is sometimes called *after-expulsion*.

It is to be noted that repression proper assumes a primal repression, so that the pattern for all later repressions is set up early in life. Later events may be assimilated to these earlier ones. The activity of repression is not, however, over at the time something is repressed.

> The process of repression is not to be regarded as something which takes place once and for all, the results of which are permanent, as when some living thing has been killed and from that time onward is dead; on the contrary, repression demands a constant expenditure of energy, and if this were discontinued the success of the repression would be jeopardized, so that a fresh act of repression would be necessary.[37]

Sears has summarized the characteristics of a repressed instinctual impulse, according to Freud, in six statements: [38]

1. It is not represented in its true form in consciousness.
2. The instinct-presentation develops in a more luxuriant fashion than it would if it were conscious.
3. The resistance of consciousness against derivatives and associations of the instinct-presentation varies in inverse proportion to their remoteness from the ideas originally repressed.
4. Repression is highly specific to each idea and substitute idea.
5. Repression is very mobile.
6. The degree of repression varies with the strength of the instinctual impulse.

The feature of repression that has appealed most to psychologists is its relation to pleasure and pain. Freud says, for example, that in repression the avoidance of pain must have acquired more strength than the pleasure of gratification.[39] Psychologists have often interpreted repression

[35] These points were made by Sears (1936a) in an able review of Freud's theory of repression and the possibilities within experimentation.
[36] Freud (1915a), page 86.
[37] Freud (1915a), page 89.
[38] Sears (1936a), pages 242–243, based on Freud (1915a).
[39] Freud (1915a), page 85. The line of development began much earlier.

quite superficially to mean that pleasurable events will be remembered and distasteful ones forgotten. The first experiments used merely affectively pleasant or unpleasant materials, such as pleasant and unpleasant odors, words such as "sugar" (pleasant) and "quinine" (unpleasant), studying whether or not such materials could be easily memorized or retained.[40] Later studies have sought in one way or another to meet more squarely the demands of psychoanalytic theory. We shall return later to a consideration of some of them.

Fixation

Fixation has two closely related meanings in psychoanalytic theory. The first meaning is that of *arrested development,* so that an adult may be fixated at an infantile or adolescent level of psychological functioning. This usually implies an object-choice (the mother; a like-sexed person) appropriate to the level of fixation, and the statement is then made that the person is fixated *at* such-and-such level and fixated *upon* such-and-such an object. The second meaning is that of *fixed habits* leading to preferred modes of solving personal problems, such as a fixation upon a particular mechanism of defense. The habit fixations discussed as forms of compulsion (pages 294–297) are fixations of this second kind. The two meanings are not clearly distinguished in psychoanalytic theory because the stage of arrested development is so intimately related to the style of life. That is, habitual modes of reacting as an adult are likely to be described in developmental terms, for example, the "anal character," the "oral character." [41]

In his review of objective studies bearing on psychoanalytic concepts, Sears treated fixation as habit strength, and listed a dozen circumstances shown experimentally to modify the strength of instrumental acts.[42] While aware of the problem, he failed to treat in any detail the qualitative features of transition from one stage of development to the next. The transition depends not only on the strength of the earlier fixation but on the hazards involved in transition to the next stage. If the next stage is attractive and non-threatening, presumably the growing individual will enter upon it even though he showed strong attachments at the earlier stage. If some residue from the earlier stage makes entrance upon the later stage painful and anxiety-producing, arrested development may oc-

[40] E.g., Gordon (1905) (1925), Tait (1913), Tolman (1917).

[41] Fenichel (1945), page 523, writes that neurotics "are not only fixated to certain levels of instinctive demands but also to certain mechanisms of defense." He also includes "character attitudes" among the items to which they are fixated.

[42] Sears (1943), pages 81–89.

cur. Habits at the different levels are not all-or-nothing affairs, for an adult who is grown up in some habits may be infantile in others. Ultimately we require a quantitative theory to account for arrested development in some aspects of personality and progressive development in others.

Regression

Regression is related to fixation in that when an act is blocked or frustrated, some substitute will occur. The substitute is quite likely to be an act once strongly fixated in the individual's repertory. Such a substitution of an earlier habit for a contemporary one represents one kind of regression.

We may distinguish three kinds of regression:

1. *Instrumental-act regression.* When the organism is prevented from using one habit, an earlier learned habit is substituted. Many animal experiments have demonstrated this to occur.[43] These results provide an analogy to *object-regression* in Freudian theory, the kind of regression in which gratification is gained by relinquishing a present object and returning to an earlier one.

2. *Age-regression.* Under some circumstances the person returns to earlier modes of behavior and obliterates future events, in a kind of *revivification.*[44] If, for example, an adult who regressed under hypnosis to an early age began to speak in a language used in childhood but no longer available to him in his adult life, we could say that he had regressed (at least in this respect) to an earlier period in his own life. Experiments under hypnosis have led to somewhat ambiguous results. Occasionally the functioning at the suggested (regressed) age resembles very closely the known historical circumstances in the person's life.[45] When regressed subjects take intelligence and personality tests, their performances differ from those of actual children at the age levels represented by the suggested regression. Hence there appears to be a certain amount of role-playing going on.[46]

3. *Primitivation.* Even though the regressed individual may not return either to instrumental acts once in his inventory of habits or to personality functioning characteristic of himself at some previous period, he may, under stress, show a kind of behavioral disorganization that can be char-

[43] E.g., Hamilton and Krechevsky (1933), Mowrer (1940a), O'Kelly (1940a) (1940b). Sears (1943), pages 89–96, has reviewed this literature.

[44] The term is used by Weitzenhoffer (1953), page 191, as one classification of regressive manifestations under hypnosis.

[45] Erickson (1937), Gill (1948), Kupfer (1945).

[46] For specimen studies with intelligence tests, see Kline (1950), Sarbin (1950). For studies with personality tests, see Sarbin and Farberow (1952), Orne (1951).

acterized as more primitive. This kind of regression has been studied with young children subjected to mild frustration.[47] They showed regression by such indices as reduced constructiveness in play following the experienced frustration.

Psychoanalysts suggest that some psychotic manifestations are regressive, particularly schizophrenia. DuBois and Forbes (1934) found little return to the fetal posture during sleep. Cameron (1938a) (1938b) failed to find childish thought patterns in schizophrenic speech. Sears points out, however, that these studies are inadequate tests of regression because they do not bear adequately on the possible *affective* indicators of regression.[48]

Aggression and Its Displacement

In his later years Freud became increasingly aware of aggression, hostility, and destructiveness. In discussing racial tensions and other intergroup antagonisms he said:

> We do not know why such sensitiveness should have been directed to just these details of differentiation; but it is unmistakable that in this whole connection men give evidence of a readiness for hatred, an aggressiveness, the source of which is unknown, and to which one is tempted to ascribe an elementary character.[49]

Freud recognized the importance of giving expression to hostility, rather than holding it back, and many contemporary analysts now give prominence to the role of repressed hostile impulses in neurosis.

While Freud thus paid increasing attention to aggressiveness in his later writings, as something inherent in man, he had earlier suggested that interference with instinctual satisfaction leads to a hostile attack upon the source of the frustration. Symptoms of neurotic illness may be so directed as to cause distress to someone in the environment who is perceived as the agent of frustration. Building upon these suggestions in Freud (1917), Dollard and his collaborators formulated the *frustration-aggression hypothesis* in a manner to make possible quantitative testing.[50] The general principle stated was that frustration leads to aggressive action; it was necessary later to correct the implication that aggression was the only (or even an inevitable) consequence.[51] The experimental evi-

[47] Barker, Dembo, and Lewin (1941).

[48] Sears (1944), page 315.

[49] Freud (1921), page 56. This "elementary character" he had assigned a year before to a "death instinct."

[50] Dollard, Doob, Miller, Mowrer, Sears, Ford, Hovland and Sollenberger (1949).

[51] Miller (1941), Sears (1941). These two papers are part of a symposium on the effects of frustration. The other papers are Rosenzweig (1941), Bateson (1941), Levy (1941), G. W. Hartmann (1941), and Maslow (1941).

dence gave abundant support to the hypothesized linkage between experienced frustration and subsequent aggressive, hostile, or destructive behavior.

If the agent responsible for frustration is unknown or inaccessible as an object of attack (absent or protected through conflicting response tendencies), another object will be chosen. This is called *displaced aggression.* The object may be as innocent as the scapegoat which in the ancient Hebrew ritual was made to bear the nation's sins.[52] The word "scapegoat" has come into general use to refer to a victim of displaced aggression.

Neal Miller and his collaborators have succeeded in relating displacement to stimulus generalization in learning theory.[53] In his original experiment, Miller taught rats to strike each other, as in fighting, when an electric shock came on. When a second rat was not present, a rat would "displace" the aggression to a celluloid doll or other object in the environment. The gain to be expected from Miller's experimental arrangement is that certain quantitative predictions can be made about the occasions for displacement, the intensity of the reaction, and so on. Miller formulated eight specific deductions from his theory, of which the following three are illustrative:

> When the direct response to the original stimulus is prevented by the absence of that stimulus, displaced responses will occur to other similar stimuli and the strongest displaced response will occur to the most similar stimulus present.
>
> When the direct response to the original stimulus is prevented by conflict, the strongest displaced response will occur to stimuli which have an intermediate degree of similarity to the original one.
>
> If the strength of the drive motivating the direct response to the original stimulus is increased, it will be possible for increasingly dissimilar stimuli to elicit displaced responses.[54]

While Miller's experiments on displacement have been with animal subjects, he shows how the principles suggested may apply to human behavior. In human beings, discriminations tend to take the form of words, so that we narrow our meanings and reduce our generalizations. The reverse holds true also, and we use words to generalize, to name classes of objects that belong together. At this point, however, we are interested in discrimination and how it breaks down. Suppose that Mr. Brown distinguishes among his new neighbors by calling them all by name. Because of a painful snub, he becomes very angry at Mr. Jones, one of these neigh-

[52] The Old Testament account of the scapegoat is in Leviticus 16:22.

[53] Miller (1948b), Miller and Kraeling (1952), Miller and Murray (1952), Murray and Miller (1952).

[54] The three statements are quoted from Miller (1948b), pages 168, 170.

bors. Because Mr. Jones's social position is more secure than Mr. Brown's, and Mr. Brown is new to the neighborhood, Mr. Brown may repress his anger. (This fits the suggestion that the expression of hostility may be prevented by conflicting tendencies.) In Miller's interpretation, what he represses is the sentence: "I am angry at Mr. Jones." Because this sentence is repressed, the anger is no longer tied directly to Mr. Jones, and it is more likely to generalize to another neighbor because discrimination through names has broken down.

Miller recognizes that the displacement problem is actually more complex than this. He points out that the *name* of Mr. Jones is not repressed when it is not in a sentence referring to anger. So Mr. Brown recognizes the neighbor's dog and says to himself: "This is Mr. Jones's dog." Because the name of Mr. Jones is attached unconsciously to hostile tendencies, he may give the dog a swift kick, which he would not do if he recalled that he was really angry at Mr. Jones, not at his dog. Thus Miller has deduced some functional differences between consciously and unconsciously determined behavior. He has restated his deduction succinctly:

> To summarize, the repression of verbal responses specifying the source of the aggression may remove a basis for discrimination and allow the illogical generalization, or displacement, of that aggression to be mediated by a different verbal response which is not repressed.[55]

Some closely related observations arise out of the study of doll play by young children. When attention is paid to aggressive behavior (fantasy aggression, in this case), the choice of object follows some of the principles of conflict outlined by Miller. That is, where anxiety is high, the object of aggression is chosen as one less similar to the person who is the source of the aggression than when anxiety is low. Consequently, as children play repeatedly in a permissive environment, their choice of object gradually shifts toward the parents, who have commonly been the authority figures responsible for some of their frustration.[56]

We may conclude this section by pointing out that on these topics (anxiety, affectivity and verbal responses, repression and recall, fixation and regression, aggression and displacement) the theories of Freud provided a stimulus to research. At the empirical level this has led to a fruitful interaction between psychoanalysis and experimental psychology.

[55] Miller (1948b), page 176.

[56] P. S. Sears (1951), R. R. Sears (1951), R. R. Sears, Whiting, Nowlis, and P. S. Sears (1953).

SUGGESTIONS FROM PSYCHOANALYSIS LITTLE REPRESENTED IN PYCHOLOGICAL STUDIES OF LEARNING

One has the feeling that a good deal of rich material from psychoanalysis has eluded the academic psychologist. This, if true, might be due either to a certain obtuseness on his part, or because the richer material is too difficult to bring under experimental control. The problem has been discussed repeatedly. Thus Sears at one time came to the conclusion:

> It seems doubtful whether the sheer testing of psychoanalytic theory is an appropriate task for experimental psychology. Its general method is estimable but its available techniques are clumsy.[57]

Kris, in a very thoughtful discussion of techniques of verification of psychoanalytic propositions, felt that a limitation of the laboratory was that the laboratory cannot produce the real dangers or deal with the basic needs which the genetic propositions of psychoanalysis encompass:

> The limitations of the laboratory to quasi needs (and quasi dangers) seriously restrict the area of propositions that can be experimentally verified. In fact, up to the present, experimental approaches have been more successful in dealing with propositions concerning substitution [58] than they have been with propositions concerning repression.[59]

Kubie, while eager to see research on psychoanalysis move forward, and even outlining a research institute in psychoanalytic psychology, deplores a certain triviality in many of the psychologists' experiments on psychoanalytic phenomena.

> It is important that any experimentalist should first make himself thoroughly familiar with phenomena as these occur in nature, ascertaining what can be proved with the unaided eye and ear before deciding what to subject to experimental verification. . . . Experimental facilities should not be wasted on issues which are already clearly proved, and to which human bias alone continues to blind us. The experimentalist should rather take up where the naturalist leaves off.[60]

Learning as Related to Stages of Development

Writers on psychoanalysis often stress that it is a *genetic* as well as a dynamic theory.[61] That is, continuities in the life of the individual must always be taken into account along with what is happening in the present.

[57] R. R. Sears (1944), page 329. The antecedent of "its" is experimental psychology.
[58] Henle (1942b) is referred to here by Kris.
[59] Kris (1947), page 255.
[60] Kubie (1952), pages 64–65.
[61] H. Hartmann and Kris (1945).

At many points the theory suggests that the very young child is unusually susceptible to influences which leave a permanent mark upon his personality, so that, for example, dreams throughout his life may be influenced by these earliest learnings. If this interpretation is true, it is important for a general psychology of learning, and the evidence needs to be specified.

While the problems have not been formulated clearly in terms of learning (i.e., why and in what way the results of childhood learning are more permanent than later learning) we are beginning to get kinds of evidence supporting the gross facts of adult consequences of early childhood experiences.

Among the experiments with animals, the best known are the experiments of Hunt (1941) on the effects of infant feeding frustration on adult hoarding in rats, and of Wolf (1943) on the effects of sensory deprivation in early life upon types of functioning under stress in later life, again with rats. While the results of these experiments are subject to some reservations, they are relevant to the genetic theory that early experiences may show their influences in the conflicts of later life.

Some conjectures about child-training practices and personality in adult life have been put to the test by Whiting and Child (1953). They went to the cross-cultural files, where anthropological reports on upwards of 200 cultures are summarized according to a great many categories. Then they asked certain questions about childhood practices and developed hypotheses about their consequences for adult experiences in those cultures. To take one illustration, they predict that socialization anxiety established in early childhood should affect the interpretation of the causes of illness in adult life. Even in our own culture, with the emphasis upon the germ theory of disease, we have many subordinate interpretations of illness: "It must have been something I ate," "I've been working too hard," "You have to suffer for your sins." Our remedies, too, show something of the magical quality: indiscriminate prescriptions of cure by rest, by liquids, by bland foods, by cathartics, by play, by suntanning, by religious observances. If a "scientific" culture such as ours has all these magical residues, it is not too much to expect that primitive interpretations of illness might be related to deep-seated anxieties.

Whiting and Child specified five kinds of anxiety and developed criteria for rating these. These five were: oral, anal, sexual, dependence, and aggression. The assumption is that severity of training and severity of punishment for infraction in these areas, or failures of gratification, would lead to anxiety. A culture might be severe in one of these areas and permissive in the others. In addition, Whiting and Child classified primitive interpretations of illness as derivatives of these anxieties.

When the childhood experience was correlated with adult interpretations of illness, some striking correspondences turned up. For example, 46 cultures could be classified with respect to degree of oral anxiety in childhood, and interpretations of illness with oral aspects, such as food poisoning. Of 20 cultures high in producing oral anxiety in children, 17 used oral interpretations of illness. Correspondingly, of 19 cultures low in oral anxiety, only 6 used oral interpretations of illness. This kind of evidence does not prove a relationship between childhood anxiety and adult behavior, but it makes such a relationship plausible.

Another important suggestion from psychoanalysis is that of childhood amnesia. In later life we appear unable to recall events that must surely have impressed us at the time, and about which we must have talked. Because these events become secondarily linked with repression sequences, they too are repressed. Memories that are recalled are often trivial, and perhaps distorted, the so-called "screen-memories," probably serving some of the purposes of repression. This whole field has been touched hardly at all by academic psychologists, who ought to be able to explore it with children, and not have to depend upon the retrospective accounts of adult patients.[62]

A further aspect of the developmental sequence posited by psychoanalysis, and relevant for learning, is the *latency period,* for it has been related to readiness for schooling (at about the age of 6) when the oedipal problems are temporarily solved and the ego is ready to feast its curiosity about the external world. After a few years adolescence produces a new threat, and learning may again be disrupted.

Most of the attempts to study the latency period by non-psychoanalysts have raised serious doubts about the existence of such a period. Blum, in reviewing the evidence up to 1952, reports that "there has been a growing trend, both within and outside psychoanalytic circles, to doubt the existence of sexual latency." [63] One very interesting experimental study has since appeared, giving results consonant with an orthodox interpretation of latency.[64] The developmental assumption is that castration anxiety will be high early (before the age of 7) and late (as adolescent development begins in the teen years). Using the method of incomplete fables,

[62] For a discussion from the psychoanalyst's viewpoint, see A. Freud (1935), pages 9–37. What data there were on the problem at the time were reviewed by G. J. Dudycha and M. M. Dudycha (1941).

[63] Blum (1953), pages 133–134.

[64] Friedman (1952).

Friedman found that between the ages of 7 to 12 his subjects more freely than younger or older children ended the stories with a strongly suggested dismemberment ending, showing reduced castration anxiety during this period. A supplementary finding was that latency by this criterion ends earlier for girls than for boys, a result that is plausible in view of the earlier onset of puberty among girls. Further material having to do with the sexual attachments of daughters for their fathers showed that from the ages of 7 to 11 the girls differed little from the boys, while from 11 onwards there was a definite increase in the kinds of fantasies interpreted as sexual feelings toward the father. A decline was possibly setting in at age 16.

While our topic is learning, not personality development, if the genetic theory of psychoanalysis contains any truth, learning will show differences from one level to another. Hence developmental stages are of possible significance for learning.

Obstacles to Learning

In case histories from child-guidance clinics we find many illustrations of obstacles to learning based on the personal history of the learner. The teacher as a parent figure may arouse false expectations or reinstate continuing battles; some symbols used in teaching may be so freighted with personal meanings as to be defended against; conflicts over authority may result in non-reading or in spelling handicaps, for no subject matter is clothed more with arbitrary authority than English pronunciation and spelling.[65]

There is little recognition within the learning laboratory of these matters so important for the kind of learning that takes place in the social environment of the home and school. At least one skilled teacher, Nathaniel Cantor (1946), has recognized that social learning at the college level is influenced by defense mechanisms. In his book on the dynamics of learning he devotes chapters to the roles of resistance, ambivalence, projection, and identification.

Psychodynamics of Thinking

The possibility of drawing upon psychoanalysis in studying the psychology of thinking has been brought strongly to the fore by the appearance of a large volume assembling papers on the organization and pa-

[65] Much of the relevant case material is reviewed by Mahler-Schoenberger (1942) and by Pearson (1952) (1954).

thology of thought.[66] Especially important for the psychoanalytic influences are the sections devoted to symbolism (including experimentally produced dreams), to motivation of thinking, fantasy thinking, and pathology of thinking.

While, as on most topics, one can find a few pioneer investigations, the suggestions from psychoanalysis have not yet been fully incorporated into the experimental study of thinking. For example, Seeman (1951) lists 23 titles as relevant to the Freudian theory of daydreams, but only seven of these use any techniques of quantification at all.

Learning at its best must include creativity, whether in the form of creative imagination embodied in the arts, or in inventiveness in science or practical affairs.[67] The hints from psychoanalysis are deserving of study.

The study of character or personality syndromes may prove useful in determining why of two people, equally intelligent, one is creative, the other not.[68] We have to be careful not to give pat answers, based on a stereotyped conception of "typical" personalities. For example, the compulsive dispositions associated with the "anal character" are not creative in essence, and may, in fact, produce mere handwashing instead of productive effort. Yet there is a certain plodding quality about scientific data-gathering which may demand *some* of this same compulsiveness. Scientific objectivity, a valuable trait, is at the same time a form of dissociation or isolation between wish and intellect, and is perhaps achieved at some cost to the individual. Some papers by Kubie [69] have stressed the personal problems of the scientist.

In the current emphasis on general-education programs in our colleges and universities we hear much about the integrative role of the arts and music. Yet as we look at artists and musicians we see some truth in the popular conception that they are somehow different, and occasionally classify as deviates. Hence the question recurs of the relationship between art and neuroticism. One form of putting it is this: Would the artist be less creative if he resolved his conflicts through psychoanalysis? Is not his neurosis precious to him? Possibly if we were successful in our mental hygiene programs we would develop a class of very uninteresting normal and contented people; perhaps we are saved from this by the ineffectiveness of our measures. There are more constructive possibilities. For one thing, artists and writers who come to analysis are those who find that

[66] Rapaport (1951). See also Rapaport (1950).
[67] For a pertinent discussion, with references, see Vinacke (1952), pages 238–261.
[68] E.g., Stein and Meer (1954).
[69] Kubie (1953) (1954).

they are afraid to practice their arts. For them, psychotherapy may give back their creativity. Again, the end of therapy is not necessarily to get rid of conflicts, but to find a way of living with them. The issues are too important to be resolved casually on the basis of a few case studies. Academic psychology ought to take its share of responsibility in the study of creativity at all levels.

Therapy as Learning

Experimental psychology will always be cut off from some of the more important aspects of psychoanalysis if it insists upon methods lying outside the psychoanalytic process itself. Without free association, the handling of the transference, and the rest that goes on within psychoanalysis, some kinds of data are simply not available. From the point of view of learning theory it is important to know *in detail* how transference operates to straighten out the confusions between past and present, between magical omnipotence and reality, so that the patient unlearns neurotic habits and acquires realistic and socially acceptable ones. To know these facts and relationships in detail is not easy, for the non-verbal communications between patient and analyst are important along with the words spoken and those subtle nuances of language that express doubt, belief, or encouragement. For a time it was thought that when Freud abandoned hypnosis he had also abandoned suggestion. As transference came increasingly into prominence as part of therapy, Freud realized that the handling of transference involved suggestion, and he did not hesitate to use the word.[70] But suggestion is a subtle process, and it is a question whether the most conscientious analyst can give an accurate retrospective account of just exactly what forms of suggestions he used with his patient, and how the patient reacted. Therefore the need of some sort of objective record is required. We probably need, in addition to the recorded interview, an immediately recorded statement from the analyst, giving what he thought he was doing, and something of his own free associations that remained unexpressed. Where the psychologist comes in will be in the analysis and interpretation of the data the analyst provides.[71]

Perhaps the main conclusion to be drawn from recognizing the unexplored areas in developmental aspects of learning, in psychodynamic

[70] Freud (1920b), page 18.

[71] For a discussion of these possibilities, see Bronner, A. F., and others (1949). The most satisfactory studies of psychotherapy at present are the investigations of client-centered therapy by Rogers and his associates, e.g., Rogers and Dymond (1954). For a treatment of psychotherapy as learning, see Shoben (1949).

obstacles to learning, in the study of thought processes and creativity, and in the understanding of the learning that goes on within psychotherapy, is that these problems can be solved only through co-operative effort. The division of labor between the academic psychologist and the psychoanalyst is not an absolute one, with the analyst doing everything that can be done within psychoanalysis, and the psychologist only that which can be done in the laboratory. If we are to achieve the ultimate understanding of the learning process not only in all its richness, but also in the form of verified propositions, there must be collaboration as well as division of labor.

EXPERIMENTS ON REPRESSION AS ILLUSTRATIVE OF THE LABORATORY USE OF PSYCHODYNAMIC CONCEPTS

As indicated earlier (page 300), psychologists were quick to pick up the suggestion from Freud that affective factors might influence recall. We shall consider two problems: the relation between affect and ease of recall, and the relation between affect and recognition thresholds. Both imply that unpleasant affect may hinder recall or recognition through events identified with or analogous to Freudian repression.

Repression and Recall

A review of the pertinent literature by Zeller (1950a) lists 93 references, enough to suggest how inviting this field has proved to be to investigators. We shall consider a few experimental reports typical of four approaches to the study of affective factors in recall.

1. *Recall of associates to affectively-toned sensory stimuli.* The most satisfactory study, following upon several earlier ones, is that of Ratliff (1938). He had subjects rate the pleasantness and unpleasantness of odors, pitches, and colors. Then the subjects associated numbers with the affective items and later were tested for recall. The results with odors were against the hypothesis of the forgetting of the unpleasant, but with pitches and colors the recall of numbers associated with the pleasant items was superior to the recall of numbers associated with unpleasant ones. Because the pleasantness and unpleasantness of sensory stimuli has little personal relevance, such experiments are no longer considered very pertinent as tests of Freudian theory.

Despite the tenuousness of the relationship to the repression theory, it is of some interest to cast up the score on experiments dealing with the recall of pleasant and unpleasant items (including words as well as sensory stimuli). Of 51 studies of this kind, 32 (63 per cent) favor more effective recall of the pleasant over the unpleasant, 14 (27 per cent) favor the reverse, and 5 (10 per cent) have neutral or ambiguous results.[72]

2. *Recall of memorized words with personal affective connotations.* In order to introduce some kind of ego threat into the laboratory-type experiment, Sharp (1938) went to the case records of neurotic subjects to find words that would be emotionally unacceptable to individual subjects, and words that for them would express gratifications. She then compared their retention of unacceptable and acceptable words, and found the unacceptable words less well recalled. Unfortunately, the only reported repetition of portions of her work did not yield confirmatory results.[73]

In an ingeniously designed experiment, Keet (1948) selected critical words from a word-association test given to each subject. One of these words was imbedded in a list to be memorized. The recall of the list was then disrupted by retroactive inhibition through new learning interpolated between memorization and recall. The disruption presumably included repression, for the critical word was more difficult to recall than the other words. Counseling procedures were used to alleviate the anxiety associated with the forgotten word, to encourage its recall much as forgotten experiences are brought to awareness in psychoanalysis. Although Keet's results were striking, those who have tried to reproduce the memorization and retroactive inhibition portions of the experiment have thus far been unsuccessful. The general logic of his experiment has so much to commend it, however, that it is to be hoped that some reproducible variant of his experiment can be discovered or invented.

Both the Sharp and the Keet experiments are more relevant to Freudian theory than the other experiments on affective materials because they selected items with a history of personal affective loading in the life of the individual outside the laboratory. Then they brought these items into the laboratory for quantitative study.

3. *Recall of affectively-toned life experiences.* In a somewhat different effort to achieve naturalness in experiments, experimenters have abandoned the memorizing of material under the artificial conditions of the laboratory and turned instead to study of the recall of actual experiences met outside the laboratory.

Meltzer (1930) asked 77 college men and 55 college women to de-

[72] The tally was made by Zeller (1950a), page 42.
[73] Heathers and Sears (1943); see Sears (1943).

scribe their Christmas vacation experiences. He not only had them list their experiences, but also asked them to rate the experiences as pleasant, unpleasant, or indifferent. Six weeks later he unexpectedly asked them to repeat the listing they had done on the day of their return. Not only did they list more pleasant than unpleasant memories immediately after returning from vacation, but after six weeks the predominance of pleasant over unpleasant memories increased. This finding is in accord with the interpretation of repression as an active process, continuing after the original event, though other interpretations are possible.[74]

A social-psychological bent was given to the naturalistic-setting recall experiment by Edwards (1941) (1942) who studied the retention of political statements by those differing in their political views. He found that his subjects tended to remember better material compatible with their political attitudes than material incompatible with them. Hence he emphasized the "frame of reference" in which remembering occurs, conflict with prevailing beliefs perhaps being more important than pleasantness and unpleasantness in controlling selective forgetting.

4. *Repression induced by experienced failure.* In a careful theoretical treatment of repression phenomena according to possibilities within stimulus-response theory, Sears (1936a) suggested a possible paradigm for the initiation of repression, and then proceeded to test it experimentally (Sears, 1937). The essential feature is that an excitatory tendency moving along a stimulus-response chain towards a consummatory response will be blocked and fail of consummation if, prior to consummation, a competing tendency is also evoked. This competing tendency violates conscience or is a threat to self-esteem, and can arouse guilt or self-criticism. Thus the arousal of an anxiety response concomitantly with an anticipatory goal response may prevent the occurrence of the goal response. This is, in short, Sear's paradigm for repression. His own experiment introduced a failure task (card sorting) between two sessions of nonsense syllable learning. The interference with the second list following failure was interpreted by Sears as an indication of repression.[75]

Discouragement induced by failure might lead to a lowering of effort and hence lead to poorer performance on a later task without any active repression. Hence, as Zeller (1950a) has pointed out, a complete test of repression ought to show recovery when the associated threat is alleviated. Several experimenters have attempted to demonstrate the two

[74] See, for example, Waters and Leeper (1936).

[75] The family resemblance between these failure-induced changes in recall and the kinds of changes in the completed-incompleted task experiment may be noted. The Zeigarnik-type experiments have already been reviewed in Chapter 8.

phases: induced repression followed by the lifting of the repression. One of the first of these was done under hypnosis (Huston, Shakow, and Erickson, 1934). Suggestions under hypnosis led to the attachment of guilt to certain words. In the waking state, while amnesic to the hypnotic experience, the subjects showed through word associations an influence on associations to the guilty words that might be interpreted as repression. Following removal of the suggestions under rehypnosis, the repressive effects disappeared. Diven (1937) used a conditioning method, following certain word pairs with shock. In the recall of the paired-associates, subjects did much better with the non-shocked than with the shocked pairs, as though recall of the "dangerous" words had been inhibited. After a "deconditioning" series, recall proved superior for the *shocked* words, hinting that an unconscious (repressed) integration may be a strong one. An attempted repetition of Diven's work has not been successful (Cannicott and Umberger, 1950). There are apparently subtleties in this kind of experiment, as suggested also by Sharp's and Keet's, that are not communicated in the description of the experimental procedures.

The initiation of repression through induced failure has been studied in an extension of Sears' type of experiment by Zeller (1950b) (1951), Russell (1952), and Aborn (1953). These experiments, with the exception of Russell's, found not only a disruption of recall, but some subsequent recovery when threat was alleviated.

Zeller used nonsense syllable learning and retention as the basic task, interpolating success and failure experiences in imitative tapping of Knox cubes. His experimental design included two tests of retention prior to the initiation of "repression," then an immediate and a delayed (48 hour) test while "repression" was active, and finally an immediate and delayed test after removal of "repression." His results for both recall and relearning corresponded to predictions from Freudian theory, though he pointed out that alternative interpretations cannot be excluded. Zeller used four conditions, so that he was able to compare the inhibiting results of failure specific to a second task with the inhibiting results of failure on a second task that had become associated with the performance of a previously learned task. Repression was not found when the failure was highly specific, but it was found when failure on the irrelevant task became associated with performance on the earlier learned one.

Aborn (1953) added another dimension by comparing the results for intentional ("set") learning with those for incidental learning. His subjects, reading the colored numbers on cards selected from the Ishahara and Dvorine tests, thought they were taking a color-blindness test. Those "set" to learn were told to remember the numbers that appeared on the cards; the "incidental" learners received no such instructions. The "ego threat" was introduced for the experimental subjects by following the series of numbered cards with others on which no numbers appeared, thus implying that the subject was color weak because he could not distinguish a number against the background of colored dots. The threat was enhanced by having him fail on some presumably related perceptual tasks,

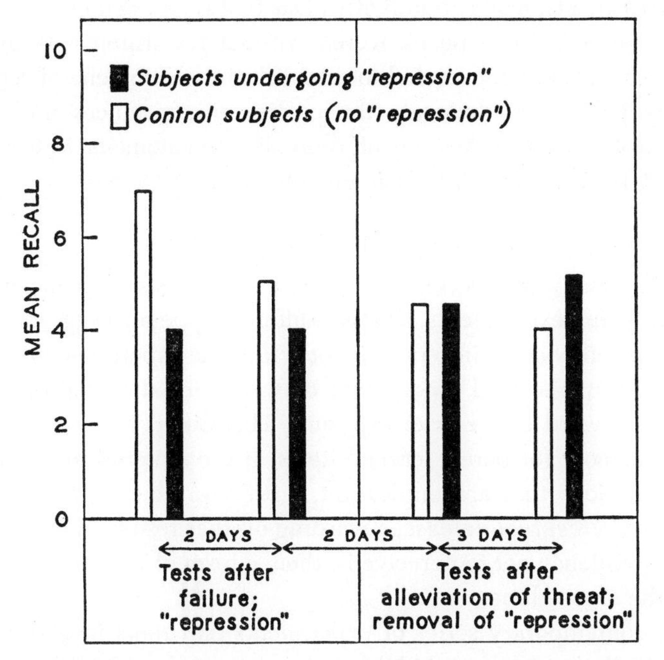

FIGURE 44. Repression and recovery in incidental learning associated with ego threat. The recall scores are of numbers learned incidentally while taking a color-blindness test. Mean, 20 subjects in each group. Replotted from the data of Aborn (1953), page 228.

stencil designs taken from the Arthur Performance Scale. As a test of memory, the subject wrote down the numbers remembered from the color test cards, then checked the numbers on a recognition test. The memory tests were unexpectedly repeated two days later. At this point the "threat" was removed by revealing the true nature of the experiment. The memory test was again given unexpectedly two days later and again after three days. The results for the incidental learners are given in Figure 44. For the control subjects there is progressive decline ("forgetting") with the passage of time. For the experimental subjects, however, there are reduced scores after failure, followed by recovery after removal of threat. The *higher* scores at the end, for the experimental subjects, correspond to Diven's finding, mentioned above. There were no differences of this kind for the subjects who had been given a set to learn; hence Aborn concludes that there are advantages in using incidental learning for this kind of study, and perhaps this fact helps to account for Russell's (1952) negative results.

Where do these studies lead us? The facts of amnesia, without additional experiments, make abundantly clear that repression occurs, and that memories once lost can be recovered without relearning.[76] While therefore experiments are not needed to establish the phenomena of repression, they may help us to delineate the precise circumstances under which repression occurs. Clarification of repression phenomena is today more important than establishing their genuineness.

Repression and Recognition Thresholds

While measures of recognition were used as tests of memory in some of the foregoing experiments, a rather different type of recognition experiment has recently come into prominence. In these experiments recognition refers to the perceptual recognition of well-learned material, as in the reading of a word under brief exposure. This differs from recognition as a test of memory for barely learned items. If the material to be perceived has connotations that are unpleasant, anxiety-producing, threatening, it may arouse *perceptual defense,* a warding off that results in higher thresholds. The tendency not to perceive is, then, a form of repression, a defense against the aroused meanings.[77]

The contemporary series of experiments had roots in earlier experiments but began most strikingly with a report by McGinnies (1949). He recorded simultaneously recognition thresholds and galvanic skin responses (GSR's) to neutral and emotional toned (taboo) words, presented by a tachistoscope. During the prerecognition interval (i.e., while the exposure time was still so short that the subject could not name the word presented) the subject produced *larger* galvanometer deflections to the words he was going to have greater difficulty in recognizing than to the words which would prove eventually to have lower thresholds. The interpretation was that the GSR revealed anxiety connected with the taboo words, and that the high threshold for verbal response represented a perceptual defense against recognition of the forbidden words.

[76] Some good cases from combat neuroses are given by Grinker and Spiegel (1945a) (1945b).

[77] Klein (1954), pages 268–270, quite properly argues against assigning *all* cognitive controls in experiments of this kind to "defense."

This study was followed almost immediately by criticisms and supplementary experiments, so that within the next three years a dozen reports appeared bearing upon it, and they have continued since.[78]

Some of the criticisms have to do with experimental logic, and some have to do with interpretations. Because all of the studies happen to treat of closely related substantive material, a review of a few of them will serve to indicate the complex causal factors that operate even within well-defined and restricted experimental contexts.

The most telling criticism against McGinnies' results as a demonstration of perceptual defense lies in the difference between his emotionally-toned taboo words and his neutral words in *frequency of use* in ordinary speech, as objectively defined by magazine word-counts. The criticism, first proposed by Howes and Solomon (1950), has led to a number of experiments demonstrating conclusively that the more common words have lower recognition thresholds than less common words, quite apart from their affective significance.[79]

Following up this criticism, Postman, Bronson, and Gropper (1952) equated critical and neutral words for frequency of ordinary use. They not only did not confirm McGinnies' finding, but obtained the very opposite result: lower thresholds for taboo words. While, therefore, the commonness of the words used must be controlled, does the total effect always disappear when that control is exercised? Not necessarily. McGinnies and Adornetto (1952) controlled word familiarity in experiments with schizophrenics, and found higher thresholds for taboo words, as in McGinnies' original experiment.

At least three additional determiners, besides frequency of word use, have been shown to affect recognition thresholds.

1. If subjects are given incomplete information about what kinds of words to expect, the difference between taboo and neutral words is greater than if information is given in advance (Lacy, Lewinger, and Adamson, 1953). Advance instructions obviously have nothing to do with experienced word frequency, though they may produce a readiness to perceive less familiar words.

2. An increase in need-relevant motivation can influence recognition thresholds for related words, whether the words are common or uncommon ones (Wispé and Drambarean, 1953). They found the recognition

[78] For a review through 1952 see Postman (1953).

[79] For further work on the relationship between frequency and threshold, see Howes and Solomon (1951), Howes (1954), McGinnies, Comer, and Lacey (1952), Postman and Schneider (1951), Solomon and Howes (1951), Solomon and Postman (1952), Wispé and Drambarean (1953).

thresholds for need-relevant words reduced after 10 and 24 hours without food and water, even though the thresholds both at high and low need states were correlated with the commonality of the words.

3. The nature of the choices confronting the subject can influence the results, apart from the familiarity of the words. Thus a forced-choice method, in which the subject was required to choose a syllable from a list to correspond to the briefly exposed one, produced more difference between thresholds for shocked and non-shocked syllables than a free-choice arrangement (Lysak, 1954).

These supplementary findings do not diminish the need to control word frequency, but they do suggest that the phenomena studied experimentally are functions of many other circumstances.

Another criticism of the McGinnies type of experiment is that deliberate *suppression* may take place, producing reduced response but for reasons differing dynamically from Freudian *repression*.[80] There may be a social hesitation to say taboo words, even though the words are recognized.

Another line of investigation is related to McGinnies' finding of GSR responses differentiating between neutral and taboo words at exposure times below threshold levels. The finding suggests renewed attack upon subthreshold perception, or *subception*, as it has come to be called. The issues are complex, but it usually turns out that there are sufficient suprathreshold features to account for most of the phenomena.[81] It is difficult even to know whether we are dealing with perception or a retrospective interpretation based on previously perceived fragmentary information (Lawrence and Coles, 1954), or whether we are dealing with perception or verbal habits (Neisser, 1954).

In the attempt to remove some of the artificiality of the taboo-word experiments, Eriksen (1951) proposed to make an independent study of personality needs and then predict what kinds of perceptual defense would occur.[82] Using a word-association test he scored his subjects (male patients in a veterans hospital) on needs related to aggression, succorance, and homosexuality. He then presented pictures tachistoscopically, with scenes related to these needs. He predicted that recognition thresholds would be raised for pictures suggesting disapproved needs. While the

[80] This criticism, and closely related ones, have been made by Howes and Solomon (1950), Lacy, Lewinger, and Adamson (1953), Lysak (1954), Postman, Bronson, and Gropper (1952), Whittaker, Gilchrist, and Fischer (1952).

[81] See, for example, Bricker and Chapanis (1953), Lazarus and McCleary (1951).

[82] This meets in part Klein's (1951) contention that we need to know more about the individual personalities of the subjects used in these experiments. In his experiments "high-interference" subjects sometimes react opposite to "low-interference" ones (Klein, 1954).

correlations obtained were not high, enough of them were significant to lend plausibility to the hypothesis that unacceptable needs tend to be defended against in perception.[83]

The phenomena of repression have not yet been very much illuminated by experiments on perceptual defense any more than they have by experiments on the ease of recall. Patience is needed, however, and it is too much to expect that as these topics are newly brought into the laboratory we can achieve at once both richness and precision.

ESTIMATE OF FREUD'S CONTRIBUTION TO LEARNING

Freud's Position on the Typical Problems

The foregoing account shows many points at which Freudian theory has impinged upon the psychology of learning. A recapitulation is in order to summarize his views as they relate to the several problems with which learning theories deal.

1. *Capacity.* As a developmental psychology, Freud's theory implies that the very young infant is most impressionable,[84] so that primary repressions occur in the first years of childhood, and character syndromes find their origins in the conflicts over food, toilet training, sex, aggression. The resolution of these conflicts takes place according to fundamental themes or styles of response, and the rest of life is spent in playing out these early themes with the assimilation, of course, of new content. Fundamental changes in the structure of the personality do not take place through ordinary education; such changes require the special kind of re-education provided by depth therapy. Alongside these modes of conduct determined by instinctual conflicts there are the conflict-free ego processes, which are the kinds dealt with in ordinary give-and-take with the real environment. At some stages of life the conflictual personal problems loom unusually large, and make difficult the adjustment to external reality implied in school learning. The easiest time for conflict-free learning should be during the "latency period," and after adolescent conflicts are resolved, but individual differences are to be expected throughout because some children do not outgrow their earlier fixations, and some conflicts remain active and disruptive at any age.

2. *Practice.* The repetition-compulsion is not a principle of learning-by-doing, for ordinarily the compulsive behavior is peculiarly resistant to change according to its consequences. The principle of learning through

[83] See also Eriksen (1952); Lazarus, Eriksen, and Fonda (1951).
[84] This may possibly be related to "imprinting," as emphasized by the ethologists.

practice is better illustrated by "working through," that aspect of therapy in which the patient faces the same conflicts over and over again in the process of re-education. Learning takes place in "working through" because the conflicts are faced from new angles, and the cues to faulty conduct become detected early enough so that the behavior can be deflected. Repetition is needed for learning, but for repetition to be effective it must be repetition with a difference.

3. *Motivation.* Freud's is chiefly a psychology of motivation, and he detected motivational control in kinds of behavior that others had thought of as trivial or accidental, such as minor forgettings and slips of speech. The first serious effort to incorporate psychoanalytic theory into general psychology recognized the Freudian wish as providing a theory of motivation.[85] The motivational concepts that have impinged most directly upon contemporary learning theory are *anxiety* (as a learned drive), and the consequences of various *ego threats,* as in the studies of regression, aggression, repression, and the defense mechanisms generally. The emphasis upon sex as a master drive has been less influential in learning theories than in other fields of personality study, although many of the ego-threatening situations used have included sexual conflicts.

4. *Understanding.* Despite Freud's preoccupation with the irrational in human behavior, his theory lays great stress upon the possibilities of cognitive control. We can even gain insight into our unconscious processes, if we work at it properly—no mean achievement for the intellect. The developing "ego psychology," playing up the "conflict-free ego sphere," allows even more room for rationality in the control of conduct.

The aim of psychoanalytic therapy is to get rid of self-deception and other blocks to rationality. To the extent that the methods are successful, they should provide some principles useful for learning and teaching.

5. *Transfer.* We must not permit verbal equivalences to lead us to assume identity where identity does not exist. "Transference" has a special meaning in psychoanalysis. It refers to the special role that the therapist plays for the patient as the therapist stands from time to time for important people in the patient's life, perhaps the mother, or father, or older brother. The patient reacts to the therapist with the emotions appropriate to these other people. Thus psychoanalytic transference does share with transfer of training the fact of generalization of responses learned in one situation to novel but related stimuli.

Problems of equivalence loom large in psychoanalysis. By way of symbols, something commonly stands for something else and provokes the

[85] Holt (1915).

responses (especially affective responses) appropriate to that something else. We have seen this process at work in displaced aggression. Other processes of symbolization and condensation are relevant to the manner in which earlier and later learning come into psychological relationship.

6. *Forgetting.* Freud long championed the view that registration of early experiences persists throughout life, that forgetting is therefore chiefly the result of repression. Forgetting is mostly a kind of amnesia, and under appropriate circumstances (as in dreams) the persistence of these memories may be detected, while under other circumstances (as in psychoanalysis) the repression may be lifted and the memories restored to waking consciousness. Although the most important repressions take place first in early childhood, the repressive process continues throughout life, maintaining the original repressions, and adding new items to the unconscious store.

Significance of Psychodynamics for Learning Theory

One influence of psychoanalytic thinking has been to broaden the *topical content* studied within the field of learning. Psychoanalytical thinking has helped to erase the boundaries between the neurotic and the normal, so that what was once relegated to "abnormal psychology" now becomes part of general psychology. Because there is a recognized continuum between the neurotic and the normal, the learning of symptoms becomes continuous with the learning of mannerisms and the acquiring of attitudes. Symbolism in night dreams makes us look for symbolism in daydreams, and in other products of creative imagination and thought. What we learn from unusual perceptual distortions, hallucinations, and amnesias influences how we think about ordinary perception in relation to the needs of the perceiver, and ordinary forgetting as related to motivation. Hence the range of topics that interest students of learning has been extended to include perceptual distortion, repression, and symbolism, all implying personal and idiosyncratic modes of expressing the results of learning.

In one form or another the conception of *unconscious determination* has made important changes in thinking about human motivation. Psychologists seeking to maintain the behavioristic orientation of the 1920's were somewhat resistant to consciousness and even more so to an unconscious consciousness. But even Watson was influenced strongly by Freudian doctrine and accepted "the unverbalized" as a substitute for the unconscious.[86] Thus the subjective-objective controversy did not turn out to be a decisive one, so far as incorporating motives of which the learner

[86] Watson (1924).

was unaware (or of which he could not speak). Freud can be credited with being the first to propose that repression leads to the inability to verbalize:

> Now, too, we are in a position to state precisely what it is that repression denies to the rejected idea in the transference neuroses—namely, the translation of the idea into words which are to remain attached to the object.[87]

Any appraisal of psychoanalytic influences would be most incomplete if it did not acknowledge the emphasis upon unconscious processes and their derivatives. This is the most obvious way in which to acknowledge the dynamic contribution of psychoanalysis.

Finally, the genetic or developmental aspects of psychoanalysis have brought to the fore the need for an adequate *ego psychology*.[88] If we are to understand the learner as he sets his goals and works realistically toward them, or as he is torn by conflicts that prevent his using his abilities, or as he burns himself out in the quest for futile objectives, we need a theory of personality organization incorporated within our general theory of learning.

The goads from psychoanalysis to broaden the content studied within learning, to recognize the range of motivational determiners, including unconscious ones, and to build toward an ego psychology are acceptable ones, and the acceptance of these challenges has already proved rewarding. A word of warning is in order. Psychoanalytic thinking is very complex and loosely formulated, so that it is not easy to find out what is essential, what is dispensable, and what internal contradictions there are in it. We need a careful, critical systematization of what appears to be best substantiated through clinical experience and through other sources of scientific evidence, so that irrelevancies and contradictions are either discarded or stated in form for decisive testing. We need to locate the most pertinent issues, and then to do our best to get adequate evidence to resolve these issues. There is much in Freud that nearly everyone will reject, such as the inheritance of acquired characteristics, and some metaphorical statements about localization of function in the brain. The problem is not to guess what Freud "really" meant and then to defend or refute him. The problem is to find out what is true, regardless of who said it. Freud uncovered some interesting hypotheses. We need to state them as carefully as we can, and then put them to the test.

[87] Freud (1915b), 133–134. Miller (1948b) has quoted these words and developed a related theory of repression in relation to displacement.

[88] See, for example, Symonds (1951). Misbach (1948), after a careful review of Freud's statements, concludes that his contributions to learning theory lie largely in the emphasis upon ego organization as the background for learning. Misbach believes the pleasure-pain (law of effect) principles in Freud to be secondary.

The Need for Collaborative Research

If psychologists are to avoid working with pallid replicas of the events dealt with in psychoanalysis, some of their work will have to be carried on in collaboration with those experienced in depth therapy. The psychologist will have to gain such sophistication as he can through personal experience with the phenomena, while he also learns the necessary methods and controls required to do research with them. Some of the problems will elude him unless he works closely (at least some of the time) with those who are dealing intimately with the more extreme manifestations of the phenomena—with emotional panic instead of the irritation of mild electric shock, with traumatic amnesia instead of the repression of mildly taboo words, with transference of hallucinatory intensity instead of a comfortable rapport, with the unusual states created under drugs and hypnosis in addition to those created by a few hours of hunger. It may be that some research problems in this field can be solved only with types of facilities that are but now coming into being.[89]

SUPPLEMENTARY READINGS

BOOKS

By Freud:

FREUD, S. (1938) *The basic writings of Sigmund Freud.* Especially for "The interpretation of dreams" (1900), and "Psychopathology of everyday life" (1904).
FREUD, S. (1920) *Beyond the pleasure principle.* Translation, 1950.
FREUD, S. (1923) *The ego and the id.* Translation, 1927.
FREUD, S. (1926) *The problem of anxiety.* Translation, 1936.
FREUD, S. (1940) *An outline of psychoanalysis.* Translation, 1949.

About Freud's views and those of others who have followed him:

FENICHEL, O. (1945) *The psychoanalytic theory of neurosis.*
FREUD, A. (1936) *The ego and mechanisms of defense.* Translation, 1937.
HALL, C. S. (1954) *A primer of Freudian psychology.*
HENDRICK, I. (1939) *Facts and theories of psychoanalysis.* Revised.
MUNROE, R. L. (1955) *Schools of psychoanalytic thought.*
SYMONDS, P. M. (1946) *The dynamics of human adjustment.*

Implications of psychoanalysis for general psychology and learning theory:

BLUM, G. S. (1953) *Psychoanalytic theories of personality.*
DOLLARD, J., and MILLER, N. E. (1950) *Personality and psychotherapy.*
HILGARD, E. R., KUBIE, L. S., and PUMPIAN-MINDLIN, E. (1952) *Psychoanalysis as science.*

[89] For a sketch of a proposed Research Institute in Psychoanalytic Psychology, see Kubie (1952), pages 113–123.

Mowrer, O. H. (1950) *Learning theory and personality dynamics.*
Mowrer, O. H. (1953) *Psychotherapy: theory and research.*
Rapaport, D. (1942) *Emotions and memory.*
Rapaport, D. (1951) *Organization and pathology of thought.*
Sears, R. R. (1943) *Survey of objective studies of psychoanalytic concepts.*

SHORTER INTRODUCTIONS AND CRITICAL APPRAISALS

Bergmann, G. (1943) Psychoanalysis and experimental psychology: a review from the standpoint of scientific empiricism. *Mind,* 52, 122–140.
Ellis, A. (1950) An introduction to the principles of scientific psychoanalysis. *Genet. Psychol. Monogr.,* 41, 147–212.
French, T. M. (1933) Interrelations between psychoanalysis and the experimental work of Pavlov. *Amer. J. Psychiat.,* 89, 1165–1203.
Frenkel-Brunswik, E. (1954) Psychoanalysis and the unity of science. *Proc. Amer. Acad. Arts and Sciences,* 80, 271–347.
Heidbreder, E. (1933) Freud and the psychoanalytic movement. In *Seven psychologies,* 376–412.
Kris, E. (1947) The nature of psychoanalytic propositions and their validation. In S. Hook and M. R. Konvitz, eds. *Freedom and experience,* pages 239–259.
Misbach, L. (1948) Psychoanalysis and theories of learning. *Psychol. Rev.,* 55, 143–156.
Sears, R. R. (1944) Experimental analysis of psychoanalytic phenomena. In J. McV. Hunt, ed. *Personality and the behavior disorders,* 306–332.
Woodworth, R. S. (1948) Psychoanalysis and related schools. In *Contemporary schools of psychology.* Revised edition, 156–212.

REPRESENTATIVE EXPERIMENTS

Blum, G. S., and Miller, D. R. (1952) Exploring the psychoanalytic theory of the "oral character." *J. Personality,* 20, 287–304.
Dudycha, G. J., and Dudycha, M. (1933) Adolescents' memories of preschool experiences. *J. genet. Psychol.,* 42, 468–480.
Eriksen, C. W. (1952) Defense against ego-threat in memory and perception. *J. abnorm. soc. Psychol.,* 47, 230–235.
Huston, P. E. Shakow, D., and Erickson, M. H. (1934) A study of hypnotically induced complexes by means of the Luria technique. *J. gen. Psychol.,* 11, 65–97.
Maier, N. R. F., Glaser, N. M., and Klee, J. B. (1940) Studies of abnormal behavior in the rat: III. The development of behavior fixations through frustration. *J. exp. Psychol.,* 26, 521–546.
Masserman, J. H., and Yum, K. S. (1946) An analysis of the influence of alcohol on experimental neuroses in cats. *Psychosom. Med.,* 8, 36–52.
Miller, N. E. (1948) Theory and experiment relating psychoanalytic displacement to stimulus-response generalization. *J. abnorm. soc. Psychol.,* 43, 155–178.
Mowrer, O. H. (1940) An experimental analogue of "regression," with incidental observations on "reaction-formation." *J. abnorm. soc. Psychol.,* 35, 56–87.
Postman, L., and Brown, D. R. (1952) Perceptual consequences of success and failure. *J. abnorm. soc. Psychol.,* 47, 213–221.
Sarbin, T. R. (1950) Mental age changes in experimental regression. *J. Personality,* 19, 221–228.

SEARS, R. R. (1951) Effects of frustration and anxiety on fantasy aggression. *Amer. J. Orthopsychiat.*, 21, 498–505.

SPENCE, K. W., and TAYLOR, J. A. (1953) The relation of conditioned response strength to anxiety in normal, neurotic, and psychotic subjects. *J. exp. Psychol.*, 45, 265–272.

FINAL NOTE

The best recent short introduction to psychoanalytic theory, with a bibliography adequate to the needs of the student of psychology, is:

HALL, C. S., and LINDZEY, G. (1954) Psychoanalytic theory and its applications in the social sciences. In G. Lindzey, ed. *Handbook of social psychology*, 143–180.

For developments in therapy, related to others aspects of psychiatry, clinical psychology, and allied fields:

ALEXANDER, F., and ROSS, H., eds. (1952) *Dynamic psychiatry.*

The student of psychoanalytic theory who wishes to gain the full flavor of its background can do no better than to get acquainted with Freud. Two books can be of great help to him:

FREUD, S. (1954) *The origins of psychoanalysis: letters to Wilhelm Fliess, drafts and notes: 1887–1902.*

These letters, edited by Marie Bonaparte, Anna Freud, and Ernst Kris, reveal Freud's personal struggle as he evolved his theory. It is unusual to have available so intimate a chronicle.

JONES, E. (1953) *The life and work of Sigmund Freud.* Vol. 1. *The formative years and the great discoveries*, 1856–1900.

JONES, E. (1955) *The life and work of Sigmund Freud.* Vol. 2. *Years of maturity*, 1901–1919.

The author is a disciple of Freud who has enough confidence in the greatness of his master so that he does not find it necessary to soft-pedal Freud's human frailties.

Most of the bridges between psychoanalysis and learning theory have thus far been built by learning theorists who devise ways of predicting Freudian phenomena from their theories. There is no fully satisfactory learning account written from the other starting point, that is, beginning with psychoanalysis and then deriving theorems about learning. There are a number of essays and books of advice about learning from the psychoanalytic viewpoint, of which the following are representative:

CANTOR, N. (1946) *Dynamics of learning.*

FREUD, A. (1935) *Psychoanalysis for teachers and parents.*

PEARSON, G. H. J. (1954) *Psychoanalysis and the education of the child.*

Chapter 10

FUNCTIONALISM

THE eight learning theories we have examined in the preceding chapters include one stimulus-response theory that antedated behaviorism (Thorndike), three varieties of stimulus-response behaviorism (Guthrie, Skinner, Hull), one "purposive" or "expectancy" behaviorism (Tolman), two variants of gestalt theory (classical gestalt and Lewin), and a psychodynamic theory (Freud). For the final major position to review, we return to the one out of which behaviorism grew but which flourished alongside it and continues to be well represented in contemporary psychology. It is the loosely formulated position known as functionalism, appropriately treated last because of its eclectic character and because its supporters have been free to learn from all of the other theories of learning.

While the name "functionalism" arose in connection with the brand of psychology developed by Angell and Carr at the University of Chicago, the name is equally applicable to the dynamic psychology that Woodworth taught at Columbia. Boring considers Woodworth "perhaps the best representative of the broad functionalism that is characteristic of American psychology." [1] Woodworth thinks of functionalism as a middle-of-the-road position, not really a "school" of psychology.[2]

GENERAL CHARACTERISTICS OF FUNCTIONALISM

Functionalism in one form or another has a long history. In Europe such men as Galton, Binet, and Claparède could be classified as functionalists. In America, James, Hall, Ladd, Baldwin, Cattell, and Seashore were all functionalists in outlook. While we turn to the University of Chicago first because it was there that functionalism became defined, functionalism early in the century was "in the air" at Clark under Hall, at Columbia

[1] Boring (1950), page 722.
[2] Woodworth (1948), page 255.

under Cattell and Woodworth, and at Yale under Ladd, Scripture, and Judd.

The Influence of John Dewey

John Dewey (1858–1952) is the "founder" of official functionalism. His famous paper on the reflex-arc concept in psychology (1896), through its clear opposition to prevailing elementarism, marked the beginning of the new protest. One might have expected him to direct his attack against sensationism, for sensation was the fundamental element in the Wundt-Titchener psychology. Instead the attack was on the reflex-arc concept, which, as Heidbreder has pointed out, was the very concept that had been introduced to move beyond a static description of elements of consciousness.[3] There was, in fact, a controversy going on between Baldwin and Titchener over reaction time (involving the reflex arc) and the first experimental paper using Dewey's formulations was a study of reaction time by Angell and Moore (1896), mediating the Baldwin-Titchener controversy.[4]

Dewey's main argument was that activity should not be thought of as starting with a stimulus, going through a central process, then emerging in a response. Instead, the activity is a complete cycle—a "reflex circuit"—in which the response may seek or "constitute" the stimulus. The relation of the response to the posterior stimulus may be as important as its relation to the anterior one.[5]

Functionalism was christened by Titchener (1898) when he attacked Dewey's position, contrasting functionalism with structuralism. The challenge was accepted by Dewey's younger colleague, James Rowland Angell (1869–1949), who became the leader of the new movement. We shall return to him presently.

Dewey turned from academic psychology to education before he left Chicago, and he went to Columbia in 1904 never again to concern himself directly with the problems of laboratory psychology. But he had already left his mark on the functional psychology that continued after he moved on. The animal laboratories and the studies of child development express the spirit of his Darwinism, with its emphasis upon the evolution of adaptive mechanisms.[6] Not much of his later writing appears in psy-

[3] Heidbreder (1933), page 212.

[4] Baldwin and Shaw (1895), Baldwin (1896); Titchener (1895a) (1895b) (1896).

[5] The same line of argument was picked up by a later Chicago psychologist, Thurstone (1923). There is a family resemblance between Dewey's position and Skinner's operant behavior, in which responses are coordinated with the stimuli to which they lead.

[6] Dewey (1920).

chology textbooks; later references in them are chiefly to his *How we think* (1910), which gave a practical and teachable account of some steps in problem-solving modeled after the steps in scientific investigations.

It would be a mistake, however, to think of Dewey's influence upon the psychology of learning as limited to the work of those who developed functional psychology within the laboratories. At least three other lines of influence can be discerned, each bearing his imprint.

The most marked of these, for its relevance to the psychology of learning, is his influence upon ways of thinking about learning as the product of schoolroom practices. This influence began with his founding of the experimental elementary school at the University of Chicago,[7] and the subsequent development known in its heyday as progressive education. His emphasis upon interest and effort, upon the child's motivation to solve his own problems, represented a dynamic innovation for which the laboratory psychologists were not yet ready. Consequently Dewey's challenge was taken up by educational philosophers rather than by psychologists.[8] Now it so happens that cousins may each resemble a common grandparent without resembling each other. Although Dewey's influence is clear in Carr's *Psychology* (1925), and in Kilpatrick's *Foundations of method* (1925), the detailed learning theories of these two books, the first a psychologist's and the second an educator's, have little in common. Progressive education, at its best, was an embodiment of the ideal of growth toward independence and self-control through interaction with an environment suited to the child's developmental level. The emphasis was upon intelligent problem-solving (*not* upon learning through play), in which each child solves his problems by selecting appropriate materials and methods and by learning to adapt these materials and methods to his ends. His interest sustains his effort as he experiments with his solutions by testing them in action. The kinds of problems solved are social as well as individual, for education is envisaged as a preparation for life in a democracy through democratic living here and now. How different this all sounds from the rules for memorizing a list of nonsense syllables in the minimum number of trials!

The second line of development, outside academic psychology, was upon sociological social psychology, by way of George Herbert Mead (1863–1931), who came with Dewey from Michigan to Chicago. Mead, whose views were very similar to those of Dewey, became the guiding

[7] For the early history of this school, with the point of view that infused it, see Mayhew and Edwards (1936).

[8] E.g., Childs (1931), Bode (1940).

spirit for developments in sociology paralleling those of Dewey in psychology and education. Mead is important for contemporary learning theory because he sponsored a form of self- or ego-psychology a whole generation before experimental psychologists were ready to take it up.[9] Mead's interpretation of the self as arising out of social interaction is close to the spirit of Dewey the social philosopher and the defender of democratic values, who saw every act as the expression of a unified self seeking to resolve its conflicts through intelligent action in a world of objects and other selves.

Finally, we have Dewey the philosopher, carrying on the pragmatic tradition of Peirce and James in a form known as *instrumentalism* or *experimentalism.* Even late in life he continued to write upon logic (1938) and upon epistemology (with A. F. Bentley, 1949), always deferring to the scientific method as the one that has helped man to acquire his firmest knowledge. He insisted that ordinary mortals, without the scientist's equipment, could learn lessons from the method of science helpful in the conduct of their daily lives.[10]

A case could be made for bringing these diverging trends into a new synthesis that would have significance for the psychology of learning. Indeed, in ill-defined ways something of the sort may already be happening, as we meet new emphases within learning theory upon ego aspects of learning, upon searching behavior and intelligent problem-solving, upon learning in social contexts. These new emphases supplement a prior preoccupation with quantification and a somewhat constricted methodology. A new synthesis, strictly in the functionalist tradition, may legitimately acknowledge Dewey in its ancestry. History has a way of moving in cycles. Shortly before Dewey's death his interpretation of perception as a *transaction* between the organism and the environment (foreshadowed in the original paper on the reflex arc) began to find its way back into the literature of psychology.[11] Possibly the rediscovery of other useful ideas may cause a re-evaluation of Dewey's place in the history of psychology.

Angell and His Successors

We return now to the main line of development of functional psychology, which went forward under Angell and his successors. Harvey

[9] Mead's influence is discernible clearly in Cottrell and Gallagher (1941), and in Newcomb (1950). One learning theorist makes direct acknowledgment to him: Muenzinger (1942).

[10] For Dewey's philosophy, see Ratner (1939).

[11] E.g., Kelley (1947), Ittleson and Cantril (1954).

Carr succeeded him at Chicago; Edward S. Robinson, a younger man, taught at Chicago before he went to Yale to carry on a similar program until accidental death cut short his career. Next to carry the mantle was John A. McGeoch, whose career, too, was ended by death at an early age. The students of Carr, Robinson, and McGeoch continue to be active, such men as Bills, Heron, Irion, McKinney, Melton, Waters, Underwood. Their students, in turn, keep the flavor of Chicago functionalism alive, although no one of those mentioned is now at Chicago, and several of them never were.

In an early clear statement of the functionalist position Angell (1907) made three points:

1. Functionalism is interested in the *how* and *why* of mental operations as well as in the *what* (i.e., descriptive content). It is a cause-and-effect psychology, or in modern terms, an input-output psychology, concerned with mental operations in their context.

2. Functionalism is essentially a psychology of the adjustment of the organism to its environment. Consciousness evolved to serve some biological purpose, to help the organism solve its problems especially when conflicts arise and habits no longer suffice. Once this position was taken, the way was open to welcome applied psychology: educational psychology, industrial psychology, mental hygiene.

3. Functionalism is interested in mind-in-body, and so studies the physiological substratum of mental events. The implied dualism is a purely practical one (as in current psychosomatic medicine) and does not imply a special position on the mind-body problem. The only position that must be rejected, if one is to stress the adaptive role of consciousness, is that known as epiphenomenalism, the view that consciousness is a useless by-product of neural activity.

Now that the quarrels within psychology have shifted somewhat, and the definition of psychology's province is no longer a matter to fight about, the word "function" has tended to return more nearly to its mathematical use, as in the expression, $y = f(x)$, ("y is a function of x"). This causes no great shift for the functionalist, for all he asked was to be free to study many sorts of contingencies, to find what depended on what, whether the dependency was upon age, species membership, prior practice, the ingestion of a drug, or accepting the experimenter's instructions. Nevertheless, the shift is away from the earlier emphasis upon adaptiveness, upon purposes served. While the functionalist is free to work on applied problems, the freedom is one of choice, and a functionalist may work with "pure" functions if he chooses. There is a kind of neutrality about the mathematical function that makes it particularly appealing to the scientist; like the correlation coefficient, it *expresses* a relationship without requiring anyone to claim that it *explains* the relationship. If it does lead to a kind of explanation, there need be nothing teleological about it; there is no implication, with Voltaire, that God must have given man a nose in order to have a support for his spectacles. If some noses support spectacles more readily than others, or if some kinds of spectacles fit more kinds of noses, that is all that the functionalist is interested in finding out.

The Background of Woodworth's Functionalism

Like Dewey, Woodworth was influenced by William James and G. Stanley Hall, although he studied only with James. His functionalism derived in part from them, and from his early association with Thorndike, Cattell, Ladd, and Sherrington. Both Angell and Woodworth became interested in imageless thought, and though they disagreed about it, the problems of imageless thought raised the question of meaning in relation to consciousness, a good functionalist topic.[12]

Woodworth's functionalism gave considerably more place to motivation than the earlier Chicago functionalism. The role of motivation was prominent in Woodworth's *Dynamic psychology* (1918), and his suggestions were heavily leaned upon when motivation became incorporated into Chicago functionalism by Carr (1925).

Apart, then, from their sharing ancestry in men like James and Hall, the developments at Chicago and at Columbia were not intimately related but were mutually congenial, and with the passing of time the differences between them have gradually faded so that we can treat the general outlook as one, particularly as that outlook is reflected in contemporary psychology.

The Flavor of Functionalism

Because contemporary functionalism is so loosely articulated, a point of view without acknowledged leadership and with few loyal and self-conscious adherents, it defies precise exposition. Hence we must be content to come to an appreciation of its flavor rather than to achieve final judgment about its principles.

1. *The functionalist is tolerant but critical.* The functionalist is free from self-imposed constraints that have shackled many other systematists.

[12] The functionalist Rahn (1914) pointed out that it was impossible to introspect a meaningless element. This was very damaging to the structuralist position of Titchener.

He uses the words from diverse vocabularies, borrowing words freely from other traditions. He is not forbidden the use of older words because today they sound subjective (e.g., "idea," "meaning," "purpose"), or because they have occasionally been given systematic connotations that he does not accept ("sensation," "image," "ego"). He does not believe that anything is gained by new terms, unless advance in knowledge justifies the further precision that new words can bring. For example, he believes it premature to call all thinking "implicit verbalization," for the objective terminology is not yet justified by what we know about thinking. Hence he holds to the older word. His definition of the field of psychology is also a tolerant one, and he is ready to accept information obtained by introspection, by objective observation, from case studies, from mental tests. He is tolerant as to method, and he is also tolerant as to content. The distinction between pure science and applied science seems to him trivial, so long as either is good science.

It is a mistake to confuse this broad tolerance with looseness, as though functionalism is merely an uncritical eclecticism. On the contrary, the functionalist is commonly a very astute critic. Because he has his eyes open for variables that may be ignored by more dogmatic systematists, he is not easily trapped into accepting "pat" systematic solutions for intricate problems. This critical attitude is expressed in a preference for *relativism* over *absolutism*.[13] Recognizing the many determiners of psychological activities, Carr deplored what he called the quest for "constants," by which he meant one-to-one correspondences, or psychological laws stated without reference to all the influential variables.

2. *The functionalist prefers continuities over discontinuities or typologies.* The mathematical statement of a functional relationship usually implies a gradual transition between the values of the dependent variable correlated with the independent variable as it increases or decreases. While extremes may differ so markedly as to appear qualitatively unlike, the functionalist looks for connecting in-between cases. This continuity of function was made the basis for a *dimensional principle* by McGeoch, and the suggestion has been elaborated by Melton.[14]

The two chief classes of variation recognized by Melton are those dependent upon experimental arrangements, which may be called *situational dimensions*, and those that depend upon the psychological functions involved, which may be called *process dimensions*.

[13] Carr (1933).

[14] McGeoch (1936), Melton (1941a) (1950). The dimensional principle was applied earlier to a modern version of the attributes of sensation by Boring (1933a).

The situational dimensions call attention to the differences between what the learner is called upon to do from one experiment to another. A very different problem is presented to the learner by a path through a maze, the rotating target of a pursuitmeter, a list of syllables on a memory drum, a reflex to be attached by conditioning to a new stimulus, and a mathematical problem to be solved by reasoning.

The process dimensions are correlated in a coarse way with the situational dimensions, but are distinguishable. They include such considerations as the amount of discovery required before the correct response is made (a distinction between *rote learning* and *problem-solving*), the involvement of motor or ideational responses (as between *motor skills* and *verbal memory*), and the relevancy of motivating conditions (*incidental learning* as against *intentional learning*).

Experiments have to be classified according to more than one dimension. Thus rote learning and reasoning experiments are alike on the dimensions verbal-nonverbal, but unlike with respect to the amount of discovery involved in the adequate response. It is important to recognize that the classification is not according to fixed types, but always according to scales that have intermediate values. Learning is not blind on the one hand and insightful on the other; there are degrees of understanding involved from a minimum at one extreme to a maximum at the other, with most cases falling between these extremes.

3. *The functionalist is an experimentalist.* In its modern form, functionalism is dedicated to the experimental method. The issues upon which the functionalist is so tolerant become a part of his science only when they are translated into experimentable form. He is free of constraint in his choice of dimensions, and may choose to set up a dimension of items graded for similarity or a dimension of tasks graded according to degree-of-understanding. He prefers to drive general issues back to specifics before he is led into controversy over them, for he believes that many linguistic difficulties fade when reference is made to the specific findings of experiments.

American psychology so generally accepts the three points which have been used to characterize functionalism that functionalism has become an almost unrecognized ground for mutual understanding. There is, however, a lingering bias detectable among leading functionalists that tempers the judgment that functionalism is neutral in respect to the major quarrels among learning theorists. This is the bias toward association theory, and the environmentalism that so often accompanies association psychologies. The affiliation with historical association theory has been recognized by leading functionalists.[15] The preference for environmentalism shows up largely in the treatment of perception, where the issue associated with the differences between Helmholtz and Hering has been kept alive in differences between gestalt psychologists and associationists. The functionalist prefers to interpret perceptual discriminations as learned.[16] Although these biases are not absolute ones, when there is room for doubt (as in some aspects of size constancy) one can predict that the functionalist will be on the side of empiricism and against nativism.

In summary, we find the functionalist tolerant but critical, favoring continuities over discontinuities, seeking to translate his problems into experimentable form. Within the free, eclectic atmosphere, he nevertheless has a preference for interpretations coherent with historical association theory as against holistic or nativistic interpretations.

FUNCTIONAL ASPECTS OF THE LEARNING PROCESS

Because the functionalist does not have a highly articulated learning theory, we can best understand his approach by following a functionalist's analysis of the problems facing an experimental psychology of learning. In what follows we shall accept Melton's (1950) summary of learning as a representative functionalist statement, using his analysis of learning and his outline of topics.

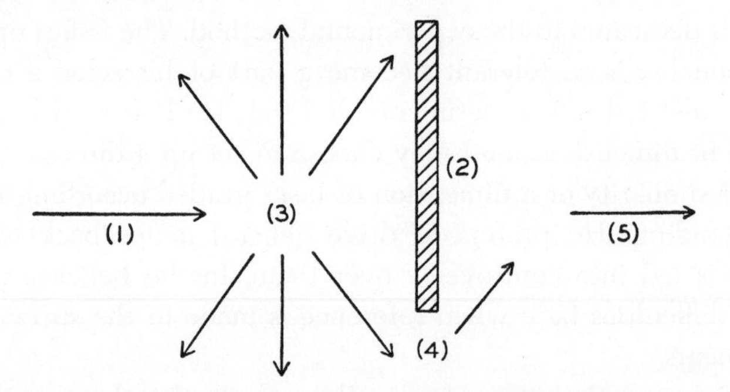

FIGURE 45. The readjustive process. After Dashiell (1949), page 26.

Melton begins with Dashiell's diagram of the readjustive process (Figure 45). The diagram shows how a problem arises when ongoing activity (1) is blocked by an obstacle (2). Eventually the organism through

[15] Carr (1931), Robinson (1932a). Melton (1950) describes his position as an "associationistic functionalism."

[16] E.g., Carr (1935). The favorite experiment quoted by functionalists has long been that of visual experiences with reversing lenses, Stratton (1896).

varied behavior (3) solves the problem (4) and proceeds on his way (5). If the process is repeated, the adequate response (4) recurs in less time, with less excess and irrelevant activity.

> Thus the learning process is primarily a matter of the discovery of the adequate response to a problem situation and the fixation of the satisfying situation-response relationship.[17]

From this analysis, Melton is led to state several major experimental problems of learning. Expressed as topics, these are:

1. Motivation
2. Initial discovery of the adequate response
3. Fixation and elimination
4. Factors determining the rate of learning
5. Transfer of training and retention

We can follow this outline in characterizing the functionalist approach to these topics.

1. *Motivation*

Woodworth was the first functionalist to give a treatment of motivation in modern form, in a small book entitled *Dynamic psychology* (1918).

It was this book that gave currency to the term "drive" as alternative to "instinct." Woodworth set the stage for the prominence that drives and motives were presently to have within psychology.

The cycle between aroused activity and quiescence is discussed according to *preparatory* and *consummatory* reactions, Woodworth crediting Sherrington[18] with the distinction. Consummatory reactions are those which satisfy basic drives or needs, activities such as eating or escaping from danger. They are directly of value to the organism. Their objective mark is that they terminate a series of acts, leading either to rest or to the turning by the organism to something else. A preparatory reaction is only indirectly or mediately of value to the organism, its value resting on the fact that it leads to or makes possible a consummatory reaction. The objective mark of the preparatory reaction is said to be that it occurs as a preliminary stage leading to the consummatory reaction.

Preparatory reactions are of two kinds. One kind represents alert attention, "a condition of readiness for a yet undetermined stimulus that may arouse further response." Another is the kind of preparatory adjustment evoked only "when the mechanism for a consummatory reaction has been aroused and is in activity." The latter sort of reaction is goal-

[17] Melton (1950), page 670.
[18] Sherrington (1906).

directed, and evokes seeking behavior, as when a hunting dog, having lost a trail, explores about in order to get back on it.

A new conception introduced is that of ongoing activity as itself a drive—activity once under way leading to its own completion. Even if the original drive under which the activity started has ceased to operate, the activity, if incomplete, may continue. The distinction between drive and mechanism breaks down when it is asserted that the mechanism (i.e., the reaction under way) may become its own drive. Allport later (1937) proposed that motives may become *functionally autonomous,* that is, completely divorced from their primal sources in basic needs of the organism. Activity leading to further activity, and functional autonomy, are very similar conceptions. Both are related to the problem of secondary reinforcement. If stimuli associated with reinforcement themselves come to have reinforcing power, it may be that a system of derived rewards may be built up which will continue to have motivating power without recourse to the satisfaction of any basic need. The increasing importance attaching to secondary reinforcement in theories like Hull's and Skinner's shows Woodworth's perspicacity in being the first to recognize that the distinction between drive and mechanism becomes less sharp as activity gets under way.

Another facet to Woodworth's motivational theory is the abiding interest that he has shown in the concept of "set," dating from his early experiments on imageless thought. It was the new emphasis brought about by the imageless thought controversy that in the first decade of this century provided functionalism's supplementation to traditional association psychology. Although Angell and Woodworth were on opposite sides of the fence on some issues concerned with the introspective contents of thought, they were in agreement on the dynamic consequences of predisposing sets and intentions.[19]

The sets and intentions emphasized by the students of imageless thought, and the preparatory reactions oriented toward consummatory responses are concepts with a similar dynamic loading. They are both directional, they are both inferred from the manner in which behavior sequences are organized. In a later development of his conception of set, Woodworth introduces what he calls the *situation-set* and the *goal-set* (1937). The situation-set refers to adjustments to environmental objects; the goal-set refers to the inner "steer" which gives unity to a series of varied but goal-directed activities.

[19] Woodworth (1906); Angell (1906).

The important suggestion in the concept of situation-set is that the environment must be brought into the psychological account in a manner not suggested by the usual stimulus-response psychology. Guthrie, for example, makes much of the fact that he is interested in movements, not in outcomes. Woodworth takes the opposite position. Movements are, to Woodworth, less important than the information about the environment to which these movements lead. The rat in the maze learns spatial relationships, not running habits; in the problem-box the cat discovers the door-opening character of the button, not a sequence of manipulatory movements. As Woodworth puts it: "The character of goodness attaches for the animal not to his movements in manipulating the button, but to the button as an object."

It is to Woodworth's credit that his long history of espousing stimulus-response concepts did not so fix his thinking that he was unable to go outside this systematic framework as he felt it necessary. The conception of situation-set presents a kind of bridge to ways of looking at psychology that have been carried out more fully by others, notably by Tolman and Brunswik. Through the years, Woodworth's use of "set" and related concepts has prevented his falling into a static system.

Carr's interpretation of motivation in his textbook (1925), was influenced by Woodworth's views, but restated the preparatory-consummatory adjustment in new terms.

Carr accepted the principle that all behavior is initiated by stimuli, so that the point of view is similar to other stimulus-response psychologies, with the difference that responses may be ideational as well as motor. He is concerned with activities, not movements. An adaptive act is described as involving a motivating stimulus, a sensory situation, and a response that alters that situation in a way that satisfies the motivating conditions. The external object by which the organism satisfies its motives is called the incentive, or the immediate objective or goal of the response. (The more remote goal, such as maintaining the life of the organism by preventing starvation, does not enter directly into the control of the act.) More specifically, a motive is described as a relatively persistent stimulus that dominates the behavior of an individual until he reacts in such a manner that he is no longer affected by it. This makes of a motive what Smith and Guthrie call a maintaining stimulus. The adaptive act is organized to obtain certain sensory consequences (i.e., the termination of the motivating stimuli) and the act can be interpreted as completed only when the consequences are attained. The interpretation of the end phase as a sensory change became Carr's way of talking about the empirical law of effect.[20]

Melton, accepting Carr's definition of motivation as a stimulating condition, points out that motivating conditions have three functions: (1) they energize the organism, making it active, (2) they direct the variable and persistent activity of the organism, and (3) they emphasize or select the activities that are repeated (fixated) and those that are not repeated (eliminated). Stated in this way, the functionalist's interpretation of motivation is consistent with Hull's, but it is coherent also with the position of Tolman and Lewin.

2. *Initial Discovery of the Adequate Response*

Melton points out that initial discovery may be the main problem in some kinds of learning (e.g., in the problem-box), while it plays little part in others (e.g., in serial rote memorization). The controversy between trial and error and insight in the interpretation of learning hinges in part on the nature of this initial discovery of the correct solution. The functionalist does not have to take sides: he waits for definitive experiments.

Melton notes that two other forms of initial discovery have played less systematic roles in learning theories, yet they should not be neglected. One of these is *guidance.* The discovery of the correct response can be facilitated by the teacher or trainer through appropriate manipulation of the environment or the learner. Hence guided learning is intermediate between rote learning (with no discovery) and problem-solving (with unguided discovery). An extensive research program on guided learning was carried out by Carr and his students and later summarized by him.[21] Such a program illustrates the freedom with which the functionalist selects his experimental variables.

The other form of initial discovery mentioned by Melton is *imitation.* He believes it can be subsumed under guidance, however, for it helps the learner to discover the solution by observing the solution by another organism.

Melton, in common with other functionalists, is willing to accept the initial discovery of solutions with insight, but, in common with other associationists, prefers interpretations emphasizing past experience:

> Insight is, however, not a term to conjure with even though it is a useful descriptive concept when employed within the framework of the major dimensions of analysis of the problem situation and the process of discovery of the correct response. In any event, the range, specific nature, and plasticity of the

[20] Carr (1938).
[21] Carr (1930).

trial behavior of the organism seem to be most profitably related to the motivating condition of the organism and to the associative spread from previous learning.[22]

3. *Fixation of Adequate Responses and Elimination of Inadequate Responses*

Melton accepts the *empirical law of effect* as stated by McGeoch: "Other things being equal, acts leading to consequences which satisfy a motivating condition are selected and strengthened, while those leading to consequences which do not satisfy a motivating condition are eliminated." [23] When it comes to *explaining* effect, Melton is cautious in choosing between a contiguity theory and a reinforcement theory:

> Two alternatives seem to be available to the student at this time: (*a*) The issue of contiguity vs. effect will be decided at some distant time in terms of the over-all fruitfulness of one or the other postulate, as judged by the application of Hull's theoretical methodology; (*b*) It may be that *mere* contiguity and reinforcement are extremes of some as yet undefined dimension of the neurophysiology of the organism, such that associations may be formed through mere contiguity *or* through reinforcement. Meanwhile, it is necessary to recognize the experimental findings which make the complete generality of one or the other untenable, for these are actually the fruits of the research on this problem during the forty years.[24]

This quotation well illustrates the functionalist's unwillingness to prejudge the outcome of a controversy whose resolution ultimately must be determined by experiment.

4. *Factors Determining the Rate of Learning*

Whatever may be the underlying principles of learning when learning is reduced to the barest essential relationships between stimulus and response, it is not difficult to arrange situations under which learning occurs. By long-established convention we plot performance scores against learning trials and come out with a "curve of learning." The search for a "typical" or "true" form of the learning curve has not proven profitable, but learning curves have helped in the search for the parameters of learning. Through a great many experiments we have learned much about the relationship between rate of learning and the amount of material to be learned, about the effects of length and distribution of practice periods, about how the characteristics of the learner affect the rate of progress. These problems have all been inviting ones to the functionalist who sets as his task the exploring of the many dimensions influencing learning.

[22] Melton (1950), page 676.
[23] McGeoch (1942), page 574.
[24] Melton (1950), page 677.

Some guiding principles are needed to establish order in an empirical program of such vast scope as accounting for everything that affects all kinds of learning by all kinds of learners under all kinds of circumstances. Some of these guiding principles were inherited from the pre-experimental association psychologists. A useful list had been provided by Thomas Brown as early as 1820. He had classified the *laws of association* (or laws of suggestion, as he called them) into *primary* or *qualitative* laws (the laws of similarity, contrast, and contiguity), and *secondary* or *quantitative* laws (frequency, vividness, emotional congruity, mental set, etc.). The primary laws represent the essential general conditions for associative formation or associative revival, whereas the secondary laws determine which of many possible associates is formed or recalled.

After Ebbinghaus (1885) had shown that associations could be studied experimentally, writers such as Müller (1911–1917) in Europe and Carr (1931) and Robinson (1932a) in America began to rewrite associative laws in quantitative form. Carr and Robinson were quite explicit that *all* associative laws could be made quantitative, and they gave lists of laws that they thought expressed our twentieth-century knowledge about associative learning.

Here is Robinson's list of laws: [25]

Law of contiguity
Law of assimilation
Law of frequency
Law of intensity
Law of duration
Law of context
Law of acquaintance
Law of composition
Law of individual differences

While in topic some of Robinson's laws sound qualitative, he attempts to show how all qualitative distinctions can be subjected to a dimensional analysis. He himself raised the question whether or not in isolating these factors as important he had really stated "laws." He summarized his discussion of "laws" as follows:

> It is my firm conviction that the facility of associative fixation is a function of all of the factors enumerated. Probably several specific relationships are involved for each named factor and almost certainly there are other factors that have not been included in this list. But, if the assumption that these factors are important determiners of association be correct, then there are "laws" of these factors whether our knowledge of them is definite or not.[26]

[25] The laws are stated in Robinson (1932a), pages 62–122.
[26] Robinson (1932a), page 124.

It turns out that Robinson's position is much like Skinner's, in that he points out the relevant variables and makes a claim for "lawfulness" rather than for "laws." Because of these limitations in the list of "laws," the Carr-Robinson laws did not catch on, even among their students, as a means of ordering the factors determining the rate of learning, although there are occasional mentions of isolated laws from the list. The issues expressed in the laws were somewhat too general. The empirical role of contiguity,[27] for example, breaks down into the study of several varieties of time relationships between events, with their corresponding gradients. Thus the separation of a conditioned and unconditioned stimulus in classical conditioning yields one kind of empirical law of contiguity, while the delay of reward at the end of a maze yields another kind. We tend to name such relationships more concretely (e.g., gradient of reinforcement, spread of effect) rather than to refer them to a more general law of contiguity. So, too, the law of frequency, as a law of relative frequency, covers too many topics, including the form of the learning curve, the form of the work curve, the effects of distributed and massed practice, the consequences of degrees of overlearning. Frequency is only a general topic, within which a number of very different laws are discoverable.

Contemporary functionalist writers, instead of setting up basic laws of learning, tend to use classificatory schemes derived directly from experimental arrangements and results. Underwood, for example, uses the following scheme to outline the factors determining the rate of learning:

a. Massed versus distributed practice
b. Type of material
(1) Intra-list similarity
(2) Meaningfulness
(3) Affectivity
c. Knowledge of performance
d. Miscellaneous (e.g., whole versus part learning; active recitation; sense modality; amount of material) [28]

While Underwood's treatment is part of a chapter in an introductory textbook on experimental psychology and is not intended to be exhaustive, his classification of variables bears a close resemblance to that used in other functionalist treatises on learning.[29] Such a classificatory scheme is not in itself a theory of learning, yet it suggests as well as the Carr-Robinson laws the kinds of variables with which functionalist systems deal.

[27] To be distinguished from the fundamental axiom of contiguity as in Guthrie's theory. The empirical problem of contiguity is a dimensional one, concerned with *degrees* of contiguity.

[28] Underwood (1949), pages 398–419.

[29] Major summaries of the literature handled functionally can be found in McGeoch and Irion (1952), Osgood (1953), Woodworth and Schlosberg (1954).

5. *Transfer of Training and Retention*

Once something has been learned it can be used, provided it has not been forgotten and provided new situations recur in which the previously learned behavior is called forth. The study of the relative permanence of learning, when tested in situations essentially duplicating those of the original learning, is the study of *retention,* while the study of the effects of old learning in new situations is often discussed as *transfer of training.* Because recurring situations always recur with differences, there is obviously an intimacy between retention and transfer. Because transfer effects may be positive, negative, or indeterminate, one view of forgetting is that it is but an illustration of negative transfer.

Melton follows McGeoch (1932a) in accepting two major laws of forgetting. The first is the *law of context* (one from Robinson's list), which asserts that the degree of retention, as measured by performance, is a function of the similarity between the original learning situation and the retention situation. The second is the *law of proactive and retroactive inhibition,* which asserts that retention is a function of activities occurring prior to and subsequent to the original learning. Proactive and retroactive inhibition have been major topics of research for several decades, ever since the problem was first opened up by Müller and Pilzecker (1900). A number of good summaries of the literature are available.[30]

The paradigm for retroactive inhibition is A—B—A, where the learning of B is interpolated between the learning and retention of A, and interferes with the retention of A. The paradigm for proactive inhibition is B—A—A, where the learning of B prior to the learning of A interferes with the later retention of A. Both retroactive and proactive interference with learning are readily demonstrable, and the empirical relationships have led to a number of hypotheses. Studying the development of one of these hypotheses will help us to understand not only retroactive inhibition but the manner in which functionalists construct their theories.

One set of problems arises over the *similarity* between the interpolated material and the material originally learned. Robinson (1927), arguing from some earlier results of his own and of Skaggs (1925), formulated a hypothesis later christened by McGeoch as the Skaggs-Robinson hypothesis. With the usual functionalist preference for stating dimensions, Robinson proposed relating the amount of retroactive inhibition to the dimen-

[30] For the earlier literature, see Britt (1935) and Swenson (1941). A general summary can be found in McGeoch and Irion (1952), 404–447.

sion of degree of similarity between the original and the interpolated material or activity.

With the similarity dimension in mind, Robinson argued that the interpolation of identical material (Material B the same as Material A) would simply provide additional practice on Material A, hence lead to increased retention on the test trials during which retroactive inhibition is usually shown. Because retroactive inhibition with dissimilar materials was already an established fact, the natural conjecture on the assumption of continuous variation is that starting with identity the amount of retroactive inhibition would increase gradually as dissimilarity was increased. Now, asks Robinson, what is likely to happen at the other end of the

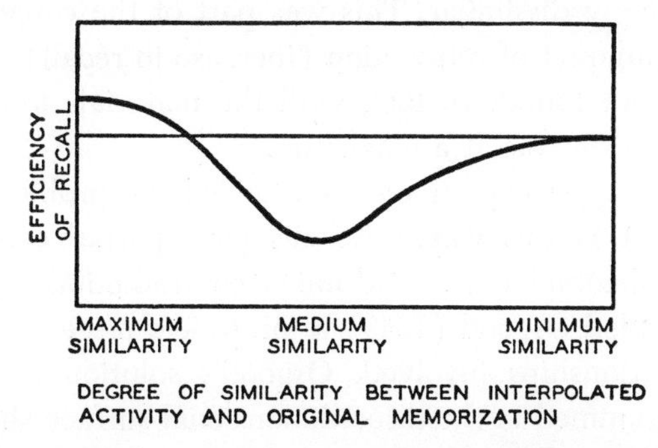

FIGURE 46. Similarity as a factor in retroactive inhibition. The curve is intended to show that retroactive inhibition bears a quantitative relationship to the degree of similarity between the interpolated activity and the material originally memorized. With maximum similarity, the interpolated activity provides positive transfer, hence increases the efficiency of recall. Maximum interference with recall is predicted to fall at some intermediate value of similarity. After Robinson (1927), page 299.

scale, as the original material (Material A) and the interpolated material (Material B) become *extremely* unlike? Presumably retroactive inhibition represents some sort of interference based on similarity between the original and interpolated activity. If there is very little similarity there should be very little retroactive inhibition. Putting all these considerations together, it is reasonable to expect a maximum of retroactive inhibition at some intermediate point of similarity between Materials A and B. Robinson formulated the whole generalization in words as follows: "As similarity between interpolation and original memorization is reduced from near identity, retention falls away to a minimum and then rises again, but with decreasing similarity it never reaches the level obtaining with maximum similarity." He expressed this graphically by the figure reproduced as Figure 46.

His own experimental test of the generalization was very simple. By the memory span method he studied the recall of the first four of a series of eight consonants as this recall was interfered with by the last four of the consonants. That is, the first four were considered to be Material A, the last four Material B, and the similarity and dissimilarity of Materials A and B were controlled. Similarity was defined as partial identity. Maximum similarity meant that the second four consonants were like the first four; maximum dissimilarity meant that all the last four differed from the first four.

The results confirmed the hypothesis only partially. Starting with near-identity, retroactive inhibition increased as the interpolated material became increasingly dissimilar. This was part of the conjecture. But the decrease in the amount of retroaction (increase in recall) with maximum unlikeness was not found. In fact, with the materials totally dissimilar, retroactive inhibition was at a maximum.

A number of later experimenters attacked the problem after Robinson formulated it in this way.[31] Results gave partial confirmation, but there was some incompleteness and minor contradictions appeared in the data. The results led Osgood (1949) to propose a more complex formulation of the relationships involved. Osgood's solution of the similarity problem is diagrammed in the three-dimensional surface shown as Figure 47.

What Osgood's surface states is that the amount of transfer in positive or negative directions is a function of shifts in similarity between learning and retention of *both* the stimulus conditions *and* the response required. Shifts in stimulus similarity are from front to rear as noted on the right-hand margin, moving from identical stimuli (S_I) through similar stimuli (S_S) to neutral stimuli (S_N). Shifts in response similarity are represented from left to right, as noted along the back margin, with identical responses (R_I) being at the left, and moving progressively through similar responses (R_S), neutral responses (R_N), partially opposite responses (R_O) to directly antagonistic responses (R_A).

The best way to practice reading the diagram is to read its edges first. The rear edge says that stimuli bearing *no* resemblance to those used in original learning lead to new responses without any transfer effect, positive or negative, regardless of the degree of resemblance between the required responses and responses that have been used in earlier experiments. The front edge says that with *identical* stimuli there will be maximum positive

[31] Mention should be made also of a more rational analysis of the form of the Skagg-Robinson function by Boring (1941).

transfer with *identical* responses (for this is merely overlearning), whereas with directly *antagonistic* responses there will be maximum interference, for the earlier responses will have to be completely unlearned or overcome. The curve moves with two inflections between these extremes, but these inflections are not actually determinate from present data. The left edge says that, with identical responses, shifts in stimulus similarity from

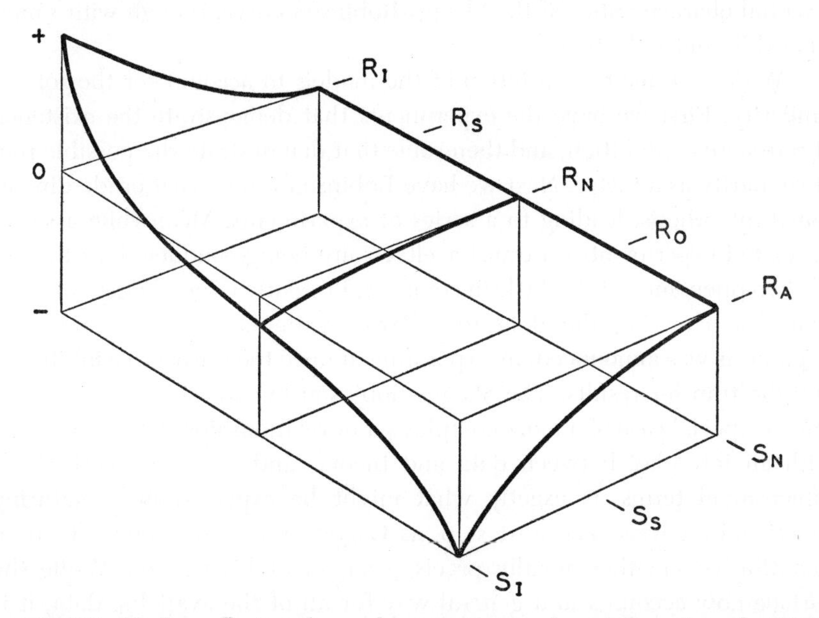

FIGURE 47. Osgood's transfer and retroaction surface (after Osgood, 1949). Vertical dimension, amount of transfer (+) or interference (−), with neutral zone represented by a plane (0). Left to right, amount of shift in response similarity between original task and new task, from identity (R_I) to antagonism (R_A). Front to rear, amount of shift in stimulus similarity between original and new task, from identify (S_I) to neutrality (S_N).

identity to neutrality will result in decreasing transfer, but no interference in new learning. The right edge says that, for antagonistic responses, shifts in stimulus similarity from identity to neutrality will produce decreasing interference, but no positive transfer. The diagram is a surface, and yields a curve wherever it is cut by a vertical plane.

In Robinson's kind of experiment the response called for varies with the stimulus, so if the stimulus changes the response also changes. (This is typically true in serial rote learning, because the response item is also a stimulus item for what follows.) Hence the Skaggs-Robinson diagram (Figure 46) can be approximated by making a diagonal slice across Osgood's surface (Figure 47), from the near left-hand corner to the rear point marked R_N. The near left-hand corner represents the Skaggs-Robinson condition of maximum task similarity (identity of both stimuli and responses between learning and testing), while the rear point represents neutrality of both stimuli and response relative to the original task. Such a diagonal curve will be high at the left, dip down into a zone of interference, and return to the neutral point at the rear, thus having the essential characteristics of the Skaggs-Robinson curve, though with somewhat different inflections.

We may trace the evolution of the models to account for the role of similarity. First we have the experiments that demonstrate the existence of retroactive inhibition, and then some that demonstrate the possible role of similarity as a factor. Next we have Robinson's somewhat crude dimensional hypothesis, leading to a series of experiments. Meanwhile a series of related experiments on transfer effects are being conducted, as though the two phenomena have little in common. Presently Osgood offers his new synthesis, covering the data that have accumulated since Robinson's hypothesis was announced, incorporating at once the retroactive inhibition and the transfer results. The Skaggs-Robinson hypothesis is seen to be a limited special case of a more complex set of relationships. This succession, with an interplay between data and theory, and a higher synthesis in dimensional terms, is exactly what might be expected in a maturing functional analysis. The next step, as Osgood points out, ought to be a quantitative (mathematically precise) model of his surface. While the surface now accounts in a general way for all of the available data, it is largely schematic, and nothing is known about the precise form it should take, or if, indeed, there is one form or a family of forms.

The discussion of Melton's topics has led us somewhat afield from the content or conclusions of his own treatment of learning, but the outline served its purpose in providing the topics for an overview of the functionalist analysis of the problems of learning.

Does this emerge as a theory of learning? Melton emphasizes in his summary that a dimensional analysis of learning, although scarcely qualifying as a theory, is not anti-theoretical. Theoretical systems, he states, help to clarify problems and they lead to the discovery of new empirical relationships. But these relationships have to be firmly established if we are to have a science of learning. We need to standardize and calibrate valid and reliable methods of investigation in order to have better data for the theorist to manipulate.

EFFECTS OF THE DISTRIBUTION OF PRACTICE AS ILLUSTRATIVE OF CURRENT FUNCTIONALISM

One of the best ways to study a scientific theory is to see it in action, that is, to note how those who hold to the theory select their topics and design their experiments and how they analyze and interpret their data. We have followed this procedure in reviewing the theories thus far discussed. We have had some introduction to the functionalist at work on the problem of retroactive inhibition. Now we are ready to examine further how functionalism works through giving more detailed consideration to some selected experimental problems.

How the General Orientation Contributes to the Planning of Experiments

When we attempt to determine how the theory directs the experiments that the functionalist chooses to perform we note two characteristics of his approach.

We discover, first, that the general theory provides only an orientation to experimentation, without providing a framework of crucial laws and postulates. The dimensional approach is a very broad frame of reference within which to work. It would be entirely unmanageable and cumbersome were it not for the guiding threads provided through years of experimentation by familiar methods upon familiar topics. Consider what would be involved in studying all the dimensions of massed and distributed practice. There are all the variables common to learning experiments (subjects, nature of materials, interrelationships within the materials, the kind of learning task), and there are the special variables specific to the problem of distribution (location of the interval between items, between trials, between banks of trials, between learning and retention, within relearning; length of the interval, whether uniform or variable; nature of the activities filling the interval). The combinations and permutations are staggering.

The second thing that we find out is that the experimenter typically narrows his task (within the broad dimensional orientation). He does this in two chief ways. First, he falls back on tasks that have familiarly been used in these studies, chiefly rote memorization and motor learning. He further restricts himself by addressing his attention to some of the "special theories" that are current or that he may himself invent. Hence the functionalist depends not only upon his general orientation but upon a body of experimental lore and a number of special theories that reduce his task to manageable proportions.

The Testing of Special Theories Related to Distributed Practice

In order to illustrate the foregoing interpretation of how the functionalist goes about his experiments, we shall examine a number of experiments studying distributed practice. One series of twelve experimental reports, by Underwood and his associates, well illustrates the nature of a systematic functionalist investigation.[32] While these investigators appear to be making a strictly dimensional analysis, the papers are in fact guided largely by several special theories, and the dimensions chosen are by no means all that might have been selected. We turn now to some of these special theories—some tested by Underwood, and others with which he was not concerned.

1. *The theory of differential forgetting* (*McGeoch*).[33] McGeoch's theory states that in the course of memorization or practice a subject learns erroneous (conflicting) responses that retard progress. Because these errors are less well learned than the correct responses, lapse of time will permit the errors to be forgotten more rapidly than the correct responses. Hence distributed practice will be advantageous over massed practice. In serial memorization some of these errors are remote associations (place-skipping tendencies). Because only the correct responses are repeatedly reinforced, the correct responses are probably better fixed than the errors. Experimenters who have looked for the forgetting of errors, as implied in McGeoch's theory, have been unable to find them. In one of the most careful direct studies of the problem, Wilson (1949) found no fewer errors in distributed than in massed practice, even though distributed practice resulted in more rapid learning, and he failed to find predicted effects in retention tests. Later studies, e.g., Underwood and Goad (1951) have also failed to substantiate McGeoch's theory.

2. *The generalization-differentiation theory* (*Gibson*).[34] Gibson assumes that in the learning of a nonsense syllable the subject has to differentiate the individual syllables from nonsense-syllables-in-general. If the subject is making some correct responses and some erroneous ones, we may say, according to this interpretation, that the correct responses have

[32] These are Underwood and Goad (1951), Underwood (1951a) (1951b), Underwood and Viterna (1951), Oseas and Underwood (1952), Underwood (1952a) (1952b) (1953a) (1953b) (1953c) (1953d) (1954a).

[33] McGeoch (1942), page 142f.; McGeoch and Irion (1952), pages 183–188.

[34] Eleanor J. Gibson (1940) (1942).

been better differentiated from syllables-in-general, while the erroneous responses still suffer from too great generalization, that is, lack of discrimination. What will be the effect of a rest interval? Because differentiation (by analogy with what goes on in conditioning experiments) involves an inhibition of alternative responses, rest should bring "spontaneous recovery" of generalization. Hence the differences in the strengths of tendency to give correct and incorrect responses should be *reduced* after rest. Thus distributed practice should prove to be *dis*advantageous as compared with massed—an implication contrary to McGeoch's hypothesis.

Experimental results are more favorable to Gibson's theory than to McGeoch's. With distributed practice, erroneous responses commonly do show an increase over those in massed practice, especially during the early trials.[35]

How difficult it is to make predictions that are genuinely unambiguous! We assumed, in stating Gibson's theory, that distributed practice should be disadvantageous. This was not really a sound assumption. It has been found that with distributed practice there are more errors, as her theory predicts, but *learning may still be more rapid under conditions of distributed practice*. It is possible that more errors are associated with a heightened set to respond that is in turn associated with more rapid learning. Part of the mystery of the finding disappears if we remember that in addition to false responses there are other kinds of inadequate responses in a serial learning experiment, such as a failure to respond, not counted as an erroneous response.

Another aspect of Gibson's generalization hypothesis has to do with the intra-list similarity of items. If items in a list are very much like each other it will be harder to differentiate them. If the process of learning is one of differentiation, it should be harder to learn a list of similar (homogeneous) items than a list of heterogeneous ones. This implication of the theory can easily be confirmed experimentally.[36] A second implication is that forgetting will be more rapid with greater intra-list similarity because of the spontaneous recovery of interfering generalizations. The interfering generalizations will, of course, be more common with more similar items. This implication does *not* receive experimental support. Because of the support of Gibson's theory in the learning and relearning data, but not in the retention data, Underwood (1954b) was led to propose some supplements to her theory.

[35] Underwood and Goad (1951), Underwood (1951b) (1952b). But not all experiments agree with the theory, e.g., Underwood (1951a).

[36] There is a family resemblance here between Gibson's theory and Köhler's. See page 246.

The results of four of Underwood's studies[37] (with both serial-syllable and paired-syllable lists) agreed substantially on the following three points: (1) The higher the intra-list similarity the more difficult the learning; (2) retention over a 24-hour interval is independent of the level of intra-list similarity; and (3) the higher the intra-list similarity the more difficult the relearning.

Underwood is called upon to account for the unexpected failure of intra-list similarity to have an effect upon retention, although it clearly affects both learning and relearning. He proposes that there may be two kinds of interference that do not reveal themselves in retention because they balance each other:

(1) If intra-list similarity is high, there is interference within the list, as predicted from Gibson's generalization hypothesis. Underwood's subjects learned and relearned three successive lists. His evidence shows a distinct trend for errors at recall to come from *within* the list when similarity of items within the list is high, and from *outside* the list when similarity of items within the list is low. Because some of these outside items came from previously learned lists, it is implied that there is *inter-list* interference when intra-list similarity is low.

(2) If intra-list similarity is high, the list being learned is more clearly differentiated from previously learned lists than if similarity is low. This accounts for less inter-list interference with high intra-list similarity.

Combining these two propositions we note that there is an inverse relationship between intra-list and inter-list interference with variations in intra-list similarity. Thus when intra-list similarity is high, the high *intra-list* interference is offset by low *inter-list* interference.[38] Provided these opposing tendencies balance each other, we have an explanation for the finding that recall is independent of the degree of intra-list similarity.

Evidence supporting these conjectures is given in Figure 48. The curves are based on the learning of successive lists of paired associates. Although early in practice the high-similarity lists are much harder to learn than the low-similarity lists, the curves converge with practice. High-similarity lists become relatively easier both because there is some learning-how-to-learn and because there is little inter-list interference. This accords with the hypothesis. Low-similarity lists become harder to learn, not because learning-how-to-learn is absent, but because there is increasing inter-

[37] The four studies are Underwood (1952b) (1953a) (1953b) (1953c).

[38] That better bounded material interferes less than loosely bounded material was shown earlier by Werner (1947).

ference (proactive inhibition) from the learning of prior undifferentiated lists. (This, too, agrees with the hypothesis.)

The interpretation is that, as one of these interferences goes up the other goes down. Hence they may balance so that retention does not show any differential effects for high or low intra-list similarity. If these are balancing functions, it ought to be possible to give one a boost over the other. In one of Underwood's experiments in this series,[39] it was found that with *extreme* similarity learning remained difficult, but retention was improved. This result, too, conforms to his hypothesis.

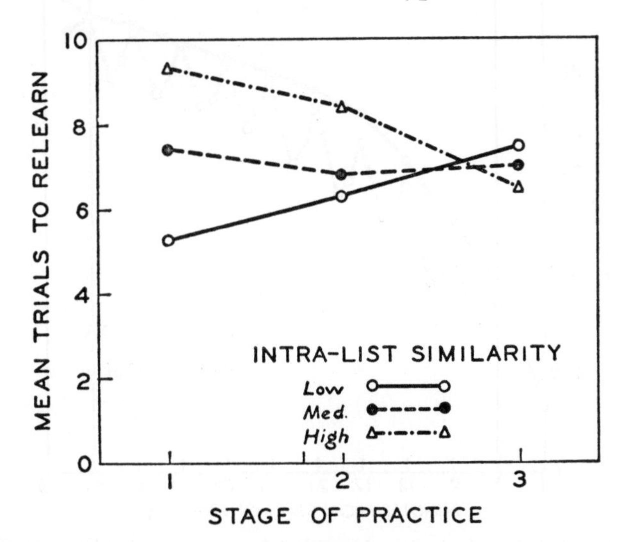

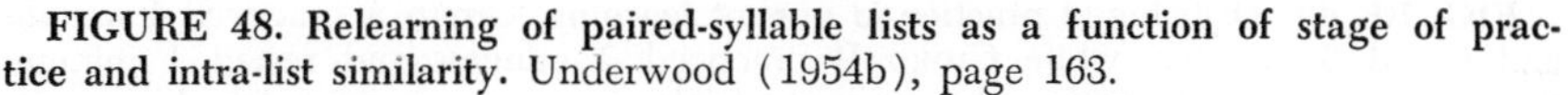
FIGURE 48. Relearning of paired-syllable lists as a function of stage of practice and intra-list similarity. Underwood (1954b), page 163.

3. *The theory of recovery from work decrement.* A very plausible theory of the advantages of distributed practice has been proposed from time to time by those who noted that massed practice had some of the characteristics of a "work curve" as well as a "learning curve." This is particularly evident in motor learning. In Figure 49, for example, we have the performance curves of two groups on a pursuit rotor, one group of subjects practicing for one minute and resting for three minutes (distributed practice), the other practicing for three minutes and resting for one minute (massed practice). Scores were recorded at the end of each minute of the 3-minute group, and these appear in the curve as a series of "work curves." The gain from practice shows as recovery over the 1-minute rests, but there is little advantage in the three times as much

[39] Underwood (1953c).

practice that this group has had. The kind of theory that these curves suggests, supplemented by "warm-up" phenomena, has been given a more formal treatment by Ammons (1947), and works reasonably well for pursuit learning.[40]

The related theory for rote memorization was elaborated by Hull and others (1940), largely around the experimental work of Ward and Hovland.[41] Here it was assumed that interferences accumulating within learn-

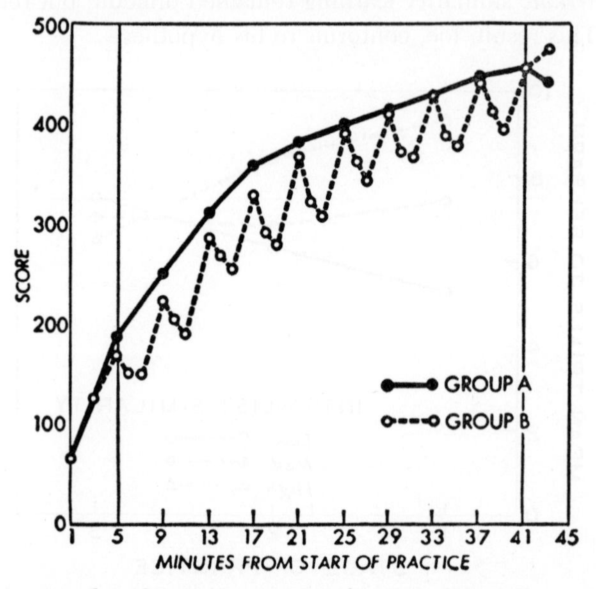

FIGURE 49. Distributed practice in pursuit learning. Group A practiced 1 minute and rested 3 minutes, while Group B practiced 3 minutes and rested 1 minute. Scores at each minute within the 3-minute trials show progressive work decrement. Doré and Hilgard (1937).

ing are of the nature of inhibitions in conditioning, and thus recover with time. A number of conjectures were borne out in the data: that there should be reminiscence after a rest following learning, that the disadvantage for items near the middle of a list should be overcome somewhat with rest, that paired associate learning should show less benefit from rest than serial learning.

The main objection to the theory was raised by one of its proponents —Hovland (1940)—when he pointed out that the theory should predict that massed practice ought to lead to better retention than distributed

[40] Further work along closely related lines has been done by a number of others, e.g., Kimble and Horenstein (1948), and Irion (1949).

[41] Ward (1937), Hovland (1938) (1939).

practice. The argument is straightforward: In order to meet a criterion of mastery under inhibitory conditions, more has to be acquired than under less inhibitory conditions. Hence the amount retained, when the inhibition vanishes, should be greater for the group that learned under a handicap, that is, the massed-practice group.

Two remarks need to be made about Hovland's objection to the theory. In the first place, the advantages of distributed practice for retention are by no means universal. In this respect some of the data gathered by others support Hovland's theory better than his own.[42] In motor learning it is not uncommon for the groups with scores depressed by massed practice to gain more following both short and overnight rests than groups with distributed practice.[43] In the second place, no single-factor theory can be expected to account for the complex data within all phases of the distributed practice problem. A theory cannot be completely validated by data that agree with it, nor can it be completely refuted by data that disagree with it. This follows if we admit that there may be competing processes operating, and in any experiment one of these processes may gain ascendancy over the other. We saw this possibility in Underwood's supplementation of Gibson's theory.

Theories of the work-interference type, whether expressed in terms of conditioned inhibition, or reactive inhibition, or in other language, are bound to have some place in the explanation of distributed practice. They account well for the similar effects found for such unlike tasks as nonsense syllable memorizing, pursuit learning, and concept formation. Direct tests have heretofore been made largely with the motor tasks, but Hovland and Kurtz (1951) have come up with an experiment in which the results of work are tested directly within a memorization experiment. If a subject does difficult mental work of another kind just before memorizing a list, more reminiscence for the list follows than if he either did not do the mental work or was permitted to rest between the mental work task and the memorization.

4. *The consolidation theory.* One of the earliest "special" theories bearing on distributed practice is that of Müller and Pilzecker (1900), known originally as the perseveration theory. The theory assumes that the benefits of practice continue for a while after practice ceases, and the results of learning are therefore not at their maximum until an appreciable time following the end of practice. Were the perseveration theory to hold,

[42] E.g., Underwood (1952b).
[43] Hilgard and Smith (1942), Cook and Hilgard (1949).

such phenomena as reminiscence and the advantages of distributed practice would be expected. Related forms of the theory attribute the consolidation effect to growth or maturation stimulated by practice.[44]

One hypothesis derived from the theory of stimulation-induced maturation is that, within the wide limits of amount of practice, learning should proceed at a rate that is a function of the learner and of the task to be learned rather than a function of the number of trials or of the actual amount of time spent in practice. Too little practice (or, at the extreme, none at all) will fail to stimulate the growth underlying the skill, while too much practice will prove to be disruptive and inefficient.

The hypothesis has been criticized because it is said that its predictions may be made "on purely empirical grounds." [45] That is, if we know that under some circumstances rest can produce as much gain as practice, there must be an intersection point at which two practice curves will overlap when plotted according to elapsed time, even though one curve is based on fewer trials than the other. While this is true, the fact that whole families of curves coincide, even within very wide ranges of difference in the spacing of practice and rest, is not so easily predicted. The two curves from Doré and Hilgard already presented (Figure 49) show how the recovery from the detrimental effects of 3-minute practice periods brings the scores to about the level reached when practice and rest are very differently spaced. The corresponding scores for the beginning and end of each of four days of practice under three widely different conditions of spacing are shown in Figure 50.[46] Whatever one's theory, it is pertinent to note that the gains within each day and the overnight losses are remarkably similar despite the accumulated differences in the number of practice trials. The ordinary trial-by-trial plot would have shown striking advantage for distributed practice without calling attention to a uniformity that no other theory predicts.

The validation or refutation of a theory is no simple matter. Although the results presented conform to the consolidation theory, other results from the same laboratory show no such correspondence to theoretical predictions.[47] When some predictions from a theory succeed and others fail, the failures mean that the theory, if not wrong, is at least incomplete.

Other suggestions. It is characteristic of the functionalist to invent

[44] Snoddy (1935), Wheeler and Perkins (1932).

[45] McGeoch and Irion (1952), page 183.

[46] Similar curves for mirror-vision co-ordination as studied by Snoddy (1945) were replotted in the first edition of this book, Hilgard (1948), page 256.

[47] Bell (1942), Wright and Taylor (1949). The latter experiment was done with verbal learning.

ad hoc theories to explain particular findings. This tendency in itself is neither good nor bad, although at some stages of knowledge it produces a great conglomeration of unrelated theories, and inconsistencies are hard to detect.

We may conclude this treatment of special theories by pointing out three suggestions not covered in the foregoing list of special theories.

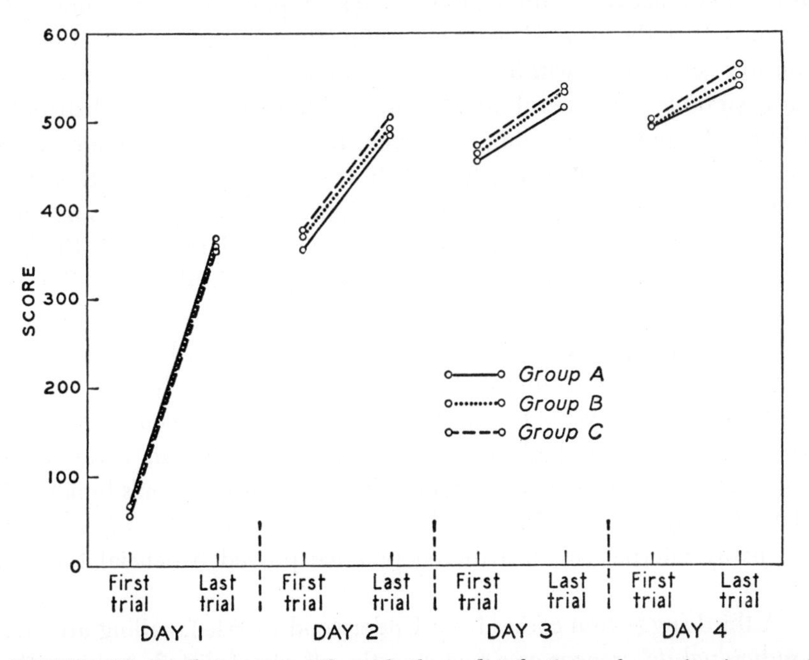

FIGURE 50. Similarity in trends with three distributions of practice in pursuit-learning. Group A by the end of the fourth day had practiced a total of 32 1-minute trials, Group B a total of 52 trials, and Group C a total of 72 trials. Data of Hilgard and Smith (1942) as plotted by Underwood (1949), page 406.

The first of these suggestions is that of Cain and Willey (1939), who studied the retention of nonsense syllables following learning to a common criterion of mastery by two groups. The massed-practice group learned the list in a single day. The distributed-practice group learned over three days, each day's practice being interrupted when the subject reached a preselected criterion short of mastery, but progressively higher each day. By the third day the distributed-practice subjects reached the same criterion of mastery that the massed-practice subjects reached in one day. The group that learned by distributed practice turned out to be far superior in retention to the massed-practice group, as tested at intervals of 1 day, 3 days and 7 days following learning. Partly because the distributed-practice group showed no advantage over the massed-practice group in trials required to learn, Cain and Willey argued from the distributed-practice group's superior retention that this group must have learned something the massed-practice group had not learned. This was to pick up the task on the following day where it had been left off many hours before, even when it had been poorly learned. In other words, the distributed-practice group had two days of practice at recalling after 24 hours that the massed-practice group did not have. While this is a plausible suggestion within the arrangements of this experiment, it is hardly suitable as a general interpretation of the advantages of distributed practice. It gives a warning, however, that qualitative changes occur when very long intervals are dealt with. It is always necessary to supplement mere scores by a psychological analysis of the activities going on.

A second suggestion was originally made and tested by Ericksen (1942). He proposed that massing of trials should lead to variability of response, through factors similar to the refractory phase that act as barriers to repetition. If this is the case, massing should be advantageous when the task is one calling for variability of attack. He found some evidence for this theory for human subjects solving a problem-box. Earlier work by Cook (1934) had found massed practice to be an advantage in early trials of puzzle-solving, a result coherent with Ericksen's hypothesis. A later test by Riley (1952) failed to find benefit from massing in a task with many alternatives; distributed practice proved beneficial throughout.

A third suggestion comes from Underwood (1954a), calling attention to *individual differences* as a factor in the effects of distributed practice. He found that retention by slow learners tended to suffer from distributed practice as shown in Figure 51. While he believes these results to account for some of the discrepant findings on the relation between distribution of practice and retention, the results do not suffice to account for all the discrepancies. The differences between the two kinds of learners are to be taken seriously, but the failure to find advantages with distributed practice even for the fast learners shows that something else is operative in these experiments.[48]

These suggestions (and they do not exhaust the possibilities) show how complex a dimensional approach would become if it were to take

[48] One possibility is that the symbol cancellation task used to fill the interval has an interfering effect upon retention, and that this interference is more severe with the slow learners. The experiments that find more advantage for distribution have used chiefly color naming, shown to be somewhat facilitating as against symbol cancellation. (Underwood, 1952a).

seriously the task of exploring in systematic variation all of the factors that have been shown by one or another experiment to be influential in experiments on the distribution of practice.

Concluding Comments on the Distribution of Practice

An examination of experiments and theories related to distributed practice has helped us to see some of the characteristics of functionalism at work. First, the general position provides an orientation towards dimen-

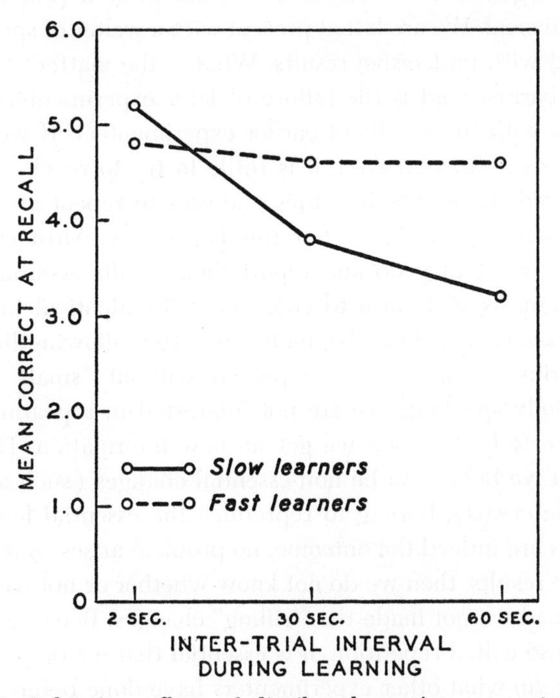

FIGURE 51. Deleterious effects of distributed practice upon retention for slow learners compared with fast learners. Underwood (1954a), page 298.

sional experimentation. If intervals are important, then we explore an orderly series of intervals; if similarity is important, then we find a way of grading similarity and we explore the effects of several degrees of similarity. Second, however, the attack is always much more specific than the general orientation alone would suggest. Not *all* or *just any* dimensions are explored, for such an approach would be too cumbersome; instead, the methods and materials used tend to be restricted largely to familiar ones, and the particular dimensions chosen for investigation are usually related to one or more of the special theories that are current. The program is very much that of science in general. It is very similar to that proposed by Skinner, to the extent that it is dimensional and seeks lawfulness rather than laws; it is related to Hull in that the tests are commonly tests of hypotheses. It lies between these two positions in that the experimenters who are functionalists usually have more respect for hypotheses than Skinner has, and they are more cautious than Hull about general systematic formulations at this stage of knowledge.

Does the approach pay off in firm scientific knowledge? The answer, at least if we generalize from studies of distributed practice, is by no means unequivocal. We are left at present with a welter of special theories, mostly tested with undecisive results. What is the matter?

One embarrassment is the failure of later experimenters to agree in their findings with the results of earlier experimenters. If we cannot find reproducible experimental data, it is futile to try to reach agreement on theoretical predictions. Possibly these failures to repeat are due to slipshod experimental procedures, but this is unlikely. Most experimenters are careful in what they do and report their results accurately. A more plausible diagnosis of failure to come up with identical findings when experiments are repeated can be made along the following lines:

1. Experiments are seldom repeated without "small" or "trifling" changes. Strictly speaking, we are not interested in repeating earlier experiments *precisely*, for then we get no new information. Hence we introduce what we believe to be non-essential changes (such as a different task in rest intervals), hoping to reproduce the essential findings. If the same findings are indeed the outcome, no problem arises. But if we do *not* find the same results, then we do not know whether or not we *would have* found them had we not made the "trifling" changes. Because of the many difficulties in so-called repetition, it is essential that we be patient enough to repeat *exactly* what other experimenters have done before we begin to make "small" changes.[49]

2. Experimental designs are permitted to become too complex, without prior psychological analysis of the processes under investigation. Experimental design is not solely a statistical problem. While of course results must be secured in a manner to make possible adequate statistical analysis, the subject's task must also be reckoned with. The counterbal-

[49] Those not close to the experimental literature have no idea how serious this nonrepeatability of experimental results has become. A notable example is the Ward-Hovland reminiscence phenomenon, which led Buxton (1943) to ascribe to it the character of "now-you-see-it-now-you-don't." Underwood (1953e) found so little evidence for it in his review of later studies that he designated it as possibly "a prewar phenomenon."

ancing of practice effects by using the same subjects in various cycles of an experiment is likely to prove *not* to be an economical procedure. Underwood's results as presented in both Figures 48 and 51 show how futile it is to try to equate effects at different stages of practice when subjects of different ability are used and when different kinds of tasks (e.g., paired associates versus serial learning) show very different effects early and late in practice. The simpler design, well represented in the experiment of Wilson (1949), in which each subject is used in but a single condition, gives all the advantages of applicability of modern analysis of variance statistics while permitting much better control of the psychological processes involved. It has the further advantage that new controls can be run without going through an elaborate counterbalanced series in which one cannot fathom what confusion has been created for the subject.

These two suggestions are related. It is too costly to repeat *exactly* very involved counterbalanced designs. If simpler designs were used, it would be possible to repeat the particular cycle in which the next experimenter was interested, in order to show that under the original conditions the original results could be obtained. Then the experimenter is free to make any changes he wants, with some assurance that his changes bear upon the modified results that he obtains.

A second source of embarrassment is that even the special theories appear to have a long life and seldom are disposed of by way of experimental evidence. The only special theory related to distributed practice that now seems ready to be dismissed is that of differential forgetting, for no experimenter has found the error items that he ought to find if the theory is true. The consolidation theory is not usually treated as very promising, yet no theory has been proposed to predict concretely the results that happen to fit it. The theories based on warm-up and recovery from work decrement satisfactorily explain some, but not all, of the results. So, too, Gibson's generalization-differentiation theory remains in the running with some substantial agreements between data and predictions, but some failures also.

It is perhaps to the functionalist's credit that he can tolerate this mass of material so loosely integrated, rather than blinding himself to some of it in order to make his theories sound more plausible. Yet it would be even more to his credit if he could invent a theory that would give a coherent account of the whole array of relationships. We may note a dilemma here. Special theories can be stated with great precision, and so they have that advantage over general theories, at least in early stages of experimentally established fact. But special theories can also be applicable more than one at a time. Hence it is almost impossible to find a crucial experiment to test a special theory. If the experiment agrees with the theory, that is fine, but we all know that you cannot prove theories through occasional agreements, but can only keep them in the running that way; if the experiment disagrees with the theory, the theory may still be true, but something else may be in conflict with it. There is no point in giving up any theory with which occasional agreement can be found until there is some more general theory that accounts for *all* the agreements. The hypothetico-deductive method is by no means as simple as at first blush it appears to be!

ESTIMATE OF FUNCTIONALISM

Current functionalism is not a unified theory such as those earlier discussed. What bounds of unity there are lie in a tolerant acceptance of a wide range of psychological phenomena and a conviction that the task before psychology is to subject the many variables to quantitative study. Such a methodological unity permits wide diversity in content.

The Functionalist Position on the Typical Problems of Learning

Within such an unstructured system there is no one clear answer to most problems of learning. The answer to be expected is that "it all depends on conditions." In practice the situation is not quite as free as this implies, for gradually there accumulate more commonly accepted generalizations.

1. *Capacity.* Robinson recognized individual and species differences in his laws of individual differences and of composition. It is in line with functional developments for McGeoch and Irion to include in their book a chapter on learning as a function of individual differences. They believe that the increase of learning ability with age is best accounted for on the basis of two hypotheses: first, organic maturation, second, changing psychological conditions (transfer, motivation, personality traits).

2. *Practice.* The law of frequency was to Robinson a law of relative frequency, which therefore recognizes the losses in score when practice is overcrowded, along with the gains when trials are more appropriately spaced. There is a tendency to emphasize the form of the learning curve and to seek the conditions under which one form rather than another is to be found. There is, however, no diatribe against a law of exercise.

3. *Motivation.* Woodworth's dynamic psychology places motivation at its core. Carr accepts in principle the preparatory-consummatory sequence, assigning motivation the role of a continuing stimulus to be terminated by the goal-response. The concept of "set" enters into the more conventional experiments on memorization and skill as a motivational supplement to the more familiar laws of association. It was the preoccupation of the early functionalist with such tasks as the learning of rote verbal series which tended to place motivation in the background rather than the foreground of theories such as Robinson's.

4. *Understanding.* While the associationist recognizes that meaningful material is more readily learned than nonsense material, degree of meaning is but one of the dimensions upon which materials can be scaled. Hence he does not believe that problem-solving or insight require interpretations beyond ordinary associative learning. The organism uses what it has learned as appropriately as it can in a new situation. If the problem cannot be solved by analogy, the behavior has to be varied until the initial solution occurs. Insight is perhaps an extreme case of transfer of training.[50]

5. *Transfer.* Following Thorndike, transfer falls chiefly under the law of assimilation. That is, transfer depends upon degree of likeness between the new situation and the old. Woodworth reinterprets the theory of identical elements to mean only that transfer is always of concrete performances.

> What the theory of identical elements demands is that transfer should be of concrete performances, whether simple or complex makes no difference to the theory.[51] . . . Perhaps anything that can be learned can be transferred. But does not everything that can be learned have the concrete character of an act or way of acting?[52]

6. *Forgetting.* The favorite theory of forgetting is that of retroactive inhibition, but the functionalist does not insist that this is the whole story. There may be some forgetting according to passive decay through disuse, and there may be forgetting through repression, as pointed out by Freud.[53]

Has Functionalism a Systematic Theory of Learning?

Functionalism is empiricist rather than systematic. It eschews inference for established experimental relationships between demonstrable

[50] McGeoch and Irion (1952), page 53.
[51] Woodworth (1938), page 177.
[52] Woodworth (1938), page 207.
[53] Robinson (1932b), pages 113–118.

variables. Its laws are quantitative, directly descriptive of data. There is a healthy respect for data, and there is a commendable urge to state issues specifically in a form subject to test. The relativism brings with it a freedom from bigotry. Before his untimely death, Robinson had turned to social problems, with the conviction that the same methods would work there. So long as people were forced to think in terms of specifics he believed that they could often reach agreement, even though on larger issues they were swayed by prejudices and preconceptions.[54]

The disadvantage of an extreme empiricism and relativism lies in its lack of articulating principles to cut across empirical laws. What results is a collection of many "laws," without hierarchial structure. There is no economical multidimensional apparatus for fitting together the various two-dimensional functional relationships, each of which is necessarily cast in the form: "other things being equal." If the dimensional program of the functionalists were fulfilled we should have a large handbook of data, with each of the several laws illustrated by a number of graphs showing the variations of associative strength under specific conditions. Empirical multidimensionality would be achieved through experimental designs testing several variables at once, but unless some simplifying steps were taken, the possible combinations and permutations of conditions would mount fabulously. Dimensional analysis puts data in order for exposition and for verification, but in itself does not connect the data into an economical scientific system. Such a system has to be logically structured as well as empirically sound.

Functionalism is in some respects an eclectic position. It is eclectic on the problem of introspection versus behavioral description, by accepting both in the account of psychological activity. A favorite illustration is that less attention to details is required after a skill is mastered. Knowledge about the representation of details in awareness requires an introspective report, while the mastery of the skill may be studied by observation of the overt movements. Functionalism is eclectic on the problem of blind versus intelligent learning, accepting a continuum between these extremes, according to the dimensional analysis of McGeoch and Melton. Any point of view which is pragmatic and pluralistic can easily incorporate concepts from alien systems; hence functionalism is well suited to play the mediating role. Functionalism is, however, an eclecticism with a bias—the bias of associationism in favor of analytic units, historical causation, environmentalism. The bias is more evident in Chicago functionalism than in that of Woodworth, who has shown him-

[54] See, for example, Robinson (1935).

self friendlier to less associationistic concepts. New data may be accepted but forced back into older concepts not fully appropriate. Thus some of the novelty of the observations made in insight experiments is lost when insight is treated as merely another illustration of the familiar transfer of training experiment. Similarly, what goes on in the reasoning process is not fully encompassed by treating reasoning as trial-and-error learning merely a little farther out on the dimension of explicit-implicit response. Those who disagree with the associationist position object to the functionalist's incorporating of new experimental findings without accepting the theoretical implications of these findings. This is a problem with which the eclectic always has to wrestle: how much can be taken over without incorporating its systematic context? The functionalist has not been greatly concerned about the inner consistency of his borrowings because he is less concerned than others about the inner consistency of his own concepts. What consistency there has been is provided by the framework of associationism within which the functionalist works.

Perhaps Melton's position is the best to take on the matter of functionalism's systematic position: the functionalist does not have an articulated system, but he would like to have one, and is not anti-theoretical. His breadth and self-criticism prevent his embracing a comprehensive system until facts are better ordered.

Whatever the systematic limitations may be, it must be recognized that great energy for experimental study has been released within the functionalist group. The books of McGeoch and Irion (1952), Osgood (1953), Woodworth and Schlosberg (1954) amply attest to this. Out of the large number of research investigations on memory and skill, done largely within this group, there has come a rich body of data and factual relationships with which anyone interested in learning must be familiar.

Convergence Toward Functionalist Interpretations

Because there is so much room within functionalism, because it is an experimentalism, because it fits the American temper, it provides a kind of framework appropriate to much of American psychology. Many of the trends in contemporary theory and experiment, not explicitly related to functionalism as a school of psychology, nevertheless are in accord with its historical orientation.

1. The scientific logic of *operationism,* whereby scientific facts and concepts are related to the concrete operations through which they are produced, has been widely espoused by psychologists of most divergent

theoretical backgrounds.[55] To the functionalist, operationism is a very natural development from James' pragmatism and Dewey's instrumentalism.

2. Mathematical models that are "neutral" with respect to many historical controversies are essentially "functional" models, in the mathematical sense of function. This mathematical sense of function is coherent with the psychological meaning of function. Hence it is not surprising to find Skinner (1953a) writing about the need for a functional analysis (meaning essentially a dimensional analysis), or to find Brunswik (1955) describing his system as a "probabilistic functionalism." The mathematical models to be described in the next chapter can properly be described as functional ones.

3. Miniature systems, in which restricted realms of data are summarized according to a few special theories, are also congenial to the functionalist. There is a heuristic pluralism involved in functionalism, not unrelated to James' pluralism. That is, in order to move forward in the interpretation of data it is sometimes necessary to accept provisional (heuristic) interpretations that permit you to move ahead with the analysis. A case in point is VTE ("vicarious trial and error") as proposed by Muenzinger and followed up by Tolman. This rather limited segment of behavior (vacillation at the point of choice) is given a name and its conditions studied. The many systematic questions (Is it vicarious? Is it trial and error?) can be postponed until some of the functional relationships are explored. At this stage there is a pluralism, because there exist *ad hoc* concepts not related by definition or equations to the fundamentals of an established system.

Contemporary psychology, to the extent that it is increasingly operational, and increasingly concerned with mathematical models and miniature systems, reflects the general outlook that, in one form or another, has all along characterized the functionalist.

SUPPLEMENTARY READINGS

BOOKS

McGeoch, J. A., and Irion, A. L. (1952) *The psychology of human learning.*
Osgood, C. E. (1953) *Method and theory in experimental psychology.*
Robinson, E. S. (1932) *Association theory today.*
Underwood, B. J. (1949) *Experimental psychology.*
Woodworth, R. S. (1918) *Dynamic psychology.*
Woodworth, R. S., and Schlosberg, H. (1954) *Experimental psychology.*

[55] E.g., Stevens (1939).

SHORTER INTRODUCTIONS

CARR, H. A. (1931) The laws of association. *Psychol. Rev.*, 38, 212–228.

HEIDBREDER, E. (1933) *Seven psychologies.* Chapter 6, Functionalism and the University of Chicago; Chapter 8, Dynamic psychology and Columbia University.

MELTON, A. W. (1950) Learning. In Monroe, W. S., ed. *Encyclopedia of educational research.*

WOODWORTH, R. S. (1930) Dynamic psychology. In Murchison, C., ed. *Psychologies of 1930.*

WOODWORTH, R. S. (1948) *Contemporary schools of psychology.* Chapter 2, Functional and structural psychology.

CRITICAL REVIEWS

BORING, E. G. (1933) Review of Robinson's *Association theory today. Psychol. Bull.*, 30, 451–455.

KÖHLER, W. (1943) Review of McGeoch's *The psychology of human learning. Amer. J. Psychol.*, 56, 455–460.

MCGEOCH, J. A. (1932) Review of Robinson's *Association theory today. J. gen. Psychol.*, 7, 231–237.

PRENTICE, W. C. H. (1954) Review of Osgood's *Method and theory in experimental psychology. Amer. J. Psychol.*, 67, 555–561.

REPRESENTATIVE EXPERIMENTS

BRUCE, R. W. (1933) Conditions of transfer of training. *J. exp. Psychol.*, 16, 343–361.

COURTS, F. A. (1939) Relations between experimentally induced muscular tension and memorization. *J. exp. Psychol.*, 25, 235–256.

IRION, A. L. (1946) Retroactive inhibition as a function of the relative serial positions of the original and interpolated items. *J. exp. Psychol.*, 36, 262–270.

LUH, C. W. (1922) The conditions of retention. *Psychol. Monogr.*, 31, No. 142.

MCCLELLAND, D. C. (1942) Studies in serial verbal discrimination learning. I. Reminiscence with two speeds of pair presentation. *J. exp. Psychol.*, 31, 44–56.

MELTON, A. W., and IRWIN, J. MCQ. (1940) The influence of degree of interpolated learning on retroactive inhibition and the overt transfer of specific responses. *Amer. J. Psychol.*, 53, 173–203.

OSGOOD, C. E. (1946) Meaningful similarity and interference in learning. *J. exp. Psychol.*, 36, 227–301.

ROBINSON, E. S., and BROWN, M. A. (1926) Effect of serial position upon memorization. *Amer. J. Psychol.*, 37, 538–552.

STROUD, J. B. (1932) Effect of complexity of material upon the form of learning curves. *Amer. J. Psychol.*, 44, 721–731.

VAN ORMER, E. B. (1932) Retention after intervals of sleep and of waking. *Arch. Psychol.*, N.Y., 21, No. 137, 49 pp.

WATERS, R. H. (1928) The influence of tuition on ideational learning. *J. gen. Psychol.*, I, 534–547.

WOODWORTH, R. S., and SELLS, S. B. (1935) An atmosphere effect in formal syllogistic reasoning. *J. exp. Psychol.*, 18, 451–460.

Chapter 11

THE EMERGENCE OF MATHEMATICAL MODELS

SCIENTIFIC description depends upon accurate observation. To make observations more precise, a scientist commonly uses recording instruments and then makes measurements with the aid of them. He records his measurements in numerical form, whether by counting, or ranking, or scaling. As he treats his data in order to discover lawful relationships among them he naturally turns to mathematics as the language designed to state relationships among the kinds of events to which numbers can be assigned. This is all so familiar, especially in the physical sciences, that mathematical expression for scientific relationships is taken for granted.

The use of mathematics in the biological and social sciences is neither so widespread nor so successful up to the present time as it has been in the physical sciences. Hence we cannot be sure that all biologists or all social scientists would today assent to the proposition that ultimately their sciences must state their laws in mathematical form. We need not seek agreement on this proposition, however, in order to study such progress as there has been in the use of mathematical models in these fields.

Learning data are well adapted to mathematical treatment. Relationships expressed in the form of learning curves or retention curves can also be expressed by equations. Because the quantitative effects of a number of variables are known, further equations can be written. We have already become acquainted with one system in which mathematical expression has been used throughout (that of Hull, in Chapter 5), and another in which an adaptation of mathematical ideas takes a central place (that of Lewin, in Chapter 8). We are ready, therefore, to review the place of mathematics in the study of learning, and to note particularly some recent developments.

EMPIRICAL AND RATIONAL CURVE-FITTING

When Ebbinghaus (1885) found that his curve of retention was roughly logarithmic in form, he fitted a logarithmic equation to it:

$$b = \frac{100k}{(\log t)^c + k} \tag{1}$$

where b = per cent retained by the savings measure
t = elapsed time
c, k = arbitrary constants obtained by curve-fitting

Thus the very first quantitative study of associative learning introduced mathematical formulation.

Ebbinghaus used the procedure that has since come to be known as *empirical curve-fitting*. When we follow this procedure, we first plot the experimental data and then look for some kind of mathematical function likely to fit it. This function represents a family of curves, say of hyperbolas, or parabolas, a growth function, or what not. Then we go through the added step of determining the constants (corresponding to the c and k of Ebbinghaus' formula) in order to find that particular member of the curve family that comes nearest to fitting the obtained data. The commonest method for doing this is known as the method of least squares. What this means is that we seek that member of the curve family that does as well as possible in passing near our experimentally determined points, the measure of success being the sum of the squares of the deviations of the curve from our data. We try to make this sum a minimum, hence the name "least squares." If we can find another curve family whose best fitting member produces a smaller sum of squared deviations, this second curve is a better fit, and is generally to be preferred.

The main point in empirical curve-fitting is that we select the curve family solely on the basis of fit, and not on the basis of any theory. Ebbinghaus set out with no assumptions and required no theory that forgetting *ought* to follow a logarithmic curve; such a function merely proved to be a convenient summary expression of the facts he discovered. Life insurance companies predict the likelihood of survival on the basis of such empirical functions; they call them *actuarial curves* because they are based upon actual recorded facts. There need be no theory whatever as to why older people are more likely to die than younger ones.

When *rational* curve-fitting is contrasted with *empirical* curve-fitting, the word "rational" implies that the family of curves is chosen according to some theory or theoretical deduction so that it is logical to expect the curve as plotted to be of a given form. Rational curves, because they arise from and test theories, are more elegant than empirical ones. A rational curve of slightly poorer fit may turn out to be more useful for purposes of science than a better-fitting empirical curve. The step of curve-fitting has to be taken with rational curves as well as with empirical ones. That is, while the form of the curve is determined by theory, the particular *member* of the curve family that fits best is determined by the method of least squares, exactly as in empirical curve-fitting. Thus the *constants* (or *parameters,* as they are called) of the rational equation are determined empirically. The rational theory demands either that these constants should be interchangeable from one experiment to another or that they should vary in some predictable manner. Hence the theory upon which the rational equation is based can be tested by the agreements or disagreements among the constants as determined empirically in different experimental settings. These constants, furthermore, have reference to variables with additional (non-mathematical) meanings.

Empirical Learning Curves

Ebbinghaus' lead was followed some twenty years later, in 1907 and 1908, by attempts to state the learning curve in mathematical form.[1] These early starts were followed from time to time by others as more men became interested in the problem.[2]

As an example of the empirical approach, let us consider some suggestions first made by Culler in 1928, then elaborated later by Culler and Girden (1951). Arguing that the complete learning curve must be S-shaped, that is, a curve of increasing gains at first, later becoming one of decreasing gains as the upper limit is approached, Culler and Girden compare the fit of the normal ogive with that of the equation for monomolecular autocatalytic functions. The normal ogive, is of course, the familiar integral of the normal probability curve. The mono-molecular autocatalytic function yields a very similar curve. When written appropriate to learning, its equation is:

$$y = \frac{be^{Ax}}{c + e^{Ax}} \qquad (2)$$

where y = a measure of learning
x = a measure of practice
A = a constant for the learner and the task
b = a limit of attainment
c = a constant of integration
e = the base for natural logarithms

[1] Schükarew (1907), Robertson (1908). See also Robertson (1923).
[2] For an able review to that date, see Gulliksen (1934).

This function,[3] as in the case of other empirical curves, does provide some hints as to what the learning process may be like. The particular mathematical expression implies that the gain per trial is *proportional to the product of the amount already learned and the amount remaining to be learned* before the limit of learning is reached. By proper choice of constants, this will yield a curve of increasing gains at first, later becoming a curve of decreasing gains. Population growth can be expressed by such a curve; [4] the conjecture is inviting that some self-limiting growth process may underlie learning. As matters stand, however, the curve is not selected because of any formal theory that learning *is* such a process. The curve is chosen merely because it fits.

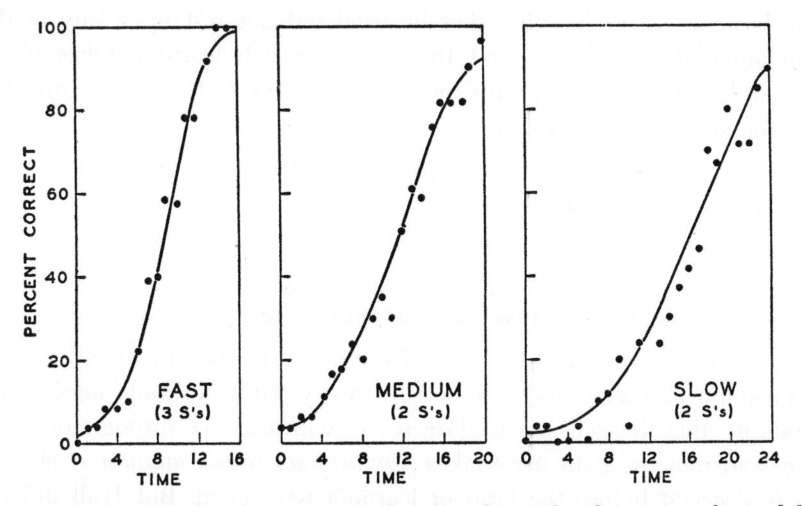

FIGURE 52. The fit of an ogive to learning data. The data were obtained by Culler from the learning of three-place symbols. Culler and Girden (1951), page 334.

Culler and Girden test both equations for a great many learning data, and find that both fit quite well. Some illustrative curves are shown in Figure 52. These are fitted with an ogive; the authors conclude that empirical considerations alone do not permit a choice to be made between the two curve forms that they tested. Culler and Girden are well aware that empirical curve-fitting is not enough, and that the choice of learning function must ultimately be made upon the basis of theory. They point out how futile it would be to obtain better-fitting curves through merely adding more parameters to an equation.[5]

[3] The mono-molecular autocatalytic reaction was first proposed as appropriate for learning by Robertson (1908). The statement in Equation (2) is as given by Gulliksen (1934).

[4] Pearl and Reed (1920).

[5] Culler and Girden (1951), page 328.

When additional parameters are used, empirical results can, of course, be very closely approximated. The formula proposed for general use by Woodrow (1942), for example, contained five parametric constants:

$$y = a + \sqrt{p^2 + k^2 - (1 - f^{x+d})^2} \tag{3}$$

His demonstration that he could fit it to a wide range of data did not make it survive as a general psychological law at all; it turned out to fit relationships of so many forms that it lost its theoretical interest. More than empirical curve-fitting is required if mathematics is to serve psychological theory.

While the deductive structure of Hull's theory is rational in form, the basic curve of learning that he used did not rest upon any of the fundamental postulates about the way in which learning takes place. Hence his curve belongs with the empirical curves. The form Hull used can be stated as follows:

$$_{S}H_{R} = M(1 - e^{-kt}) \tag{4}$$

where $_{S}H_{R}$ = habit strength
M = upper limit of habit strength
t = trials
k = a constant expressing learning rate
e = the base of natural logarithms

Such a curve (as in the case of the autocatalytic one) can be given a meaning that suggests some sort of theory. Hull's formula implies, for example, that the gain per trial decreases with practice throughout learning, and that the gain per trial *is proportional to the amount remaining to be learned* before the limit of learning is reached. But Hull did not state why this should be so.

Rational Learning Curves

An advance in the application of mathematical thinking to learning was made by Thurstone (1930a)(1930b) when he based his equations on a theory as to how learning takes place. The psychological assumptions are not very complex, and he did not pay any attention to the mechanisms underlying learning. What happens, according to Thurstone, is that the animal (or other learner) performs a number of acts per unit of time. His attainment can be stated as the probability that one of these acts will be successful. Thurstone introduced law-of-effect assumptions (without calling them that), for he proposed that successful performances led to further successes with practice, and unsuccessful performances led to a dropping out of errors.

If the learner at any one time has available to him s successful acts and e erroneous ones, his probability of success is simply the proportion of successful acts:

$$p = \frac{s}{s + e} \tag{5}$$

Similarly, the probability of failure will be:

$$q = 1 - p = \frac{e}{s + e} \tag{6}$$

If learning takes place with practice, we may write a differential equation to describe the increase in probability of success with time, introducing the constant k to describe the learning rate:

$$\frac{ds}{dt} = kp = \frac{ks}{s + e} \tag{7}$$

Error elimination can be expressed similarly, the negative sign indicating that errors are reduced with practice:

$$\frac{de}{dt} = -kq = \frac{-ke}{s + e} \tag{8}$$

Another learning constant is required, reflecting the difficulty or complexity of the task. Thurstone shows by computations based on equations (7) and (8) that the following equation must hold:

$$m = s \times e \tag{9}$$

That is, the product of errors and successes available at one time will be a constant (m). When the task is complex, this product will be large; when the task is simple, this product will be small.

Without any further psychological assumptions, Thurstone is able to perform an integration yielding the following curve of learning:

$$\frac{2p - 1}{\sqrt{p - p^2}} = \frac{kt}{\sqrt{m}} + z \tag{10}$$

where p = probability of success per unit of time (the measure of attainment)
k = constant reflecting learning ability
m = constant reflecting task complexity
t = time in the units over which probability is measured
z = constant of integration

By strict mathematical transformations, Thurstone (1930b) was able to make some predictions from his equation, in addition to fitting ordinary learning curves. He predicted, for example, the relationship between length of task and learning time under varied circumstances and found a satisfactory relationship between his prediction and existing data.

Gulliksen (1934) generalized Thurstone's theory another step and arrived at another rational equation that proved quite satisfactory in fitting learning data (Figure 53). The constants in his final equation included the initial strengths of correct and incorrect responses, a constant for the strength added by repeating and rewarding a correct response, and a constant for the strength subtracted by repeating and punishing an incorrect response. Later Gulliksen and Wolfle (1938) ex-

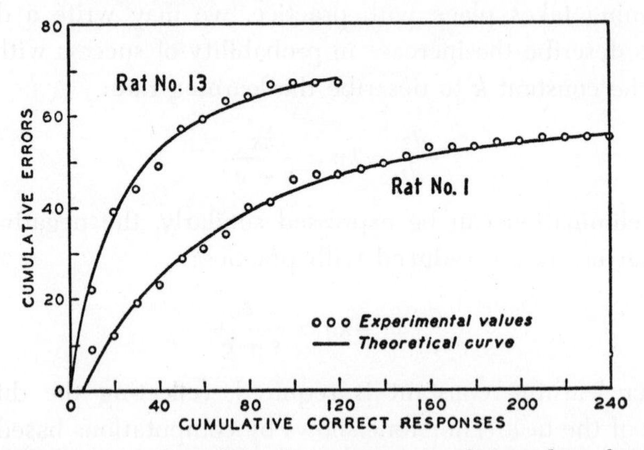

FIGURE 53. Success of Gulliksen's equation in fitting data from individual rats trained in visual discrimination by Lashley's jumping technique. Gulliksen (1934), page 420.

tended the equation to cover discrimination learning and subjected it to experimental test. The papers of Thurstone, Gulliksen, and Gulliksen and Wolfle represent a kind of succession, in which each equation is somewhat more general than the preceding one, and the earlier equations can be considered special cases of the later ones.

This is about where the matter was left before World War II. There were other developments in the mathematics of learning, particularly by Rashevsky and his students and colleagues, but psychologists had not shown themselves ready to pay much heed to them.[6] The painstaking volume by Hull and his collaborators entitled "Mathematico-deductive theory of rote learning" appeared in 1940, calling strongly to the attention of the psychological world the possibility of a forward step in rigorous theorizing, including not only derivations in ordinary mathematics but in

[6] Rashevsky had dealt mathematically with learning problems in American psychological journals as early as 1931, and his 1938 volume on *Mathematical biophysics* contained chapters on conditioned reflexes, the discrimination of relations, error elimination, rational learning and thinking.

symbolic logic as well. The stage was well set for new mathematical approaches after the disruptions of the war years, based, to be sure, in part upon developments that wartime demands brought about.

SOME MODELS FROM OTHER FIELDS POTENTIALLY USEFUL FOR LEARNING THEORY

In the last few years it has become customary to refer to some kinds of formal scientific theories as corresponding to one or another "model." The notion of making a model to represent a theory is a very old one. Most of us have seen colored balls arranged on wires to represent the atoms in a molecule or crystal, though we know very well that the molecule under a microscope would not look like that. Yet the model does represent certain relationships. Or in describing the operation of the Organ of Corti and the basilar membrane we may have learned of a hydraulic model. Helmholtz' resonance theory used a harp as a model. The model represents a series of relationships—mathematical, physical, conceptual—which appear to be appropriate for the understanding of some realm of data. There must be a kind of "fit" between the data and the model. The adequacy of the model can be judged by its success in ordering data, and in making verifiable predictions from the data.

The more formally a model is worked out, the more likely it is to be a mathematical one. A mathematical model consists of a set of relationships and transformations that can be made consistently according to the definitions and rules of the particular kind of mathematics. Data of many kinds and from many fields of science may be treated according to the rules of any one kind of mathematics. Thus the same rules of differentiation and integration apply within calculus whether one is investigating the action of an electronic circuit, an airplane wing under stress, the transmission of a nervous impulse or the behavior of a crowd.

While a mathematical model can therefore be used with a variety of data, models tend to be developed in close conjunction with the solution of particular kinds of problems, and they show some of the history of their origins in the form they take. Whether or not these models will prove useful within learning theory may depend upon some analogies between the substantive problems in the field in which the model developed and in the field of learning.

Three types of model from other fields are worth mentioning here: the feedback model, the information-theory model, and the theory-of-games model.

The Feedback Model

The science of *cybernetics* was christened by Wiener (1948), who encouraged the application of some principles coming from communication engineering to physiological and social problems. The word "cybernetics" comes from a Greek word meaning steersman or governor, and cybernetics can be thought of as the study of control processes in machines, in organisms, in social groups. It is a mechanism of control that provides the model for these various activities.

One of the central concepts of cybernetics, "feedback," has gained wide currency in psychological discussion. Let us examine the analogy between adaptive behavior and a thermostatic control system. When the heat comes on and warms the room the thermostat records the rise in temperature. When the temperature reaches a critical point, the thermostat sends a "message" back to the furnace and turns off the heat. The furnace is thus controlled by a "feedback" from the consequences of the furnace's operation. A man walking down a path has a "feedback" from his muscles, tendons, and joints, so that he makes corrective movements if the ground is uneven or if his foot strikes an obstacle. The awkward gait in *tabes dorsalis* arises because part of this feedback is missing, and the placing of the feet has to be controlled visually—thus using a less satisfactory feedback device.

Is feedback a possible model for learning theory? Consider trial-and-error learning, especially in the form of approximation-and-correction. What the learner does on successive trials is regulated by the consequences of his activity. The old problem of the circularity of the law of effect can perhaps be resolved in terms of feedback.

Another name for the feedback mechanism is *servomechanism,* and a large literature is now available, much of it expressed in mathematical form.[7]

The feedback model as such has thus far been little used in learning theory. Ellson (1949) showed how some of the input-output formulations of operational analysis might prove useful in the psychology of learning, but he failed to combine the feedback concept with the input-output one. Leavitt and Mueller (1951) show how the old problem of knowledge of results can be treated in the language of "feedback." The instructor tries to communicate to a student a geometrical form, using only words. Success is much greater if the student is free to ask questions and to receive answers in the form of "feedback." This seems fairly ob-

[7] For example, MacColl (1945); Truxal (1955).

vious, yet there are some interesting possibilities in quantifying the amount of feedback and its consequences for learning.

The Information-Theory Model

Both the feedback model and the information-theory model have their origins in the study of communication. Yet information-theory has had a somewhat distinctive formulation, with a clear influence upon psychology.[8]

The communication model suggests that psychological events can be understood through analogy with the events that occur when a message is transmitted through an electronic transmission system (e.g., a long-distance teletype system). The communication paradigm developed by Shannon [9] is reproduced in Figure 54.

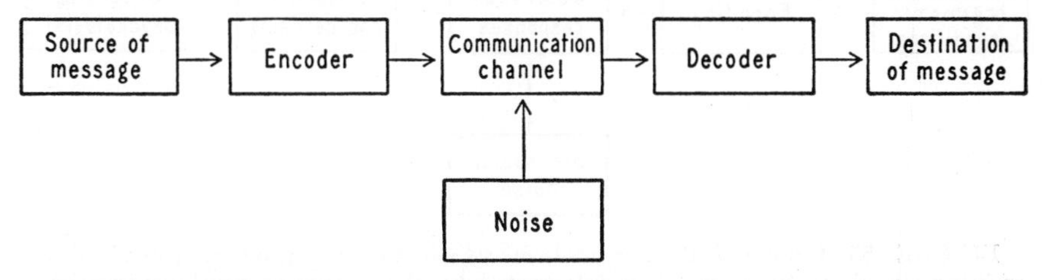

FIGURE 54. Model for a communication system. After Shannon. Reproduced from Grant, 1954, page 63.

Information in the form of a message enters at the source and is converted to a code suitable for the given transmission system. A teletype machine converts the typist's strokes into patterns of dots and dashes suitable for sending as electrical impulses. These go through the communication channel as electrical impulses, or perhaps as radio waves or light waves. They have to be decoded at the receiving end, and appear as letters typed by the teletype receiving machine at the other end. Noise (static, etc.) may enter the message in the process of transmission, and the message may be somewhat garbled before it is typed at the destination. In military practice a special coding process may be introduced, so that the ordinary decoding done by the teletype machine will not suffice, and the original message can be yielded only if the code is known (or is broken by a cryptoanalyst).

In what respects are psychological events similar to the events in such a communication system? One way of picturing them is shown in

[8] The standard work on information-theory is Shannon and Weaver (1949). Useful introductions for psychologists are the papers by Miller (1953) and Grant (1954).
[9] See Shannon and Weaver (1949).

Figure 55. The organism here corresponds to the communication channel, transmitting information to the psychologist by way of its behavior. The observable responses make their appearance only as complex resultants of prior conditions as these are "encoded" (perceived? reacted to?) by the organism. The responses may be modified by non-essential circumstances (here "biosocial noise"), so that the observing psychologist has a difficult task in interpreting ("decoding") the subject's behavior. This is but one way of using the communication model to describe psychological events, and other analogies are permissible. For example, the conversation between two people can be described according to the successive processes of encoding, transmitting, and decoding messages.[10]

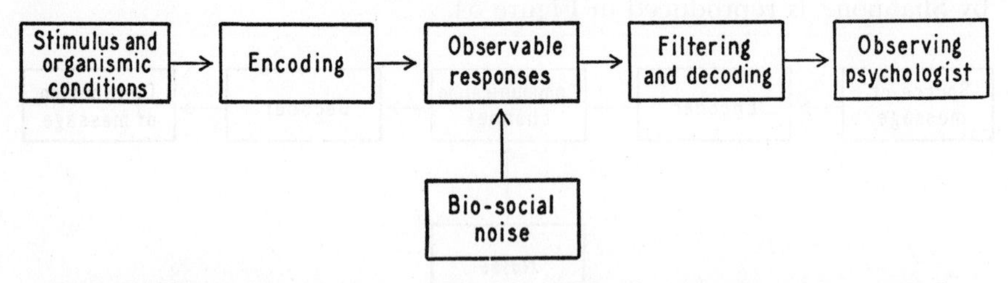

FIGURE 55. Communication model in which the organism is conceived as emitting signals to be received or interpreted by the observing psychologist. From Grant, 1954, page 65.

The service to psychology of the communication model has thus far come largely through some special considerations relating to information in its quantitative aspects.

Information is, of course, a very familiar concept. We receive information when we get our questions answered; we use information when we find our way about; the dictionary, the telephone directory, the encyclopedia, are full of information. But when we turn aside from the rich substance of information to consider only *amount* of information, and to find a *unit* by which to describe the quantity of information, we enter the province of information-theory. The basic notion is that information is discriminative; it answers the question: "Which of a number of alternatives is this?" The more alternatives there are, the more information is conveyed by the answer. If you give a person's name you give more information about him than if you give merely his sex, because through his name you have identified him among many alternatives, while by giving his sex you have identified him among only two alternatives.

[10] For parallels between physical communication systems and various problems of human intercommunication, see Schramm (1954), pages 3–26.

The relation of information to number of alternatives is given more formal expression: the amount of information yielded by specifying one of a number of alternatives increases as the logarithm of the number of alternatives.

Where does this logarithmic relationship come from? The simplest way to look at it is that we can communicate information in a formal sense by reducing alternatives one half at a time. Suppose you were trying to guess a number between 1 and 32 and can ask questions answered only by "yes" or "no." The most information you could get from your first question by an orderly approach would be whether or not the number was 16 or less, or above 16, thus reducing your alternatives by half. By continuing this process, you would arrive at your number. How many questions would you have to ask? It is not hard to prepare a little table to see how this works:

Range Within Which Number Lies	*Number of Guesses Required*
1–2	1
1–4	2
1–8	3
1–16	4
1–32	5

We may say that specifying a number from among a larger set of numbers gives more information than specifying a number from among a smaller set. The relationship between our two columns can be expressed as follows:

$$\text{Number of guesses required} = \log_2 \text{number of alternatives}$$

This is the model used for information theory. The unit of information is called the "bit," which is a clever adoption of a familiar way of talking about small amounts of information, combined with a condensation of "binary digit." The "bit" of information is the unit of information gained whenever the number of alternatives is reduced by one-half. If a message reduces the number of alternatives k to some fraction k/x, then the amount of information in the message is $\log_2 x$ bits.

Information-theory deals with such problems as the disturbance of a message as it goes through a transmission system. The system contains random interference ("noise") which requires that the message have some "redundancy" in order that it may be understood at the end. The English language is said to be about 50 per cent redundant. That permits a message to be somewhat garbled as it comes from the telegraph office and still be understood. Because of noise the amount of *unavailable* information at the end of a transmission system is greater than at the beginning, suggesting a parallel to the physical notion of *entropy.* In the transformation of energy, some is always dissipated as heat, and no machine is 100 per cent efficient. The second law of thermodynamics states this principle as an increase in entropy. So, too, in communication some available information tends to be lost and unavailable information increases.

Because learning involves input and output, with processes of discrimination, variability,[11] and interference between stimulus and response, the information-theory model might presumably find useful applications. This has indeed proved to be the case.

There is a familiar demonstration experiment in psychology in which we show how much easier it is to learn a list of related words than a list of unrelated ones, and how, in turn, the unrelated words are easier to learn than a list of nonsense syllables. While the results may be stated quantitatively (showing a statistically significant difference between each pair of lists) the differences between the lists, as materials to be memorized, remain qualitative ("related," "unrelated," "nonsense"). Here information-theory comes to our help because it is possible to show on the basis of the statistical characteristics of the English language the amount of information that has to be acquired in order to learn each list. A familiar word conforms to English language practice in following one letter by another in non-random fashion. (An extreme illustration is always following *q* by *u,* but a *t* is also followed by an *h* beyond chance, a *j* seldom followed by a *c,* and so on.) Nonsense syllables are constructed out of more nearly random sequences of letters, so that more information has to be acquired in learning them than in learning meaningful words. Word sequences also have their probabilities in English, so that less information has to be acquired to learn "related" words than to learn "unrelated" ones. This is particularly true if the related words form a sentence, thus capitalizing on non-random features of familiar sentence construction in English.

It would be difficult to take the typical demonstration experiment as ordinarily used and make the necessary computations to assign difficulty in terms of the amount of information that has to be acquired to learn each of the three kinds of lists, but, in principle, it could be done.

[11] Information measurement can be interpreted in terms of variance and covariance. Large variance corresponds to a large amount of unassimilated information (i.e., ignorance). Covariance or correlation corresponds to the relationship between input and output, that is, to the amount of transmitted information. These points are made by G. A. Miller (1955).

Closely related experiments, however, have been designed and performed.

Miller and Selfridge (1950), for example, constructed materials with different degrees of approximation to the statistical structure of English. A random selection of words from the Thorndike-Lorge list of the 30,000 commonest words provided the "sentence" most unlike English. This they called the zero-order approximation to English. The next, or first-order approximation, was a random selection from the words produced by the subjects in the higher-order sentences about to be described. Then followed a series of approximations each constructed in similar fashion. The next approximation (second-order) was obtained by constructing a "sentence" one word at a time by giving the first word to one subject who responded with a single word, then giving his one-word response to another subject who added one more word, and so on until the "sentence" was constructed. This procedure goes beyond the purely random list in preserving some of the word-association sequences of English. The next order of approximation gave as the context for response the two preceding words in the sentence. The procedure was followed through 7-word sequences. Finally, the authors selected a passage from current fiction or biography as a meaningful English text to determine how close the higher orders of approximation were coming to "meaningful" material. Results for passages of different length constructed in this way are shown in Figure 56. It is quite clear that as the passages come nearer to the structure of English they are more readily recalled. To a rough approximation, the amount of information recalled was constant. Hence difficulty was in reality not a function of "meaningfulness" per se, but of quantity of information that had to be acquired.

Inspection of Figure 56 shows that a 50-word passage at the fifth order of approximation is learned as readily as a fully "meaningful" passage of text. Are we to assume then that the fifth order of approximation is really meaningful text? Here is an illustration of such a passage:

> House to ask for is to earn our living by working towards a goal for his team in old New-York was a wonderful place wasn't it even pleasant to talk about and laugh hard when he tells lies he should not tell me the reason why you are is evident.[12]

It appears that there are kinds of nonsense as easy to recall as passages taken from a novel. The nonsense is easy if it preserves the learned structure of the language, even though it remains nonsense. The struc-

[12] Miller and Selfridge (1950), pages 182–183.

ture can be treated quantitatively according to information-theory. Thus information-theory provides a powerful new analytic tool.

Hovland (1952b) has furnished another illustration of the usefulness of the information-theory approach. He reanalyzed the concept formation studies by Smoke (1932)(1933). Smoke had found that in the acquiring of concepts through presenting various embodiments of the concept along with irrelevant cues, "positive instances" in which the essential characteristics of the concept were included facilitated learning

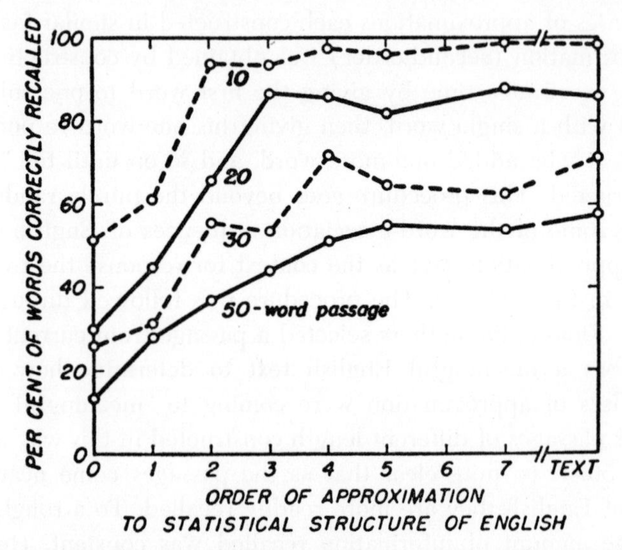

FIGURE 56. Amount retained after equivalent practice with materials of different degrees of approximation to English. Miller and Selfridge (1950), page 181.

much more than "negative instances" in which some characteristics essential to the concept were lacking. Hovland questioned the generality of Smoke's conclusion because of two possibilities: subjects might be reacting to differences in information in positive and negative instances, or they might for some reason find it more difficult to assimilate the information given by negative instances. If the second possibility is the true one, Smoke's conclusion would be acceptable as an important generalization about concept formation. If, however, the first possibility is correct, and negative instances furnish less information than positive ones, stimulus presentation would have to be blamed for the finding, and the generalization about negative and positive instances would have little psychological meaning.

It should be noted in passing that these questions can also be raised about some cases testing the positive and negative aspects of the law of effect, in which verbal "punishment" was sometimes found less effective than verbal "reward." It will usually turn out that saying *Wrong* eliminates fewer possibilities than saying *Right.* In that event the generalization about the asymmetry between reward and punishment takes on new meaning.

Hovland's analysis of the amount of information conveyed by positive and negative instances in the concept experiment shows that the amount varies greatly. In general, as the total number of possible responses increases, the minimum number of negative instances needed to convey the concept increases, even when the necessary number of positive instances remains constant. In the most extreme case, a minimum of *two* positive instances sufficed to convey the concept, while 625 negative instances were required!

The experimental test conducted by Hovland and Weiss (1953) showed that human subjects do not behave as a machine would which was built according to the laws of information-theory. Even when the amount of information yielded by positive and negative instances was equated, they learned better from positive instances than from negative ones. While thus showing the simple information-theory model not sufficient to account for concept learning, there was some gain in having equated the information for positive and negative instances. There was at least *some* learning from negative instances, a result Smoke had not found.

It is evident that in the studies by Miller and Selfridge (1950) and of Hovland (1952b), information-theory has provided a useful tool. Many other studies are currently appearing. They will help to define the range of this usefulness.[13]

The Theory-of-Games Model

The appearance in 1944 of von Neumann and Morgenstern's *Theory of games and economic behavior* marked the beginning of a very rapid development, especially among economists, of a type of model of potential usefulness in other fields of social science, including psychology. The mathematics employed leans heavily upon concepts originating in set theory and linear geometry, branches of mathematics until recently little studied by social scientists.

[13] Thus far quantitative aspects of information ("bits") have been used almost exclusively in the description of the stimulus. The sequential aspects of communication, including the interesting problems of encoding and decoding, are just beginning to be brought into the psychological laboratory.

As its name implies, the theory attempts to define the optimum strategy in competitive games, such as simplified poker games or modified chess games. A player makes his moves against uncertainty, either the uncertainties of chance events (such as the order of the cards in a well-shuffled deck), or the uncertainties of the moves of the opponent. The game provides a simplified model of economic behavior, in which the decisions of an entrepreneur are made according to his predictions of an uncertain market and the moves of his competitors. The original theory-of-games model assumes that the players are thoroughly rational, and that they always make the best decision that the available information allows. In the game of tick-tack-toe, for example, it is possible to master the rational strategy, so that the outcome of the game is predictable for expert players. But we know that in many instances the rational course is not chosen. We shall meet an illustration on page 390, in which it will be pointed out that in guessing against a 75:25 odds, subjects commonly guess in the 75:25 pattern, while theory-of-games would easily show that hits would be maximized by always guessing on the 75 side, that is, guessing in a 100:0 pattern.

In addition to the estimation of probabilities of outcome, the individual playing a game *prefers* one outcome to another. In the language of theory of games, one outcome has higher *utility* than another. In other words, decisions are based upon *value systems* as well as upon *prediction systems.*[14] Utility and value are essentially motivational terms, and hence relevant to psychology. Some empirical investigations have been made to translate assumed utility systems into measures of utility as expressed through individual behavior.[15]

A game usually involves more than one player, so that the theory of games tends to be applied to group decisions, although, of course, individual choice is involved.[16] Some learning theorists, however, have attempted to bring game-theory into relationship with individual learning. A relevant example is that of Flood (1954) who entitles his paper "On game-learning theory and some decision-making experiments."

Flood attempts to show how a player can learn to improve his strategy during a sequence of plays. He accepts basic assumptions from both the von Neumann-Morgenstern game theory and the Bush-Mosteller learning theory to be discussed later in this chapter. Among the assumptions is one that learning can be described by the special type of

[14] A very helpful elementary introduction to these notions is contained in Bross (1953).

[15] E.g., Mosteller and Nogee (1951).

[16] E.g., Arrow (1951b).

stochastic process known as a Markov process, in which only the immediately preceding event is used in making predictions about the one that follows it. The author admits that this assumption will probably not prove adequate.[17]

There is likely to be a greater interplay between the theory-of-games model and psychology within the next few years, but it is already quite clear that the model will have to undergo some modifications to move from the assumption of rational behavior to more appropriate assumptions based on the actual behavior of individuals. This need is widely recognized. For example, Estes in reporting individual behavior in the face of uncertainty concludes that "in a simple decision process the human subject tends to behave in accordance with the principles of associative learning and not, in general, in the most rational manner as 'rational' is conventionally defined."[18] Similarly, Hoffman, Festinger, and Lawrence (1954), in a study of coalitions in a competitive situation, are able to specify motivational changes affecting the coalitions in a manner to deny the symmetrical utility function required by game theory. Davis has taken the position that their situation is gamelike, but probably better treated as general psychology than as game-theory.[19] Davis' position is little likely to lead to a unified theory of social behavior.

These brief introductions to feedback models, information-theory models, and theory of games, suffice as a background for the model-building activity of contemporary learning theories. There is a family resemblance among all these models. They all deal with sequential behavior, they all deal with uncertainty and decision-making. While these three models were developed in contexts other than psychology, it is clear that they are gradually influencing contemporary psychological theorizing.

MATHEMATICAL MODELS IN CONTEMPORARY LEARNING THEORY

We have already seen, in a preliminary way, how mathematics has been used in relation to learning data. Empirical curve-fitting uses a loosely defined model: merely a family of curves selected according to convenience and without theoretical justification. When some new data are better fitted by a curve from a different family, the old model is

[17] Markov processes were first mentioned in the interpretation of learning by Miller and Frick (1949), and they are assumed in most of the later mathematical treatments.

[18] Estes (1954a), page 136.

[19] Davis (1954), page 15.

abandoned in favor of a new one. Rational curve-fitting corresponds more closely to contemporary model-building, for the nature of the curve is fixed by the theory, and predictions follow.

Models Based Largely upon Differential Calculus

The success of calculus in handling so many problems of physics and engineering has made it the standard fare of most college mathematical sequences. Because calculus deals with rates of change, it appears to be an appropriate mathematics to try out in relation to problems of learning.

Models depending largely upon differential calculus have been extensively used by Rashevsky and his colleagues and students in studies over many years. While the models are usually referred to the nervous system, little of neuroanatomical detail is involved, so that the model is, in fact, more largely mathematical than anatomical or physiological. Despite the ingenuity displayed, and the mathematical sophistication, these models have had relatively little influence within psychology. Their neglect must be due only in part to the inability of psychologists to follow the mathematics, for other difficult mathematical models have been understood by at least a few psychologists. Some of the neglect may have been due to the lack of interest in neurophysiological speculation by learning theorists. Possibly more important is the social fact that no one has attempted a consistent experimental program tied to the systematic developments. It is not enough that the mathematical consequences satisfactorily fit old data. For psychologists to become interested, new and relevant data must be predicted. The failure of anyone to pick up the threads of the Rashevsky theories may be merely a kind of historical accident, for the possibilities appear to be there.[20]

We saw in Equations (7) and (8), page 373, how Thurstone began by setting up differential equations and then through integration arrived at his learning-curve equation. Many models begin in this way. To illustrate the naturalness of this approach to the construction of a mathematical model, we may consider a very sketchy model recently proposed by Simon (1954). He called it a "Berlitz model," after the self-instruction method of learning a foreign language. He makes the following assumptions about a person starting out to learn French by this method:

[20] For a review making the Rashevsky models somewhat more accessible, see Coleman (1954). These models deal with social behavior, rather than with learning, but the review reveals the type of logic employed.

1. The individual is free to practice as much or as little as he wishes.
2. As he practices, the activity becomes easier for him.
3. The pleasantness of the activity increases as it becomes easier for him.
4. The more pleasant the activity, the more he engages in it; the less pleasant the activity, the less he engages in it.

It takes very few additional assumptions to express these verbal statements in a mathematical model.

First, the rate according to which difficulty decreases as practice continues can be expressed by the following differential equation:

$$\frac{dD}{dt} = -aDx \qquad (11)$$

where D = level of difficulty at any one time
x = rate at which practice takes place
a = a constant based on the learner's capacity to learn
t = elapsed time

This means, in words, that the rate of change in difficulty decreases as the product of the difficulty level at the time and the rate of practice at the time. With this equation as the starting point, we will come out with a logarithmic decrease of difficulty with practice when the differential is integrated. Thus the statement that practice reduces difficulty has become *more precise* as we use a mathematical model instead of the verbal one; whether or not it is *true* remains a matter for empirical testing.

A second differential equation expresses the motivational assumption that the task becomes more pleasant with practice, and that, as it becomes more pleasant, there will be a tendency to practice more:

$$\frac{dx}{dt} = -b\,(x - \overline{x}) \qquad (12)$$

where x = rate at which practice takes place
$\overline{x}$ = satiation level of practice for any level of difficulty
Less practice is pleasant, more practice is unpleasant
$-b$ = a constant based on the learner's motivation
t = elapsed time

Put into words, this says that the amount of practice will decrease proportionately to the amount that the rate of practice exceeds the satiation level.

Even as simple a model as this permits predictions of time paths of practice and difficulty, provided the original values of difficulty (D_0), the initial practice rate (x_0), and the satiation level ($\overline{x}$) are known. Here are examples of some common-sense predictions based on the model. These predictions follow strictly, however, from the mathematical implications of the model:

a. If the initial values of D_0 and x_0 are very high, it can be predicted that the decrease in x will be more rapid than the decrease in D, so that the student will give up his practice before learning French.

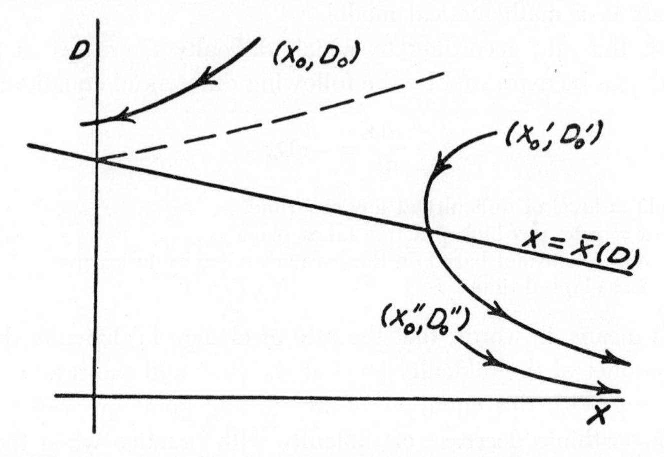

FIGURE 57. Some implications of Simon's "Berlitz" model. Simon (1954), page 403.

b. With intermediate values of D_0 and x_0 there will be temporary discouragement and slowing up of practice, because practice of difficult material is unpleasant, and unpleasantness slows practice. The mathematical model shows, however, that there is a critical point, and if difficulty falls below this point before practice stops, practice will become pleasant and learning will proceed to mastery.

c. If difficulty is low, and initial rate of practice also low, learning, according to this model, will proceed smoothly.

These three conditions are illustrated in the curves of Figure 57.

Even the student entirely unfamiliar with calculus will perceive a certain naturalness in the attempt to fit this model to a learning situation. The model is proposed by Simon for purposes of illustration, and he does not think of it as sufficiently developed to be used to design empirical research.

Stochastic Models

Psychologists have long been familiar with probability concepts as underlying psychological measurements. They have also recognized the possibility of extending probability concepts to sequential data of the sort found in learning. Thus Thurstone (1930a), with a background in psychophysical measurement, found it appropriate to use probability concepts in developing his rational curve equation, although the mathematical procedures used were those of differential and integral calculus.

The kind of model based on probability mathematics rather than upon differential calculus [21] has come to be called a stochastic model. A stochastic process is defined as a sequence of events together with the probabilities of these sequences. Thus for the older notion of a casual chain we now have the related concept of stochastic process—a chain with uncertainty at every link. These uncertain but possible events at each link are expressed according to the mathematics of probability. Perhaps the Tolman and Brunswik (1935) expression "causal texture" can be appropriately substituted for "causal chain" when we deal with stochastic processes.

We shall turn now to two illustrations of stochastic models within learning theory.

Estes' Statistical-Association Model

Estes (1950) presented a statistical model with psychological assumptions very similar to those of Guthrie. As general background theory he assumed that the stimulus complex consists of a "finite population of relatively independent environmental events." Only a sample from this population is effective at any given time. Responses, too, fall into classes, and response instances occur and enter into experiments as the dependent variables. To develop a probability model, response probability has to be defined. Estes defined response probability as the average frequency of occurrence of members of a response class relative to the maximum possible frequency under the conditions of the experiment. The basic learning assumption is that association occurs through contiguity. That is, if a stimulus element is present once along with a response occurrence, the association is formed at full strength through this single occurrence. Response probability for the class of responses being learned increases with practice because more stimulus elements become conditioned to it on succeeding trials, and more elements become alienated from their association with other response classes. This is, of course, Guthrie's theory, expressed by Estes in mathematical form. These psychological

[21] This does not mean that calculus is not used in the course of developing these models, for you do not avoid calculus in probability theory any more than you avoid algebra in calculus. The main point is that calculus deals with regularities, while probability deals with measures that contain some degree of uncertainty.

assumptions suffice to permit equations to be written, predictions made, and agreements or disagreements with data determined.

The theory first proposed by Estes (1950) has been refined mathematically and applied to new problems by Estes and Burke (1953) and Estes (1953) (1954a).

Let us consider, first of all some data to which the developed model is appropriate. The experiment is one by Grant, Hake, and Hornseth (1951), extending a kind of experiment introduced by Humphreys (1939b).

Two lights are mounted on a board before the subject. The subject is asked to guess, while the left light is on, whether or not the second light will flash on. The guess is recorded, and the subject notes whether or not his guess was correct. The experiment was so arranged that for different groups of subjects the percentages of second flashes varied. The percentages of trials on which the second light flashed on were 0, 25, 50, 75, and 100 per cent. Results are plotted in Figure 58. Note that after 60 trials subjects tended to be guessing at about the percentage at which the lights were flashing.

Although these results appear plausible enough, a little reflection will show that they are *not* the results that would be given by a "rational" decision-maker, as implied, say, in game-theory. Consider the cases in which lights come on 75 per cent of the time and are off 25 per cent of the time. Any gambler knows that if the odds are 3:1 that one event will occur rather than another, once he detects these odds he will maximize his hits by always betting on the more frequent event. Yet the subjects somehow "preferred" to match the stimulus probabilities with their guesses rather than to maximize their hits. Many similar experiments have yielded similar results.[22]

We need to examine a little more carefully the sense in which Estes' theory is a contiguity theory similar to Guthrie's. The events in this light-guessing experiment are conceived by Estes to parallel classical conditioning as follows:

1. Conditioned stimulus = signal light (left light).
2. (Conditioned response = saying "on" or "off" in anticipation of what is going to happen on the right.)

[22] The reader must be warned that these are experiments in guessing without risk. If there are penalties for errors, the described experimental results are no longer found. When Humphreys' (1939a) subjects received a puff of air to the eye following 50 per cent of the conditioned stimuli, they approached the same asymptote for their conditioned eye-blinks (and at the same rate) as though they received the air-puff 100 per cent of the time. The over-reaction to the 50 per cent reinforcement presumably depended upon the threat involved in not responding.

3. Unconditioned stimulus = right light "on" or "off."
4. Unconditioned response = saying "on" of "off" according to what happens on the right.

In a contiguity theory the conditioned response is unimportant except as an indicator of the state of the learned-response system, and as furnishing some of the components of the stimulus situation present when the unconditioned stimulus and response occur. The conditioned

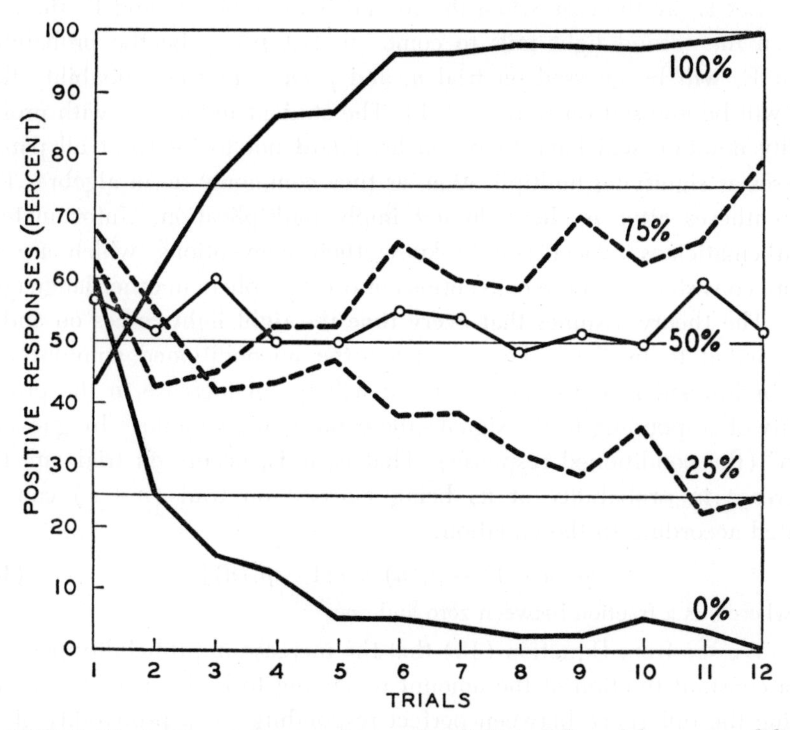

FIGURE 58. Positive responses when a first light is followed by a second light in specified percentages of the trials. Note that the limit approached tends to correspond to the percentage of times that the light appears. The trials are numbered in blocks of five. After Grant, Hake, and Hornseth (1951).

response as such is not important in determining the terminal events that are responsible for what is learned. The contiguous items in Estes' system are the conditioned stimulus, the unconditioned stimulus, and the unconditioned response. The conditioned response (the "guess" as to whether or not the light is coming on, or which light in some cases) does not enter the equations as a modifier of the influence of the unconditioned stimulus. Thus there is no "confirmation" of a correct guess and no "correction" of an erroneous one. All that really matters is the occurrence or non-occurrence of a light and the verbal response to it in the presence of cues (the effective conditioned stimulus). Thus the interpretation is strictly a contiguous association one, without reinforcement or extinction of a *prior* response, as in reinforcement-type theories.

Now to return to Estes and Burke. We shall see something of the construction of their theory in relation to the experiment previously described. In this we follow Estes (1953).

Let E_1 be the case when the second light comes on and E_2 the case when the second light fails to come on. Let $p_1(n)$ be the probability that E_1 will be guessed on trial n, and $p_1(n+1)$ the probability that E_1 will be guessed on trial $(n+1)$. The student unfamiliar with probability notation will have to be on his guard not to interpret all parentheses as signifying multiplication, as they commonly do in algebra. The parentheses after p_1, here do *not* imply multiplication. Unfortunately, mathematicians expect you to know their conventions, which are no more consistent than the conventions of orthographers in other languages.

The theory assumes that every time the right light comes on and is responded to by "on" (i.e., whenever the unconditioned stimulus and unconditioned response occur) there will be an increase in the probability of responding to the signal (the conditioned stimulus) by guessing "on" (the conditioned response). That is, if E_1 occurs on trial (n) the increase in probability of its being guessed on trial $(n+1)$ can be stated according to the equation:

$$p_1(n+1) - p_1(n) = \theta[1 - p_1(n)] \tag{13}$$

where θ is a fraction between zero and one.

We see from Equation (13) that the increase in probability per trial is a constant fraction of the amount remaining to be learned, $1 - p_1(n)$ being the difference between perfect responding (at a probability of 1) and the present probability, $p_1(n)$. This will obviously yield the same form of learning curve as that adopted by Hull (see page 372).

Now if E_2 (absence of light) occurs, the probability of predicting E_1 diminishes because by association theory it is the response to E_2 that should be favored on the next trial. This diminution of probability is expressed by the following equation:

$$p_1(n+1) - p_1(n) = -\theta p_1(n) \tag{14}$$

These two equations are known as *operator* or *difference equations.* They merely state in precise form the assumption that probabilities of repeating one of a pair of alternative responses increase with positive cases and decrease with negative cases. The constant θ has to be determined empirically, but once determined it should hold through many variations of the experiment.

The fraction of trials that the light comes on (when E_1 occurs) can be expressed as π (Greek letter pi), and the trials on which it is omitted (when E_2 occurs) as $(1 - \pi)$. We know what happens when E_1 occurs from Equation (13) and what happens when E_2 occurs from Equation (14). Because we know the relative frequencies of E_1 and E_2, we can combine Equations (13) and (14) directly:

$$p_1(n+1) - p_1(n) = \pi(\theta[1 - p_1(n)]) + (1 - \pi)[-\theta p_1(n)] \tag{15}$$

This equation looks difficult to the mathematical novice because of the parentheses and brackets, a subscript, some Greek letters, and uncertainty as to which parentheses are really subscripts and which mean multiplication. Anyone with high school algebra can carry out the multiplication and combine terms. When this is done, the following equation results:

$$p_1(n+1) - p_1(n) = \theta[\pi - p_1(n)] \tag{16}$$

Comparing Equation (16) with Equation (13), we see that π has replaced 1. In other words, the limit of learning has changed from 1 to π.

Equation (16) gives us the expected change of p_1 from any one trial to the next. Now we skip some mathematical steps leading from Equation (16) to a derived learning-curve equation. It can be shown rigorously that beginning with trial 0 and going to trial *n*, we have as the probability of guessing E_1 on any trial *n*:

$$p_1(n) = \pi - [\pi - p_1(0)](1 - \theta)^n \tag{17}$$

This is a derived learning-curve equation, and in form it looks very much like many others in the literature, for example, that of Hull, Equation 4, page 372. But the constants have a special meaning in this case. Just as Hull's curve approaches M as a limit, so this curve approaches π as a limit. This follows because the second term in Equation (17) becomes negligible for very large values of *n*. But π is the relative frequency with which E_1 occurs.

Now we come back to our experimental findings. The mathematical theory has predicted exactly the result found by Grant, Hake, and Hornseth (1951), and other experimenters, for the asymptote of the guesses in these experiments tends to be π, the relative frequency with which the second light comes on.

While this is a most incomplete account of Estes' theory, it serves at least as an introduction to it.

Bush and Mosteller's Linear-Operator Model

Bush and Mosteller (1951a) were the first to propose a linear-operator model for learning theory, although such operators were later incorporated into the Estes and Burke model just described. We shall see presently how mathematically similar the two models are, but first we may examine the similarities and differences in psychological assumptions.

Bush and Mosteller make essentially the same assumptions as Estes with respect to stimulus and response. Their assumptions are stated with particular clarity in their second paper.[23] In this paper they use the notation of "set theory" in mathematics. For both Estes and Bush and Mosteller the organism perceives (or reacts to) some fraction of the total stimuli available. Whereas Estes describes this fraction in terms of the proportion of elements in a totality, Bush and Mosteller speak of the "measure" of the elements. The "measure" is a kind of sum of weighted elements, and serves the same purpose as Estes' number of elements. The set-theoretic model in this second paper is used to derive the linear operators of the earlier paper. Because the psychological assumptions are unchanged in this more elegant mathematical treatment, we return now to the original psychological assumptions.

The basic difference between the psychological assumptions of Bush and Mosteller and of Estes rests on interpretation of reinforcement. Estes follows a contiguous association theory, not requiring the operation of reinforcement or of extinction as fundamental principles. Bush and Mosteller adopt principles of learning more like those of Hull and Skinner, accepting one parameter (a) for the positive influence of reinforcement, and another parameter (b) for the negative influence of punishment or of work required in responding, that is, a work interpretation of extinction.

Their basic operator, in their notation, is:

$$Q_p = p + a(1 - p) - bp \qquad (18)$$

where Q_p = the operator Q operating on p, the probability that a response will occur during a specified time
a = parameter associated with reward
b = parameter associated with punishment or work required
p = probability of response

This is the linear operator that gives the model its name.[24]

[23] Bush and Mosteller (1951b).

[24] We may rewrite Equation (18) in a form to show more clearly that it is a linear function: $Q_p = (1 - a - b)p + a$. Because $(1 - a - b)$ and (a) are constants, the equation is in typical linear form, e.g., $y = ax + b$.

We may define the isolated effect of reinforcement by setting $b = 0$ in Equation (18):

$$Q_1 p = p + a(1 - p) \tag{19}$$

Similarly, the isolated effect of extinction can be studied by setting $a = 0$ in Equation (18):

$$Q_2 p = p - bp \tag{20}$$

Now we have two equations from Estes, Equations (13) and (14) and two from Bush and Mosteller, Equations (19) and (20). How are these related? In the case of flashing lights we may assume that the effect of saying "on" to a light that has appeared will affect the next performance in an amount equal to the effect of saying "off" to a light that has not come on (although, of course, the effects are in opposite directions). That is, we may set the parameters all equal, $a = b = \theta$. Then we can show that the Estes and the Bush and Mosteller equations are equivalent. They may be written in parallel as follows:

$$p_1(n+1) = p_1(n) + \theta[1 - p_1(n)] \quad \text{From Equation (13)}$$
$$Q_1 p = p + \theta[1 - p] \quad \text{From Equation (19)}$$

$$p_1(n+1) = p_1(n) - \theta p_1(n) \quad \text{From Equation (14)}$$
$$Q_2 p = p - \theta p \quad \text{From Equation (20)}$$

The only remaining differences are in notation.

This coincidence of two models based on quite different psychological assumptions is significant, but the case illustrated here is a special one, without risk, with the assumption of equal consequences of alternative occurrences, and without any assumption of work involved in responding. When these several assumptions are not met, the two models may yield different predictions.

Let us now look at a single illustration of the Bush and Mosteller model in use. Consider the course of learning in a Skinner box. One measure of learning is the total number of responses to extinction following various numbers of reinforcements. Data are available from the work of Williams (1938) for responses after 5, 10, 30, and 90 reinforcements. These are plotted in Figure 59. The smooth curve is the one predicted from the Bush and Mosteller model, but we need to retrace the steps to see how it was arrived at.

Beginning with the operator in Equation (18), the change of rate of responding with time can be computed on the assumption that, starting with any probability p, the rate will increase according to this probability changed by the operator. According to the mathematics of differential and integral calculus, appropriate to changes of rate in a free-response situation of this kind, an expression can be derived for the maximum rate of responding.[25] This turns out to be:

$$V_{max} = \frac{\omega}{1 + b/a} \tag{21}$$

where V_{max} = rate of responding with infinite time
ω = maximum possible rate of responding when $p = 1$; "activity level"
b/a = ratio of the constants from the operator

What does this maximum mean? The final rate of responding increases with a, hence with the amount of reinforcement, and decreases with b, the amount of work required in responding (or other negative influences). Under most circumstances the maximum possible rate (ω)

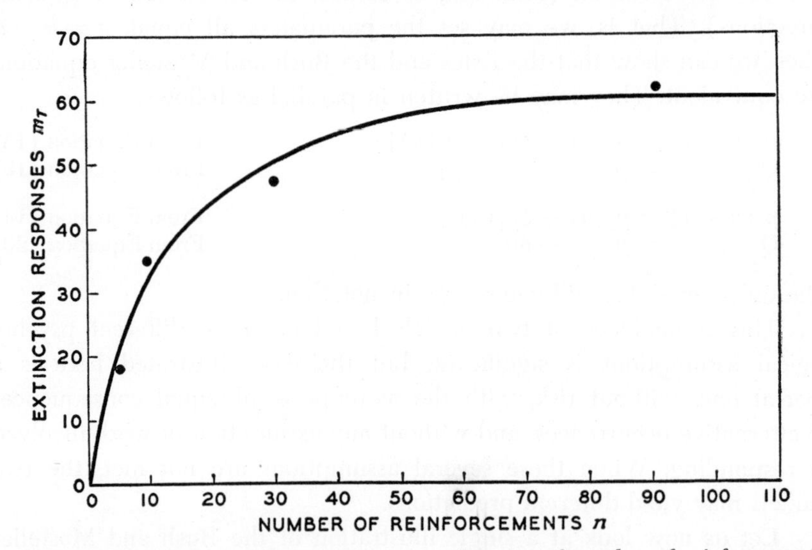

FIGURE 59. Total extinction responses as a function of number of reinforcements. Data from Williams (1938). Smooth curve as derived from Bush and Mosteller's learning model. After Bush and Mosteller (1951a), page 320.

will not be approached, even with long-continued practice. For example, when $a = b$, the maximum rate will be $V_{max} = 0.5\omega$. This formulation is missing from the Estes-Burke model, which does not take into account the work required in responding.

By similar mathematical processes it is possible to derive an equation for the total number of responses to some criterion of extinction,

[25] Details of the derivations here summarized very sketchily are found in Bush and Mosteller (1951a), pages 317–319.

provided only the rate of responding at the beginning of extinction (V_e) is known. This turns out:

$$m_T = \frac{1}{b} \log \frac{V_e}{V_f} \tag{22}$$

where m_T = total responses to a criterion of extinction
b = constant from the operator
V_e = rate of response at beginning of extinction
V_f = final rate at "end" of extinction (i.e., criterion for empirically "completed" extinction)

Equation (22) fits the data of Skinner-type extinction curves. But we wish to go one step further in fitting the Williams data of Figure 59. We must express the total number of extinction responses as a function of n, the number of reinforcements.

The original operator, if repeatedly applied, produces a curve of acquisition very similar to that of Estes and Burke in Equation (16). In the notation of Bush and Mosteller we have:

$$Q^n p = \left(\frac{a}{a+b}\right) - \left(\frac{a}{a+b} - p\right)(1 - a - b)^n \tag{23}$$

where $Q^n p$ = probability of response after n reinforcements.
a, b = the constants from the operator
n = number of reinforcements
p = probability of response at the beginning of reinforcement

A transformation involving some additional steps that need not concern us rewrites Equation (23) in terms of rates of response at the beginning (V_0), when extinction is undertaken (V_e), and at the maximum (V_{max}):

$$V_e = V_{max} - (V_{max} - V_0)(1 - a - b)^n \tag{24}$$

Note that to produce identity between the Estes Equation (17) and the Bush and Mosteller Equation (24) we need only make the following assumptions:

$V_{max} = \pi$
$a = \theta$
$b = 0$ (for Estes does not consider the work factor)

We return now to the problem of fitting the Williams data. The main relationships are contained in Equations (22) and (24). The second of these relates the rate of responding at the time extinction is begun to the number of prior reinforcements, while the first predicts how many extinction responses will follow this level of responding. All we need to do is substitute Equation (24) into Equation (22) and we have our required equation. We have:

$$m_{\mathrm{T}} = \frac{1}{\mathrm{b}} \log \left\{ \frac{\mathrm{V}_{\max}}{\mathrm{V}_f} - \left[\frac{\mathrm{V}_{\max}}{\mathrm{V}_f} - \frac{\mathrm{V}_0}{\mathrm{V}_f} \right] (1 - a - b)^n \right\} \tag{25}$$

Inspection of the Williams data led Bush and Mosteller to set $\mathrm{V}_{\max}/\mathrm{V}_f = 5$, and $\mathrm{V}_0 = \mathrm{V}_f$. After this gross empirical step, the constants a and b were determined by curve-fitting, yielding $a = .014$ and $b = .026$. Substituting these values, Equation (25) reduces to the following:

$$m_{\mathrm{T}} = \frac{1}{.026} \log \left\{ 5 - [4](.96)^n \right\} \tag{26}$$

It is now clear that we have an equation in which m_{T}, the total responses to extinction, can be computed by substituting a value for n, the number of reinforcements. This is the computation that produced the points from which the smooth curve of Figure 59 was constructed. The fit, as we see by inspection, is satisfactory.

This one specimen can serve as the barest introduction to the Bush and Mosteller models, which have recently been published in book form.[26]

Relative Success of Stochastic Models

The models of Estes, Estes and Burke, and of Bush and Mosteller have been quite successful in predicting the course of events within lever-pressing problems, simple runway problems, discrimination, and reactions to uncertainty. Data have been derived from both animal and human experimentation.

Because of the common choice of an exponential function (essentially of the form Hull found so convenient in his extensive curve-fitting), theories derived from a variety of assumptions are all rather successful in fitting empirical data. Hence success in curve-fitting does not permit choice from among the theories. A more penetrating question to be asked of them is whether or not the *constants* that show up in their equations are consistent. The real test of a "rational" equation begins with the interchangeability of the constants from one situation to another. (If constants vary systematically, the varied constants must also be interchangeable.) A further test (for which contemporary theories are not yet ready) is to provide independent justification and measurement of the constants. For example, the speed of light shows up as a constant in many physical

[26] Bush and Mosteller (1955). The book had not yet appeared when this chapter was written.

equations. But the speed of light can be measured, and thus can give independent justification for identifying the constant with the speed of light. If Estes' constant θ represents some fraction of the total stimulus elements effective at once, there ought to be some way of demonstrating this directly. Similarly, Bush and Mosteller's constants a and b ought to have independent justification through quantitative studies of motivation and work, independent of learning. But this more searching analysis of the theories can wait until the success with interchangeable constants is demonstrated.

Mosteller (1953) has presented a table showing the value of Estes and Burke's θ as derived from a number of symmetrical two-choice situations, resembling the experiment of Grant, Hake, and Hornseth previously described, but also including some experiments arranged as a gambling set-up, in which the subject had to pay to play, and thus had additional motivation for desiring to win. Mosteller's table is reproduced as Table 6.

Two things need to be said about this table:

1. Of 22 determinations with rats, high school students, and college students, under a variety of conditions including many pay-off frequencies, the value of θ is either .03 or .04 in 14 cases, and only four cases lie outside the range of .02 to .05. This is rather interesting agreement, considering that all the data are fitted in accordance with a single parameter.

A word of caution is in order. At the asymptote π (or V_{max}) the term that includes θ (or a and b in the other system) approaches zero, so that the prediction of the *value* of the asymptote is independent of θ. The value of θ specifies the *rate* at which the asymptote is approached, and a slight change in θ may make a great change in the number of trials required to approach the asymptote. For example, let us set the quantity $(1 - \theta)^n = .01$. Then by substituting values of θ and solving for n we can see what difference θ makes in the number of trials required to approach to within a standard distance of the asymptote. By this calculation the range of trials required to approach the asymptote with a θ of .05 is 90 trials, whereas with a θ of .02 the corresponding value is 228 trials. Hence very small changes in θ may produce significant differences in the number of trials required to reach some criterion of mastery.[27]

[27] Dr. Douglas H. Lawrence, who called my attention to the importance of small differences in θ, also points out that θ varies more widely if the usual method of least squares is abandoned in favor of the method of maximum likelihood in fitting curves

TABLE 6. Value of Estes' θ Computed from a Number of Symmetric Two-Choice Situations. After Mosteller, 1953, page 42.

Pay-off Frequencies	*Experimenter, Subjects, Conditions*	*Value of θ*
100:0	Stanley (rats in T-maze)	.04
	Jarrett (Harvard students)	
	—pay to play	.11
	—free play	.05
50:0	Stanley (rats in T-maze)	.04
	Jarrett (Harvard students)	
	—pay to play	.04
	—free play	.02
	Robillard (students)	
	—rewards of 0-cents	.04
	—rewards of 1-cent	.03
	—rewards of 5-cents	.03
	Cards (high school students)	.04
	(Harvard students)	.07
75:25	Stanley (rats in T-maze)	.04
	Jarrett (Harvard students)	
	—pay to play	.03
	Estes (students)	.04
	Jarvik (students)	.05
100:50	Jarrett (Harvard students)	
	—pay to play	.07
80:0	Robillard (students)	
	—no rewards	.06
80:40	Robillard (students)	
	—no rewards	.03
67:33	Jarvik (students)	.03
60:40	Jarvik (students)	.02
60:30	Robillard (students)	
	—no rewards	.03
30:0	Robillard (students)	
	—no rewards	.03

2. The four cases in which the parameter disagrees strikingly with the rest are psychologically interesting, and pose important problems for theory.

For example, in the 100:0 problem it makes a real difference whether or not the Harvard students had to pay one cent to operate a slot machine in order to win one cent. Also the fact that 100:50 has consequences

to empirical data. The method of maximum likelihood is more appropriate than the method of least squares because it weights more heavily the approach to the asymptote. The approach to the asymptote best tests the constancy of θ.

different from 50:0 is psychologically interesting. From a probability point of view these are alike (provided we weight positive and negative cases equally): certainty on one side and a 50:50 chance on the other. Yet they are unlike in the pattern of responses they call out from the subject. These discordant results show that some supplementary assumptions are needed before the theories can be considered completely general.

The models described are, of course, unfinished ones. The original model-builders are carrying on with them, and others have come along with new suggestions. For example, Restle (1955) has presented a variation of the model in which θ is interpreted as the proportion of *relevant* cues.[28] This turns out to be a simplifying assumption, so far as discrimination is concerned, and leads to some satisfactory predictions. Restle's work comes nearer to providing an independent measure of what is essentially Estes' θ, and shows circumstances under which θ values change.

THE PLACE OF MATHEMATICS IN LEARNING

With the advance of psychology as a science there will inevitably be an increased use of mathematics. Mathematics is the language of measurement, of precision, of prediction. Yet there is no royal road to scientific achievement and mathematics must remain subservient to observation and reflection. Instruments of precision in the laboratory are also the means of scientific progress, but we all know that in the wrong hands they may lead to narrowness and triviality instead of to advance. Therefore we need to examine mathematics critically as a powerful tool, but not a magical one.

The Improvement of Data

The relationship between theory and data is circular: without theories we do not know what data to look for, and without good data we cannot test our theories.

We have been greatly helped in the improvement of our data through that branch of applied mathematics known as statistics. We have learned how to test the significance of differences, how to express reliability and validity of scores, how to use correlation as a measure of relationship, and factor analysis to comprehend a table of intercorrelations. We

[28] The concept of relevant and irrelevant cues is discussed by Lawrence (1950), with experimental justification for the distinction.

have gone ahead to learn more about the design of experiments so that results can be secured both economically and in a form suitable for statistical treatment. Statisticians have helped us also in the construction of scales by which data can be ordered, and we have learned to distinguish between interval scales and ratio scales.

These services of statistics are reflected throughout the experimental study of learning. Because through the better application of statistical methods the yield of data is better, the learning theorist is helped. He needs satisfactory data if he is to test with any precision the predictions from his theories.

The Improvement of Theory

Theory has often had a rather bad name, being associated with "idle speculation." Modern theory, closely in contact with data, is essential to the advance of psychology as a science. Just as statistics helps the experimenter to go about his business, so the contemporary mathematical models help the theorist who wishes to bring order out of existing data and make it possible for him to suggest new experiments that need doing.

The advantages of models have been summarized by Estes (1953) as follows:

1. Information incorporated in a model is in a form suitable for prediction.

2. The results of different experiments often become more nearly comparable when referred to the same formal model.

3. The quantitative analysis of data may be facilitated by the model. Hidden or confounded variables can often be unraveled if the mathematical model is a good one.

4. Because of the rigor engendered by the model, theoretical assumptions can be given more precise test than without the model.

Mosteller (1953), in commenting on Estes' paper, goes further into the advantages of mathematical models over ordinary curve-fitting. He points out that with a good model a great many questions can be answered on the basis of a very few numbers (perhaps as few as two or three computed parameters). Some types of questions that he says might be answered are:

1. What is the average trial number of the last failure?

2. What is the average length of runs of failures?

3. What is the standard deviation of the trial number on which the tenth success is achieved?

4. What is the probability that a man who has failed on trials 7, 8, and 10 will succeed on trial 14?

He points out that routine curve-fitting would require new calculations direct from data in order to answer each of these questions. He concludes: "Thus, in a reasonable sense the few constants plus the model can contain nearly all the useful information in the original data."

The purpose of the model is clear enough. It provides a formal theoretical structure into which data can be fitted, and it permits the statement of testable scientific propositions about the relationships among the data.

Some Cautions

The fascination and promise of mathematical theories are so great that a word or two of caution may be appropriate. That is, we need to keep all developments in proper perspective. It is not a question of being for or against the development of mathematical models. They should most certainly be developed, but in their appropriate relationship to other aspects of science. The following statements call attention to some of the considerations that ought to be kept in mind as mathematical theories are evaluated.

1. The history of science tells us that some of the most important developments in the relation of mathematics to science came about with very simple mathematics. Thus chemistry and atomic theory generally were enormously advanced by the law of combining proportions (Gay-Lussac's law), which stated simply that the combining volumes of gases entering into compounds could be stated as simple whole numbers. Thus the ratio of hydrogen and oxygen combining to form water is 2:1. What mathematics could be simpler? Another advance in atomic theory was Mendeleev's periodic arrangement of the elements. He noted a kind of periodicity in which, with elements arranged in order of increasing atomic weights, certain elements resembled earlier ones in valence and other properties. Again, the simplest of mathematics, with the most profound results. Or, to choose another field, consider Mendel's famous ratio of 3:1 for the types showing up after a given kind of mating. Here is the background for the modern science of genetics. What these examples suggest is that scientific advance comes when the right concepts are discovered. The right concepts may prove to be beautifully simple and capable of very simple mathematical expression. The complicated mathematics becomes more useful later, after work goes on within the right concept system.

This is not, of course, a complete history of science, and sometimes it has required real mathematical genius to bring scientific advance. Had Kepler not been a skilled mathematician he could not have brought order out of the very complex mass of data left by Tycho Brahé. When by a series of curve-fitting attempts he found that he could fit the path of Mars with an elipse, his "model" created a kind of order until the more satisfactory "model" of Newton succeeded his. The fact remains, however, that the search for the most appropriate concepts by which to harmonize scientific data often may not require complex mathematics.

2. The verification of a scientific theory is a slow process, and a few successes do not suffice to assure the enduring value of the theory. As we have seen, theories starting out with different assumptions may account for some of the same data. As long as competing hypotheses are in the running, further tests are needed to permit choice among them. A really poor model gets rejected early, but a plausible model may survive for some time before it is discarded in favor of a better one.

3. A model is appropriate to a limited range of phenomena at most. This fact is ignored in two ways. The first way in which the limitations are ignored is by the model-builder who is tempted to generalize the applicability of his model beyond the data to which it is appropriate. This is all right, provided he is as cautious in his extrapolations as he is in his model-building, but the temptation is great to argue by analogy without testing the analogy as carefully as it needs to be tested. The second way in which these limitations are ignored is by the critic who brings in as a refutation of the model some data that the model does not propose to handle.[29]

4. Models starting with unlike assumptions may be complementary rather than competitive. A model such as that of Pitts (1943), which follows the Rashevsky pattern in making assumptions about the nervous system as the basis for a model of conditioning and learning, may complement a model such as that of Bush and Mosteller that is concerned with events going on at the level of learning data. In other words, it may turn out that more than one model is "true," in the sense that it fairly represents reality when that reality is abstracted in a certain way.

5. Mathematical models are not foolproof, even when the mathematics used is elegant and accurate. Mathematical arguments have to be scrutinized for fallacies just as verbal arguments do. It is usually easier to detect the error in mathematics than in verbal statement, but not always. The mathematical system is self-contained, but its appropriate-

[29] This point has been made by Spence (1952b).

ness for a given set of data always involves assumptions, some of which may be far from obvious. For example, more than one process may be symbolized by a common parameter. We have seen how the parameter b in the Bush and Mosteller model stands for inhibitory processes such as punishment and work. But this is a large order! Whenever b appears in an equation it is appropriately multiplied or divided or squared, but if punishment and work are not processes that act alike, this parameter does not fully represent them. Estes' model is supposed to get along without assumptions about reinforcement or extinction, yet the operators distinguish between success and failure in a manner that looks suspiciously as though some kind of "feedback" is implied. The mathematical model is not going to save us from theoretical arguments, although it may perhaps save us from foolish ones.

6. Because mathematical models are useful ones, it does not follow that they will pre-empt the field, and that no other kind of theory will be worth listening to. Guthrie's theory, which provides the background of assumptions for Estes, was derived without benefit of mathematics. Freud's various theories, possibly the most influential of all in the psychology of the twentieth century, were developed by observations unaided with either instruments or mathematics. While mathematical models deserve prestige, they need not lead to the neglect of other kinds of theorizing.

SUPPLEMENTARY READINGS

BOOKS

Relevant mathematical models from non-psychological fields

ARROW, K. J. (1951) *Social choice and individual values.*
BROSS, I. D. J. (1953) *Design for decision.*
MORSE, P., and KIMBALL, G. (1951) *Methods in operations research.*
RASHEVSKY, N. (1938) *Mathematical biophysics.*
SHANNON, C. E., and WEAVER, W. (1949) *The mathematical theory of communication.*
TRUXAL, J. G. (1955) *Automatic feedback system synthesis.*
VON NEUMANN, J., and MORGENSTERN, O. (1947) *Theory of games and economic behavior.*
WIENER, N. (1948) *Cybernetics.*

Mathematical models in psychology and learning theory

BUSH, R. R., and MOSTELLER, F. (1955) *Stochastic models for learning.*
HOUSEHOLDER, A. S., and LANDAHL, H. D. (1945) *Mathematical biophysics of the central nervous system.*
HULL, C. L., and others (1940) *Mathematico-deductive theory of rote learning.*

Lazarsfeld, P. F., ed. (1954) *Mathematical thinking in the social sciences.*
Thrall, R. M., Coombs, C. H., and Davis, R. L., eds. (1954) *Decision processes.*

SHORTER INTRODUCTIONS

Arrow, K. J. (1951) Mathematical models in the social sciences. In D. Lerner and H. D. Lasswell, eds. *The policy sciences.* 129–154.

Bertalanffy, L. von (1951) Theoretical models in biology and psychology. *J. Personality,* 20, 24–38.

Coombs, C. H., Raiffa, H., and Thrall, R. M. (1954) Some views on mathematical models and measurement theory. *Psychol. Rev.,* 61, 132–144.

Ellson, D. G. (1949) Application of operational analysis to human motor behavior. *Psychol. Rev.,* 56, 9–17.

Grant, D. A. (1954) The discrimination of sequences in stimulus events and the transmission of information. *Amer. Psychologist,* 9, 62–68.

Miller, G. A. (1953) What is information measurement? *Amer. Psychologist,* 8, 3–11.

Mowrer, O. H. (1954) Ego psychology, cybernetics, and learning theory. In Kentucky Symposium. *Learning theory, personality theory, and clinical research,* 81–90.

Spence, K. W. (1952) Mathematical formulations of learning phenomena. *Psychol. Rev.,* 59, 152–160.

REPRESENTATIVE PAPERS ON MATHEMATICAL MODELS FOR LEARNING TESTED AGAINST EMPIRICAL FINDINGS

Bush, R. R., Mosteller, F., and Thompson, G. L. (1954) A formal structure for multiple-choice situations. In R. M. Thrall, C. H. Coombs, and R. L. Davis, eds. *Decision processes,* 99–126.

Estes, W. K. (1954) Individual behavior in uncertain situations: an interpretation in terms of statistical association theory. In R. M. Thrall, C. H. Coombs, and R. L. Davis, eds. *Decision processes,* 127–137.

Flood, M. M. (1954) On game-learning theory and some decision-making experiments. In R. M. Thrall, C. H. Coombs, and R. L. Davis, eds. *Decision processes,* 139–158.

Frick, F. C., and Miller, G. A. (1951) A statistical description of operant conditioning. *Amer. J. Psychol.,* 64, 20–36.

Graham, C. H., and Gagné, R. M. (1940) The acquisition, extinction, and spontaneous recovery of a conditioned operant response. *J. exp. Psychol.,* 26, 251–281.

Gulliksen, H., and Wolfle, D. L. (1938) A theory of learning and transfer. *Psychometrika,* 3, 127–149; 225–261.

Hovland, C. I., and Weiss, W. (1953) Transmission of information concerning concepts through positive and negative instances. *J. exp. Psychol.,* 45, 175–182.

Miller, G. A., and McGill, W. J. (1952) A statistical description of verbal learning. *Psychometrika,* 17, 369–396.

Pitts, W. (1943) A general theory of learning and conditioning. *Psychometrika,* 8, 1–18; 131–140.

Restle, F. (1955) A theory of discrimination learning. *Psychol. Rev.,* 62, 11–19.

Spence, K. W. (1936) The nature of discrimination learning in animals. *Psychol. Rev.,* 43, 427–449.

Thurstone, L. L. (1933) The error function in maze learning. *J. gen. Psychol.,* 9, 288–301.

Chapter 12

CURRENT DEVELOPMENTS: I. REINFORCEMENT AND DRIVE

IN an active field of research, with continuous interaction between experimentation and theorizing, we do not expect the younger generation to remain loyal to the past. In other words, we cannot expect the students of Thorndike to remain simply Thorndikian, those of Guthrie simply Guthrian, or those of Tolman merely Tolmanian. Yet we do find some of the preoccupations of the newer generation reflecting a background of training under one or another of the earlier systematists. Contemporary developments can best be understood if they are reflected against a thorough understanding of the earlier systems. One role of history is so to familiarize us with persistent and recurrent issues that we gain perspective on the conflicts and quarrels of the present. Recent history is no less important for this purpose than more remote history. Here lies the justification for the treatment of the separate systems in the earlier chapters of this book. In the process of historical development some of the earlier cleavages will become blurred as newer controversies take the center of the stage, and eventually there may be entirely new alignments.

It is instructive to review a listing of learning theories made in 1926 by Perrin and Klein.[1] They listed (1) pleasure-pain theory, (2) modified pleasure-pain (Thorndike), (3) confirmation-inhibition (Hobhouse), (4) congruity theory (Holmes), (5) drive or motor-set theory (Woodworth, Tolman), (6) completeness of response (Peterson), (7) frequency-recency (Watson), (8) intensity (Carr), and (9) conditioned-reflex theory (Smith and Guthrie). Many of the issues dealt with in these theories of 1926 are still current, and many of the same names continue to appear in theoretical discussion today. But the lines of demarcation by which the theories could be grouped into major families had not yet become clear. Gestalt learning theory had not yet become influential in America, Tol-

[1] Perrin and Klein (1926), pages 218–243.

man had not yet sharpened his views, and the positions of Hull and Skinner were still unborn. It may very well happen that in a few years from now the chapter divisions of this book will be as inappropriate to newer issues as the divisions of 1926 are today. The recent distinction between the two families of theories, stimulus-response theories and cognitive theories, is already in the process of breaking down, partly because of increased interest all around in problems of perception, partly because of the emergence of information-theory as a device for objectifying some aspects of cognitive processes, partly because of the awkward number of qualifications in respect to present theories, necessitated by the unceasing impact of new experimental data.

Because of the rapidity of developments, a chapter of this kind cannot serve either as a thorough or an up-to-date review of the contemporary literature.[2] All it can do is to call attention to some lines of development that appear promising or important, citing a few theoretical and experimental articles as indicative of the trends.

THE INTERPRETATION OF REINFORCEMENT

Within stimulus-response theories a basic issue has been the interpretation of reinforcement, dividing the systematists within the group into contiguity-theorists and reinforcement-theorists. These differences are often referred to the two patterns of conditioned response: *classical conditioning* and *instrumental* or *operant conditioning*. These paradigms are in turn correlated with two classes of laboratory experiment, that of Pavlov ("classical") and that of Skinner ("instrumental," "operant"). An experiment seldom provides a "pure case" representing a theoretical model, and the existence of the two kinds of conditioning experiments does not necessarily require two theoretical explanations of conditioning. Some psychologists, such as Guthrie, who adopt a theory more appropriate to classical conditioning as a paradigm, believe that a response that occurs gets conditioned merely because stimulus and response are contiguous. Others, such as Hull, adopting the other paradigm, believe that contiguous occurrence of stimulus and response leads to conditioning only when followed by another event: reinforcement. An out-and-out contiguity theorist will *derive* the results of reinforcement from his theory. Guthrie's solution, we recall, is to show that reward (reinforcement) merely prevents unlearning what was learned through contiguous association. An out-and-out reinforcement theorist will deny *mere* con-

[2] This purpose is served better by the reviews appearing in the *Psychological Bulletin* and the *Annual Review of Psychology*.

tiguous conditioning by arguing that *some* reinforcement (primary or secondary) is always present when learning occurs, even under the experimental arrangements of classical conditioning. Pavlov's dog, after all, was hungry and ate after salivating. A third position, advanced by others (e.g., Skinner, Schlosberg, Mowrer) is that the two kinds of conditioning may require two kinds of theory, one typified by learning under contiguity alone, the other by learning under reinforcement. These several possibilities all lie within stimulus-response theory.[3]

Not all reinforcement-systematists have a "theory" of reinforcement. That is, one can accept the fact that certain kinds of events are reinforcing because they lead to the appearance of conditioned responses or to increase of habit strength, and let it go at that.[4] A learning theorist such as Skinner or Spence who is not interested in the physiological substratum of learning does not deny that learning goes on in the body. He may simply turn the problems of the physiology of learning over to someone else. So, too, the theorist interested in interrelationships among learning data may not concern himself about the intimate relationship between reinforcement and physiological needs. The commonest interpretation of reinforcement, however, can be traced back to Sherrington's preparatory and consummatory response. It now goes by the name of the *drive-reduction* theory. We have, of course, met this before, particularly in Hull's theory. The basic sequence is that deprivation produces a state of need in the organism. This need finds representation psychologically as a tension state known as drive, a state that energizes into action and produces stimuli associated with it. Thus the food-deprived animal shows the restless activity characteristic of the hunger drive, and the stimuli associated with the drive lead to food-seeking. This restless state of tension is brought to an end when food is ingested, because food is "consummatory." That is, food restores the bodily depletion, reduces drive, and removes the associated stimuli, bringing the cycle to an end. Primary reinforcement is interpreted as related to the last portion of the deprivation-activity-satiation cycle. That is, a primary reinforcing state of affairs is one that reduces drive through satisfying need. We shall see that not all re-

[3] The issues are met so differently by cognitive theorists that it would be very difficult to treat their views in this section.

[4] The term "reinforcement" may be used broadly or narrowly. We have favored the broadest and most nearly neutral definition of reinforcement, permitting it to refer to the presentation of the stimulus that serves as the unconditioned stimulus in classical conditioning or as the rewarding stimulus in instrumental conditioning. This broad use permits speaking of the number of reinforcements necessary before a conditioned response appears in classical conditioning. MacCorquodale (1955), page 48, recommends a narrower meaning, for he requires an antecedent response before it is permissible to speak of reinforcement. More specialized meanings of reinforcement in what follows will be clear from the context.

inforcement theorists hold that drive reduction is necessary for learning, yet drive reduction remains the basic paradigm for explaining why a reinforcing event is reinforcing.

In the recent literature of reinforcement theory, secondary reinforcement has come to play an increasing role. Even in Hull's (1943) drive-reduction interpretation, secondary reinforcement did not have to be drive-reducing. Its effectiveness, however, was said to wear off unless it was sustained by association with primary reinforcement. Hence the mechanism of primary reinforcement remained of central interest.

In the early 1950's a number of investigators began to report the results of experiments designed to study the reinforcement process more directly than it had been studied before. Suspicion became aroused that much that had been classed as primary reinforcement was really secondary. For example, it takes a long time after eating before the food produces nutritive changes in the body that will alter materially the tissue state associated with food depletion. Yet the reinforcing action is more prompt than this. Possibly even food—the standard incentive for "primary" reinforcement—is actually yielding relationships based on secondary reinforcement, or, as an alternative interpretation, possibly need reduction is not essential even to primary reinforcement. These doubts and queries have led to a variety of experiments and a variety of interpretations.

Sheffield's Prepotent-Response Interpretation

In order to test the need-reduction theory of reinforcement, Sheffield and his collaborators designed experiments in which the incentive used as the reinforcement could be responded to but without satisfying the physiological need to which that incentive was appropriate. Sheffield and Roby (1950) showed that the non-nutritive sweet taste of saccharin could serve as a reward in rat learning, even though no *metabolic* relief of hunger was involved. Later experiments showed that the reinforcing value of a sweet taste depended primarily on the amount of evoked consummatory activity (Sheffield, Roby, and Campbell, 1954). Sheffield, Wulff, and Backer (1951) showed similarly that naive male rats would learn to run and leap over hurdles in order to copulate with receptive females even though no ejaculation was permitted. The rate of learning depended upon the amount of copulation, so that prepotent act of copulation was important in the reinforcement sequence, even though the release of physiological sexual tensions through ejaculation did not occur. These experiments seriously question the importance for reinforcement of satisfying primary drives either through making up depletions (as in satisfying hunger) or through relieving excess tensions (as in discharges from the male sex organs).

Sheffield, in offering the theory of prepotent responses, is very close to Guthrie, whose views he has often defended. He has used these experiments, in fact, in support of a contiguity interpretation of learning.[5]

Neal E. Miller's Theory of Stimulus-Intensity Reduction

Because, for Miller, any strong stimulus can become a drive and impel to action, his drive-reduction theory of reinforcement is really a *stimulus-intensity-reduction* theory.[6]

We have learned that it is too much to expect to find a crucial experiment that will resolve our disputes once and for all. Miller's reply to Sheffield's experiments is contained in the results of a series of experiments in which the consequences of food in the mouth can be compared with food in the stomach as reinforcing agents. If food injected into the stomach is reinforcing, this is obviously a threat to Sheffield's prepotent response theory. For example, using the stomach-fistula method, Miller and Kessen (1952) taught rats a simple T-maze when milk followed choice of the correct side and normal saline solution followed choice of the incorrect side. When the incentive substances were received by mouth the animals learned faster, but they also learned when the reinforcement was received by stomach (Figure 60).[7] The authors believe that their results support the drive-reduction theory and refute Sheffield's prepotent-response hypothesis. That learning was faster by mouth would be expected from the support given to the learning via secondary reinforcement.

In developing his form of drive-reduction theory, Miller has struggled particularly with the problems created by learned drive (fear) based upon pain. The empirical situation is well established. It is possible to shock a rat in the white compartment of a two-compartment box, and arouse fear. Placed again in the box, without shock, he shows all the signs of a "conditioned" fear. Given an opportunity to jump a hurdle, turn a wheel, or in some other manner find his way out of the compartment to a "safe" one in which he has not been shocked, he "learns" this

[5] Sheffield (1951).

[6] Miller and Dollard (1941), Dollard and Miller (1950), Miller (1951a) (1951b).

[7] Saccharin has been shown to reduce subsequent food consumption when taken by mouth, but not by stomach fistula, by Miller, Murray, and Roberts (1955).

mode of escape. The drive reduction that serves as the reinforcement is the reduction of fear.[8] To hold consistently to a drive-reduction theory of reinforcement, it is necessary to account for the rat's fear of the compartment in which he was shocked. It does not do to fall back upon classical conditioning and to account for the rat's agitation as a substitution of the

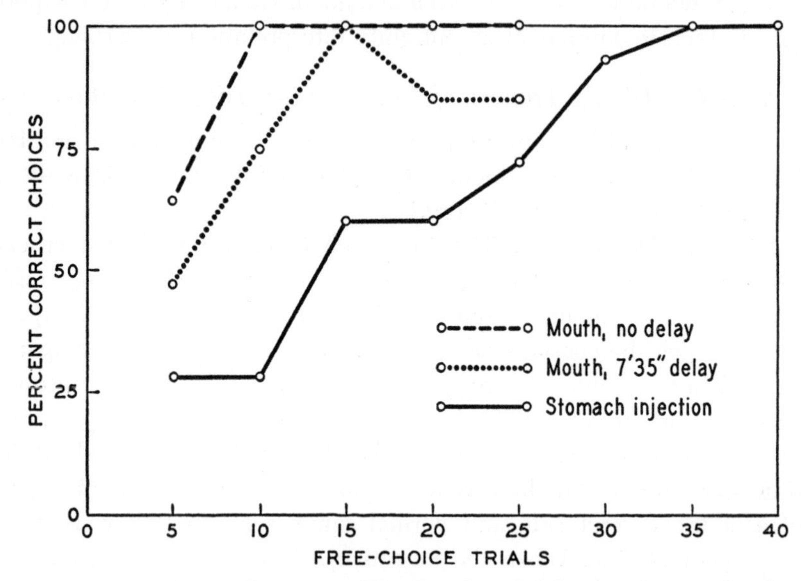

FIGURE 60. Correct choices to milk side when fed by mouth immediately and with delay, and when fed by fistula. Miller and Kessen (1952), page 560.

previously neutral compartment for the shock that caused the agitation in the box-shock trials. Miller recognizes that in order to be consistent he must assume that the agitated responses are reinforced as all other responses are, namely, by stimulus reduction, hence in this case by *termination* of the painful stimulus. He adopts this interpretation of what happens, though he confesses some uneasiness about it.[9]

Because strong stimulation is not necessarily based upon a need state, Miller's theory has a genuine advantage over Hull's in that it yields a unified interpretation of primary and learned drives and of primary and secondary reinforcement. In his words:

> Thus the basic mechanism of motivation (strong stimulation) is the same for primary and learned drives, and the basic mechanism of reinforcement (a reduction in strong stimulation) is the same for primary and learned rewards.[10]

[8] Miller (1948a). See also Brown and Jacobs (1949).
[9] Miller (1951a), page 375.
[10] Miller (1951b), page 440. The attempt to provide a demonstration of a learned drive based on hunger has not proved successful, Myers and Miller (1954).

Mowrer's Two-Factor Theory

Mowrer early saw the possibility that much learning could be accounted for on the basis of reinforcement motivated by acquired fear, or by anxiety, as he then called it. His was the first clear statement of the anxiety-reduction or fear-reduction theory of reinforcement.[11] Reflecting upon the same problem that bothered Miller, the problem of how fear is acquired via pain, Mowrer later came to reject the drive-reduction theory, and returned to the familiar stimulus-substitution theory of classical conditioning. But he saved the drive-reduction theory for instrumental learning, and thus came to espouse a *two-factor* theory.[12]

The interpretation of learning as a dual process was not new. We met it in Thorndike's associative shifting and learning under the law of effect. We met it also in Skinner's two types, Type S and Type R. A somewhat similar proposal had been made by Schlosberg (1937). Mowrer's espousal of the dual theory was important, however, because it represented a conversion to the position by one who had been rather closely identified with the drive-reduction unified theory. He thus set himself in direct opposition to the views of Miller, although both men were producing related experimental results.

Mowrer, in elaborating the two-factor theory, has used the term *sign learning* for simple conditioning of the stimulus-substitution or associative-shifting variety, and *solution learning* for trial-and-error learning under reinforcement. He writes:

> In order to make a two-factor theory work, "conditioning," it now appears, must be restricted to the process whereby emotions, meanings, attitudes, appetites, and cognitions are acquired, with "solution learning" applying to all cases of overt instrumental habit formation.[13]

Mowrer believed that he found support for his theory in the differences in function between the autonomic and the central nervous system. Emotional responses, of which fear is an example, are largely involuntary and are chiefly under the control of the autonomic system. Problem-solving responses, instrumental responses, are largely voluntary, skeletal, under the control of the central nervous system. Hence it would not be surprising if in the course of evolution different principles of learning

[11] The early paper is Mowrer (1939). It is reproduced with later comments by its author in Mowrer (1950). He and Miller have long been concerned about very similar problems, and while they were together at Yale they collaborated on a demonstration apparatus to exhibit the learned behavior in which they were both interested, Mowrer and Miller (1942).

[12] Mowrer (1947) (1950) (1951) (1954b).

[13] Mowrer (1951), page 352.

might have developed, their dissimilarities showing in the differing activities of these two systems.

The issue is sharp between Mowrer's interpretation and Miller's. The latter, holding to his unified theory, runs somewhat up against the intuitions of ordinary experience. That is, we seem ordinarily to be apprehensive about the expected *onset* of pain, and it is hard to believe that our fears are strengthened because pain subsides quickly. In order to refute the theory that conditioning of fear depends upon the termination of pain, Mowrer and Suter [14] performed an experiment in which a flickering light served as the conditioned stimulus. The subject could avoid a shock by running to the opposite end of the apparatus during the first 5 seconds of the persisting conditioned stimulus. If however, the shock came on (as it did at the end of 5 seconds) there was no way to escape it, and it continued for 10 seconds. The two conditions of the experiment were (1) terminating the conditioned stimulus at the *onset* of the shock, and (2) terminating the conditioned stimulus at the *end* of the shock. Mowrer argued that Miller's theory should produce greater conditioning under condition (2), since the end of shock is reinforcing; whereas his theory would predict no difference in the two methods, since coincidence with onset is common to both, and is all that matters. The results confirmed Mowrer's deductions from his theory, in that there was no significant difference between the two groups.

Miller (1951a) rejected the interpretation of the Mowrer and Suter experiment, basing his case in part on criticisms by Kendler (1951) and Sheffield (1951), and on some results of Sullivan (1950) that appear to support his own theory. We must leave this issue as unresolved.[15]

Mowrer's theory is currently undergoing revision, but the new theory is too recent for critical exposition here. The two factors of the original version have given way to two new factors: *incremental* fear conditioning (secondary motivation), and *decremental* fear conditioning (secondary reinforcement). In the new theory, all learning is sign learning.[16]

Spence's Interpretation of the Role of Reinforcement

In his recent formulation of his position in the Silliman Lectures at Yale, Spence (1955) has reiterated his lack of active interest in how reinforcement works, for example, whether or not it is drive-reducing or

[14] Reported in Mowrer (1950), pages 278–287.

[15] For additional evidence on Mowrer's theory, see Mowrer and Solomon (1954) and Mowrer and Aiken (1954). On Miller's side, see Zeaman, Deane, and Wegner (1954).

[16] Mowrer (1955).

need-reducing. He has preferred all along to adopt the empirical law of effect (in this agreeing with Skinner) and then to deal with quantitative relationships, using (unlike Skinner) an approach via intervening variables.

Because Spence's views are commonly held to be close to those of Hull, he is careful to point out what differences there are between his general theoretical preferences and those of Hull. He makes four points:

1. In the first place, the formal hypothetico-deductive style, as used by Hull and others (1940), did not appeal to him as appropriate at this stage of learning theory. Along with Bergmann [17] he showed that Hull's theoretical successes lay rather in the intervening-variable approach, and it was the article in which they pointed this out (and the extensive correspondence then being carried on between Hull and Spence) that led Hull in his 1943 book to characterize his method in terms of intervening variables and to borrow this term from Tolman.

2. Spence felt that Hull went farther than necessary in attempting to give neurophysiological specification to his intervening variables. Although Spence prefers to remain neutral with respect to physiological interpretations, he would have no objection, of course, to genuinely *fruitful* physiological concepts.

3. Whereas Hull adopted reduction in drive strength (or reduction in drive stimuli) as essential to reinforcement, Spence did not commit himself on these issues, holding instead merely to the empirical law of effect.

4. Finally, Spence prefers to develop his position step-by-step, with his ventures into theorizing always very close to data. Hull was rather more willing than he to make guesses in the form of "postulates" on the basis of minimum empirical evidence. Spence's objectives are stated thus:

> That is, the initial objective is to develop a set or system of concepts and postulated interrelationships which, in combination with the different initial and boundary conditions specific to each experimental situation, will provide for the deduction of the several kinds of conditioning laws that have been obtained. It is hoped further that this theory, along with the necessary additional composition rules, will permit one to account for more complex learning phenomena.[18]

Spence indicates two reasons why, over the years, he was not actively interested in the mechanism of reinforcement. The first was his interest in quantification, which he repeatedly pointed out did not require a theory of reinforcement.[19] The second was the difficulty that showed up in

[17] Bergmann and Spence (1941).
[18] Spence (1955), quoted from manuscript (Lecture 3).
[19] E.g., Spence (1952b).

experiments on latent learning of ever finding an experimental situation totally free of reinforcing events. It was the effort to explain the various things happening in latent-learning experiments that led to an interpretation of reinforcement important in Spence's contemporary theorizing.[20]

The contemporary theory accepts the association of stimuli and responses through their contiguous occurrence. Events at the goal are important. The conditioning that takes place in the goal-box is reinforced (as Pavlov's dog's salivation is reinforced) and no special theory of this reinforcement is presented. That is, for conditioning to occur, the subject must respond to the goal-object either by consuming it, or by perceiving it. This reinforcing act produces the conditioning of fractional goal responses (r_G) to stimulus cues throughout the response chain of the activity prior to the goal, and these conditioned responses (r_G) and the stimuli they produce (s_G) serve as important integrators of behavior, as they do in Hull's theory. The instrumental responses themselves, in this chain, are strengthened merely because they occur, and *not* because they are reinforced through some act at the end of the chain. The reinforcing act at the end of the chain strengthens the r_G's, and these affect earlier links of the chain as motivators rather than as contributors to habit strength. Thus the r_G-s_G mechanism becomes identified in Spence's theory with Hull's incentive motivation (K) rather than with habit strength (H). Differences in reaction potential of responses at different distances from the reinforcement end of the behavior chain are thus due to differences in the K factor rather than to differences in H.

Because reinforcement may be necessary for classical conditioning and is not decisive for instrumental learning, Spence toys with the notion (without committing himself to it) that he may have a two-factor theory just the opposite of Mowrer's:

> It is interesting to note that *if* one were to adopt a theory that reinforcement (e.g., need reduction) plays a decisive role in the acquisition of habit strength of classical conditioned responses but not in the case of instrumental conditioned responses, one would have a two-factor theory that is exactly the opposite of the well known two-factor theory espoused by Schlosberg, Mowrer and others.[21]

Because Spence's theory is becoming a major competitor to other theories, and is already leading to relevant experimental work, it is de-

[20] The theory has been developing over some years, and has been mentioned in the writings of some of Spence's students (e.g., Kendler, 1946). It was first elaborated more fully in Spence, Bergmann, and Lippitt (1950). See also Spence (1954a) (1954b).

[21] Spence (1955), quoted from manuscript (Lecture 5).

sirable to see an example of how it works out in quantitative studies. The theory does not, in fact, commit Spence to an interpretation of the *mechanism* of reinforcement for classical conditioning. It does, however, require that he demonstrate that the K factor (based on anticipatory goal responses) acts as drive does upon excitatory potential rather than as habit strength does.

If K acts as a drive, it will have a multiplicative relationship to H in the determination of E. That is, other things being equal,

$$E = H \times K \tag{1}$$

where E is reaction potential
H is habit strength
and K is the incentive motivator based on the fractional goal response

Equation (1) above is written in terms of intervening variables. What are the experimental variables correlated with these intervening variables? The diagram in Figure 61 shows how experimental variables and resulting behavior are related to the intervening variables.

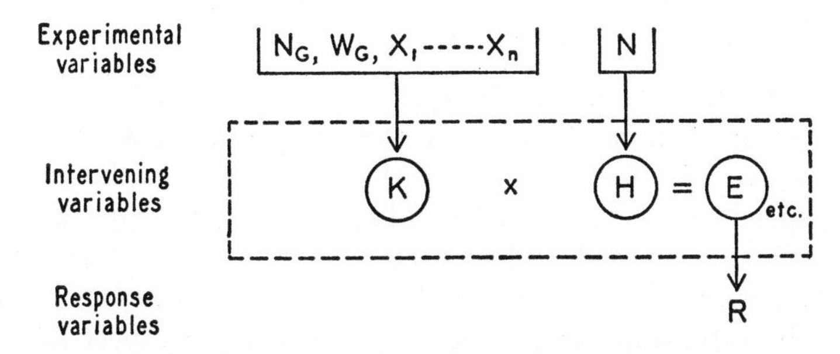

FIGURE 61. Relation of experimental variables to intervening variables in the determination of K as a multiplier of habit strength. Spence (1955), Lecture 5.

Habit strength is assumed to be related only to N, the number of response occurrences, whether goal responses or not. Hence we are interested primarily in the determiners of K, if we are to understand E. These are as follows:

N_G = the number of classical conditioning trials, i.e., the number of times the subject enters the goal-box and responds to (consumes or sees) the goal-object.

W_G = amount of goal substance consumed (number of pellets, weight or volume of food).

$X_1 \ldots X_N$ = a number of as yet unknown variables that presumably determine the vigor of the consummatory response, e.g., the sweetness of the object, the amount of sucking effort required to obtain the object in the case of liquids, possibly the hardness of the goal-object, and so on.

The presumption is that experimental variations of reinforcing agents can be shown, by way of properly devised experimental tests, to affect the nature of K. If the habit strength of r_G is increased, K should be increased. The relevant K may also be affected by the vigor of the particular r_G that is strengthened, that is, the particular component that gets conditioned from out of all the activity going on in the goal box.

The theory implies that the differences in reaction potential of responses at different distances from reinforcement will be due to differences in K rather than in H, and this theory leads to a number of deductions. In order to see how these deductions are submitted to test, we shall follow through one of Spence's deductions.

The theory, as it takes more specific form, assumes that K and D are additive (not multiplicative, as for Hull). This choice of addition rather than multiplication is not purely arbitrary, and if the wrong choice were made it would be corrected by the experimental consequences. The reasons for the choice need not now concern us, for the results will provide an indirect verification. The assumption may be stated:

$$E = H(D + K) \quad (2)$$

Now we turn to an experiment. Suppose we are interested in the running speed of a rat in a 1-foot section of a straight runway, the section beginning 1 foot from the start, and 4 feet from the goal. This running speed is either reinforced as a habit by what happens in the goal box (Hull), or it is sustained by D and K, its habit strength being independent of events in the goal box (Spence). If the section, the same distance from the start, is 10 feet from the goal, we expect somewhat less reinforcement (and also somewhat less r_G and hence K), so that running speed will be reduced there, as compared with the section beginning 4 feet from the goal. Expressed thus crudely, the Hull and Spence theories seem to lead to the same deduction. But the importance of a quantitative theory is well illustrated here, for the *quantitative* deductions of the two theories differ.

Expressed in reinforcement terms (Hull's 1943 theory), the excitatory potentials for shorter and longer distances from the goal will be:

$$E_S = H_S \times D \quad (3)$$

$$E_L = H_L \times D \quad (4)$$

Subtracting the two equations, we find:

$$E_S - E_L = D \times (H_S - H_L) \quad (5)$$

Equation (5) shows that the differences in excitatory potential, at a given level of practice, will be a function of drive. Because running speed is assumed to be a linear function of excitatory potential, this could be tested experimentally. If (in appropriate units) drive level doubles, running speed should also double. This would be a simple Hullian inference.

If we go through similar steps in accordance with Spence's theory, we come out with a different inference. According to Spence:

$$E_S = H \times (D + K_S) \tag{6}$$

$$E_L = H \times (D + K_L) \tag{7}$$

Subtracting these two equations, we have:

$$E_S - E_L = H \times (K_S - K_L) \tag{8}$$

Equation (8), by contrast with Equation (5), shows that at different levels of practice (represented by H) the differences in reaction potential between the shorter and longer path will be *independent* of drive level, and a function solely of differences in K.

The experimental test to determine whether Equation (5) or Equation (8) holds is straightforward. Run the rats with two delays under two drive levels, holding everything else constant, and see whether the differences in running speed under the two delays diverge or remain constant with changes in drive. If they diverge, the change with drive is more likely to be due to H, as implied in Hull's theory and Equation (5). If the differences remain constant, support is given to Equation (8) and to the interpretation that running speed depends on K rather than H. A preliminary test run in Spence's laboratory yielded the results shown in Figure 62, confirming his views, as implied in Equation (8). The figure shows the results for 9 rats per group on the first daily trial over the last three training days (days 10, 11, and 12) for the four groups of subjects.

We shall meet some other derivations from this theory in the next chapter. For the present, this suffices to indicate how the theory is translated into experimentable form.

How can Spence's theory best be characterized, in relation to other reinforcement theories? Let us quote his own words:

> This theory is, then, a reinforcement theory so far as excitatory potential is concerned; that is, the presence or absence of a reinforcer, and differences in its properties when present, do make a difference in the strength of the instrumental response. It is not, however, a reinforcement theory in the traditional sense of the term, for the habit or associative factor is not assumed to vary with variations in reinforcement.[22]

[22] Spence (1955), quoted from manuscript (Lecture 5).

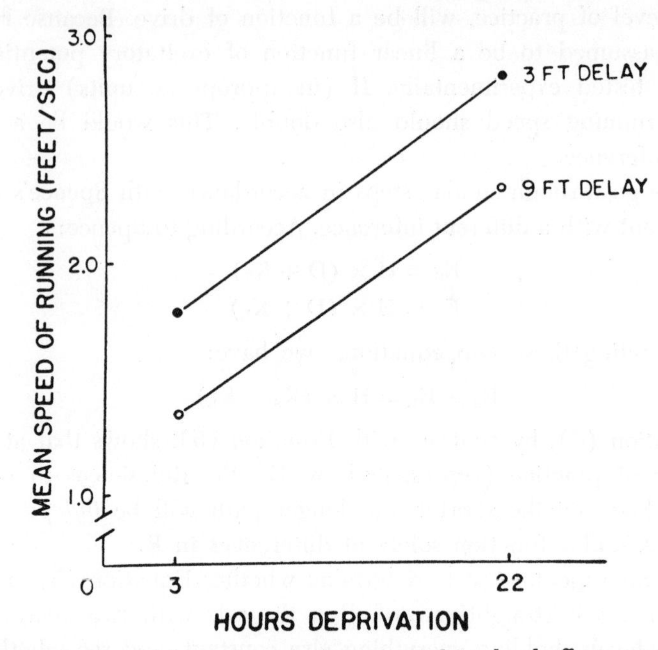

FIGURE 62. Test to determine whether or not drive level affects amount of discrimination between two delays. Because the differences at low and high drive remain constant, Spence's theory that D and K are additive is supported. Spence (1955), Lecture 5.

Seward's Two-Moment Theory of Motivated Learning

In a series of theoretical papers beginning in 1950,[23] Seward has attempted to unravel the problems of drive and goal response in the learning of instrumental behavior under both appetitive and aversive drives.

The early statement of his theory had very much in common with Spence's recent interpretation of reinforcement because the emphasis was upon the fractional goal response as a mediator, its role being *facilitation* rather than *association.* This is roughly what Spence came out with: the incentive motivation is a component of drive, and hence acts as a multiplier of habit strength rather than a producer of it. Seward took as his point of departure Hull's (1950a) revised postulates and Spence's (1947) interpretation of delayed-reward learning. Because he, like Spence, was worried about latent learning, it is not too surprising that with these common starting points they should come out with similar theories.

Seward's general position is as follows:

[23] The chief papers in the series are Seward (1950) (1951) (1952) (1953).

1. All learning is based on a simple law of association, without reference to reinforcement.

2. Conditioning of the fractional goal response is a special case of such learning, limited by the amount and delay of reward.

3. This conditioning of the fractional goal response results in a construct (at first called *tertiary motivation,* but the term was later dropped) which enters into the equation for $_{S}E_{R}$ as a multiplier along with D and $_{S}H_{R}$.

Because this multiplier facilitates the act in progress, instrumental activity is affected by what happens at the goal.

The modifications of Hull's position by Spence and by Seward are readily seen to be very similar. Drive-reduction reinforcement of instrumental responses is dropped by both, and fractional goal responses enter as components of motivation. Beyond that the theories differ.

Seward (1952) ran into trouble in applying his theory symmetrically to learning based on either appetitive or aversive drives.[24] He introduced a modification in the form of a *two-moment* theory of motivation. As he reviewed the events in a cycle of motivated behavior, it appeared to him that most activity begins with something aversive and ends with something satisfying. This is, of course, coherent with a common interpretation of the need-drive-incentive pattern, for drive is conceived as a state of disturbed homeostasis, while the incentive restores the equilibrium. The problem reduces, then, to two subproblems: how *drives* are acquired and how *goals* are acquired, with the implications for appetitive and aversive learning. Through ordinary conditioning processes, a *drive surrogate* (rs_D) is acquired as well as a *goal surrogate* (rs_G). These are the two *moments* of motivation which are now said to contribute to *stimulus-intensity dynamism* of a motive (V_m), as follows:

$$V_m = a(rs_G + rs_D) + k$$

This V_m is a multiplier of habit strength, as in Hull's equations.[25]

The advantage of the two-moment theory is that relative weights can be assigned to rs_G and to rs_D to account for appetitive and aversive problems. In problems such as escape from pain and pain avoidance, emphasis is placed upon rs_D, with rs_G playing a minor role. The interpretation of

[24] Spence has not yet dealt specifically with escape and avoidance learning in the development of his theory.

[25] All varieties of stimulus, whether produced by external events, by the organism's movements, or by drive, must have both cue aspects and stimulus-intensity dynamism aspects. Hence a great deal of arbitrariness enters into terms such as D, K, and V in Hull's system or any derivatives from it. Seward could have chosen to tie his terms to K, as Spence does, instead of to V.

experiments such as those of Miller (1948a) and Brown and Jacobs (1949) rests almost entirely on acquired fear, a form of rs_D. But in the case of instrumental learning for reward, as in food-rewarded hunger, there has been little success in finding learned drives (rs_D),[26] so that most of the burden is taken on by learning related to the goal response (rs_G). The separation of these two moments of motivation is a very natural development from familiar interpretations of drive and goal, and it appears to open up a useful line of investigation in harmonizing learning under reward and punishment.

Concluding Remarks on Reinforcement

We come out with post-Hullian interpretations of reinforcement as follows:

1. Single-factor theories
   a. Contiguity only (Sheffield, Seward)
   b. Drive reduction only (N. E. Miller)
2. Dual theories
   a. Drive reduction for instrumental acts only (Mowrer)
   b. Drive reduction for classical conditioning only (Spence) (?)

It is evident that agreement has not yet been achieved!

NEEDS, DRIVES, AND INCENTIVES

We have seen that the problems that have arisen in connection with the reinterpretation of reinforcement are also problems in the interpretation of motivation.

The need-drive-incentive pattern, in its simplest form, asserts that physiological needs are created by deprivation (or by tissue injury, as in noxious stimulation), and that these needs give rise to drives. A drive, in turn, goads to activity, and may also guide activity, until an incentive (goal-object) is encountered. Response to the incentive reduces the drive by satisfying the need, that is, by making up for the deprivation or by getting rid of the noxious stimulation. It is possible to hold to this general pattern of events as a model of the motivational cycle whether or not one accepts a reinforcement theory of learning. While this pattern serves as a crude approximation to what actually happens, recent studies show that the details are very complex indeed, and there are some who have come to believe that, as a motivational model, the need-drive-incentive pattern is actually misleading.

[26] Seward (1951), Myers and Miller (1954).

Drives as Correlates of Physiological Needs

We may define "need" as the physiological state of deprivation or of tissue injury, and "drive" as the psychological consequence of this state. We know, in general, that the longer we have abstained from food, the hungrier we get, and that rats deprived of food tend to run faster in an activity cage than well-fed rats. As we examine the details of the need-drive correlation, however, we find that we cannot assume a one-to-one correspondence between need level and drive level.

We have already seen how Hull (1952a) introduced an inanition factor to account for the fact that as animals become weakened by deprivation their food-seeking drives are also weakened. Prolonged starvation is thus one exceptional condition that disturbs the relationship between need and drive.

Other qualifications of the need-drive correlation are shown by the experiments on artificial drive reduction, where need is not satisfied (as in saccharin feeding), or where a common amount of need reduction leads to varying amounts of drive reduction (as in the fistula-feeding experiments).[27]

There must be some sort of "feedback" mechanism within the nervous system that tells the organism when it has had enough to eat or to drink, prior to the metabolic assimilation of the food or liquid. The search for such mechanisms helps to throw light upon the relationship between need and drive. We have met the suggestion by Heron (1949) that distention of the stomach, whether by water or by food, seemed to be one basis for drive reduction (somewhat independent of need reduction). If Heron's theory were true, it would not deny the usual correlation between need and drive, for usually the stomach distention would be produced by substances appropriate to the satisfaction of need. But doubts concerning the generality of Heron's results have been raised by Miller and Kessen (1954), who inserted a small balloon on the end of the stomach fistula of rats prepared as in their previous experiments. They could now compare the behavior of the rats when the stomach was distended by milk with their behavior when the stomach was distended by the inflated balloon. They found in experiments with a T-maze that the results did not support Heron's claims. The milk served as a reward,

[27] In addition to the experiments by Miller and Kessen (1952), already cited, we may note the related experiments by Hull, Livingston, Rouse, and Barker (1951), Kohn (1951), Berkun, Kessen and Miller 1952). The experiments have been repeated for the thirst drive by Sampliner and Woodrow, in Miller's laboratory (unpublished).

and led to the choice of that arm of the T that was followed by milk injection; the inflated balloon served as a punishment, and led to avoidance of the side that led to balloon inflation. Hence stomach distention alone is not the condition resulting in drive reduction of either hunger or thirst.

Another feedback mechanism has been located in the region of the hypothalamus, clearly affecting the thirst drive. Andersson (1953) showed that the injection of a saline solution into the third ventricle of the brain (the region of the hypothalamus) produced excessive drinking in goats. The experiment has been repeated and extended in Miller's laboratory with cats as subjects.[28] Hypertonic saline solution (2 per cent NaCl) injected into the ventricle produced excessive water consumption, while pure water produced a minimum of drinking. Isotonic salt solution fell between the two. The amounts injected were very small (0.15 cc. of sterile solution). This suggests a sort of "detector" mechanism in the nervous system that may prove to give important clues as to how the organism adjusts its liquid input to its needs.

Drives as Goads to Activity

It has usually been assumed that restless activity is associated with heightened drive, and the activity-cage performance has sometimes been used as an indicator of drive level. The relationship has been studied anew by Campbell and Sheffield (1953). They kept twelve rats in a constant environment with unvarying external stimulating conditions for seven days, four days with food always present and three days deprived of all food. In such a constant environment there was very little change in general activity as a result of food deprivation. When, however, sounds were introduced or changing visual stimuli were provided, the activity level increased, and the amount of increase was noticeably affected by the level of deprivation, as shown in Figure 63. The authors conclude that hunger drive produces lower thresholds of response rather than internal stimulation to activity. The result is plausible in view of the well-established findings that bodily deficiencies result in selective food preferences, a result that might come about through a lowering of thresholds for specific kinds of stimulation. Total prolonged absence of food would correspondingly lower thresholds for almost any kind of stimulation.

[28] Richter and Southwick (unpublished).

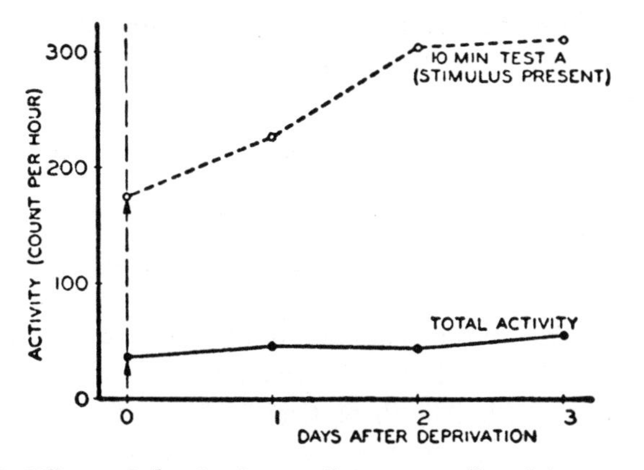

FIGURE 63. Effects of deprivation on "spontaneous" activity as compared with activity when an environmental change is introduced. Campbell and Sheffield (1953), page 321.

Drives as Cues to Differential Response

In addition to whatever drives do to reduce thresholds or to stimulate activity, they also help to direct activity through providing various differential cues. For example, an animal can be taught to turn one way when hungry, another way when thirsty. Bailey and Porter (1955) have taught cats to perform one instrumental response to get water when thirsty, and another to get food when hungry. Eight of nine cats were highly successful in making the discrimination.

Bailey (1954) performed an experiment with rats to determine whether or not hunger or thirst could provide differential cues for a discrimination rewarded not by food or water but by escape from intense light. The rats had to press one of two panels in order to turn off the light. Which panel was correct was determined by which drive was active. Thus the drives served as cues exactly as if they were different figures on the panels. Three groups were able to discriminate (*a*) thirst from hunger, (*b*) thirst from satiation, and (*c*) hunger from satiation.

In the same series of experiments, Bailey also used the presence or absence of a 10,000 cycle tone as a cue for the differential response to the panels. If the tone was presented shortly before the time of response, results were very similar to those with drive discrimination. If the tone began to stimulate the rat a long time before he was placed in the apparatus, he did not learn. The difference between the long-delay and short-delay tone is used to interpret the difficulty sometimes found in drive-discrimination experiments, because drives are long-persistent stimuli. The argument that long-persistent stimuli are hard to discriminate is weakened by the finding that drive discriminations were no more difficult than short-delay tone discriminations. Supplementary conjectures are required, possibly about cue distinctiveness, if the original argument is to hold.

Drive Interaction and General Drive Level

Though drives provide differential cues, all drives may have something in common. Each may contribute its share to a general drive level, as implied in the theories of Hull and of Spence. This general drive level (D) is the multiplier used in their equations to produce reaction potential from habit strength. The theoretical problem of a general drive level contributed to by specific drives is subject to a variety of experimental approaches.

Verplanck and Hayes (1953) conducted a series of experiments on food and water deprivation in rats in which the animals later, under conditions varying from experiment to experiment, had an opportunity to eat and drink. They found a very complex picture of drive interaction as measured by consummatory activity. For example, the amount of food eaten by water-deprived rats is some 60 per cent of the amount eaten by those which have had continuous access to water, while the amount of water drunk by food-deprived rats is only 40 per cent of that drunk by animals which have had continuous access to food. If the animal is allowed to drink, after being deprived of water for 22 hours, so that its water needs are satisfied, it is motivated to *eat* about as much food as if it had been deprived of food for the same period. Similarly, termination of a fast, without water deprivation, leads to water consumption approaching that of water drunk after a like period of water deprivation. The authors believe these results to be significant for studies of latent learning, which often try to distinguish too sharply between "hungry" and "thirsty" rats.

Considerable success has been achieved in studies originating at the University of Iowa, and largely carried out there, which treat some generalized human motives according to the intervening variable (D), and then make predictions as to consequences for conditioning, discrimination, and verbal learning. Most of the studies have used a measure of "anxiety," based on Taylor's anxiety scale.[29] Others have used a measure of achievement motive in somewhat the same way.[30] Farber

[29] A number of these studies have been listed in Footnote 32, Chapter 9. Theoretical summaries, in relation to drive theory, can be found in Farber (1954), Spence (1955).
[30] E.g., Hurley (1953). Cited by Farber (1953).

(1953) points out that possibly achievement scores should not be used as indicative of drive level, but rather as indicative of a general response tendency influencing performance in a variety of situations. He suggests that it might possibly be referred to as an "achievement-oriented habit."

In his very thoughtful review of anxiety as a drive state, Farber (1954) rightly points out the successes that have been achieved through treating anxiety parsimoniously as generalized drive (D). He notes, however, that anxiety must be a special kind of D; it could not be claimed that just any heightened drive would lead to precisely the same consequences. His doubts about the status of achievement motive are perhaps equally applicable to anxiety. The detailed studies which show how test-measured anxiety acts as a cue or specific set of response tendencies (in addition to its enhancement effect as generalized drive) have not yet been reported.[31]

In developing the relationship between reaction potential, drive, and habit formation, the later theorizing of both Hull and Spence limited the effect of drive (D) to an influence upon reaction potential, not upon habit strength. An experiment by Campbell and Kraeling (1954) calls this into question. Rats trained to run in a straight alley under high and low strengths of hunger drive were tested in extinction trials according to two measures: resistance to extinction (measured by trials) and amplitude (measured by running speed). The Hull-Spence position was confirmed when resistance to extinction was used as a criterion, but with amplitude there was greater response strength during extinction with stronger training drive level, regardless of the drive level during extinction. This experiment is merely one more showing how uncertain are our generalizations based on the drive-reinforcement paradigm.[32]

The Positive Role of Incentives

The words "goal," "lure," "incentive" seem to imply some kind of directional orientation toward a state or condition that is attractive. We say that organisms strive toward goals. By a curious chain of circum-

[31] Spence (1955) reports some experiments to determine whether anxiety of this kind acts as if it were a generalized excitement or whether it acts more as if it merely lowered the threshold for emotional experiences. Experiments in Eysenck's laboratory in London have shown selective effects for different personality types—contrasting a "neurasthenic" type with a "hysterical" type.

[32] Campbell and Kraeling point out that their experimental result also criticizes Hull's use of resistance-to-extinction and amplitude of response as alternative measures of reaction potential, for the functional relationship of experimental variables to response differ depending upon which measure is used.

stances, this rather primitive nature of goal-experiences was largely lost sight of in the theorizing of the last decade or two. To be sure, it could not be ignored entirely, but striving and goal-seeking had to be derived from more primitive principles before the familiar facts could be recognized as valid. The circumstances that led away from attributing positive qualities to incentives probably arose historically through the turn toward objectivity and away from conceptions that appeared tainted with animism or teleology.

There is little doubt that the drive-reduction theory of motivation led to a predominantly negative role for incentives. According to this interpretation, food is eaten not because it tastes good but because it ends hunger-pangs. A compartment in which the rat is *not* shocked is reinforcing not because of anything attractive about its size, color, temperature, or fittings, but because it provides relief from a compartment in which shock has been given or is threatened. This negative position moved into the interpretation of human motivation as well. "At the level of ego-psychology," writes Mowrer (1952), "there may be said to be only one master motive: anxiety" (p. 423). Not something positive, like love, or avarice, or ambition, to spur one on—just anxiety from which we seek to escape.

A rather one-sided position of this kind often gains wide currency because of controversies that develop *among those who hold the position*, so that this point of agreement is not questioned. For example, this issue does not arise between Guthrie's contiguity theory and Hull's drive-reduction theory. Guthrie, too, was negative about the role of rewards, since all they did was change the situation. Psychoanalysis, which might be thought of as a somewhat competing position, tended also to describe adjustment negatively, adjustment depending upon anxiety reduction or escape from feelings of guilt. Even Lewin's theory, which recognized the positive valences of some incentives, looked to tension reduction as the basis for motivated action. Support was given also through Cannon's doctrine of homeostasis, which made it easy to view the function of motivation as the restoration of equilibrium through reduced tension. If all these factions accepted some form of tension reduction or stimulus reduction or mere change toward equilibrium as the basis for understanding motivated action, it is not surprising that the role of incentives remained essentially negative. Concessions are always made to reality, so that it can be pointed out that there were *some* positive features assigned incentives in each of these positions. That is not the point: the *Zeitgeist* favored our seeing incentives not as providing something sought after for what was inherent in the incentive, but something providing relief. The incentive was seen as an avenue of escape from pain, anxiety, tension.

The drive-reduction theory or tension-reduction theory, predominant in mid-century, has been coming under increasing attack and reexamination by its friends as well as by its enemies.

1. There have, of course, been critics of the drive-reduction theory all along. Because of its inviting nature and its acceptance by otherwise conflicting factions among the learning theorists, most of those who objected were "voices crying in the wilderness." They failed to get much of a hearing. McDougall (1923) argued that striving toward a goal was satisfying, and reaching it was relatively unimportant; Allport (1937) (1946) never did like the law of effect or the motivational theory related to it; Murphy (1947) wanted sensory and activity drives added to visceral ones; Anderson (1941) wrote on the externalization of drive; Young (1949) felt that we paid too little attention to appetites in our overattention to drives. These views did not do very much to stem the tide of the prevailing theory, though they may have sown dormant seeds of doubt that have more recently sprouted.

2. A rather important feature of the background for the present questioning of the drive-reduction theory has come from within the camp of reinforcement theorists. The entering wedge came through experiments on secondary reinforcement, as when Wolfe's (1936) chimpanzees accepted poker-chips as rewards instead of food. When Hull in 1943 did not require drive reduction in order for a secondary reinforcing agent to strengthen habit, he opened a way for recognizing the positive roles of incentives, though he was reluctant to follow this path. Instead, by 1952 he had made secondary reinforcers also stimulus-intensity reducers. He later introduced (K), incentive motivation, as a further move in the same direction, although K applied to primary incentives only.

Spence's incentive motivation, related to Hull's K, while supposedly separable from the general drive level (D), is additive to D, and hence functions exactly as a component of drive. Spence's theory gives recognition to a somewhat neglected role of incentives: their *drive-enhancing* role as well as their drive-reducing role. At least for perceived incentives, naturalistic observation tells us that they can enhance drive, as when a male dog is aroused by a receptive female in the neighborhood. Previously experienced incentives, as in Spence's theory, act similarly through the arousal of fractional anticipatory responses, even though the incentive is not directly perceived. The incentive, in its role of enhancing drive, takes on qualities not suggested in its role as a drive reducer.

The drive-reduction theory is naturally strained if the same object can both enhance drive and reduce it. The paradox is partially resolved, however, if we recognize that more than one response is possible to the same object. Thus the smell of fresh bread may increase appetite, while eating the bread may reduce it. In the case of secondary rewards the problem is more difficult, for they are obviously not need-reducing, so their drive-enhancing and their drive-reducing qualities are harder to distinguish. Miller (1951a), struggling with this problem, suggested that perhaps the two effects alternated in some manner. Mowrer (1947), facing the same problem, found it necessary to give up the drive-reduction interpretation as a unitary one, and go to his two-factor theory.

We have already seen how the experimental evidence makes confident assertions about the need-drive-incentive pattern less possible now than a few years ago. With this weakening of the orthodox position, the way is opened for a hearing from those who offer new interpretations.

3. Some psychologists with strong physiological orientation have turned their backs on the orthodox drive theory of motivated behavior.

Hebb (1949) favors an interpretation of hunger as an organized neural activity in the cortico-diencephalic system. It can be aroused (1) by the sight and smell of food, and the act of eating, (2) by stomach contractions, and (3) conceptually. Because these several determiners may summate, hunger can be aroused or increased by an attractive appearance of food, or by its smell and taste. He thus emphasizes the drive-enhancing role of incentives beyond their drive-reducing role. By emphasizing a "central motive state" (Morgan, 1943), the precise physiological condition of need becomes less significant and perceived incentives become more important.

Harlow (1953)(1954) has come to emphasize curiosity as a motive, on the basis of observations on monkeys in his laboratory. He finds that when he puts complicated devices in their cages they learn to take them apart, even though no "bait" (no obvious reinforcement) is used. They show a great deal of curiosity and will work hard merely for an opportunity to "look." [33]

Reflections upon these experiments have led Harlow to make strong statements against drive reduction and physiological states as the basis for motivation:

> There are logical reasons why a drive-reduction theory of learning, a theory which emphasizes the role of internal, physiological-state motivation, is entirely untenable as a motivational theory of learning.

[33] Butler (1953); Harlow and McClearn (1954).

> The condition of strong drive is inimical to all but very limited aspects of learning—the learning the ways to reduce tension. . . . The hungry child is a most uncurious child, but after he has eaten and become thoroughly sated, his curiosity and all the learned responses associated with his curiosity take place.[34]

He interprets the evidence with monkeys to indicate that strong drive is quite as likely to inhibit learning as to facilitate it. These criticisms, coming from a physiologically-oriented psychologist, represent one of the extreme reactions to the position that shortly before was being so widely endorsed.

It is possible that Harlow has gone too far. Events are complicated, and possibly some drive-incentive conditions are appropriately treated according to the drive-reduction pattern while others may not be. Furthermore, boredom may arouse a tension state that is relieved by any change in the environment, so that satisfying curiosity may be boredom-relieving, and thus drive-reducing.[35]

Montgomery has performed a number of experiments on the exploratory drive in rats, a drive closely related to curiosity. While exploratory drive interacts with other drives such as hunger, thirst, and fear, it cannot be explained by them. Novel stimuli, for example, may arouse both fear and exploration, but after the prolonged exposure has reduced fear the exploratory drive may persist. Montgomery's hypothesis is simply that novel stimuli arouse the exploratory drive that motivates exploratory behavior.[36]

A position like Harlow's and the related one of Montgomery's receives some support from Woodworth (1947), who recognized that a motive to perceive was a prevalent one, and from Nissen (1954), who accepts a "biogenic drive to explore, to perceive, to know." Another way that Nissen puts it is that capacity is its own motivation; an organism goes about functioning in the ways it is prepared to function.[37]

Still another support from the camp of physiological psychologists for a more positive interpretation of what happens at the goal comes from the experiments of Olds and Milner (1954) on positive reinforcement through electrical stimulation of part of the rat's brain, the septal area below the corpus callosum and between the two lateral ventricles.

[34] Harlow (1953), page 25.

[35] This is, as might be expected, Miller's reply to Harlow, e.g., Myers and Miller (1954). See also Brown (1953).

[36] Montgomery (1952) (1953a) (1953b) (1953c), Montgomery and Monkman (1955).

[37] The amazing disturbances in human subjects restricted experimentally to an unstimulating environment shows something of this need for interplay with the environment, Bexton, Heron, and Scott (1954).

Electrodes permanently imbedded could be made to deliver an alternating current to this area if the rat pressed the lever of a Skinner box. The "shock" was found to be positively reinforcing. That is, the rat would press the lever as if being rewarded, provided the current was turned on. When the current was turned off, and pressing the lever had no effect, typical extinction ensued. (Other areas of the brain can be found mildly rewarding, some neutral, some punishing.)[38]

The experiment demonstrates that it is possible to reward an animal without satisfying a physiological need or withdrawing a noxious stimulus. Thus reward appears to be separable from need and drive. Further work along these lines may prove helpful in determining just how reward and punishment work.[39] At this point the significance of the finding is that incentives may have properties requiring their definition independently of need and drive. It is possible that the role of Olds's electrical stimulation was that of affective arousal, that the stimulation produced a state that the rat found "pleasant." If so, the study gives some physiological support for the theory next to be considered.

4. A clear statement of the positive role of incentives, and a reinterpretation of the motivational sequence, has been given by McClelland and his collaborators.[40] It is a theory of affective arousal, a pleasure-pain theory, thus returning, in some sense, to a "law of affect" rather than a "law of effect." It cannot be dismissed simply as old-fashioned hedonism, for there is a genuine effort to deal with the problem of objectifying affective arousal. A motive is defined as "the redintegration of a cue by the change in an affective situation."[41] A less cryptic definition, published earlier, defined a motive as "a strong affective association, characterized by an anticipatory goal reaction and based on past association of certain cues with pleasure or pain."[42]

McClelland's criticism of drive-reduction theories of motivation is of what we have called above their negative character, that is, their failure to take account of active pleasures and comforts as well as the relief of pain and discomfort. If we seek thrills, excitement, adventure, esthetically satisfying experiences, because of the quality of experience they invoke, McClelland believes we do well to reintroduce the affective as-

[38] Delgado, Roberts, and Miller (1954) have confirmed with cats learning through electrical stimulation of parts of the tectal area, thalamus, and hippocampus, but the mechanism appeared to be the arousal of fear (or pain).

[39] Olds (1955) has examined some of these possibilities.

[40] McClelland (1951), McClelland, Atkinson, Clark, and Lowell (1953), Atkinson (1954).

[41] McClelland and others (1953), page 28.

[42] McClelland (1951), page 466.

pects of motivation. That is, he returns to the common-sense notion that we seek activities that are pleasurable because we enjoy the pleasurable state that they excite in us, and we dislike and avoid other activities precisely because they are annoying or unpleasant to experience. Having taken this general position, he is not willing merely to turn back the hands of the clock to an earlier hedonism. Instead he is attempting to build a new theory on scientific props of the same order of objectivity and validity as those supporting the drive-reduction theory. One of the facets of his theory is that *slight* changes in intensity of stimulation tend to arouse pleasant affect, *extreme* changes unpleasant affect.

The main point is that McClelland has substituted affective arousal for drive reduction, and all motives are said to be cued by changes in affective situations. Furthermore, all motives are learned. The two master motives recognized by McClelland are *appetite* and *anxiety.* Continuity with the prevailing theories is there, so far as anxiety is concerned, but *added to it* are the positive motives summarized under appetite.

However the many suggestions and counter-suggestions will finally come out, we may be sure that the need-drive-incentive pattern will not emerge in uncomplicated form. Some satisfactory solution will have to be found for the treatment of positive wants and desires that impel men to heroic and daring action. Only a few men see in the passive Nirvana state the true bliss for which they long.

Summary of Reinforcement and Drive

The confident espousal of a need-drive-incentive conception of motivated behavior, and of a drive-reduction theory of reinforcement has given way to a searching analysis of the circumstances under which learning occurs, whether through contiguous stimulation, drive reduction, stimulus-intensity reduction, some combination of these, or through some process as yet not understood. Secondary motivation and secondary reinforcement studies are very important in these analyses.

The most significant new direction in the study of motivation is away from tension-reduction interpretations to an emphasis upon the positive aspects of behavior related to preferred incentives or activities.

SUPPLEMENTARY READINGS

A list of supplementary readings on current developments is provided following Chapter 13.

Chapter 13

CURRENT DEVELOPMENTS: II. SOME PERSISTING ISSUES

THE issues around the need-drive-incentive pattern, as discussed in the preceding chapter, are all central to stimulus-response theories. The quarrels between stimulus-response theories and cognitive theories are somewhat more clearly represented in other issues. One of these, which experimenters have actively investigated for twenty years, has to do with the nature of discrimination learning in animals. This issue has been selected for review because it is not only central, but currently alive.

Stimulus-response psychologists have often shown impatience with cognitive theorists, charging them with lack of precision in the statement of their theories. We shall therefore consider some recent attempts to make up the deficiency in formal statement of cognitive theories.

Finally, there has been a renewal of interest in the old problem of the contribution of neurophysiology to learning theory. This is the third of the current developments selected for review.

DISCRIMINATION LEARNING IN ANIMALS

Although discrimination learning in animals had long been the subject of laboratory study, new interest in the problem developed after Köhler (1918) (1925) called attention to the theoretical importance of relational discrimination and transposition, and another dimension of interest was added as Krech began to write about "hypotheses" in the presolution period in discrimination learning by rats.[43]

The theoretical issues between these interpretations and those of stimulus-response psychology were sharpened by Spence in two important papers which have led to a considerable literature of experiment and theory.

The first of these [44] took up the problem raised by Krech, and showed

[43] Krechevsky (1932a) (1932b).
[44] Spence (1936).

how reinforcement and extinction could account for the non-random features of presolution learning. This paper led to distinction between two viewpoints that have come to be known as the *continuity* and *non-continuity* theories of discrimination learning. Continuity theory accounts for the present in terms of past associative learning. Non-continuity theory predicts sharp breaks in learning as the animal learner shifts from one systematic mode of behavior to another, or achieves insight. The continuity theory may predict sharp breaks also, under specified conditions, but they are always predictable on the basis of the prior experiences of the learner. Spence was on the side of continuity, Krech on the side of non-continuity.

The second of Spence's theoretical papers [45] was concerned with the issue of discrimination based on the *absolute* versus the *relative* properties of the discriminated stimuli, as brought to the fore by Köhler's transposition experiments. Spence showed very ingeniously how the overlapping gradients of generalization of excitatory and inhibitory tendencies resulting from reinforcing responses to the positive member of the stimulus pair and extinguishing responses to the negative member could account for transposition with similar stimuli.

The nature of Spence's analysis is illustrated by Figure 64. The tests for transposition are made after the gradients in the figure have been set up through reinforcing responses to 160 (the positive stimulus) and extinguishing responses to 100 (the negative stimulus). Transposition can be tested by selecting any pair of neighboring stimuli. If response is then to the larger of the two stimuli, transposition is demonstrated because the original training required response to the larger of the stimuli. Suppose we select the pair of stimuli 160 and 256. We learn from the diagram that the response tendency to 160 has a strength of 51.7 and to 256 a strength of 72.1. Hence the tendency to respond to the larger stimulus (256) is greater than the tendency to respond to the smaller stimulus (160), even though the smaller (160) was the positive stimulus during training. Thus the *fact* of transposition is accounted for without any assumption of reaction to the relationship "larger-than."

Spence's theory has the virtue over Köhler's that it can also predict the known failure of transposition with extreme stimuli. Suppose stimuli 409 and 655 are selected as test stimuli. Transposition (reaction to the larger) would require response to 655. But we learn from Figure 64 that the tendency to respond to 655 is 18.5, while the tendency to respond to 409 is 52.1. Thus transposition will break down, and response will be to the smaller of the two stimuli.

[45] Spence (1937).

Because Spence's gradients were generated entirely on the basis of the *absolute* (specific) characteristics of the individual stimuli, he set himself against theories of discrimination based on *relative* characteristics.[46]

These two problems (continuity versus discontinuity; absolute versus relative discrimination) are closely related, but they are sufficiently separable for us to consider independently the status of the issues they represent.

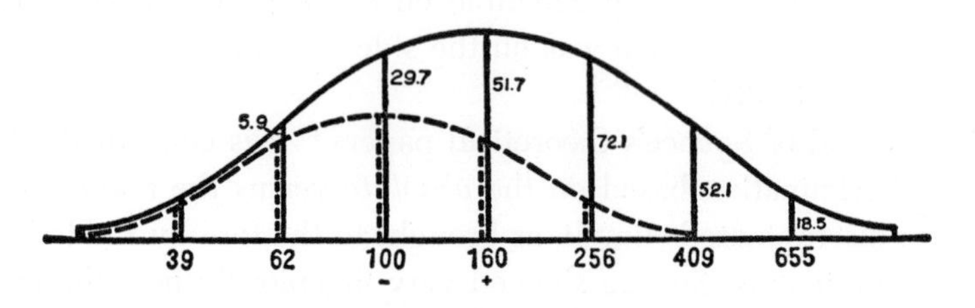

FIGURE 64. Spence's theory of transposition (Spence, 1942). The visual stimuli to be discriminated in either training or testing are scaled along the baseline according to their areas.

Reinforcement of responses to stimulus 160 during training produces the generalization curve represented by the solid line. That is, the tendency to respond is increased not only for responses to stimulus 160 but to neighboring stimuli in proportion to their proximity to 160.

Non-reinforcement (extinction) of responses to stimulus 100 produces the corresponding inhibitory gradient represented by the broken line.

The tendency to respond positively to any stimulus along the baseline can be computed by subtracting the length of the dotted vertical line from that of the solid vertical line at that position along the baseline. The results of this computation are indicated by the numerical values above each stimulus size.

The text explains how the diagram is used to explain transposition.

Current Status of the Continuity and Non-continuity Issue

The original paper of Spence (1936), denying the discontinuity between presolution performance and solution learning, has been followed by many experimental pro's and con's, of which only the more recent will be reviewed here.[47]

Ehrenfreund (1948) conducted two experiments, the data of the first appearing to support the non-continuity theory, while the second supported the continuity theory. In the first experiment, rats were ulti-

[46] He later granted that some circumstances might *force* discrimination on the basis of relative characteristics (Spence, 1952c), but only if the relationships could *not* be learned more readily on the basis of the absolute characteristics of the component patterns. In this connection, see Nissen (1953).

[47] A few of the more important earlier references, which cite the other literature, are: Krechevsky (1938), McCulloch (1939), Lashley (1942), Spence (1940) (1945).

mately required to learn to discriminate between an upright and an inverted triangle, having first been given 40 trials in which responses to the (later) negative stimulus were rewarded. They learned the ultimate problem as rapidly as a control group whose prior practice was not contradictory. Hence there appeared to be some discontinuity between the presolution learning and the ultimate discrimination. In the second experiment, however, the experimental group was retarded in its later learning by its earlier contradictory practice. The apparent paradox was resolved by Ehrenfreund by pointing out that the arrangements of the first experiment precluded discriminably different retinal excitations from the later-to-be-discriminated stimulus cards during the presolution period. The later-to-be-discriminated stimuli appeared on the upper portion of the cards, and the animals during the presolution period were forming position habits without "paying attention" to the figures. The second experiment, by contrast, required attention to the cards, because the jumping stand was raised and the rat jumped against the later-to-be-discriminated figures during the presolution period. Under the circumstances of the second experiment the reinforcements during the presolution period modified the later discrimination learning, as continuity theory would predict. Ehrenfreund concluded that his findings as a whole supported the continuity theory.

The implied importance of "attention to the stimuli" has been given further study by Lawrence (1949) (1950), who makes a distinction between "relevant" and "irrelevant" stimuli, and who believes that his results mediate some of the differences between continuity and non-continuity theories. A *relevant* cue is one consistently correlated with reward or punishment, whether alone or in combination with other cues. Thus Ehrenfreund's cues in the presolution period were relevant ones because, for the experimental group, only one of the pair of figures was ever reinforced. An *irrelevant* cue is one that is presented inconsistently, sometimes with reward and sometimes with punishment. The stimulus cards during presolution were irrelevant cues in Ehrenfreund's control groups. Lawrence found that when an animal learns to discriminate between a pair of cues in one situation there is transfer to a new situation, even though entirely different instrumental responses are required. The cues acquire distinctiveness, so that new responses to them can be learned more readily.[48] These new responses include reversals of habit, so that an oversimplified continuity theory is not applicable. Lawrence's inter-

[48] Lawrence has really restated and given new evidence for Robinson's law of acquaintance (Robinson, 1932a, page 118).

pretation is in stimulus-response terms, but implies a mediating response learned to the cues. This mediating response makes the cues distinctive, so that a new association is more readily established between them and instrumental responses. Lawrence and Mason (1955) have reported a somewhat elaborately designed experiment involving three sets of cue-dimensions (black-white, high and low hurdles, and spatial position). They showed that with two cue-dimensions present, one may remain non-functional while the animal is responding to the other; when the first has become relevant again, the discrimination is picked up as though the reinforcement and non-reinforcement of these cues did not matter while the other cues were relevant. When three dimensions were involved, there was a tendency to fall into systematic position preferences when the cue relationships to reward were changed. The authors suggest that the greater the number of irrelevant stimulus aspects during habit reversal, the greater the likelihood of systematic runs to dimensions that do not lead to solution.

As so often happens after the heat of controversy cools, the atmosphere of debate is changed to one of search for the conditions under which various experimental results are found.[49] It often turns out that the original issue was a somewhat artificial one. The suggestion that cues may acquire distinctiveness through prior experience supports some aspects of continuity theory, but also moves the theory somewhat closer to the claims of the non-continuity theorists.

Another suggestion, bearing on the continuity and non-continuity problem, has been provided by the experiments of Harlow on "learning-how-to-learn" or what he calls "learning sets." [50] He finds in experiments with monkeys that, after practice, discrimination reversals can be made following a single trial. Because this "insightful" performance is achieved gradually, Harlow believes he has demonstrated a "continuity" relationship between insight and prior experience. He writes:

> The field theorists, unlike the Neo-behaviorists, have stressed insight and hypothesis in their description of learning. The impression these theorists give is that these phenomena are properties of the innate organization of the individual. If such phenomena appear independently of a gradual learning history, we have not found them in the primate order.[51]

While this statement of Harlow's somewhat distorts the insight problem, which has to do with how experience is utilized rather than with the non-necessity of experience, his experiments are useful additions to

[49] See, for example, Blum and Blum (1949).

[50] E.g., Harlow (1949). See also Bateson (1942) on deutero-learning, as a "learning to learn."

[51] Harlow (1949), page 65.

the literature on continuity and the modifications brought about by prolonged experiences with related problems.

As an illustration of the trend to treat the discrimination problem on the basis of experimental variation, and at a relatively non-controversial level, Spence's mathematical study of the effects of drive level and delayed reinforcement on several varieties of discrimination learning provides a good case.[52]

He is able to show by a manipulation of his intervening variables that sometimes drive level will be important in discrimination, sometimes not. For example, if, by some kind of forcing, responses to the positive and negative stimuli are kept equal, discrimination should be independent of drive level:

$$E_{+} = H \times (D + K) \quad (1)$$

$$E_{-} = (H \times D) - I \quad (2)$$

$$E_{+} - E_{-} = KH + I, \text{ the D's cancelling} \quad (3)$$

In free responding, habit strength to the positive stimulus will gradually exceed that to the negative stimulus. Then we have:

$$E_{+} = H_{+} \times (D + K) \quad (4)$$

$$E_{-} = (H_{-} \times D) - I \quad (5)$$

$$E_{+} - E_{-} = D(H_{+} - H_{-}) + (H_{+}K + I) \quad (6)$$

According to Equation (6), the influence of drive upon the discrimination will depend upon the stage of practice. The relationship can become quite complicated. Spence points out how important it is to specify the initial and boundary conditions, as well as the laws and hypotheses of a theory, when that theory is applied to a particular set of experimental relationships.

Spence (1955) has been very successful in applying his quantitative approach to a variety of discrimination data. The analysis of the two-bar problem, when responses to one bar are reinforced twice as often as the other, serves as a convenient illustration. The apparatus used in the experiment was similar to that used by Logan (1952), and the data were unpublished from Ramond (1954). This discrimination problem does not involve non-reinforcement (extinction), so that it is conveniently studied according to D and K, without the complication of I (inhibition). What happens is that, in free-choice trials, the bar whose responses have been more frequently reinforced (hereafter called the more frequently reinforced bar) is chosen more often than the bar whose re-

[52] Spence (1955), lecture 7. See also Spence (1954a).

sponses have been less frequently reinforced, up to a maximum discrimination. But as the training continues, reinforcements on the favored bar no longer add the increment that reinforcements on the less frequently reinforced bar do, so the responses to the second bar "catch up," and the discrimination becomes poorer. Responses to the more frequently reinforced bar under two levels of drive are given in Figure 65. Note that under both levels of drive the maximum is at the same stage of training. This agrees with the theory, in that the maximum at any one drive level is determined by the *differences* in growth rates of H to the two bars, which is a function solely of the number of reinforcements.

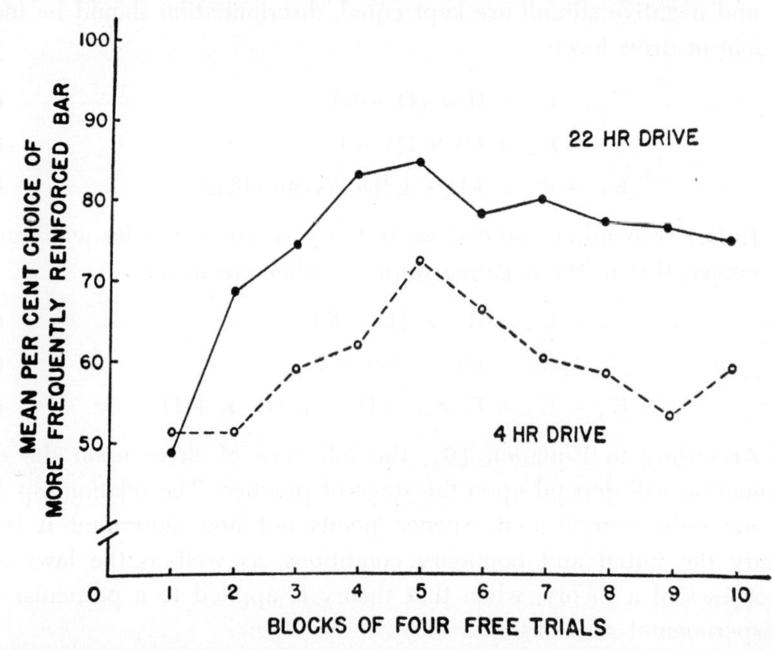

FIGURE 65. Responses to the more frequently reinforced of two bars under two levels of drive. Spence (1955), Lecture 7.

In the approach to their respective maximum values, the responses to the more frequently reinforced bar proceed at somewhat different rates under the two levels of drive, so there is a stage at which the *difference* between the two response levels is a maximum. This falls in the fifth block of free trials of Figure 65, and represents the point at which there have been 36 reinforcements of the more frequently reinforced bar. Spence designates the maximum value (here 36) as N_A.

Now to return to the quantitative theory. Spence has computed the point at which N_A should occur according to the theory, and it turns out for this problem (where one bar is reinforced twice as often as the other) to be a function solely of *i*, the coefficient of the exponent used in plotting the acquisition curve:

$$N_A = \frac{2 \log 2}{i} \qquad (1)$$

Because N_A has been determined empirically from the data ($N_A = 36$), it is possible to compute *i*, which turns out to be .0167. Hypothetical growth curves, using this exponent, can be drawn for responses to the more frequently reinforced bar under the two conditions of drive, as shown in Figure 66, using the value of *i* determined from N_A.

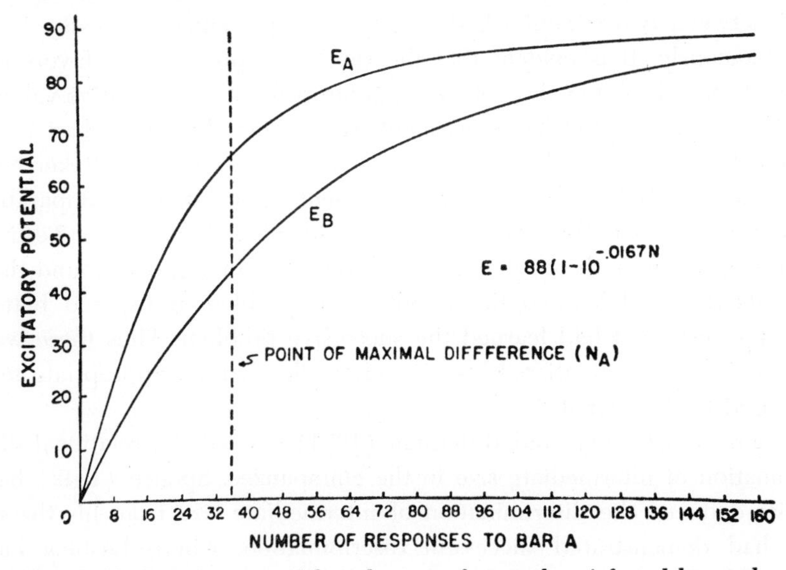

FIGURE 66. Reaction potential to the more frequently reinforced bar under two conditions of drive (theoretical, but based on $N_A = 36$). After Spence (1955), Lecture 7.

The theory can now be put to a severe test. Will this *i*, determined from these data, fit latency data obtained in the forced trials to the more frequently reinforced bar presented alone? Latency is first converted to running speed. Then using the relationship between E and running speed, as previously determined theoretically (Spence, 1954b), and plotting Ramond's data accordingly, an acquisition curve with the exponential coefficient $i = .0167$ turns out to fit satisfactorily. This then meets the desire for stable interchangeable constants pointed out in the chapter on mathematical models.

This mathematical extension of Spence's discrimination theory remains a continuity theory, in that separate equations are written for responses to the positive and negative stimuli, and no discontinuous emergent is anywhere implied.

Current Status of the Issue Whether Discrimination Is Based on Absolute or Relative Properties of Stimuli

Spence's second paper (1937) contained the careful description of intersecting gradients of generalization and was therefore expressed in a form well subject to testing. Again a substantial literature collected, of which only the most recent papers will be reviewed here.[53]

Grice (1949) showed that rats could learn to discriminate equally well between two stimuli whether they were presented successively or simultaneously. It is evident that the successive presentation favors reaction to the absolute values of the stimulus rather than to relative values, so that he interpreted his experiment as showing that there had been no reaction to relationship in the simultaneous presentation. Baker and Lawrence (1951), building their experiment upon his, got comparable results, except that they carried the experiment a step further. Testing for transposition with novel stimuli not used in training, they found that the rats that had learned the simultaneous problem transposed better than the ones that had learned the successive problem. Thus there was some evidence for relational learning after all, when an appropriate test was used to discover it.[54]

Gonzalez, Gentry, and Bitterman (1954) studied the relational discrimination of intermediate size in the chimpanzee. Spence (1942) had earlier deduced the discrimination of intermediate size from his theory and had demonstrated successful discrimination, where Lashley had previously failed. Gonzalez, Gentry, and Bitterman went on to demonstrate transposition, with successful results which they say "point unmistakably to the operation of a relational process in the discrimination of intermediate size by the chimpanzee."

Lawrence and De Rivera (1954) developed a new type of transposition experiment likely to prove fruitful in further studies of relational

[53] For some of the follow-ups of this paper see Hull (1939a), Tolman (1939) (1941), Spence (1942), Kuenne (1946), Lashley and Wade (1946), Hull (1947b) (1950b).

[54] Unfortunately the two experiments were not exactly equivalent, and so the conclusion remains somewhat in doubt. The simultaneous-successive type of discrimination, in a different form, has been studied by Weise and Bitterman (1951), Bitterman and Wodinsky (1953), and others in their laboratory. A flurry of papers related to these studies appeared in the *Psychological Review* following a paper by Nissen (1950), in which he argued that approach-avoidance was the fundamental dimension according to which discrimination should be described. The papers are worth reading for the experiments described, but the points at issue were not very well clarified.

learning. Because of its novelty and potential fruitfulness it is worth describing in some detail. In this experiment the animal learner always faced two identical cards exposed in the Lashley jumping apparatus. Each card was divided into an upper and lower half. The lower half during training always consisted of an intermediate gray (No. 4 in a scale from 1 to 7, with 1 being lightest). The upper half was either No. 1, 2, or 3, lighter grays, or 5, 6, or 7, darker grays. The animal had to learn to jump to the *right* if the top half was *lighter* than the bottom half, and to the *left* if the top half was *darker* than the bottom half. Note that it would conceivably be possible to ignore the bottom half of the card. It was entirely indifferent, so far as reward and punishment were concerned. Furthermore, the top halves of the cards *could* have been learned according to their absolute brightness, for 1, 2, and 3 were always reinforced when jumping was to the right, and 5, 6, and 7 when jumping was to the left. Thus the situation is not one that *forces* relational learning, although it of course permits it.

We may raise the question: When the rats solved this problem (as they did), was it on the basis of absolute or relative stimulus characteristics? The experimenters went on to a test with the grays in different combinations. Consider the simple expedient of placing the cards upside down, with No. 4 gray always on top. Now with the lighter Nos. 1, 2, or 3 on the bottom, the top card is *darker*, and so jumping should be to the left (if cues are relational) while jumping should be to the *right* if cues remain absolute. Correspondingly the darker Nos. 5, 6, 7, if on the bottom, make the top card relatively *lighter*, so relative response would lead to jumping to the right, while absolute cues would suggest jumping to the left. This particular form of transposition test yielded 74 per cent of the jumps *relationally* determined, well beyond the .01 level of significance. Some of the transposition tests lead to the same prediction by both the absolute and the relative theories. For example, suppose gray 1 is placed above gray 3. Then the top is lighter, and both components have been associated with reward for jumping to the right. With such stimuli, 94 per cent of the jumps were in predicted direction. A third set of relationships, such as No. 2 over No. 5 and No. 6 over No. 3 makes prediction from the specific stimulus (absolute) theory ambiguous, for one stimulus component is associated with jumps to the right, one with jumps to the left. In such cases, instead of chance choices, 95 per cent were in keeping with the relational hypothesis.[55]

These recent experiments show that responses to relationships are

[55] This particular high-success level may also be accounted for on another basis. Because in original learning only the top half of the cards was significant, the top half

clearly possible under circumstances in which specific stimulus cues are minimized and relational cues emphasized. Again an old controversy dissolves in favor of a statement of the conditions under which one or another form of response occurs. Rats can react *either* to the absolute characteristics of specific stimuli *or* to stimuli in relation to each other. It is the circumstances that are important in determining which they will do. Spence (1952c) has accepted what is essentially this position.

The mathematical treatment of discrimination does not require favoring either absolute or relational discrimination. While Spence's theory (1937) was based on the absolute qualities of the stimuli, the mathematical treatment by Gulliksen and Wolfle (1938) was based on the relative qualities of the stimuli.

The details of Spence's theory of overlapping gradients have been subjected to recent criticism. Spence (1937) and Hull (1939a) (1950b) adopted gradients differing in curvature, Spence's being concave downward and Hull's concave upward. Lawrence (1952) studied the transfer of discrimination along a continuum. He found that learning was more efficient if training was first given on an easy discrimination and then shifted to the test discrimination *than if all the training was given directly with the test stimuli.* He found also that best results were obtained when the test discrimination was approached gradually. The results suggest that discrimination learning comes about not only through the generation of habit strength through reinforcement of specific stimuli, but through the isolation of functionally relevant stimulus dimensions.[56] In a theoretical treatment of his results, Lawrence (1955) has shown difficulties in the attempt to apply either Spence's or Hull's form of gradient. Although some form of supplement or modification of Spence's theory may prove to be applicable, Lawrence was unable to provide a consistent set of statements about generalization gradients applicable to his own study as well as to other studies of discrimination learning.

Several experimenters have followed their predecessors in extending the methods originating in animal experiments to the study of discrimination and transposition in children.[57] These experiments help somewhat in mediating the problem of absolute versus relative discrimi-

may have become "distinctive." A top half prediction conforms to a relative prediction for these stimuli, so that *one* aspect of reaction to specific stimuli corresponds to reaction to relations, and hence a high per cent of successes might be anticipated.

[56] See in this connection the argument by Gibson and Gibson (1955) that in man perceptual learning comes about by differentiation of cues.

[57] For earlier studies, see, for example, Ivanov-Smolensky (1927), Jackson and Dominguez (1939). The later ones include Kuenne (1946), Alberts and Ehrenfreund (1951), Stevenson and Iscoe (1954), Stevenson, Iscoe, and McConnell (1955).

nation by showing that, in general, transposition is easier as the children become older. Some importance is attributed to the development of language, but the causal factors are obscure and alternative hypotheses are possible. One curious finding [58] is that a size-discrimination was much easier progressively from preschool years to the fifth grade, but then became more difficult up to the college years. The only plausible interpretation was that the older students were looking for a more difficult problem and overlooked the very simple demands of the discrimination. This suggests (for human learning at least) theories emphasizing "set" or acquired cue distinctiveness over those based merely on the rewarding and punishing of specific responses.

These recent studies leave the problem of discrimination at a maturer level for analysis, beyond the stage of polemical debate in which one side or another scores a "victory." There are systematic modes of solution emphasized by the non-continuity exponents, and there are the cumulative results of experience emphasized by the continuity exponents. There are responses to specific stimulus components as advocated by those building their theories upon them, but there are also responses to stimulus characteristics defined in relational terms.

THE FORMALIZATION OF EXPECTANCY THEORY

Because of its more precise formal structure, stimulus-response theory has guided more research and theory construction in recent years than cognitive theory. Many of the *problems* set for stimulus-response psychologists, however, were posed by those from the other camp: for example, the distinction between learning and performance, latent learning, transposition, systematic modes of problem solution, secondary reinforcement (in the form of sign learning), incentive motivation (the valence of perceived incentives). As stimulus-response experimentation and theorizing has become more developed many of the challenging problems which cognitive theorists first called attention to have taken on new interest for the stimulus-response theorists. For example, instead of denying latent learning, new stimulus-response derivations are required to account for it; instead of denying relational discrimination, earlier theories are modified to include it. This is entirely wholesome, and in the end may lead to the kind of unification of psychological theory that we all wish to see.

A few psychologists, many of them trained in stimulus-response ap-

[58] Stevenson, Iscoe, and McConnell (1955).

proaches, have become increasingly aware that the cognitive theorists were talking about psychological reality, even though their formalization of certain phenomena was inadequate. Some of them have turned their attention to the formalization of cognitive theories in a manner more nearly consonant with the kind of systematic treatment that stimulus-response theories have been getting.

The fact that something may not yet have been done does not mean that it cannot be done. Miller (1949) has repeated the invitation of Hull (1930) to those friendly to gestalt psychology to do for cognitive theories what has been done for stimulus-response theory. Yet it must be remembered that little was done to formalize Thorndike's theory between 1898 and 1930. The motivations of psychologists have to be taken into account as well as the ripeness of their theories. Here lie some interesting problems for the historian of science.

Osgood (1950), acknowledging a preference for stimulus-response theories, tried his hand at applying Tolman's theory to avoidance learning. He suggested four postulates consonant with Tolman's theory, and believed that they could be used satisfactorily to derive avoidance learning.

Olds (1954) set up a neural model for Tolman's theory, based on Hebb's (1949) discussion of cell assemblies. The model is sufficiently precise to allow for experimental testing, and one experimental study based on it has been reported (Olds, 1953).

MacCorquodale and Meehl's Postulate System

The most careful attempt to date to develop a Hull-like set of postulates for a Tolman-like expectancy theory is that of MacCorquodale and Meehl (1953) (1954). Without arguing its truth-value they have taken the task of making explicit what expectancy theory would be like were it formalized.

To begin with, an expectancy is said always to have three terms: (1) something initially perceived, called an *elicitor* of the expectancy (S_1); (2) something to be done following this perception, a response (R_1); and then something that will be perceived, as the goal of the expectancy, the *expectandum* (S_2). The process can be symbolized as S_1-R_1-S_2 in the defining of an expectancy just as the process S-R is used to define an association. The best way to remember the process is to think of some ordinary sentence, such as: "When this *button* (S_1) is *pressed* (R_1), I *expect* to hear the *ringing doorbell* (S_2)." This total process, prior to doing anything to the button right now, is the expectancy.

If ringing the doorbell becomes a goal (becomes *valenced*), then the expectancy is *activated*. I *push* the button only if I want to ring the doorbell; I may have the expectancy ($S_1R_1S_2$) without doing anything about it.

Capital letters are used to describe the significant environmental events S_1-R_1-S_2, and the same letters may be used for the inferred construct, the expectancy ($S_1R_1S_2$). The letters are enclosed in parentheses when reference is to the construct rather than to events themselves. But whenever capital letters are used, whether in describing events or the inferred expectancy, it is appropriate to use physical-stimulus language. That is, S_1 and S_2 are objects in the environment, with their ordinary characteristics, and R_1 is a physical response. The specification of the terms of an expectancy in physical language permits not only objective verification, but also clear statements about confirmed and unconfirmed expectancies. (The logic of the physical language is no different from that used in assigning dimensions to Hull's ${}_SH_R$.) [59]

Twelve postulates are stated, often with guesses as to the form of mathematical function involved. For a briefer introduction to the flavor of the system, the postulates are here paraphrased, with much of the quantitative detail omitted.

1. *Mnemonization*. The occurrence of the sequence S_1-R_1-S_2 results in an increase in the strength of an expectancy ($S_1R_1S_2$). The *rate* of growth increases with the valence of S_2. The *limit* of growth depends on the probability (P) with which S_2 regularly follows S_1-R_1. That is, growth approaches P as a limit.

This is the basic acquisition postulate. It is a contiguity theory, in that mere occurrence of the sequences presumably leads to increase in expectancy. But it is also a kind of reinforcement theory, because the expectancy is influenced by the valence of the terminal item (S_2) in the sequence. It is not, however, a stimulus-response theory in the usual sense. MacCorquodale and Meehl point out that by their accepting specified parameters for rate and limit of growth they have not made concessions to some form of non-expectancy theory.

2. *Extinction*. The occurrence of a sequence S_1-R_1, if not followed by S_2, tends to produce a decrement in the expectancy.

Two cases have to be distinguished. If P has been 1.00 (that is, S_1-R_1 always followed by S_2) a single omission of S_2 will lead to a

[59] Meehl and MacCorquodale allow for a central state called the *expectant* ($s_1r_1s_2$), but they make no use of it in their preliminary formalization. Presumably if one were to turn to neurophysiological explanations there would be some translations between the neurophysiological language of ($s_1r_1s_2$) and the physical language of ($S_1R_1S_2$).

prompt decrement, depending both on the current strength of $(S_1R_1S_2)$ and the valence of S_2. If, however, P has been less than 1.00, the course of decrement will be slower, and, if P shifts to a lower P′, the expectancy will approach the new value of P′ as an asymptote.[60]

3. *Primary-stimulus generalization.* When an expectancy $(S_1R_1S_2)$ has been strengthened, other expectancies $(S'_1R_1S_2)$ will also have received some strength, depending upon the similarity of the elicitors S'_1 and S_1.

Similarity gradients are an empirical matter, and there is no point in trying to distinguish the functions from those used by stimulus-response psychologists. Tolman (1939) recognized this when he built Spence's (1937) gradients into his "schematic sowbug."

4. *Inference.* When an expectancy $(S_1R_1S_2)$ exists at some strength, the presence of a valenced object S^* in close contiguity with S_2 gives rise to a new expectancy $(S_1R_1S^*)$.

5. *Generalized inference.* Even though $(S_1R_1S_2)$ is originally of zero strength, the occurrence of a valenced object S^* in close contiguity with S_2 may give rise to a new expectancy $(S_1R_1S^*)$, provided $(S_1R_1S'_2)$ is of some strength, and S'_2 is similar to S_2.

These are the kinds of postulates said by MacCorquodale and Meehl to contribute heavily to the identification of an expectancy theory. They give the basis for latent learning and for the interpretation of experiments modeled after Maier's reasoning experiments.

The next six postulates have to do with motivation, described according to needs, cathexes, and valences. I am taking the liberty of renumbering them for expository purposes. They can easily be identified in the original source because their titles are unchanged. The three following postulates state the fundamental position with respect to motivation.[61]

6. *Cathexis.* The cathexis (C^*) of a valenced stimulus situation (S^*) is a function of the number of contiguous occurrences between it and the consummatory response.

7. *Need strength.* The need (D) for a cathected stimulus (S^*) is an increasing function of the time interval since satiation for it.

8. *Valence.* The valence of a stimulus S^* is a multiplicative function of the correlated need D and the cathexis C^* attached to S^*.

[60] We know from Humphreys' (1939b) experiment that following a P of .50 there may be an increasing level of $(S_1R_1S_2)$ for a few trials if S_2 is regularly omitted. The MacCorquodale-Meehl postulate is incomplete, as they were the first to admit. Yet it is a few points, such as this increase in response in the first few trials of extinction, that provide some of the greatest support for an expectancy interpretation over other interpretations.

[61] The treatment covers rewarding (appetitive) motivation only. Pain and avoidance are not treated.

Postulates 6 to 8 imply a fairly complex theory of motivation, generated (as Spence's recent theory was) by the problems of latent learning. The *sight* of food leads to food-seeking because of the correlation of sight of food with consummatory response (eating). This is the meaning of cathexis. Food thus gains a certain attractiveness (*cathexis*) through prior experiences of eating, but its present pulling power as an incentive (its *valence*) depends also on how hungry the organism is (its *need* level). Need is a function of deprivation; cathexis is a function of experienced satisfactions in the past; valence is a product of both. There is a striking parallel with Hull and Spence's D and K, which act together (as a product or as a sum) to influence reaction potential.

Now we are ready for some postulates (actually earlier in the original list) concerning some further relationships between experience and cathexis.

9. *Secondary cathexis.* The contiguity of S_2 and S^* (a valenced stimulus) increases the cathexis of S_2.

This is a kind of "secondary reinforcement" or acquired incentive value, whereby the valence of one expectandum is given to a contiguous expectandum.

10. *Induced elicitor-cathexis.* The acquisition of valence by an expectandum S_2 belonging to an existing expectancy ($S_1R_1S_2$), induces a cathexis in the elicitor S_1.

11. *Confirmed elicitor-cathexis.* The confirmation of an expectancy ($S_1R_1S_2$), when S_2 has a positive valence, increases the cathexis of S_1.

These two postulates mean that an elicitor, as a discriminative stimulus, comes to have reinforcing power. It is easily demonstrated that cues at a choice-point, if similar to cues in the goal-box, facilitate learning. While usually interpreted according to secondary reinforcement, the notion of acquired elicitor cathexis is roughly equivalent.[62]

The difference between "induction" and "confirmation" is that between introducing food after satiated runs, and learning while hungry.

12. *Activation.* The reaction potential $_SE_R$ of a response R_1 in the presence of S_1 is a multiplicative function of the strength of the expectancy ($S_1R_1S_2$) and the valence of the expectandum.

This final postulate gets around the jibe of Guthrie (1952, page 143) that Tolman leaves the rat buried in thought. The parallel with the Hull-Spence basic formulation is striking:

[62] Bauer and Lawrence (1953) show that the problem of choice-point cues and goal cues is complex. Conditioned inhibition may turn out to be as relevant as secondary reinforcement.

Hull-Spence
$_{S}E_{R} = f(_{S}H_{R}) \times f(D, K)$
MacCorquodale-Meehl
$_{S}E_{R} = f(S_1R_1S_2) \times f(D, C^*)$

As one goes on to specify in more detail the relations between reaction potential and response, there remain the problems of thresholds, oscillation, and the like. MacCorquodale and Meehl point out that there is no reason to handle these further matters differently in the expectancy model and the stimulus-response model.

How successful are these postulates in deducing the experimental phenomena of learning? MacCorquodale and Meehl (1953) illustrate the procedure by deducing the phenomena from several experiments representing subvarieties of latent learning.[63] They succeed reasonably well in accounting for the data through manipulation of the postulates.

The postulate set is avowedly weak on some matters that have been of particular interest to expectancy or cognitive theorists, such as the problems of multiple paths, systematic modes of solution ("hypotheses"), perceptual patterning. The authors believe that they have chosen a course more fruitful than that of Tolman himself in his emphasis on "maps" and "perceptions." It is a useful beginning in showing, first, how a theory of this kind can be made explicit, including notational reference to response within an expectancy setting, and second, when made explicit, that there are large areas of agreement between a theory of this kind and stimulus-response theory.

Rotter's Social-Learning Theory

Rotter (1954), in a book designed to provide a theory for clinical psychology, has evolved an expectancy-reinforcement theory with many points of resemblance to the MacCorquodale and Meehl model.

His basic formula for *behavior potential* (B.P.), the equivalent of reaction potential, makes it a function of *expectancy of reinforcement* (E), and the *reinforcement value* (R.V.) of the expected reinforcement. That is:

$$B.P. = f(E, R.V.)$$

It will be recalled that in other systems the motivational term commonly has two components, one reflecting need or drive, the other reflecting goal-activity or incentive value. Rotter's theory concentrates upon

[63] The experiments are those of Kendler (1946), Meehl and MacCorquodale (1948), and Tolman and Gleitman (1949).

the incentive value, and the reinforcement value (R.V.) is measured directly by the *preference* for one goal-object over another when the possibilities of occurrence are equal. Something similar to Allport's functional autonomy of motives is implied: social goals are learned ones, and they need not be referred back to physiological needs. Instead, present reinforcements are best understood in relation to prior reinforcements:

> *We find it a sufficient basis for prediction to state that behavior directed toward the attainment of a learned goal or external reinforcement may be predicted through a knowledge of the situation the organism is in and from a knowledge of his past learning experiences.* It appears as if a theory that attempted to predict meaningful behavior through description of the organism's physiological drive condition at a particular moment would hold not only no advantages but many disadvantages.[64]

The theory has a rather different flavor from the familiar ones because of its social, hence more molar, reference. For example, the list of six major needs brings newcomers to learning theory: recognition-status, protection-dependency, dominance, independence, love and affection, physical comfort.[65]

Another new concept is that of *freedom of movement*, which is related to psychological need. It is defined as: The mean expectancy of obtaining positive satisfactions as a result of a set of related behaviors directed toward the accomplishment of a group of functionally-related reinforcements.[66] What this means is that high freedom of movement implies an expectancy of success for many different kinds of behavior in many different situations related to a family of common goals. Low freedom of movement, of course, implies the opposite.

Rotter's theory has been subjected to a number of experimental tests in relation to its quantitative assumptions, but few of the results have yet reached publication, so that critical appraisal in relation to other learning theories must be postponed.[67] It is a significant effort at theory construction, however, and should be seriously considered because of its attempt to broaden the boundaries encompassed by our present quantitative theories.

[64] Rotter (1954), page 116.
[65] Rotter (1954), page 132.
[66] Rotter (1954), page 194.
[67] Some studies have appeared at the time of writing, e.g., Crandall (1951), Schroder and Rotter (1952), Rotter, Fitzgerald, and Joyce (1954). Other previously unpublished dissertations are appearing currently.

NEUROPHYSIOLOGICAL INTERPRETATIONS OF LEARNING

Among the systematists whose views are presented in Chapters 2 through 10, only Thorndike, Köhler, and Freud gave any appreciable attention to the neural correlates of their theories. Thorndike's early "synaptic resistance" theory seemed no longer important to him in his later years. Freud's influence has been functional rather than neuroanatomical. Only Köhler has continued to attempt to find physiological support for his principle of isomorphism.

This relative lack of interest by learning theorists in the nervous system, particularly in the period of 1930 to 1950, is again a problem for the historian. No one denied the importance of the nervous system in learning. The denial had to do only with its importance for *theories* of learning. Possibly one influence was a certain disillusionment about progress in neuroanatomy and neurophysiology after the breakdown of the localization doctrine under many lines of evidence, including Head's studies of aphasia and Lashley's cortical ablation studies. If nobody really knew anything about how the brain worked, what help could present neurophysiology be to the learning theorist? So the argument ran. Perhaps another influence was the tendency for objective studies to favor "peripheral" rather than "central" interpretations. Guthrie and Hull were making the case for fractional anticipatory responses and movement-produced stimuli; Skinner was arguing that we stick to the data and avoid the c.n.s. ("conceptual nervous system"). When even a "centralist" such as Tolman had little interest in the nervous system, it was not surprising that the non-physiological position temporarily won the day.

A reaction has now begun to be felt, and the relation of the nervous system to learning is awakening renewed interest. Although, to be sure, the interest had never fully died out, the renewal of widespread interest among the theorists can be dated by the appearance of Hebb's (1949) neuropsychological theory. Hebb brought a freshness of approach, capitalizing on recent developments in neurophysiology and introducing some daring speculations in a non-polemical manner that invited tractable consideration. Two specific events that marked the reaction away from the non-physiological period are some remarks in a discussion by Tolman (1949c) pleading for a more explicit neurological model, and a subsequent insistence by Krech (1950) that we think of every hypothetical construct in psychology in purely neurological terms.

The Experimental Contributions of Neurophysiology to an Understanding of Learning

A great many experiments have been devised through the years in an effort to locate the parts of the brain essential for carrying out learned activities. While results of interest have been secured, they have not led to any significant generalizations about the precise mechanisms of learning.[68]

Although the new interest in neurophysiological theories of learning also has thus far led to little that is of genuine explanatory value, a number of leads have been opened. Without attempting to appraise the vast literature, we may mention a few of the developments as indicative of some of the directions in which research is moving.

1. Electrical exploration of the brain of human subjects under local anesthetics (especially with epileptic patients) has located some sites, particularly in the temporal lobe region, where vivid memories appear to be re-enacted under stimulation.[69]

2. The temporal lobes, particularly the amygdaloid nuclei, have become of special interest not only in studies of emotion, but also in the affective control of learning. Cats with these nuclei ablated required more trials to learn an avoidance response than cats with control lesions, but their retention was unaffected.[70]

3. Recent work, in part using the electroencephalograph, has called attention to a diffuse system by which the midbrain affects the cortex other than through anatomically defined sensory pathways. This diffuse system operates via the reticular substance, and permits incoming sensory stimulation, acting at a subcortical level, to waken the organism and incite it to activity.[71]

4. Working with amplifiers that can record resting potentials or slowly varying ones, it is possible to detect changes of potential on the surface of the skull at the occipital lobes corresponding in some ways to the patterning of visual stimuli. These results appear to give some support for Köhler's field theory of excitation.[72]

5. Imbedded electrodes worn while animals engage in learning are

[68] Useful summaries of the major findings may be found in reviews by Marquis (1951), Morgan (1951), and Osgood (1953).

[69] Penfield and Jasper (1954).

[70] Brady and others (1954). The problem was opened up by Klüver and Bucy (1939). For a review of temporal lobe function see Milner (1954).

[71] E.g., Lindsley and others (1950), Magoun (1952).

[72] Köhler and Held (1949), Köhler, Held, and O'Connell (1952). The theory supported has been criticized experimentally by Lashley, Chow and Semmes (1951).

being used to study the effects on learning of stimulating various portions of the brain.[73]

6. Some chemical differences are found in the brain tissue of rats high in "hypothesis" behavior as contrasted with those low in "hypothesis" behavior.[74]

Interesting as these various leads are, they are mostly rather remote from the central problems of learning, although some of them bear on the problems of motivation and the nature of reinforcement.

Hebb's Speculative Neuropsychological Model

Because of its influence in renewing interest in neurophysiological speculation, Hebb's (1949) theory deserves special mention.[75]

Hebb recognizes that the basic problem is to understand *thought*, the something that intervenes between sensory and motor processes and is not fully controlled by environmental stimulation. He wishes to explain thought in neurological terms and of course to do so without any shade of animism. He has no truck with a little man in the head who *wants* or *disapproves* or *guides*. Hence, while Hebb wishes a theory adequate to the phenomena of a cognitive psychology, he wants no softness in it, and so ties it as closely as possible to what we know about neurones, their interconnections, and their functioning. The "central process" in the cortex must be better specified than in the telephone switchboard analogy of connectionists, or in the distribution of potentials across a homogeneous surface as implied by cortical-field theorists.

Hebb's two concepts most important for understanding cortical processes are the *cell assembly* and the *phase sequence*.

A cell assembly arises through frequently repeated particular stimulation. It corresponds roughly to the persisting neural counterpart ("engram") of a simple association. It is a diffuse structure comprising cells in the cortex and subcortical centers. When the particular stimulation again occurs, the cell assembly is aroused. Going into action as a closed system, it facilitates other systems and usually facilitates motor response. A cell assembly can thus be activated by another activated cell assembly, by sensory stimulation, or by both at once.

The neuronic basis for a persisting reverberating circuit is speculative. Hebb suggests that stimulation repeated often enough to have a

[73] E.g., Olds and Milner (1954), Delgado, Roberts and Miller (1954).

[74] Krech and others (1954).

[75] No attempt is made here to review the many speculative models that have appeared, e.g., Ashby (1952), Coburn (1951) (1953), McReynolds (1950) (1953), Wolpe (1949) (1953).

lasting influence results in the growth of "synaptic knobs" that increase the area of contact between the axon and the tissue into which it fires. This comes only after repetition; the primary process creating the cell assembly depends on convergences of excitation in a rather diffuse neurone network, as a consequence of contiguous stimulation. Some "equipotentiality" is implied, because once a cell assembly is set up, fewer fibers have to be active at once in order to traverse the synapses necessary to arouse the cell assembly.

A *phase sequence* is constituted by the arousal of a series of cell assemblies. For example, looking successively at the three corners of a triangle arouses the cell assemblies appropriate to each corner, and these facilitate each other. Thus the whole triangle may be perceived while attending to any one corner. Even the act of perceiving a triangle involves rather complex cortical facilitation, both sensory and motor; for example, we can anticipate ("expect") the change that will come about by changing fixation from corner A to corner B. Thus the *phase sequence* is the thought process.

At birth there is an *intrinsic organization* to cortical activity, indicated by the large slow waves of the infant's electroencephalogram. For learning to take place, sensory processes have to interrupt this intrinsic organization and gain control of association-area activity. Hence the larger the association area (relative to the sensory areas), the more difficult it is for the young to learn. Hebb accounts on this basis for the slowness of learning by the human infant as compared with lower animals.

The first stage of learning is the establishing of cell assemblies and their related phase sequences. At first this comes about slowly, and slow-increment learning is characteristic of childhood. But the results of such learning endure and are influential throughout life.

Adult learning is essentially conceptual, often prompt and insightful. Such learning is possible, according to Hebb, only when the stimulation sets off well-organized phase sequences.

This is the theory in broad outlines. Hebb's book has been influential not only because of its neurophysiological ideas but because of the wealth of psychological observations reported in it. Unfortunately it is impossible to convey this richness of detail in a few paragraphs.

CONCLUDING REMARKS ON CURRENT DEVELOPMENTS

The theoretical positions developed in the first half of the century have had their fruits not in the final triumph of any one system but in a more sophisticated approach to both experimentation and refinement of theory. The vast volume of experimental work now appearing is almost all oriented to the checking of one or more hypotheses, and these hypotheses are imbedded in larger theoretical contexts. This kind of development tends at once to soften the clashes between systematists as they attempt soberly to face common facts, and to improve fact-gathering by experimenters. The newer facts, oriented to more precise theories, are more likely to be additive than they were in the past.

We have reviewed the kinds of searching criticisms that are going on in current studies of reinforcement, of motivational aspects of learning, and of the problems of learned discrimination. The efforts to systematize "expectancy" interpretations come in recognition of the cognitive and directional aspects of learning. Neurophysiological speculation is again welcomed. These developments have not yet reached any climax, and no mediator has yet appeared to enlist agreement on some kind of harmonious interpretation of all the phenomena of learning. Yet progress is being made, and there is reason to hope that we are moving toward the unification of theory.

SUPPLEMENTARY READINGS

SYMPOSIA ON CURRENT VIEWS

ESTES, W. K., and others (1954) *Modern learning theory.*

Kentucky Symposium (1954) *Learning theory, personality theory, and clinical research.*

MCCLELLAND, D. C., ed. (1955) *Studies in motivation.*

Nebraska Symposium on Motivation (1953) *Current theory and research in motivation,* I.

Nebraska Symposium on Motivation, M. R. Jones, ed. (1954) *Current theory and research in motivation,* II.

Nebraska Symposium on Motivation, M. R. Jones, ed. (1955) *Current theory and research in motivation,* III.

RECENT BOOKS ON PARTICULAR THEORIES

DOLLARD, J., and MILLER, N. E. (1950) *Personality and psychotherapy.*

HEBB, D. O. (1949) *The organization of behavior.*

MCCLELLAND, D. C., and others (1953) *The achievement motive.*

MAIER, N. R. F. (1949) *Frustration: the study of behavior without a goal.*

MOWRER, O. H. (1950) *Learning theory and personality dynamics.*

MOWRER, O. H. (1955) *Two-factor learning theory: reviewed, revised, and extended.* (Mimeographed.)

ROTTER, J. B. (1954) *Social learning and clinical psychology.*

SPENCE, K. W. (1955) *Behavior theory and conditioning.* (Silliman lectures).

Chapter 14

RETROSPECT AND PROSPECT

THE array of theories we have examined may be thought to present an unfavorable picture of the state of systematic knowledge about learning. How can psychologists be helpful to other social scientists or to those who wish to apply their findings if they disagree among themselves on these fundamental matters? It seems to us that there are several considerations which temper this adverse judgment. For one thing, there is a great deal of empirical knowledge about learning which is unrelated to the differences among the major points of view. For another, there are, in addition to the general theories, a number of special theories, more closely related to particular experimental situations. These special theories are tested and corrected in a matter-of-fact manner, cutting across the preferences of rival theoretical positions. Finally, discipleship in one or another of the major schools is not characteristic of most psychologists working in the field of learning. There are strong tendencies toward mediating positions. Many writers have found the major contributions of the different schools largely reconcilable.[1]

The disadvantages of conflicting points of view are balanced to some extent by the motivation which a strong position provides its proponent and by the challenge it presents to its adversary. Out of the heat of controversy there is eventually scientific advance.[2] Even in the midst of controversy, it is not necessary for the theorist to set aside reasonableness or critical powers. Theoretical differences show up most markedly where the data remain ambiguous, so that preferences hold sway over evidence. As the data become more securely established, it becomes increasingly possible to translate one system into another.

While the state of knowledge is not therefore as bad as the parade of points of view makes it out to be, it is still rather unsatisfactory. There are no laws of learning which can be taught with confidence. Even

[1] E.g., Dashiell (1935), Kellogg (1938), McConnell (1942).
[2] Boring (1929).

the most obvious facts of improvement with practice and the regulation of learning under reward and punishment are matters of theoretical dispute.

TOWARD A MORE SATISFACTORY THEORY

A generally satisfactory theory awaits a set of concepts which will be appropriate to all that is known about learning. While each major theorist believes his concepts to be the appropriate ones, their pertinence often derives from the fact that the theorist's interest is primarily in some segment or aspect of the total learning situation. Some are interested in the initial adjustment, as in insight or problem-solving, others are interested in the predictability of performance under varied conditions of motivation, and so on. We need a more careful delineation of the *kinds* of learning which take place (each of which may have "laws" of its own), and an acceptable fractionation of the *aspects* of learning which make demands upon theory. Some theories are different largely because they are concerned with different problems to begin with. This search for the appropriate concepts is not merely an exercise in definition or classification. It requires a high order of theory construction, based on open-minded acceptance of demonstrated relationships, and in addition contributing to the ordering of such relationships into a system.

There is no single direction for theory to take. In fact, it is useful to recognize a division of labor in theory construction just as there is a division of labor in experimentation. Here are some of the needed directions, and theory can be advanced by good work in any one of them:

1. *More precise formulation and quantification.* Ultimately science must be exact and quantitative. We have had occasion to review some of the newer model-building efforts in Chapter 11, where we cited both the advantages and limitations of this approach.

2. *Greater specification of mediating processes.* The intervening-mediator type of theory has been forced into prominence by the factual relationships found within behavior. Simple correlations with end-terms do not suffice to account for the kinds of variation discovered in these relationships.

Because this is so, two possibilities remain open. One is to stay with the functional analysis and to specify the intervening process solely in terms of the conditions that give rise to it. The mediating concept remains intangible, but it must be "triangulated" so as to be specified and measured. It must have units of measurement that derive from the operations giving rise to it. MacCorquodale and Meehl (1948) named this kind of mediating process an "intervening variable."

The other possibility is to give the intervening process tangible or substantial status, and then search for it directly. MacCorquodale and Meehl call this kind of tangible intermediary a "hypothetical construct." The experiments concerned with the need-reduction theory of reinforcement are of this sort; they are not studying the place of reinforcement in the *equations* of Hull, but they are going at the *substance* of a reinforcement postulate. Similarly, the direct attacks on drive in relation to food deprivation can be launched without worrying about drive as a multiplier of habit strength. The fractional anticipatory goal response is substantive and ought to be directly observable in appropriate experiments. A neurophysiological theory, provided it leads to concrete experiments, can give a substantive basis for the mediating processes in either the peripheralist or centralist theories.

3. *Greater inclusiveness.* Spence (1953) has given us a diagram showing six levels of lawful relationships within learning data, to which correspond six first-level theories, close to these varieties of data. Above these in a logical hierarchy are second-level theories that co-ordinate the first-level theories, and then there may be more general theories at the third level. It is his contention that we must work up from the fields in which the data are best quantified, and where the interrelationships of variables have been most thoroughly explored. At present, our most precise theories deal with conditioning, selective learning, and serial learning. Our first-level theories are very weak in the study of skills, problem-solving, and group learning. Spence's diagram is reproduced as Figure 67.

We may accept Spence's analysis as historically accurate, without being entirely bound by it. Some theorists, for example, instead of *waiting* for the better lawful relationships to be established in the fields of skill, problem-solving, and group learning, will wish to set up models to help in the design of experiments that will result in studies revealing lawful relationships in these areas. Spence's diagram has the virtue that it does not prejudge the question as to which kind of learning is more *fundamental,* for the six kinds of learning are all at Level 1. The fact that the situations at the left are somewhat *simpler,* in terms of the control of experimental variables and the gathering of data, need not imply that any more fundamental psychological processes are involved.

The search for greater inclusiveness is one direction for theory to take, and this search does not have to wait.

4. *A more exact applied psychology of learning.* This scarcely sounds like theory at all, yet a high order of theoretical work will be necessary to arrive at a set of practical rules that will make general psychological laws of learning applicable to teaching and training. It is one of the challenging tasks confronting the psychology of learning, and able talents are needed for it.

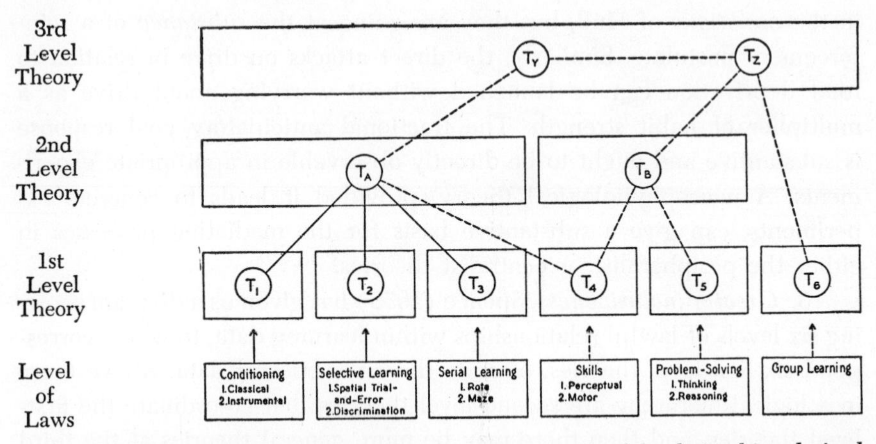

FIGURE 67. Levels of learning theory in relation to lawful relationships derived from experiments. Spence (1953).

These several directions of advance suggest how much there is to be done, and how defeatist it would be to wait for the "brilliant theorist," the Newton or the Einstein who will solve all of our problems for us.

SPECIAL PROBLEMS THAT LEARNING THEORIES FACE

Next in our retrospect we turn to some of the typical problems that were used to summarize the several systems, and to some related questions that arise as we consider the problems the theorists tried to solve.

Learning Capacities

The extreme form of generalization from comparative studies is that there are no differences, except quantitative ones, between the learning of lower mammals and man. Hull stated this quite clearly:

The natural-science theory of behavior being developed by the present author and his associates assumes that all behavior of the individuals of a given species and that of all species of mammals, including man, occurs according to the same set of primary laws.[3]

While such a position is more often implied than asserted, it is strange that the opposite point of view is not more often made explicit—that at the human level there have emerged capacities for retraining, reorganizing, and foreseeing experiences which are not approached by the lower animals, including the other primates. No one has seriously proposed that animals can develop a set of ideals that regulate conduct around long-range plans, or that they can invent a mathematics to help them keep track of their enterprises. Because a trained dog shows some manifestations of shame, or a chimpanzee some signs of co-operation, or a rat a dawning concept of triangularity, it does not follow that these lower organisms, clever as they are, have anything comparable to the richness of human mental activity.

The problem of emerging types of learning ability must be pushed farther back. Language in man is perhaps the clearest of the emergents which carries with it a forward surge in what may be learned. It seems plausible enough that other advances in the ability to learn must have come about as the nervous system evolved through successive stages below man. The prevailing learning theories have had remarkably little to say about the different processes which together make up the functional changes which are classified together as learning.[4] There are probably a number of different kinds of learning which have emerged at different evolutionary periods, with the more highly evolved organisms using several of them. It is quite probable that these different kinds of learning follow different laws, and it is foolhardy to allow our desire for parsimony to cause us to overlook persisting differences.

Learning capacity can be assigned a quantitative meaning only when the several learning capacities are identified, and when we know more about the ways in which these capacities are modified. To what extent can the ceiling of ability itself be modified by training? It is evident that without appropriate prior experiences there are things to be learned that are quite within a man's capacity which he will never acquire. Without appropriate linguistic or mathematical tools, for example, there are kinds of problems he cannot solve, regardless of how much native intelligence he has. After these tools are acquired, his learning ability rises, without any necessary inference that the *ceiling* of his ability was raised.

The obstacle to a precise scientific statement of the problem lies in

[3] Hull (1945), page 56.
[4] Maier (1939a, 1939b) and Tryon (1940) have stressed similar points.

the difficulty of assigning such a limit until one is approached. The notion of a physiological or psychological limit as taught in our elementary textbooks is a convenient fiction. The records of athletic contests suffice to show how impractical it is to assign definite limits, because records are made by improving methods, and are not set solely by the speed of conduction of neural impulses. When the bamboo pole was introduced into pole-vaulting, for example, records increased by a full foot, but improvements in technique have led to their continued improvement beyond this. Kantor [5] has made much of the *interbehavioral* meaning of abilities. He would argue that typewriters must enter into the equations defining typing speed and poles into vaulting records. The difficulty exists, and must be taken account of. There is, however, an asymmetry between the learner and his instrument. The typewriter or the pole does not learn, and there ought to be some way of getting at what the limit would be for a given typist with a given typewriter or a given vaulter with a given pole. Until the ceiling of ability gets a satisfactory theoretical-empirical definition, such problems as the effect of practice on individual differences can receive only superficial answers.

Simple Conditioning

The theory of simple conditioning is an inviting one. It says in effect that partial cues reinstate past stimulus-response situations, that what was *done* in the presence of the stimuli tends to recur in their presence. Despite all the attention commonly given to simple conditioning in learning theory, the evidence for it is very fragmentary. There is no doubt that learning takes place under the arrangements of the conditioned-response experiment, but the results may usually be given alternative explanations. The fact is that *there is little evidence that the simultaneous or nearly simultaneous occurrence of an incidental stimulus and an unconditioned response is the sufficient condition for establishing a sensori-motor association between them.*

The repeated failures to obtain pupillary conditioning through pairing of sounds with illumination changes is one of the most damaging bits of evidence against the conventional pattern assigned to simple conditioning, for the unconditioned pupillary responses occur with regularity, but conditioned responses do not follow.[6]

[5] E.g., Kantor (1947).

[6] To the earlier failures must be added those of Hilgard, Dutton, and Helmick (1949), and F. A. Young (1954). Successful conditioning of the pupil in human subjects has been reported by Mihama and Kotake (1954). Their results were so unstable that one would scarcely wish to base a theory of learning upon them.

If simple conditioning is not accepted as the rule, the alternative is to find the contingencies which give rise to results looking like simple conditioning. The usual solution is to find the stimulus-response sequences related to an ongoing goal-directed activity, whether this be described as proximity to a reinforcing state of affairs, or as part of a field tension-system. It is undeniable that in many instances the learner will do what he last did in the presence of given stimuli because similar motives are operating, and what he did last time achieved the goal.

Some types of direct action release—weeping at a letter bearing sad news, fainting at the sight of blood—appear to conform to a simple conditioning formula, but the full consideration of what is happening involves motives like anxiety, making these cases not unlike other illustrations of learning with tension release. Action systems that seem to be directly released by perceived stimuli usually have either a low threshold or are supported by strong motives. Some people weep easily, so that tears to a letter would be a matter of low thresholds; others would weep only if the letter reported the loss of someone deeply loved. Some reaction systems, such as salivation and neurocirculatory changes, are in unstable equilibrium most of the time, so that they are easily disturbed by a wide range of perceptual experiences. Because these actions can occur without environmental support, they may be activated independently of dominant ongoing activity at the time.

While allowance must be made for some relatively automatic associated movements released by perceived stimuli, in the more usual case these movements are integrated with goal-directed activity. This follows because the motives which support the goal-seeking activity serve also to lower the thresholds for the perceptually-aroused concomitants. Hence the hungry dog is likely to salivate while nosing up the lid to the food-box. Because the dog is hungry the threshold for salivation is low, and the sight of food or food-related objects is likely to lead to salivation.

Hence, as alternative to the simple conditioning notion of associative learning we may consider several possibilities: (1) the aroused perception may serve as an intermediary between the conditioned stimulus and the conditioned response; (2) sometimes the appearance of the conditioned response will be a matter of facilitation rather than of association; (3) goal-directed activity may provide an important background for what appears to be simple conditioning.

Stimulus, Response, and Mediating Processes

Stimulus and response concepts have a long history in psychology. The original S-R psychology was not that of learning theory at all: it began with reaction time, as psychologists measured the time between the signal and the response to it, and then tried in various ways to fractionate this time. Even at the start, it was clear that there were intermediate processes beyond merely the speed of impulse transmission. In his early criticism of the reflex-arc theory, Dewey (1896) had in mind these reaction-time experiments and the generalizations that were being made from them. Woodworth, a student of the neuro-physiologist Sherrington, urged strongly that the S-R motto be hung on the walls of the psychological laboratory as a reminder to the student to think in stimulus-response terms. Woodworth later modified his S-R motto to read S-O-R, recognizing that the mediating processes in the organism always had to be taken into account in the correlation between stimulus and response.

It is meaningless to approve or disapprove of stimulus-response in general, because all psychology can be translated into stimulus-response terms. Before expressing approval or disapproval it is important to specify *what kind* of stimulus-response theory is under consideration.

Two kinds of stimulus-response theory are worth distinguishing. One of these we shall call a *substantive* S-R theory, the other a *functional* S-R theory.

By a *substantive* S-R theory we shall mean the kind of theory that says that the only facts of interest to a psychologist are facts of physical stimulation and measurable responses (muscular movements and glandular secretions). Not only is the theory tied to S's and R's, but all inferences are to S's and R's, *including inferences to mediating processes.* For this reason, such theories are also called *peripheralist.* Hull's fractional anticipatory goal response (r_G) is a good representative of a substantive intermediary.

A *functional* S-R theory is anchored to stimuli and responses as points of reference, in giving operational definition to the measurements used in the theory. That is, the theory always *points* to S's and R's in describing its experimental results or in beginning its theory construction. Mediating processes, however, need not be conceived in S-R terms, and they may have purely functional characteristics. The drive level (D) in the theories of Hull and Spence is a concept of this kind. It is given operational definition in physical terms, according to maintenance schedule and hours of food deprivation, but D itself is characterized by a mere number, a multiplying constant without any dimensions of its own, unless we infer it to have the dimensions of reaction potential. Thus a system such as Hull's or Spence's may be substantive in some parts and functional in others.

The *functional* S-R theory is generally congenial to the functionalist psychologists, whereas the *substantive* S-R theory is more common among neo-behaviorists. Thus the stimuli used in a memorization experiment may be classified by the functionalist according to degree of meaningfulness. Because degree of meaning can be specified denotatively by reference to the material used in the experiment, the difficulty of defining the material in strictly physical stimulus energy terms does not worry him, although it should worry the *substantive* S-R theorist. The functional S-R position permits further specification of the mediating processes, but these need not be specified in S-R terms. Thus the mediators can be brain states, if evidence can be found for them.[7]

MacCorquodale and Meehl (1953) have shown that an expectancy theory can be written in *functional* S-R terms, so that the main difference between their theory and one such as Hull's or Spence's is the difference that I have indicated between *substantive* S-R theories and *functional* S-R theories.

If this analysis is correct, the issues between the theories arise largely over the nature of and specification of the mediating processes. The factual results are going to be accepted in the end by any theory that survives, so that there is no point in looking for a crucial experiment at the level of learned behavior. It is only experiments that bear crucially on the mediating processes that will make possible a choice between competing theories of learning. Once inferred intermediaries appear to account satisfactorily for the relationships found in experiments, experiments designed to study these intermediaries as directly as possible will prove helpful. We do not have enough such experiments today to force the impartial judge to select one general theory over another.

Perception and Learning

The problem of perceptual discrimination is a central one for learning theory. There is some uncertainty as to the manner in which perception is natively organized, but at a primitive level there are undoubtedly some

[7] Thus either *substantive* S-R theorists or *functional* S-R theorists may use *hypothetical constructs* in the terminology of MacCorquodale and Meehl (1948), but the substantive S-R theorist puts them in S-R terms, if he is consistent. Osgood's (1953) mediation hypothesis appears to me to fit the pattern of hypothetical constructs within a functional S-R theory.

discriminations of continuity and discontinuity, of change and succession, of boundary phenomena, of proximity and remoteness. There is an old controversy between those who believe that the organization of perception is essentially unlearned, and those who believe that practically everything within perception is learned.[8] It is not necessary to enter this controversy in order to point out that the learning theorist must be aware of the learning within perception as well as of the role of perception in learning.

The perception of objects suffices to show that there is at least some learning in perception. A cake of ice *looks* cold; the red tip of the poker *looks* hot. The properties of cold and hot, not present to the senses, are present in the perception as a result of prior experiences. They are not judgments or deliberate inferences from perceptual data, but are given as immediately as any other of the properties of the perceived objects.

The process whereby identifying signs are used to represent a total situation previously experienced in called *redintegration*.[9] The ice looks cold because the previous experiences of felt cold are redintegrated by its appearance. The paramnesic experience (sometimes referred to as *déjà vu*) is probably of this sort. That the process occurs is evident, but its explanation is not easy.

If we accept the fact of perceptual learning, and we believe in some sort of goal orientation in learning, can we discover any goals in perception that might control perceptual learning? I have elsewhere suggested two possible perceptual goals: (1) *the achievement of environmental stability,* and (2) *the achievement of clarity and definiteness in perception.*[10]

The organism seeks a perceptually stable environment in a fashion somewhat parallel to that in which it seeks an internally stable environment. There is a kind of environmental homeostasis parallel to physiological homeostasis. The equilibrium is a dynamic one, and the external environment, like the internal one, is ever changing. The organism tolerates perceptual differences between night and day as it does physiological differences between waking and sleeping, but it does not accept an environment that distorts too rapidly. If a man's perceived environment distorts too rapidly he gets upset or seasick.

In normal perception the goal of stability accounts for many of our perceptual achievements. For example, were it not for this achieved

[8] The contrasting positions are represented by Koffka (1930) and Carr (1935).
[9] Hollingworth (1928).
[10] Hilgard (1951). The next few paragraphs borrow heavily from this source.

stability, the visual world would move as we move our heads from side to side. That such stability is an achievement is easily demonstrated by seeing what happens when you view the world through reversing lenses. When the visual world is unfamiliar, as it is through reversing lenses, the line of regard is the anchoring point, and when you move your head the world races by in the direction opposite to the movement of your line of regard. Stratton (1896) (1897) found that after wearing the lenses for a while the visual scene no longer would swing with head movements: stability had again been achieved.[11]

The goals of stability and of definiteness are similar, but they can be distinguished. In reversible geometrical figures, for example, definiteness is achieved at the price of stability. Stability might be better achieved if a geometrical figure were perceived as only so many lines on the paper. Instead we see it as a *something,* even though it is ambiguous, and so the "somethings" it represents tend to alternate.

Woodworth felt convinced that there is a fundamental motive to perceive clearly. As he put it: "To see, to hear—to see clearly, to hear distinctly—to make out what it is one is seeing or hearing—moment by moment, such concrete, immediate motives dominate the life of relation with the environment." [12]

Recent emphasis upon "curiosity" as a motive for learning suggests that such "curiosity" may also be a motive within the learning of perceptual responses themselves.[13]

There is a strong tendency to construct concrete things out of the patterns we perceive, for concrete things have definiteness. Hebb distinguishes three kinds of perceptual unity: a primitive, sensorily determined unity, as that of a splash of black ink on a white card; a unity affected by experience, as in the perception of familiar geometrical figures such as squares and circles; and a unity of *identified* figures or objects.[14] Once a perceptual pattern is identified as a familiar object, the perception of the object remains remarkably constant, and the so-called object-constancies apply.[15]

These conjectures suggest the possibility of further experiments on

[11] Some fascinating new experiments with inverted vision have recently come from Innsbruck, substantiating and extending Stratton's findings, e.g., Kohler (1953). For a discussion of them, see Werner and Wapner (1955).

[12] Woodworth (1947), page 123.

[13] The experiments of Butler (1953) (1954) on curiosity and Montgomery's experiments on exploratory drive, Montgomery (1952) and later, have already been cited.

[14] Hebb (1949), 19–35.

[15] E.g., Brunswik (1944) (1955).

the learned features of perception, in line with other studies of motivated learning.[16]

The relationship between perception and learning is a reciprocal one. So far we have considered the role of learning in perception. Now we may consider the role of perception in learning. The cognitive theories all assign an important place to perception and perception-like processes in learning; some even have gone to the extreme of identifying learning with perceptual restructuring.[17] Currently S-R psychologists are paying more attention to perception in learning. Spence (1955) includes "looking at" the food in the goal-box as a feature of reinforcement. Lawrence (1949) (1950) emphasizes acquired distinctiveness of cues as a part of discrimination learning. Wickens (1954) decides that the stimuli in learning experiments arouse perceptual responses that are the intermediaries to which overt movement responses are made.

A complete learning theory must incorporate perceptual processes as part of the main body of theory. Secondary reinforcement, increasingly prominent in S-R theories, is mediated largely by something akin to perception. These relationships cannot be permitted to remain unexamined by the theorist.

Motivation

In Chapter 12 we had occasion to review some of the studies concerned with the details of drive and reinforcement, and with the current criticisms of the need-drive-incentive conception of motivation. An important contemporary trend is to supplement the tension-reduction theory (escape from food tensions, escape from pain or fear or anxiety) with more positive incentives, such as exploration and curiosity, or the arousal of positive (pleasurable) affect.

That there are goal tensions, and that the goal situation is an end-state that makes a change (either toward relaxation or elation) cannot be denied. In that sense, everyone must accept a reinforcement principle, meaning nothing more by it than that rewards and punishments matter for learning. This has come to be called *the empirical law of effect.* Its incorporation into quantitative theories may remain at this level, but its further theoretical explanation raises a number of additional questions.

[16] The many recent studies of perceptual distortion by way of needs and persistent personality characteristics are also relevant even though somewhat controversial. See summaries by Bruner (1951), Klein (1954), Postman (1953). Against a learning theory of perceptual change, see Gibson and Gibson (1955).

[17] Krech and Crutchfield (1948).

The necessary distinction between performance and learning, between *facilitation* and *association,* as Seward (1952a) puts it, does not require that motivation be assigned to one of the terms and not to the other. Everybody agrees that motivation affects performance, but there are arguments over the extent to which it affects the learning of habits or of cognitive structures. The problem is an empirical one, but the goals of the learner almost surely affect *both* learning and performance. Motivation determines attention, and attention is related to cognitive restructuring, the form of learning that is supposed to be most detached from performance. The effect of motivation upon learning and performance is not symmetrical. A starved person may be motivated to eat but not to learn new table manners. Table manners are probably better learned when the hunger drive is less strongly aroused.

The introduction of personality variables into conceptions of drive (e.g., anxiety or need for achievement as measured by tests) suggests an important aspect of motivation long neglected in learning theories: the relation of the given circumstances to the more persistent goals of the individual. If there is any teaching that has come to be generally accepted as a result of Freudian psychology (and related conceptions of personality), it is that motives are organized in some sort of hierarchy within the individual, resulting in a value-system expressed in behavior. This system may go by such names as "ego" or "character-structure," but whatever it is called, it becomes very important for the learning of that individual. A sophisticated learning theory, however it conceives its primary data or principles, must take into account the organization of motives in the individual. Hence concepts such as ego involvement and level of aspiration, as introduced by Lewin and his followers, become important supplements to theories of reward and punishment in the interpretation of motivated learning.

Reinforcement, Provisional Try, and Feedback

Many learning problems require the selection of one or another possible mode of action in order to reach a goal. Because alternative responses appear one after another until the correct one is stumbled upon, this learning is commonly described as trial and error. This designation is descriptively appropriate to several standard laboratory experiments. In motor-skill experiments, acceptable responses have to be discovered within a range of movement possibilities; in the problem-box, there is usually one correct response among many unspecified possibilities; in discrimination experiments, selection is to be made from among fixed alternatives; in the maze and multiple-discrimination experiments, successive choices must be integrated in proper order.

Two main theoretical problems arise: the problem of the nature of the original adjustment ending in the correct act, and the problem as to how this adjustment is facilitated when the situation is repeated.

Thorndike's explanation has tended to separate the two problems. The initial adjustment is a result of the tendency of the organism to vary its responses ("law of multiple response"). The acts within its repertory run off more or less by chance until the correct one is hit upon. Then the second principle comes into play. The correct response is stamped in ("law of effect"). When the situation recurs, the rewarded response has a favored position in relation to the rest of the possible multiple responses, and tends to occur earlier than before. Because prior experiences will have established preferential orders of response even in a situation relatively novel, the multiple responses will never, in fact, be purely random. Hull has worked out a theory like Thorndike's, giving an orderly account of these possibilities.

The alternative is that the original behavior is *not* the running off of earlier habits in the new situation, but is a genuine attempt at discovering the route to the goal. Past experience is used, but in a manner appropriate to the present. Such an interpretation makes the original adjustment a *provisional try*, to be confirmed or denied by its success or failure. What is here being called a provisional try corresponds to what Tolman and Krech have called "hypothesis" behavior. The theory supposes that a provisional behavior route is kept in suspension until its consequences change its provisional status; if it is confirmed it is an appropriate path of action to be followed under like circumstances.

When the *provisional try* was first suggested as appropriate for much behavior classified as trial and error,[18] the concept of *feedback mechanisms* had not yet gained wide currency. All that the provisional try implies is a feedback that corrects the provisional responses according to their consequences. The conception of provisional try, and of feedback, suggests that the role of reinforcement is essentially *informative,* more or less what Thorndike implied when he talked of the confirming or "O.K." response.

There are some consequences for quantitative theories if the informative role of reinforcement is accepted. The relationship between the *informative* role of a stimulus and its *facilitating* role is not one-to-one. The word "yes" is discriminated from "no" when the words are spoken

[18] In the first edition of this book, Hilgard (1948).

softly as well as when they are shouted (though there are some differences, as every army recruit and army sergeant knows!). Hull theorized that habit strength requires some (unspecified) minimum of drive-reducing reinforcement, but is not dependent on the amount of drive reduction beyond the necessary minimum. Hull's position can be assimilated to an information theory. The minimum reinforcement necessary for habit strength is that required for information, for feedback; excesses beyond that affect reaction potential but not habit.

The conception of the provisional try is especially appropriate when the movement called for is not clearly specified by the apparatus. In mirror drawing or pursuit learning or ball tossing the performance called for is a pattern of movements correct in direction and (in some cases) in rhythm. The general character of the correct movement is understood at the outset, but it cannot be produced without considerable fumbling. This fumbling is a real try. The learner does not act in chance fashion, no matter how clumsy his movements may be. In this kind of situation either Dodge's designation *approximation and correction* or Woodworth's *trial-and-check* is appropriate.[19] Theories of spontaneous movement and of conditioning of previous responses have never been successful in dealing with the detailed movements that occur in manual skill. The suggestion that any new movements must be compromises between movements elicited as old responses to familiar stimuli does not take the problem seriously. The movements are new integrations at first crudely adapted to the situation at hand, presently becoming better adapted.

It may be that an organism at some early stage in its development has to learn how to try,[20] but by the time it is ready for the usual laboratory experiments it has learned, and its behavior is probably not greatly unlike the human learner acquiring a skill. The cat's behavior in the problem-box is best described by saying that the cat is trying to get out of the box. When the cat quits trying, and, as Lewin would say, "goes out of the field," its not-trying is evident also. It may lie down, lick itself, appear to be relaxed, then suddenly return to a state of tension and again begin to try.

The many experiments currently under way on visual tracking[21] (that is, manually following a visual target that moves in either a regular

[19] Dodge (1931), page 113, Woodworth (1947).

[20] Hull (1937) shows the possibility of deriving "striving" from more elementary principles.

[21] The experiments have been encouraged by the need for this performance in military activities, e.g., in tracking a moving target with a gunsight. See Chapanis, Garner, and Morgan (1949), pages 264–295

or an irregular path) require for their explanation: (1) the goal of remaining on the target, and (2) the perception of discrepancies from the target, resulting in corrective movements. This is provisional-try behavior, corrected by feedback from the consequence of the attempted positional movements.

The "tracking" behavior of a hunting dog gives a naturalistic illustration of similar behavior. Woodworth, for example, long ago used the behavior of the dog as an illustration of "seeking" behavior:

> That there is a persistent inner tendency towards the consummatory reaction is seen when, for instance, a hunting dog loses the trail; if he were simply carried along from one detail of the hunting process to another by a succession of stimuli calling out simple reflexes, he would cease hunting as soon as the trail ceased, or follow it back again; whereas what he does is to explore about, seeking the trail, as we say. This seeking, not being evoked by any external stimulus (but rather by the absence of an external stimulus), must be driven by some internal force; and the circumstances make it clear that the inner drive is directed toward the capture of the prey.[22]

This behavior, controlled by some sort of "fit" between the perceived environment and the goal-seeking behavior of the organism, involves the assimilation of feedback information along the route as well as at the end. It descriptively justifies a concept such as that of the provisional try. The incorporation of this behavior into a more general theory requires further steps that have not as yet been taken.

Overlearning and Stereotypy

A theory which assumes that behavior is regulated reasonably on the basis of available information is put to it to account for the persistence of habits in situations in which they are no longer adaptive.

One kind of stereotypy, normally adaptive, is a consequence of overlearning. By overlearning is meant the facilitation of response with repetition *after* the essential learning has been mastered. Memorization furnishes convenient illustrations. A series of digits can be learned in a single presentation so that it can be correctly repeated if recall is immediate. But if the series is long enough to be near the limit of immediate memory, more repetitions are needed to fix the list so that it can be recalled after greater lapse of time. The most evident effect of overlearning is this one upon recall. It provides the explanation for the long retention of overlearned skills such as swimming or bicycle riding.

But overlearning has other consequences than guaranteeing retention. These have been little studied, and only a few suggestions are

[22] Woodworth (1918), page 41.

available. One possible result is a mechanization of habit, leading to a loss of "docility." Oft-repeated activities take on some measure of goal-character, perhaps through a process like secondary reinforcement. The learner is then "blinded" to new possibilities.[23] Rats which have learned a path including a jump appear to prefer that path to other more economical ones after they have been overtrained on it.[24] Maier and his associates interpret some of their data as showing that habits learned in accordance with original preferences are more easily altered than habits built up against original preferences.[25] If this be generally true, it may account in part for the persistent preferences by adults for highly artificial ways of doing things learned as children.[26]

The familiar way of doing things is commonly economical, and there is no special mystery about its persistence. It has had motivational support according to any theory. There are other instances of stereotyped fixations, however, which have had no such history of support as adaptive habits. Their occurrence raises additional problems.

One source of fixated behavior is the insoluble problem. There is no way in which to make a reasonable adjustment, because the order of events in the environment is chaotic. There is no basis for choice, and a ritualistic fixed choice is adopted. Such a ritualistic performance represents a giving up of the attempt to predict the occurrence of reward on the basis of "correct" behavior. The environment is unresponsive to the trying by the learner. It is not surprising that such a pattern of behavior persists against punishment. Maier's finding that there was evidence that positive and negative cards were in fact discriminated, even though the position habit remained fixed, means in cognitive terms only that the organism finds the situation too difficult. The problems which experimenters set animals are often fairly complex when translated into our own experiences. In this situation the animal learner, in adopting the fixated habit, has rejected the second window as no better than the first, since its provisional tries were frustrated as frequently at one place as the other. Because there now develops a pattern of predictable success and failure at the first window does not mean that things would be any better at the other one. A human parallel might be as follows. Suppose that in long experience the front door and the rear door of the laboratory had always been unlocked together. Even though one knows about both

[23] Luchins (1942), Wertheimer (1945).

[24] Gilhousen (1931).

[25] Maier, Glaser, and Klee (1940).

[26] Holt (1931) attributes this fixity of familiar ways of doing things to "canalization" in childhood. His position has been adopted and extended by Murphy (1947).

doors, he might sit a long time before the front door, waiting for it to be opened, before trying the back door, even though on that day a careless attendant had unlocked one door and neglected the other. Fixated behavior need not be interpreted as a compulsion to which the learner is a slave. An alternative is that the situation is misinterpreted in the light of the learner's experience, and the sense of alternative has been lost. The ease with which the alternative can be brought back into the animal learner's behavior field was shown by Maier when, through manual guidance, he quickly restored the animal's discriminatory responses.

Another source of fixated behavior is excessive punishment at the moment of choice. The general frustration probably interferes in this case with orderly cognitive processes, so that the learner falls back on stereotyped responses. The reduction in cognitive clearness under intense emotion is what is proposed in the expression "blind with rage." [27]

Still another form of stereotypy is that in the Guthrie and Horton experiment, for it is not based on overlearning or insolvability or frustration. The two features of the Guthrie and Horton situation which may have given rise to stereotyped behavior are that the task is (1) easy, in the sense of being promptly solved, and (2) baffling, in the sense that the response being made is unclearly related to its consequences. The most economical behavior in a situation that is confusing but successful is to do what worked the last time. If a door that is stuck opens promptly when you happen to raise up the knob, the tendency will be great to repeat that behavior the next time without inquiring into the physics of the situation. Maybe it would also open if you pushed down, but there is no need to try the alternative if the prior solution came quickly. The cats that responded directly to the pole, while facing it and the door, transferred more readily to new pole positions than the cats that backed into the pole. The direct tries of practically all of the cats were oriented toward the escape door. The pole was struck in a posture that was door-related, not pole-related, especially by those cats that were backing up. If the relations were unclear, but the solutions prompt, the stereotyped performance would follow, according to the conjectures we have advanced here.

Overlearned, fixated, and stereotyped behavior can be made coherent with the theory of the provisional try if two assumptions are accepted. One assumption is that after sufficient overlearning the learner

[27] The complex role of emotion in learned activity deserves more detailed study than it has been given. See, for example, Brady and Hunt (1955).

no longer tries, unless something dramatic again arouses his searching behavior. Otherwise the old ways of doing things are preferred. The other assumption is that stereotypy results when situations are cognitively too difficult. Here again the organism stops trying, and adopts a patterned mode of response without regard to the environmental consequences.[28]

Understanding, Problem-Solving, and Inventive Ideation

Because learning is to some extent under cognitive control we must not suppose that it always proceeds with full understanding. A correct response may be made time and again in a situation without the learner's awareness of what is being done. The probabilities of a situation may be estimated without the learner's making any computations. The experiments of Thorndike and his collaborators on learning without awareness are of this sort.[29] The subjects made discriminations on the basis of the probabilities of the situation, but could not tell what they had done. Yet their responses were predictable in terms of the arrangements of the learning situation. The experiments were used to substantiate a blind law-of-effect interpretation, but they may be explained equally well on the basis of cumulative discriminations among real tries.

While there is a tendency to achieve clarity and to learn with understanding when that is possible, there is a limit to the learner's curiosity, and it is not true as implied in some gestalt writings that learning takes place with all the understanding which the situation and the capacities of the learner permit. The understanding which the learner wishes in a problematic situation is knowledge of the essentials to economical goal-achievement, and nothing more can be counted on. The mistake is sometimes made in teaching school children (or college students) of assuming that they wish to understand what lies behind a process which is for them just a tool. They wish to know how to use the tool to reach immediate goals; the further curiosity is related to different goals, which may be goals for the teacher but not for them.

Because all learning is to some extent cognitively controlled, the distinction between blind learning and learning with understanding becomes one of degree. There is a point, however, at which understanding takes on new prominence. That is in the kind of creative attack on a problem in which experience does not provide solutions ready-made, but

[28] Note in this connection the falling back on position habits when too many discriminatory cues are involved, Lawrence and Mason (1955).

[29] E.g., Thorndike and Rock 1934). For a different sort of criticism, see Irwin, Kauffman, Prior, and Weaver (1934).

the solutions have to be discovered or invented through a reconstruction of experience appropriate to the problem at hand. This is not completely specified by experiments on insight, but it is suggested by them.

There are several alternatives. One is to treat all problem-solving and reasoning as a form of trial-and-error learning, with some transfer to account for short-cut solutions. This is the position of Carr (1925), endorsed by McGeoch (1942). This position fails to grant any reality to the reconstruction of experience present in the act of reasoning which makes the "try" something other than the running off of varying habits. A second alternative, that of Hull (1935c), is to recognize that the mechanism for assembling prior experiences appropriate to problem solution has in it characteristics different from ordinary trial-and-error learning. Hull attempts to derive such behavior from other processes. This derivation depends upon discrimination among the fractional anticipatory responses that are common to several experiences and have to be integrated in order to solve the problem.

Stimulus-response psychologists, under the restraint of Lloyd Morgan's principle of parsimony,[30] have assigned as little as possible to ideation, but they have usually recognized that some behavior is controlled by ideas. Thorndike called ideas by that name and granted their occurrence; Hunter recognized a "symbolic process" necessary to account for behavior in delayed-action and double-alternation experiments; [31] Hull inferred "pure-stimulus acts," that is, responses whose sole function is to furnish stimuli to guide or integrate behavior sequences; Guthrie's position is about like Hull's, with great emphasis upon movements (especially implicit speech) as the substance of thought. Tolman, in behaviorist spirit, makes of ideation a "mere 'behavior-feint' at running-back-and-forth," without specifying the precise nature of the feint.

Is there any gain, having accepted ideation, in seeking a movement basis for ideas? To assert that the organism can discriminate between the sensory consequences of two kinds of anticipatory salivation more readily than between two perceptual redintegrations is no great gain, except for the logical possibility of discovering by separate techniques the presence of two kinds of salivation. Because both perceptual redintegrations and stimuli from anticipatory responses are, in fact, inferred, it is as possible to be logically strict about one as the other—*and the evidence used in the inference for one has to be as good as the evidence for the other.* The benefit of the doubt need not go to the one preferring

[30] Morgan (1894).
[31] Hunter (1924).

movements. There is some concealing of ignorance in attributing specific stimulus-response bases for psychological functions such as drives, sets, images, and thoughts. If we are critical about accepting the results of experiments, then stomach contractions are *not* the basis of appetite, eye movements are *not* the cause of the Müller-Lyer illusion, kinesthetic cues are *not* the preferred ones in maze learning, tongue movements are *not* the basis for thinking. The burden of proof is on those who believe otherwise. That there are some movement concomitants of thought is insufficient evidence that these movements (and their consequences) are the sufficient condition for the occurrence of the thought. The argument that inferring movements will make easier the task of the neurophysiologist does not hold. It is no harder to make a brain model for perceptual redintegration than for the pattern of discrimination among the proprioceptive consequences of anticipatory responses.

The alternative to trial-and-error and reinforcement theories is to make allowance for a genuine reconstruction of experience appropriate to problem solution, as proposed by Tolman (1932b) in his principle of creative instability and by Maier (1931) in his separation of reasoning from other kinds of learning. An organism capable of functioning at different levels does not keep his abilities in abeyance to be brought out to suit the convenience of an experimenter. Therefore if a given ability is shown in clear outline in one experimental situation, it may be supposed that if looked for it might also be found in other situations in which it is not as clearly exhibited.[32] Thus the reconstruction of experience goes on to some extent in every act of redintegration. When ice is seen as cold, or a distant object as a motorcycle, the perceptions are not photographic, nor are they simply revivals of past experiences. They are perceptual achievements molded out of past experience and present sensory discriminations. It is only the more striking recombinations of previous experiences and present perceptions that we call reasoning. These more striking instances reveal aspects of the process which might otherwise be overlooked.

One aspect of the detour or roundabout experiment emphasized by Köhler is the turning away from the ends of action to the means. The direct path to the goal may be blocked. A stupid animal will continue to make a direct attack, but a more intelligent one is able to turn its back and to take the long way around. Discovering a long route which

[32] Note this inversion of Lloyd Morgan's canon. As now inverted it might be paraphrased: "An organism capable of ideational problem-solving may also use ideas in learning situations in which they would be theoretically unnecessary."

already exists is one way of solving such a problem. It is trial-and-error behavior, but in a direction against the attraction of the goal. Another solution is that of discovering or creating some sort of tool which then becomes a means to the goal. This often requires a reconstruction of experience, perhaps by putting some familiar object to unfamiliar use: making a pliers into a pendulum-bob, a clamp into a hat-hanger, a Bunsen-burner tube into a blow-pipe, and so on. It is this reconstruction aspect rather than the detour aspect which is most significant in reasoning experiments.

The reconstruction of experience follows certain lines of solution which Maier calls "direction." If there is a flame to be blown out, one "direction" is to find some way to direct a jet of air upon it, another direction is to use water, still another is to smother it with something solid. Each of these suggestions directs the search for appropriate objects to convert into means. In one of the psychological laboratories during World War II a glass plate was being used in a piece of apparatus in such a way that it was to be looked through and also used as a mirror, somewhat as in the Dodge tachistoscope. There were troublesome double images of a small fixation object due to reflections from both the front and the back surfaces of the glass. The first hypothesis was that the glass could be made so thin that the images would fuse. Successively thinner sheets of glass were used in following out this "direction," but without solving the problem. The idea emerged of making the glass much thicker, so that the images could be drawn apart and one of them screened off. This worked. The direction "if we can make it thin enough" was one hypothesis used until the other hypothesis "if we can make it thick enough" supervened.[33] This sudden restructuring gives the subjective experience of insight.

Understanding and inference may be used in unsuccessful solutions as well as in successful ones. The flash of insight is not evidence of unusual heights to which intelligence has soared, but of an aptness of the solution suggested. A solution may be achieved with understanding without any such experience of insight. For example, in fitting mathematical functions to a given set of points it is often necessary to try out curves from several families to see which will achieve the best fit. Such a solution to a problem goes on at a high level of skill and of understanding, but when the best fit is found there is no necessary experience of insight. Insight is experienced only when there is an integration of experiences,

[33] I am indebted to S. Smith Stevens for this illustration.

a restructuring, a seeing of things in a new light, appropriate to the problem at hand.

Because the integration and reconstruction of experience go on in many acts of learning, reasoning need not be made a separate category as done by Maier. This does not mean that there may not be one or more special capacities involved in reasoning ability and in other sorts of creativity. But there may be different learning processes below the reasoning level as well. In order to avoid artificial boundaries, it is preferable to include together in one family of processes all forms of problem-solving and reasoning, subject to later determination of the kinds and number of processes involved.

To What Kind of Theory Would the Foregoing Comments Lead?

The comments on the several kinds of problems facing learning theorists do not in themselves constitute a theory of learning, yet they express certain desiderata for a theory. If they were to be co-ordinated with any one of the preceding viewpoints, they would fit best with the tolerant functionalism recommended by Woodworth.

The merit of the broad functionalist position is the willingness to accept new dimensions as they are discovered, to tolerate some theoretical inconsistencies rather than fly in the face of well-demonstrated experimental relationships. Such a positivistic attitude has worked well in other sciences. Even the elegant science of physics has stumbled along for a good while with inconsistent theories such as the wave theory and the quantum theory of light. Biologists do not worry too much that their gene theories and their theories of embryological development are not yet satisfactorily integrated.

The difficulty with functionalism is that it does not satisfy the esthetic desire for a neat system. The motivation to seek for a few postulates, to find interchangeable constants, to be able to move logically from one part of the system to another has worked well in the physical sciences, and there is every reason to expect it to work well in psychology also. Functionalism has no quarrel with this possibility, and it is entirely possible to seek systematic elegance within the tolerance of a functionalist position. In the end, we shall know more and find more convenient ways both of expressing what we know and of finding out still more. That is ultimately what we are after, however that end is achieved.

AN EXPERIMENTAL PROGRAM

In the foregoing suggestions toward a theory of learning the erroneous impression may easily be given that the concepts represent a return to the pre-experimental period of psychologizing about learning. Acceptance of such a point of view might be interpreted to mean turning our backs upon the advances which have come through rejecting mentalistic and mystical concepts in favor of objective behavioral ones. In order to allay such fears and correct misapprehensions, I wish to propose what appear to me to be some directions in which contemporary research upon learning might move.

Naturalistic Observations

Because the search must continue for the most appropriate concepts to be used in the study and description of learning, it is desirable to keep the approaches flexible and to welcome novelty as well as precision. In urging consideration for a concept like the provisional try, I have not intended to discard the results of experimentation which have been obtained under other concepts, but only to break through the rigidity which makes us think of nonsense syllable lists, mazes, conditioning experiments, and target practice as exhausting the phenomena of learning.

The common acknowledgment of the ingenuity and originality of the experiments by Lewin and his students (even by those most devastatingly critical of his conceptual system) leads to a search for the roots of this freshness of approach. The answer probably lies in Lewin's tendency to pick problems out of real life situations, instead of choosing examples which would fit a previously learned method of study. It is out of real life one finds problems such as the forgetting of an intention, the tendency to resume interrupted tasks, and so on. Such problems are not thought up by students whose only concern is to counterbalance practice effects in a standard experiment in such a manner as to add an additional decimal point to the determination.

Somewhat the same thing might be said about Freud's contributions. Because Freud was listening to real people in their efforts to recall and to come to grips with their recollections, he discovered facts about repression and distortion in memory which were unknown to the followers of Ebbinghaus.

It would probably be worth while for someone to do for learning what Brunswik has been doing for perception and Barker for child development[34]—that is, take a notebook and follow a child around for hours at a time. What are the circumstances under which he learns? What performances provide for recall? for recognition? for problem-solving? What tasks are left half-finished? What kinds of forgetting are there? What motives can be inferred? Such observations would be like a breath of fresh air in most learning laboratories. To be sure, many observers would see only what they were taught to see. Some would find nothing but trial and error, others would see the child doing only what he last did, others would be impressed by the child's insight. But of a group who started out in this manner one or two would probably come back with suggestions as fertile as those of Lewin and his students. Such suggestions would help break the sterility of contemporary learning theories, and would help in the search for appropriate new concepts.

Physiological Changes Concomitant with Learning

No one should infer because this book has largely neglected physiology[35] that it is anti-physiological. On the contrary, it is a blot upon our scientific ingenuity that after so many years of search we know as little as we do about the physiological accompaniments of learning.

Learning theories may be developed at a molar level, independent of neurophysiology. It is preferable that the division of labor between psychology and physiology be recognized, and that psychological theories be developed objectively and self-consistently at the molar level, without recourse to a hypothetical neurology or a physiology not grounded in demonstrated relationships. Once, however, the possibility of such a learning theory is granted—and there appears to be increasing agreement on this point—then an appropriate position with respect to neurophysiology can be established. The learning theorist does not have to *wait* for physiology in order to go ahead on firm scientific ground, but this does not mean that he will not welcome any advance in knowledge in this field, nor that he will not wish to contribute to such knowledge through appropriate experiments.

One of the most crying needs is for a crucial experiment identifying specifically a change occurring in neural tissues (or in bio-electrical fields related to such tissue) as learning takes place. Possibly the first task is to find an organism as appropriate for this purpose as the fruit-fly has been for genetics. The white rat is probably too complicated. Perhaps a

[34] Brunswik (1944). Barker and Wright (1954).
[35] Except for the brief discussion in Chapter 13.

simpler organism like amblystoma should be chosen, in which the nervous elements are few enough to be under direct inspection with modern techniques. It is possible to teach larval amblystoma simple habits,[36] and it ought to be possible to find out what sort of "trace" these habits leave. To refuse to search for such a change would be like refusing to look for the micro-organism causing malaria just because an objective plot of the temperature fluctuations in the patient could be made a means of identifying the disease. It can be stated with reasonable confidence that there are changes in the nervous system accompanying learning, and, if there are, then there are surely no insurmountable obstacles to detecting such changes. It is a surprising thing that, with all the interest in learning, this direct identifying step has not been taken more successfully.

The other possibilities, besides the study of the simpler organism, include the study of special preparations, such as the spinal animal. Electrical methods of exploring the cortex may succeed, but they, like behavioral studies, are likely to be at a molar level from which the identifying steps still have to be made inferentially.

Much that is known and can be found out about learning will not be altered by changes in neurophysiological knowledge. This is the basis of the argument for learning theories which dispense with physiology, and it is sound. But it would be foolhardy to suppose that a knowledge of the physical substratum of learning would not be helpful in further advancing our theories and in achieving control over the learning process. Such knowledge is indeed so important that psychologists interested in learning will wish to continue in the future, as they have in the past, to share with physiologists and neurologists in experimentation designed to get at the changes in the organism which go along with manifest behavior.

Standardization of Methods and Measures

Scientific facts ought to be gathered in such a way that later workers can move ahead on the secure foundation of fact accumulated by earlier workers. In more advanced sciences, such as chemistry and physics, large handbooks are devoted to tables and formulas conserving this accepted body of knowledge.

The handbooks of psychology are not of this kind. While they serve as a storehouse of important experimentation and theory, they contain relatively few tables of measurements or constants that can be used as starting points for later work. Suppose, for example, a student comes to

[36] Moore and Welch (1940).

one of us and asks: "Will you please measure my reaction time, and tell me how I compare with others?" Of course we know how to connect a telegraph key in circuit with a sounder and an electric timer. But do we know how to secure results that can be compared with norms? How many practice trials, or perhaps sessions of so many trials each, should there be before we begin to count? How many measurements do we need for a stable value? A ready signal? The interval between ready signal and stimulus? If an auditory stimulus, how loud? A useful start was made by those who assembled what relevant material they could find in a *Handbook of human engineering data,*[37] but the very limitations in what they could find helped to show how inadequate most of our standardization is. The two studies of simple auditory reaction time that they report yielded means of 192 msec. and 153 msec., the second mean being a full standard deviation below the first. Of course the conditions differed, but that is why we would have difficulty in measuring our student's reaction time and knowing whether it was long or short, unless we troubled to run our own normative group.

If we are to make advances in quantitative theories of learning we need data that are comparable, and this means more standardization than has yet been achieved.

Two arguments are used against standardization:

1. Standardization may prove wasteful until our conceptual systems have settled to the point where we know what we want to measure. If we proceed to standardize now we may spend a great deal of effort on the trivial, or on some device or method tied to outworn concepts. For example, we might finally achieve a calibrated set of nonsense syllables, just to find that those working on rote memorization prefer to use meaningful words in their experiments.

2. Standardization, because it demands conformity, might put a damper on originality, and hence achieve comparability at too great a cost. The "trained observer" of early introspective psychology ran this danger, and some suspected that students observed the same things as their masters simply as a result of this "standardization" of what was permissible in a report.

Both of these arguments are somewhat misleading. Consider first whether or not standardization is premature. Nobody would attempt large-scale standardization of equipment and methods except in fields in which there is widespread current activity. If the fields later became inactive, that would not prove that standardization was a mistake. It

[37] Tufts College Institute for Applied Experimental Psychology (1952).

conceivably might have helped to settle some issues that had previously remained open. Furthermore, without standardization as much effort might have been spent in the meantime on unstandardized procedures with less definitive results.

The second argument, that standardization cripples novelty and imagination, does not necessarily hold. Suppose that one wishes to introduce a new-style memory drum, or to introduce a new material to be learned, after standardization has been achieved with an old-style drum, with other material. All that is necessary is to perform calibration experiments to show that the two drums give comparable results (if they do) with the original material. Then the new drum can be recommended if it is more convenient. The new materials then need to be standardized also, against the norms of the previously standardized material. Thus the new equipment and materials, if they merit it, can be added to the store of standardized materials, and normative data can be published where such data are accessible.[38]

Without standardization, failure to repeat earlier results commonly leads to the excuse that conditions may have differed. This excuse needs to be eliminated, so that we *can* repeat experimental data when we try to. Then we can go on to a new experiment, *with specified modifications*, and criticize the interpretation of the earlier data. Standardization thus need not prevent originality. The gain is that results under novel conditions can be compared confidently with results under standard conditions, so that the new results can fit into the historically accumulating body of scientific knowledge.

Broadening the Boundary Conditions

For some workers, the process of standardization, because it takes time and requires controls, is likely to result in a narrowing of the initial and boundary conditions of some varieties of experiment through specifying pretraining, apparatus dimensions, and the like. But again we must recognize a division of labor, so that the experimenter does not have to be coerced into doing what he does not find congenial. For some experimenters, the most inviting task is to broaden the boundary conditions of both experiment and theory. This is, of course, a reason for encouraging naturalistic observations. But these observations will not serve well unless they are translated into experimentable form. For example, even now new

[38] The parallel with intelligence test standardization and revision is obvious. Such tests, because their norms are taken seriously, have been better "calibrated" than much laboratory apparatus

richness is being introduced into learning experiments by including motives formerly little studied in the laboratory. So many human motives are personal—emulative, defiant, aggressive, appealing—that a social psychology of learning is sure to develop eventually.[39]

RELATION BETWEEN LEARNING AND THE PRACTICAL DEMANDS OF INSTRUCTION AND TRAINING

Theories serve more than one purpose: they attempt to organize existing knowledge, they attempt to provide guiding threads or hypotheses toward new knowledge, and they may also furnish principles by which what is known can be used.[40] This practical outcome is seldom central in the thinking of the constructor of theory, and it is not surprising, therefore, that the person seeking advice from the learning theorist often comes away disappointed. For example, Newman, writing on the contemporary status of learning theory, says that for many practical skills such as those required in batting a home run, fencing, boxing, fancy diving, or dancing, "a rabbit's foot is worth as much as the psychologist's sage advice."[41] While Newman's skepticism here is extreme, he at least puts us on notice not to expect from the learning theorist too much that is practical.

Some Agreement on Practical Matters

It turns out, however, that many of the quarrels of the theorists are internal ones, not very important in relation to immediate practical problems; there are, in fact, a great many practically important experimental relationships upon which the theorists are in substantial agreement. That is, they accept the facts as demonstrated, even though they disagree about the interpretations of these facts. If the theoretical differences are irreconcilable, and one position eventually wins out over the other, there will ultimately be an effect upon practice. But advice for practical people today need not wait for the resolution of these theoretical controversies.

Here are a few statements upon which I would expect a majority of learning theorists to agree. It would be too much to ask for perfect agreement, for some statements require many qualifications, and there are always a few theorists who are sticklers for wording.

[39] For a serious beginning, see Rotter (1954).
[40] Much of this section is adapted from Hilgard (1953b).
[41] Newman (1951), page 411.

1. In deciding who should learn what, the capacities of the learner are very important. Brighter people can learn things less bright ones cannot learn; in general, older children can learn more readily than younger ones; the decline of ability with age, in the adult years, depends upon what it is that is being learned.

2. A motivated learner acquires what he learns more readily than one who is not motivated.[42] The relevant motives include both general and specific ones, for example, desire to learn, need for achievement (general), desire for a certain reward or to avoid a threatened punishment (specific).

3. Motivation that is too intense (especially pain, fear, anxiety) may be accompanied by distracting emotional states, so that excessive motivation may be less effective than moderate motivation for learning some kinds of tasks, especially those involving difficult discriminations.

4. Learning under the control of reward is usually preferable to learning under the control of punishment. Correspondingly, learning motivated by success is preferable to learning motivated by failure. Even though the theoretical issue is still unresolved, the practical outcome must take into account the social by-products, which tend to be more favorable under reward than under punishment.

5. Learning under intrinsic motivation is preferable to learning under extrinsic motivation.

6. Tolerance for failure is best taught through providing a backlog of success that compensates for experienced failure.

7. Individuals need practice in setting realistic goals for themselves, goals neither so low as to elicit little effort nor so high as to foreordain to failure. Realistic goal-setting leads to more satisfactory improvement than unrealistic goal-setting.

8. The personal history of the individual, for example, his reaction to authority, may hamper or enhance his ability to learn from a given teacher.

9. Active participation by a learner is preferable to passive reception when learning, for example, from a lecture or a motion picture.

10. Meaningful materials and meaningful tasks are learned more readily than nonsense materials and more readily than tasks not understood by the learner.

[42] There may be theoretical argument whether motivation helps performance or habit strength, but this is an illustration where the practical outcome does not depend on the theoretical answer. Possibly the motivated learner merely practices more (Kimble, 1953); even so, he acquires what he needs to learn more readily than if he were not motivated.

11. There is no substitute for repetitive practice in the overlearning of skills (for instance, the performance of a concert pianist), or in the memorization of unrelated facts that have to be automatized.

12. Information about the nature of a good performance, knowledge of his own mistakes, and knowledge of successful results, aid learning.

13. Transfer to new tasks will be better if, in learning, the learner can discover relationships for himself, and if he has experience during learning of applying the principles within a variety of tasks.

14. Spaced or distributed recalls are advantageous in fixing material that is to be long retained.

These points are neither systematic nor comprehensive. They are listed merely in order to add concreteness to the suggestion that there are a number of useful generalizations about which students of learning are in substantial agreement.

Improving the Contributions of Psychology to the Practical Understanding and Control of Learning

If psychology is to be of greater help in gearing itself to problems of training and to the other practical problems of learning, there are a few suggestions that can be offered.

1. *Validate the principles developed in the laboratory in real life situations.* A theoretical principle cannot simply be borrowed and used to guide practice. It must be first tried out under the conditions of actual life. In real life, learning occurs in a social setting, with constraints of time and personnel and equipment. An instructor teaching a course, because he does not have complete charge of his students, is not free to do everything he would like to do. Hence a laboratory learning principle has to be tried out in the classroom before we can be sure that it is useful.

2. *Be tolerant of negative results.* If two methods of teaching or training are to be tried out experimentally, we ought to accept for trial only methods that have a good deal to commend them, for example, skilled teachers who favor them. Under these circumstances we are very likely to come out with differences that are not significant statistically, even though the experiment is well designed and the sample adequate. Instead of being disappointed with such a finding, and concealing it, the result is well worth knowing. Within the practical limitations of classroom teaching it is quite possible that alternative methods *are* equally acceptable, and this may prove very comforting to teachers who prefer one or the other method.

3. *Enlist the co-operation of inventive practical people.* Theories in

the psychology of learning do not automatically design or invent teaching methods. Very often experienced teachers have a flair for finding ways to motivate students, to gain their participation, to suit learning tasks to their ability levels. The psychologist seeking to give practical help will seek to collaborate with such persons, using his own methods, to be sure, to validate their procedures, but capitalizing on their inventiveness and experience in a situation with many features not present in his laboratory.

4. *Lean more heavily on studies of problem-solving and creativity than on studies of rote learning.* The old "principles of economy" in memorization and in acquiring skill depended very largely on studies of rote learning, and hence emphasized massed and distributed practice, learning by parts or by wholes, consequences of warm-up and fatigue, the effects of recitation, and so on. While these principles have some relevance for learning, they are not very applicable in practice. The boy learning to ride his bicycle does not need advice on distributing practice. If he assembles a motor car, he doesn't need to be taught to space his reviews in order to remember the name of the carburetor or generator.

Of far more practical importance is the ability to make relevant use of past experience in facing new problems, of maintaining motivation until a difficult task is completed or a baffling problem solved, of gaining confidence in oneself as a creative person, of learning how to diagnose a problem, how to fill gaps in necessary knowledge, how to call on experts when necessary. In a rapidly changing culture such as ours in America, learning how to go about learning in the face of new demands is more important than learning to commit serial passages to memory. Let me not be misunderstood: you cannot think without information. The point is that you have to learn how to *use* information in relation to presented problems.

A closer integration of theory with practice is desirable, and it is hoped that an increasing number of psychologists will find this task attractive.

Pure versus Applied Research

The foregoing discussion raises some of the old controversies over pure and applied research. A study of the history of science will show that there is no uniform relationship between pure and applied science as they develop. The practice of extracting ores preceded the appropriate understanding of chemistry by centuries. Diets upon which people grew to maturity were chosen for ages before there was a science of nutrition. As theoretical and experimental science mature, the relationship between science and invention becomes more intimate. Gunpowder could be invented before physical science was far advanced, but the atomic bomb could not have been made without calling upon the resources of pure science. The scientific study of learning is today in an intermediate position. While its results can be helpful to educators and parents, there are many problems in the practical guidance of learning which cannot yet be handled upon the basis of well-established principles.

At any one time, scientists in experimental and theoretical fields can work only on the problems upon which they are prepared to work with the conceptual and material tools at hand. These may or may not be appropriate to the practical problem calling for solution. Mothers must feed and rear their children as best they can while the children are growing up, and physicians have to treat their patients when they are ill. Practical pursuits cannot wait. Hence some sorts of adjustment are made in the practical world, while the scientists go about their business. Children may have rickets because at the time nothing is known about vitamins, and patients may die because a new curative drug has not yet emerged from the laboratory. Scientists could not be blamed if their science had not yet discovered vitamins or was not yet prepared to synthesize the new drug.

Because scientists have to develop appropriate methods and concepts before their results can become efficient regulators of practice, their concerns for a time may appear to be remote from practical affairs, and some of their disputes will seem to be quibbles over distinctions that do not matter. All this suggests the need for patience and tolerance toward experimentation which pushes back the boundaries of the known and toward theory construction which attempts to sharpen the conceptual tools with which scientists can work.

One faulty interpretation of the relationship between pure and applied science is to be avoided. This is the interpretation that applications, if they are to have any verifiable basis, must wait until there is a pure science ready to be applied. A corollary of this interpretation is the confident hope that once the pure science is in order, applications will follow automatically. Neither the interpretation nor the corollary corresponds to reality, for it is quite possible to do applied research before the problems of pure science are settled, and it is seldom if ever possible to apply scientific principles directly to practical situations without some empirical tailoring to make them fit.

An adequate research program in the applied psychology of learning would rest in part upon the findings in the experimental studies of learning, but it would consist in much more than the making of suggestions on the basis of general principles. There must finally be experimental testing in the school, or on the playground, or in the shop—wherever the application is to be made.

If in the end a principle has to be experimented upon at the point of application, it might be asked, why do laboratory research at all? If what we do with animals has to be repeated with children, why not work with children in the first place? There are several answers. For one thing, we do some things with animals which we cannot do with children. For another thing, we make many false starts in the laboratory, and it would be wasteful to subject school children to all the things we try in the laboratory. Again, in the laboratory we are able to control conditions as we are not able to control them in the school. *A principle once discovered in a better controlled situation can be validated in a less-well-controlled one.*[43] Even though the sole aim of learning experimentation were practical, it might prove economical to work in the laboratory in order to find the leads worth testing in practice.

Research on practical problems, if well done, not only adjusts theory to practice, but contributes to substantiating, refuting, or extending theoretical knowledge. It is a mistake to distinguish too sharply between pure and applied research, if both are good research. It is true, however, that much applied research is necessarily concerned with problems bound to specific times and places, and so lacks the universality of pure research. It is these local and temporary features which lead to the judgment that applied research is inferior, and tend to reduce the prestige of the applied scientist relative to the pure scientist. When the relationships between pure and applied research are properly worked out, the requisite skills are of a high order however the labor is divided, and there is no reason why prestige should not be more equitably distributed.

SUPPLEMENTARY READINGS

ECLECTICISM IN LEARNING THEORY

DASHIELL, J. F. (1935) A survey and synthesis of learning theories. *Psychol. Bull.*, 32, 261–275.

[43] This is well illustrated by experiments on diet. It would be difficult to start out to detect dietary deficiencies by analyzing the whole bill of fare of subjects with a varied diet, but once dietary essentials have been discovered in the laboratory it is possible to supplement otherwise varied diets (lacking in some essentials) and so validate the laboratory findings that this factor is indeed essential.

KELLOGG, W. N. (1938) An eclectic view of some theories of learning. *Psychol. Rev.*, 45, 165–184.
MCCONNELL, T. R. (1942) Reconciliation of learning theories. Chapter 7 in *The psychology of learning.* Natl. Soc. Stud. Educ., 41st Yearbook, Part II, 243–286.
MELTON, A. W. (1950) Learning. In W. S. Monroe, ed. *Encyclopedia of educational research.* Revised edition, 668–690.

THE NATURE OF THEORY CONSTRUCTION RELATED TO THE PSYCHOLOGY OF LEARNING

ADAMS, D. K. (1954) Learning and explanation. In the Kentucky Symposium. *Learning, theory, personality theory, and clinical research.* 66–80.
BRUNSWIK, E. (1952) *The conceptual framework of psychology. Int. Encycl. unified Sci.*, 1, No. 10.
BRUNSWIK, E. (1955) Representative design and probabilistic theory in a functional psychology. *Psychol. Rev.*, 62, 193–217.
KOCH, S. (1951) Theoretical psychology, 1950: an overview. *Psychol. Rev.*, 58, 295–301.
MAIER, N. R. F. (1954) The premature crystallization of learning theory. In The Kentucky Symposium. *Learning theory, personality theory, and clinical research.* 54–65.
SKINNER, B. F. (1950) Are theories of learning necessary? *Psychol. Rev.*, 57, 193–216.
SPENCE, K. W. (1950) Cognitive versus stimulus-response theories of learning. *Psychol. Rev.*, 57, 159–172.
VERPLANCK, W. S. (1955) Since learned behavior is innate and vice versa, what now? *Psychol. Rev.*, 62, 139–144.

PROBLEMS IN THE APPLIED PSYCHOLOGY OF LEARNING

BLAIR, G. M. (1948) The psychological basis of the modern curriculum: 6. How learning theory is related to curriculum organization. *J. educ. Psychol.*, 39, 161–166.
BRAY, C. W. (1948) *Psychology and military proficiency.*
GAGNÉ, R. M. (1954) Training devices and simulators: some research issues. *Amer. Psychologist*, 9, 95–107.
HOBAN, C. F., Jr., and VAN ORMER, E. B. (1950) *Instructional film research, 1918–1950.*
SKINNER, B. F. (1954) The science of learning and the art of teaching. *Harv. educ. Rev.*, 24, 86–97.
STROUD, J. B. (1940) Experiments on learning in school situations. *Psychol. Bull.*, 37, 777–807.
WOLFLE, D. L. (1951) Training. In S. S. Stevens, ed. *Handbook of experimental psychology.* 1267–1286.

REPRESENTATIVE EXPERIMENTS IN THE APPLIED STUDY OF LEARNING

BOECK, C. H. (1951) The inductive-deductive compared to the deductive-descriptive approach to laboratory instruction in high school chemistry. *J. exp. Educ.*, 19, 247–254.
BROWNELL, W. A., and MOSER, H. E. (1949) Meaningful versus mechanical learning: a study in Grade 3 subtraction. *Duke Univ. Res. Stud. Educ.*, No. 8.
CHILD, I. L., POTTER, E. H., and LEVINE, E. M. (1946) Children's textbooks and

personality development: an exploration in the social psychology of education. *Psychol. Monogr.*, 60, No. 3.

Gagné, R. M. (1950) Learning and transfer of training in two forms of rudder control task. *USAF Hum. Resourc. Res. Cent., Res. Note P&MS*, 50–1.

Herr, S. E. (1946) The effect of pre-first-grade training upon reading readiness and reading achievement among Spanish-American children. *J. educ. Psychol.*, 37, 87–102.

Lindahl, L. G. (1945) Movement analysis as an industrial training method. *J. appl. Psychol.*, 29, 420–436.

Melton, A. W., Feldman, N. G., and Mason, C. W. (1936) *Experimental studies of the education of children in a museum of science.* Washington, D.C.: Publ. Amer. Assn Museums, New Series, No. 15.

Pressey, S. L. (1950) Development and appraisal of devices providing immediate automatic scoring of objective tests and concomitant self-instructions. *J. Psychol.*, 29, 417–447.

Rudolf, K. B. (1949) The effect of reading instruction on achievement in eighth grade social studies. *Teach. Coll. Contr. Educ.*, No. 945.

Thompson, G. G., and Hunnicutt, C. W. (1944) Effects of repeated praise or blame on the work achievement of introverts and extroverts. *J. educ. Psychol.*, 35, 257–266.

Vander Meer, A. W. (1950) *Relative effectiveness of instruction by: films exclusively, films plus study guides, and standard lecture methods.*

REFERENCES AND AUTHOR INDEX

The numbers in italics following each reference give the text pages on which the paper is cited. Citations in the text are made by author and date of publication.

ABEL, T. M. (1938) Neuro-circulatory reaction and the recall of unfinished and completed tasks. *J. Psychol.*, 6, 377–383.—*283*

ABORN, M. (1953) The influence of experimentally induced failure on the retention of material acquired through set and incidental learning. *J. exp. Psychol.*, 45, 225–231.—*316, 317*

ACH, N. (1910) *Über den Willensakt und das Temperament: Eine experimentelle Untersuchung*. Leipzig: Quelle and Meyer.—*258*

ADAMS, D. K. (1929) Experimental studies of adaptive behavior in cats. *Comp. Psychol. Monogr.*, 6, No. 27.—*65*

ADAMS, D. K. (1933) Three theories of learning. *J. gen. Psychol.*, 8, 485–497. —*220*

ADAMS, D. K. (1948) Review of Guthrie and Horton's *Cats in a puzzle box*. *Psychol. Bull.*, 45, 548–550.—*81*

ADAMS, D. K. (1954) Learning and explanation. In the Kentucky Symposium. *Learning theory, personality theory, and clinical research.* New York: Wiley, 66–80.—*491*

ADAMSON, J. F. *See* Lacy, Lewinson, and Adamson (1953).

ADAMSON, R. E., and TAYLOR, D. W. (1954) Functional fixedness as related to elapsed time and set. *J. exp. Psychol.*, 47, 122–126.—*256*

ADLER, D. L., and KOUNIN, J. (1939) Some factors operating at the moment of resumption of interrupted tasks. *J. Psychol.*, 7, 255–267.—*284*

ADORNETTO, J. *See* McGinnies and Adornetto (1952).

AESCHLIMAN, B. *See* Ritchie, Aeschliman, and Peirce (1950).

AIKEN, E. G. *See* Mowrer and Aiken (1954).

ALBERTS, E., and EHRENFREUND, D. (1951) Transposition in children as a function of age. *J. exp. Psychol.*, 41, 30–38.—*444*

ALEXANDER, F., and ROSS, H., eds. (1952) *Dynamic psychiatry*. Chicago: Univ. Chicago Press.—*327*

ALLPORT, G. W. (1930) Change and decay in the visual memory image. *Brit. J. Psychol.*, 21, 134–148.—*243*

ALLPORT, G. W. (1937) *Personality: a psychological interpretation.* New York, Holt.—*96, 338, 429*

ALLPORT, G. W. (1946) Effect: a secondary principle of learning. *Psychol. Rev.*, 53, 335–347.—*285, 429*

ALLPORT, G. W., and POSTMAN, L. (1947) *The psychology of rumor.* New York: Holt.—*245*

ALPER, T. G. (1946) Task-orientation vs. ego-orientation in learning and retention. *Amer. J. Psychol.*, 59, 236–248.—*283*

ALPER, T. G. (1948) Memory for completed and incompleted tasks as a function of personality: correlation between experimental and personality data. *J. Personality*, 17, 104–137.—*283*

Alper, T. G. (1952) The interrupted task method in studies of selective recall: a reevaluation of some recent experiments. *Psychol. Rev.*, 59, 71–88.—*283*

Ammons, R. B. (1947) Acquisition of motor skill: I. Quantitative analysis and theoretical formulation. *Psychol. Rev.*, 54, 263–281.—*354*

Anderson, E. E. (1941) The externalization of drive. I. Theoretical considerations. *Psychol. Rev.*, 48, 204–224.—*429*

Andersson, B. (1953) The effect of injections of hypertonic solutions in parts of the hypothalamus of goats. *Acta Physiol. Scand.*, 28, 188–201.—*424*

Angell, J. R. (1906) Review of *Studies in philosophy and psychology* (Garman Commemorative Volume). *J. Phil. Psychol. sci. Meth.*, 3, 637–643.—*338*

Angell, J. R. (1907) The province of functional psychology. *Psychol. Rev.*, 14, 61–91.—*332*

Angell, J. R., and Moore, A. W. (1896) Reaction-time: a study in attention and habit. *Psychol. Rev.*, 3, 245–258.—*329*

Antonitis, J. J. *See* Schoenfeld, Antonitis, and Bersh (1950a) (1950b).

Arnold, W. J. (1947) Simple reaction chains and their integration. I. Homogeneous chaining with terminal reinforcement. *J. comp. physiol. Psychol.*, 40, 349–363.—*105, 155*

Arrow, K. J. (1951a) Mathematical models in the social sciences. In D. Lerner and H. D. Lasswell, eds. *The policy sciences.* Stanford, Calif.: Stanford Univ. Press, 129–154.—*406*

Arrow, K. J. (1951b) *Social choice and individual values.* New York: Wiley.—*384, 405*

Ashby, W. R. (1952) *Design for a brain.* New York: Wiley.—*454*

Atkinson, J. W. (1953) The achievement motive and recall of interrupted and completed tasks. *J. exp. Psychol.*, 46, 381–390.—*283*

Atkinson, J. W. (1954) Exploration using imaginative thought to assess the strength of human motives. In the Nebraska Symposium on Motivation, M. R. Jones, ed. *Current theory and research in motivation.* Lincoln, Nebr.: Univ. of Nebraska Press, 56–112.—*432*

Atkinson, J. W. *See also* McClelland and Atkinson (1948), McClelland and others (1953).

Bailey, C. J. (1954) *The efficiency of drives as cues.* Unpublished Ph.D. dissertation, Yale University.—*425*

Bailey, C. J., and Porter, L. W. (1955) Relevant cues in drive discrimination in cats. *J. comp. physiol. Psychol.* In press.—*425*

Baker, R. A., and Lawrence, D. H. (1951) The differential effects of simultaneous and successive stimuli presentation on transposition. *J. comp. physiol. Psychol.*, 44, 378–382.—*442*

Baldwin, J. M. (1896) The "type-theory" of reaction. *Mind, N.S.*, 5, 81–89.—*329*

Baldwin, J. M., and Shaw, W. J. (1895) Types of reaction. *Psychol. Rev.*, 2, 259–273.—*329*

Ball, J. *See* Lashley and Ball (1929).

Ballachey, E. L. *See* Buel and Ballachey (1934).

Barker, A. N. *See* Hull and others (1951).

Barker, R. G. (1942) An experimental study of the resolution of conflict by children: time elapsing and amount of vicarious trial-and-error behavior occurring. In Q. McNemar and M. A. Merrill, eds. *Studies in personality; Contributed in honor of Lewis M. Terman.* McGraw-Hill, 13–34.—*267, 288*

BARKER, R. G. (1946) An experimental study of the relationship between certainty of choice and the relative valence of the alternatives. *J. Personality,* 16, 41–52.—*267*

BARKER, R. G., DEMBO, T., and LEWIN, K. (1941) Frustration and regression: a study of young children. *Univ. Ia. Stud. Child Welf.,* 18, No. I.—*273, 288, 304*

BARKER, R. G., KOUNIN, J., and WRIGHT, H. F. (1943) *Child behavior and development.* New York: McGraw-Hill.—*286*

BARKER, R. G., and WRIGHT, H. F. (1954) *Midwest and its children.* Evanston, Ill.: Row, Peterson.—*481*

BARTEL, H. (1937) Über die Abhängigkeit spontaner Reproduktionen von Feldbedingungen. *Psychol. Forsch.,* 22, 1–25.—*246*

BARTLETT, F. C. (1932) *Remembering.* Cambridge, Cambridge Univ. Press.—*244, 245*

BATESON, G. (1941) The frustration-aggression hypothesis and culture. *Psychol. Rev.,* 48, 350–355.—*304*

BATESON, G. (1942) Social planning and the concept of "deutero-learning." *Science, philosophy and religion.* New York: Conference on Science, Philosophy, and Religion. 81–97.—*438*

BAUER, F. J., and LAWRENCE, D. H. (1953) Influence of similarity of choice-point and goal cues on discrimination learning. *J. comp. physiol. Psychol.,* 46, 241–248.—*449*

BAVELAS, A. (1942) Morale and the training of leaders. In G. Watson, ed. *Civilian morale.* Boston: Houghton Mifflin, 143–165.—*279*

BAVELAS, A. *See also* Seashore and Bavelas (1941).

BELL, H. M. (1942) Rest pauses in motor learning as related to Snoddy's hypothesis of mental growth. *Psychol. Monogr.,* 54, No. 243.—*356*

BENDIG, A. W. (1952) Latent learning in a water maze. *J. exp. Psychol.,* 43, 134–137.—*212*

BENNETT, E. L. *See* Krech and others (1954).

BENTLEY, A. F. *See* Dewey and Bentley (1949).

BERGMANN, G. (1943) Psychoanalysis and experimental psychology: a review from the standpoint of scientific empiricism. *Mind,* 52, 122–140.—*326*

BERGMANN, G. *See also* Spence, Bergmann, and Lippitt (1950).

BERGMANN, G., and SPENCE, K. W. (1941) Operationism and theory in psychology. *Psychol. Rev.,* 48, 1–14.—*415*

BERKUN, M. M., KESSEN, M. L., and MILLER, N. E. (1952) Hunger-reducing effects of food by stomach fistula versus food by mouth measured by a consummatory response. *J. comp. physiol. Psychol.,* 45, 550–554.—*423*

BERNSTONE, A. H. *See* Muenzinger, Bernstone, and Richards (1938).

BERSH, P. J. (1951) The influence of two variables upon the establishment of a secondary reinforcer for operant responses. *J. exp. Psychol.,* 41, 62–73.—*95*

BERSH, P. J. *See also* Schoenfeld, Antonitis, and Bersh (1950a) (1950b), Notterman, Schoenfeld, and Bersh (1952), Schoenfeld and Bersh (1952).

BERTALANFFY, L. von. (1951) Theoretical models in biology and psychology. *J. Personality,* 20, 24–38.—*406*

BEXTON, W. H., HERON, W., and SCOTT, T. H. (1954) Effects of decreased variation in the environment. *Canad. J. Psychol.*, 8, 70–76.—*431*

BINDRA, B., PATERSON, A. L., and STRZELECKI, J. (1955) On the relation between anxiety and conditioning. *Canadian J. Psychol.*, 9, 1–6.—*300*

BIRCH, H. G. (1945a) The role of motivational factors in insightful problem-solving. *J. comp. Psychol.*, 38, 295–317.—*256*

BIRCH, H. G. (1945b) The relation of previous experience to insightful problem-solving. *J. comp. Psychol.*, 38, 367–383.—*234, 256*

BIRENBAUM, J. (1930) Das Vergessen einer Vornahme. *Psychol. Forsch.*, 13, 218–284.—*253, 288*

BITTERMAN, M. E. *See* Gonzales, Gentry, and Bitterman (1954), Weise and Bitterman (1951).

BITTERMAN, M. E., and HOLTZMAN, W. H. (1952) Conditioning and extinction of the galvanic skin response as a function of anxiety. *J. abnorm. soc. Psychol.*, 47, 615–623.—*300*

BITTERMAN, M. E., and WODINSKY, J. (1953) Simultaneous and successive discrimination. *Psychol. Rev.*, 60, 371–376.—*442*

BLACKWELL, M. G., Jr. *See* Wallace, Blackwell, and Jenkins (1941).

BLAIR, G. M. (1948) The psychological basis of the modern curriculum: 6. How learning theory is related to curriculum organization. *J. educ. Psychol.*, 39, 161–166.—*491*

BLODGETT, H. C. (1929) The effect of the introduction of reward upon the maze performance of rats. *Univ. Calif. Publ. Psychol.*, 4, 113–134.—*209, 211, 220*

BLODGETT, H. C., and MCCUTCHAN, K. (1947) Place versus response-learning in the simple T-maze. *J. exp. Psychol.*, 37, 412–422.—*194*

BLODGETT, H. C., and MCCUTCHAN, K. (1948) The relative strength of place and response learning in the T-maze. *J. comp. physiol. Psychol.*, 41, 17–24. —*194*

BLUM, G. S. (1953) *Psychoanalytic theories of personality.* New York: McGraw-Hill.—*309, 325*

BLUM, G. S., and MILLER, D. R. (1952) Exploring the psychoanalytic theory of the "oral character." *J. Personality*, 20, 287–304.—*326*

BLUM, J. S. *See* Blum, R. A., and Blum, J. S. (1949).

BLUM, R. A., and BLUM, J. S. (1949) Factual issues in the "continuity" controversy. *Psychol. Rev.*, 56, 33–50.—*438*

BODE, B. H. (1940) *How we learn.* Boston: Heath.—*330*

BOECK, C. H. (1951) The inductive-deductive compared to the deductive-descriptive approach to laboratory instruction in high school chemistry. *J. exp. Educ.*, 19, 247–254.—*491*

BORING, E. G. (1929) The psychology of controversy. *Psychol. Rev.*, 36, 97–121.—*457*

BORING, E. G. (1930) The gestalt psychology and the gestalt movement. *Amer. J. Psychol.*, 42, 308–315.—*256*

BORING, E. G. (1933a) *The physical dimensions of consciousness.* New York, Appleton-Century-Crofts.—*334, 367*

BORING, E. G. (1933b) Review of Robinson's *Association theory today. Psychol. Bull.*, 30, 451–455.—*367*

BORING, E. G. (1941) Communality in relation to proaction and retroaction. *Amer. J. Psychol.*, 54, 280–283.—*346*

BORING, E. G. (1950) *A history of experimental psychology.* Second edition. New York: Appleton-Century-Crofts.—*128, 290, 328*

BRADY, J. V., and HUNT, H. F. (1955) An experimental approach to the analysis of emotional behavior. *J. Psychol.*, 40, 313–324.—*474*

BRADY, J. V., SCHREINER, L., GELLER, I., and KLING, A. (1954) Subcortical mechanisms in emotional behavior: the effect of rhinencephalic injury upon the acquisition and retention of a conditioned avoidance response in cats. *J. comp. physiol. Psychol.*, 47, 179–186.—*453*

BRALY, K. W. (1933) The influence of past experience in visual perception. *J. exp. Psychol.*, 16, 613–643.—*230*

BRAY, C. W. (1948) *Psychology and military proficiency.* Princeton: Princeton Univ. Press.—*491*

BRELAND, K., and BRELAND, M. (1951) A field of applied animal psychology. *Amer. Psychologist,* 6, 202–204.—*88*

BRELAND, M. *See* Breland, K., and Breland, M. (1951).

BRETNALL, E. P. *See* Tolman, Hall, and Bretnall (1932).

BRICKER, P. D., and CHAPANIS, A. (1953) Do incorrectly perceived tachistoscopic stimuli convey some information? *Psychol. Rev.*, 60, 181–188.—*320*

BRITT, S. H. (1935) Retroactive inhibition: a review of the literature. *Psychol. Bull.*, 32, 381–440.—*344*

BRONNER, A. F. (Chmn.) (1949) The objective evaluation of psychotherapy. Round Table, 1948. *Amer. J. Orthopsychiat.*, 19, 463–491.—*312*

BRONSON, W. C. *See* Postman, Bronson, and Gropper (1952).

BROSS, I. D. J. (1953) *Design for decision.* New York: Macmillan.—*384, 405*

BROWN, D. R. *See* Postman and Brown (1952).

BROWN, F. D. *See* Pechstein and Brown (1939).

BROWN, J. F. (1929) The methods of Kurt Lewin in the psychology of action and affection. *Psychol. Rev.*, 36, 200–221.—*261*

BROWN, J. F. (1936) *Psychology and the social order.* New York: McGraw-Hill.—*286*

BROWN, J. F., and FEDER, D. D. (1934) Thorndike's theory of learning as gestalt psychology. *Psychol. Bull.*, 31, 426–437.—*28, 46*

BROWN, J. S. (1942) The generalization of approach responses as a function of stimulus intensity and strength of motivation. *J. comp. Psychol.*, 33, 209–226.—*168*

BROWN, J. S. (1948) Gradients of approach and avoidance responses and their relation to levels of motivation. *J. comp. physiol. Psychol.* 41, 450–465.—*168, 183*

BROWN, J. S. (1953) Comments on Professor Harlow's paper. In the Nebraska Symposium on Motivation. *Current theory and research in motivation.* Lincoln, Nebr.: Univ. of Nebraska Press, 49–55.—*431*

BROWN, J. S. *See also* Miller, Brown, and Lipofsky (1943).

BROWN, J. S., and JACOBS, A. (1949) The role of fear in the motivation and acquisition of responses. *J. exp. Psychol.*, 39, 747–759.—*412, 422*

BROWN, M. A. *See* Robinson and Brown (1926).

BROWN, T. (1820) *Lectures on the philosophy of the human mind.* 16th edition, 4 vols. Edinburgh: William Tait, 1846.—*342*

BROWN, W. (1935) Growth of 'memory images.' *Amer. J. Psychol.*, 47, 90–102. —*243*

BROWN, W. L. *See* Gentry, Brown, and Kaplan (1947).

BROWN, W. O. *See* Muenzinger and others (1952).

BROWNELL, W. A., and MOSER, H. E. (1949) Meaningful versus mechanical learning: a study in Grade 3 subtraction. *Duke Univ. Res. Stud. Educ.*, No. 8.—*491*

BRUCE, R. W. (1933) Conditions of transfer of training. *J. exp. Psychol.*, 16, 343–361.—*367*

BRUNER, J. S. (1951) Personality dynamics and the process of perceiving. In R. R. Blake and G. V. Ramsey, eds. *Perception, an approach to personality.* New York: Ronald Press, 121–147.—*468*

BRUNSWIK, E. (1939) Probability as a determiner of rat behavior. *J. exp. Psychol.*, 25, 175–197.—*197, 198, 294*

BRUNSWIK, E. (1944) Distal focussing of perception: Size-constancy in a representative sample of situations. *Psychol. Monogr.*, 56, No. 254.—*467*

BRUNSWIK, E. (1952) *The conceptual framework of psychology.* Chicago: Univ. Chicago Press. *Int. Encycl. unified Sci.*, 1, No. 10.—*491*

BRUNSWIK, E. (1955) Representative design and probabilistic theory in a functional psychology. *Psychol. Rev.*, 62, 193–217.—*366, 467, 491*

BRUNSWIK, E. *See also* Tolman and Brunswik (1935).

BRYAN, W. L., and HARTER, N. (1897) Studies in the physiology and psychology of the telegraphic language. *Psychol. Rev.*, 4, 27–53.—*1*

BRYAN, W. L., and HARTER, N. (1899) Studies on the telegraphic language. The acquisition of a hierarchy of habits. *Psychol. Rev.*, 6, 345–375.—*1*

BUCY, P. C. *See* Klüver and Bucy (1939).

BUEL, J., and BALLACHEY, E. L. (1934) Choice-point expectancy in the maze running of the rat. *J. genet. Psychol.*, 45, 145–168.—*220*

BURKE, C. J. *See* Estes and Burke (1953).

BUSH, R. R., and MOSTELLER, F. (1951a) A mathematical model for simple learning. *Psychol. Rev.*, 58, 313–323.—*394, 396*

BUSH, R. R., and MOSTELLER, F. (1951b) A model for stimulus generalization and discrimination. *Psychol. Rev.*, 58, 413–423.—*394*

BUSH, R. R., and MOSTELLER, F. (1955) *Stochastic models for learning.* New York: Wiley.—*398, 405*

BUSH, R. R., MOSTELLER, F., and THOMPSON, G. L. (1954) A formal structure for multiple-choice situations. In R. M. Thrall, C. H. Coombs, and R. L. Davis, eds. *Decision processes.* New York: Wiley, 99–126.—*406*

BUTLER, R. A. (1953) Discrimination learning by rhesus monkeys to visual-exploration motivation. *J. comp. physiol. Psychol.*, 46, 95–98.—*430, 467*

BUTLER, R. A. (1954) Incentive conditions which influence visual exploration. *J. exp. Psychol.*, 48, 19–23.—*467*

BUXTON, C. E. (1940) Latent learning and the goal gradient hypothesis. *Contrib. psychol. Theor.*, 2, No. 6.—*211*

BUXTON, C. E. (1943) The status of research on reminiscence. *Psychol. Bull.*, 40, 313–340.—*360*

CAIN, L. F., and WILLEY, R. deV. (1939) The effect of spaced learning on the curve of retention. *J. exp. Psychol.*, 25, 209–214.—*357*

CAMERON, N. (1938a) Reasoning, regression, and communication in schizophrenics. *Psychol. Monogr.*, 50, No. 1.—*304*

CAMERON, N. (1938b) A study of thinking in senile deterioration and schizophrenic disorganization. *Amer. J. Psychol.*, 51, 650–664.—*304*

CAMPBELL, A. A. *See* Hilgard and Campbell (1936).

CAMPBELL, B. A., and KRAELING, D. (1954) Response strength as a function of drive level during training. *J. comp. physiol. Psychol.*, 47, 101–103.—*427*

CAMPBELL, B. A., and SHEFFIELD, F. D. (1953) Relation of random activity to food deprivation. *J. comp. physiol. Psychol.*, 46, 320–322.—*424, 425*

CAMPBELL, R. K. *See* Hilgard, Campbell, and Sears (1938).

CANNICOTT, R. G., and UMBERGER, J. P. (1950) An investigation of the psychoanalytic "mechanism" of repression: the retention of verbal material associated with noxious stimulation. *Proc. Okla. Acad. Sci.*, 31, 176–178.—*316*

CANTOR, N. (1946) *Dynamics of learning.* Buffalo, N.Y.: Foster and Stewart.—*327*

CANTRIL, H. *See* Ittleson and Cantril (1954).

CARMICHAEL, L. (1936) Review of Guthrie's *The psychology of human learning. J. gen. Psychol.*, 14, 490–492.—*81*

CARMICHAEL, L., HOGAN, H. P., and WALTER, A. A. (1932) An experimental study of the effect of language on the reproduction of visually perceived form. *J. exp. Psychol.*, 15, 73–86.—*243*

CARR, H. A. (1925) *Psychology, a study of mental activity.* New York, Longmans.—*330, 333, 339, 476*

CARR, H. A. (1930) Teaching and learning. *J. genet. Psychol.*, 37, 189–219.—*340*

CARR, H. A. (1931) The laws of association. *Psychol. Rev.*, 38, 212–228.—*336, 342, 367*

CARR, H. A. (1933) The quest for constants. *Psychol. Rev.*, 40, 514–532.—*334*

CARR, H. A. (1935) *An introduction to space perception.* New York, Longmans.—*336, 466*

CARR, H. A. (1938) The law of effect. *Psychol. Rev.*, 45, 191–199.—*340*

CARTER, L. F. (1936) Maze learning with a differential proprioceptive cue. *J. exp. Psychol.*, 19, 758–762.—*81*

CARTER, L. F. (1941) Intensity of conditioned stimulus and rate of conditioning. *J. exp. Psychol.*, 28, 481–490.—*81*

CARTWRIGHT, D. (1942) The effect of interruption, completion, and failure upon the attractiveness of activities. *J. exp. Psychol.*, 31, 1–16.—*284*

CASON, H. (1932) Review of Thorndike's *Human learning. J. abnorm. soc. Psychol.*, 27, 214–222.—*46*

CASON, H. *See also* Trowbridge and Cason (1932).

CHAPANIS, A. *See* Bricker and Chapanis (1953).

CHAPANIS, A., GARNER, W. R., and MORGAN, C. T. (1949) *Applied experimental psychology.* New York: Wiley.—*471*

CHILD, I. L. *See* Whiting and Child (1953).

CHILD, I. L., POTTER, E. H., and LEVINE, E. M. (1946) Children's textbooks and personality development: an exploration in the social psychology of education. *Psychol. Monogr.*, 60, No. 3.—*491*

CHILDS, J. L. (1931) *Education and the philosophy of experimentalism.* New York: Appleton-Century-Crofts.—*330*

CHOW, K. L. *See* Lashley, Chow, and Semmes (1951).

CHRISTIE, R. (1951) The role of drive discrimination in learning under irrelevant motivation. *J. exp. Psychol.*, 42, 13–19.—*212*

CHRISTIE, R. (1952) The effect of some early experiences in the latent learning of adult rats. *J. comp. physiol. Psychol.*, 43, 281–288.—*212*

CLARK, R. A. See McClelland and others (1953).

COBURN, H. E. (1951) The brain analogy. *Psychol. Rev.*, 58, 155–178.—*454*

COBURN, H. E. (1953) The brain analogy: transfer of differentiation. *Psychol. Rev.*, 60, 413–422.—*454*

COFER, C. N. *See* Rosenthal and Cofer (1948).

COHEN, L. H., HILGARD, E. R., and WENDT, G. R. (1933) Sensitivity to light in a case of hysterical blindness studied by reinforcement-inhibition and conditioning methods. *Yale J. Biol. Med.*, 6, 61–67.—*73*

COLEMAN, J. S. (1954) An expository analysis of some of Rashevsky's social behavior models. In P. Lazarsfeld, ed. *Mathematical thinking in the social sciences*. Glencoe, Ill.: Free Press, 105–165.—*386*

COLES, G. R. *See* Lawrence and Coles (1954).

COMBS, A. W. *See* Snygg and Combs (1949).

COMER, P. B. *See* McGinnies, Comer, and Lacey (1952).

CONRAD, D. G. *See* Muenzinger and Conrad (1953).

COOK, B. S., and HILGARD, E. R. (1949) Distributed practice in motor learning: Progressively increasing and decreasing rests. *J. exp. Psychol.*, 39, 169–172.—*355*

COOK, S. W., and SKINNER, B. F. (1939) Some factors influencing the distribution of associated words. *Psychol. Rec.*, 3, 178–184.—*107*

COOK, T. W. (1934) Massed and distributed practice in puzzle solving. *Psychol. Rev.*, 41, 330–355.—*358*

COOMBS, C. H. *See* Thrall, Coombs, and Davis (1954).

COOMBS, C. H., RAIFFA, H., and THRALL, R. M. (1954) Some views on mathematical models and measurement theory. *Psychol. Rev.*, 61, 132–144.—*406*

COTTRELL, L. S. Jr., and GALLAGHER, R. (1941) Important developments in American social psychology during the past decade. *Sociometry*, 4, 107–139.—*331*

COURTS, F. A. (1939) Relations between experimentally induced muscular tension and memorization. *J. exp. Psychol.*, 25, 235–256.—*367*

COWLES, J. T., and NISSEN, H. W. (1937) Reward expectancy in delayed responses of chimpanzees, *J. comp. Psychol.*, 24, 345–358.—*192*

CRANDALL, V. J. (1951) Induced frustration and punishment-reward expectancy in thematic apperception stories. *J. consult. Psychol.*, 15, 400–404.—*451*

CROW, W. J. *See* Muenzinger and others (1952).

CRUTCHFIELD, R. S. (1939) The determiners of energy expenditure in string-pulling by the rat. *J. Psychol.*, 7, 163–178.—*220*

CRUTCHFIELD, R. S. *See also* Krech and Crutchfield (1948).

CULLER, E. (1928) Nature of the learning curve. *Psychol. Bull.*, 34, 742–743.—*370*

CULLER, E., and GIRDEN, E. (1951) The learning curve in relation to other psychometric functions. *Amer. J. Psychol.*, 64, 327–349.—*370, 371*

CUNNINGHAM, L. M. *See* Jenkins and Cunningham (1949).

DASHIELL, J. F. (1935) A survey and synthesis of learning theories. *Psychol. Bull.*, 32, 261–275.—*457, 490*

DASHIELL, J. F. (1949) *Fundamentals of general psychology*. Third edition. Boston: Houghton Mifflin.—*336*

DATEL, W. E. *See* Seward, Datel, and Levy (1952).

DAUB, C. T. (1933) The effect of doors on latent learning. *J. comp. Psychol.*, 15, 49–58.—*211*

DAVIS, R. H. *See* Denny and Davis (1951).

DAVIS, R. L. (1954) Introduction to "Decision processes." In R. M. Thrall, C. H. Coombs, and R. L. Davis, eds. *Decision processes*. New York: Wiley, 1–18.—*385*

DAVIS, R. L. *See also* Thrall, Coombs, and Davis (1954).

DEANE, G. *See* Zeaman, Deane, and Wegner (1954).

DEESE, J. (1952) *The psychology of learning.* New York: McGraw-Hill.—*14*

DELGADO, J. M. R., ROBERTS, W. W., and MILLER, N. E. (1954) Learning motivated by electrical stimulation of the brain. *Amer. J. Physiol.*, 179, 587–593.—*432, 454*

DEMBO, T. (1931) Der Ärger als dynamischen Problem. *Psychol. Forsch.*, 15, 1–144.—*288*

DEMBO, T. *See also* Barker, Dembo, and Lewin (1941), Lewin and others (1944).

DENNY, M. R., and DAVIS, R. H. (1951) A test of latent learning for a non-goal significate. *J. comp. physiol. Psychol.*, 44, 590–595.—*213*

DERIVERA, J. *See* Lawrence and DeRivera (1954).

DEUTSCH, M. (1954) Field theory in social psychology. In G. Lindzey, ed. *Handbook of social psychology.* Cambridge, Mass.: Addison-Wesley, 181–222.—*265, 289*

DEVALOIS, R. L. *See* Walker, Knotter, and DeValois (1950).

DEWEY, J. (1896) The reflex arc concept in psychology. *Psychol. Rev.*, 3, 357–370.—*464*

DEWEY, J. (1910) *How we think.* Boston: Heath.

DEWEY, J. (1920) *Influence of Darwin on philosophy.* New York: Holt.—*329*

DEWEY, J. (1938) *Logic: the theory of inquiry.* New York: Holt.—*331*

DEWEY, J., and BENTLEY, A. F. (1949) *Knowing and the known.* Boston: Beacon Press.—*331*

DIESENROTH, C. F., and SPENCE, K. W. (1941) An investigation of latent learning in the white rat. *Psychol. Bull.*, 38, 706. (Abstract)—*212*

DINSMOOR, J. A. (1950) A quantitative comparison of the discriminative and reinforcing functions of a stimulus. *J. exp. Psychol.*, 40, 458–472.—*120*

DIVEN, K. (1937) Certain determinants in the conditioning of anxiety reactions. *J. Psychol.*, 3, 291–308.—*316*

DODGE, R. (1911) A working hypothesis for inner psychophysics. *Psychol. Rev.*, 18, 167–185.—*128*

DODGE, R. (1931) *Conditions and consequences of human variability.* New Haven, Yale Univ. Press.—*236, 471*

DOLLARD, J. *See* Miller and Dollard (1941).

DOLLARD, J., DOOB, L. W., MILLER, N. E., MOWRER, O. H., SEARS, R. R., FORD, C. S., HOVLAND, C. I., and SOLLENBERGER, R. T. (1939) *Frustration and aggression.* New Haven: Yale Univ. Press.—*304*

DOLLARD, J., and MILLER, N. E. (1950) *Personality and psychotherapy.* New York: McGraw-Hill.—*292, 293, 295, 299, 325, 411, 456*

DOMINGUEZ, K. *See* Jackson and Dominguez (1939).

DOOB, L. W. *See* Dollard and others (1939).

DORÉ, L. R., and HILGARD, E. R. (1937) Spaced practice and the maturation hypothesis. *J. Psychol.*, 4, 245–259.—*354, 356*

DRAMBAREAN, N. C. *See* Wispé and Drambarean (1953).

DUBOIS, P. H., and FORBES, T. W. (1934) Studies of catatonia: III. Bodily postures assumed while sleeping. *Psychiat. Quart.*, 8, 546–552.—*304*

DUDYCHA, G. J., and DUDYCHA, M. M. (1941) Childhood memories: a review of the literature. *Psychol. Bull.*, 38, 668–682.—*309, 326*

DUDYCHA, M. M. *See* Dudycha, G. J., and Dudycha, M. M. (1941).

DUNCAN, C. P. (1951) Stimulus-generalization and spread of effect. *Amer. J. Psychol.*, 64, 585–590.—*38*

DUNCKER, K. (1938) Experimental modification of children's food preferences through social suggestion. *J. abnorm. soc. Psychol.*, 33, 489–507.—*279*

DUNCKER, K. (1945) On problem-solving. Trans. by L. S. Lees from the 1935 original. *Psychol. Monogr.*, 58, No. 270.—*242, 256*

DURKIN, H. E. (1937) Trial-and-error, gradual analysis, and sudden reorganization: An experimental study of problem-solving. *Arch. Psychol.*, N.Y., No. 210.—*256*

DUTTON, C. E. *See* Hilgard, Dutton, and Helmick (1949).

DYMOND, R. F. *See* Rogers and Dymond (1954).

EBBINGHAUS, H. (1885) *Memory*. Trans. by H. A. Ruger and C. E. Bussenius. New York: Teachers College, 1913.—*1, 342, 369*

EDGREN, R. D. *See* Hilgard, Edgren, and Irvine (1954).

EDWARDS, A. C. *See* Mayhew and Edwards (1936).

EDWARDS, A. L. (1941) Political frames of reference as a factor influencing recognition. *J. abnorm. soc. Psychol.*, 36, 34–61.—*315*

EDWARDS, A. L. (1942) The retention of affective experiences—a criticism and restatement of the problem. *Psychol. Rev.*, 49, 43–53.—*315*

EDWARDS, A. L. *See also* Guthrie and Edwards (1949).

EHRENFREUND, D. (1948) An experimental test of the continuity theory of discrimination learning with pattern vision. *J. comp. physiol. Psychol.*, 41, 408–422.—*436*

EHRENFREUND, D. *See also* Alberts and Ehrenfreund (1951).

ELLIOTT, M. H. (1928) The effect of change of reward on the maze performance of rats. *Univ. Calif. Publ. Psychol.*, 4, 19–30.—*192*

ELLIOTT, M. H. (1929) The effect of appropriateness of rewards and of complex incentives on maze performance. *Univ. Calif. Publ. Psychol.*, 4, 91–98.—*211*

ELLIS, A. (1950) An introduction to the principles of scientific psychoanalysis. *Genet. Psychol. Monogr.*, 41, 147–212.—*326*

ELLIS, W. D. (1938) *A source book of gestalt psychology*. New York: Harcourt, Brace.—*255*

ELLSON, D. G. (1938) Quantitative studies of the interaction of simple habits. I. Recovery from specific and generalized effects of extinction. *J. exp. Psychol.*, 23, 339–358.—*183*

ELLSON, D. G. (1939) The concept of reflex reserve. *Psychol. Rev.*, 46, 566–575.—*86*

ELLSON, D. G. (1949) Application of operational analysis to human motor behavior. *Psychol. Rev.*, 56, 9–17.—*376, 406*

ERICKSEN, S. C. (1942) Variability in attack in massed and distributed practice. *J. exp. Psychol.*, 31, 339–345.—*358*

ERICKSON, M. H. (1937) Development of apparent unconsciousness during hypnotic reliving of a traumatic experience. *Arch. Neurol. Psychiat.*, 38, 1282–1288.—*303*

ERICKSON, M. H. *See also* Huston, Shakow, and Erickson (1934).

ERIKSEN, C. W. (1951) Perceptual defense as a function of unacceptable needs. *J. abnorm. soc. Psychol.*, 46, 557–564.—*320*

ERIKSEN, C. W. (1952) Defense against ego-threat in memory and perception. *J. abnorm. soc. Psychol.*, 47, 230–235.—*321, 326*

ERIKSEN, C. W. *See also* Lazarus, Eriksen, and Fonda (1951).

ERIKSON, E. H. (1950) *Childhood and society.* New York: Norton.—*294*

ESTES, W. K. (1944) An experimental study of punishment. *Psychol. Monogr.*, 57, No. 263, iii, 40 pp.—*98, 109–112*

ESTES, W. K. (1949) A study of motivating conditions necessary for secondary reinforcement. *J. exp. Psychol.*, 39, 306–310.—*120*

ESTES, W. K. (1950) Toward a statistical theory of learning. *Psychol. Rev.*, 57, 94–107.—*74, 389*

ESTES, W. K. (1953) Models for learning theory. In *Symposium on psychology of learning basic to military training problems.* Washington, D.C.: Committee on Human Resources, Research and Development Board, HR-HTD 201/1, 21–38.—*390, 392, 402*

ESTES, W. K. (1954a) Individual behavior in uncertain situations: an interpretation in terms of statistical association theory. In R. M. Thrall, C. H. Coombs, and R. L. Davis, eds. *Decision processes.* New York: Wiley, 127–137.—*385, 406*

ESTES, W. K. (1954b) Kurt Lewin. In W. K. Estes and others. *Modern learning theory.* New York: Appleton-Century-Crofts, 317–344.—*274, 287, 289*

ESTES, W. K., and BURKE, C. J. (1953) A theory of stimulus variability in learning. *Psychol. Rev.*, 60, 276–286.—*390, 392*

ESTES, W. K., KOCH, S., MACCORQUODALE, K., MEEHL, P. E., MUELLER, C. G., Jr., SCHOENFELD, W. N., and VERPLANCK, W. S. (1954) *Modern learning theory.* New York: Appleton-Century-Crofts.—*14, 456*

ESTES, W. K., and SKINNER, B. F. (1941) Some quantitative properties of anxiety. *J. exp. Psychol.*, 29, 390–400.—*120*

EVANS, S. (1936) Flexibility of established habit. *J. gen. Psychol.*, 14, 177–200. —*195*

FAGAN, C. A., and NORTH, A. J. (1951) A verification of the guessing sequence hypothesis about spread of effect. *J. exp. Psychol.*, 41, 349–351.—*35*

FAJANS, S. (1933a) Die Bedeutung der Entfernung für die Stärke eines Aufforderungscharakters beim Säugling und Kleinkind. *Psychol. Forsch.*, 17, 215–267.—*267*

FAJANS, S. (1933b) Erfolg, Ausdauer, und Aktivität beim Säugling und Kleinkind. *Psychol. Forsch.*, 17, 268–305.—*267*

FARBER, I. E. (1953) Motivational factors in verbal learning. In *Symposium on psychology of learning basic to military training problems.* Washington, D.C.: Committee on Human Resources, Research and Development Board, HR-HTO 201/1, 127–144.—*426, 427*

FARBER, I. E. (1954) Anxiety as a drive state. *Current theory and research on motivation.* In the Nebraska Symposium on Motivation, M. R. Jones, ed. Lincoln, Nebr.: Univ. Nebraska Press, 1–46.—*299, 300, 426, 427*

FARBER, I. E. *See also* Spence and Farber (1953) (1954).

FARBER, I. E., and SPENCE, K. W. (1953) Complex learning and conditioning as a function of anxiety. *J. exp. Psychol.*, 45, 120–125.—*300*

FARBEROW, N. L. *See* Sarbin and Farberow (1952).

FECHNER, G. T. (1873) *Einige Ideen zur Schöpfungs—und Entwicklungsgeschichte der Organismen.* Leipzig. Cited by Freud, 1920.—*291*

FEDER, D. D. *See* Brown and Feder (1934).

FEHRER, E. (1951) Latent learning in the sophisticated rat. *J. exp. Psychol.*, 42, 409–416.—*212*

FELDMAN, N. G. *See* Melton, Feldman, and Mason (1936).

FELSINGER, J. M. *See* Gladstone and others (1947), Hull and others (1947), Yamaguchi and others (1948).

FELSINGER, J. M., GLADSTONE, A. I., YAMAGUCHI, H. G., and HULL, C. L. (1947) Reaction latency ($_{S}t_{R}$) as a function of the number of reinforcements (N). *J. exp. Psychol.*, 37, 214–228.—*146*

FENICHEL, O. (1945) *The psychoanalytic theory of neurosis.* New York: Norton.—*295, 297, 302, 325*

FERSTER, C. B. (1953) The use of the free operant in the analysis of behavior. *Psychol. Bull.*, 50, 263–274.—*85*

FERSTER, C. B. (1954) Use of the blackout in the investigation of temporal discrimination in fixed-interval reinforcement. *J. exp. Psychol.*, 47, 69–74. —*120*

FESTINGER, L. (1942) Wish, expectation, and group standards as factors influencing level of aspiration. *J. abnorm. soc. Psychol.*, 37, 184–200.—*288*

FESTINGER, L. *See also* Hoffman, Festinger, and Lawrence (1954), Lewin and others (1944).

FINAN, J. L. (1940) Review of Skinner's *The behavior of organisms. J. gen. Psychol.*, 22, 441–447.—*119*

FINGER, F. W. (1954) Review of Skinner's *Science and human behavior. Psychol. Bull.*, 51, 86–88.—*119*

FISCHER, J. W. *See* Whittaker, Gilchrist, and Fischer (1952).

FITCH, E. E. *See* Smith and Fitch (1935).

FITCH, F. B. *See* Hull and others (1940).

FITZGERALD, B. J. *See* Rotter, Fitzgerald, and Joyce (1954).

FLETCHER, F. M. *See* Muenzinger and Fletcher (1936) (1937).

FLOOD, M. M. (1954) On game-learning theory and some decision-making experiments. In R. M. Thrall, C. H. Coombs, and R. L. Davis, eds. *Decision processes.* New York: Wiley, 139–158.—*384, 406*

FONDA, C. P. *See* Lazarus, Eriksen, and Fonda (1951).

FOORD, E. N. *See* Hebb and Foord (1945).

FORBES, T. W. *See* DuBois and Forbes (1934).

FORD, C. S. *See* Dollard and others (1949).

FRANK, J. D. (1941) Recent studies of the level of aspiration. *Psychol. Bull.*, 38, 218–226.—*278*

FRANK, L. K. (1939) Time perspectives. *J. soc. Phil.*, 4, 293–312.—*272*

FRENCH, T. M. (1933) Interrelations between psychoanalysis and the experimental work of Pavlov. *Amer. J. Psychiat.*, 89, 1165–1203.—*326*

FRENKEL-BRUNSWIK, E. (1954) Psychoanalysis and the unity of science. *Proc. Amer. Acad. Arts and Sciences,* 80, 271–347.—*326*

FREUD, A. (1935) *Psychoanalysis for teachers and parents.* New York: Emerson Books.—*309, 327*

FREUD, A. (1936) *The ego and mechanisms of defense.* Translation, 1937. London: Hogarth Press.—*294, 325*

FREUD, S. (1911) Formulations regarding the two principles in mental functioning. In *Collected papers.* London: Hogarth Press, 1925, IV, 13–21.—*293*

FREUD, S. (1915a) Repression. In *Collected papers.* London: Hogarth Press, 1925, IV, 84–97.—*293*

FREUD, S. (1915b) The unconscious. In *Collected papers.* London: Hogarth Press, 1925, IV, 98–136.—*324*

FREUD, S. (1920a) *A general introduction to psychoanalysis.* New York: Boni and Liveright.—*298, 325*

FREUD, S. (1920b) *Beyond the pleasure principle.* Translation, 1950. New York: Liveright.—*291, 292, 295, 312*

FREUD, S. (1921) *Group psychology and the analysis of the ego.* Translation, 1922. New York: Liveright.—*304*

FREUD, S. (1923) *The ego and the id.* Translation, 1927. London: Hogarth Press.—*325*

FREUD, S. (1926) *The problem of anxiety.* Translation, 1936. New York: Norton.—*298, 325*

FREUD, S. (1938) *The basic writings of Sigmund Freud.* New York: Modern Library.—*325*

FREUD, S. (1940) *An outline of psychoanalysis.* Translation, 1949. New York: Norton.—*325*

FREUD, S. (1954) *The origins of psychoanalysis: letters to Wilhelm Fliess, drafts and notes: 1887–1902.* New York: Basic Books.—*327*

FRICK, F. C. (1948) An analysis of an operant discrimination. *J. Psychol.,* 26, 93–123.—*120*

FRICK, F. C. *See also* Miller and Frick (1949).

FRICK, F. C., and MILLER, G. A. (1951) A statistical description of operant conditioning. *Amer. J. Psychol.,* 64, 20–36.—*406*

FRIEDMAN, S. M. (1952) An empirical study of the castration and oedipus complexes. *Genet. Psychol. Monogr.,* 46, 61–130.—*309*

GAGNÉ, R. M. (1950) Learning and transfer of training in two forms of rudder control task. *USAF Hum. Resourc. Res. Cent., Res. Note P & MS,* 50–1.—*492*

GAGNÉ, R. M. (1954) Training devices and simulators: some research issues. *Amer. Psychologist,* 9, 95–107.—*491*

GAGNÉ, R. M. *See also* Graham and Gagné (1940).

GALLAGHER, R. *See* Cottrell and Gallagher (1941).

GARNER, W. R. *See* Chapanis, Garner, and Morgan (1949).

GATES, A. I. (1942) Connectionism: Present concepts and interpretations. Chapter 4 in *The psychology of learning.* Natl. Soc. Stud. Educ., 41st Yearbook, Part II, 141–164.—*46*

GEIER, F. M., LEVIN, M., and TOLMAN, E. C. (1941) Individual differences in emotionality, hypothesis formation, vicarious trial and error, and visual discrimination learning in rats. *Comp. Psychol. Monogr.,* 17, Serial No. 87.—*196, 220*

GELB, A., and GOLDSTEIN, K. (1918) Zur Psychologie des optischen Wahrnehmungs- und Erkennungsvorganges. *Z. ges. Neurol. Psychiat.,* 41, 1–143. Condensed and translated as "Analysis of a case of figural blindness" in Ellis (1938), pages 315–325.—*254*

GELLER, I. *See* Brady and others (1954).

GENGERELLI, J. A. (1928) Preliminary experiments on the causal factors in animal learning. *J. comp. Psychol.,* 8, 435–457.—*49*

GENTRY, G. V. *See* Gonzales, Gentry, and Bitterman (1954).

GENTRY, G., BROWN, W. L., and KAPLAN, S. J. (1947) An experimental analysis of the spatial location hypothesis in learning. *J. comp. physiol. Psychol.,* 40, 309–322.—*194*

GIBSON, E. J. (1940) A systematic application of the concepts of generalization and differentiation to verbal learning. *Psychol. Rev.*, 47, 196–229.—*350*

Gibson, E. J. (1942) Intra-list generalization as a factor in verbal learning. *J. exp. Psychol.*, 30, 185–200.—*350*

Gibson, E. J. *See also* Gibson, J. J., and Gibson, E. J. (1955).

Gibson, J. J. (1929) The reproduction of visually perceived forms. *J. exp. Psychol.*, 12, 1–39.—*243*

Gibson, J. J., and Gibson, E. J. (1955) Perceptual learning: Differentiation or enrichment? *Psychol. Rev.*, 62, 32–41.—*444, 468*

Gilchrist, J. C. (1952) Characteristics of latent and reinforcement learning as a function of time. *J. comp. physiol. Psychol.*, 45, 198–203.—*213*

Gilchrist, J. C. *See also* Whittaker, Gilchrist, and Fischer (1952).

Gilhousen, H. C. (1931) An investigation of "insight" in rats. *Science*, 73, 711–712.—*296, 473*

Gill, M. (1948) Spontaneous regression on the induction of hypnosis. *Bull. Menninger Clin.*, 12, 41–48.—*303*

Ginsberg, A. (1954) Hypothetical constructs and intervening variables. *Psychol. Rev.*, 61, 119–131.—*12, 219*

Girden, E. *See* Culler and Girden (1951).

Gladstone, A. I. *See* Felsinger and others (1947), Hull and others (1947), Yamaguchi and others (1948).

Gladstone, A. I., Yamaguchi, H. G., Hull, C. L., and Felsinger, J. M. (1947) Some functional relationships of reaction potential ($_SE_R$) and related phenomena. *J. exp. Psychol.*, 37, 510–526.—*146*

Glaser, N. M. *See* Maier, Glaser, and Klee (1940).

Gleitman, H. (1950) Studies in motivation and learning: II. Thirsty rats trained in maze with food but not water; then run hungry. *J. exp. Psychol.*, 40, 169–174.—*212*

Gleitman, H. *See also* Tolman and Gleitman (1949).

Glixman, A. F. (1948) An analysis of the use of the interruption technique in experimental studies of "repression." *Psychol. Bull.*, 45, 491–506.—*283*

Glixman, A. F. (1949) Recall of completed and incompleted activities under varying degrees of stress. *J. exp. Psychol.*, 39, 281–295.—*283, 288*

Goad, D. *See* Underwood and Goad (1951).

Goldmeier, E. (1941) Progressive changes in memory traces. *Amer. J. Psychol.*, 54, 490–503.—*244*

Goldstein, K. (1939) *The organism: A holistic approach to biology derived from pathological data in man.* New York: American Book.—*254*

Goldstein, K. (1940) *Human nature.* Cambridge: Harvard Univ. Press.—*254*

Goldstein, K. (1948) *Language and language disturbances.* New York: Grune and Stratton.—*254*

Goldstein, K. *See also* Gelb and Goldstein (1918).

Gonzalez, R. C., Gentry, G. V., and Bitterman, M. E. (1954) Relational discrimination of intermediate size in the chimpanzee. *J. comp. physiol. Psychol.*, 47, 385–388.—*442*

Gordon, K. (1905) Über das Gedächtnis für aftektiv bestimmte Eindrücke. *Arch. ges. Psychol.*, 4, 437–458.—*302*

Gordon, K. (1925) The recollection of pleasant and unpleasant odors. *J. exp. Psychol.*, 8, 225–239.—*302*

Gottschaldt, K. (1926) Über den Einfluss der Erfahrung auf die Wahrnehmung von Figuren, I. *Psychol. Forsch.*, 8, 261–317. Translated and condensed as "Gestalt factors and repetition" in Ellis (1938), pages 109–122.—*230, 256*

GRAHAM, C. H., and GAGNÉ, R. M. (1940) The acquisition, extinction, and spontaneous recovery of a conditioned operant response. *J. exp. Psychol.*, 26, 251–281.—*120, 406*

GRANT, D. A. (1954) The discrimination of sequences in stimulus events and the transmission of information. *Amer. Psychologist*, 9, 62–68.—*377, 378, 406*

GRANT, D. A. *See also* Hake, Grant, and Hornseth (1951).

GRANT, D. A., HAKE, H. W., and HORNSETH, J. P. (1951) Acquisition and extinction of a verbal conditioned response with differing percentages of reinforcement. *J. exp. Psychol.*, 42, 1–5.—*200, 390, 391, 393, 399*

GRICE, G. R. (1940) An experimental test of the expectation theory of learning. *J. comp. physiol. Psychol.*, 41, 137–143.—*212*

GRICE, G. R. (1949) Visual discrimination learning with simultaneous and successive presentation of stimuli. *J. comp. physiol. Psychol.*, 42, 365–373.—*183, 442*

GRINKER, R. R., and SPIEGEL, J. P. (1945a) *Men under stress.* New York: Blakiston.—*318*

GRINKER, R. R., and SPIEGEL, J. P. (1945b) *War neuroses.* New York: Blakiston.—*318*

GROPPER, G. L. *See* Postman, Bronson, and Gropper (1952).

GULLIKSEN, H. (1934) A rational equation of the learning curve based on Thorndike's law of effect. *J. gen. Psychol.*, 11, 395–434.—*370, 371, 374*

GULLIKSEN, H., and WOLFLE, D. L. (1938) A theory of learning and transfer. *Psychometrika*, 3, 127–149; 225–251.—*374, 406, 444*

GUTHRIE, E. R. (1930) Conditioning as a principle of learning. *Psychol. Rev.* 37, 412–428.—*74, 80*

GUTHRIE, E. R. (1933) Association as a function of time interval. *Psychol. Rev.*, 40, 355–367.—*81*

GUTHRIE, E. R. (1935) *The psychology of learning.* New York: Harper.—*53, 56–64, 74–80, 237, 261*

GUTHRIE, E. R. (1936a) Psychological principles and scientific truth. *Proc. 25th Anniv. Celebr. Inaug. Grad. Stud.*, Univ. Southern Calif., 104–115.—*63*

GUTHRIE, E. R. (1936b) Thorndike's concept of "belonging." *Psychol. Bull.*, 33, 621.—*28*

GUTHRIE, E. R. (1938) *The psychology of human conflict.* New York: Harper.—*57, 80*

GUTHRIE, E. R. (1940) Association and the law of effect. *Psychol. Rev.*, 47, 127–148.—*58*

GUTHRIE, E. R. (1942) Conditioning: A theory of learning in terms of stimulus, response, and association. Chapter 1 in *The psychology of learning.* Natl. Soc. Stud. Educ., 41st Yearbook, Part II, 17–60.—*58*

GUTHRIE, E. R. (1952) *The psychology of learning.* Revised. New York: Harper.—*2, 53, 57, 69, 79, 80, 449*

GUTHRIE, E. R. *See also* Smith and Guthrie (1921), Yacorzynski and Guthrie (1937).

GUTHRIE, E. R., and EDWARDS, A. L. (1949) *Psychology: A first course in human behavior.* New York: Harper.—57

GUTHRIE, E. R., and HORTON, G. P. (1946) *Cats in a puzzle box.* New York: Rinehart.—*57, 58, 64, 67, 68, 237, 239*

GUTHRIE, E. R., and POWERS, F. F. (1950) *Educational psychology.* New York: Ronald Press.—*57*

GWINN, G. T. (1949) The effects of punishment on acts motivated by fear. *J. exp. Psychol.*, 39, 260–269.—*60*

HAKE, H. W. *See* Grant, Hake, and Hornseth (1951).

HAKE, H. W., GRANT, D. A., and HORNSETH, J. P. (1951) Resistance to extinction and pattern of reinforcement: III. The effect of trial pattern in verbal "conditioning." *J. exp. Psychol.*, 41, 221–225.—*200*

HALL, C. S. (1954) *A primer of Freudian psychology.* Cleveland: World Publ. Co.—*298, 325*

HALL, C. S. *See also* Tolman, Hall, and Bretnall (1932).

HALL, C. S., and LINDZEY, G. (1954) Psychoanalytic theory and its applications in the social sciences. In G. Lindzey, ed. *Handbook of social psychology.* Cambridge, Mass.: Addison-Wesley, 143–180.—*327*

HALL, M. *See* Hull and others (1940).

HAMILTON, G. V. (1916) A study of perseverance reactions in primates and rodents. *Behav. Monogr.*, 3, No. 13, 65 pp.—*68*

HAMILTON, J. A., and KRECHEVSKY, I. (1933) Studies in the effect of shock upon behavior plasticity in the rat. *J. comp. Psychol.*, 16, 237–253.—*303*

HANAWALT, N. G. (1937) Memory traces for figures in recall and recognition. *Arch. Psychol.*, New York: No. 216.—*244*

HANAWALT, N. G. (1952) The method of comparison applied to the problem of memory change. *J. exp. Psychol.*, 43, 37–42.—*244, 256*

HANAWALT, N. G., and POST, B. E. (1942) Memory trace for color. *J. exp. Psychol.*, 30, 216–227.—*244*

HANDLON, J. P., Jr. *See* Seward, Levy, and Handlon (1950).

HANEY, G. W. (1931) The effect of familiarity on maze performance of albino rats. *Univ. Calif. Publ. Psychol.*, 4, 319–333.—*211*

HARE, R. *See* Ritchie, Hay, and Hare (1951).

HARLOW, H. F. (1949) The formation of learning sets. *Psychol. Rev.*, 56, 51–65.—*438*

HARLOW, H. F. (1953) Mice, monkeys, men, and motives. *Psychol. Rev.*, 60, 23–32.—*430, 431*

HARLOW, H. F. (1954) Motivational forces underlying learning. In the Kentucky Symposium. *Learning theory, personality theory, and clinical research.* New York: Wiley, 36–53.—*430*

HARLOW, H. F., and MCCLEARN, G. E. (1954) Object discriminations learned by monkeys on the basis of manipulation motives. *J. comp. physiol. Psychol.*, 47, 73–76.—*430*

HARSH, C. M. (1937) Disturbance and "insight" in rats. *Univ. Calif. Publ. Psychol.*, 6, 163–168.—*195*

HARTER, N. *See* Bryan and Harter (1897) (1899).

HARTMANN, G. W. (1935) *Gestalt psychology.* New York: Ronald Press.—*255*

HARTMANN, G. W. (1941) Frustration phenomena in the social and political sphere. *Psychol. Rev.*, 48, 362–363.—*304*

HARTMANN, G. W. (1942) The field theory of learning and its educational consequences. Chapter 5 in *The psychology of learning.* Natl. Soc. Stud. Educ., 41st Yearbook, Part II, 165–214.—*256*

HARTMANN, H. (1950) Comments on the psychoanalytic theory of the ego.

In *The psychoanalytic study of the child.* New York: International Universities Press, V, 74–96.—*294*

Hartmann, H., and Kris, E. (1945) The genetic approach in psychoanalysis. *Psychoanal. Stud. Child,* 1, 11–30.—*307*

Hay, A. *See* Ritchie, Hay, and Hare (1951).

Hayes, J. R. *See* Verplanck and Hayes (1953).

Heathers, L. B., and Sears, R. R. (1943) Experiments on repression. II. The Sharp technique. (Unpublished: see Sears, 1943).—*314*

Hebb, D. O. (1949) *The organization of behavior: a neuropsychological theory.* New York: Wiley.—*430, 446, 452, 454, 456, 467*

Hebb, D. O., and Foord, E. N. (1945) Errors of visual recognition and the nature of the trace. *J. exp. Psychol.,* 35, 335–348.—*245*

Heidbreder, E. (1933) *Seven psychologies.* New York: Appleton-Century-Crofts.—*256, 326, 329, 367*

Heidbreder, E. (1937) Review of Lewin's *Principles of topological psychology. Psychol. Bull.,* 34, 584–604.—*288*

Heineman, C. *See* Schlosberg and Heineman (1950).

Held, R. *See* Köhler and Held (1944), Köhler, Held, and O'Connell (1952).

Helmick, J. S. *See* Hilgard, Dutton, and Helmick (1949).

Hendrick, I. (1939) *Facts and theories of psychoanalysis.* Revised. New York: Knopf.

Henle, M. (1942a) An experimental investigation of past experience as a determinant of visual form perception. *J. exp. Psychol.,* 30, 1–22.—*230*

Henle, M. (1942b) The experimental investigation of the dynamic and structural determinants of substitution. *Contr. Psychol. Theor.,* 2, No. 3.—*307*

Henle, M. *See also* Wallach and Henle (1941) (1942).

Herb, F. H. (1940) Latent learning—non-reward followed by food in blinds. *J. comp. Psychol.,* 29, 247–256.—*211*

Heron, W. *See* Bexton, Heron, and Scott (1954).

Heron, W. T. (1949) Internal stimuli and learning. *J. comp. physiol. Psychol.,* 42, 486–492.—*212, 213*

Heron, W. T., and Skinner, B. F. (1940) The rate of extinction in maze-bright and maze-dull rats. *Psychol. Rec.,* 4, 11–18.—*120*

Herr, S. E. (1946) The effect of pre-first-grade training upon reading readiness and reading achievement among Spanish-American children. *J. educ. Psychol.,* 37, 87–102.—*492*

Hilgard, E. R. (1931) Conditioned eyelid reactions to a light stimulus based on the reflex wink to sound. *Psychol. Monogr.,* 41, No. 184.—*73*

Hilgard, E. R. (1933) Modification of reflexes and conditioned reactions. *J. gen. Psychol.,* 9, 210–215.—*137*

Hilgard, E. R. (1935) Review of Guthrie's *The psychology of learning. Psychol. Bull.,* 32, 306–309.—*81*

Hilgard, E. R. (1938) An algebraic analysis of conditioned discrimination in man. *Psychol. Rev.,* 45, 472–496.—*260*

Hilgard, E. R. (1939) Review of Skinner's *The behavior of organisms. Psychol. Bull.,* 36, 121–125.—*119*

Hilgard, E. R. (1940) Review of *Mathematico-deductive theory of rote learning:* The psychological system. *Psychol. Bull.,* 37, 808–815.—*173, 183*

Hilgard, E. R. (1942) Success in relation to level of aspiration. *Sch. & Soc.,* 55, 423–428.—*276*

HILGARD, E. R. (1948) *Theories of learning*. New York: Appleton-Century-Crofts.—*126, 161, 225, 356, 470*

HILGARD, E. R. (1951) The role of learning in perception. In R. R. Blake and G. V. Ramsey, eds. *Perception, an approach to personality*. New York: Ronald Press, 95–120.—*466*

HILGARD, E. R. (1953a) Educational research: some friendly suggestions. *Calif. J. educ. Res.*, 4, 51–55.—*286*

HILGARD, E. R. (1953b) Theories of human learning and problems of training. *Symposium on psychology of learning basic to military training problems*. Washington, D.C.: Research and Development Board, 3–13.—*485*

HILGARD, E. R. *See also* Cohen, Hilgard, and Wendt (1933) Cook and Hilgard (1949), Doré and Hilgard (1937).

HILGARD, E. R., and CAMPBELL, A. A. (1936) The course of acquisition and retention of conditioned eyelid responses in man. *J. exp. Psychol.*, 19, 227–247.—*56*

HILGARD, E. R., CAMPBELL, R. K., and SEARS, W. N. (1938) Conditioned discrimination: the effect of knowledge of stimulus-relationships. *Amer. J. Psychol.*, 51, 498–506.—*198*

HILGARD, E. R., DUTTON, C. E., and HELMICK, J. S. (1949) Attempted pupillary conditioning at four stimulus intervals. *J. exp. Psychol.*, 39, 683–689. *85, 462*

HILGARD, E. R., EDGREN, R. D., and IRVINE, R. P. (1954) Errors in transfer following learning with understanding: further studies with Katona's card-trick experiments. *J. exp. Psychol.*, 47, 457–464.—*251*

HILGARD, E. R., IRVINE, R. P., and WHIPPLE, J. E. (1953) Rote memorization, understanding, and transfer: an extension of Katona's card-trick experiments. *J. exp. Psychol.*, 46, 288–292.—*251*

HILGARD, E. R., JONES, L. V., and KAPLAN, S. J. (1951) Conditioned discrimination as related to anxiety. *J. exp. Psychol.*, 42, 94–99.—*300*

HILGARD, E. R., KUBIE, L. S., and PUMPIAN-MINDLIN, E. (1952) *Psychoanalysis as science*. Stanford, Calif.: Stanford Univ. Press.—*325*

HILGARD, E. R., and MARQUIS, D. G. (1940) *Conditioning and learning*. New York: Appleton-Century-Crofts.—*14, 52, 54, 85, 90, 91, 93, 153, 159, 161*

HILGARD, E. R., and SMITH, M. B. (1942) Distributed practice in motor learning: score changes within and between daily sessions. *J. exp. Psychol.*, 30, 136–146.—*355, 357*

HILGARD, J. R. (1953) Anniversary reactions in parents precipitated by children. *Psychiatry*, 16, 73–80.—*297*

HILL, L. M. *See* Keller and Hill (1936).

HOBAN, C. F., Jr., and VAN ORMER, E. B. (1950) *Instructional film research, 1918–1950*. Pennsylvania State College, Instructional Film Research Reports, P-977.—*491*

HOGAN, H. P. *See* Carmichael, Hogan, and Walter (1932).

HOFFMAN, P. J., FESTINGER, L., and LAWRENCE, D. H. (1954) Tendencies toward group comparability in competitive bargaining. In R. M. Thrall, C. H. Coombs, and R. L. Davis, eds. *Decision processes*. New York: Wiley, 231–253.—*385*

HOLLAND, M. A. *See* Seward, Dill, and Holland (1944).

HOLLINGWORTH, H. L. (1928) General laws of redintegration. *J. gen. Psychol.*, 1, 79–90.—*466*

HOLLINGWORTH, H. L. (1931) Effect and affect in learning. *Psychol. Rev.*, 38, 153–159.

HOLMBERG, A. R. (1950) Nomads of the Long Bow: the Siriono of Eastern Bolivia. *The Smithsonian Institute of Social Anthropology*, Washington, D.C., Publication No. 10.—*292*

HOLT, E. B. (1915) *The Freudian wish and its place in ethics.* New York: Holt.—*322*

HOLT, E. B. (1931) *Animal drive and the learning process.* New York: Holt. —*473*

HOLTZMAN, W. H. *See* Bitterman and Holtzman (1952).

HONZIK, C. H. (1936) The sensory basis of maze learning in rats. *Comp. Psychol. Monogr.*, 13, No. 64.—*54*

HONZIK, C. H. *See also* Krechevsky and Honzik (1932), Tolman and Honzik (1930a) (1930b).

HONZIK, C. H., and TOLMAN, E. C. (1936) The perception of spatial relations by the rat: a type of response not easily explained by conditioning. *J. comp. Psychol.*, 22, 287–318.—*220*

HOPPE, F. (1930) Erfolg und Misserfolg. *Psychol. Forsch.*, 14, 1–62.—*277, 289*

HORENSTEIN, B. R. *See* Kimble and Horenstein (1948).

HORNSETH, J. P. *See* Grant, Hake, and Hornseth (1951), Hake, Grant, and Hornseth (1951).

HORTON, G. P. *See* Guthrie and Horton (1946).

HOUSEHOLDER, A. S., and LANDAHL, H. D. (1945) *Mathematical biophysics of the central nervous system.* Bloomington, Ind.: Principia Press.—*405*

HOVLAND, C. I. (1936) "Inhibition of reinforcement" and phenomena of experimental extinction. *Proc. nat. Acad. Sci.*, Washington, D.C., 22, 430–433.—*137*

HOVLAND, C. I. (1937) The generalization of conditioned responses: IV. The effects of varying amounts of reinforcement upon the degree of generalization of conditioned responses. *J. exp. Psychol.*, 21, 261–276.—*146*

HOVLAND, C. I. (1938) Experimental studies in rote-learning theory. III. Distribution of practice with varying speeds of syllable presentation. *J. exp. Psychol.*, 23, 172–190.—*354*

HOVLAND, C. I. (1939) Experimental studies in rote-learning theory. IV. Comparison of reminiscence in serial and paired associate learning. *J. exp. Psychol.*, 24, 466–484.—*354*

HOVLAND, C. I. (1940) Experimental studies in rote-learning theory: VI. Comparison of retention following learning to same criterion by massed and distributed practice. *J. exp. Psychol.*, 26, 568–587.—*354*

HOVLAND, C. I. (1952a) Clark Leonard Hull, 1884–1952. *Psychol. Rev.*, 59, 347–350.—*146*

HOVLAND, C. I. (1952b) A "communication analysis" of concept learning. *Psychol. Rev.*, 59, 461–472.—*382, 383*

HOVLAND, C. I. *See also* Dollard and others (1939), Hull and others (1940), Sears and Hovland (1941).

HOVLAND, C. I., and KURTZ, K. H. (1951) Experimental studies in rote-learning theory: IX. Influence of work-decrement factors on verbal learning. *J. exp. Psychol.*, 42, 265–272.—*355*

HOVLAND, C. I., and SEARS, R. R. (1938) Experiments on motor conflict. I.

Types of conflict and their modes of resolution. *J. exp. Psychol.*, 23, 477–493.—*267*

Hovland, C. I., and Weiss, W. (1953) Transmission of information concerning concepts through positive and negative instances. *J. exp. Psychol.*, 45, 175–182.—*383, 406*

Howes, D. (1954) On the interpretation of word frequency as a variable affecting speed of recognition. *J. exp. Psychol.*, 48, 106–112.—*319*

Howes, D. L. *See also* Solomon and Howes (1951).

Howes, D. H., and Solomon, R. L. (1950) A note on McGinnies' "Emotionality and perceptual defense." *Psychol. Rev.*, 57, 229–234.—*319, 320*

Howes, D. H., and Solomon, R. L. (1951) Visual duration threshold as a function of word probability. *J. exp. Psychol.*, 41, 401–410.—*319*

Hudson, B. B. (1950) One-trial learning in the domestic rat. *Genet. Psychol. Monogr.*, 41, 99–146.

Hull, C. L. (1917) The formation and retention of associations among the insane. *Amer. J. Psychol.*, 28, 419–435.—*143*

Hull, C. L. (1920) Quantitative aspects of the evolution of concepts: an experimental study. *Psychol. Monogr.*, 28, No. 123.—*125*

Hull, C. L. (1928) *Aptitude testing.* Yonkers-on-Hudson, New York: World Book.—*204*

Hull, C. L. (1930) Simple trial and error learning: a study in psychological theory. *Psychol. Rev.*, 37, 241–256.—*446*

Hull (1931) Goal attraction and directing ideas conceived as habit phenomena. *Psychol. Rev.*, 38, 487–506.—*124*

Hull, C. L. (1932) The goal gradient hypothesis and maze learning. *Psychol. Rev.*, 39, 25–43.—*135, 159*

Hull, C. L. (1933) Differential habituation to internal stimuli in the albino rat. *J. comp. Psychol.*, 16, 255–273.—*268*

Hull, C. L. (1934) The concept of the habit-family hierarchy and maze learning. *Psychol. Rev.*, 41, 33–54; 134–152.—*160*

Hull, C. L. (1935a) The conflicting psychologies of learning—a way out. *Psychol. Rev.*, 42, 491–516.—*122, 126, 182*

Hull, C. L. (1935b) The influence of caffeine and other factors on certain phenomena of rote learning. *J. gen. Psychol.*, 13, 249–274.—*183*

Hull, C. L. (1935c) The mechanism of the assembly of behavior segments in novel combinations suitable for problem solution. *Psychol. Rev.*, 42, 219–245.—*476*

Hull, C. L. (1935d) Special review of Thorndike's *The fundamentals of learning. Psychol. Bull.*, 32, 807–823.—*31, 41, 46*

Hull, C. L. (1937) Mind, mechanism, and adaptive behavior. *Psychol. Rev.*, 44, 1–32.—*122, 126, 149, 160, 471*

Hull, C. L. (1938) The goal-gradient hypothesis applied to some "field-force" problems in the behavior of young children. *Psychol. Rev.*, 45, 271–299.—*159, 161*

Hull, C. L. (1939a) The problem of stimulus equivalence in behavior theory. *Psychol. Rev.*, 46, 9–30.—*140, 442, 444*

Hull, C. L. (1939b) Simple trial and error learning—an empirical investigation. *J. comp. Psychol.*, 27, 233–258.—*162, 163*

Hull, C. L. (1942) Conditioning: outline of a systematic theory of learning. Chapter 2 in *The psychology of learning.* Natl. Soc. Stud. Educ., 41st Yearbook, Part II, 61–95.—*142, 183*

HULL, C. L. (1943) *Principles of behavior.* New York: Appleton-Century-Crofts.—*2, 126–147, 151, 159, 176, 183, 410, 415, 418, 429*

HULL, C. L. (1945) The place of innate individual and species differences in a natural-science theory of behavior. *Psychol. Rev.,* 52, 55–60.—*148, 174, 204, 461*

HULL, C. L. (1947a) Reactively heterogeneous trial-and-error learning with distributed trials and terminal reinforcement. *J. exp. Psychol.,* 37, 118–135.—*184*

HULL, C. L. (1947b) The problem of primary stimulus generalization. *Psychol. Rev.,* 54, 120–134.—*140, 442*

HULL, C. L. (1949) Stimulus intensity dynamism (V) and stimulus generalization. *Psychol. Rev.,* 56, 67–76.—*140*

HULL, C. L. (1950a) Behavior postulates and corollaries—1949. *Psychol. Rev.,* 57, 173–180.—*126, 183, 420*

HULL, C. L. (1950b) Simple qualitative discrimination learning. *Psychol. Rev.,* 57, 303–313.—*140, 442, 444*

HULL, C. L. (1951) *Essentials of behavior.* New Haven: Yale Univ. Press.—*125–148, 151, 183*

HULL, C. L. (1952a) *A behavior system: An introduction to behavior theory concerning the individual organism.* New Haven: Yale Univ. Press.—*124–149, 155–159, 163–170, 173, 174, 177, 183, 269, 423*

HULL, C. L. (1952b) Autobiography. In *A history of psychology in autobiography,* IV. Worcester, Mass.: Clark Univ. Press.—*184*

HULL, C. L. *See also* Felsinger and others (1947), Gladstone and others (1947), Yamaguchi and others (1948).

HULL, C. L., FELSINGER, J. M., GLADSTONE, A. I., and YAMAGUCHI, H. G. (1947) A proposed quantification of habit strength. *Psychol. Rev.,* 54, 237–254.—*146*

HULL, C. L., HOVLAND, C. I., ROSS, R. T., HALL, M., PERKINS, D. T., and FITCH, F. G. (1940) *Mathematico-deductive theory of rote learning.* New Haven: Yale Univ. Press.—*126, 143, 182, 183, 354, 374, 405, 415*

HULL, C. L., LIVINGSTON, J. R., ROUSE, R. O., and BARKER, A. N. (1951) True, sham, and esophageal feeding as reinforcements. *J. comp. physiol. Psychol.,* 44, 236–245.—*423*

HULL, C. L., and LUGOFF, L. S. (1921) Complex signs in diagnostic free association. *J. exp. Psychol.,* 4, 111–136.—*300*

HUMPHREYS, L. G. (1939a) The effect of random alternation of reinforcement on the acquisition and extinction of conditioned eyelid reactions. *J. exp. Psychol.,* 25, 141–158.—*198, 390*

HUMPHREYS, L. G. (1939b) Acquisition and extinction of verbal expectations in a situation analogous to conditioning. *J. exp. Psychol.,* 25, 294–301.—*199, 200, 390*

HUNNICUTT, C. W. *See* Thompson and Hunnicutt (1944).

HUNT, H. F. *See* Brady and Hunt (1955).

HUNT, J. MCV. (1941) The effects of infant feeding-frustration upon adult hoarding in the albino rat. *J. abnorm. soc. Psychol.,* 36, 338–360.—*308*

HUNTER, W. S. (1924) The symbolic process. *Psychol. Rev.,* 31, 478–497.—*476*

HURLEY, J. R. (1953) *Verbal learning as a function of instructions and achievement motivation.* Unpublished Ph.D. dissertation, University of Iowa.—*426*

HUSTON, P. E., SHAKOW, D., and ERICKSON, M. H. (1934) A study of hypnotically induced complexes by means of the Luria technique. *J. gen. Psychol.*, 11, 65–97.—*316, 326*

IREY, E. *See* Muenzinger, Koerner, and Irey (1929).

IRION, A. L. (1946) Retroactive inhibition as a function of the relative serial positions of the original and interpolated items. *J. exp. Psychol.*, 36, 262–270.—*367*

IRION, A. L. (1949) Reminiscence in pursuit-rotor learning as a function of length of rest and of amount of pre-rest practice. *J. exp. Psychol.*, 39, 492–499.—*354*

IRION, A. L. *See also* McGeoch and Irion (1952).

IRVINE, R. P. *See* Hilgard, Edgren, and Irvine (1954), Hilgard, Irvine, and Whipple (1953).

IRWIN, F. W., KAUFFMAN, K., PRIOR, G., and WEAVER, H. B. (1934) On "Learning without awareness of what is being learned." *J. exp. Psychol.*, 17, 823–827.—*475*

IRWIN, F. W., and ROVNER, H. (1937) Further study of the method of comparison applied to the problem of memory changes. *J. exp. Psychol.*, 21, 533–544.—*244*

IRWIN, F. W., and SEIDENFELD, M. A. (1937) The application of the method of comparison to the problem of memory change. *J. exp. Psychol.*, 21, 363–381.—*244*

IRWIN, J. McQ. *See* Melton and Irwin (1940).

ISCOE, I. *See* Stevenson and Iscoe (1954), Stevenson, Iscoe, and McConnell (1955).

ITTLESON, W. H., and CANTRIL, H. (1954) *Perception: A transactional approach.* New York: Doubleday.—*331*

IVANOV-SMOLENSKY (1927) On the methods of examining the conditioned food reflexes in children and in mental disorders. *Brain*, 50, 138–141.—*444*

IWAHARA, S., and MARX, M. (1950) Cognitive transfer in discrimination learning. *Amer. Psychologist*, 5, 479. (Reported by title only.)—*213*

JACKSON, L. L. (1943) VTE on an elevated maze. *J. comp. Psychol.*, 36, 99–107.—*196*

JACKSON, T. A. (1942) Use of the stick as a tool by young chimpanzees. *J. comp. Psychol.*, 34, 223–235.—*235*

JACKSON, T. A., and DOMINGUEZ, K. (1939) Studies in the transposition of learning by children: II. Relative vs. absolute choice with multi-dimensional stimuli. *J. exp. Psychol.*, 24, 630–639.—*444*

JACOBS, A. *See* Brown and Jacobs (1949).

JAMES, W. (1890) *The principles of psychology.* New York: Holt.—277

JARRETT, R. F. *See* Postman and Jarrett (1952).

JASPER, H. *See* Penfield and Jasper (1954).

JENKINS, G. *See* Wallace, Blackwell, and Jenkins (1941).

JENKINS, W. O. (1943) Studies in the spread of effect. *J. comp. Psychol.*, 35, 41–72.—*41*

JENKINS, W. O. *See also* Sheffield and Jenkins (1952).

JENKINS, W. O., and CUNNINGHAM, L. M. (1949) The guessing-sequence hypothesis, the "spread of effect," and number-guessing habits. *J. exp. Psychol.*, 39, 158–168.—*35*

JENKINS, W. O., and POSTMAN, L. (1948) Isolation and 'spread of effect' in serial learning. *Amer. J. Psychol.*, 61, 214–221.—37

JENKINS, W. O., and SHEFFIELD, F. D. (1946) Rehearsal and guessing habits as sources of the "spread of effect." *J. exp. Psychol.*, 36, 316–330.—*35, 41*

JENKINS, W. O., and STANLEY, J. C., Jr. (1950) Partial reinforcement: a review and critique. *Psychol. Bull.*, 47, 193–234.—*118, 200*

JONES, E. (1953) *The life and work of Sigmund Freud. Vol. 1. The formative years and the great discoveries.* New York: Basic Books.

JONES, E. (1955) *The life and work of Sigmund Freud, Vol. 2. Years of maturity.* New York: Basic Books.—*327*

JONES, H. M. *See* Mowrer and Jones (1943).

JONES, L. V. *See* Hilgard, Jones, and Kaplan (1951).

JOYCE, J. *See* Rotter, Fitzgerald, and Joyce (1954).

JUDD, C. H. (1908) The relation of special training to general intelligence. *Educ. Rev.*, 36, 28–42.—*252*

KALISH, D. *See* Tolman, Ritchie, and Kalish (1946) (1947).

KANNER, J. H. (1954) A test of whether the "nonrewarded" animals learned as much as the "rewarded" animals in the California latent learning study. *J. exp. Psychol.*, 48, 175–183.—*214*

KANNER, J. H. *See also* Kendler and Kanner (1950).

KANTOR, J. R. (1947) *Problems of physiological psychology.* Bloomington, Ind.: Principia Press.—*462*

KAPLAN, S. J. *See* Gentry, Brown, and Kaplan (1947), Hilgard, Jones, and Kaplan (1951).

KARASIK, A. D. *See* Kendler, Karasik, and Schrier (1954).

KARN, H. W., and PORTER, J. M. Jr. (1946) The effects of certain pre-training procedures upon maze performance and their significance for the concept of latent learning. *J. exp. Psychol.*, 36, 461–469.—*211*

KARSTEN, A. (1928) Psychische Sättigung. *Psychol. Forsch.*, 10, 142–254.—*274, 279, 289*

KATONA, G. (1940) *Organizing and memorizing.* New York: Columbia Univ. Press.—*231, 249, 250*

KATONA, G. (1942) Organizing and memorizing: a reply to Dr. Melton. *Amer. J. Psychol.*, 55, 273–275.—*251*

KATZ, D. (1950) *Gestalt psychology, its nature and significance.* New York: Ronald Press.—*257*

KAUFFMAN, K. *See* Irwin and others (1934).

KEET, C. D. (1948) Two verbal techniques in a miniature counseling situation. *Psychol. Monogr.*, 62, No. 204.—*314*

KEISTER, M. E. (1937) The behavior of young children in failure: an experimental attempt to discover and to modify undesirable responses of preschool children to failure. *Univ. Ia. Stud. Child Welf.*, 14, 28–82.—*280*

KELLER, F. S. (1941) Light-aversion in the white rat. *Psychol. Rec.*, 4, 235–250.—*120*

KELLER, F. S. (1954) *Learning (Reinforcement theory).* Garden City, N.Y.: Doubleday.—*119*

KELLER, F. S., and HILL, L. M. (1936) Another "insight" experiment. *J. genet. Psychol.*, 48, 484–489.—*195*

KELLER, F. S., and SCHOENFELD, W. N. (1950) *Principles of psychology.* New York: Appleton-Century-Crofts.—*82, 94, 95, 104, 105, 107, 115, 116, 119*

KELLEY, E. C. (1947) *Education for what is real.* New York: Harper.—*331*

KELLOGG, W. N. (1938) An eclectic view of some theories of learning. *Psychol. Rev.*, 45, 165–184.—*457, 491*

KENDALL, J. W., Jr. *See* Kimble and Kendall (1953).

KENDLER, H. H. (1946) The influence of simultaneous hunger and thirst drives upon the learning of two opposed spatial responses of the white rat. *J. exp. Psychol.*, 36, 212–220.—*184, 416, 450*

KENDLER, H. H. (1947a) A comparison of learning under motivated and satiated conditions in the white rat. *J. exp. Psychol.*, 37, 545–549.—*212*

KENDLER, H. H. (1947b) An investigation of latent learning in a T-maze. *J. comp. physiol. Psychol.*, 40, 265–270.—*212*

KENDLER, H. H. (1951) Reflections and confessions of a reinforcement theorist. *Psychol. Rev.*, 58, 368–374.—*414*

KENDLER, H. H. (1952) Some comments on Thistlewaite's perception of latent learning. *Psychol. Bull.*, 49, 47–51.—*211*

KENDLER, H. H., and KANNER, J. H. (1950) A further test of the ability of rats to learn the location of food when motivated by thirst. *J. exp. Psychol.*, 40, 762–765.—*212*

KENDLER, H. H., KARASIK, A. D., and SCHRIER, A. M. (1954) Studies of the effect of change of drive: III. Amounts of switching produced by shifting drive from thirst to hunger and from hunger to thirst. *J. exp. Psychol.*, 47, 179–182.—*212*

KENDLER, H. H., and LEVINE, S. (1953) A more sensitive test of irrelevant-incentive learning under conditions of satiation. *J. comp. physiol. Psychol.*, 46, 271–273.—*212*

KENDLER, H. H., and MENCHER, H. C. (1948) The ability of rats to learn the location of food when motivated by thirst—an experimental reply to Leeper. *J. exp. Psychol.*, 38, 82–88.—*212*

KENTUCKY SYMPOSIUM (1954) *Learning theory, personality theory, and clinical research.* New York: Wiley.—*456*

KESSEN, M. L. *See* Berkun, Kessen, and Miller (1952), Miller and Kessen (1952) (1954).

KILPATRICK, W. L. (1925) *Foundations of method.* New York: Macmillan.—*330*

KIMBALL, G. *See* Morse and Kimball (1951).

KIMBALL, L. T. *See* Kimball, R. C., Kimball, L. T., and Weaver (1953).

KIMBALL, R. C., KIMBALL, L. T., and WEAVER, H. E. (1953) Latent learning as a function of the number of differential cues. *J. comp. physiol. Psychol.*, 46, 274–280.—*211*

KIMBLE, G. A. (1947) Conditioning as a function of the time between conditioned and unconditioned stimuli. *J. exp. Psychol.*, 37, 1–15.—*54, 127*

KIMBLE, G. A. (1949) An experimental test of a two-factor theory of inhibition. *J. exp. Psychol.*, 39, 15–23.—*138, 184*

KIMBLE, G. A. (1953) Comments on "Theories of human learning and problems of training." *Symposium on psychology of learning basic to military training problems.* Washington, D.C.: Research and Development Board, 15–19.—*486*

KIMBLE, G. A., and HORENSTEIN, B. R. (1948) Reminiscence in motor learning as a function of length of interpolated rest. *J. exp. Psychol.*, 38, 239–244.—*354*

KIMBLE, G. A., and KENDALL, J. W., Jr. (1953) A comparison of two methods of producing experimental extinction. *J. exp. Psychol.*, 45, 87–90.—*75*

KLEE, J. B. *See* Maier, Glaser, and Klee (1940).

KLEIN, D. B. *See* Perrin and Klein (1926).

KLEIN, G. S. (1951) The personal world through perception. In R. R. Blake and G. V. Ramsey, eds. *Perception: an approach to personality.* New York: Ronald Press, 328–355.—*320*

KLEIN, G. S. (1954) Need and regulation. In the Nebraska Symposium on Motivation, M. R. Jones, ed. *Current theory and research in motivation.* Lincoln, Nebr.: Univ. Nebraska Press, 224–274.—*318, 320, 468*

KLINE, M. V. (1950) Hypnotic age regression and intelligence. *J. genet. Psychol.*, 77, 129–132.—*303*

KLING, A. *See* Brady and others (1954).

KLÜVER, H., and BUCY, P. C. (1939) Preliminary analysis of functions of the temporal lobes in monkeys. *Arch. Neurol. Psychiat.: Chicago*, 42, 979–1000.—*453*

KNOTTER, M. C. *See* Walker, Knotter, and DeValois (1950).

KNOWLES, W. B. *See* Lindsley and others (1950).

KOCH, S. (1944) Review of Hull's *Principles of behavior. Psychol. Bull.*, 41, 269–286.—*183*

KOCH, S. (1951) Theoretical psychology, 1950: an overview. *Psychol. Rev.*, 58, 295–301.—*491*

KOCH, S. (1954) Clark L. Hull. In W. K. Estes and others. *Modern learning theory.* New York: Appleton-Century-Crofts, 1–176.—*166, 183, 184*

KOCH, S. *See also* Estes and others (1954).

KOERNER, L. *See* Muenzinger, Koerner, and Irey (1929).

KOFFKA, K. (1924) *The growth of the mind.* Trans. by R. M. Ogden. London: Kegan Paul, Trench, Trubner & Co., Ltd.—*222, 224, 228, 255*

KOFFKA, K. (1925) Mental development. In C. Murchison, ed. *Psychologies of 1925.* Worcester, Mass., Clark Univ. Press, 130–143.—*256*

KOFFKA, K. (1930) Some problems of space perception. In C. Murchison, ed. *Psychologies of 1930.* Worcester, Mass., Clark Univ. Press, 161–187.—*466*

KOFFKA, K. (1933) Review of Tolman's *Purposive behavior in animals and men. Psychol. Bull.*, 30, 440–451.—*217, 220*

KOFFKA, K. (1935) *Principles of gestalt psychology.* New York: Harcourt, Brace.—*225, 227–233, 253, 255*

KOHLER, I. (1953) Umgewöhnung im Wahrnehmungsbereich. *Die Pyramide*, 5, 92–95; 6, 109–113.—*467*

KÖHLER, W. (1917) *Intelligenzprufungen an Menschenaffen. See* Köhler, 1925.—*222*

KÖHLER, W. (1918) Nachweis einfacher Strukturfunktionen beim Schimpansen und beim Haushuhn. *Abb. d. königl. Preuss. Ak. d. Wissen,* Phys. Math. Klasse, Nr. 2, 1–101. Translated and condensed as "Simple structural functions in the chimpanzee and in the chicken" in Ellis (1938), pages 217-227.—*256, 434*

KÖHLER, W. (1925) *The mentality of apes.* Trans. by E. Winter. New York: Harcourt, Brace.—*222, 255, 434*

KÖHLER, W. (1929) *Gestalt psychology.* New York: Liveright.—*256*

KÖHLER, W. (1930) Some tasks of gestalt psychology. In C. Murchison, ed. *Psychologies of 1930.* Worcester, Mass.: Clark Univ. Press, 143–160.—*256*

KÖHLER, W. (1938) *The place of value in a world of facts.* New York: Liveright.—*231, 246, 254*

KÖHLER, W. (1940) *Dynamics in psychology.* New York: Liveright.—*246, 249, 256*

KÖHLER, W. (1941) On the nature of associations. *Proc. Amer. phil. Soc.*, 84, 489–502.—*227, 229*

KÖHLER, W. (1943) Review of McGeoch's *The psychology of human learning. Amer. J. Psychol.*, 56, 455–460.—*367*

KÖHLER, W. (1947) *Gestalt psychology.* New York: Liveright.—*240, 254, 256*

KÖHLER, W., and HELD, R. (1949) The cortical correlate of pattern vision. *Science*, 110, 414–419.—*453*

KÖHLER, W., HELD, R., and O'CONNELL, D. L. (1952) An investigation of cortical currents. *Proc. Amer. phil. Soc.*, 96, 290–330.—*453*

KÖHLER, W., and RESTORFF, H. VON (1935) Analyse von Vorgängen im Spurenfeld. *Psychol. Forsch.*, 21, 56–112.—*246, 248, 256*

KOHN, M. (1951) Satiation of hunger from food injected directly into the stomach versus food ingested by mouth. *J. comp. physiol. Psychol.*, 44, 412–422.—*423*

KOTAKE, Y. *See* Mihama and Kotake (1954).

KOTAKE, Y., and MIHAMA, H. (1951) Conditioning of pupillary reflex in man. *Jap. J. Psychol.*, 22, 77–88.—*85*

KOUNIN, J. (1941) Experimental studies of rigidity. I. The measurement of rigidity in normal and feeble-minded persons. *Character & Pers.*, 9, 251–272.—*284*

KOUNIN, J. *See also* Adler and Kounin (1939), Barker, Kounin, and Wright (1943).

KRAELING, D. *See* Campbell and Kraeling (1954), Miller and Kraeling (1952).

KRECH, D. (1950) Dynamic systems, psychological fields, and hypothetical constructs. *Psychol. Rev.*, 57, 283–290.—*452*

KRECH, D., and CRUTCHFIELD, R. S. (1948) *Theory and problems of social psychology.* New York: McGraw-Hill.—*245, 468*

KRECH, D., ROSENZWEIG, M. R., BENNETT, E. L., and KRUECKEL, B. (1954) Enzyme concentrations in the brain and adjustive behavior-patterns. *Science*, 120, 994–996.—*454*

KRECHEVSKY, I. (1932a) 'Hypotheses' in rats. *Psychol. Rev.*, 39, 516–532.—*196, 201, 433*

KRECHEVSKY, I. (1932b) 'Hypotheses' versus 'chance' in the presolution period in sensory discrimination-learning. *Univ. Calif. Publ. Psychol.*, 6, 27–44.—*201, 221, 433*

KRECHEVSKY, I. (1933a) Hereditary nature of 'hypotheses.' *J. comp. Psychol.*, 16, 99–116.—*201*

KRECHEVSKY, I. (1933b) The docile nature of 'hypotheses.' *J. comp. Psychol.*, 15, 429–443.—*201*

KRECHEVSKY, I. (1938) A study of the continuity of the problem-solving process. *Psychol. Rev.*, 45, 107–133.—*436*

KRECHEVSKY, I. (1939) Review of Skinner's *The behavior of organisms. J. abnorm. soc. Psychol.*, 34, 404–407.—*119*

KRECHEVSKY, I. *See also* Hamilton and Krechevsky (1933).

KRECHEVSKY, I., and HONZIK, C. H. (1932) Fixation in the rat. *Univ. Calif. Publ. Psychol.*, 6, 13–26.—*216*

KRIS, E. (1947) The nature of psychoanalytic propositions and their validation. In S. Hook and M. R. Konvitz, eds. *Freedom and experience.* Ithaca, N.Y.: Cornell Univ. Press, 239–259. Also in Marx (1951), pages 332–351.—*307*

KRIS, E. *See also* Hartmann and Kris (1945).

KRUECKEL, B. *See* Krech and others (1954).

KUBIE, L. S. (1952) Problems and techniques of psychoanalytic validation and progress. In E. R. Hilgard, L. S. Kubie, and E. Pumpian-Mindlin. *Psychoanalysis as science.* Stanford, Calif.: Stanford Univ. Press, 46–124. —*307, 325*

KUBIE, L. S. (1953) Some unsolved problems of the scientific career. I. *Amer. Scientist,* 41, 596–613.—*311*

KUBIE, L. S. (1954) Some unsolved problems of the scientific career. II. *Amer. Scientist,* 42, 104–112.—*311*

KUBIE, L. S. *See also* Hilgard, Kubie, and Pumpian-Mindlin (1952).

KUENNE, M. R. (1946) Experimental investigation of the relation of language to transposition behavior in young children. *J. exp. Psychol.,* 36, 471–490.—*442, 444*

KUO, Z. Y. (1937) Forced movement or insight? *Univ. Calif. Publ. Psychol.,* 6, 169–188.—*195*

KUPFER, H. I. (1945) Psychic concomitants in wartime injuries. *Psychosom. Med.,* 7, 15–21.—*303*

KURTZ, K. H. *See* Hovland and Kurtz (1951).

LACEY, O. L. *See* McGinnies, Comer, and Lacey (1952).

LACY, O. W., LEWINGER, N., and ADAMSON, J. F. (1953) Foreknowledge as a factor affecting perceptual defense and alertness. *J. exp. Psychol.,* 45, 169–174.—*319, 320*

LAMBERT, W. W. (1954) Stimulus-response contiguity and reinforcement theory in social psychology. In G. Lindzey, ed. *Handbook of social psychology.* Cambridge, Mass.: Addison-Wesley, I, 65–71.—*183*

LANDAHL, H. D. *See* Householder and Landahl (1945).

LASHLEY, K. S. (1918) A simple maze: with data on the relation of the distribution of practice to rate of learning. *Psychobiol.,* 1, 353–367.—*211*

LASHLEY, K. S. (1929) Learning: I. Nervous mechanisms in learning. In C. Murchison, ed. *The foundations of experimental psychology.* Worcester, Mass., Clark Univ. Press, 524–563.—*202*

LASHLEY, K. S. (1942) An examination of the "continuity theory" as applied to discriminative learning. *J. gen. Psychol.,* 26, 241–265.—*436*

LASHLEY, K. S., and BALL, J. (1929) Spinal conduction and kinesthetic sensitivity in the maze habit. *J. comp. Psychol.,* 9, 71–105.—*193*

LASHLEY, K. S., CHOW, K. L., and SEMMES, J. (1951) An examination of the electrical field theory of cerebral integration. *Psychol. Rev.,* 58, 123–136. —*453*

LASHLEY, K. S., and WADE, M. (1946) The Pavlovian theory of generalization. *Psychol. Rev.,* 53, 72–87.—*442*

LAWRENCE, D. H. (1949) Acquired distinctiveness of cues: I. Transfer between discriminations on the basis of familiarity with the stimulus. *J. exp. Psychol.,* 39, 770–784.—*437, 468*

LAWRENCE, D. H. (1950) Acquired distinctiveness of cues: II. Selective association in a constant stimulus situation. *J. exp. Psychol.,* 40, 175–188.—*401, 437, 468*

LAWRENCE, D. H. (1952) The transfer of a discrimination along a continuum. *J. comp. physiol. Psychol.*, 45, 511–516.—*444*

LAWRENCE, D. H. (1955) The applicability of generalization gradients to the transfer of a discrimination. *J. gen. Psychol.*, 52, 37–48.—*444*

LAWRENCE, D. H. *See also* Baker and Lawrence (1951), Bauer and Lawrence (1953), Hoffman, Festinger, and Lawrence (1954).

LAWRENCE, D. H., and COLES, G. R. (1954) Accuracy of recognition with alternatives before and after the stimulus. *J. exp. Psychol.*, 47, 208–214.—*320*

LAWRENCE, D. H., and DERIVERA, J. (1954) Evidence for relational discrimination. *J. comp. physiol. Psychol.*, 47, 465–471.—*442*

LAWRENCE, D. H., and MASON, W. A. (1955) Systematic behavior during discrimination reversal and change of dimensions. *J. comp. physiol. Psychol.*, 48, 1–7.—*438, 475*

LAZARSFELD, P. F., ed. (1954) *Mathematical thinking in the social sciences.* Glencoe, Ill.: Free Press.—*406*

LAZARUS, R. S., ERIKSEN, C. W., and FONDA, C. P. (1951) Personality dynamics and auditory perceptual recognition. *J. Personality*, 19, 471–482.—*321*

LAZARUS, R. S., and MCCLEARY, R. A. (1951) Autonomic discrimination without awareness: a study of subception. *Psychol. Rev.*, 58, 113–122.—*320*

LEAVITT, H. J., and MUELLER, R. A. H. (1951) Some effects of feedback on communication. *Hum. Relat.*, 4, 401–410.—*376*

LEEPER, R. (1935a) The role of motivation in learning; a study of the phenomenon of differential motivational control of the utilization of habits. *J. genet. Psychol.*, 46, 3–40.—*268, 269*

LEEPER, R. (1935b) A study of a neglected portion of the field of learning—the development of sensory organization. *J. genet. Psychol.*, 46, 41–75.—*226*

LEEPER, R. (1943) *Lewin's topological and vector psychology, a digest and a critique.* Eugene, Ore.: Univ. Oregon Press.—*265, 268, 271, 287, 288*

LEEPER, R. (1944) Dr. Hull's *Principles of behavior. J. genet. Psychol.*, 65, 3–52.—*183, 187*

LEEPER, R. (1952) Review of Hull's *Essentials of behavior. Amer. J. Psychol.*, 65, 478–491.—*183*

LEEPER, R. *See also* Waters and Leeper (1936).

LEVIN, M. *See* Geier, Levin, and Tolman (1941).

LEVINE, E. M. *See* Child, Potter, and Levine (1946).

LEVINE, S. *See* Kendler and Levine (1953).

LEVY, N. *See* Seward, Datel, and Levy (1952), Seward, Levy, and Handlon (1950).

LEVY, D. M. (1941) The hostile act. *Psychol. Rev.*, 48, 356–361.—*304*

LEWIN, K. (1917) Die psychische Tätigkeit bei der Hemmung vons Willensvorgängen und das Grundgesetz der Assoziation. *Z. Psychol.*, 77, 212–247.—*259*

LEWIN, K. (1922) Das Problem der Willensmessung und das Grundgesetz der Assoziation. *Psychol. Forsch.*, I, 65–140; 191–302.—*259*

LEWIN, K. (1926) Vorsatz, Wille, und Bedürfnis (Mit Vorbemerkungen über die psychischen Kräfte und Energien und die Struktur der Seele). *Psychol. Forsch.*, 7, 294–385. Translated and condensed as "Will and needs" in Ellis (1938), pages 283–299.—*261, 280*

LEWIN, K. (1933a) Environmental forces. In C. Murchison, ed. *A handbook of child psychology.* Worcester, Mass.: Clark Univ. Press, 590–625.—*159, 286*

Lewin, K. (1933b) Vectors, cognitive processes, and Mr. Tolman's criticism. *J. gen. Psychol.*, 8, 318–345.—*217*

Lewin, K. (1935) *A dynamic theory of personality.* Trans. by D. K. Adams and K. E. Zener, New York: McGraw-Hill.—*159, 265, 266, 278, 288*

Lewin, K. (1936) *Principles of topological psychology.* Trans. by F. Heider and G. M. Heider, New York: McGraw-Hill.—*262, 264, 266, 288*

Lewin, K. (1937) Psychoanalysis and topological psychology. *Bull. Menninger Clin.*, I, 202–211.—*285*

Lewin, K. (1938) The conceptual representation and measurement of psychological forces. *Contr. Psychol. Theor.*, I. No. 4.—*262, 267–270, 288*

Lewin, K. (1942) Field theory and learning. Chapter 4 in *The psychology of learning.* Natl. Soc. Stud. Educ., 41st Yearbook, Part II, 215–242.—*262, 271, 275, 276, 279, 288*

Lewin, K. (1943) Defining the 'field at a given time.' *Psychol. Rev.*, 50, 288–290; 292–310.—*272, 287*

Lewin, K. (1946) Behavior and development as a function of the total situation. In L. Carmichael, ed. *Manual of child psychology.* New York, Wiley, 791–844.—*275, 286, 288*

Lewin, K. (1948) *Resolving social conflicts.* New York: Harper.—*286, 288*

Lewin, K. (1951) *Field theory in social science.* New York: Harper.—*286, 288*

Lewin, K. *See also* Barker, Dembo, and Lewin (1941).

Lewin, K., Dembo, T., Festinger, L., and Sears, P. S. (1944) Level of aspiration. In J. McV. Hunt, ed. *Personality and the behavior disorders.* New York: Ronald Press, 333–378.—*278*

Lewin, K., Lippitt, R., and White, R. K. (1939) Patterns of aggressive behavior in experimentally created 'social climates.' *J. soc. Psychol.*, 10, 271–299.—*289*

Lewinger, N. *See* Lacy, Lewinger, and Adamson (1953).

Libby, A. (1951) Two variables in the acquisition of depressant properties by a stimulus. *J. exp. Psychol.*, 42, 100–107.—*54*

Lindahl, L. G. (1945) Movement analysis as an industrial training method. *J. appl. Psychol.*, 29, 420–436.—*492*

Lindsley, D. B., Schreiner, L. H., Knowles, W. B., and Magoun, H. W. (1950) Behavioral and EEG changes following chronic brain stem lesions in the cat. *EEG clin. Neurophysiol.*, 2, 483–498.—*453*

Lindzey, G. *See* Hall and Lindzey (1954).

Lipofsky, H. *See* Miller, Brown, and Lipofsky (1943).

Lippitt, R. *See* Lewin, Lippitt, and White (1939), Spence, Bergmann, and Lippitt (1950), Spence and Lippitt (1940) (1946).

Littman, R. A. (1950) Latent learning in a T-maze after two degrees of training. *J. comp. physiol. Psychol.*, 43, 135–147.—*212*

Livingston, J. R. *See* Hull and others (1951).

Logan, F. A. (1952) The role of delay of reinforcement in determining reaction potential. *J. exp. Psychol.*, 43, 393–399.—*439*

London, I. D. (1944) Psychologists' misuse of the auxiliary concepts of physics and mathematics. *Psychol. Rev.*, 51, 266–291.—*263, 287*

Lorenz, K. Z. (1952) *King Solomon's ring.* New York: Crowell.—*3*

Lorge, I. (1936) Irrelevant rewards in animal learning. *J. comp. Psychol.*, 21, 105–128.—*47*

LORGE, I. *See also* Thorndike and Lorge (1935).

LOWELL, E. L. *See* McClelland and others (1953).

LOWENSTEIN, R. M. (1954) Some remarks on defenses, autonomous ego, and psychoanalytic technique. *Int. J. Psychoanal.*, 35, 1–6.—*294*

LUCHINS, A. S. (1942) Mechanization in problem solving. The effect of *Einstellung. Psychol. Monogr.*, 54, No. 248.—*233, 473*

LUCHINS, A. S. (1951) An evaluation of some current criticisms of gestalt psychological work on perception. *Psychol. Rev.*, 58, 69–95.—*229*

LUGOFF, L. S. *See* Hull and Lugoff (1921).

LUH, C. W. (1922) The conditions of retention. *Psychol. Monogr.*, 31, No. 142. —*367*

LYSAK, W. (1954) The effects of punishment upon syllable recognition thresholds. *J. exp. Psychol.*, 47, 343–350.—*320, 321*

MCALLLISTER, W. R. (1953) Eyelid conditioning as a function of the CS-US interval. *J. exp. Psychol.*, 45, 417–422.—*54*

MCCLEARN, G. E. *See* Harlow and McClearn (1954).

MCCLEARY, R. A. *See* Lazarus and McCleary (1951).

MCCLELLAND, D. C. (1942) Studies in serial verbal discrimination learning. I. Reminiscence with two speeds of pair presentation. *J. exp. Psychol.*, 31, 44–56.—*367*

MCCLELLAND, D. C. (1951) *Personality.* New York: Sloane.—*432*

MCCLELLAND, D. C., ed. (1955) *Studies in motivation.* New York: Appleton-Century-Crofts.—*456*

MCCLELLAND, D. C., and ATKINSON, J. W. (1948) The projective expression of needs: I. The effects of different intensities of the hunger drive on perception. *J. Psychol.*, 25, 205–223.—*292*

MCCLELLAND, D. C., ATKINSON, J. W., CLARK, R. A., and LOWELL, E. L. (1953) *The achievement motive.* New York: Appleton-Century-Crofts.—*432*

MACCOLL, L. A. (1945) *Fundamental theory of servomechanisms.* New York: Van Nostrand.—*376*

MCCONNELL, C. *See* Stevenson, Iscoe, and McConnell (1955).

MCCONNELL, T. R., and others (1942) *The psychology of learning.* Natl. Soc. Stud. Educ., 41st Yearbook, Part II.—*14, 457, 491*

MACCORQUODALE, K. (1955) Learning. *Ann. Rev. Psychol.*, 6, 29–62.—*409*

MACCORQUODALE, K. *See also* Estes and others (1954), Meehl and MacCorquodale (1948) (1951).

MACCORQUODALE, K., and MEEHL, P. E. (1948) On a distinction between hypothetical constructs and intervening variables. *Psychol. Rev.*, 55, 95–107. —*12, 218, 459, 465*

MACCORQUODALE, K., and MEEHL, P. E. (1951) On the elimination of culentries without obvious reinforcement. *J. comp. physiol. Psychol.*, 44, 367–371.—*211, 212*

MACCORQUODALE, K., and MEEHL, P. E. (1953) Preliminary suggestions as to a formalization of expectancy theory. *Psychol. Rev.*, 60, 55–63.—*446, 450, 465*

MACCORQUODALE, K., and MEEHL, P. E. (1954) Edward C. Tolman. In W. K. Estes and others, *Modern learning theory.* New York: Appleton-Century-Crofts, 177–266.—*211, 215, 221, 446*

MCCULLOCH, T. L. (1939) Comment on the formation of discrimination habits. *Psychol. Rev.*, 46, 75–85.—*436*

McCutchan, K. *See* Blodgett and McCutchan (1947) (1948).

McDougall, W. (1923) *Outline of psychology*. New York: Scribner.—*285, 429*

McGeoch, J. A. (1932a) Forgetting and the law of disuse. *Psychol. Rev.*, 39, 352–370.—*344*

McGeoch, J. A. (1932b) Review of Robinson's *Association theory today. J. gen. Psychol.*, 7, 231–237.—*367*

McGeoch, J. A. (1933) Review of Thorndike's *The fundamentals of learning. J. gen. Psychol.*, 8, 285–296.—*46*

McGeoch, J. A. (1936) The vertical dimensions of mind. *Psychol. Rev.*, 43, 107–129.—*334*

McGeoch, J. A. (1942) *The psychology of human learning*. New York: Longmans.—*341, 350, 476*

McGeoch, J. A., and Irion, A. L. (1952) *The psychology of human learning*. Revised. New York: Longmans.—*14, 205, 283, 343, 344, 350, 356, 363, 365, 366*

McGill, W. J. *See* Miller and McGill (1952).

McGinnies, E. M. (1949) Emotionality and perceptual defense. *Psychol. Rev.*, 56, 244–251.—*318*

McGinnies, E. M., and Adornetto, J. (1952) Perceptual defense in normal and schizophrenic observers. *J. abnorm. soc. Psychol.*, 47, 833–837.—*319*

McGinnies, E. M., Comer, P. B., and Lacey, O. L. (1952) Visual recognition thresholds as a function of word length and word frequency. *J. exp. Psychol.*, 44, 65–69.—*319*

McKinney, F. (1935) Studies in the retention of interrupted learning activities. *J. comp. Psychol.*, 19, 265–296.—*283*

MacLeod, R. B. (1947) The phenomenological approach to social psychology. *Psychol. Rev.*, 54, 193–210.—*254*

MacLeod, R. B. (1951) The place of phenomenological analysis in social psychological theory. In J. H. Rohrer and M. Sherif, eds. *Social psychology at the crossroads*. New York: Harper, 215–241.—*254*

MacLeod, R. B. (1952) Review of Tolman's *Collected papers in psychology. Psychol. Bull.*, 49, 274–276.—*220*

McReynolds, P. (1950) Logical relationships between memorial and transient functions. *Psychol. Rev.*, 57, 140–144.—*454*

McReynolds, P. (1953) Thinking conceptualized in terms of interacting moments. *Psychol. Rev.*, 60, 319–330.—*454*

Macfarlane, D. A. (1930) The role of kinesthesis in maze learning. *Univ. Calif. Publ. Psychol.*, 4, 277–305.—*193*

Magoun, H. W. (1952) An ascending reticular activating system in the brain stem. *A.M.A. Arch. Neurol. Psychiat.*, 67, 145–154.—*453*

Magoun, H. W. *See also* Lindsley and others (1950).

Mahler-Schoenberger, M. (1942) Pseudoimbecility: a magic cap of invisibility. *Psychoanalyt. Quart.*, 11, 149–164.—*310*

Maier, N. R. F. (1929) Reasoning in white rats. *Comp. Psychol., Monogr.*, 6, No. 29.—*213*

Maier, N. R. F. (1930) Reasoning in humans. I. On direction. *J. comp. Psychol.*, 10, 115–143.—*235, 237*

Maier, N. R. F. (1931) Reasoning and learning. *Psychol. Rev.*, 38, 332–346.—*6, 477*

MAIER, N. R. F. (1939a) Qualitative differences in the learning of rats in a discrimination situation. *J. comp. Psychol.*, 27, 289–331.—*461*

MAIER, N. R. F. (1939b) The specific processes constituting the learning function. *Psychol. Rev.*, 46, 241–252.—*461*

MAIER, N. R. F. (1949) *Frustration, the study of behavior without a goal.* New York: McGraw-Hill.—*296, 456*

MAIER, N. R. F. (1954) The premature crystallization of learning theory. In the Kentucky Symposium. *Learning theory, personality theory, and clinical research.* New York: Wiley, 54–65.—*491*

MAIER, N. R. F., GLASER, N. M., and KLEE, J. B. (1940) Studies of abnormal behavior in the rat: III. The development of behavior fixations through frustration. *J. exp. Psychol.*, 26, 521–546.—*326, 473*

MALTZMAN, I. M. (1950) An experimental study of learning under an irrelevant need. *J. exp. Psychol.*, 40, 788–793.—*212*

MALTZMAN, I. (1952) The Blodgett and Haney types of latent learning experiment: Reply to Thistlewaite. *Psychol. Bull.*, 49, 52–60.—*211*

MARHENKE, P. (1940) Review of *Mathematico-deductive theory of rote learning:* The logical system. *Psychol. Bull.*, 37, 815–817.—*183*

MARQUIS, D. G. (1951) The neurology of learning. In C. P. Stone, ed. *Comparative psychology.* Third edition. New York: Prentice-Hall, 292–315.—*453*

MARQUIS, D. G. *See also* Hilgard and Marquis (1940).

MARROW, A. J. (1938) Goal tensions and recall. *J. gen. Psychol.*, 19, 3–35, 37–64.—*281, 283*

MARTENS, D. (1946) Spread of effect in verbal serial learning. (Abstract.) *Amer. Psychologist*, I, 448–449.—*32*

MARTIN, J. R. (1940) Reminiscence and gestalt theory. *Psychol. Monogr.*, 52, No. 235.—*283*

MARX, M. H., ed. (1951a) *Psychological theory: contemporary readings.* New York: Macmillan.—*14*

MARX, M. H. (1951b) Intervening variable or hypothetical construct? *Psychol. Rev.*, 58, 235–247.—*12, 219*

MARX, M. *See also* Iwahara and Marx (1950).

MASLOW, A. H. (1941) Deprivation, threat, and frustration. *Psychol. Rev.*, 48, 364–366.—*304*

MASON, C. W. *See* Melton, Feldman, and Mason (1936).

MASON, W. A. *See* Lawrence and Mason (1955).

MASSERMAN, J. H., and YUM, K. S. (1946) An analysis of the influence of alcohol on experimental neuroses in cats. *Psychosom. Med.*, 8, 36–52.—*326*

MAY, R. (1950) *The meaning of anxiety.* New York: Ronald Press.—*298*

MAYHEW, K. C., and EDWARDS, A. C. (1936) *The Dewey School: the laboratory school at the University of Chicago, 1896–1903.* New York: Appleton-Century.—*330*

MAZE, J. R. (1954) Do intervening variables intervene? *Psychol. Rev.*, 61, 226–234.—*12, 219*

MEEHL, P. E. (1950) On the circularity of the law of effect. *Psychol. Bull.*, 47, 52–75.—*47*

MEEHL, P. E. *See also* Estes and others (1954), MacCorquodale and Meehl (1948) (1951) (1953) (1954).

MEEHL, P. E., and MACCORQUODALE, K. (1948) A further study of latent learning in the T-maze. *J. comp. physiol. Psychol.*, 41, 372–396.—*212, 450*

MEEHL, P. E., and MACCORQUODALE, K. (1951) A failure to find the Blodgett effect, and some secondary observations on drive conditioning. *J. comp. physiol. Psychol.*, 44, 178–183.—*211*
MEER, B. *See* Stein and Meer (1954).
MELTON, A. W. (1941a) Learning. In W. S. Monroe, ed. *Encyclopedia of educational research.* New York: Macmillan, 667–686.—*334*
MELTON, A. W. (1941b) Review of Katona's *Organizing and memorizing. Amer. J. Psychol.*, 54, 455–457.—*251*
MELTON, A. W. (1950) Learning. In W. S. Monroe, ed. *Encyclopedia of educational research.* Revised. New York: Macmillan, 668–690.—*334, 336, 337, 341, 367, 491*
MELTON, A. W., FELDMAN, N. G., and MASON, C. W. (1936) *Experimental studies of the education of children in a museum of science.* Washington, D.C.: Publ. Amer. Assn. Museums, New Series, No. 15.—*492*
MELTON, A. W., and IRWIN, J. McQ. (1940) The influence of degree of interpolated learning on retroactive inhibition and the overt transfer of specific responses. *Amer. J. Psychol.*, 53, 173–203.—*367*
MELTZER, H. (1930) Individual differences in forgetting pleasant and unpleasant experiences. *J. educ. Psychol.*, 21, 399–409.—*314*
MENCHER, H. C. *See* Kendler and Mencher (1948).
MIHAMA, H. *See* Kotake and Mihama (1951).
MIHAMA, H., and KOTAKE, Y. (1954) The conditioned pupillary light-reflex in man and its verbal control. *Annual Studies, Vol. II* (Department of Humanities Series, No. 1). Nishinomiya-shi, Japan: Kwansei Gakuin University, 1–20.—*85, 462*
MILES, W. R. *See* Miller and Miles (1935).
MILLER, D. R. *See* Blum and Miller (1952).
MILLER, G. A. (1953) What is information measurement? *Amer. Psychologist*, 8, 3–11.—*377, 406*
MILLER, G. A. (1955) *The magical number seven, plus-or-minus two, or, some limits on our capacity for processing information.* Address at Eastern Psychological Association, April 15, 1955. Dittoed.—*381*
MILLER, G. A. *See also* Frick and Miller (1951).
MILLER, G. A., and FRICK, F. C. (1949) Statistical behavioristics and sequences of responses. *Psychol. Rev.*, 56, 311–324.—*385*
MILLER, G. A., and MCGILL, W. J. (1952) A statistical description of verbal learning. *Psychometrika*, 17, 369–396.—*406*
MILLER, G. A., and SELFRIDGE, J. A. (1950) Verbal context and the recall of meaningful material. *Amer. J. Psychol.*, 63, 176–185.—*381–383*
MILLER, N. E. (1935) A reply to "Sign-Gestalt or conditioned reflex?" *Psychol. Rev.*, 42, 280–292.—*181*
MILLER, N. E. (1941) The frustration-aggression hypothesis. *Psychol. Rev.*, 48, 337–342.—*304*
MILLER, N. E. (1944) Experimental studies in conflict. In J. McV. Hunt, ed. *Personality and the behavior disorders.* New York: Ronald Press, 431–465.—*168, 169*
MILLER, N. E. (1948a) Studies of fear as an acquired drive. I. Fear as motivation and fear-reduction as reinforcement in the learning of new responses. *J. exp. Psychol.*, 38, 89–101.—*129, 299, 412, 422*
MILLER, N. E. (1948b) Theory and experiment relating psychoanalytic dis-

placement to stimulus-response generalization. *J. abnorm. soc. Psychol.*, 43, 155–178.—*305, 306, 324, 326*

MILLER, N. E. (1949) Review of Hilgard's *Theories of learning. Psychol. Bull.*, 46, 529–532.—*184, 446*

MILLER, N. E. (1951a) Comments on multiple-process conceptions of learning. *Psychol. Rev.*, 58, 375–381.—*411, 412, 430*

MILLER, N. E. (1951b) Learnable drives and rewards. In S. S. Stevens, ed. *Handbook of experimental psychology.* New York: Wiley, 435–472.—*129, 137, 411, 412*

MILLER, N. E. *See also* Berkun, Kessen, and Miller (1952), Delgado, Roberts, and Miller (1954), Dollard and Miller (1950), Dollard and others (1939), Mowrer and Miller (1942), Murray and Miller (1952), Myers and Miller (1954).

MILLER, N. E., BROWN, J. S., and LIPOFSKY, H. (1943) A theoretical and experimental analysis of conflict behavior: III. Approach-avoidance conflict as a function of strength of drive and strength of shock. (Unpublished: *see* Miller, 1944.)—*168*

MILLER, N. E., and DOLLARD, J. C. (1941) *Social learning and imitation.* New Haven: Yale Univ. Press.—*123, 137, 411*

MILLER, N. E., and KESSEN, M. L. (1952) Reward effects of food via stomach fistula compared with those of food via mouth. *J. comp. physiol. Psychol.*, 45, 555–564.—*412, 413*

MILLER, N. E., and KESSEN, M. L. (1954) Is distension of the stomach via balloon rewarding or punishing? *Amer. Psychologist,* 9, 430–431.—*423*

MILLER, N. E., and KRAELING, D. (1952) Displacement: greater generalization of approach than avoidance in a generalized approach-avoidance conflict. *J. exp. Psychol.*, 43, 217–221.—*305*

MILLER, N. E., and MILES, W. R. (1935) Effect of caffeine on the running speed of hungry, satiated, and frustrated rats. *J. comp. Psychol.*, 20, 397–412.—*155*

MILLER, N. E., and MURRAY, E. J. (1952) Displacement and conflict: learnable drive as a basis for the steeper gradient of avoidance than of approach. *J. exp. Psychol.*, 43, 227–231.—*305*

MILLER, N. E., MURRAY, E. J., and ROBERTS, W. W. (1955) Temporary reduction of hunger by saccharin. (Unpublished.)—*411*

MILNER, B. (1954) Intellectual function of the temporal lobes. *Psychol. Bull.*, 51, 42–62.—*453*

MILNER, P. *See* Olds and Milner (1954).

MINIUM, E. *See* Tolman and Minium (1942).

MISBACH, L. (1948) Psychoanalysis and theories of learning. *Psychol. Rev.*, 55, 143–156.—*324, 326*

MONKMAN, J. A. *See* Montgomery and Monkman (1955).

MONTAGUE, E. K. (1953) The role of anxiety in serial rote learning. *J. exp. Psychol.*, 45, 91–96.—*300*

MONTGOMERY, K. C. (1952) Exploratory behavior and its relation to spontaneous alternation in a series of maze exposures. *J. comp. physiol. Psychol.*, 45, 50–57.—*431*

MONTGOMERY, K. C. (1953a) Exploratory behavior as a function of "similarity" of stimulus situations. *J. comp. physiol. Psychol.*, 46, 129–133.—*431*

MONTGOMERY, K. C. (1953b) The effect of hunger and thirst drives upon exploratory behavior. *J. comp. physiol. Psychol.*, 46, 315–319.—*431*

MONTGOMERY, K. C. (1953c) The effect of activity deprivation upon exploratory behavior. *J. comp. physiol. Psychol.*, 46, 438–441.—*431*

MONTGOMERY, K. C., and MONKMAN, J. A. (1955) The relation between fear and exploratory behavior. *J. comp. physiol. Psychol.*, 48, 132–136.—*431*

MOORE, A. R., and WELCH, J. C. (1940) Associative hysteresis in larval amblystoma. *J. comp. Psychol.*, 29, 283–292.—*482*

MOORE, A. W. *See* Angell and Moore (1896).

MOORE, M. G. (1930) Gestalt vs. experience. *Amer. J. Psychol.*, 42, 453–455.—*230*

MORGAN, C. L. (1894) *Introduction to comparative psychology.* London: Scott.—*476*

MORGAN, C. T. (1943) *Physiological psychology.* New York: McGraw-Hill.

MORGAN, C. T. (1951) The psychophysiology of learning. In S. S. Stevens, ed. *Handbook of experimental psychology.* New York: Wiley, 758–788.

MORGAN, C. T. *See also* Chapanis, Garner, and Morgan (1949).

MORGENSTERN, O., *See* Von Neumann and Morgenstern (1944).

MORSE, P., and KIMBALL, G. (1951) *Methods in operations research.* New York: Wiley.—*405*

MOSER, H. E. *See* Brownell and Moser (1949).

MOSTELLER, F. (1953) Comments on "Models for human learning." In *Symposium on psychology of learning basic to military training problems.* Washington, D.C.: Committee on Human Resources, Research and Development Board, HR-HTD 201/1, 39–42.—*399, 400, 402*

MOSTELLER, F. *See also* Bush and Mosteller (1951a) (1951b) (1955), Bush, Mosteller, and Thompson (1954).

MOSTELLER, F., and NOGEE, P. (1951) An experimental measurement of utility. *J. polit. Econ.*, 59, 371–404.—*384*

MOWRER, O. H. (1938) Preparatory set (expectancy): a determinant in motivation and learning. *Psychol. Rev.*, 45, 62–91.—*292*

MOWRER, O. H. (1939) A stimulus-response analysis of anxiety and its role as a reinforcing agent. *Psychol. Rev.*, 46, 553–565.—*299, 413*

MOWRER, O. H. (1940a) An experimental analogue of "regression" with incidental observations on "reaction-formation." *J. abnorm. soc. Psychol.*, 35, 56–87.—*303, 326*

MOWRER, O. H. (1940b) Anxiety reduction and learning. *J. exp. Psychol.*, 27, 497–516.—*299*

MOWRER, O. H. (1946) The law of effect and ego psychology. *Psychol. Rev.*, 53, 321–334.—*285*

MOWRER, O. H. (1947) On the dual nature of learning: a re-interpretation of "conditioning" and "problem-solving." *Harvard educ. Rev.*, 17, 102–148.—*413, 430*

MOWRER, O. H. (1950) *Learning theory and personality dynamics.* New York: Ronald Press.—*293, 295, 296, 299, 326, 413, 414, 456*

MOWRER, O. H. (1951) Two-factor learning theory: summary and comment. *Psychol. Rev.*, 58, 350–354.—*413*

MOWRER, O. H. (1952) Motivation. *Ann. Rev. Psychol.*, 3, 419–438.—*428*

MOWRER, O. H. (1953) *Psychotherapy: theory and research.* New York: Ronald Press.—*326*

MOWRER, O. H. (1954a) Ego psychology, cybernetics, and learning theory. In the Kentucky Symposium. *Learning theory, personality theory, and clinical research.* New York: Wiley, 81–90.—*406*

MOWRER, O. H. (1954b) Learning theory: historical review and re-interpretation. *Harvard educ. Rev.*, 24, 37–58.—*413*

MOWRER, O. H. (1955) *Two-factor learning theory: reviewed, revised, and extended.* Urbana, Ill. (Mimeographed.)—*414, 456*

MOWRER, O. H. *See also* Dollard and others (1939).

MOWRER, O. H., and AIKEN, E. G. (1954) Contiguity vs. drive-reduction in conditioned fear: temporal variations in conditioned and unconditioned stimulus. *Amer. J. Psychol.*, 67, 26–38.—*414*

MOWRER, O. H., and JONES, H. M. (1943) Extinction and behavior variability as functions of effortfulness of task. *J. exp. Psychol.*, 33, 369–386.—*137, 139*

MOWRER, O. H., and MILLER, N. E. (1942) A multi-purpose learning-demonstration apparatus. *J. exp. Psychol.*, 31, 163–170.—*413*

MOWRER, O. H., and SOLOMON, L. N. (1954) Contiguity vs. drive-reduction in conditioned fear: the proximity and abruptness of drive-reduction. *Amer. J. Psychol.*, 67, 15–25.—*414*

MOWRER, O. H., and ULLMAN, A. D. (1945) Time as a determinant in integrative learning. *Psychol. Rev.*, 52, 61–90.—*299*

MUELLER, C. G., Jr. (1950) Theoretical relationships among some measures of conditioning. *Proc. nat. Acad. Sci.*, Washington, D.C., 36, 123–130.—*147*

MUELLER, C. G., Jr. *See also* Estes and others (1954).

MUELLER, C. G., Jr., and SCHOENFELD, W. N. (1954) Edwin R. Guthrie. In W. K. Estes and others. *Modern learning theory.* New York: Appleton-Century-Crofts, 345–379.—*68, 79–81*

MUELLER, R. A. H. *See* Leavitt and Mueller (1951).

MUENZINGER, K. F. (1935a) Motivation in learning. I. Electric shock for correct response in the visual discrimination habit. *J. comp. Psychol.*, 17, 267–277.—*202*

MUENZINGER, K. F. (1934b) Motivation in learning. II. The function of electric shock for right and wrong responses in human subjects. *J. exp. Psychol.*, 17, 439–448.—*202*

MUENZINGER, K. F. (1938) Vicarious trial and error at a point of choice. I. A general survey of its relation to learning efficiency. *J. genet. Psychol.*, 53, 75–86.—*202*

MUENZINGER, K. F. (1942) *Psychology: The science of behavior.* New York: Harper.—*331*

MUENZINGER, K. F., BERNSTONE, A. H., and RICHARDS, L. (1938) Motivation in learning. VIII. Equivalent amounts of electric shock for right and wrong responses in a visual discrimination habit. *J. comp. Psychol.*, 26, 177–185.—*202*

MUENZINGER, K. F., BROWN, W. O., CROW, W. J., and POWLOSKI, R. F. (1952) Motivation in learning. XI. An analysis of electric shock for correct responses into its avoidance and accelerating components. *J. exp. Psychol.*, 43, 115–119.—*202*

MUENZINGER, K. F., and CONRAD, D. G. (1953) Latent learning observed through negative transfer. *J. comp. physiol. Psychol.*, 46, 1–8.—*214*

MUENZINGER, K. F., and FLETCHER, F. M. (1936) Motivation in learning. VI. Escape from electric shock compared with hunger-food tension in the visual discrimination habit. *J. comp. Psychol.*, 22, 79–91.—*202*

MUENZINGER, K. F., and FLETCHER, F. M. (1937) Motivation in learning. VII. The effect of an enforced delay at the point of choice in the visual discrimination habit. *J. comp. Psychol.*, 23, 383–392.—*202*

MUENZINGER, K. F., KOERNER, L., and IREY, E. (1929) Variability of an habitual movement in guinea pigs. *J. comp. Psychol.*, 9, 425–436.—*69*

MUENZINGER, K. F., and NEWCOMB, H. (1935) Motivation in learning. III. A bell signal compared with electric shock for right and wrong responses in the visual discrimination habit. *J. comp. Psychol.*, 20, 85–93.—*202*

MUENZINGER, K. F., and NEWCOMB, H. (1936) Motivation in learning. V. The relative effectiveness of jumping a gap and crossing an electric grid in a visual discrimination habit. *J. comp. Psychol.*, 21, 95–104.—*202*

MUENZINGER, K. F., and POWLOSKI, R. F. (1951) Motivation in Learning. X. Comparison of electric shock for correct turns in a corrective and non-corrective situation. *J. exp. Psychol.*, 42, 118–124.—*202*

MUENZINGER, K. F., and VINE, D. O. (1941) Motivation in learning. IX. The effect of interposed obstacles in human learning. *J. exp. Psychol.*, 1941, 29, 67–74.—*202*

MUENZINGER, K. F., and WOOD, A. (1935) Motivation in learning. IV. The function of punishment as determined by its temporal relation to the act of choice in the visual discrimination habit. *J. comp. Psychol.*, 20, 95–106.—*202*

MÜLLER, G. E. (1911) Zur Analyse der Gedächtnistätigkeit und des Vorstellungsverlaufes, Vol. I. *Z. Psychol.*, Ergänzungs-Bd. 5.—*342*

MÜLLER, G. E. (1913) Zur Analyse der Gedächtnistätigkeit und des Vorstellungsverlaufes, Vol. III. *Z. Psychol.*, Ergänzungs-Bd. 8.—*342*

MÜLLER, G. E. (1917) Zur Analyse der Gedächtnistätigkeit und des Vorstellungsverlaufes, Vol. II. *Z. Psychol.*, Ergänzungs-Bd. 9.—*342*

MÜLLER, G. E., and PILZECKER, A. (1900) Experimentelle Beiträge zur Lehre vom Gedächtnis. *Z. Psychol.*, Erbgd. I.—*344, 355*

MÜLLER, I. (1937) Zur Analyse der Retentionsstörung durch Häufung. *Psychol. Forsch.*, 22, 180–210.—*246*

MUNROE, R. L. (1955) *Schools of psychoanalytic thought.* New York: Dryden. —*325*

MURPHY, G. (1947) *Personality.* New York: Harper.—*296, 429, 473*

MURRAY, E. J. *See* Miller and Murray (1952), Miller, Murray, and Roberts (1955).

MURRAY, E. J., and MILLER, N. E. (1952) Displacement: steeper gradient of generalization of avoidance than of approach with age of habit controlled. *J. exp. Psychol.*, 43, 222–226.—*305*

MURRAY, H. A. (1938) and others. *Explorations in Personality.* New York: Oxford Univ. Press.—*187*

MYERS, A. K., and MILLER, N. E. (1954) Failure to find a learned drive based on hunger; evidence for learning motivated by "exploration." *J. comp. physiol. Psychol.*, 47, 428–436.—*412, 422, 431*

Nebraska Symposium on Motivation (1953) *Current theory and research in motivation,* I. Lincoln, Nebr.: Univ. of Nebraska Press.—*456*

Nebraska Symposium on Motivation, M. R. Jones, ed. (1954) *Current theory and research in motivation,* II. Lincoln, Nebr.: Univ. of Nebraska Press.—*456*

Nebraska Symposium on Motivation, M. R. Jones, ed. (1955) *Current theory and research on motivation.* III. Lincoln, Nebr.: Univ. of Nebraska Press. —*456*

NEISSER, U. (1954) An experimental distinction between perceptual process and verbal response. *J. exp. Psychol.*, 47, 399–402.—*320*

NEWCOMB, H. *See* Muenzinger and Newcomb (1935) (1936).

NEWCOMB, T. M. (1950) *Social psychology.* New York: Dryden.—*331*

NEWMAN, E. B. (1939) Forgetting of meaningful material during sleep and waking. *Amer. J. Psychol.*, 52, 65–71.—*257*

NEWMAN, E. B. (1951) *Learning.* In H. Helson, ed. *Theoretical foundations of psychology.* New York: Van Nostrand, 390–451.—*485*

NISSEN, H. W. (1950) Description of the learned response in discrimination learning. *Psychol. Rev.*, 57, 121–131.—*442*

NISSEN, H. W. (1953) Sensory patterning versus central organization. *J. Psychol.*, 36, 271–287.—*436*

NISSEN, H. W. (1954) The nature of the drive as innate determinant of behavioral organization. In the Nebraska Symposium on Motivation, II, M. R. Jones, ed. *Current theory and research in motivation.* Lincoln, Nebr.: Univ. of Nebraska Press, 281–321.—*431*

NISSEN, H. W. *See also* Cowles and Nissen (1937).

NOGEE, P. *See* Mosteller and Nogee (1951).

NOLAN, C. Y. *See* Webb and Nolan (1953).

NORTH, A. J. *See* Fagan and North (1951).

NOTTERMAN, J. M. (1951) A study of some relations among aperiodic reinforcement, discrimination training, and secondary reinforcement. *J. exp. Psychol.*, 41, 161–169.—*120*

NOTTERMAN, J. M., SCHOENFELD, W. N., and BERSH, P. J. (1952) A comparison of three extinction procedures following heart rate conditioning. *J. abnorm. soc. Psychol.*, 47, 674–677.—*85*

NOWLIS, H. H. (1941) The influence of success and failure on the resumption of an interrupted task. *J. exp. Psychol.*, 28, 304–325.—*284*

NOWLIS, V. *See* Sears and others (1953).

NUTTIN, J. (1949) 'Spread' in recalling failure and success. *J. exp. Psychol.*, 39, 690–699.—*40*

NUTTIN, J. (1953) *Tâche, réussite et échec.* Louvain, Belgium: Publications Univ. de Louvain.—*40, 47, 283*

NYSWANDER, D. B. *See* Stone and Nyswander (1927).

O'CONNELL, D. L. *See* Köhler, Held, and O'Connell (1952).

O'KELLY, L. I. (1940a) An experimental study of regression. I. Behavioral characteristics of the regressive response. *J. comp. Psychol.*, 30, 41–53.—*303*

O'KELLY, L. I. (1940b) An experimental study of regression. II. Some motivational determinants of regression and perseveration. *J. comp. Psychol.*, 30, 55–95.—*303*

OLDS, J. (1953) The influence of practice on the strength of secondary approach drives. *J. exp. Psychol.*, 46, 232–236.—*446*

OLDS, J. (1954) A neural model for sign-gestalt theory. *Psychol. Rev.*, 61, 59–72.—*446*

OLDS, J. (1955) A physiological study of reward. In D. C. McClelland, ed. *Studies in motivation.* New York: Appleton-Century-Crofts, 134–143.—*432*

OLDS, J., and MILNER, P. (1954) Positive reinforcement produced by electrical stimulation of septal area and other regions of rat brain. *J. comp. physiol. Psychol.*, 47, 419–427.—*431, 454*

ORNE, M. T. (1951) The mechanism of hypnotic age regression: an experimental study. *J. abnorm. soc. Psychol.*, 46, 213–225.—*303*

OSEAS, L., and UNDERWOOD, B. J. (1952) Studies of distributed practice: V. Learning and retention of concepts. *J. exp. Psychol.*, 43, 143–148.—*350*

OSGOOD, C. E. (1946) Meaningful similarity and interference in learning. *J. exp. Psychol.*, 36, 227–301.—*367*

OSGOOD, C. E. (1949) The similarity paradox in human learning: a resolution. *Psychol. Rev.*, 56, 132–143.—*346, 347*

OSGOOD, C. E. (1950) Can Tolman's theory of learning handle avoidance training? *Psychol. Rev.*, 57, 133–137.—*446*

OSGOOD, C. E. (1953) *Method and theory in experimental psychology.* New York: Oxford Univ. Press.—*14, 243, 246, 343, 365, 366, 453, 465*

OVSIANKINA, M. (1928) Die Wiederaufnahme unterbrochener Handlungen. *Psychol. Forsch.*, II, 302–379.—*260, 284, 289*

PACHAURI, A. R. (1935) A study of gestalt problems in completed and interrupted tasks. *Brit. J. Psychol.*, 25, 447–457.—*283*

PATERSON, A. L. *See* Bindra, Paterson, and Strzelecki (1955).

PAVLOV, I. P. (1927) *Conditioned reflexes.* London: Oxford Univ. Press.—*51, 121*

PAVLOV, I. P. (1928) *Lectures on conditioned reflexes.* Trans. by W. H. Gantt, New York: International.—*51*

PEAK, H. (1933) Reflex and voluntary reactions of the eyelid. *J. gen. Psychol.*, 8, 130–156.—*83*

PEARL, R., and REED, L. J. (1920) On the rate of growth of the population in the United States since 1790 and its mathematical representation. *Proc. nat. Acad. Sci.*, 6, 275–288.—*371*

PEARSON, G. H. J. (1952) A survey of learning difficulties in children. *Psychoanal. Stud. Child*, 7, 322–386.—*310*

PEARSON, G. H. J. (1954) *Psychoanalysis and the education of the child.* New York: Norton.—*310, 327*

PECHSTEIN, L. A., and BROWN, F. D. (1939) An experimental analysis of the alleged criteria of insight learning. *J. educ. Psychol.*, 30, 38–52.—*238*

PEIRCE, P. *See* Ritchie, Aeschliman, and Peirce (1950).

PENFIELD, W., and JASPER, H. (1954) *Epilepsy and the functional anatomy of the human brain.* Boston: Little, Brown.—*453*

PERIN, C. T. (1942) Behavior potentiality as a joint function of the amount of training and the degree of hunger at the time of extinction. *J. exp. Psychol.*, 30, 93–113.—*139, 179, 184*

PERKINS, D. T. *See* Hull and others (1940).

PERKINS, F. T. (1932) Symmetry in visual recall. *Amer. J. Psychol.*, 44, 473–490.—*243, 257*

PERKINS, F. T. *See also* Wheeler and Perkins (1932).

PERRIN, F. A. C., and KLEIN, D. B. (1926) *Psychology; its methods and principles.* New York: Holt.—*407*

PERRY, R. B. (1918) Docility and purposiveness. *Psychol. Rev.*, 25, 1–20.—*187*

PETERSON, J. (1922) Learning when frequency and recency factors are negative. *J. exp. Psychol.*, 5, 270–300.—*49*

PIERS, G., and SINGER, M. B. (1953) *Shame and guilt.* Springfield, Ill.: Thomas.—*298*

PILZECKER, A. *See* Müller and Pilzecker (1900).

PITTS, W. (1943) A general theory of learning and conditioning. *Psychometrika*, 8, 1–18; 131–140.—*406*

PLATT, C. E. *See* Wickens and Platt (1954).
PORTER, J. M., Jr. *See* Karn and Porter (1946).
PORTER, L. W. *See* Bailey and Porter (1955).
POST, B. E. *See* Hanawalt and Post (1942).
POSTMAN, L. (1947) The history and present status of the Law of Effect. *Psychol. Bull.*, 44, 489–563.—*47*
POSTMAN, L. (1953) The experimental analysis of motivational factors in perception. In the Nebraska Symposium on Motivation. *Current theory and research in motivation, I.* Lincoln, Nebr.: Univ. of Nebraska Press, 59–108.—*319, 468*
POSTMAN, L. *See also* Allport and Postman (1947), Jenkins and Postman (1948), Solomon and Postman (1952).
POSTMAN, L., BRONSON, W. C., and GROPPER, G. L. (1952) Is there a mechanism of perceptual defense? *J. abnorm. soc. Psychol.*, 48, 215–224.—*319, 320*
POSTMAN, L., and BROWN, D. R. (1952) Perceptual consequences of success and failure. *J. abnorm. soc. Psychol.*, 47, 213–221.—*326*
POSTMAN, L., and JARRETT, R. F. (1952) An experimental analysis of 'learning without awareness.' *Amer. J. Psychol.*, 65, 244–255.—*47*
POSTMAN, L., and SCHNEIDER, B. (1951) Personal values, visual recognition and recall. *Psychol. Rev.*, 58, 271–284.—*319*
POSTMAN, L., and TUMA, A. H. (1954) Latent learning in human subjects. *Amer. J. Psychol.*, 67, 119–123.—*214*
POTTER, E. H. *See* Child, Potter, and Levine (1946).
POWERS, F. F. *See* Guthrie and Powers (1950).
POWLOSKI, R. F. *See* Muenzinger and others (1952), Muenzinger and Powloski (1951).
PRATT, C. C. (1936) Review of Koffka's *Principles of gestalt psychology. Amer. J. Psychol.*, 48, 527–531.—*256*
PRENTICE, W. C. H. (1944) The interruption of tasks. *Psychol. Rev.*, 51, 329–340.—*283*
PRENTICE, W. C. H. (1954) Review of Osgood's *Method and theory in experimental psychology. Amer. J. Psychol.*, 67, 555–561.—*367*
PRESSEY, S. L. (1950) Development and appraisal of devices providing immediate automatic scoring of objective tests and concomitant self-instructions. *J. Psychol.*, 29, 417–447.—*492*
PRIOR, G. *See* Irwin and others (1934).
PUMPIAN-MINDLIN, E. *See* Hilgard, Kubie, and Pumpian-Mindlin (1952).
RADNER, L. *See* Zeaman and Radner (1953).
RAHN, C. L. (1914) The relation of sensation to other categories in contemporary psychology. *Psychol. Monogr.*, 16, No. 67.—*333*
RAIFFA, H. *See* Coombs, Raiffa, and Thrall (1954).
RAMOND, C. K. (1953) Anxiety and task as determiners of verbal performance. *J. exp. Psychol.*, 46, 120–124.—*300*
RAMOND, C. K. (1954) Performance in instrumental learning as a joint function of delay of reinforcement and time of deprivation. *J. exp. Psychol.*, 47, 248–250.—*439*
RAMSAY, A. O. (1951) Familial recognition in domestic birds. *Auk*, 68, 1–16.—*3*
RAPAPORT, D. (1942) *Emotions and memory.* Baltimore: Williams and Wilkins. (Second unaltered edition, 1950. New York: International Universities Press.)—*280, 326*

RAPAPORT, D. (1950) On the psychoanalytic theory of thinking. *Int. J. Psychoanal.*, 31, 1–10.—*311*

RAPAPORT, D. (1951) *Organization and pathology of thought.* New York: Columbia Univ. Press.—*311, 326*

RASHEVSKY, N. (1931) Learning as a property of physical systems. *J. gen. Psychol.*, 5, 207–229.—*374*

RASHEVSKY, N. (1938) *Mathematical biophysics.* Chicago: Univ. of Chicago Press.—*374, 405*

RATLIFF, M. M. (1938) The varying function of affectively toned olfactory, visual, and auditory cues in recall. *Amer. J. Psychol.*, 51, 695–699.—*313*

RATNER, J. (1939) *Intelligence in the modern world: John Dewey's philosophy.* New York: Modern Library.—*331*

RAZRAN, G. (1949) Stimulus generalization of conditioned responses. *Psychol. Bull.*, 46, 337–365.—*140*

REED, L. J. *See* Pearl and Reed (1920).

RESTLE, F. (1955) A theory of discrimination learning. *Psychol. Rev.*, 62, 11–19.—*401, 406*

RESTORFF, H. VON (1933) Analyse von Vorgängen im Spurenfeld. I. Über die Wirkung von Bereichsbildungen im Spurenfeld. *Psychol. Forsch.*, 18, 299–342.—*41, 246*

RESTORFF, H. VON. *See also* Köhler and Restorff (1935).

RETHLINGSHAFER, D. (1941) Measures of tendency-to-continue. *J. genet. Psychol.*, 59, 109–124; 125–138.—*284*

REYNOLDS, B. (1945a) The acquisition of a trace conditioned response as a function of the magnitude of the stimulus trace. *J. exp. Psychol.*, 35, 15–30.—*54, 127*

REYNOLDS, B. (1945b) A repetition of the Blodgett experiment on 'Latent learning.' *J. exp. Psychol.*, 35, 504–516.—*211*

RICE, P. B. (1946) The ego and the law of effect. *Psychol. Rev.*, 53, 307–320. —*285*

RICHARDS, I. A. (1943) *Basic English and its uses.* New York: Norton.—*44*

RICHARDS, L. *See* Muenzinger, Bernstone, and Richards (1938).

RICHARDS, M. E. *See* Skinner, Solomon, Lindsley, and Richards (1954).

RICHARDSON, H. M. (1932) The growth of adaptive behavior in infants: an experimental study at seven age levels. *Genet. Psychol. Monogr.*, 12, 195–359.—*234*

RICKERS-OVSIANKINA, M. (1937) Studies on the personality structure of schizophrenic individuals. II. Reaction to interrupted tasks. *J. gen. Psychol.*, 16, 179–196.—*284*

RILEY, D. A. (1952) Rote learning as a function of distribution of practice and the complexity of the situation. *J. exp. Psychol.*, 43, 88–95.—*358*

RITCHIE, B. F. (1944) Hull's treatment of learning. *Psychol. Bull.*, 41, 640–652.—*183*

RITCHIE, B. F. (1948) Studies in spatial learning. VI. Place orientation and direction orientation. *J. exp. Psychol.*, 38, 659–669.—*195, 196*

RITCHIE, B. F. *See also* Tolman, Ritchie, and Kalish (1946) (1947).

RITCHIE, B. F., AESCHLIMAN, B., and PEIRCE, P. (1950) Studies in spatial learning. VIII. Place performance and the acquisition of place dispositions. *J. comp. physiol. Psychol.*, 43, 73–85.—*194*

RITCHIE, B. F., HAY, A., and HARE, R. (1951) Studies in spatial learning: IX. A dispositional analysis of response performance. *J. comp. physiol. Psychol.*, 44, 442–449.—*221*

ROBERTS, W. W. *See* Delgado, Roberts, and Miller (1954), Miller, Murray, and Roberts (1955).

ROBERTSON, T. B. (1908) Sur la dynamique chimique de systeme nerveux central. *Arch. int. de Physiol.*, 6, 388–454.—*370, 371*

ROBERTSON, T. B. (1923) *The chemical basis of growth and senescence.* Philadelphia: Lippincott.—*370*

ROBINSON, E. S. (1927) The 'similarity' factor in retroaction. *Amer. J. Psychol.*, 39, 297–312.—*344, 345*

ROBINSON, E. S. (1930) Review of Köhler's *Gestalt psychology. J. genet. Psychol.*, 37, 431–450.—*256*

ROBINSON, E. S. (1932a) *Association theory today.* New York: D. Appleton-Century.—*336, 342, 366, 437*

ROBINSON, E. S. (1932b) *Man as psychology sees him.* New York: Macmillan. —*363*

ROBINSON, E. S. (1935) *Law and the lawyers.* New York: Macmillan.—*364*

ROBINSON, E. S., and BROWN, M. A. (1926) Effect of serial position upon memorization. *Amer. J. Psychol.*, 37, 538–552.—*367*

ROBY, T. B. *See* Sheffield and Roby (1950), Sheffield, Roby, and Campbell (1954).

ROCK, R. T., Jr. (1935) The influence upon learning of the quantitative variation of after-effects. *Teach. Coll. Contr. Educ.*, No. 650.—*47*

ROCK, R. T., Jr. (1940) Thorndike's contributions to the psychology of learning. *Teach. Coll. Rec.*, 41, 751–761.—*46*

ROCK, R. T., Jr. *See also* Thorndike and Rock (1934).

ROGERS, C. R., and DYMOND, R. F., eds. (1954) *Psychotherapy and personality change.* Chicago: Univ. Chicago Press.—*312*

ROSENTHAL, D., and COFER, C. N. (1948) The effect on group performance of an indifferent and neglectful attitude shown by one group member. *J. exp. Psychol.*, 38, 568–577.—*289*

ROSENZWEIG, M. R. *See* Krech and others (1954).

ROSENZWEIG, S. (1933) Preferences in the repetition of successful and unsuccessful activities as a function of age and personality. *J. genet. Psychol.*, 42, 423–441.—*283*

ROSENZWEIG, S. (1941) Need-persistive and ego-defensive reactions to frustration as demonstrated by an experiment on repression. *Psychol. Rev.*, 48, 347–349.—*283, 304*

ROSENZWEIG, S. (1943) An experimental study of "repression" with special reference to need-persistive and ego-defensive reactions to frustration. *J. exp. Psychol.*, 32, 64–74.—*283*

ROSENZWEIG, S. *See also* Shakow and Rosenzweig (1940).

ROSENZWEIG, S., and MASON, G. (1934) An experimental study of memory in relation to the theory of repression. *Brit. J. Psychol.*, 24, 247–265.—*283*

ROSS, H. *See* Alexander and Ross (1952).

ROSS, R. T. *See* Hull and others (1940).

ROTTER, J. B. (1954) *Social learning and clinical psychology.* New York: Prentice-Hall.—*450, 451, 456, 485*

ROTTER, J. B. *See also* Schroder and Rotter (1952).

ROTTER, J. B., FITZGERALD, B. J., and JOYCE, J. (1954) A comparison of some objective measures of expectancy. *J. abnorm. soc. Psychol.*, 49, 111–114. —*451*

ROUSE, R. O. *See* Hull and others (1951).

ROVNER, H. *See* Irwin and Rovner (1937).

RUDOLF, K. B. (1949) The effect of reading instruction on achievement in eighth grade social studies. *Teach. Coll. Contr. Educ.*, No. 945.—*492*

RUSSELL, W. A. (1952) Retention of verbal material as a function of motivating instructions and experimentally-induced failure. *J. exp. Psychol.*, 40, 411–422.—*316, 318*

SANDIFORD, P. (1942) Connectionism: Its origins and major features. Chapter 3 in *The psychology of learning.* Natl. Soc. Stud. Educ., 41st Yearbook, Part II, 97–140.—*46*

SANFORD, R. N. (1946) Age as a factor in the recall of interrupted tasks. *Psychol. Rev.*, 53, 234–240.—*283*

SARBIN, T. R. (1950) Mental age changes in experimental regression. *J. Personality*, 19, 221–228.—*303, 326*

SARBIN, T. R., and FARBEROW, N. L. (1952) Contributions to role-taking theory: a clinical study of self and role. *J. abnorm. soc. Psychol.*, 47, 117–125.—*303*

SCHEERER, M. (1954) Cognitive theory. In G. Lindzey, ed. *Handbook of social psychology.* Cambridge: Addison-Wesley, 91–137.—*257*

SCHLOSBERG, H. (1937) The relationship between success and the laws of conditioning. *Psychol. Rev.*, 44, 379–394.—*413*

SCHLOSBERG, H. *See also* White and Schlosberg (1952), Woodworth and Schlosberg (1954).

SCHLOSBERG, H., and HEINEMAN, C. (1950) The relationship between two measures of response strength. *J. exp. Psychol.*, 40, 235–247.—*300*

SCHMULLER, A. M. *See* Thorpe and Schmuller (1954).

SCHNEIDER, B. *See* Postman and Schneider (1951).

SCHOENFELD, W. N. *See* Estes and others (1954), Keller and Schoenfeld (1950), Mueller and Schoenfeld (1954), Notterman, Schoenfeld, and Bersh (1952).

SCHOENFELD, W. N., ANTONITIS, J. J., and BERSH, P. J. (1950a) A preliminary study of training conditions necessary for secondary reinforcement. *J. exp. Psychol.*, 40, 40–45.—*95*

SCHOENFELD, W. N., ANTONITIS, J. J., and BERSH, P. J. (1950b) Unconditioned response rate of the white rat in a bar-pressing apparatus. *J. comp. physiol. Psychol.*, 43, 41–48.—*120, 145*

SCHOENFELD, W. N., and BERSH, P. J. (1952) Review of Hull's *Essentials of behavior. Psychol. Bull.*, 49, 628–636.—*183*

SCHRAMM, W., ed. (1954) *The process and effects of mass communication.* Urbana, Ill.: Univ. of Illinois Press.—*378*

SCHREINER, L. H. *See* Lindsley and others (1950).

SCHREINER, L. *See* Brady and others (1954).

SCHRIER, A. M. *See* Kendler, Karasik, and Schrier (1954).

SCHRODER, H. M., and ROTTER, J. B. (1952) Rigidity as learned behavior. *J. exp. Psychol.*, 44, 141–150.—*451*

SCHÜKAREW, A. (1907) Über die energetischen Grundlagen des Gesetzes von Weber-Fechner und der Dynamik des Gedächtnisses. *Ann. d. Naturphil.*, 6, 139–149.—*370*

SCHWARZ, G. (1927) Über Rückfälligkeit bei Umgewohnung. *Psychol. Forsch.*, 9, 86–158.—*289*

SCOTT, T. H. *See* Bexton, Heron, and Scott (1954).

SEARS, P. S. (1940) Levels of aspiration in academically successful and unsuccessful children. *J. abnorm. soc. Psychol.*, 35, 498–536.—*278, 280*

SEARS, P. S. (1941) Level of aspiration in relation to some variables of personality: clinical studies. *J. soc. Psychol.*, 14, 311–336.—*278, 280*

SEARS, P. S. (1951) Doll play aggression in normal young children: influence of sex, age, sibling status, father's absence. *Psychol. Monogr.*, 65, No. 6. —*306, 326*

SEARS, P. S. *See also* Lewin and others (1944), Sears, R. R., and others (1953).

SEARS, R. R. (1936a) Functional abnormalities of memory with special reference to amnesia. *Psychol. Bull.*, 33, 229–274.—*280, 301, 315*

SEARS, R. R. (1936b) Review of Lewin's *A dynamic theory of personality. Psychol. Bull.*, 33, 548–552.—*288*

SEARS, R. R. (1937) Initiation of the repression sequence by experienced failure. *J. exp. Psychol.*, 20, 570–580.—*315*

SEARS, R. R. (1939) Review of Guthrie's *The psychology of human conflict. Psychol. Bull.*, 36, 829–830.—*81*

SEARS, R. R. (1941) Non-aggressive reactions to frustration. *Psychol. Rev.*, 48, 343–346.—*304*

SEARS, R. R. (1943) *Survey of objective studies of psychoanalytic concepts.* New York: Social Science Research Council.—*302, 303, 314, 326*

SEARS, R. R. (1944) Experimental analysis of psychoanalytic phenomena. In J. McV. Hunt, ed. *Personality and the behavior disorders.* New York: Ronald Press, 306–332.—*304, 307, 326*

SEARS, R. R. (1951) Effects of frustration and anxiety on fantasy aggression. *Amer. J. Orthopsychiat.*, 21, 498–505.—*190, 306*

SEARS, R. R. *See also* Dollard and others (1939), Heathers and Sears (1943), Hovland and Sears (1938).

SEARS, R. R., and HOVLAND, C. I. (1941) Experiments on motor conflict. II. Determination of mode of resolution by comparative strengths of conflicting responses. *J. exp. Psychol.*, 28, 280–286.—*267*

SEARS, R. R., WHITING, J. W. M., NOWLIS, V., and SEARS, P. S. (1953) Some child-rearing antecedents of aggression and dependency in young children. *Genet. Psychol. Monogr.*, 47, 135–236.—*306*

SEARS, W. N. *See* Hilgard, Campbell, and Sears (1938).

SEASHORE, H., and BAVELAS, A. (1941) The functioning of knowledge of results in Thorndike's line-drawing experiment. *Psychol. Rev.*, 48, 155–164. —*26*

SEEMAN, W. (1951) The Freudian theory of daydreams: an operational analysis. *Psychol. Bull.*, 48, 369–382.—*311*

SEIDENFELD, M. A. (1938) Time as a factor in the recognition of visually perceived figures. *Amer. J. Psychol.*, 51, 64–82.—*244*

SEIDENFELD, M. A. *See also* Irwin and Seidenfeld (1937).

SELFRIDGE, J. A. *See* Miller and Selfridge (1950).

SELLS, S. B. *See* Woodworth and Sells (1935).

SEMMES, J. *See* Lashley, Chow, and Semmes (1951).

SEWARD, J. P. (1942) An experimental study of Guthrie's theory of reinforcement. *J. exp. Psychol.*, 30, 247–256.—*75*

SEWARD, J. P. (1949) An experimental analysis of latent learning. *J. exp. Psychol.*, 39, 177–186.—*213*

SEWARD, J. P. (1950) Secondary reinforcement as tertiary motivation: a revision of Hull's revision. *Psychol. Rev.*, 57, 362–374.—*420*

SEWARD, J. P. (1951) Experimental evidence for the motivating function of reward. *Psychol. Bull.*, 48, 130–149.—*420, 422*

SEWARD, J. P. (1952a) Delayed reward learning. *Psychol. Rev.*, 59, 200–201. —*469*

SEWARD, J. P. (1952b) Introduction to a theory of motivation. *Psychol. Rev.*, 59, 405–413.—*420, 421*

SEWARD, J. P. (1953) How are motives learned? *Psychol. Rev.*, 60, 99–110.—*420*

SEWARD, J. P. (1954) Hull's system of behavior: an evaluation. *Psychol. Rev.*, 61, 145–159.—*183*

SEWARD, J. P. (1955) The constancy of the I-V: a critique of intervening variables. *Psychol. Rev.*, 62, 155–168.—*218*

SEWARD, J. P., DATEL, W. E., and LEVY, N. (1952) Tests of two hypotheses of latent learning. *J. exp. Psychol.*, 43, 274–280.—*213*

SEWARD, J. P., DILL, J. B., and HOLLAND, M. A. (1944) Guthrie's theory of learning: a second experiment. *J. exp. Psychol.*, 34, 227–238.—*75*

SEWARD, J. P., LEVY, N., and HANDLON, J. P., Jr. (1950) Incidental learning in the rat. *J. comp. physiol. Psychol.*, 43, 240–251.—*212*

SHAKOW, D. *See* Huston, Shakow, and Erickson (1934).

SHAKOW, D., and ROSENZWEIG, S. (1940) The use of the tautophone ("verbal summator") as an auditory apperceptive test for the study of personality. *Character and Pers.*, 8, 216–226.—*107*

SHANNON, C. E., and WEAVER, W. (1949) *The mathematical theory of communication.* Urbana, Ill.: Univ. of Illinois Press.—*377, 405*

SHARP, A. A. (1938) An experimental test of Freud's doctrine of the relation of hedonic tone to memory revival. *J. exp. Psychol.*, 22, 395–418.—*614*

SHAW, M. E., and WATERS, R. H. (1950) An experimental test of latent learning in a relatively free-choice situation. *J. genet. Psychol.*, 77, 283–292. —*212*

SHAW, W. J. *See* Baldwin and Shaw (1895).

SHEFFIELD, F. D. (1948) Avoidance training and the contiguity principle. *J. comp. physiol. Psychol.*, 41, 165–177.—*81*

SHEFFIELD, F. D. (1949a) Hilgard's critique of Guthrie. *Psychol. Rev.*, 56, 284–291.—*60, 62, 81*

SHEFFIELD, F. D. (1949b) "Spread of effect" without reward or learning. *J. exp. Psychol.*, 39, 575–579.—*35, 37*

SHEFFIELD, F. D. (1951) The contiguity principle in learning theory. *Psychol. Rev.*, 58, 362–367.—*411*

SHEFFIELD, F. D. *See also* Campbell and Sheffield (1953), Jenkins and Sheffield (1946).

SHEFFIELD, F. D., and JENKINS, W. O. (1952) Level of repetition in the "spread of effect." *J. exp. Psychol.*, 44, 101–107.—*33, 35, 38, 39, 41*

SHEFFIELD, F. D., and ROBY, T. B. (1950) Reward value of a non-nutritive sweet taste. *J. comp. physiol. Psychol.*, 43, 471–481.—*59, 60, 410*

SHEFFIELD, F. D., ROBY, T. B., and CAMPBELL, B. A. (1954) Drive reduction versus consummatory behavior as determinants of reinforcement. *J. comp. physiol. Psychol.*, 47, 349–354.—*410*

SHEFFIELD, F. D., and TEMMER, H. W. (1950) Relative resistance to extinction of escape training and avoidance training. *J. exp. Psychol.*, 40, 287–298.—*81*

Sheffield, F. D., Wulff, J. J., and Backer, R. (1951) Reward value of copulation without sex drive reduction. *J. comp. physiol. Psychol.*, 44, 3–8.—*81, 410*

Sheffield, V. F. (1949) Extinction as a function of partial reinforcement and distribution of practice. *J. exp. Psychol.*, 39, 511–526.—*75*

Sheffield, V. F. (1950) Resistance to extinction as a function of the distribution of extinction trials. *J. exp. Psychol.*, 40, 305–313.—*81*

Sherrington, C. S. (1906) *The integrative action of the nervous system.* New Haven, Yale Univ. Press.—*62, 337*

Shoben, E. J., Jr. (1949) Psychotherapy as a problem in learning theory. *Psychol. Bull.*, 46, 366–392.—*312*

Simmons, R. (1924) The relative effectiveness of certain incentives in animal learning. *Comp. Psychol. Monogr.*, 1924, 2, 1–79.—*211*

Simon, H. A. (1954) Some strategic considerations in the construction of social science models. In P. Lazarsfeld, ed. *Mathematical thinking in the social sciences.* Glencoe, Ill.: Free Press, 388–415.—*386, 388*

Singer, E. A. (1911) Mind as an observable object. *J. Phil. Psychol. sci. Meth.*, 8, 180–186.—*48*

Singer, M. B. *See* Piers and Singer (1953).

Skaggs, E. B. (1925) Further studies in retroactive inhibition. *Psychol. Monogr.*, 34, No. 161.—*344*

Skinner, B. F. (1933) 'Resistance to extinction' in the process of conditioning. *J. gen. Psychol.*, 9, 420–429.—*87*

Skinner, B. F. (1935) Two types of conditioned reflex and a pseudo type. *J. gen. Psychol.*, 12, 66–77.—*116*

Skinner, B. F. (1936) The verbal summator and a method for the study of latent speech. *J. Psychol.*, 2, 71–107.—*107*

Skinner, B. F. (1937) The distribution of associated words. *Psychol. Rec.*, 1, 71–76.—*107*

Skinner, B. F. (1938) *The behavior of organisms: an experimental analysis.* New York: Appleton-Century-Crofts.—*82, 84–87, 91, 93, 98–101, 104, 119*

Skinner, B. F. (1939) The alliteration in Shakespeare's sonnets: A study in literary behavior. *Psychol. Rec.*, 3, 186–192.—*107*

Skinner, B. F. (1941) A quantitative estimate of certain types of sound-patterning in poetry. *Amer. J. Psychol.*, 54, 64–79.—*107*

Skinner, B. F. (1944) Review of Hull's *Principles of behavior. Amer. J. Psychol.*, 57, 276–281.—*183*

Skinner, B. F. (1948a) "Superstition" in the pigeon. *J. exp. Psychol.*, 38, 168–172.—*120*

Skinner, B. F. (1948b) *Walden two.* New York: Macmillan.—*106, 120*

Skinner, B. F. (1950) Are theories of learning necessary? *Psychol. Rev.*, 57, 193–216.—*56, 86, 89, 92, 96, 117–119, 147, 491*

Skinner, B. F. (1951) How to teach animals. *Sci. Amer.*, 185, December, 26–29.—*88*

Skinner, B. F. (1953a) *Science and human behavior.* New York: Macmillan.—*82, 87–90, 93, 95–97, 103, 107, 108, 114–116, 119, 120, 366*

Skinner, B. F. (1953b) Some contributions of an experimental analysis of behavior to psychology as a whole. *Amer. Psychologist*, 8, 69–78.—*94, 119*

SKINNER, B. F. (1954) The science of learning and the art of teaching. *Harvard educ. Rev.*, 24, 86–97.—*106, 491*

SKINNER, B. F. *See also* Cook and Skinner (1939), Estes and Skinner (1941), Heron and Skinner (1940).

SKINNER, B. F., SOLOMON, H. C., LINDSLEY, O. R., and RICHARDS, M. E. (1954) *Studies in behavior therapy. Status Report II.* Research under contract with the Office of Naval Research. (Mimeographed.)—*109*

SKOLNICK, A. *See* Wedell, Taylor, and Skolnick (1940).

SMITH, M. B. *See* Hilgard and Smith (1942).

SMITH, M. H., Jr. (1949) Spread of effect is the spurious result of non-random response tendencies. *J. exp. Psychol.*, 39, 355–368.—*35, 41*

SMITH, S., and FITCH, E. E. (1935) Skill and proprioceptor pattern. *J. genet. Psychol.*, 46, 303–310.—*81*

SMITH, S., and GUTHRIE, E. R. (1921) *General psychology in terms of behavior.* New York: Appleton.—*50, 57, 62*

SMOKE, K. L. (1932) An objective study of concept formation. *Psychol. Monogr.*, 42, No. 4.—*382*

SMOKE, K. L. (1933) Negative instances in concept learning. *J. exp. Psychol.*, 16, 583–588.—*382*

SNODDY, G. S. (1935) *Evidence for two opposed processes in mental growth.* Lancaster, Pa.: Science Press.—*356*

SNODDY, G. S. (1945) Evidence for a universal shock factor in learning. *J. exp. Psychol.*, 35, 403–417.—*356*

SNYGG, D., and COMBS, A. W. (1949) *Individual behavior: A new frame of reference for psychology.* New York: Harper.—*254*

SOLLENBERGER, R. T. *See* Dollard and others (1939).

SOLOMON, H. C. *See* Skinner, Solomon, Lindsley, and Richards (1954).

SOLOMON, L. N. *See* Mowrer and Solomon (1954).

SOLOMON, R. L. *See* Howes and Solomon (1950) (1951).

SOLOMON, R. L., and HOWES, D. H. (1951) Word frequency, personal values, and visual duration thresholds. *Psychol. Rev.*, 58, 256–270.—*319*

SOLOMON, R. L., and POSTMAN, L. (1952) Frequency of usage as a determinant of recognition thresholds for words. *J. exp. Psychol.*, 43, 195–201.—*319*

SPENCE, K. W. (1936) The nature of discrimination learning in animals. *Psychol. Rev.*, 43, 427–449.—*140, 406, 433, 436*

SPENCE, K. W. (1937) The differential response in animals to stimuli varying within a single dimension. *Psychol. Rev.*, 44, 430–444.—*140, 435, 442, 444, 448*

SPENCE, K. W. (1939) A reply to Dr. Razran on the transposition of response in discrimination experiments. *Psychol. Rev.*, 46, 88–91.—140

SPENCE, K. W. (1940) Continuous versus non-continuous interpretations of discrimination learning. *Psychol. Rev.*, 47, 271–288.—*436*

SPENCE, K. W. (1941) Review of Köhler's *Dynamics in psychology. Psychol. Bull.*, 38, 886–889.—*256*

SPENCE, K. W. (1942) The basis of solution by chimpanzees of the intermediate size problem. *J. exp. Psychol.*, 31, 257–271.—*140, 184, 436, 442*

SPENCE, K. W. (1945) An experimental test of the continuity and non-continuity theories of discrimination learning. *J. exp. Psychol.*, 35, 253–266.—*436*

SPENCE, K. W. (1947) The role of secondary reinforcement in delayed reward learning. *Psychol. Rev.*, 54, 1–8.—*136, 154, 420*

SPENCE, K. W. (1948) The postulates and methods of 'behaviorism.' *Psychol. Rev.*, 55, 67–78.—*220*

SPENCE, K. W. (1950) Cognitive versus stimulus-response theories of learning. *Psychol. Rev.*, 57, 159–172.—*491*

SPENCE, K. W. (1951a) Theoretical interpretations of learning. In C. P. Stone, ed. *Comparative psychology*. Third edition. New York: Prentice-Hall, 239–291.—*132, 183, 220*

SPENCE, K. W. (1951b) Theoretical interpretations of learning. In S. S. Stevens, ed. *Handbook of experimental psychology*. New York: Wiley, 690–729.—*183*

SPENCE, K. W. (1952a) Clark Leonard Hull: 1884–1952. *Amer. J. Psychol.*, 65, 639–646.—*122*

SPENCE, K. W. (1952b) Mathematical formulations of learning phenomena. *Psychol. Rev.*, 59, 152–160.—*404, 406, 415*

SPENCE, K. W. (1952c) The nature of the response in discrimination learning. *Psychol. Rev.*, 59, 89–93.—*436, 444*

SPENCE, K. W. (1953) Résumé of symposium. *Symposium on psychology of learning basic to military training problems*. Washington, D.C.: Research and Development Board, 185–189.—*459, 460*

SPENCE, K. W. (1954a) Current interpretations of learning data and some recent developments in stimulus-response theory. In the Kentucky Symposium. *Learning theory, personality theory, and clinical research*. New York: Wiley, 1–21.—*416, 439*

SPENCE, K. W. (1954b) The relation of response latency and speed to the intervening variables and *N* in S-R theory. *Psychol. Rev.*, 61, 209–216. —*416, 441*

SPENCE, K. W. (1955) *Behavior theory and conditioning*. Silliman Lectures, Yale University. To be published by Yale Univ. Press.—*414–417, 419, 420, 426, 427, 439–441, 456, 468*

SPENCE, K. W. *See also* Bergmann and Spence (1941), Diesenroth and Spence (1941), Farber and Spence (1953), Taylor and Spence (1952).

SPENCE, K. W., BERGMANN, G., and LIPPITT, R. A. (1950) A study of simple learning under irrelevant motivational-reward conditions. *J. exp. Psychol.*, 40, 539–551.—*184, 212, 416*

SPENCE, K. W., and FARBER, I. E. (1953) Conditioning and extinction as a function of anxiety. *J. exp. Psychol.*, 45, 116–119.—*300*

SPENCE, K. W., and FARBER, I. E. (1954) The relation of anxiety to differential eyelid conditioning. *J. exp. Psychol.*, 47, 129–134.—*300*

SPENCE, K. W., and LIPPITT, R. (1940) "Latent" learning of a simple maze problem with relevant needs satiated. *Psychol. Bull.*, 37, 429. (Abstract)—*212*

SPENCE, K. W., and LIPPITT, R. (1946) An experimental test of the sign-gestalt theory of trial and error learning. *J. exp. Psychol.*, 36, 491–502.—*212*

SPENCE, K. W., and TAYLOR, J. A. (1951) Anxiety and strength of the UCS as determiners of the amount of eyelid conditioning. *J. exp. Psychol.*, 42, 183–188.—*300*

SPENCE, K. W., and TAYLOR, J. A. (1953) The relation of conditioned response strength to anxiety in normal, neurotic, and psychotic subjects. *J. exp. Psychol.*, 45, 265–272.—*300, 327*

SPIEGEL, J. P. *See* Grinker and Spiegel (1945a) (1946b).

STANLEY, J. C., Jr. *See* Jenkins and Stanley (1950).
STEIN, M. I., and MEER, B. (1954) Perceptual organization in a study of creativity. *J. Psychol.*, 37, 39–43.—*311*
STEPHENS, J. M. (1934) A change in the interpretation of the law of effect. *Brit. J. Psychol.*, 24, 266–275.—*31, 41*
STEPHENS, J. M. (1941) The influence of symbolic punishment and reward upon strong and upon weak associations. *J. gen. Psychol.*, 25, 177–185. —*33*
STEVENS, S. S. (1939) Psychology and the science of science. *Psychol. Bull.*, 36, 221-263.—*366*
STEVENS, S. S., ed. (1951) *Handbook of experimental psychology.* New York: Wiley.—*14*
STEVENSON, H. W. (1954) Latent learning in children. *J. exp. Psychol.*, 47, 17–21.—*214*
STEVENSON, H. W., and ISCOE, I. (1954) Overtraining and transposition in children. *J. exp. Psychol.*, 47, 251–255.—*444*
STEVENSON, H. W., ISCOE, I., and MCCONNELL, C. (1955) A developmental study of transposition. *J. exp. Psychol.*, 49, 278–280.—*444, 445*
STOLUROW, L. M., ed. (1953) *Readings in learning.* New York: Prentice-Hall. —*14*
STONE, C. P., and NYSWANDER, D. B. (1927) Reliability of rat learning scores from the multiple T-maze as determined by four different methods. *J. genet. Psychol.*, 34, 497–524.—*210*
STONE, G. R. (1948) Hilgard on the dominant laws of learning. *Psychol. Rev.*, 55, 342–344.—*47*
STONE, G. R. (1953) The effect of negative incentives in serial learning: VII. Theory of punishment. *J. gen. Psychol.*, 48, 133–161.—*41, 47*
STRANGE, J. R. (1950) Latent learning under conditions of high motivation. *J. comp. physiol. Psychol.*, 43, 194–197.—*212*
STRASSBURGER, R. C. (1950) Resistance to extinction of a conditioned operant as related to drive level at reinforcement. *J. exp. Psychol.*, 40, 473–487.— *97, 120, 141*
STRATTON, G. M. (1896) Some preliminary experiments on vision without the inversion of the retinal image. *Psychol. Rev.*, 3, 611–617.—*336, 467*
STRATTON, G. M. (1897) Vision without inversion of the retinal image. *Psychol. Rev.*, 4, 341–360, 463–481.—*467*
STRAUGHAN, J. H. *See* Estes and Straughan (1954).
STROUD, J. B. (1932) Effect of complexity of material upon the form of learning curves. *Amer. J. Psychol.*, 44, 721–731.—*367*
STROUD, J. B. (1940) Experiments on learning in school situations. *Psychol. Bull.*, 37, 777–807.—*491*
STRZELECKI, J. *See* Bindra, Paterson, and Strzelecki (1955).
SULLIVAN, J. J. (1950) *Some factors affecting the conditioning of the galvanic skin response.* Unpublished Ph.D. dissertation, University of Iowa.—*414*
SWENSON, E. J. (1941) *Retroactive inhibition: a review of the literature.* Minneapolis, Univ. Minnesota Press.—*344*
SYMONDS, P. M. (1946) *The dynamics of human adjustment.* New York: Appleton-Century-Crofts.—*325*
SYMONDS, P. M. (1951) *The ego and the self.* New York: Appleton-Century-Crofts.—*324*

SZYMANSKI, J. S. (1918) Versuche über die wirkung der Factoren, die als Antrieb zum Erlernen einer Handlung dienen können. *Pflüg. Arch. ges. Physiol.*, 171, 374–385.—*212*

TAIT, W. D. (1913) The effect of psycho-physical attitudes on memory. *J. abnorm. Psychol.*, 8, 10–37.—*302*

TAYLOR, D. W. *See* Adamson and Taylor (1954), Wright and Taylor (1949).

TAYLOR, F. V. *See* Wedell, Taylor, and Skolnick (1940).

TAYLOR, J. A. (1951) The relationship of anxiety to the conditioned eyelid response. *J. exp. Psychol.*, 41, 81–92.—*299*

TAYLOR, J. A. (1953) A personality scale of manifest anxiety. *J. abnorm. soc. Psychol.*, 48, 285–290.—*300*

TAYLOR, J. A. *See also* Spence and Taylor (1951) (1953).

TAYLOR, J. A., and SPENCE, K. W. (1952) The relationship of anxiety level to performance in serial learning. *J. exp. Psychol.*, 44, 61–66.—*300*

TEMMER, H. W. *See* Sheffield and Temmer (1950).

TENNIES, L. G. (1942) Memory trace and perception in the blind. *J. exp. Psychol.*, 30, 23–39.—*244*

THISTLETHWAITE, D. L. (1951a) A critical review of latent learning and related experiments. *Psychol. Bull.*, 48, 97–129.—*211*

THISTLETHWAITE, D. L. (1951b) An experimental test of a reinforcement interpretation of latent learning. *J. comp. physiol. Psychol.*, 44, 431–441.—*208, 212*

THISTLETHWAITE, D. L. (1952a) Reply to Kendler and Maltzman. *Psychol. Bull.*, 49, 61–71.—*211*

THISTLETHWAITE, D. L. (1952b) Conditions of irrelevant incentive learning. *J. comp. physiol. Psychol.*, 45, 517–525.—*212, 221*

THOMPSON, G. G., and HUNNICUTT, C. W. (1944) Effects of repeated praise or blame on the work achievement of introverts and extroverts. *J. educ. Psychol.*, 35, 257–266.—*492*

THOMPSON, G. L. *See* Bush, Mosteller, and Thompson (1954).

THORNDIKE, E. L. (1898) Animal intelligence: an experimental study of the associative processes in animals. *Psychol. Rev., Monogr. Suppl.*, 2, No. 8.—*1, 16*

THORNDIKE, E. L. (1903) *Educational psychology.* New York: Lemcke and Buechner.—*24*

THORNDIKE, E. L. (1908) The effect of practice in the case of a purely intellectual function. *Amer. J. Psychol.*, 19, 374–384.—*47*

THORNDIKE, E. L. (1910) Practice in the case of addition. *Amer. J. Psychol.*, 21, 483–486.—*47*

THORNDIKE, E. L. (1911) *Animal intelligence.* New York: Macmillan.—*16, 46*

THORNDIKE, E. L. (1913a) *The original nature of man.* (Educational psychology, I.) New York: Teachers College.—*16, 18*

THORNDIKE, E. L. (1913b) *The psychology of learning.* (Educational psychology, II.) New York: Teachers College.—*16, 17, 19–23, 45, 46, 204*

THORNDIKE, E. L. (1922) *The psychology of arithmetic.* New York: Macmillan.—*46*

THORNDIKE, E. L. (1924) Mental discipline in high school studies. *J. educ. Psychol.*, 15, 1–22; 83–98.—*47*

THORNDIKE, E. L. (1927) The influence of primacy. *J. exp. Psychol.*, 10, 18–29.—*47*

THORNDIKE, E. L. (1932a) *The fundamentals of learning.* New York: Teachers College.—*25, 27–29, 46*

THORNDIKE, E. L. (1932b) Reward and punishment in animal learning. *Comp. Psychol. Monogr.*, 8, No. 39.—*26, 27, 47*

THORNDIKE, E. L. (1933a) A proof of the law of effect. *Science,* 77, 173–175. —*29*

THORNDIKE, E. L. (1933b) An experimental study of rewards. *Teach. Coll. Contr. Educ.*, No. 580.—*29, 38, 47*

THORNDIKE, E. L. (1933c) A theory of the action of the after-effects of a connection upon it. *Psychol. Rev.*, 40, 434–439.—*28*

THORNDIKE, E. L. (1935) *The psychology of wants, interests and attitudes.* New York: D. Appleton-Century.—*22, 25, 27, 29, 46*

THORNDIKE, E. L. (1940) *Human nature and the social order.* New York: Macmillan.—*26, 46*

THORNDIKE, E. L. (1949) *Selected writings from a connectionist's psychology.* New York: Appleton-Century-Crofts.—*40, 46*

THORNDIKE, E. L., and others (1927) *The measurement of intelligence.* New York: Teachers College.—*42*

THORNDIKE, E. L., and others (1928) *Adult learning.* New York: Macmillan.—*46*

THORNDIKE, E. L., and LORGE, I. (1935) The influence of relevance and belonging. *J. exp. Psychol.*, 18, 574–584.—*47*

THORNDIKE, E. L., and ROCK, R. T., Jr. (1934) Learning without awareness of what is being learned or intent to learn it. *J. exp. Psychol.*, 17, 1–19.—*47, 475*

THORNDIKE, E. L., and WOODWORTH, R. S. (1901) The influence of improvement in one mental function upon the efficiency of other functions. *Psychol. Rev.*, 8, 247–261, 384–395, 553–564.—*24*

THORPE, L. P., and SCHMULLER, A. M. (1954) *Contemporary theories of learning, with applications to education and psychology.* New York: Ronald Press.—*14*

THRALL, R. M., COOMBS, C. H., and DAVIS, R. L., eds. (1954) *Decision processes.* New York: Wiley.—*406*

THURSTONE, L. L. (1923) The stimulus-response fallacy in psychology. *Psychol. Rev.*, 30, 354–369.—*329*

THURSTONE, L. L. (1930a) The learning function. *J. gen. Psychol.*, 3, 469–493. —*372, 389*

THURSTONE, L. L. (1930b) The relation between learning time and length of task. *Psychol. Rev.*, 37, 44–53.—*372, 373*

THURSTONE, L. L. (1933) The error function in maze learning. *J. gen. Psychol.*, 9, 288–301.—*406*

TILTON, J. W. (1939) The effect of "right" and "wrong" upon the learning of nonsense syllables in multiple choice arrangement. *J. educ. Psychol.*, 30, 95–115.—*31, 41*

TILTON, J. W. (1945) Gradients of effect. *J. genet. Psychol.*, 66, 3–19.—*31, 32, 41*

TINBERGEN, N. (1951) *The study of instinct.* London: Oxford Univ. Press.—*3*

TINKLEPAUGH, O. L. (1928) An experimental study of representative factors in monkeys. *J. comp. Psychol.*, 8, 197–236.—*192*

TITCHENER, E. B. (1895a) Simple reactions. *Mind, N.S.*, 4, 74–81.—*329*

TITCHENER, E. B. (1895b) The type-theory of simple reactions. *Mind, N.S.*, 4, 506–514.—*329*

TITCHENER, E. B. (1896) The 'type-theory' of the simple reaction. *Mind, N.S.*, 5, 236–241.—*329*

TITCHENER, E. B. (1898) Postulates of a structural psychology. *Philos. Rev.*, 7, 449–465.—*329*

TOLMAN, E. C. (1917) Retroactive inhibition as affected by conditions of learning. *Psychol. Monogr.*, 25, No. 107.—*216, 302*

TOLMAN, E. C. (1922) A new formula for behaviorism. *Psychol. Rev.*, 29, 44–53.—*219*

TOLMAN, E. C. (1932a) Lewin's concept of vectors. *J. gen. Psychol.*, 7, 3–15.—*217*

TOLMAN, E. C. (1932b) *Purposive behavior in animals and men.* New York: D. Appleton-Century (Reprinted, Univ. of California Press, 1949.)—*185, 203–205, 220, 477*

TOLMAN, E. C. (1934) Theories of learning. In F. A. Moss ed. *Comparative psychology.* New York: Prentice-Hall, 367–408.—*206*

TOLMAN, E. C. (1936) Connectionism; wants, interests, and attitudes. *Character & Pers.*, 4, 245–253.—*41, 46*

TOLMAN, E. C. (1937) The acquisition of string-pulling by rats—conditioned response or sign-gestalt? *Psychol. Rev.*, 44, 195–211.—*206*

TOLMAN, E. C. (1938a) The determiners of behavior at a choice point. *Psychol. Rev.*, 45, 1–41.—*15, 187*

TOLMAN, E. C. (1938b) The law of effect. *Psychol. Rev.*, 45, 165–203.—*15, 187*

TOLMAN, E. C. (1939) Prediction of vicarious trial and error by means of the schematic sowbug. *Psychol. Rev.*, 46, 318–336.—*189, 190, 442, 448*

TOLMAN, E. C. (1941) Discrimination vs. learning and the schematic sowbug. *Psychol. Rev.*, 48, 367–382.—*189, 442*

TOLMAN, E. C. (1942) *Drives toward war.* New York: D. Appleton-Century.—*185, 216, 220*

TOLMAN, E. C. (1943) Identification and the postwar world. *J. abnorm. soc. Psychol.*, 38, 141–148.—*185*

TOLMAN, E. C. (1945) A stimulus-expectancy need-cathexis psychology. *Science*, 101, 160–166.—*215*

TOLMAN, E. C. (1948a) Kurt Lewin, 1890–1947. *Psychol. Rev.*, 55, 1–4.—*217, 289*

TOLMAN, E. C. (1948b) Cognitive maps in rats and men. *Psychol. Rev.*, 55, 189–208.—*196, 220*

TOLMAN, E. C. (1949) There is more than one kind of learning. *Psychol. Rev.*, 56, 144–155.—*206, 207, 208*

TOLMAN, E. C. (1949c) Discussion. *J. Personality*, 18, 48–50.—*452*

TOLMAN, E. C. (1951a) *Collected papers in psychology.* Berkeley, Calif.: Univ. of Calif. Press.—*220*

TOLMAN, E. C. (1951b) A psychological model. In T. Parsons and E. A. Shils, eds. *Toward a general theory of action.* Cambridge, Mass.: Harvard Univ. Press, 279–361.—*189, 191, 219, 221*

TOLMAN, E. C. (1952a) Autobiography. In H. S. Langfeld and others. *A history of psychology in autobiography.* Vol. IV. Worcester, Mass.: Clark Univ. Press.—*221*

TOLMAN, E. C. (1952b) A cognition motivation model. *Psychol. Rev.*, 59, 389–400.—*189, 202, 220*

TOLMAN, E. C. *See also* Geier, Levin, and Tolman (1941), Honzik and Tolman (1936).

TOLMAN, E. C., and BRUNSWIK, E. (1935) The organism and the causal texture of the environment. *Psychol. Rev.*, 42, 43–77.—*185, 197, 389*

TOLMAN, E. C., and GLEITMAN, H. (1949) Studies in learning and motivation: I. Equal reinforcements in both end-boxes, followed by shock in one end-box. *J. exp. Psychol.*, 39, 810–819.—*213, 221, 450*

TOLMAN, E. C., HALL, C. S., and BRETNALL, E. P. (1932) A disproof of the law of effect and a substitution of the laws of emphasis, motivation and disruption. *J. exp. Psychol.*, 15, 601–614.—*41, 201, 221*

TOLMAN, E. C., and HONZIK, C. H. (1930a) "Insight" in rats. *Univ. Calif. Publ. Psychol.*, 4, 215–232.—*194*

TOLMAN, E. C., and HONZIK, C. H. (1930b) Introduction and removal of reward, and maze performance in rats. *Univ. Calif. Publ. Psychol.*, 4, 257–275.—*209, 211*

TOLMAN, E. C., and MINIUM, E. (1942) VTE in rats: overlearning and difficulty of discrimination. *J. comp. Psychol.*, 34, 301–306.—*221*

TOLMAN, E. C., RITCHIE, B. F., and KALISH, D. (1946) Studies in spatial learning. II. Place learning versus response learning. *J. exp. Psychol.*, 36, 221–229.—*193*

TOLMAN, E. C., RITCHIE, B. F., and KALISH, D. (1947) Studies in spatial learning. V. Response learning vs. place learning by the non-correction method. *J. exp. Psychol.*, 37, 285–292.—*193*

TROWBRIDGE, M. H., and CASON, H. (1932) An experimental study of Thorndike's theory of learning. *J. gen. Psychol.*, 7, 245–258.—*26*

TRUXAL, J. G. (1955) *Automatic feedback system synthesis.* New York: McGraw-Hill.—*376, 405*

TRYON, R. C. (1940) Studies in individual differences in maze ability: VII. The specific components of maze ability, and a general theory of psychological components. *J. comp. Psychol.*, 30, 283–335.—*461*

Tufts College Institute of Applied Experimental Psychology (1952) *Handbook of human engineering data.* Medford, Mass.: Tufts College.—*483*

TUMA, A. H. *See* Postman and Tuma (1954).

ULLMAN, A. D. *See* Mowrer and Ullman (1945).

UMBERGER, J. P. *See* Cannicott and Umberger (1950).

UNDERWOOD, B. J. (1949) *Experimental psychology: an introduction.* New York: Appleton-Century-Crofts.—*343, 357, 366*

UNDERWOOD, B. J. (1951a) Studies of distributed practice: II. Learning and retention of paired-adjective lists with two levels of intralist similarity. *J. exp. Psychol.*, 42, 153–161.—*350, 351*

UNDERWOOD, B. J. (1951b) Studies of distributed practice: III. The influence of stage of practice in serial learning. *J. exp. Psychol.*, 42, 291–295.—*350, 351*

UNDERWOOD, B. J. (1952a) Studies of distributed practice: VI. The influence of rest-interval activity in serial learning. *J. exp. Psychol.*, 43, 329–340.—*350, 358*

UNDERWOOD, B. J. (1952b) Studies of distributed practice: VII. Learning and retention of serial nonsense lists as a function of intralist similarity. *J. exp. Psychol.*, 44, 80–87.—*350, 352, 355*

UNDERWOOD, B. J. (1953a) Studies of distributed practice: VIII. Learning and retention of paired nonsense syllables as a function of intralist similarity. *J. exp. Psychol.*, 45, 133–142.—*350, 352*

UNDERWOOD, B. J. (1953b) Studies of distributed practice: IX. Learning and retention of paired adjectives as a function of intralist similarity. *J. exp. Psychol.*, 45, 143–149.—*350, 352*

UNDERWOOD, B. J. (1953c) Studies of distributed practice: X. The influence of intralist similarity on learning and retention of serial adjective lists. *J. exp. Psychol.*, 45, 253–259.—*350, 352, 353*

UNDERWOOD, B. J. (1953d) Studies of distributed practice: XI. An attempt to resolve conflicting facts on retention of serial nonsense lists. *J. exp. Psychol.*, 45, 355–359.—*350*

UNDERWOOD, B. J. (1953e) Learning. *Ann. Rev. Psychol.*, 4, 31–58.—*360*

UNDERWOOD, B. J. (1954a) Studies of distributed practice: XII. Retention following varying degrees of original learning. *J. exp. Psychol.*, 47, 294–300.—*350, 358, 359*

UNDERWOOD, B. J. (1954b) Intralist similarity in verbal learning and retention. *Psychol. Rev.*, 61, 160–166.—*353*

UNDERWOOD, B. J. *See also* Oseas and Underwood (1952).

UNDERWOOD, B. J., and GOAD, D. (1951) Studies of distributed practice: I. The influence of intralist similarity in serial learning. *J. exp. Psychol.*, 42, 125–134.—*350, 351*

UNDERWOOD, B. J., and VITERNA, R. O. (1951) Studies of distributed practice: IV. The effect of similarity and rate of presentation in verbal discrimination learning. *J. exp. Psychol.*, 42, 296–299.—*350*

VANDER MEER, A. W. (1950) *Relative effectiveness of instruction by: films exclusively, films plus study guides, and standard lecture methods.* Pennsylvania State College Instructional Film Research Program. Special Devices Center. ONR, Human Engineering Report SDC 269–7–13.—*492*

VAN ORMER, E. B. (1932) Retention after intervals of sleep and waking. *Arch. Psychol.*, N.Y., 21, No. 137.—*367*

VAN ORMER, E. B. *See* Hoban and Van Ormer (1950).

VERNON, P. E. (1935–1936) Review of Koffka's *Principles of gestalt psychology. Character & Pers.*, 4, 92–94.—*256*

VERPLANCK, W. S. (1954) Burrhus F. Skinner. In Estes and others. *Modern learning theory.* New York: Appleton-Century-Crofts, 267–316.—*117, 118, 120*

VERPLANCK, W. S. (1955) Since learned behavior is innate, and vice versa, what now? *Psychol. Rev.*, 62, 139–144.—*491*

VERPLANCK, W. S. *See also* Estes and others (1954).

VERPLANCK, W. S., and HAYES, J. R. (1953) Eating and drinking as a function of maintenance schedule. *J. comp. physiol. Psychol.*, 46, 327–333.—*426*

VINACKE, W. E. (1952) *The psychology of thinking.* New York: McGraw-Hill. —*311*

VINE, D. O. *See* Muenzinger and Vine (1941).

VITERNA, R. O. *See* Underwood and Viterna (1951).

VOEKS, V. W. (1948) Postremity, recency, and frequency as bases for prediction in the maze situation. *J. exp. Psychol.*, 38, 495–510.—*53, 71*

VOEKS, V. W. (1950) Formalization and clarification of a theory of learning. *J. Psychol.*, 30, 341–362.—*53, 70*

VOEKS, V. W. (1954) Acquisition of S-R connections: a test of Hull's and Guthrie's theories. *J. exp. Psychol.*, 47, 137–147.—*72, 73, 81*

VON NEUMANN, J., and MORGENSTERN, O. (1944) *Theory of games and economic behavior.* Revised edition, 1947. Princeton: Princeton Univ. Press. —*383, 405*

WALKER, E. L. (1948) Drive specificity and learning. *J. exp. Psychol.*, 38, 39–49.—*212*

WALKER, E. L. (1951) Drive specificity and learning: Demonstration of a response tendency acquired under a strong irrelevant drive. *J. comp. physiol. Psychol.*, 44, 596–603.—*212*

WALKER, E. L., KNOTTER, M. C., and DEVALOIS, R. L. (1950) Drive specificity and learning: The acquisition of a spatial response to food under conditions of water deprivation and food satiation. *J. exp. Psychol.*, 40, 161–168.—*212, 213*

WALLACE, S. R., Jr., BLACKWELL, M. G., Jr., and JENKINS, G. (1941) Pre-reward and post-reward performance in the "latent learning" of an elevated maze. *Psychol. Bull.*, 38, 694. (Abstract.)—*211*

WALLACH, H., and HENLE, M. (1941) An experimental analysis of the law of effect. *J. exp. Psychol.*, 28, 340–349.—*33, 36, 40*

WALLACH, H., and HENLE, M. (1942) A further study of the function of reward. *J. exp. Psychol.*, 30, 147–160.—*36*

WALTER, A. A. *See* Carmichael, Hogan, and Walter (1932).

WAPNER, S. *See* Werner and Wapner (1955).

WARD, L. B. (1937) Reminiscence and rote learning. *Psychol. Monogr.*, 49, No. 220.—*354*

WATERS, R. H. (1928) The influence of tuition on ideational learning. *J. gen. Psychol.*, 1, 534–547.—*367*

WATERS, R. H. *See also* Shaw and Waters (1950).

WATERS, R. H., and LEEPER, R. (1936) The relation of affective tone to the retention of experiences in everyday life. *J. exp. Psychol.*, 19, 203–215.—*315*

WATSON, J. B. (1907) Kinesthetic and organic sensations: their role in the reactions of the white rat to the maze. *Psychol. Monogr.*, 8, No. 33.—*49*

WATSON, J. B. (1913) Psychology as the behaviorist views it. *Psychol. Rev.*, 20, 158–177.—*48*

WATSON, J. B. (1914) *Behavior. An introduction to comparative psychology.* New York: Holt.—*49*

WATSON, J. B. (1916) The place of the conditioned reflex in psychology. *Psychol. Rev.*, 23, 89–116.—*50*

WATSON, J. B. (1919) *Psychology from the standpoint of a behaviorist.* Philadelphia: Lippincott.—*50*

WATSON, J. B. (1924) The unverbalized in human behavior. *Psychol. Rev.*, 31, 273–280.—*323*

WEAVER, H. B. *See* Irwin and others (1934).

WEAVER, W. *See* Shannon and Weaver (1949).

WEBB, W. B., and NOLAN, C. Y. (1953) Cues for discrimination as secondary reinforcing agents: a confirmation. *J. comp. physiol. Psychol.*, 46, 180–181.—*95*

WEDELL, C. H., TAYLOR, F. V., and SKOLNICK, A. (1940) An attempt to condition the pupillary response. *J. exp. Psychol.*, 27, 517–551.—*85*
WEGNER, N. *See* Zeaman, Deane, and Wegner (1954).
WEISE, P., and BITTERMAN, M. E. (1951) Response-selection in discriminative learning. *Psychol. Rev.*, 58, 185–195.—*442*
WEISS, W. *See* Hovland and Weiss (1953).
WEITZENHOFFER, A. M. (1953) *Hypnotism*. New York: Wiley.—*303*
WELCH, J. C. *See* Moore and Welch (1940).
WENDT, G. R. (1937) Two and one-half year retention of a conditioned response. *J. gen. Psychol.*, 17, 178–180.—*56*
WERNER, H. (1947) The effect of boundary strength on interference and retention. *Amer. J. Psychol.*, 60, 598–607.—*248, 352*
WERNER, H. (1948) *Comparative psychology of mental development*. Second edition. Chicago: Follett.—*254*
WERNER, H., and WAPNER, S. (1955) The Innsbruck studies on distorted visual fields in relation to an organismic theory of perception. *Psychol. Rev.*, 62, 130–138.—*467*
WERTHEIMER, M. (1923) Untersuchungen zur Lehre von der Gestalt, II. *Psychol. Forsch.*, 4, 301–350. Translated and condensed as "Laws of organization in perceptual forms" in Ellis (1938), pages 71–88.—*227*
WERTHEIMER, M. (1925) Über Schlussprozesse im produktiven Denken. *Drei Abhandlungen zur Gestalttheorie*. Berlin: Erlangen, 164–184. Translated and condensed as "The syllogism and productive thinking" in Ellis (1938), pages 274–282.—*257*
WERTHEIMER, M. (1945) *Productive thinking*. New York: Harper.—*240–242, 256, 473*
WHEELER, R. H. (1929) *The science of psychology*. New York: Crowell.—*225*
WHEELER, R. H. (1932) *The laws of human nature*. New York: Appleton.—*225, 230*
WHEELER, R. H. (1940) *The science of psychology*. Second edition. New York: Crowell.—*225*
WHEELER, R. H., and PERKINS, F. T. (1932) *Principles of mental development*. New York: Crowell.—*225, 356*
WHIPPLE, J. E. *See* Hilgard, Irvine, and Whipple (1953).
WHITE, C. T., and SCHLOSBERG, H. (1952) Degree of conditioning of the GSR as a function of the period of delay. *J. exp. Psychol.*, 43, 357–362.—*54*
WHITE, R. K. (1943) The case for the Tolman-Lewin interpretation of learning. *Psychol. Rev.*, 50, 157–186.—*217*
WHITE, R. K. *See also* Lewin, Lippitt, and White (1939).
WHITING, J. W. M. *See* Sears and others (1953).
WHITING, J. W. M., and CHILD, I. L. (1953) *Child training and personality*. New Haven: Yale Univ. Press.—*308*
WHITTAKER, E. M., GILCHRIST, J. C., and FISCHER, J. W. (1952) Perceptual defense or response suppression? *J. abnorm. soc. Psychol.*, 47, 732–733.—*320*
WICKENS, D. D. (1954) Stimulus-response theory as applied to perception. In the Kentucky Symposium. *Learning theory, personality theory, and clinical research*. New York: Wiley, 22–35.—*468*
WICKENS, D. D., and PLATT, C. E. (1954) Response termination of the cue

stimulus in classical and instrumental conditioning. *J. exp. Psychol.*, 47, 183–186.—*75*

WIENER, N. (1948) *Cybernetics.* New York: Wiley.—*376, 405*

WILCOXON, H. C. (1952) "Abnormal fixation" and learning. *J. exp. Psychol.*, 44, 324–333.—*296*

WILLEY, R. DEV. *See* Cain and Willey (1939).

WILLIAMS, K. A. (1929) The reward value of a conditioned stimulus. *Univ. Calif. Publ. Psychol.*, 4, 31–55.—*211*

WILLIAMS, S. B. (1938) Resistance to extinction as a function of the number of reinforcements. *J. exp. Psychol.*, 23, 506–521.—*139, 395, 396*

WILSON, J. T. (1949) The formation and retention of remote associations in rote learning. *J. exp. Psychol.*, 39, 830–838.—*361*

WISPÉ, L. G., and DRAMBAREAN, N. C. (1953) Physiological need, word frequency, and visual duration thresholds. *J. exp. Psychol.*, 46, 25–31.—*319*

WODINSKY, J. *See* Bitterman and Wodinsky (1953).

WOLF, A. (1943) The dynamics of the selective inhibition of specific functions in neurosis. *Psychosom. Med.*, 5, 27–38.—*308*

WOLFE, J. B. (1934) The effect of delayed reward upon learning in the white rat. *J. comp. Psychol.*, 17, 1–21.—*154*

WOLFE, J. B. (1936) Effectiveness of token-reward for chimpanzees. *Comp. Psychol. Monogr.*, 12, No. 60.—*429*

WOLFLE, D. L. (1951) Training. In S. S. Stevens, ed. *Handbook of experimental psychology.* New York: Wiley, 1267–1286.—*491*

WOLFLE, D. L. *See also* Gulliksen and Wolfle (1938).

WOLPE, J. (1949) An interpretation of the effects of combinations of stimuli (patterns) based on current neurophysiology. *Psychol. Rev.*, 56, 277–283.—*454*

WOLPE, J. (1953) Theory construction for Blodgett's latent learning. *Psychol. Rev.*, 60, 340–344.—*454*

WOOD, A. *See* Muenzinger and Wood (1935).

WOODBURY, C. B. (1950) Double, triple, and quadruple repetition in the white rat. *J. comp. physiol. Psychol.*, 43, 490–502.—*184*

WOODROW, H. (1942) The problem of general quantitative laws in psychology. *Psychol. Bull.*, 39, 1–27.—*372*

WOODWORTH, R. S. (1906) Imageless thought. *J. Phil. Psychol. sci. Meth.*, 3, 701–708.—*338*

WOODWORTH, R. S. (1918) *Dynamic psychology.* New York: Columbia Univ. Press.—*62, 285, 333, 337, 366, 472*

WOODWORTH, R. S. (1929) *Psychology.* Revised edition. New York: Holt.—*122*

WOODWORTH, R. S. (1930) Dynamic psychology. In C. Murchison, ed. *Psychologies of 1930.* Worcester, Mass.: Clark Univ. Press, 327–336.—*367*

WOODWORTH, R. S. (1937) Situation- and goal-set. *Amer. J. Psychol.*, 50, 130–140.—*338*

WOODWORTH, R. S. (1947) Reinforcement of perception. *Amer. J. Psychol.*, 60, 119–124.—*431, 467, 471*

WOODWORTH, R. S. (1948) *Contemporary schools of psychology.* Revised edition. New York: Ronald Press.—*256, 326, 328, 367*

WOODWORTH, R. S. (1949) Review of Hilgard's *Theories of learning. J. abn. soc. Psychol.*, 44, 124–129.—*47*

WOODWORTH, R. S. *See also* Thorndike and Woodworth (1901).

WOODWORTH, R. S., and SCHLOSBERG, H. (1954) *Experimental psychology.* Revised. New York: Holt.—*14, 243, 343, 365, 366*

WOODWORTH, R. S., and SELLS, S. B. (1935) An atmosphere effect in formal syllogistic reasoning. *J. exp. Psychol.,* 18, 451–460.—*367*

WRIGHT, H. F. *See* Barker, Kounin, and Wright (1943), Barker and Wright (1954).

WRIGHT, S. T. H., and TAYLOR, D. W. (1949) Distributed practice in verbal learning and the maturation hypothesis. *J. exp. Psychol.,* 39, 527–531.—*356*

WULF, F. (1922) Über die Veränderung von Vorstellungen (Gedächtnis und Gestalt). *Psychol. Forsch.,* I, 333–373. Translated and condensed as "Tendencies in figural variation" in Ellis (1938), pages 136–148.—*231, 243, 257*

WULFF, J. J. *See* Sheffield, Wulff, and Backer (1951).

YACORZYNSKI, G. K., and GUTHRIE, E. R. (1937) A comparative study of involuntary and voluntary conditioned responses. *J. gen. Psychol.,* 16, 235–257.—*81*

YAMAGUCHI, H. G. (1951) Drive (D) as a function of hunger (h). *J. exp. Psychol.,* 42, 108–117.—*132*

YAMAGUCHI, H. G. (1952) Gradients of drive stimulus (S_D) intensity generalization. *J. exp. Psychol.,* 43, 298–304.—*141, 184*

YAMAGUCHI, H. G. *See also* Felsinger and others (1947), Gladstone and others (1947), Hull and others (1947).

YAMAGUCHI, H. G., HULL, C. L., FELSINGER, J. M., and GLADSTONE, A. I. (1948) Characteristics of dispersions based on the pooled momentary reaction potentials (${}_S\dot{E}_R$) of a group. *Psychol. Rev.,* 55, 216–238.—*146*

YERKES, R. M. (1916) The mental life of monkeys and apes: a study of ideational behavior. *Behav. Monogr.,* 3, No. 12.—*224*

YERKES, R. M. (1927) The mind of a gorilla: I. *Genet. Psychol. Monogr.,* 2.—*237, 238*

YERKES, R. M. (1943) *Chimpanzees: A laboratory colony.* New Haven: Yale Univ. Press.—*236*

YOUNG, F. A. (1954) An attempt to obtain pupillary conditioning with infrared photography. *J. exp. Psychol.,* 48, 62–68.—*85, 462*

YOUNG, P. T. (1933) Review of Tolman's *Purposive behavior in animals and men. Amer. J. Psychol.,* 45, 177–178.—*220*

YOUNG, P. T. (1949) Food-seeking drive, affective process, and learning. *Psychol. Rev.,* 56, 98–121.—*429*

YOUNG, P. T. (1952) The role of hedonic processes in the organization of behavior. *Psychol. Rev.,* 59, 249–262.—*292*

YUM, K. S. (1946) *See* Masserman and Yum (1946).

ZEAMAN, D., DEANE, G., and WEGNER, N. (1954) Amplitude and latency characteristics of the conditioned heart response. *J. Psychol.,* 38, 235–250.—*414*

ZEAMAN, D., and RADNER, L. (1953) A test of the mechanisms of learning proposed by Hull and Guthrie. *J. exp. Psychol.,* 45, 239–244.—*75*

ZEIGARNIK, B. (1927) Das Behalten erledigter und unerledigter Handlungen, *Psychol. Forsch.,* 9, 1–85. Translated and condensed as "On finished and unfinished tasks" in Ellis (1938), pages 300–314.—*260, 280, 289*

ZELLER, A. F. (1950a) An experimental analogue of repression: I. Historical summary. *Psychol. Bull.*, 47, 39–51.—*313–315*

ZELLER, A. F. (1950b) An experimental analogue of repression: II. The effect of individual failure and success on memory measured by relearning. *J. exp. Psychol.*, 40, 411–422.—*316*

ZELLER, A. F. (1951) An experimental analogue of repression: III. The effect of induced failure and success on memory measured by recall. *J. exp. Psychol.*, 42, 32–38.—*316*

ZIRKLE, G. A. (1946a) Success and failure in serial learning. I. The Thorndike effect. *J. exp. Psychol.*, 36, 230–236.—*34*

ZIRKLE, G. A. (1946b) Success and failure in serial learning. II. Isolation and the Thorndike effect. *J. exp. Psychol.*, 36, 302–315.—*36, 37, 41*

SUBJECT INDEX